The Law and Practice of Banking

Volume 1
BANKER AND CUSTOMER

To Bill Monaghan

with Best wishes

Calum Johnston

1991.

The Law and Practice of Banking

Volume I
BANKER AND CUSTOMER

J. Milnes Holden, LL.B., PhD, LL.D
of Lincoln's Inn, Barrister
Emeritus Professor of Business Law at the University of Stirling
Honorary Fellow of the Chartered Institute of Bankers

Fifth Edition

Pitman

Pitman Publishing
128 Long Acre, London WC2E 9AN

A Division of Longman Group UK Limited

© J. Milnes Holden, 1970, 1974, 1982, 1986, 1991

First published in Great Britain, 1970
Third Edition, 1982
Reprinted 1982 and 1983
Fourth Edition, 1986
Reprinted 1987
Fifth Edition 1991

British Library Cataloguing in Publication Data

Holden, J. Milnes (James Milnes) *1918–*
    The law and practice of banking. — 5th ed.
    Vol. 1, Banker and customer.
    1. Great Britain. Banking. Law
    I. Title
    344.10682

ISBN 0-273-03134-1

ISBN (ELBS) 0-273-03271-2

Printed and bound in Singapore.

CONTENTS

Preface to Fifth Edition   ix
Preface to First Edition   xi
Table of Cases   xiii
Table of Statutes   xlii
Table of Statutory Instruments   lxiv
Table of Abbreviations   lxvii

PART I: RELATIONSHIP OF BANKER AND CUSTOMER

I Introductory
Section
1 Banks and banking businesses   2
2 Starting and conducting a banking business   12
3 Meaning of customer   24
4 Types of account   26
5 The Financial Services Act 1986   31

2 Contract between banker and customer
Section
1 General relationship between banker and customer   50
2 Limitation of actions   58
3 Banker's right to charge for his services   68
4 Banker's right of set-off   71
5 Appropriation of payments   78
6 Banker's duty of secrecy   86
7 Customer's duties to his banker   103
8 Statement of account or passbook   106
9 Wrongful dishonour of cheques   110

3 Determination of contract between banker and customer
Section
1 Closure of account   116
2 Death of customer   121
3 Mental incapacity of customer   124
4 Bankruptcy of customer   128
5 Winding-up of company customer   131
6 Winding-up of bank   131
7 Garnishee orders and summonses   132
8 Writs of sequestration   142
9 Outbreak of war   142

PART 2: BANKING OPERATIONS

4 Negotiable instruments
Section
1 Characteristics of negotiable instruments 146
2 Types of negotiable and quasi-negotiable instruments 148

5 The drawing, issue and negotiation of cheques
Section
1 Essentials of a cheque 154
2 Crossings on cheques 160
3 Issuing a cheque 168
4 Negotiation of cheques 171
5 Holder of a cheque 178
6 Defences to a claim on a cheque 186
7 Liabilities of parties to a cheque 199

6 Collection of cheques
Section
1 The clearing system 206
2 Collecting banker's duties 213
3 Bank as holder for value 216
4 Claims by third parties against collecting bankers 219
5 Statutory defence 224
6 Defence of estoppel 245
7 Defence of contributory negligence 246
8 Defence that bank acquired a good title to cheque 247
9 Defence of *ex turpi causa non oritur actio* 249
10 Bank's right to an indemnity 250

7 Payment of cheques
Section
1 Paying banker's duties 253
2 Statutory protection of paying banker 273
3 Claims by third parties against paying bankers 283

8 Bills of exchange
Section
1 Legal principles 287
2 The bill in action 312

9 Other instruments handled by bankers
Section
1 Dividend and interest warrants 324
2 Bankers' drafts 328

3 Instruments payable to wages or order, or cash or order   331
4 Conditional orders   334
5 Non-transferable cheques   336
6 Promissory notes   336
7 Postal orders   342

10 Other banking operations
Section
1 The bank giro system   344
2 Girobank   353
3 Cheque cards, credit cards and cash dispensers   356
4 Status opinions   361
5 Safe custody   368
6 Customers' investments   374
7 Ancillary financial services   387

PART 3: ACCOUNTS OF CUSTOMERS

11 Accounts of customers
Section
1 Accounts of individual customers   392
2 Accounts of minors   406
3 Accounts of married women   411
4 Joint accounts   412
5 Partnership accounts   420
6 Accounts of customers in the professions   431
7 Accounts of executors and administrators   439
8 Accounts of trustees   446
9 Accounts of trustees in bankruptcy   454
10 Accounts of trustees under deeds of arrangement   455
11 Accounts of companies   457
12 Accounts of receivers for debenture holders   503
13 Accounts of liquidators   506
14 Accounts of building societies   509
15 Accounts of friendly societies   512
16 Accounts of industrial and provident societies   513
17 Accounts of parochial church councils   515
18 Accounts of local authorities   516
19 Accounts of clubs and societies   518

Appendix 1   Circulars issued by the Committe of London Clearing Bankers   522

Appendix 2 Terms of Reference of, and Recommendations by, the Review Committee on Banking Services Law and the Government's Response 529

Appendix 3 Addendum on Reform of the *Ultra Vires* Rule 543

Index 550

PREFACE TO FIFTH EDITION

Many developments in the law and practice of banking have taken place during the four years which have elapsed since I wrote the preface to the fourth edition of the book.

Parliament has passed a number of statutes affecting bankers, the chief among them being the Financial Services Act 1986, the Insolvency Act 1986, the Banking Act 1987 and the Companies Act 1989. The Financial Services Act 1986, with special reference to its implications for bankers, is considered in paragraphs 1-78 to 1-93 of Chapter 1. The Act has made a considerable impact upon the provision of financial advice by bankers and others. The Banking Act 1987 strengthened the provisions of the Banking Act 1979, which it replaced. I have referred to the relevant provisions of the Banking Act 1987 in Chapter 1, paragraphs 1-39 to 1-51.

There have been a number of relevant legal decisions, including two cases involving the loss or theft of a large amount of travellers' cheques, namely, *Braithwaite* v. *Thomas Cook Travellers Cheques Ltd* [1989] 1 All ER 235 and *Elawadi* v. *Bank of Credit and Commerce International SA* [1989] 1 All ER 242. In the former case, the plaintiff's claim for reimbursement failed, whereas in the latter case the claim succeeded.

Electronic banking has received considerable publicity recently as a result of the introduction of EFTPOS (Electronic Funds Transfer at Point of Sale), which I have described in Chapter 10, paragraphs 10-32B to 10-32E. This system enables a customer at a supermarket, or other point-of-sale purchaser of goods or services, to make payment from his bank or building society account without the need for the transmission of paper vouchers. Electrical impulses are sent in encrypted form over the EFTPOS network to the card issuer.

Electronic banking is not a recent development. As long ago as 1967 cash dispensers were introduced at a few of the larger offices of the clearing banks. They are now known as automated teller machines (ATMs), and their use is explained in Chapter 10, paragraphs 10-50A to 10-50C. No vouchers are required. When a customer obtains cash from an ATM, the amount of his withdrawal is electronically transmitted over the network, and his account is debited.

The company now known as BACS Limited provides an automated money transfer service. The transactions which it handles include the majority of standing orders, salary and pension payments and direct debits. These transactions are recorded on magnetic tape and, as a general rule, vouchers are not used. I have described the system in Chapter 10, paragraph 10-32.

The system known as CHAPS (Clearing House Automated Payments System) came into operation in 1984 for the purpose of making high-value payments of £10,000 or over anywhere within the United Kingdom. The system, which now allows for payments of £7,000 or more, provides an electronic sterling credit transfer service, with 'same-day settlement'. I have described the system in Chapter 10, paragraph 10-32A.

In Appendix 2 I have set out the Terms of Reference of, and Recommendations by, the Review Committee on Banking Services Law. The Report of the Review Committee, whose Chairman was Professor R. B. Jack, CBE, was presented to Parliament by the Chancellor of the Exchequer as a Blue Paper in February 1989. Chapter 1 of the Report stated that the need for an enquiry into banking services law and practice did not stem from deep public disquiet which had been growing over a period of years or which had emerged in the wake of some dramatic event. Rather it was a need that had arisen because of the recent emergence of certain developments on the banking scene including the growth of new technology, the increasingly international scope of banking, the deregulation of banking services, and the growing formalization of the banker–customer relationship. Also in Appendix 2 I have referred to the White Paper, Cm. 1026, published in March 1990, responding to the Report of the Jack Committee.

In an Addendum which is published in Appendix 3 I have given an account of those provisions of the Companies Act 1989 which relate to the reform of the *ultra vires* rule.

For assistance in regard to specific parts of the book, I am indebted to Mr Laurence Shurman, the Banking Ombudsman; Mr J. Byllam-Barnes, FIB, a Head Office Inspector, Central Inspection Department, Law Section, Barclays Bank; Mrs Jenny Smith, Guidance Executive, Professional Ethics Division, The Law Society; Mr E. W. Stubbs, the Chief Inspector of the Clearing House; and Dr Enid A. Marshall, Reader in Business Law at the University of Stirling.

Finally, I record my thanks to Miss Elissa Elings for her assistance in seeing this edition through the press.

I have endeavoured to state the law as at the date of this preface, although it has been possible to include some more recent material.

J. Milnes Holden

The University of Stirling,
Stirling, FK9 4LA
1 November 1989

PREFACE TO FIRST EDITION

The theme of the Institute of Bankers' second Cambridge Seminar held at Christ's College in March 1969 was 'Bank Management – Recruitment and Training'. In the course of his paper on 'Bank Management in the 1970s', Mr M. T. Wilson, MBE, Chief General Manager, Lloyds Bank Ltd, said: 'Seen in broad perspective, the fifties were a time of adaptation to post-war conditions ... By comparison, the sixties have been years of exciting and progressive change ... We are experiencing the computer revolution; many important innovations such as cheque and credit cards, dollar and sterling CDs; environmental changes such as the growth of the Eurocurrency market and the launching of the National Giro; and last but not least, the recent mergers.'

The truth of Mr Wilson's remarks has been apparent to me during the preparation of this book. I started work on it ten years ago, and after some six or seven years, I was obliged to alter the structure of the book considerably. Certain aspects of banking law and practice which traditionally find a place in books on this subject had to be jettisoned in order to make room for some of the exciting changes to which Mr Wilson referred.

My day-to-day work has brought me into close contact with many of these changes. After some twelve years' experience in one of the clearing banks and a short period engaged in research and university teaching, I was called to the Bar where I practised for sixteen years. Most of my work consisted of advisory work in regard to commercial and financial problems. In March 1969 I retired from the Bar in order to take up a full-time appointment with the Inter-Bank Research Organisation, established recently by the Committee of London Clearing Bankers.

When a new edition of my book *Securities for Bankers' Advances* (now in its fourth edition) is required, it will become Volume 2 of this present work. Both volumes will be indexed by reference to paragraph numbers instead of to pages. It is hoped that this will assist readers when using the general index, and the tables of cases and statutes. Instead of having to look through a whole page in order to find a particular point, their attention will be directed to a specific paragraph. Thus, para. 2-17 refers to Chapter 2, paragraph 17.

One of the duties of an author is to thank those who have assisted him. I place on record, first, my gratitude to my friend, the late Mr T. J. Cogar, an Inspector of Barclays Bank Ltd. He and I had agreed to write this work jointly, but ill-health obliged him to ask the publishers to release him from his commitment. This they did, but until his death in

September 1966, whilst still in the service of Barclays Bank, Mr Cogar read each section of each chapter as I completed it, and gave me the benefit of his wide knowledge and experience. The work had then proceeded as far as Chapter 8. I am very grateful to one of his colleagues, Mr F. W. Weir, then an Inspector of Barclays Bank Ltd, and now an Assistant General manager of Barclays Bank (London and International) Ltd, who very kindly read the remaining sections of the book as I completed them.

I also record my thanks to Mr R. McC. M. Adams, Resident Solicitor, National Westminster Bank Ltd, and to Mr G. E. Belk, Manager, Midland Bank Ltd, Boston, each of whom read the proofs, and offered many useful suggestions.

For assistance in regard to specific parts of the book, I am indebted to Dr N. L. Armstrong, Assistant Manager, Services Section, General Administration Department, National Westminster Bank Ltd; Mr R. J. Foster, Area Officer, Harrow, National Westminster Bank Ltd; Mr R. B. Stevenson, Manager, Commercial Information Section, National Westminster Bank Ltd; Mr P. I. Twelvetree, the General Manager, Surrey Trustee Savings Bank; and Mr E. A. Young, the Deputy Inspector of the Bankers' Clearing House.

Much of the material for the book has been obtained at the Library of the Institute of Bankers, and I record my appreciation of the assistance given to me by the Librarian, Mr P. Spiro.

I must also thank numerous members of the Institute of Bankers who, by posing questions at lectures which I have been privileged to deliver at local centres of the Institute, have caused me to deal with problems which I might otherwise have omitted to consider.

Finally, it would be ungallant of me to omit to mention my wife, without whose help and encouragement throughout the last ten years the book would not have been written; Miss Gwen Bingham, who typed the manuscript; and Miss Sally Keen who helped me with the proof reading, and with the preparation of the index, and the tables of cases and statutes.

J. Milnes Holden

10 Lombard Street
London, EC3
1 November 1969

TABLE OF CASES

*References to paragraphs in which some account of the facts of a case
is given are printed in bold type*

Para.

A and another *v.* C and others [1980] 2 All ER 347; [1981]
2 WLR 629; [1980] 2 Lloyd's Rep 200   2-105A

A'Court *v.* Cross (1825) 3 Bing 329; 11 Moore 198; 4 LJ
(OS) CP 79   2-22

Adair, *Ex parte, see* Gross, *Re, Ex parte* Adair   7-44

Adamson *v.* Jarvis (1827) 4 Bing 66; 12 Moore, CP 241   6-140

Addis *v.* Burrows [1948] 1 KB 444; [1948] 1 All ER 177;
[1948] LJR 1033; 205 LT Jo 61; 64 TLR 169; 92 Sol Jo
124   9-41

Akrokerri (Atlantic) Mines Ltd *v.* Economic Bank [1904] 2
KB 465; 73 LJKB 742; 91 LT 175; 20 TLR 564; 48 Sol Jo
545; 9 Com Cas 281; 2 LDB 63   5-47, 6-111, 7-6

Alliance Bank Ltd *v.* Kearsley (1871) LR 6 CP 433; 40
LJCP 249; 24 LT 552; Chorley and Smart's *Leading
Cases* (5th ed.) 190   11-114

Alliston Creamery *v.* Grosdanoff and Tracy (1962) 34 DLR
(2d.) 189   5-187

Aluminium Industrie Vaasen BV *v.* Romalpa Aluminium
Ltd [1976] 1 WLR 676; [1976] 2 All ER 552; 120 Sol Jo
95; Chorley and Smart's *Leading Cases* (5th ed.) 371   **11-320**

Anon. (1697) 1 Comyns 43   4-6

Anon. (1699) 1 Salk 126; 3 Salk 71; 1 Ld Raym 738   4-6

Arab Bank Ltd *v.* Barclays Bank (Dominion Colonial and
Overseas) Ltd [1952] WN 529; [1952] TLR 920; on appeal [1953] 2 QB 527, CA; [1953] 2 All ER 263; 103 LJ
398; 97 Sol Jo 420; affirmed [1954] AC 495; [1954] 2 All
ER 226; 104 LJ 344; 98 Sol Jo 350; 6 LDB 429   2-12, 3-82, **3-86**

Arab Bank Ltd *v.* Ross [1952] 2 QB 216; [1952] 1 All ER
709; [1952] 1 TLR 811; 96 SJ 229; 6 LDB 286; Chorley
and Smart's *Leading Cases* (5th ed.) 50

    5-84, **5-87/8**, 5-90, 5-107, 5-112

Ardern *v.* Bank of New South Wales [1956] VLR 569;
[1956] ALR 1210; 7 LDB 85   11-71

Arnold *v.* Cheque Bank (1876) 1 CPD 578; 45 LJQB 562;
34 LT 729; 40 JP 711   6-54, 6-59

Para.

Ashbury Railway Carriage and Iron Co. *v.* Riche (1875) LR
7 HL 653; 44 LJ Ex 185; 33 LT 450; 24 WR 794   11-277

Atkinson *v.* Bradford Third Equitable Benefit Building
Society (1890) 25 QBD 377; 59 LJQB 360; 62 LT 857   2-26

Attorney-General *v.* Great Eastern Railway Co. (1880) 5
App Cas 473; 49 LJ Ch 545; 42 LT 810   11-227

Attorney-General *v.* National Provincial Bank Ltd (1928) 44
TLR 701; 4 LDB 194   **2-106**

Aucteroni and Co. *v.* Midland Bank Ltd [1928] 2 KB 294;
97 LJKB 625; 139 LT 344; 44 TLR 441; 72 Sol Jo 337; 33
Com Cas 345; 4 LDB 164   7-10, 8-140

Australia and New Zealand Bank Ltd *v.* Ateliers de Constructions Electriques de Charleroi [1967] AC 86   6-112

Babanaft International Co. SA *v.* Bassatne and another
[1989] 2 WLR 232; [1989] 1 All ER 433   7-42F

Baden, Delvaux and Lecuit *v.* Société Générale pour
Favoriser le Développement du Commerce et de L'In-
dustrie en France SA [1983] BCLC 325; affirmed [1985]
BCLC 258 n.   7-45A

Bagley *v.* Winsome and National Provincial Bank Ltd
[1952] 2 QB 236; [1952] 1 All ER 637; 96 Sol Jo 607; 6
LDB 265   3-67

Baines *v.* National Provincial Bank Ltd (1927) 96 LJKB 801;
137 LT 631; 32 Com Cas 216; 4 LDB 87; Chorley and
Smart's *Leading Cases* (5th ed.) 94   2-13, 7-9, **7-51**

Baker *v.* Australia and New Zealand Bank Ltd [1958]
NZLR 907; 7 LDB 186   2-142, **2-147**, 2-150

Baker *v.* Barclays Bank Ltd [1955] 1 WLR 822; [1955] 2 All
ER 571; 99 Sol Jo 491; 7 LDB 26
   6-95, **6-126/8**, 6-138, 6-141, 11-9

Ballman, *Re, Ex parte* Garland (1804) 10 Ves 110; 1 Smith
KB 220   11-183

Balmoral Supermarket Ltd *v.* Bank of New Zealand [1974]
2 NZLR 155   **2-8**

Banbury *v.* Bank of Montreal [1918] AC 626; 87 LJKB
1158; 119 LT 446; 34 TLR 518; 62 Sol Jo 665; 23 Com Cas
337; 3 LDB 189   10-68

Bank of Australasia *v.* Breillat (1847) 6 Moo PCC 152   11-105

Bank of Baroda Ltd *v.* Punjab National Bank Ltd [1944]
AC 176; [1944] 2 All ER 83; 114 LJPC 1; 60 TLR 412;
88 Sol Jo 225; 5 LDB 377   **7-101**, 8-20

Para.

Bank of Ceylon *v.* Kulatilleke (1957) 59 Ceylon NLR 188;
7 LDB 163   6-77

Bank of Chettinad Ltd *v.* Commissioners of Income Tax
[1948] AC 378; [1948] LJR 1925; 92 SJ 602   1-22

Bank of England *v.* Vagliano Brothers [1891] AC 107; 60
LJQB 145; 64 LT 353; 7 TLR 333; 1 LDB 130; Chorley
and Smart's *Leading Cases* (5th ed.) 40   7-10, 8-139/40

Bank of Montreal *v.* Dominion Gresham Guarantee and
Casuality Co. Ltd [1930] AC 659; 99 LJPC 202; 144 LT
6; 46 TLR 575; 36 Com Cas 28; 4 LDB 248   **9-16**

Bank Polski *v.* K. J. Mulder and Co. [1942] 1 KB 497;
[1942] 1 All ER 396; 111 LJKB 481; 166 LT 259; 58 TLR
178: 86 Sol Jo 161; 5 LDB 328   8-34

Bankers Trust Company *v.* Shapira and others [1980] 3 All
ER 353   **2-105A**

Barclays Bank Ltd *v.* Astley Industrial Trust Ltd [1970] 2
QB 527; [1970] 1 All ER 719   6-41

Barclays Bank plc *v.* Bank of England [1985] 1 All ER 385   **6-29A**

Barclays Bank Ltd *v.* Beck [1952] 2 QB 47; [1952] 1 TLR
595; [1952] 1 All ER 549; 96 Sol Jo 194; 6 LDB 258;
Chorley and Smart's *Leading Cases* (5th ed.) 289   **2-38**

Barclays Bank Ltd *v.* Harding (1962) *Journal of the Institute of Bankers*, Vol. 83, p. 109   6-39

Barclays Bank Ltd *v.* Okenarhe [1966] 2 Lloyd's Rep 87   2-61

Barclays Bank Ltd *v.* Quistclose Investments Ltd [1970]
AC 567; [1968] 3 All ER 651; 112 Sol Jo 903   **2-60A**, 2-70

Barclays Bank Ltd *v.* W. J. Simms & Cooke (Southern) Ltd
and another [1980] 2 WLR 218; [1979] 3 All ER 522;
[1980] 1 Lloyd's Rep 225   7-37A

Barclays Bank plc *v.* Quincecare Ltd and Unichem Ltd
[1988] FLR 166; [1988] 1 FTLR 507   7-45A

Barclays Bank plc (trading as Barclaycard) *v.* Taylor.
Trustee Savings Bank of Wales and Border Counties *v.*
Taylor, [1989] 3 All ER 563   2-107D

Barclays Bank plc *v.* Walters and another, *The Times*, 20
October 1988   2-39

Barker *v.* Wilson [1980] 2 All ER 81; [1980] 1 WLR 884;
124 Sol Jo 326   **2-104A**

Barker's Trusts, *Re* (1875) 1 Ch 43; 45 LJ Ch 52   11-229

Barnes *v.* Addy (1874) LR 9 Ch App 244; 43 LJ Ch 513; 30
LT 4   7-47A

Barnes, *In the Goods of*, Hodson *v.* Barnes (1926) 96 LJP
26; 136 LT 380; 43 TLR 71   5-12

Para.

Batts Combe Quarry Co. *v.* Barclays Bank Ltd (1931) 48
  TLR 4; 4 LDB 271   10-65
Bavins, Junr & Sims *v.* London and South Western Bank
  Ltd [1900] 1 QB 270; 69 LJQB 164; 81 LT 655; 16 TLR
  61; 1 LDB 293; Chorley and Smart's *Leading Cases* (5th
  ed.) 39   5-8, 6-55, 6-124, 6-140, **9-34**, 9-37
Baxendale *v.* Bennett (1878) 3 QBD 525; 47 LJQB 624   5-70
Beauforte (Jon) (London) Ltd, *Re*, Grainger Smith & Co.
  (Builders) Ltd, Wright (John) & Son (Veneers) Ltd, and
  Lowell Baldwin Ltd's Applications [1953] Ch 131; [1953]
  1 All ER 634; 97 Sol Jo 152; 6 LDB 357   11-279
Beavan, *Re*, Davies, Banks & Co. *v.* Beavan [1912] 1 Ch
  196; 81 LJ Ch 113; 105 LT 784   3-35
Beckham *v.* Drake (1841) 9 M & W 79; on appeal 11 MW
  315   11-106
Belfast Banking Co. *v.* Doherty (1879) 4 LR Ir 124   5-139, 11-44
Bellamy *v.* Marjoribanks (1852) 7 Ex 389; 21 LJ Ex 70; 18
  LTOS 277   5-46, 7-75
Belmont Finance Corporation *v.* Williams Furniture Ltd
  (No. 2) [1980] 1 All ER 393; Chorley and Smart's
  Leading Cases (5th ed.) 73   11-275A
Benson *v.* Parry (1780) cited 2 TR 52 and 15 Ves 121   2-44
Berkeley *v.* Hardy (1826) 5 B & C 355; 8 Dow & Ry KB 102;
  4 LJOS(KB) 184   11-19
Bevan *v.* National Bank Ltd (1906) 23 TLR 65; 2 LDB 135   6-109
Bird & Co. *v.* Thomas Cook & Son Ltd [1937] 2 All ER 227;
  156 LT 415; 5 LDB 21   5-84, 5-150
Birkbeck Permanent Benefit Building Society, *Re* [1912] 2
  Ch 183; 81 LJ Ch 769; 106 LT 968; 28 LTR 451; affirmed
  sub. nom. Sinclair *v.* Brougham [1914] AC 398; 83 LJ
  Ch 465; 111 LT 1; 30 TLR 315; 58 Sol Jo 302, HL
                                          1-19, 1-22, 11-279
Bishop, *Re*, National Provincial Bank Ltd *v.* Bishop [1965]
  Ch 450; [1965] 1 All ER 249; 109 Sol Jo 107   11-87
Bissell and Co. *v.* Fox Brothers and Co. (1884) 51 LT 663;
  on appeal (1885) 53 LT 193; 1 TLR 452; 1 LDB 67   6-112
Blades *v.* Free (1829) 9 B & C 167; 7 LJOS(KB) 211   3-24, 11-24
Blake, *Re* [1887] WN 173   11-226
Boehm *v.* Sterling (1797) 7 TR 423   5-5
Bolt & Nut Co. (Tipton) Ltd *v.* Rowlands Nicholls & Co.
  Ltd [1964] 2 QB 10; [1964] 1 All ER 137; 107 Sol Jo 909   5-181
Bonalumi *v.* Secretary of State for the Home Dept. [1985]

Para.

QB 675; [1985] 1 All ER 797; [1985] 2 WLR 722; (1985) 129 Sol Jo 223 — **1-60**

Borden (UK) Ltd *v.* Scottish Timber Products Ltd [1981] Ch 25; [1979] 3 All ER 961; [1980] 1 Lloyd's Rep 160; 123 Sol Jo 688 — **11-321**

Bottomgate Industrial Co-operative Society, *Re* (1891) 65 LT 712; 56 JP 216 — 1-22

Bower *v.* Foreign and Colonial Gas Co. Ltd, Metropolitan Bank, Garnishees (1874) 22 WR 740 — 2-66, 3-63, 11-318

Box *v.* Midland Bank Ltd [1979] 2 Lloyd's Rep 291; [1981] 1 Lloyd's Rep 434, CA — 1-70

Boyd *v.* Emmerson (1834) 2 A & E 184; 4 LJKB 43 — 6-32, 7-52

Boynton (A.) Ltd, *Re*, Hoffman *v.* Boynton (A.) Ltd [1910] 1 Ch 519; 79 LJ Ch 247; 102 LT 273; 26 TLR 294; 54 Sol Jo 308 — 11-368

Bradford Old Bank Ltd *v.* Sutcliffe (1981) 23 Com Cas 299 and, on appeal, [1918] 2 KB 833; 88 LJKB 85; 119 LT 727; 34 TLR 619; 62 Sol Jo 753; 24 Com Cas 27; 3 LDB 195; Chorley and Smart's *Leading Cases* (5th ed.) 284 — 2-42, **2-90**

Bradley Egg Farm Ltd *v.* Clifford [1943] 2 All ER 378 — 11-438

Brady *v.* Brady [1988] 2 All ER 617; [1988] 2 WLR 1308; [1988] 2 FTLR 181; [1988] BCLC 579 — 11-275B

Braithwaite *v.* Thomas Cook Travellers Cheques Ltd [1989] 3 WLR 212; [1989] 1 All ER 235; [1988] BTLC 327 — **4-11A**

Brettel *v.* Williams (1849) 4 Exch 623; 19 LJ Ex 121; 14 LTOS 255 — 11-105

Brewer *v.* Westminster Bank Ltd and Another [1952] 2 All ER 650; [1952] 2 TLR 568; 96 Sol Jo 531; on appeal *The Times*, 5 February 1953; 6 LDB 344 — 2-136, 11-71

Brighton Empire and Eden Syndicate *v.* London and County Bank (1904) *The Times*, 24 March — 7-70

Britannia Electric Lamp Works Ltd *v.* D. Mandler and Co. Ltd [1939] 2 KB 129; [1939] 2 All ER 469; 108 LJKB 823; 160 LT 587; 55 TLR 655; 5 LDB 206 — 5-187

British American Elevator Co. Ltd *v.* Bank of British North America [1919] AC 658; 88 LJPC 118; 121 LT 100; 3 LDB 208 — 11-231

British & North European Bank *v.* Zalstein [1927] 2 KB 92; 96 KJKB 539; 137 LT 127; 43 TLR 299; 4 LDB 76; Chorley and Smart's *Leading Cases* (5th ed.) 158 — **2-135**

British Guiana Bank *v.* Official Receiver (1911) 104 LT 754; 27 TLR 454 — **2-60**

Para.

British Power Traction and Lighting Co. Ltd, *Re*, Halifax
Joint Stock Banking Co Ltd *v.* British Power Traction
and Lighting Co. Ltd (No. 2) [1907] 1 Ch 528; 76 LJ Ch
423; 97 LT 198   11-369

British Thomson-Houston Co Ltd *v.* Federated European
Bank Ltd [1932] 2 KB 176; 101 LJKB 690; 147 LT 345   11-293

British Trade Corporation, *Re* [1932] 2 Ch 1; 101 LJ Ch
273; 147 LT 46: 4 LDB 310   9-54, 9-56

Brown *v.* Black (1873) 8 Ch App 939; 42 LJ Ch 814; 29 LT
362   11-56

Brown *v.* Westminster Bank Ltd [1964] 2 Lloyds List 187;
8 LDB 286   2-131

Brown's Estate, *Re* [1893] 2 Ch 300; 62 LJ Ch 695; 69 LT
12; 37 Sol Jo 354   2-23

Bryant, Powis and Bryant Ltd *v.* La Banque du Peuple
[1893] AC 170; 62 LJPC 68; LT 546; 9 TLR 322   11-34

Buckingham (Earl) *v.* Drury (1762) 2 Eden 60   11-46

Buckingham & Co. *v.* London and Midland Bank Ltd
(1895) 12 TLR 70; 1 LDB 219; Chorley and Smart's
Leading Cases (5th ed.) 222   **2-64**, 2-67, **3-6**

Bucknell *v.* Bucknell [1969] 1 WLR 1204; [1969] 2 All ER
998; 113 Sol Jo 586   3-81

Burchfield *v.* Moore (1854) 3 E & B 683; 23 LJQB 261; 23
LTOS 143; 18 Jur 727   5-147

Burn *v.* Boulton (1846) 2 CB 476; 15 LJCP 97   2-76

Burnett *v.* Westminster Bank Ltd [1966] 1 QB 742; [1965]
3 All ER 81; 109 Sol Jo 533; [1965] 2 Lloyd's Rep 218;
8 LDB 424   **5-31**

Bute (Marquess) *v.* Barclays Bank Ltd [1955] 1 QB 202;
[1954] 3 All ER 365; 98 Sol Jo 805, 6 LDB 467; Chorley
and Smart's *Leading Cases* (5th ed.) 142

        6-51, 6-55, 6-65, 6-100, **6-106**, 6-132

Calder *v.* Rutherford (1822) 3 Brod & Bing 302; 7 Moore CP
158   9-50

Calico Printers' Association *v.* Barclays Bank Ltd and
Anglo-Palestine Co. Ltd (1931) 36 Com Cas 71 and 197;
145 LT 51; 39 LlLR 51; 4 LDB 262   8-108

Capital and Counties Bank Ltd *v.* Gordon [1903] AC 240;
72 LJKB 451; 88 LT 574; 19 TLR 462; 2 LDB 35; Chorley
and Smart's *Leading Cases* (5th ed.) 121   5-8, 6-65

Capper's Case (1868) 3 Ch App 458   11-56

Carlon *v.* Ireland (1856) 5 E & B 765; 25 LJQB 113   7-75

Para.

Carpenters' Company *v.* British Mutual Banking Co. Ltd
 [1938] 1 KB 511; [1937] 3 All ER 811; 107 LJKB 11; 157
 LT 329; 53 TLR 1040; 43 Com Cas 38; 81 Sol Jo 701; 5
 LDB 57; Chorley and Smart's *Leading Cases* (5th ed.) 90
         6-116, 7-59, **7-71/4**, 7-76
Carr *v.* Carr (1811) 1 Mer 541 n.   **2-5**
Carter *v.* White (1883) 25 Ch D 666; 54 LJ Ch 138; 50 LT
 670; 1 LDB 36   2-43
Caswell *v.* Powell Duffryn Associated Colleries Ltd [1940]
 AC 152; [1939] 3 All ER 722; 108 LJKB 779; 161 LT 374;
 55 TLR 1004; 83 Sol Jo 976   6-134
Catlin *v.* Cyprus Finance Corporation (London) Ltd [1983]
 QB 759; [1983] 1 All ER 809; (1982) 126 Sol Jo 744 11-71
Caunt *v.* Thompson (1849) 18 LJCP 125; 7 CB 400; 6 D &
 L 261; 13 Jur 495   8-62
Chambers *v.* Miller (1862) 13 CBNS 125; 32 LJCP 30; 7 LT
 856   **7-50**
Chapman *v.* Smethurst [1909] 1 KB 73; reversed [1909] 1
 KB 927; 78 LJKB 654; 10 LT 465; 215 TLR 383; 53 Sol
 Jo 340; 14 Com Cas 94; 2 LDB 183   5-187
Charge Card Services Ltd, *Re* [1988] 3 All ER 702; [1988]
 3 WLR 764; [1988] BCLC 711   **10-47B**
Charles *v.* Blackwell (1877) 2 CPD 151; 46 LJCP 368; 36 LT
 195   5-34, 5-181, 7-58, 7-79
Chartered Bank *v.* Dickson (1871) LR 3 PC 574 9-57
Chatterton *v.* London and County Bank (1890). *The Miller*,
 5 May 1890 (first trial); *The Miller*, 7 July 1890 and *The
 Times*, 27 June 1890 (Divisional Court); *The Miller*, 3
 November 1890 (Court of Appeal); *The Miller*, 2
 February 1891 and *The Times*, 21 January 1891 (second
 trial); 1 LDB 110; Chorley and Smart's *Leading Cases*
 (5th ed.) 152   **2-136**
Chetwynd's Settlement, *Re*, Scarisbrick *v.* Nevinson [1902]
 1 Ch 692; 71 LJ Ch 352; 86 LT 216; 18 TLR 348; 46 Sol
 Jo 296   11-227
Chief Constable of Kent *v.* V. [1983] QB 34; [1982] 3 All
 ER 36; Chorley and Smart's *Leading Cases* (5th ed.) 89 **7-42**
Choice Investments Ltd *v.* Jeromnimon, Midland Bank
 Ltd, Garnishees [1981] QB 149; [1981] 1 All ER 225; 124
 Sol Jo 883; Chorley and Smart's *Leading Cases* (5th ed.)
 84   3-69B
City Equitable Fire Insurance Co., *Re* [1930] 2 Ch 293; 99
 LJ Ch 536; 143 LT 444   **2-60**

Para.

Clare & Co. *v.* Dresdner Bank [1915] 2 KB 576; 84 LJKB
1443; 113 LT 93; 31 TLR 278; 21 Com Cas 62   2-12/13

Clark *v.* Pigot (1699) 1 Salk 126   4-3, 5-76

Clayton's Case (1816) 1 Mer 572; Chorley and Smart's
Leading Cases (5th ed.) 158
2-80/1, **2-85/6**, 2-87/98, 11-90, 11-136, 11-142,
11-144, 11-302, 11-359

Clements *v.* London and North Western Railway Co.
[1894] 2 QB 482; 63 LJQB 837; 70 LT 896; 10 TLR 539;
38 Sol Jo 562   11-40

Clifton Place Garage Ltd, *Re* [1970] Ch at p. 486; [1970]
1 All ER 353; 113 Sol Jo 895   11-328

Clough Mill Ltd *v.* Martin [1985] 1 WLR 111; [1984] 3 All
ER 982; (1984) 128 Sol Jo 850   11-321

Coldman *v.* Hill [1919] 1 KB 443; 88 LJKB 491; 120 LT
412; 35 TLR 146; 63 Sol Jo 166   10-84, 10-86

Cole *v.* Milsome [1951] 1 All ER 311; [1951] WN 49; 211
LT Jo 53; 6 LDB 171   5-17, 9-28

Coleman *v.* Bucks and Oxon Union Bank [1897] 2 Ch 243;
66 LJ Ch 564; 76 LT 684; 41 Sol Jo 491   6-57, 7-45

Collinson *v.* Lister (1855) 20 Beav 356   11-133

Commercial Banking Co. Ltd *v.* Hartigan and Others (1952)
86 ILTR 109   1-22

Commercial Banking Co. of Sydney Ltd *v.* R. H. Brown &
Co. [1972] ALJR 297: [1972] 2 Lloyd's Rep 360   10-69

Commissioners of the State Savings Bank of Victoria *v.*
Permewan Wright & Co. Ltd (1914) 19 CLR 457   1-22, 6-97

Commissioners of Taxation *v.* English, Scottish and
Australian Bank Ltd [1920] AC 683; 89 LJPC 181; 123
LT 34; 36 TLR 305; 3 LDB 220; Chorley and Smart's
Leading Cases (5th ed.) 26   1-67/8, 6-97

Company, *Re* a (No. 00175 of 1987) [1987] BCLC 467   11-332

Construction Ltd, T. W. *Re* [1954] 1 WLR 540; [1954] 1
All ER 744; 98 Sol Jo 216; 6 LD 423   11-350

Consumer and Industrial Press Ltd, *Re* [1988] BCLC 177;
[1988] PCC 436   11-330

Cooper *v.* Brayne (1858) 27 LJ Ex 446; 31 LTOS 265   3-48

Cory Brothers & Co. *v.* Mecca Turkish SS (Owners). The
Mecca [1897] AC 286; 66 LJP 86; 76 LT 579; 13 TLR 339   2-89

Coutts & Co. *v.* Irish Exhibition in London (1891) 7 TLR
313; 1 LDB 127   **11-438**

Para.

Crears *v.* Hunter (1887) 19 QBD 341; 56 LJQB 518; 57 LT
554   5-126

Crouch *v.* The Crédit Foncier Co. (1873) LR 8 QB 374; 42
LJQB 183; 29 LT 259   4-1, 5-107

Crumplin *v.* London Joint Stock Bank Ltd (1913) 30 TLR
99, 109 LT 856; 19 Com Cas 69; 3 LDB 69; Chorley and
Smart's *Leading Cases* (5th ed.) 147   6-107, **6-129**

Currie *v.* Misa (1875) LR 10 Ex 153; affirmed *sub. nom.*
Misa *v.* Currie (1876) 1 App Cas 554   5-181

Curtice *v.* London City and Midland Bank Ltd [1908] 1 KB
293; 77 LJKB 341; 98 LT 190; 24 TLR 176; 52 Sol Jo 130;
2 LDB 156; Chorley and Smart's *Leading Cases* (5th ed.)
101   **7-35**

Curwen *v.* Milburn (1889) 42 Ch D. 424; 62 LT 278   2-43

Cutbush *v.* Cutbush (1839) 1 Beav 184; 8 LJ Ch 175   11-183

Davidson *v.* Barclays Bank Ltd [1940] 1 All ER 316; 164 LT
25; 56 TLR 343; 84 Sol Jo 117; 5 LDB 232; Chorley and
Smart's *Leading Cases* (5th ed.) 106   2-146, 2-149

Debtor A. (No. 564 of 1949), *Re, Ex parte* Commissioners
of Customs and Excise *v.* Debtor [1950] Ch 282; [1950]
1 All ER 308; 66 TLR 313; 94 Sol Jo 113   11-59

Deeley *v.* Lloyds Bank Ltd [1912] AC 756; 81 LJ Ch 697;
107 LT 465; 29 TLR 1; 56 Sol Jo 734; 2 LDB 230; 3 LDB
26   2-78, 2-95

Derby & Co. Ltd *v.* Weldon (No. 1) [1989] 1 All ER 469   7-42F

Derby & Co. Ltd *v.* Weldon (No. 3) [1989] 1 All ER 1002;
[1989] 2 WLR 276; [1989] 1 Lloyd's Rep 122; (1989) 133
Sol Jo 83   7-42F

Derry *v.* Peek (1889) 14 App Cas 337; 58 LJ Ch 864; 61 LT
265   10-67

Deutsche Bank und Disconto-Gesellschaft *v.* Banque des
Marchands de Moscou (1931) 4 LDB 293   3-23

Devaynes *v.* Noble (1816) 1 Mer 529; Chorley and Smart's
Leading Cases (5th ed.) 158   2-5

Devitt *v.* Kearney (1883) 13 LR Ir 45   11-187

Dickie *v.* Singh, 1974 SLT (Notes) 3   9-44

Director of Public Prosecutions *v.* Turner [1974] AC 357;
[1973] 3 All ER 124; 117 Sol Jo 664   1-70

Para.

District Savings Bank, *Re, Ex parte* Coe (1861) 31 LJ Bank
8; 3 De GF & J 335; 5 LT 566   1-19, 1-22

Douglass *v*. Lloyds Bank Ltd (1929) 34 Com Cas 263; 4
LDB 220; Chorley and Smart's *Leading Cases* (5th ed.)
175   **2-30**

Down *v*. Halling (1825) 4 B & C 330   6-54

Dowse *v*. Gorton [1891] AC 190; 60 LJ Ch 745; 64 LT 809   11-186

Drew *v*. Nunn (1879) 4 QBD 661; 48 LJQB 591; 40 LT 671
    3-31, 3-34, 11-24

Dunnicliffe *v*. Johnson and another (1934) *Journal of the
Institute of Bankers*, Vol. LV, p. 129   **10-126**

Durham Fancy Goods Ltd *v*. Michael Jackson (Fancy
Goods) Ltd and another [1968] 3 WLR 225; [1968] 2 All
ER 987   5-188

Dutton *v*. Marsh (1871) LR 6 QB 361; 40 LJQB 175; 24 LT
470   5-186

Eaglehill Ltd *v*. J. Needham Builders Ltd [1972] 2 QB 8;
[1972] 1 All ER 417; [1972] 1 Lloyd's Rep 128; 116 Sol
Jo 95; reversed [1973] AC 992; [1972] 3 All ER 895; 122
NLJ 990   8-75

East, *Re, Re* Bellwood's Will Trusts (1873) 8 Ch App 735;
42 LJ Ch 480   11-226

East, *Re*, London County and Westminster Banking Co.
Ltd *v*. East (1914) 111 LT 101; 58 Sol Jo 513   11-186

Eckman and others *v*. Midland Bank Ltd and another
[1973] 1 QB 519; [1973] ICR 71; [1973] 1 All ER 609;
[1973] 1 Lloyd's Rep 162   **3-81**

Edelstein *v*. Schuler & Co. [1902] 2 KB 144; 71 LJKB 572;
97 LT 204; 18 TLR 597; 46 Sol Jo 500   4-13

Elawadi *v*. Bank of Credit and Commerce International SA
[1989] 1 All ER 242; [1989] 3 WLR 220   **4-11B**

Elliott *v*. Bax-Ironside [1925] 2 KB 301; 94 LJKB 807; 133
LT 624; 41 TLR 631   5-184, 5-186

Ellis *v*. Pond [1898] 1 QB 426; 67 LJQB 345; 78 LT 125;
14 TLR 152   6-141

Emerson *v*. American Express Co. (1952) 90 *Atlantic
Reporter*, 2nd series, 236; 6 LDB 337   4-11

Employers' Liability Assurance Corporation *v*. Skipper &
East (1887) 4 TLR 55   5-80

Ertel Bieber & Co. *v*. Rio Tinto Co. Ltd [1918] AC 260; 87
LJKB 531; 118 LT 181; 34 TLR 208   3-82

Etlin (H.B.) Co. Ltd *v*. Asselstyne (1962) 34 DLD (2d) 191   5-187

Para.

Evans (D.B.) (Bilston) Ltd *v.* Barclays Bank Ltd (1961) *The Times*, 17 February; 7 LDB 283   **11-352**

Farley *v.* Turner (1857) 26 LJ Ch 710; 29 LTOS 257; 3 Jur NS 532   2-79

Farrow *v.* Wilson (1869) LR 4 CP 744; 38 LJCP 326; 20 LT 810   3-15

Fern *v.* Bishop & Co. Ltd and another (1980) *Guardian Gazette*, 26 November; Chorley and Smart's *Leading Cases* (5th ed.) 84   3-64

Fernandey *v.* Glynn (1808) 1 Camp 426 n.   6-3

Fine Art Society Ltd *v.* The Union Bank of London Ltd (1886) 17 QBD 705; 56 LJQB 70; 55 LT 536; 2 TLR 883; LDB 70   4-16, **6-49**, 6-132, 9-66

Fisher *v.* Roberts (1890) 6 TLR 354   5-42

Fisher *v.* Tayler (1843) 2 Hare 218; on appeal, 2 LTOS 205   11-105

Flach *v.* London and South Western Bank Ltd (1915) 31 TLR 334; 3 LDB 123   2-145, 1-150

Flanders *v.* Clarke (1747) 3 Atk 509; 1 Ves Sen 9   11-188

Flower (C.) and Metropolitan Board of Works, *Re, Re* M. Flower and Metropolitan Board of Works (1844) 27 Ch D 592; 53 LJ Ch 955; 51 LT 257   11-204

Foley *v.* Hill (1848) 2 HL Cas 28; Chorley and Smart's *Leading Cases* (5th ed.) 1   **2-6**, 2-9, 2-11

Forman *v.* Bank of England (1902) 18 TLR 339; 2 LDB 21   **6-29**

Foster *v.* Bank of London (1862) 3 F & F 214   2-99

Foster *v.* Mackinnon (1869) LR 4 CP 704; 38 LJCP 310; 20 LT 887   **5-154**, 5-115

Foxton *v.* Manchester and Liverpool District Banking Co. (1881) 44 LT 406   7-45

Freeman and Lockyer *v.* Buckhurst Park Properties (Mangal) Ltd [1964] 2 QB 480; [1964] 1 All ER 630; 108 Sol Jo 96; Chorley and Smart's *Leading Cases* (5th ed.) 203   11-293

Friend *v.* Young [1897] 2 Ch 421; *sub nom. Re* Friend, Friend, *v.* Friend (Young), 66 LJ Ch 737; 77 LT 50; 41 Sol Jo 607   2-77

Frixione *v.* Tagliaferro & Sons (1856) 10 Moo PCC 175; 27 LTOS 21   6-140

Garnett *v.* M'Kewan (1872) LR 8 Ex 10; 42 LJ Ex 1; 27 LT 560; 21 WR 57   **2-61**

Garrett *v.* Noble (1834) 6 Sim 504; 3 LJ Ch 159   11-183

Para.

General Auction Estate and Monetary Co. *v.* Smith [1891]
3 Ch 432; 60 LJ Ch 723; 65 LT 188   11-278, 11-372

General Estates Co., *Re, Ex parte* City Bank (1868) LR 3
Ch App 758; 18 LT 894   11-372

Gibbon *v.* Budd (1863) 2 H & C 92; 32 LJ Ex 182; 8 LT 321   2-47

Gibbons *v.* Westminster Bank Ltd [1939] 2 KB 882; [1939]
3 All ER 577; 108 LJKB 841; 161 LT 61; 55 TLR 888; 83
Sol Jo 674; 5 LDB 219   **2-143/4**

Giblin *v.* McMullen (1896) LR 2 PC 317; 38 LJPC 25; 21 LT
214; Chorley and Smart's *Leading Cases* (5th ed.) 329   10-81

Gillman *v.* Gillman (1946) 174 LT 272   5-155

Glynn *v.* Margetson & Co. [1893] AC 351; 62 LJQB 466;
69 LT 1; 9 TLR 437   9-41

Goodman *v.* J. Eban Ltd [1954] 1 QB 550; [1954] 1 All ER
763; 98 SJ 214   5-14

Gore *v.* Gibson (1845) 13 M & W 623; 14 LJ Ex 151   5-142

Gorgier *v.* Mieville (1824) 3 B & C 45   4-13

Grant *v.* United Kingdom Switchback Railways Co. (1880)
40 Ch D 135; 58 LJ Ch 211; 60 LT 525   11-291

Grant *v.* Vaughan (1764) 3 Burr 1516   5-5

Gray *v.* Johnston (1868) LR 3 HL 1; Chorley and Smart's
Leading Cases (5th ed.) 166   7-44, 11-193, 11-230

Gray's Inn Construction Co. Ltd, *Re*, [1980] 1 WLR 711;
[1980] 1 All ER 814   **11-359**

Great Western Railway Co. *v.* London and County Banking
Co. Ltd [1899] 2 QB 172; on appeal [1900] 2 QB 464; 69
LJQB 741; 82 LT 746; 16 TLR 453; 5 Com Cas 282;
reversed [1901] AC 414; 70 LJKB 915, 85 LT 152; 17
TLR 700; 45 Sol Jo 690; 6 Com Cas 275; 2 LDB 10;
Chorley and Smart's *Leading Cases* (5th ed.) 26
     1-66/7, 5-45, 6-61/2, 6-107

Green *v.* Whitehead [1930] 1 Ch 38; 99 LJ Ch 153; 142 LT
1; 46 TLR 11; 4 LDB 228   11-209

Greenhalgh (W.P.) and Sons *v.* Union Bank of Manchester
[1924] 2 KB 153; 93 LJKB 844; 131 LT 637; 3 LDB 341
     2-61, 2-68, 2-79, **2-84**

Greenwood *v.* Martins Bank Ltd [1932] 1 KB 371; 101
LJKB 33; 146 LT 32; 47 TLR 607; 37 Com Cas 1, CA; affirmed [1933] AC 51; 101 LJKB 623; 147 LT 441; 48 TLR
601; 76 Sol Jo 544; 38 Com Cas 54, HL; 4 LDB 337;
Chorley and Smart's *Leading Cases* (5th ed.) 98
     2-18, **2-128**, 2-131, 5-146, 7-12

Para.

Gregory-Salisbury Metal Products, Inc. *v.* Whitney National Bank (1964) 160 So 2d 813   6-78

Griffiths *v.* Dalton [1940] 2 KB 264; 109 LJKB 656; 163 LT 359; 56 TLR 784; 84 SJ 467; 5 LDB 247; Chorley and Smart's *Leading Cases* (5th ed.) 59   5-18, 7-14

Grose (George) Ltd, *Re* (1969) *The Financial Times*, 23 May   11-357

Gross, *Re, Ex parte* Adair (1871) 24 LT 198; affirmed *sub. nom. Re* Gross, *Ex parte* Kingston (1871) 6 Ch App 632; 25 LT 250; Chorley and Smart's *Leading Cases* (5th ed.) 162   2-69, 7-44

Guerrine (otherwise Roberts) *v.* Guerrine [1959] 1 WLR 760; [1959] 2 All ER 594; 103 Sol Jo 678   3-81

Gurney *v.* Behrend (1854) 3 E & B 622; 23 LJQB 265; 23 LTOS 89; 18 Jur 856; 2 WR 425   4-17

Hadley (Felix) & Co. Ltd *v.* Hadley [1898] 2 Ch 680; 67 LJ Ch 694; 79 LT 299   5-181

Halifax Union *v.* Wheelwright (1875) LR 10 Ex 183; 44 LJ Ex 121; 32 LT 802   1-19, 1-22

Hall (William) (Contractors) Ltd, *Re* [1967] 1 WLR 948; [1967] 2 All ER 1150; 111 Sol Jo 472   **11-307**

Hallett's Estate *Re*, Knatchbull *v.* Hallett (1880) 13 Ch D 696; 49 LJ Ch 415; 42 LT 421; Chorley and Smart's *Leading Cases* (5th ed.) 170   2-88

Halstead *v.* Patel [1972] 1 WLR 661; [1972] 2 All ER 147; 116 Sol Jo 218   **1-69**

Hamilton Finance Co. Ltd *v.* Coverley Westray Walbaum & Tosetti Ltd and Portland France Co. Ltd [1969] 1 Lloyd's Rep 53   8-76

Hampstead Guardians *v.* Barclays Bank Ltd (1923) 39 TLR 229; 67 Sol Jo 440; 3 LDB 282   **11-6/7**

Hancock *v.* Smith (1889) 41 Ch D 456; 58 LJ Ch 725; 61 LT 341; 5 TLR 459   3-76

Hannan's Lake View Central Ltd *v.* Armstrong & Co. (1900) 16 TLR 236; 5 Com Cas 188; 1 LDB 301   6-119

Harding *v.* London Joint Stock Bank Ltd (1914) *The Times*, 21 January; 3 LDB 81   **11-15**

Hardy *v.* Veasey (1868) LR 3 Exch 107; 37 LJ Ex 76; 17 LT 607   2-99

Hare *v.* Henty (1861) 10 CB (NS) 65; 30 LJCP 302; 4 LT 363; 7 Jur NS 523; 25 JP 678   6-32

Para.

Harris Simons Construction Ltd, *Re* [1989] 1 WLR 368;
  [1989] BCLC 202; [1989] PCC 229; (1989) 133 Sol Jo 122   **11-330**
Harrison *v.* Jackson (1797) 7 Term Rep 207   11-105
Harrods *v.* Tester [1937] 2 All ER 236; 157 LT 7; 81 Sol Jo
  376; 5 LDB 31   3-76
Hay *v.* Ayling (1851) 16 QB 423; 20 LJQB 171   5-166
Hedley *v.* Bainbridge (1842) 3 QB 316; 2 Gal & Dav 483; 11
  LJQB 293   11-105
Hedley Byrne & Co. Ltd *v.* Heller & Partners Ltd (1960)
  The Times, 21 December, McNair, J; [1962] 1 QBD 396,
  CA; [1964] AC 465; [1963] 2 All ER 575; 107 Sol Jo 454;
  [1963] 1 Lloyd's Rep 485; 8 LDB 155   2-121, 10-52, 10-53, **10-65**
Helson *v.* McKenzies Ltd [1950] NZLR 878   6-135
Hely-Hutchinson *v.* Brayhead Ltd [1968] 1 QB 549; [1967]
  2 All ER 14; 111 Sol Jo 329; affirmed [1968] 1 QB 573;
  [1967] 3 All ER 98; 111 Sol Jo 830   11-293
Heppenstall *v.* Jackson, Barclays Bank Ltd, Garnishees
  [1939] 1 KB 585; [1939] 2 All ER 10, 108 LJKB 266; 160
  LT 261; 55 TLR 489; 83 Sol Jo 276; 5 LDB 197   3-59
Hibernian Bank Ltd *v.* Gysin and Hanson [1939] 1 KB 483;
  [1939] 1 All ER 166; 108 LJKB 214; 160 LT 233; 55 TLR
  347; 83 Sol Jo 113; 44 Com Cas 115; 5 LDB 194   5-42
Hirschorn *v.* Evans, Barclays Bank Ltd, Garnishees [1938]
  2 KB 801; [1938] 3 All ER 491; 107 LJKB 756; 159 LT
  405; 54 TLR 1069; 82 Sol Jo 664; 5 LDB 155   3-71, 11-95
Hirst *v.* West Riding Banking Co. Ltd [1901] 2 KB 560; 70
  LJKB 828; 85 LT 3; 17 LTR 629   **10-69**
Hodgson, *Re*, Beckett *v.* Ramsdale (1885) 31 Ch D 177; 55
  LJ Ch 241; 54 LT 222; 34 WR 127; 2 TLR 73   9-49
Hodson, *Re, Ex parte* Richardson (1818) 3 Madd 138; Buck
  202; affirmed (1819) Buck 421   11-183
Holland *v.* Manchester and Liverpool Banking Co. Ltd
  (1909) 14 Com Cas 241; 25 TLR 386; 2 LDB 221; Chorley
  and Smart's *Leading Cases* (5th ed.) 155   2-134
Holland *v.* Russell (1863) 4 B & S 14; 32 LJQB 297; 8 LT 468   6-52
Holt *v.* Markham [1923] 1 KB 504; 92 LJKB 406; 128 LT
  719; 67 Sol Jo 314; 3 LDB 293   2-134
Houghland *v.* R. R. Low (Luxury Coaches) Ltd [1962] 1
  QB 694; [1962] 2 All ER 159; 106 Sol Jo 243; 8 LDB 48   **10-82**
Houghton & Co. *v.* Nothard, Lowe and Wills Ltd [1927] 1
  KB 246; 96 LJKB 25; 136 LT 140; affirmed [1928] AC 1;
  97 LJKB 76; 138 LT 210; 44 TLR 76; 4 LDB 133   11-293, 11-297
House Property Co. of London Ltd *v.* London County and

Para.

Westminster Bank (1915) 84 LJKB 1846; 113 LT 817; 31
TLR 479; 3 LDB 126; Chorley and Smart's *Leading Cases*
(5th ed.) 145   **6-109**

Howard *v.* Beall (1889) 23 QBD 1; 58 LJQB 384; 60 LT 637   2-104

Howatson *v.* Webb [1907] 1 Ch 537; affirmed [1908] 1 Ch
1; 77 LJ Ch 32; 97 LT 730; 52 Sol Jo 11   5-155

Howes *v.* Bishop [1909] 2 KB 390; 78 LJKB 796; 100 LT
826; 25 TLR 533   5-162

Hughes (C. W. and A. L.) Ltd, *Re* [1966] 1 WLR 1369;
[1966] 2 All ER 702; 110 Sol Jo 404; 116 LJ 836   11-305

Husband *v.* Davis (1851) 10 CB 645; 2 LM & P 50; 20 LJCP
118   11-70

Hussey *v.* Jacob (1696) 1 Comyns 4   4-6

Hutley *v.* Peacock (1913) 30 TLR 42   5-139, 11-44

Imperial Loan Co. Ltd *v.* Stone [1892] 1 QB 599; 61 LJQB
499; 66 LT 556   5-141

Importers Co. Ltd *v.* Westminster Bank Ltd [1927] 2 KB
297; 96 LJKB 919; 137 LT 693; 43 TLR 639; 32 Com Cas
369; 4 LDB 118   1-69, 6-110, 6-138

International Sales and Agencies Ltd. *v.* Marcus [1982] 3
All ER 551; Chorley and Smart's *Leading Cases* (5th ed.)
73   11-279

Introductions Ltd *v.* National Provincial Bank Ltd [1968]
2 All ER 1221; on appeal [1970] Ch 199; [1969] 1 All ER
887; 113 Sol Jo 122   **11-281**

Jackson *v.* White and Midland Bank Ltd [1967] 2 Lloyd's
Rep 68   11-71

Jacobs *v.* Morris [1902] 1 Ch 816; 71 LJ Ch 363; 86 LT 275;
18 TLR 384; 46 Sol Jo 315   11-21

Jayson *v.* Midland Bank Ltd [1967] 2 Lloyd's Rep 563;
[1968] 1 Lloyd's Rep 409 CA   2-150

Jeffryes *v.* Agra and Masterman's Bank Ltd (1866) 35 LJ Ch
686; LR 2 Eq 674; 35 LJ Ch 686; 14 WR 889   2-66

Jenkin *v.* Pharmaceutical Society of Great Britain [1921] 1
Ch 392; 90 LJ Ch 47; 124 LT 309; 37 LTR 54; 65 Sol Jo
116   11-312

Jeune *v.* Ward (1818) 1 B & Ald 653   8-49

Joachimson *v.* Swiss Bank Corporation [1921] 3 KB 110; 90
LJKB 973; 125 LT 338; 37 TLR 534; 65 Sol Jo 434; 26
Com Cas 196, CA; 3 LDB 233; Chorley and Smart's
Leading Cases (5th ed.) 1   2-10/13, **2-27**, 2-35, 2-41, 3-7, 3-67

Para.

Jones *v.* Gordon (1877) 2 App Cas 616; 37 LT 477   5-121

Jones *v.* Merionethshire Building Society [1892] 1 Ch 173;
61 LJ Ch 138; 65 LT 685   5-165

Jones & Co. *v.* Coventry [1909] 2 KB 1029; 79 LJKB 41; 101
LT 281; 25 TLR 736; 53 Sol Jo 734   3-64

Jones (R.E.) Ltd *v.* Waring and Gillow Ltd [1926] AC 670;
95 LJKB 913; 135 LT 548; 42 TLR 644; 70 Sol Jo 756; 32
Com Cas 8; 4 LDB 37   5-119, 5-178

K (Enduring Powers of Attorney), *In re* [1988] Ch 310;
[1988] 1 All ER 358; (1987) 137 Sol Jo 1488   **11-38G**

Kayford Ltd, *Re* [1975] 1 WLR 279; [1975] 1 All ER 604;
118 Sol Jo 752   2-60A

Keene *v.* Beard (1860) 8 CB (NS) 372; 29 LJCP 287; 6 Jur
(NS) 1248; LT 240   5-5, 7-68

Keever, A Bankrupt, *Re, Ex parte* the Trustee of the Property of the Bankrupt *v.* Midland Bank Ltd [1967] Ch 182;
[1966] 3 All ER 631; [1966] 2 Lloyd's Rep 475; 110 Sol
Jo 847   6-41

Kepitigalla Rubber Estates Ltd *v.* National Bank of India
Ltd [1909] 2 KB 1010; 78 LJKB 964; 100 LT 516; 25 TLR
402; 53 Sol Jo 377; 14 Com Cas 116; 2 LDB 186   2-137

Kettle *v.* Dunster and Wakefield (1927) 43 TLR 770; 138 LT
158   5-187

King and Boyd *v.* Porter [1925] NI 107   5-133, 7-97

Kingston, *Ex parte, see* Gross *Re, Ex parte* Kingston

Kleinwort, Sons & Co. *v.* Comptoir National D'Escompte
de Paris [1894] 2 QB 157; 63 LJQB 674; 10 TLR 424; 1
LDB 198   6-49

Knight and Searle *v.* Dove [1964] 2 QB 631; [1963] 2 All ER
307; 108 Sol Jo 320   1-4

Koch *v.* Mineral Ore Syndicate, London and South Western
Bank Ltd, Garnishees (1910) 54 Sol Jo 600; 2 LDB 264   3-57

Kreditbank Cassel GmbH *v.* Schenkers Ltd [1927] 1 KB
826; 96 LJKB 501; 136 LT 716; 43 TLR 237; 71 Sol Jo
141; 32 Com Cas 197; 4 LDB 64   11-293, 11-297

Krige *v.* Willemse (1908) 25 Cape SC 180   5-155

Kulatilleke *v.* Mercantile Bank of India (1958) 59 Ceylon
NLR 190; 7 LDB 166   2-125

Kymer *v.* Laurie (1849) 18 LJQB 218; 13 Jur 426   8-139

Lacave & Co. *v.* Crédit Lyonnais [1897] 1 QB 148; 66 LJQB
226; 75 LT 514; 13 TLR 60; 2 Com Cas 17; 1 LDB 245   1-67, 6-49

Ladbroke *v.* Todd (1914) 111 LT 43; 30 TLR 433; 19 Com Cas 256; 3 LDB 89   1-68, 6-103, **11-5**

Lamprell *v.* Guardians of Billericay Union (1849) 3 Exch 283; 18 LJ Ex 282   2-77

Lancaster Motor Company (London) Ltd *v.* Bremith Ltd, Barclays Bank Ltd, Garnishees [1941] 1 KB 675; [1941] 2 All ER 11; 110 LJKB 398; 165 LT 134; 57 TLR 418; 5 LDB 310   3-74

Landes *v.* Marcus and Davids (1909) 25 TLR 478; 2 LDB 203   **5-186/7**

Langtry *v.* Union Bank of London (1896) *Journal of the Institute of Bankers*, Vol XVII, p. 338; 1 LDB 229   **10-80**

Lazarus Estates Ltd *v.* Beasley [1956] 1 QB 703; [1956] 1 All ER 341; 100 Sol Jo 131   5-14

Leadbitter *v.* Farrow (1816) 5 M & S 345   5-185

Lemann's Trust, *Re* (1883) 22 Ch D 633; 52 LJ Ch 560; 48 LT 389   11-226

Leonard *v.* Wilson (1834) 2 Cr & M 589; 3 LJ Ex 171   5-84

Leslie (R.) Ltd *v.* Sheill [1914] 3 KB 607; 83 LJKB 1145; 111 LT 106; 30 TLR 460; 58 Sol Jo 453; Chorley and Smart's *Leading Cases* (5th ed.) 179   11-48

Levy (A.I.) (Holdings) Ltd, *Re* [1964] Ch 19; [1963] 2 All ER 556; 107 Sol Jo 416   **11-334**

Lewes Sanitary Steam Laundry Co. Ltd *v.* Barclay, Bevan & Co. Ltd (1906) 11 Com Cas 255; 95 LT 444; 22 TLR 737   2-137

Lewis *v.* Alleyne (1888) 4 TLR 560   11-51

Lilley *v.* Rankin (1886) 56 LJQB 248; 55 LT 814   **5-167**

Lipkin Gorman *v.* Karpnale Ltd and Lloyds Bank plc [1987] 1 WLR 987; [1986] FLR 271; reversed in part [1988] 6 JIBL N-209; [1989] FLR 137   **7-45A**

Lloyd *v.* Grace Smith & Co. [1912] AC 716; 81 LJKB 1140; 107 LT 531; 28 TLR 547; 56 Sol Jo 723   10-89

Lloyds Bank Ltd *v.* Brooks (1950) *Journal of the Institute of Bankers*, Vol. LXXII, p. 114; 6 LDB 161   **2-134**

Lloyds Bank Ltd *v.* The Chartered Bank of India, Australia and China [1929] 1 KB 40; 97 LJKB 609; 139 LT 126; 44 TLR 534; 33 Com Cas 306; 4 LDB 171; Chorley and Smart's *Leading Cases* (5th ed.) 132   6-48, 6-53, 6-96, 6-100, **6-117**

Lloyds Bank Ltd *v.* Dolphin (1920) *The Times*, 2 December; 3 LDB 230   6-35

Lloyds Bank Ltd *v.* Hornby (1933) *The Financial Times*, 5 July; *Journal of the Institute of Bankers*, Vol. LIV, p. 372   6-39

Para.

Lloyds Bank Ltd *v*. Margolis and others [1954] 1 WLR 644;
[1954] 1 All ER 734; 98 Sol Jo 250; 6 LDB 416; Chorley
and Smart's *Leading Cases* (5th ed.) 291 **2-41**

Lloyds Bank Ltd *v*. E. B. Savory and Co. [1933] AC 201;
102 LJKB 224; 148 LT 291; 49 TLR 116; 38 Com Cas
115; 44 LlL Rep 231; 4 LDB 368; Chorley and Smart's
Leading Cases (5th ed.) 124
6-94/5, 6-98, 6-100, 6-103, 6-112/13, **6-116**, 6-133, 11-11

London and County Banking Co. *v*. Groome (1881) 8 QBD
288; 51 LJQB 224; 46 LT 60; LDB 40 5-114

London and Montrose Shipbuilding and Repairing Co. Ltd
v. Barclays Bank Ltd (1926) 31 Com Cas 67; (on appeal)
31 Com Cas 182; 4 LDB 31 6-120

London and Provincial Bank *v*. Golding (1918) 3 LDB 161 9-68

London City and Midland Bank Ltd *v*. Gordon [1903] AC
240; 72 LJKB 451; 88 LT 574; 19 TLR 462; 2 LDB 35;
Chorley and Smart's *Leading Cases* (5th ed.) 35
4-10, 6-66, 7-58, 7-59, 9-22

London Joint Stock Bank *v*. Macmillan and Arthur [1918]
AC 777; 119 LT 387; 34 TLR 509; 62 Sol Jo 650, HL; 3
LDB 165; Chorley and Smart's *Leading Cases* (5th ed.) 75
2-13, 2-16, **2-125**, 7-18, 7-20

London Provincial and South-Western Bank Ltd *v*. Buszard
(1918) 35 TLR 142; 63 Sol Jo 246; 3 LDB 204 7-33

Lovell and Christmas *v*. Beauchamp [1894] AC 607; 63
LJQB 802; 71 LT 587 11-54

Lumsden & Co. *v*. London Trustee Savings Bank [1971] 1
Lloyd's Rep 114 6-135, 11-10

Macdonald *v*. North of Scotland Bank, 1942 SC 369 2-28

McDonald (Gerald) & Co. *v*. Nash & Co. [1924] AC 625;
93 LJKB 610; 131 LT 428; 40 TLR 530; 68 Sol Jo 594; 29
Com Cas 313; 3 LDB 331 7-68

M'Lean *v*. Clydesdale Banking Co. (1883) 9 App Cas 95; 50
LT 457; 1 LDB 53 **6-40**

McEvoy *v*. Belfast Banking Co. Ltd [1935] AC 24; 103
LJPC 137; 151 LT 501; 40 Com Cas 1; 4 LDB 447;
Chorley and Smart's *Leading Cases* (5th ed.) 184 **11-84**, 11-88

M'Neillie *v*. Acton (1853) 4 De GM & G 744; 23 LJ Ch 11;
22 LTOS 111 11-187

Manches *v*. Trimborn [1946] WN 62; 115 LJKB 305; 174
LT 344; 90 Sol Jo 223 5-141

Manning *v*. Westerne (1707) 2 Vern 606 2-76

Para.

Marchant *v.* Morton Down & Co. [1901] 2 KB 829; 70
LJKB 820; 85 LT 169; 17 TLR 640   11-105

Mareva Compania Naviera SA *v.* International Bulkcarriers
SA [1975] 2 Lloyd's Rep 509; also reported in a Note at
[1980] 1 All ER 213; Chorley and Smart's *Leading Cases*
(5th ed.) 86   **7-42A**

Marfani & Co. Ltd *v.* Midland Bank Ltd [1968] 1 WLR
956; [1968] 2 All ER 573; [1968] 1 Lloyd's Rep 411; 112
Sol Jo 396   6-95, 6-98, 6-100A, **11-10**

Marryatts *v.* White (1817) 2 Stark 101   2-76

Marshal *v.* Crutwell (1875) LR 20 Eq 328; 44 LJ Ch 504   11-87

Martin *v.* Gale (1876) 4 Ch D 428; 46 LJ Ch 84; 36 LT 357   11-51

Master *v.* Miller (1791) 4 TR 320; affirmed 5 TR 367   5-147

Matthews *v.* Williams, Brown & Co. (1894) 63 LJQB 494;
10 TLR 386; 1 LDB 200   1-67/8

May *v.* Chapman (1847) 16 M & W 355; 8 LTSO 369   5-121/2

Mellon National Bank *v.* Citizens Bank & Trust Co. 8 Cir.
1937, 88 F. 2d 128   4-11

Mersey Steel and Iron Co. *v.* Naylor, Benzon & Co. (1884)
9 App Cas 434; 53 LJQB 497; 51 LT 637; 32 WR 989
    2-60, 11-329, 11-353

Metropolitan Police Commissioner *v.* Charles [1977] AC
177; [1976] 3 All ER 112; 120 Sol Jo 588   10-44A

Meyappan *v.* Manchanayake [1961] Ceylon NLR 529   5-14

Midland Bank Ltd *v.* Charles Simpson Motors Ltd (1961)
Journal of the Institute of Bankers, Vol. 82, p. 38; 7 LDB
251   6-39

Midland Bank Ltd *v.* Conway Corporation [1965] 1 WLR
1165; [1965] 2 All ER 972; 109 SJ 494; 8 LDB 416   2-7

Midland Bank Ltd *v.* R. V. Harris Ltd [1963] 1 WLR 1021;
[1963] 2 All ER 685; 8 LDB 150   5-61, 6-39

Midland Bank Ltd *v.* Reckitt [1933] AC 1; 102 LJKB 297;
148 LT 374; 48 TLR 271; 76 Sol Jo 165; 37 Com Cas 202;
4 LDB 298; Chorley and Smart's *Leading Cases* (5th ed.)
137   5-121, 6-94, **6-105**

Midland Bank plc *v.* Shephard [1988] 3 All ER 17; [1988]
BTLC 395   **11-93A**

Miller *v.* Huddlestone (1882) 22 Ch D 233; 52 LJ Ch 208;
47 LT 570   3-81

Miller *v.* Mynn (1859) 1 E & E 1075; 28 LJQB 324; 33 LTOS
184   11-95

Mills *v.* Fowkes (1839) 5 Bing NC 455; 7 Scott 444; 8 LJCP
276; 3 Jur 406   2-77

Para.

Molton *v.* Camroux (1849) 4 Ex 17; 18 LJ Ex 356   5-142

Momm *v.* Barclays Bank International Ltd [1977] QB 790;
[1977] 2 WLR 407; [1976] 3 All ER 588; (1976) 120 Sol
Jo 486; [1976] 2 Lloyd's Rep 341; Chorley and Smart's
Leading Cases (5th ed.) 97   3-65

Moore *v.* Mourgue (1776) 2 Cowp 479   10-81

Morel (E.J.) (1934) Ltd, *Re* [1962] 1 Ch 21; [1961] 1 All
ER 796; 105 Sol Jo 156; 7 LDB 272   **2-91**, 1-304

Morison *v.* London County and Westminster Bank Ltd
[1914] 3 KB 356; 83 LJKB 1202; 111 LT 114; 30 TLR 481;
58 Sol Jo 453; 19 Com Cas 273; 3 LDB 91; Chorley and
Smart's *Leading Cases* (5th ed.) 133   5-45

Morris *v.* Kanssen [1946] AC 459; [1946] 1 All ER 586; 115
LJ Ch 177; 174 LT 353; 62 TLR 306   11-292

Mortimer (Thomas) Ltd, *Re* (1925) reported in a Note in
[1965] Ch 186; 4 LDB 3   2-97A

Motor Traders Guarantee Corporation Ltd *v.* Midland
Bank Ltd [1937] 4 All ER 90; 157 LT 498; 54 TLR 10; 81
Sol Jo 865; 5 LDB 68; Chorley and Smart's *Leading
Cases* (5th ed.) 138   **6-125**

Nash *v.* Hodgson (1855) 6 De GM & G 474; 25 LJ Ch 186;
1 Jur (NS) 946   2-76

Nash *v.* Inman [1908] 2 KB 1; 77 LJKB 626; 98 LT 658; 24
TLR 401; 52 Sol Jo 335   11-40

Nathan *v.* Ogdens Ltd (1905) 94 LT 126; 22 TLR 57   9-35

National Bank *v.* Silke [1891] 1 QB 435; 60 LJQB 199; 63
LT 787; 1 LDB 118   5-48, 5-71, **6-39**, 6-111

National Bank of New Zealand *v.* Grace (1890) 8 NZLR 706   2-61

National Bank of South Africa Ltd *v.* Paterson [1909]
Transvaal L.R. Part II, p. 322   5-73

National Permanent Benefit Building Society, *Re, Ex parte*
Williamson (1869) 5 Ch App 309; 22 LT 284   11-51, 11-279

National Provincial Bank Ltd *v.* Freedman and Rubens
(1934) *Journal of the Institute of Bankers*, Vol. LV, p.
392; 4 LDB 44; Chorley and Smart's *Leading Cases* (5th
ed.) 377   2-98, 11-303

National Westminster Bank Ltd *v.* Barclays Bank International Ltd [1975] QB 654; [1974] 3 All ER 834; [1974]
2 Lloyd's Rep 506; 118 Sol Jo 627   7-12

National Westminster Bank Ltd *v.* Halesowen Presswork
and Assemblies Ltd [1972] AC 785; [1972] 1 All ER 641;
[1972] 1 Lloyd's Rep 101; 122 NLJ 105; 116 Sol Jo 1383   2-60

Para.

Nimemia Maritime Corporation *v.* Trave Schiffahrtsgesellschaft mbH & Co., KG, The Niedersachen
[1984] 1 All ER 398; [1983] 1 WLR 1412   7-42E

North and South Insurance Corporation Ltd *v.* National
Provincial Bank Ltd [1936] 1 KB 328; 105 LJKB 163; 154
LT 255; 52 TLR 71; 80 Sol Jo 111; 41 Com Cas 80; 4 LDB
489   5-17, 9-26, 9-32

Norton *v.* Ellam (1837) 2 M & W 461; 6 LJ Ex 121   2-23, 2-35

Nottingham Permanent Benefit Building Society *v.*
Thurstan [1903] AC 6; 72 LJ Ch 134; 87 LT 529; 19 TLR
54   11-49

Nu-Stilo Footwear Ltd *v.* Lloyds Bank Ltd (1956) *The
Times*, 19 June; *Journal of the Institute of Bankers*, Vol.
77, p. 239; 7 LDB 121   6-103, 6-126, **11-8/9**

Oakeley *v.* Ooddeen (1861) 2 F & F 656   5-121

Ogden *v.* Benas (1874) LR 9 CP 513; 43 LJCP 259; 30 LT
683   6-54, **6-59/61**

Operator Control Cabs Ltd, *Re* [1970] 3 All ER 657n   11-358

Orbit Mining & Trading Co. Ltd *v.* Westminster Bank Ltd
[1963] 1 QB 794; [1962] 3 All ER 565; 106 SJ 937;
Chorley and Smart's *Leading Cases* (5th ed.) 36
    5-17, 6-98, 6-113, 6-132, 9-25/7, 9-29

Overweg, *Re*, Haas *v.* Durant [1901] 1 Ch 209; 69 LJ Ch
225; 81 LT 776; 16 TLR 70   3-24, 11-24

Oxley, *Re*, Hornby (John) & Sons *v.* Oxley [1914] 1 Ch 604;
83 LJ Ch 442; 110 LT 626; 30 TLR 327; 58 Sol Jo 319   11-186

Parker *v.* Marchant (1843) 1 Ph 356   2-5

Parr's Bank Ltd *v.* Thomas Ashby and Co. (1898) 14 TLR
563; 1 LDB 268   **7-48**

Parr's Banking Co. *v.* Yates [1898] 2 QB 460; 67 LJQB 851;
79 LT 321; 1 LDB 276   2-32

Parsons *v.* Barclay and Co. Ltd and Goddard (1910) 103 LT
196; 26 TLR 628; 2 LDB 248   2-118, 10-53, 10-59

Paul & Frank Ltd and another *v.* Discount Bank (Overseas)
Ltd and another [1967] Ch 348; [1966] 2 All ER 922; 110
Sol Jo 423   8-114

Penmount Estates Ltd *v.* National Provincial Bank Ltd
(1945) 173 LT 344; 89 Sol Jo 566; 5 LDB 418
    6-96, 6-107, 6-109, **6-121**

Pennington *v.* Crossley & Son (1897) 77 LT 43; 13 TLR 513;
1 LDB 249   5-32

Para.

Peters *v.* Anderson (1814) 5 Taunt 596; 1 Marsh 238   2-76

Plunkett *v.* Barclays Bank Ltd [1936] 2 KB 107; [1936] 1
All ER 653; 105 LJKB 379; 154 LT 465; 52 TLR 353; 80
Sol Jo 225; 4 LDB 495; Chorley and Smart's *Leading
Cases* (5th ed.) 79   2-146, **3-76/7**, 11-153, 11-164

Pollard, *Re*, Pollard *v.* Pollard [1902] WN 144; 87 LT 61;
18 TLR 717   3-81

Pollock *v.* Bank of New Zealand (1902) 20 NZLR 174   7-16

Pollock *v.* Garle [1898] 1 Ch 1; 66 LJ Ch 788; 77 LT 415;
14 TLR 16; 42 Sol Jo 32   2-104

Pool *v.* Pool (1889) 58 LJP 67; 61 LT 401   3-24, 11-24

Price *v.* Hong Kong Tea Co. (1861) 2 F & F 466   2-47

Primrose (Builders) Ltd, *Re* [1950] 1 Ch 561; [1950] 2 All
ER 334; 210 LT Jo 13; 66 (Pt. 2) TLR 99; 6 LDB 128 **2-98**, 11-303

Prince *v.* Oriental Bank (1878) 3 App Cas 325; 47 LJCP 42;
38 LT 41   6-3

Prinz Adalbert, The [1917] AC 586; 86 LJPC 165; 116 LT
802; 33 TLR 490; 61 Sol Jo 610   4-17

Produce Marketing Consortium Ltd, *Re* [1989] 3 All ER 1;
[1989] 1 WLR 745; (1989) 133 Sol Jo 945; [1989] BCLC
513   **11-361A**

Prosperity Ltd *v.* Lloyds Bank Ltd (1923) 39 TLR 372; 3
LDB 287; Chorley and Smart's *Leading Cases* (5th ed.)
338   **3-8/13**

Pyke *v.* Hibernian Bank Ltd [1950] IR 195; 6 LDB 33   2-146

R *v.* Andover Justices, *Ex parte* Rhodes (1980) *The Times*,
14 June   2-104

R *v.* Bevan (1987) 84 Cr App R 143   **10-44B**

R *v.* Bigg (1716) 1 Str 18; 2 East PC 882; 3 P Wms 419   5-81

R *v.* Crown Court of Manchester, *Ex parte* Taylor [1988]
2 All ER 769; [1988] 1 WLR 705   **2-107C**

R *v.* Davenport [1954] 1 All ER 602; [1954] 1 WLR 569;
98 Sol Jol 217   2-11

R *v.* Financial Intermediaries Managers and Brokers
Regulatory Association, *ex parte* Cochrane (1989) *The
Times*, 23 June   **1-87**

R *v.* Industrial Disputes Tribunal, *ex parte* East Anglian
Trustee Savings Bank [1954] 1 WLR 1093; [1954] 2 All
ER 730; 104 L Jo 586; 218 LT Jo 70; 98 Sol Jo 558   1-22

R *v.* Kinghorn [1908] 2 KB 949; 78 LJKB 33, 99 LT 794; 72
JP 478; 25 TLR 219; 21 Cox CC 727   1-59

Para.

R *v*. Kupfer [1915] 2 KB 321; 84 LJKB 1021; 112 LT 1138;
31 TLR 223   11-124

R *v*. Lambie [1982] AC 449; [1981] 2 All ER 776; Chorley
and Smart's *Leading Cases* (5th ed.) 215   10-46B

R *v*. Leicester Crown Court, *ex parte* Director of Public
Prosecutions [1987] 3 All ER 654; [1987] 1 WLR 1361;
131 Sol Jo 1390   **2-107B**

R *v*. Navvabi [1986] 3 All ER 102; [1986] 1 WLR 1311; 83
Cr App R 271   **10-44C**

Rama Corporation Ltd *v*. Proved Tin and General Investments Ltd [1952] 2 QB 147; [1952] 1 All ER 554;
[1952] 1 TLR 709; 96 Sol Jo 197   11-293

Rampgill Mill Ltd, *Re* [1967] Ch 1138; [1967] 1 All ER 56;
[1966] 2 Lloyd's Rep 527; 110 Sol Jo 130   2-98, **11-302**

Randleson, *Ex parte* (1833) 2 Deac & Ch 534   2-77

Raphael *v*. Bank of England (1855) 17 CB 161; 25 LJCP 33;
Chorley and Smart's *Leading Cases* (5th ed.) 92   5-121

Redmond *v*. Allied Irish Banks PLC [1987] 2 FTLR 264;
[1987] FLR 307   **6-142**

Rekstin *v*. Severo Sibirsko Gosudarstvennoe Akcionernoe
Obschestvo Komseverputj, and The Bank for Russian
Trade Ltd [1933] 1 KB 47; 102 LJKB 16; 147 LT 231; 48
TLR 578; 76 Sol Jo 494; 4 LDB 328   **3-65**

Republic of Haiti *v*. Duvalier [1989] 1 All ER 456; [1989]
2 WLR 261   7-42F

Richards *v*. Heather (1817) 1 B & Ald 29   9-50

Richardson *v*. Richardson, National Bank of India Ltd,
Garnishees [1927] P 228; 96 LJP 125; 137 LT 492; 43
TLR 631; 71 Sol Jo 695; 4 LDB 80   3-79

Robarts *v*. Tucker (1851) 16 QB 560; 20 LJQB 270; Chorley
and Smart's *Leading Cases* (5th ed.) 110   7-57, 8-140

Robinson *v*. Midland Bank Ltd (1925) 41 TLR 170; on
appeal, 402; 4 LDB 19   1-65, **11-2/4**

Robinson Printing Co. Ltd. *v*. Chic Ltd [1905] 2 Ch 123;
74 LJ Ch 399; 93 LT 262; 21 TLR 446   11-372

Rogers *v*. Whiteley [1898] AC 118; 61 LJQB 512; 66 LT
303; 8 TLR 418; 1 LDB 181; Chorley and Smart's
Leading Cases (5th ed.) 79   **3-49**

Rolin *v*. Steward (1854) 14 CB 595; 23 LJCP 148; 23 LTOS
114   **2-142**

Roscorla *v*. Thomas (1842) 3 QB 234; 11 LJQB 214; 6 Jur
929   **5-127**

Para.

Ross *v.* London County, Westminster, and Parr's Bank Ltd
[1919] 1 KB 678; 88 LJKB 927; 120 LT 636; 3 LDB 205;
Chorley and Smart's *Leading Cases* (5th ed.) 140   4-10, 6-123

Rouse *v.* Bradford Banking Co. Ltd [1894] AC 586; 63 LJ
Ch 890; 71 LT 522   2-13

Rowlandson *v.* National Westminster Bank Ltd [1978] 1
WLR 798; [1978] 3 All ER 370; [1978] 1 Lloyd's Rep
523; 122 Sol Jo 347   7-44, **11-231A**

Royal Bank of Ireland Ltd *v.* O'Rourke [1962] IR 159   6-32

Royal Bank of Scotland *v.* Christie (1840) 8 Cl & Fin 214   2-94

Royal Bank of Scotland *v.* Tottenham (1894) 2 QB 715; 64
LJQB 99; 71 LT 168; 10 TLR 569; 38 Sol Jo 615; 1 LDB
201   6-35

Royal British Bank *v.* Turquand (1856) 6 E & B 327;
Chorley and Smart's *Leading Cases* (5th ed.) 203
    11-284, 11-292/4

Russian Commercial and Industrial Bank, *Re* [1955] 1 Ch
148; [1955] 1 All ER 75; 99 Sol Jo 44   **3-45**

Rutherford (James R.) & Sons Ltd, *Re* [1964] 1 WLR 1211;
[1964] 3 All ER 137; 108 Sol Jo 563   2-98, 11-301

St Peter, Roydon, *Re* [1969] 2 All ER 1233; [1969] 1 WLR
1849   11-419

Saunders (Executrix of the Will of Rose Maud Gallie,
deceased) *v.* Anglia Building Society [1971] AC 1004;
[1970] 3 All ER 961; 120 NLJ 1058; 114 Sol Jo 885   5-155

Savory (E.B.) & Co. *v.* Lloyds Bank Ltd [1932] 2 KB 122.
See also Lloyds Bank Ltd *v.* E. B. Savory & Co   6-95

Sawers, *Re, Ex parte* Blain (1879) 12 Ch D 522; 41 LT 46   11-100

Scarth *v.* National Provincial Bank Ltd (1930) 4 LDB 241   **3-36**

Scottish and Newcastle Breweries Ltd *v.* Blair and others.
1967 SLT 72   5-188

Securities and Investment Board *v.* Pantell SA [1989] 2 All
ER 673; [1989] 3 WLR 698   **1-83A**

Serrell *v.* Derbyshire Railway Co. (1850) 9 CB 811; 19 LJCP
371; 15 LTOS 254   5-114

Seymour *v.* Pickett [1905] 1 KB 715; 74 LJKB 413; 92 LT
519; 21 TLR 302   2-78

Shaw *v.* Picton (1825) 4 B & C 715; 7 D & R 201; 4 LJ (OS)
KB 29   2-76

Shields' Estate, *Re* [1901] IR 172   1-22

Shurey, *Re* Savory *v.* Shurey [1918] 1 Ch 263; 87 LJ Ch 245;
118 LT 355; 34 TLR 171   11-39

Para.

Sim *v*. Stretch [1936] 2 All ER 1237; 52 TLR 669; 80 Sol Jo
703   2-145
Sims *v*. Bond (1833) 5 B & Ad 389; 2 Nev & MKB 608   2-5
Simson *v*. Ingham (1823) 2 B & C 65; 3 Dow & Ry KB 249;
1 LJOS (KB) 234   2-74
Sinclair *v*. Brougham [1914] AC 398; 83 LJ Ch 465; 111 LT
1; 30 TLR 315; 58 Sol Jo 302, HL   1-19, 1-22, 11-279
Skyring *v*. Greenwood (1825) 4 B & C 281; 6 Dow & Ry KB
401   2-134
Slingsby *v*. District Bank Ltd [1932] 1 KB 544; 101 LJKB
281; 146 LT 377; 48 TLR 114; 27 Com Cas 39; 41 Lloyds
LR 138; 4 LDB 275; Chorley and Smart's *Leading Cases*
(5th ed.) 56   **2-127**, 6-78, 7-64, 7-88
Slingsby *v*. Westminster Bank Ltd (No. 1) [1931] 1 KB 173;
100 LJKB 195; 144 LT 369; 47 TLR 1; 36 Com Cas 54;
4 LDB 252   9-1
Slingsby *v*. Westminster Bank Ltd (No. 2) [1931] 2 KB 583;
36 Com Cas 61; 4 LDB 258   **6-78**
Smally *v*. Smally (1700) 1 Eq Cas Abr 283   11-53
Smith *v*. King [1892] 2 QB 543; 67 LT 420; 36 Sol Jo 489
                                                                            5-139, 11-44
Smith *v*. Milles (1786) 1 Term Rep 475   3-17
Smith *v*. Prosser [1907] 2 KB 735; 77 LJKB 71; 97 LT 155;
51 SJ 551; 2 LDB 151   5-70
Smith and Baldwin *v*. Barclays Bank Ltd (1944) *Journal of
the Institute of Bankers*, Vol. LXV, p. 171; 5 LDB 370   **6-122**
Smout *v*. Ilbery (1842) 10 M & W 1; 12 LJ Ex 357   3-24, 11-24
Solicitor, A, *Re* [1952] Ch 328; [1952] 1 All ER 133; 96 Sol
Jo 59   11-161
Soltykoff, *Re, Ex parte* Margrett [1891] 1 QB 413; 60 LJQB
339; 7 TLR 197   5-139, 11-40
Souchette Ltd *v*. London County Westminster and Parr's
Bank Ltd (1920) 36 TLR 195; 3 LDB 215   6-116
Space Investments Ltd *v*. Canadian Imperial Bank of Com-
merce Trust Co. (Bahamas) Ltd [1986] 3 All ER 75;
[1986] 1 WLR 1072; 130 Sol Jo 612   **2-7A**
Spencer *v*. Wakefield (1887) 4 TLR 194   **2-46**
Stapelberg *v*. Barclays DCO 1963 (3) SA 120   7-70
Steane's (Bournemouth) Ltd, *Re* [1950] 1 All ER 21; [1949]
WN 490; 208 LT Jo 377   11-350
Steinberg *v*. Scala (Leeds) Ltd [1923] 2 Ch 452; 92 LJKB
944; 129 LT 624; 39 TLR 542; 67 Sol Jo 656   11-43
Stevenson (Hugh) & Sons Ltd *v*. Akstiengesellschaft für

Para.

Cartonnagen Industrie [1918] AC 239; 87 LJKB 416; 118
LT 126; 34 TLR 206; 62 Sol Jo 290   11-128

Stocks *v.* Wilson [1913] 2 KB 235; 82 LJKB 598; 108 LT
834; 29 TLR 352   11-41

Stoney Stanton Supplies (Coventry) Ltd *v.* Midland Bank
Ltd [1966] 2 Lloyd's Rep 373; 8 LDB 342   11-2

Strickland *v.* Symons (1883) 22 Ch D 666; on appeal 26 Ch
D 245; 53 LJ Ch 582; 5 LT 406   11-183

Sunderland *v.* Barclays Bank Ltd (1938), *The Times*, 24 and
25 November; 5 LDB 163   **2-117**, 2-119

Sutton's Hospital Case (1612) 10 Co Rep 1a, 23a   11-312

Swift *v.* Jewsbury and Goddard (1874) LR 9 QB 301; 43
LJQB 56; 30 LT 31   10-69

T. W. Construction Ltd, *Re* [1954] 1 WLR 540; [1954] 1
All ER 744; 98 Sol Jo 216; 6 LDB 423   11-350

Tai Hing Cotton Mill Ltd *v.* Liu Chong Hing Bank [1985]
2 All ER 947   **2-138**

Talbot *v.* von Boris [1911] 1 KB 854; 80 LJKB 661; 104 LT
524; 27 TLR 266; 55 Sol Jo 290   5-158

Tapp *v.* Jones (1875) LR 10 QB 591; 44 LJQB 127; 33 LT
201   3-62

Tarn *v.* The Commercial Banking Company of Sydney
(1884) 12 QBD 294; 50 LT 365; 1 LDB 56   **3-18**

Tassell *v.* Cooper (1850) 9 CB 509; 14 LTSO 466; Chorley
and Smart's *Leading Cases* (5th ed.) 174   2-99, 7-41

Tate *v.* Wilts and Dorset Bank (1899) 1 LDB 286   6-52

Tatung (UK) Ltd *v.* Galex Telesure Ltd [1989] 5 BCC 25   11-321

TCB Ltd *v.* Gray [1986] Ch 621; [1986] 1 All ER 587;
[1986] BCLC 113   **11-279A**

Thackwell *v.* Barclays Bank plc [1986] 1 All ER 676   6-100A, **6-139A**

Thairlwall *v.* Great Northern Railway Co [1910] 2 KB 509;
79 KJKB 924; 1203 LT 186; 26 TLR 555; 54 Sol Jo 652
    5-9, 9-3, 9-12/13, 9-36

Thomson *v.* Clydesdale Bank Ltd [1893] AC 282; 62 LJPC
91; 69 LT 156; Chorley and Smart's *Leading Cases* (5th
ed.) 169   11-166

Tidd, Tidd *v.* Overell, *Re* [1893] 3 Ch 154; 62 LJ Ch 915;
69 LT 255; 9 TLR 550; 37 Sol Jo 618   2-26

Totterdell *v.* Fareham Blue Brick and Tile Co. (1866) LR 1
CP 674; 35 LJCP 278; 12 Jur (NS) 901; 14 WR 919   11-297

Tournier *v.* National Provincial and Union Bank of

Para.

England Ltd [1924] 1 KB 461; 93 LJKB 449; 130 LT 682;
40 TLR 214; 68 Sol Jo 441; 29 Com Cas 129, CA; 3 LDB
305; Chorley and Smart's *Leading Cases* (5th ed.) 6
2-100/3, 2-113, 2-116, 2-118, 2-121, 3-14
Twibell *v.* London Suburban Bank [1869] WN 127   11-71

Underwood (A. L.) Ltd *v.* Bank of Liverpool and Martins,
Same *v.* Barclays Bank Ltd [1924] 1 KB 775; 93 LJKB
690; 157 LT 106; 40 TLR 302; 68 Sol Jo 716; 29 Com Cas
182; 3 LDB 323   6-49, 6-98, 6-109, **6-119**, 6-138, 11-310
Union Bank of Australia Ltd *v.* Murray-Aynsley [1898] AC
693; 67 LJPC 123; 1 LDB 274   **2-70**
Union Bank of Australia Ltd *v.* Schultz [1914] VLR 183   5-43
Unit 2 Windows Ltd, *Re* [1985] 3 All ER 647; [1985] 1
WLR 1383   **11-307A**
United Australia Ltd *v.* Barclays Bank Ltd [1941] AC 1;
[1940] 4 All ER 20; 109 LJKB 919; 164 LT 139; 57 TLR
13; 46 Com Cas 1; 5 LDB 274   6-55, 6-120
United Dominions Trust Ltd *v.* Kirkwood [1966] 1 QBD
783; [1965] 2 All ER 992; on appeal [1966] 2 QBD 431;
[1966] 1 All ER 968; [1966] 1 Lloyd's Rep 418; 110 Sol
Jo 169; 8 LDB 490; Chorley and Smart's *Leading Cases*
(5th ed.) 23   1-23/4, **1-28**
United Overseas Bank *v.* Jiwani [1976] 1 WLR 964; [1977]
1 All ER 733; 120 Sol Jo 329   2-135
United Service Co., *Re* Johnston's Claim (1871) 6 Ch App
212; 40 LJ Ch 286; 24 LT 115; Chorley and Smart's
Leading Cases (5th ed.) 253   10-88
Uttamchandami *v.* Central Bank of India (1989) 139 NLJ
222; (1989) 133 Sol Jo 262   **2-72A**

Vaisey *v.* Reynolds (1828) 5 Russ 12; 6 LJOS Ch 172   2-5
Valentini *v.* Canali (1889) 24 QBD 166; 59 LJQB 74; 61 LT
731; 6 TLR 75   11-41
Vincent *v.* Horlock (1808) 1 Camp 442   5-76

Wakefield *v.* Alexander (1901) 17 TLR 217   **5-85**
Walkden *v.* Hartley and Cavell (1866) 2 TLR 767   11-51
Walker and Another *v.* Manchester and Liverpool District
Banking Co. Ltd (1913) 29 TLR 492; 108 LT 728; 57 Sol
Jo 478; 3 LDB 55   2-137
Walter *v.* Everard [1891] 2 QB 369; 60 LJQB 738; 65 LT
443; 7 TLR 469   11-51

Para.

Walton *v.* Mascall (1844) 13 M & W 452; 14 LJ Ex 54   2-23

Warwick *v.* Rogers (1843) 15 M & G 340   6-3

Wauthier *v.* Wilson (1912) 28 TLR 239   5-140

Webb *v.* Adkins (1854) 14 CB 401; 23 LJCP 96; 22 LTOS
260   3-18

Webb *v.* Earle (1875) LR 20 Eq 556; 44 LJ Ch 608   10-101

Weeks *v.* Propert (1873) LR 8 CP 427; 42 LJCP 129; 21 WR
676   11-291

Welch *v.* Bank of England [1955] Ch 508; [1955] 1 All ER
811; 99 Sol Jo 236; 7 LDB 4   11-71

Weld-Blundell *v.* Stephens [1920] AC 956; 89 LJKB 705;
123 LT 593; 36 TLR 640; 64 Sol Jo 529   2-113

Westminster Bank Ltd *v.* Cond (1940) 46 Com Cas 60; 5
LDB 263   2-96

Westminster Bank Ltd *v.* Hilton (1926) 43 TLR 124; 136 LT
315; 70 Sol Jo 1196; 4 LDB 47; Chorley and Smart's
Leading Cases (5th ed.) 78   2-7, **7-36**

Westminster Bank Ltd *v.* Zang [1966] AC at p. 196; [1965]
1 All ER 1023; [1965] 1 Lloyd's Rep 183; 109 Sol Jo 191,
CA; affirmed [1966] AC at p. 211; [1966] 1 All ER 114;
[1966] 1 Lloyd's Rep 49; 109 Sol Jo 1009, HL; 8 LDB
267; Chorley and Smart's *Leading Cases* (5th ed.) 119
    6-37, 6-39, 6-41, 6-85

Weston's Case (1870) 5 Ch App 614; 39 LJ Ch 753; 23 LT
287   11-56

Wilkinson *v.* Parry (1828) 4 Russ 272   11-224

Williams *v.* Griffith (1839) 5 M & W 300   2-77

Williams and others *v.* Summerfield [1972] 2 QB 512;
[1972] 2 All ER 1334; 122 NLJ 473; 116 Sol Jo 413   2-104

Williams *v.* Williams [1987] 3 All ER 257; [1988] QB 161   **2-104A**

Williams & Glyn's Bank Ltd *v.* Barnes [1981] Com LR 205;
Chorley and Smart's *Leading Cases* (5th ed.) 210   1-70, 2-15A

Williamson *v.* Johnson (1823) 1 B & C 146   11-105

Wilson *v.* Midland Bank Ltd (1961) *The reading Standard*
13 October   2-151, **3-2**

Wilson *v.* United Counties Bank Ltd [1920] AC 102; 88
LJKB 1033; 122 LT 76   2-142

Wilson and Meeson *v.* Pickering [1946] KB 422; [1946] 1
All ER 394; [1947] LJR 18; 175 LT 65; 62 TLR 223   5-42

Wise *v.* Perpetual Trustee Co [1903] AC 139; 72 LJPC 31;
19 TLR 125   11-438

Para.

Woods *v.* Martins Bank Ltd [1959] 1 QB 55; [1958] 3 All
 ER 166; 102 Sol Jo 655; 7 LDB 192; Chorley and Smart's
 Leading Cases (5th ed.) 335   **1-66, 10-127/9**
Wookey *v.* Pole (1820) 4 B & Ald 1   4-12
Woolf *v.* Hamilton [1898] 2 QB 337; 67 LJQB 917; 79 LT
 49   5-166
Woolley *v.* Clark (1822) 5 B & Ald 744; 1 Dow & Ry KB 409   3-17
Wright *v.* Laing (1824) 3 B & C 165; 4 D & R 783   2-77

Yates, *Ex parte* (1857) 27 LJ Bcy 9; 2 De G & J 191; 30
 LTOS 282   5-81
Yeoman Credit Ltd *v.* Gregory [1963] 1 WLR 343; [1963]
 1 All ER 245; 107 Sol Jo 315   5-135, 8-42, **8-44, 8-76**
Yeovil Glove Co. Ltd, *Re* [1965] Ch 148; [1964] 2 All ER
 849; 108 Sol Jo 499; 8 LDB 267   2-90A
Young *v.* Grote (1827) 4 Bing 253; 12 Moore, CP 484; 5
 LJOSCP 165   2-125
Young and another *v.* Sealey [1949] Ch 278; [1949] 1 All
 ER 92; 6 LDB 8; Chorley and Smart's *Leading Cases* (5th
 ed.) 187   11-86

Z Ltd *v.* A and others [1982] QB 558; [1982] 1 All ER 556;
 126 Sol Jo 100; Chorley and Smart's *Leading Cases* (5th
 ed.) 85   7-42C

TABLE OF STATUTES

		Para.
7 & 8 Will. III, c. 31	Exchequer Bills 1696	4-12
20 Geo. II, c. 42	Wales and Berwick Act 1746	
	s. 3	11-270
9 Geo. IV, c. 14	Statute of Frauds Amendment Act 1828	
	s. 6	10-68
4 & 5 Will. IV, c. 41	Gaming Act 1835	5-166
7 Will. IV & Vict., c. 26	Wills Act 1837	
	s. 7	11-58
	s. 11	11-58
7 & 8 Vict., c. 32	Bank Charter Act 1844	9-60
	s. 11	9-18
8 & 9 Vict., c. 109	Gaming Act 1845	
	s. 18	5-167
16 & 17 Vict., c. 59	Stamp Act 1853	
	s. 1	7-56
	s. 19	7-58/60, 7-64, 7-72/3, 9-22, 9-39
	Sched.	7-56
18 & 19 Vict., c. 111	Bills of Lading Act 1855	
	s. 1	4-17
19 & 20 Vict., c. 25	Crossed Cheques Act 1856	5-37
22 & 22 Vict., c. 79	Crossed Cheques Act 1858	5-37
25 & 26 Vict., c. 89	Companies Act 1862	
	Table A	11-287
33 & 34 Vict., c. 71	National Debit Act 1870	9-1
37 & 38 Vict., c. 62	Infants' Relief Act 1874	
	s. 1	11-41, 11-48/9
	s. 2	11-44
38 & 39 Vict., c. 77	Supreme Court of Judicature Act 1875	
	s. 10	2-60
39 & 40 Vict., c. 48	Bankers' Books Evidence Act 1876	1-56
39 & 40 Vict., c. 81	Crossed Cheques Act 1876	5-37, 6-62/3, 6-91
	s. 9	7-79/80
	s. 12	5-42, 6-60

		Para.
40 & 41 Vict., c. 2	Treasury Bills Act 1877	4-12
42 & 43 Vict., c. 11	Bankers' Books Evidence	
	Act 1879	1-25
	s. 3	1-56
	s. 4	1-56
	s. 5	1-56
	s. 6	1-57
	s. 7	1-59, 2-104
	s. 9	1-56
	s. 10	1-56
45 & 46 Vict., c. 61	Bills of Exchange Act 1982	
	s. 2	1-20, 4-2, 5-11, 5-60/3, 5-73, 5-96, 5-116, 7-55, 7-68, 7-81
	s. 3(1)	4-10, 5-6, 6-70, 7-64, 8-2, 8-19, 8-62, 9-14, 9-26
	s. 3(2)	4-10, 8-2, 9-14
	s. 3(3)	5-10, 8-3
	s. 3(4)	4-18, 5-60, 5-111, 7-14, 8-4
	s. 4(1)	8-14/15
	s. 4(2)	8-14
	s. 5(1)	8-5
	s. 5(2)	4-10, 5-13, 6-70, 8-62, 9-14
	s. 7(2)	5-82
	s. 7(3)	5-39
	s. 8(1)	5-71, 5-103, 6-111, 9-40
	s. 8(3)	5-77, 5-96, 9-40
	s. 8(4)	5-71
	s. 9(1)	8-10, 9-46
	s. 9(2)	5-16, 7-17
	s. 9(3)	8-10
	s. 10(1)	5-15, 8-7
	s. 11	8-8
	s. 12	8-9, 8-30
	s. 13(2)	5-19
	s. 14(1)	8-12A, 8-22
	s. 14(2)	8-13
	s. 14(3)	8-13
	s. 14(4)	8-13
	s. 16(1)	5-85, 5-177
	s. 16(2)	5-86

Para.

45 & 46 Vict., c. 61, Bills of Exchange Act 1882 *contd.*

s. 17(1)	8-30
s. 17(2)	8-30
s. 18	8-31
s. 18(2)	8-55
s. 19(1)	8-34
s. 19(2)	8-34
s. 20(1)	5-18, 7-14
s. 20(2)	5-68
s. 21(2)	5-65/6, 5-70, 5-91, 5-144
s. 22(1)	5-138
s. 22(2)	5-140, 11-45
s. 24	4-5, 5-38, 5-87, 5-109, 5-145, 6-45
s. 25	5-80
s. 26(1)	5-184, 5-186
s. 26(2)	5-184
s. 27(1)	5-128, 6-38, 6-40
s. 27(2)	5-116, 5-119, 5-131
s. 27(3)	5-118, 6-41, 8-117
s. 28(1)	5-189
s. 28(2)	5-189
s. 29	5-39, 5-60, 5-66, 5-88, 5-104, 5-108, 5-111, 5-116, 6-137, 7-14, 8-109, 9-28
s. 29(1)	5-18, 5-119, 5-125, 5-148 5-156, 9-53
s. 29(2)	5-121, 6-53
s. 29(3)	5-122
s. 30(1)	5-130
s. 30(2)	5-123
s. 31	5-119, 9-28
s. 31(1)	5-72
s. 31(2)	4-2, 5-72, 5-74, 9-58
s. 31(3)	4-2, 5-72, 5-75, 9-58
s. 31(4)	5-72, 5-97, 5-183
s. 31(5)	5-85, 5-177
s. 32(1)	5-79
s. 32(2)	5-82
s. 32(3)	5-83
s. 32(4)	5-84
s. 33	5-91
s. 34(1)	5-74

Para.

45 & 46 Vict., c. 61, Bills of Exchange Act 1882 *contd.*

s. 34(2)	5-75
s. 34(3)	5-82
s. 34(4)	5-76, 5-100, 5-150
s. 35(1)	5-92, 5-103
s. 35(2)	5-95
s. 35(3)	5-95
s. 36(2)	5-168, 9-59
s. 36(3)	5-114
s. 36(5)	5-169
s. 38(2)	5-156, 5-162, 5-164
s. 39(1)	8-28
s. 39(2)	8-28
s. 40(1)	8-38
s. 41(1)	8-39
s. 41(2)	8-38/9, 8-41, 8-54
s. 41(3)	8-41
s. 42	8-49
s. 42(1)	8-54
s. 43(1)	8-50, 8-54
s. 43(2)	8-52
s. 44(1)	8-36, 8-51, 8-54
s. 44(2)	8-36, 9-57
s. 44(3)	8-36
s. 45	5-132, 8-21, 8-42/3
s. 45(2)	6-32
s. 45(8)	7-11
s. 46(1)	8-45
s. 46(2)	8-46
s. 47(1)	8-56
s. 47(2)	8-57
s. 48	5-135, 6-33, 8-60
s. 48(1)	8-60
s. 48(2)	8-61
s. 49	5-106
s. 49(1)	8-64
s. 49(2)	8-65
s. 49(3)	8-66
s. 49(4)	8-67
s. 49(5)	8-68
s. 49(6)	6-33, 8-69
s. 49(7)	8-70
s. 49(8)	8-71

Para.

45 & 46 Vict., c. 61, Bills of Exchange Act 1882 *contd.*

s. 49(9)	8-72
s. 49(10)	8-73
s. 49(11)	8-74
s. 49(12)	5-135, 6-33, 8-75
s. 49(13)	5-136, 8-77
s. 49(14)	6-33, 8-78
s. 49(15)	8-79
s. 50(1)	8-80
s. 50(2)	5-106, 5-137, 8-62
s. 51	8-16
s. 51(1)	8-87
s. 51(2)	8-89
s. 51(3)	8-90
s. 51(4)	8-92
s. 51(6)	8-95
s. 51(7)	8-84
s. 51(8)	8-86
s. 51(9)	8-94, 8-96
s. 52(1)	8-42
s. 52(2)	8-42
s. 52(3)	8-59, 8-61, 8-91
s. 52(4)	8-43
s. 53(1)	8-32
s. 54	8-32
s. 55(1)(a)	5-171, 8-110, 9-55
s. 55(1)(b)	5-174, 8-110, 9-55
s. 55(2)	5-110, 5-146, 9-55
s. 55(2)(a)	5-135, 5-175
s. 55(2)(b)	5-176
s. 55(2)(c)	5-176
s. 56	5-178
s. 58(1)	5-180
s. 58(2)	5-180
s. 58(3)	5-180
s. 59(1)	7-54, 7-61/2, 7-95, 8-140
s. 60	7-10/11, 7-25, 7-59, 7-62/4, 7-69/70, 7-72/4, 7-76/8, 7-80, 7-82/8, 7-90, 7-98, 8-24
s. 64(1)	5-147, 7-19, 7-64, 7-88
s. 64(2)	5-150, 7-14, 7-64, 7-88
s. 69	5-102, 9-13
s. 70	9-13

Para.

45 & 46 Vict., c. 61, Bills of Exchange Act 1882 *contd.*

s. 71	8-16
s. 72(4)	8-11
s. 73	5-6, 7-47, 7-64, 8-5, 8-18/19, 9-14, 9-26
s. 74(1)	5-133, 7-97, 8-21
s. 74(2)	6-32
s. 74(3)	5-133, 7-97
s. 75	3-22, 3-24, 7-30
s. 76	5-37, 5-50/2, 6-63/4, 6-70 7-80, 8-23, 9-7
s. 77(1)	5-50
s. 77(2)	5-53, 5-101
s. 77(3)	5-54, 5-101
s. 77(4)	5-55, 5-101
s. 77(5)	5-56
s. 77(6)	5-57
s. 78	5-37, 5-58, 5-150, 6-63/4, 6-70, 7-80, 9-7
s. 79	1-26, 5-37, 6-63/4, 6-70, 7-4, 7-75, 7-79/80, 9-7
s. 79(2)	7-4, 7-21, 7-99
s. 80	1-26, 5-37, 6-63/4, 6-70, 7-25, 7-73, 7-79/86, 7-90, 7-98, 8-24, 9-7, 9-22, 9-33, 9-39
s. 81	5-37, 5-42, 6-39, 6-44, 6-63/4, 6-70, 6-139, 7-80, 8-23, 9-7
s. 82	6-53, 6-63/4, 6-66/8, 6-70, 6-73/4, 6-76/7, 6-101, 6-103, 6-109, 6-112, 6-116, 6-119, 6-122/3, 6-128, 7-72/3, 7-80, 11-5/6, 11-8
s. 83(1)	9-44
s. 83(2)	9-47
s. 83(3)	9-47
s. 83(4)	9-47
s. 84	9-46
s. 85(1)	9-48
s. 85(2)	9-48
s. 86(1)	9-57
s. 86(2)	9-57
s. 86(3)	9-59

Para.

45 & 46 Vict., c. 61, Bills of Exchange Act 1882 *contd.*

	s. 87(1)	9-54
	s. 87(2)	9-56
	s. 87(3)	9-56
	s. 88	9-53
	s. 89(1)	9-55, 9-58
	s. 89(2)	9-55
	s. 90	5-120, 6-92, 7-65, 7-76, 7-92
	s. 91(1)	5-79
	s. 92	5-135, 8-39, 8-75
	s. 93	8-92
	s. 94	8-85
	s. 95	9-1, 9-7
	s. 96	6-63, 7-80
	s. 97(3)(d)	9-5/6
	Sched. I	8-85
	Sched. II	6-63, 7-80
46 & 47 Vict., c. 55	Revenue Act 1883	
	s. 17	6-64/5, 6-73, 6-79, 6-124, 9-29, 9-32, 9-34, 9-37
47 & 48 Vict., c. 62	Revenue Act 1884	
	s. 11	3-18, 11-169
53 & 54 Vict., c. 39	Partnership Act 1890	
	s. 1(1)	11-97, 11-112
	s. 4(1)	11-97
	s. 4(2)	11-100
	s. 5	5-83, 11-103/4
	s. 8	11-104
	s. 9	11-106, 11-122/3
	s. 14(1)	11-9
	s. 17(1)	11-141
	s. 17(2)	11-144
	s. 32	11-129
	s. 33(1)	11-130/1
	s. 33(2)	11-133
	s. 34	11-128
	s. 35	11-134
	s. 45	11-97, 11-112
55 & 56 Vict., c. 4	Betting and Loans (Infants) Act 1892	
	s. 5	5-140, 11-42, 11-48

		Para.
63 & 64 Vict., c. 51	Moneylenders Act 1900	1-28/9
6 Edw. VII, c. 17	Bills of Exchange (Crossed	
	Cheques) Act 1906	6-66/9, 6-73/4
	s. 1	6-68
Edw. VII, c. 69	Companies (Consolidation)	
	Act 1908	
	s. 212	2-97A
	Table A, Art. 73	11-288
4 & 5 Geo. V, c. 47	Deeds of Arrangement Act	
	1914	11-239
	s. 2	11-242
	s. 3(1)	11-242
	s. 3(4)	11-242
	s. 5	11-242
	s. 11(4)	11-240
	s. 24(2)	11-241
7 & 8 Geo. V, c. 48	Bills of Exchange (Timing	
	of Noting) Act 1917	
	s. 1	8-92
7 & 8 Geo. V, c. 58	Wills (Soldiers and Sailors)	
	Act 1918	
	s. 1	11-58
	s. 2	11-58
	s. 5(2)	11-58
8 & 9 Geo. V. c, 40	Income Tax Act 1918	
	s. 103	2-106
15 & 16 Geo. V, c. 19	Trustee Act 1925	
	s. 11	1-30
	s. 16(1)	11-214
	s. 16(2)	11-214
	s. 17	11-215
	s. 18(1)	11-221
	s. 18(2)	11-221
	s. 23	11-209
	s. 25	11-210
	s. 34(1)	11-198
	s. 36(1)	11-226
	s. 39(1)	11-225
	s. 57(1)	11-217
	s. 68	6-57
15 & 16 Geo. V, c. 20	Law of Property Act 1925	
	s. 1(6)	11-55

		Para.
15 & 16 Geo. V, c. 23	Administration of Estates Act 1925	
	s. 2(1)	11-181
	s. 7(1)	11-189
	s. 9	3-17
	s. 27(1)	3-21
	s. 27(2)	3-21
	s. 39	11-181
	s. 55(1)(xv)	3-17
15 & 16 Geo. V, c. 28	Administration of Justice Act 1925	
	s. 22(1)	11-242
15 & 16 Geo. V, c. 49	Supreme Court of Judicature (Consolidation) Act 1925	
	s. 45	7-42A
	s. 165(1)	11-57
17 & 18 Geo. V, c. 21	Moneylenders Act 1927	1-28/9
18 & 19 Geo. V, c. 93	Agricultural Credits Act 1928	
	s. 5(1)	1-31
	s. 5(7)	1-31
	s. 9	11-404
	s. 14	11-404
19 & 20 Geo. V, c. 23	Companies Act 1929 Sched. I, Table A, Art. 69	11-288
20 & 21 Geo. V, c. 23	Mental Treatment Act 1930	
	s. 20(5)	3-26
22 & 23 Geo. V, c. 44	Bills of Exchange Act (1882) Amendment Act 1932	6-71, 6-73, 6-80
	s. 1	6-70, 9-17
22 & 24 Geo. V, c. 24	Solicitors Act 1933	
	s. 8	11-153
24 & 25 Geo. V, c. 41	Law Reform (Miscellaneous Provisions) Act 1934	
	s. 1(1)	9-50, 11-78
25 & 26 Geo. V, c. 30	Law Reform (Married Women and Tortfeasors) Act 1935	
	s. 1	11-61
	s. 3	2-130

l

Para.

2 & 3 Geo. VI, c. 16	Prevention of Fraud (Investments) Act 1939	1-78
8 & 9 Geo. VI, c. 28	Law Reform (Contributory Negligence) Act 1945	
	s. 1	6-134
	s. 4	6-134
9 & 10 Geo. VI, c. 27	Bank of England Act 1946	
	s. 4(3)	1-32, 1-35
	s. 4(6)	1-32, 1-35
10 & 11 Geo. VI, c. 47	Companies Act 1947	
	s. 123	1-29
11 & 12 Geo. VI, c. 38	Companies Act 1948	
	s. 28(1)	11-251
	s. 54	11-275
	s. 95	8-114, 11-321
	s. 227	11-353, 11-356/7
	Sched. I	11-286
	Table A	
	Art. 79	11-289/90
	Art. 100	11-308/9
	Art. 102	11-297
	Art. 121	9-12
	Table D	11-260
1 & 2 Eliz. II, c. 36	Post Office Act 1953	
	s. 21(3)	9-69
4 & 5 Eliz. II, c. 46	Administration of Justice Act 1956	
	s. 38	3-49
	s. 38(1)	3-68
	s. 38(2)	3-69
5 & 6 Eliz. II, c. 36	Cheques Act 1957	6-72, 7-73
	s. 1(1)	7-26, 7-70, 7-89/91, 7-94/5, 7-98, 8-24
	s. 1(2)	7-26, 7-60
	s. 1(2)(a)	5-8, 5-17, 9-31, 9-33, 9-38
	s. 1(2)(b)	9-20, 9-22
	s. 2	5-183, 6-36/7, 6-138
	s. 3	7-28

Para.

5 & 6 Eliz. II, c. 36, Cheques Act 1957 *contd.*

	s. 4	1-27, 1-64, 6-90/1, 6-101,
		6-135, 6-141, 7-72/3, 8-25,
		9-29, 11-10/11, 11-13
	s. 4(1)	6-53, 6-69, 6-74, 6-94, 9-19
	s. 4(2)	6-65, 6-71, 6-75, 6-79
	s. 4(2)(a)	6-76, 9-19
	s. 4(2)(b)	5-8, 5-17, 6-79, 9-27,
		9-29/30, 9-37
	s. 4(2)(c)	6-79
	s. 4(2)(d)	6-80, 9-7, 9-19
	s. 4(3)	6-82
	s. 5	5-8, 5-17, 5-42, 9-7,
		9-17, 9-22, 9-27, 9-33, 9-39
	s. 6(1)	6-92, 7-92
	s. 6(3)	6-63, 6-65, 6-69, 6-71, 6-73,
		9-17, 9-29, 9-32, 9-34, 9-37
	Sched.	6-63, 6-65, 6-69, 6-71, 6-73,
		9-17, 9-29, 9-32, 9-34, 9-37

6 and 7 Eliz. II, c. 45	Prevention of Fraud	
	(Investments) Act 1958	1-78
7 & 8 Eliz. II, c. 72	Mental Health Act 1959	
	s. 5	3-28
	s. 147(1)	3-28
	s. 149(2)	3-26
	Sched. VIII	3-26
8 & 9 Eliz. II, c. 37	Payment of Wages Act	
	1960	10-18
8 & 9 Eliz. II, c. 58	Charities Act 1960	
	s. 1(1)	11-199
	s. 1(2)	11-199
	s. 34	11-200, 11-203
	s. 35(1)	11-201
	Sched. I	11-199
1963, c. 16	Protection of Depositors	
	Act 1963	11-150
1964, c. 4	Trustee Savings Banks Act	
	1964	1-5
1965, c. 12	Industrial and Provident	
	Societies Act 1965	
	s. 3	11-410
	s. 5(2)	11-410

Para.

1965, c. 12, Industrial and Provident Societies Act 1965 *contd.*
	s. 5(5)	11-410
	s. 30(1)	11-414
	s. 74	11-411
	Sched. I	11-411

1965, c. 31 — Solicitors Act 1965
| | s. 8 | 11-148 |

1967 c. 15 — Post Office (Borrowing Powers) Act 1967
| | s. 2 | 10-36 |

1967, c. 48 — Industrial and Provident Societies Act 1967
| | s. 1(1) | 11-416 |
| | s. 1(2) | 11-416 |

1967, c. 80 — Criminal Justice Act 1967
| | s. 9 | 1-59 |

1967, c. 81 — Companies Act 1967
| | s. 2 | 11-261A |
| | s. 123 | 1-29 |

1968, c. 19 — Criminal Appeal Act 1968 1-60

1968, c. 60 — Theft Act 1968
| | s. 15 | 1-69 |
| | s. 16(1) | 10-44A/B, 10-46B |

1968, c. 64 — Civil Evidence Act 1968
	s. 5(1)	1-62
	s. 5(2)	1-62
	s. 5(4)	1-62
	s. 5(5)	1-62

1969, c. 46 — Family Law Reform Act 1969
	s. 1	11-39
	s. 9	11-39
	s. 12	11-39

1969, c. 48 — Post Office Act 1969
| | s. 7(1) | 10-35 |

1970, c. 9 — Taxes Management Act 1970
| | s. 13 | 2-106 |
| | s. 17 | 2-107 |

1970, c. 24 — Finance Act 1970
| | s. 32 | 2-65, 5-20, 8-12 |
| | Sched. 7 | 2-65, 5-20, 8-12 |

		Para.
1970, c. 31	Administration of Justice Act 1970	
	s. 1(6)	3-17
	s. 4	6-29A
1971, c. 27	Powers of Attorney Act 1971	
	s. 1(1)	11-28
	s. 1(2)	11-28
	s. 3	11-28
	s. 4(1)	11-36
	s. 5(1)	11-37
	s. 5(2)	11-38
	s. 9	11-210
	s. 10(1)	11-29
	s. 10(2)	11-29
	Sched. 1	11-29
1971, c. 80	Banking and Financial Dealings Act 1971	
	s. 3	8-12A, 8-22, 8-39
1972, c. 70	Local Government Act 1972	
	s. 1(1)	11-420
	s. 2	11-422
	s. 9	11-423
	s. 20(1)	11-421
	s. 21	11-422
	s. 27	11-423
	s. 151	11-425
1974, c. 39	Consumer Credit Act 1974	
	s. 8	1-52
	s. 21	1-48
	s. 49	1-53
	s. 51(1)	1-54, 10-46A
	s. 74(4)	1-52
	s. 75(1)	10-47A
	s. 75(2)	10-47A
	s. 75(5)	10-47A
	s. 145(8)	10-53
	s. 192(3)	1-29
	Sched. 5	1-29
1974, c. 46	Friendly Societies Act 1974	
	s. 8(1)	11-404
	s. 24(1)	11-404
	s. 24(2)	11-404
	s. 52(1)	11-409

Para.

1974, c. 47	Solicitors Act 1974	
	s. 32	11-150
	s. 35	11-158, 11-163
	s. 36(1)	11-162
	s. 85	11-152, 11-153
	s. 86	1-56
	s. 87(1)	11-150
	Sched. I	11-158, 11-163
1975, c. 45	Finance (No. 2) Act 1975	
	s. 74	11-150
1975, c. 60	Social Security Pensions Act 1975	
	Sched. 3	11-299
1976, c. 4	Trustee Savings Banks Act 1976	
	s. 1(2)	1-6
	s. 9(1)	1-7
1976, c. 10	Post Office (Banking Services) Act 1976	
	s. 1(1)	10-35
1976, c. 34	Restrictive Trade Practices Act 1976	10-109
1977, c. 32	Torts (Inferference with Goods) Act 1977	
	s. 11(1)	6-136
1977, c. 46	Insurance Brokers (Registration) Act 1977	
	s. 11	11-167
1977, c. 50	Unfair Contract Terms Act 1977	
	s. 2(2)	10-66
	s. 11(5)	10-66
1978, c. 30	Interpretation Act 1978	
	s. 22	11-270
	Sched. 2	11-270
1978, c. 47	Civil Liability (Contribution) Act 1978	9-49
1979, c. 37	Banking Act 1979	1-38/40
	s. 47	6-136
	s. 51(1)	1-56, 11-150, 11-363
	Sched. 6	
	Para. 1	1-56, 2-104A
	Para. 6	11-363

			Para.
1979, c. 37, Banking Act 1979 *contd.*			
		Para. 9	11-150
		Para. 16	11-396
1979, c. 38	Estate Agents Act 1979		
		s. 14	11-167
1979, c. 54	Sale of Goods Act 1979		
		s. 3(2)	5-139, 11-40
		s. 22	4-4
1980, c. 22	Companies Act 1980		
		s. 1(2)	11-248, 11-260
		s. 88	11-251
		Sched. 4	11-251
1980, c. 58	Limitation Act 1980		
		s. 2	6-56
		s. 5	2-23, 2-32, 2-42, 5-134, 9-54
		s. 8(1)	2-42
		s. 20(1)	2-39
		s. 20(2)	2-41
		s. 20(3)	2-40
		s. 20(4)	2-41
		s. 20(5)	2-39
		s. 21(1)	6-57
		s. 29(5)	2-24, 2-36
		s. 29(7)	2-24
		s. 30(1)	2-24
		s. 30(2)	2-24
		s. 38(1)	6-57
1981, c. 54	Supreme Court Act 1981		
		s. 18(1)	1-60
		s. 37(1)	7-42D, 7-42E
		s. 37(3)	7-42B, 7-42E
1981, c. 65	Trustee Savings Bank Act 1981		1-9
1982, c. 29	Supply of Goods and Services Act 1982		
		s. 13	2-47, 10-129A
		s. 15(1)	2-47
		s. 15(2)	2-47
1982, c. 51	Mental Health (Amendment) Act 1982		3-26

		Para.
1983, c. 20	Mental Health Act 1983	3-26
	s. 93	3-30
	s. 94	3-30
	s. 95(1)	3-30
	s. 95(2)	3-30
	s. 99(1)	3-31
	s. 99(3)	3-31
1984, c. 35	Data Protection Act 1984	
	s. 21	2-16A
1984, c. 60	Police and Criminal	
	Evidence Act 1984	1-59
	s. 9(1)	2-107A/C
	s. 14	2-107A
	Sched. 1	2-107A
1985, c. 6	Companies Act 1985	
	s. 1(2)	11-258
	s. 1(3)	11-248, 11-250, 11-258, 11-270
	s. 1(4)	11-248, 11-260
	s. 2	11-270
	s. 4	11-280
	s. 7	11-286
	s. 8(2)	11-286
	s. 13(1)	11-267
	s. 13(6)	11-267
	s. 13(7)	11-267
	s. 17	11-280
	s. 25(1)	11-252
	s. 26(1)	11-253
	s. 26(3)	11-252
	s. 27(4)	11-252
	s. 30	11-259
	s. 35(1)	11-279, 11-279A
	s. 35(2)	11-279, 11-279A
	s. 36(3)	11-266
	s. 81(1)	11-250
	s. 101(1)	11-249
	s. 117(1)	11-254, 11-268
	s. 117(2)	11-249
	s. 117(7)	11-268
	s. 118	11-249

		Para.
1985, c. 6, Companies Act 1985 *contd*.		
	s. 121	10-104
	s. 151(1)	11-275B
	s. 151(2)	11-275B
	s. 153(1)	11-275B
	s. 153(3)	11-275B
	s. 153(4)	11-275B
	s. 155	32-78
	s. 182(2)	10-106
	s. 196(1)	11-299, 11-300
	s. 196(5)	11-300
	s. 228(1)	1-33
	s. 241(4)	11-261A
	s. 282	11-253
	s. 349(1)	5-188
	s. 370	11-309
	s. 371	11-308
	s. 395	8-114, 11-321
	s. 405	11-316
	s. 425	11-330
	s. 431	2-108
	s. 432	2-108
	s. 434(1)	2-108
	s. 434(4)	2-108
	s. 716(1)	11-101, 11-262
	s. 716(2)	11-101
	s. 716(3)	11-101
	Sched. 9	
	Para. 27	1-33
1985, c. 7	Business Names Act 1985	
	s. 1	11-107
	s. 2	11-108
	s. 4	11-109
1985, c. 9	Companies Consolidation (Consequential Provisions) Act 1985	
	s. 31(2)	11-108
1985, c. 29	Enduring Powers of Attorney Act 1985	
	s. 1	11-38B
	s. 2(1)	11-38C
	s. 2(7)	11-38F
	s. 3(1)	11-38D

		Para.
1985, c. 29, Enduring Powers of Attorney Act 1985 *contd.*		
	s. 4	11-38E
	s. 6	11-38E
1985, c. 58	Trustee Savings Banks Act 1985	
	s. 3	1-9
	Sched. 4	1-9
1986, c. 32	Drug Trafficking Offences Act 1986	
	s. 7	2-110
	s. 8	2-110
	s. 24	2-110A
	s. 27	2-110B
	s. 31	2-110B
1986, c. 48	Wages Act 1986	
	s. 11	10-18
1986, c. 45	Insolvency Act 1986	
	s. 8	11-330
	s. 9(1)	11-331
	s. 9(2)	11-330, 11-332
	s. 9(3)	11-331
	s. 9(4)	11-331
	s. 10(1)	11-333
	s. 10(2)	11-333
	s. 11	11-332, 11-334
	s. 14	11-335
	s. 15	11-336
	s. 18(1)	11-339
	s. 18(2)	11-339
	s. 19	11-341
	s. 21(1)	11-337
	s. 22	11-338
	s. 23(1)	11-339
	s. 23(2)	11-339
	s. 29(2)	11-322
	s. 35(1)	11-372
	s. 41(1)(b)	11-375
	s. 42(1)	11-323, 11-373
	s. 42(3)	11-323
	s. 43(1)	11-324
	s. 43(2)	11-324
	s. 43(3)	11-324
	s. 44(1)	11-325
	s. 46(1)	11-326

			Para.
1986, c. 45, Insolvency Act 1986 *contd.*			
	s. 47		11-327
	s. 48(1)		11-328
	s. 48(2)		11-328
	s. 48(3)		11-328
	s. 74(1)		11-261
	s. 74(2)		11-261
	s. 85		11-324
	s. 86		11-344
	s. 89		11-344
	s. 91(1)		11-344
	s. 91(2)		11-344
	s. 98(1)		11-344
	s. 100(2)		11-345
	s. 103		11-345
	s. 122		11-348
	s. 123		11-330, 11-348
	s. 127	11-350, 11-355,	11-360
	s. 129		11-350
	s. 165(3)		11-380, 11-384
	s. 167(1)		11-388
	s. 175		11-299
	s. 214(1)		11-361
	s. 214(2)		11-361
	s. 214(3)		11-361
	s. 214(7)		11-362
	s. 218		2-109
	s. 219		2-109
	s. 221		11-132
	s. 222		11-132
	s. 223		11-132
	s. 224		11-132
	s. 230(1)		11-331
	s. 231		11-381, 11-389
	s. 245		2-97
	s. 251		11-362
	s. 264		3-38
	s. 267		3-38
	s. 268		3-38
	s. 278		3-39
	s. 283(3)		11-161
	s. 284		3-40
	s. 292(2)		11-232

Para.

1986, c. 45, Insolvency Act 1986 *contd.*

	s. 292(3)	11-232
	s. 306	3-41
	s. 307	3-41/2
	s. 310	3-42
	s. 312(3)	3-41
	s. 314(1)	11-236
	s. 323	2-59, 2-66
	s. 382	3-40
	s. 382(3)	2-66
	s. 386	11-299
	s. 388(2)	11-240
	s. 390	11-232
	s. 391	11-232
	Sched. 1	11-323, 11-335, 11-373
	Sched. 4	11-349, 11-353, 11-357
	Sched. 5	11-236
	Sched. 6	11-299
1986, c. 53	Building Societies Act 1986	
	s. 5(8)	11-392
	s. 7	11-400
	s. 34	1-70, 11-393, 11-399
	s. 97(1)	11-394
	Sched. 2	11-392/3, 11-400
	Sched. 8	1-70, 11-393, 11-399
1986, c. 60	Financial Services Act 1986	
	s. 3	1-82/3A
	s. 6	1-83A
	s. 96	1-83
	s. 97	1-83
	s. 98	1-83
	s. 99	1-83
	s. 100	1-83
	s. 101	1-83
	s. 102	1-84
	s. 105	2-111
	s. 114(1)	1-80
	s. 114(2)	1-80
	s. 117	2-111A
	Sched. 1	1-82
	Sched. 2	1-85
	Sched. 9	
	Para. 2	1-80

		Para.
1987, c. 22	Banking Act 1987	
	s. 1(3)	1-51
	s. 2(2)	1-46
	s. 2(3)	1-46
	s. 2(6)	1-46, 1-51
	s. 3(1)	1-41
	s. 4(1)	1-41
	s. 6(1)	1-41
	s. 8	1-42
	s. 12	1-44
	s. 21(1)	1-47
	s. 22(1)	1-47
	s. 24(1)	1-47
	s. 24(2)	1-47
	s. 24(3)	1-47
	s. 26(1)	1-47
	s. 26(2)	1-47
	s. 26(3)	1-47
	s. 26(7)	1-47
	s. 27(3)	1-47
	s. 32(1)	1-42
	s. 37(1)	1-47
	s. 37(2)	1-47
	s. 38(1)	1-48
	s. 38(9)	1-48
	s. 39(1)	1-42
	s. 39(11)	1-43
	s. 46(1)	1-45
	s. 46(2)	1-45
	s. 47	1-45
	s. 50(1)	1-50
	s. 52(1)	1-50
	s. 58(1)	1-50
	s. 60(1)	1-50
	s. 67	1-49
	s. 70(1)	1-49
	s. 70(3)	1-49
	s. 71(5)	1-49
	s. 105(4)	1-47
	s. 106	1-42
	Sched. 2	1-41
	Sched. 3	1-42

		Para.
1987, c. 38	Criminal Justice Act 1987	
	s. 1	2-112
	s. 2	2-112
1988, c. 1	Income and Corporation Taxes Act 1988	
	s. 414	11-256
	s. 415	11-256
	s. 419	11-257
	s. 421	11-257
1989, c. 4	Prevention of Terrorism (Temporary Provisions) Act 1989	
	s. 1(1)	2-113
	s. 9(1)	2-113A
	s. 9(2)	2-113A
	s. 9(3)	2-113A
	s. 10	2-113B
	s. 11(1)	2-113C
	s. 11(2)	2-113C
	s. 12(1)	2-113D
	s. 12(2)	2-113D
	Sched. 1	2-113
1989, c. 40	Companies Act 1989	
	s. 72	1-92
	s. 73	1-92
	s. 74	1-92
	s. 75	1-92
	s. 76	1-92
	s. 108(1)	Appendix 3
	s. 110	Appendix 3

TABLE OF STATUTORY INSTRUMENTS

Para.

SR & O 1906, No. 596/L.15	Order of the Board of Trade substituting a new Table A for that contained in the Companies Act 1862	11-288
SI 1956, No. 1191	Rules of the Supreme Court (No. 2) Order 1956	3-68
SI 1957, No. 1780	Post Office Annuity Amendment (No. 1) Regulations 1957 Regulation 2	6-81
SI 1968, No. 1222	Partnerships (Unrestricted Size) No. 1 Regulations 1968	11-101
SI 1970, No. 835	Partnerships (Unrestricted Size) No. 2 Regulations 1970	11-101
SI 1970, No. 992	Partnerships (Unrestricted Size) No. 3 Regulations 1970	11-101
SI 1970, No. 1319	Partnerships (Unrestricted Size) No. 4 Regulations 1970	11-101
SI 1971, No. 782	Limited Partnerships (Unrestricted Size) No. 1 Regulations 1971	11-101
SI 1972, No. 583	Trustee Savings Bank Regulations 1972 Regulation 4	11-46
SI 1972, No. 641	Savings Certificates Regulations 1972 Regulation 7(2)	6-81
SI 1972, No. 764	National Savings Bank Regulations 1972 Regulation 21(5)	6-81

		Para.
SI 1972, No. 765	Premium Savings Bonds Regulations 1972	
	Regulation 8(2)	6-81
SI 1976, No. 2012	National Savings Stock Register Regulations 1976	
	Regulation 22(2)	6-81
SI 1979, No. 489	Insurance Brokers Registration Council (Accounts and Business Requirements) Rules Approval Order 1979	11-167
SI 1980, No. 54	Consumer Credit (Advertisements) Regulations	1-55
SI 1980, No. 55	Consumer Credit (Quotations) Regulations 1980	1-55
	Sched. 1	1-55
SI 1981, No. 1520	Estate Agents (Accounts) Regulations 1981	11-167
SI 1981, No. 1630	Insurance Brokers Registration Council (Accounts and Business Requirements) (Amendment) Rules Approval Order 1981	11-167
SI 1981 No. 1685	Company and Business Names Regulations 1981	11-108
SI 1982, No. 530	Partnerships (Unrestricted Size) No. 5 Regulations 1982	11-101
SI 1983, No. 1553	Consumer Credit (Agreements) Regulations 1983	
	Regulation 2(1)	1-55
	Regulation 2(3)	1-55
	Regulation 2(7)	1-55
	Regulation 6(2)	1-55
	Sched. 1	1-55
	Sched. 2	1-55
	Sched. 5	1-55
SI 1983, No. 1878	Consumer Credit (Increase of Monetary Limits) Order 1983	1-55

Para.

SI 1985, No. 805	Companies (Tables A to F Regulations 1985	
	Table A	
	Regulation 70	11-290A
	Regulation 72	11-297
	Regulation 90	11-308
	Regulation 106	9-12
	Table C	11-286
SI 1986, No. 126	Enduring Powers of Attorney (Prescribed Form) Regulations 1986	11-38C
SI 1986, No. 1925	Insolvency Rules 1986	
	Rule 2	11-332
	Rule 4.11	11-350
	Rule 4.90	2-60
SI 1986, No. 1994	Insolvency Regulations 1986	
	Regulation 4	11-233, 11-386
	Regulation 6(1)	11-233, 11-386
	Regulation 6(3)	11-234, 11-387
	Regulation 6(6)	11-235, 11-387
SI 1986, No. 2142	Insolvent Partnerships Order 1986	
	Article 9	11-132
	Article 10	11-132

TABLE OF ABBREVIATIONS

AC	Appeal Cases	1891–current
Ad & E	Adolphus and Ellis	1834–40
All ER	All England Reports	1936–current
App Cas	Appeal Cases	1875–90
Asp MC	Aspinall's Maritime Law Cases	1871–1943
Atk	Atkyns	1736–55
B & Ald	Barnewall and Alderson	1817–22
B & C	Barnewall and Cresswell	1822–30
B & P	Bosanquet and Puller	1796–1804
B & S	Best and Smith	1861–70
BCLC	Butterworths Company Law Cases	1983–current
Beav	Beavan	1838–66
Bli (NS)	Bligh, New Series	1827–37
Bro CC	Brown (by Belt)	1778–94
BTLC	Butterworths Trading Law Cases	1986–88
Buck	Buck	1816–20
C & P	Carrington and Payne	1823–41
CB (NS)	Common Bench, New Series	1856–65
Cas in Ch	Cases in Chancery	1660–97
Ch	Chancery Division	1891–current
Ch App	Chancery Appeal Cases	1865–75
Ch D	Chancery Division	1875–90
Chorley and Smart's *Leading Cases*	*Leading Cases in the Law of Banking* by Lord Chorley and P. E. Smart	
Cl & Fin	Clark and Finnelly	1831–46
Com Cas	Commercial Cases	1896–1941
Com LR	Commercial Law Reports	1980–current
Cox CC	Cox's Criminal Cases	'1843–1943
Cox Eq Cas	Cox's Equity	1783–96
CP	Common Pleas Cases	1865–75
CPD	Common Pleas Division	1875–80
Cr App R	Criminal Appeal Reports	1908–current
Cro Eliz	Croke	1582–1603
De G & Sm	De Gex and Smale, temp. Knight-Bruce and Parker	1846–52

De G F & J	De Gex, Fisher and Jones, temp. Campbell	1860–62
De G M & G	De Gex, Macnaghten & Gordon	1851–57
Deac	Deacon	1836–39
Dow & Ry (KB)	Dowling and Ryland, King's Bench	1821–27
Drewr	Drewry Reports, temp. Kindersley	1852–59
E & B	Ellis and Blackburn	1851–58
East	East's Term Reports	1801–12
Eq	Equity Cases	1866–75
Esp	Espinasse	1793–1807
Exch	Exchequer Reports (Welsby, Hurlstone and Gordon)	1847–56
FLR	Financial Law Reports	1985–current
FTLR	Financial Times Law Reports	1982–88
Giff	Giffard	1857–65
H & C	Hurlstone and Coltman	1862–66
Har & W	Harrison and Wollaston	1835–36
Hare	Hare	1841–53
HLC	Clark's Reports, House of Lords	1847–66
JIBL	Journal of International Banking Law	1982–current
JP	Justice of the Peace and Local Government Review	1837–1945
Jur	Jurist Reports	1837–54
Jur (NS)	Jurist Reports, New Series	1855–66
K & J	Kay and Johnson	1854–58
KB	King's Bench	1901–52
LDB	*Legal Decisions Affecting Bankers*	
LlL Rep	Lloyds List Reports	1919–current
LJ (Bcy)	Law Journal Reports, Bankruptcy	1831–80
LJ Ch	Law Journal Reports, Chancery	1831–1949
LJCP	Law Journal Reports, Common Pleas	1831–80
LJ Ex	Law Journal Reports, Exchequer	1831–75
LJKB	Law Journal Reports, King's Bench	1831–37, 1901–47
LJOS (KB)	Law Journal Reports, Old Series, King's bench	1822–30
LJPC	Law Journal Reports, Privy Council	1831–1947
LJQB	Law Journal Reports, Queen's Bench	1837–1900
LJR	Law Journal Reports	1947–49
LRCP	Law Reports, Common Pleas Cases	1865–75
LR Eq	Law Reports, Equity Cases	1865–75
LR Ex	Exchequer Cases	1865–75

LRHL	House of Lords, English and Irish Appeals	1866–75
LT	Law Times Reports	1859–1947
LT News	Law Times Newspaper	1843–1965
LTOS	Law Times, Old Series	1843–59
M & Gr	Manning and Granger	1840–44
M & W	Meeson and Welsby	1836–47
Mer	Merivale	1815–17
Moo & M	Moody and Malking	1826–30
Moo & R	Moody and Robinson	1830–44
New & M (KB)	Neville and Manning	1832–36
NZLR	New Zealand Law Reports	1883–current
PCC	Palmer's Company Cases	1985–current
Peake Ad Cas	Peake's Additional Cases	1795–1812
QB	Queen's Bench	1891–1900, 1952–current
QBD	Queen's Bench Division	1875–90
RR	Revised Reports	1785–1866
RSC	Rules of the Supreme Court	
Russ	Russell	1823–29
SC	Session Cases	1906–current
SC (HL)	Session Cases (House of Lords)	1907–current
SLT	Scots Law Times	1893–current
Scott (NR)	Scott's New Reports	1840–45
Sim	Simons	1826–49
Sol Jo	Solicitor's Journal	1857–current
Str	Strange	1716–49
TLR	Times Law Reports	1884–1952
TR	Term Reports (by Durnford and East)	1785–1800
Tax Cas	Tax Cases	1875–1945
Vern	Vernon	1681–1720
Ves	Vesey Junior's Reports	1789–1816
Wils KB	Wilson's King's Bench Reports	1742–74
WLR	Weekly Law Reports	1953–current
WN	Weekly Notes	1866–1952
WR	Weekly Reports	1853–1906
Wm Bl	Sir William Blackstone	1746–80
Y & C Ch Cas	Younge and Collyer, temp. Bruce	1841–43

PART I

Relationship of banker and customer

1

Introductory

In this chapter it is proposed to consider first the various types of banks and banking businesses, secondly the legal requirements governing the commencement and the operation of a banking business, thirdly the principles which determine whether a person is a customer of a bank, fourthly the different types of account that are available to customers, and finally the Financial Services Act 1986.

Section 1
BANKS AND BANKING BUSINESSES

The Bank of England

1-1 The Bank of England is the central bank of the United Kingdom. As such, it is concerned with the nation's money in that it issues and manages the currency, advising the government on the direction of policy likely to affect its value. The Bank acts as banker to the other banks in the United Kingdom and to the government. As agent for the government, it arranges for the issue, servicing and redemption of government securities and assists the government by raising the finance necessary to meet any day-to-day shortfall in the level of receipts over payments. It operates in the security and short-term money markets, buying and selling government debt so as to stabilize and, from time to time, influence the level of interest rates. In all these operations the Bank keeps closely in touch with government on the one hand and with City institutions on the other.[1]

Savings banks

1-2 The principal savings banks in the United Kingdom are (a) the trustee savings banks, and (b) the National Savings Bank.

1 See W. M. Acres, *The Bank of England from Within 1694–1900* (1931); K. Rosenberg and R. T. Hopkins, *The Romance of the Bank of England* (1933); Sir John Clapham, *The Bank of England* (1944); R. S. Sayers, *The Bank of England, 1819–1944*, three volumes (1976).

(a) Trustee Savings Banks

1-3 The trustees savings banks have a long and interesting history. They 'were founded in Scotland in the early nineteenth century to fulfil a basic need for a small savings medium',[2] and they soon spread to England. In 1817 the first Savings Bank Bill was introduced in the House of Commons. These banks were originally known as *trustee* savings banks, because the persons who were responsible for managing the business of the banks were the trustees.

1-4 There used to be some uncertainty as to whether a trustee savings bank was a legal entity, capable of being sued in its own name. However, it was held in 1964 that an action for damages for conversion could be brought against a trustee savings bank in its own name.[3]

1-5 Deposits bearing interest may be made in savings accounts, whilst deposits in investment accounts and in premium accounts attract a higher rate of interest, which varies from time to time. The Trustee Savings Banks Act 1964 empowered these banks, for the first time, to provide current account facilities, thus enabling their customers to use cheque books.

1-6 The Committee to Review National Savings (the 'Page Committee') reported in 1973. Its principal recommendation relating to trustee savings banks was that they should be entitled to operate full banking functions.[4]

1-7 The Trustee Savings Bank Act 1976 granted to each trustee savings bank the power 'to carry on the business of banking'.[5] This provision gave effect to the recommendation of the Page Committee that such banks should be entitled to operate full banking functions. Thus trustee savings banks now grant overdrafts and loans, including personal loans, bridging facilities (bridging the financial gap between the sale of an existing house and the purchase of a new one), and home improvement loans. They issue cheque cards, and they provide travellers' cheques and, since 1978, they have provided VISA credit cards under the name 'Trustcard'. In 1982 they moved into corporate lending.

1-8 In addition to the banking facilities already described, trustee savings banks offer certain additional financial facilities. Thus unit

2 J. F. D. Miller, 'The Trustee savings banks in transition', *Journal of the Institute of Bankers*, Vol. 98 (1977), pp. 174–7. At the time when Mr Miller contributed this very interesting article, he was the deputy chief general manager, Trustee Savings Banks Central Board. See also H. Oliver Horne, *A History of Savings Banks* (1947).
3 *Knight and Searle* v. *Dove* [1964] 2 QB 631.
4 Cmnd. 5273 (1973), para. 269.
5 S. 9(1).

trusts,[6] insurance services, instalment credit services and vehicle rental services are provided.

1-9 As a result of amalgamations, there are now only four trustee savings banks serving, respectively, England and Wales, Scotland, Northern Ireland and the Channel Islands. The Trustee Savings Bank Act 1985 made provision for these banks to be gathered together under a holding company, TSB Group plc.[7] In 1986 the shares of TSB Group plc were offered for sale to the public.

(b) National Savings Bank

1-10 This bank, which until 1969 was known as the Post Office Savings Bank, was established by the Post Office Savings Bank Act 1861. Business may be conducted at any post office. On ordinary accounts the bank pays interest at $2\frac{1}{2}$ per cent per annum, but for balances of £500 or more interest at 5 per cent is paid. Deposits in investment accounts attract a higher rate of interest, which varies from time to time. It has no power to make loans, or to grant overdrafts, or to operate current accounts upon which cheques may be drawn.

Commercial Banks

1-11 These banks are usually limited companies operating for profit under the Companies Acts, though a few unlimited companies still carry on a banking business.[8] Commercial banks may be divided into three categories: (a) banks of deposit, (b) merchant banks and (c) industrial bankers.

(a) Deposit banks

1-12 The primary business of deposit banks is to receive sums of money lent to them by their customers on current or deposit account, and to employ such funds profitably by lending them by way of loan or overdraft, by discounting bills of exchange, and by investing in short- or medium-dated gilt-edged securities. Most of the deposit banking business in England is concentrated in the clearing banks. There are, in addition, other large banks with their head offices in London which

---

6 *Post*, paras 10-112/116A.

7 S. 3. The Act also repealed the Trustee Savings Banks Act 1981, which had consolidated the Trustee Savings Banks Acts 1969 to 1978: see s. 3 and Sched. 4.

8 For the history of a bank which used to be conducted as a partnership and is now an unlimited company, see *Hoare's Bank, A Record 1673–1955*, published by Messrs. C. Hoare and Co.

operate a network of branches overseas, and there are many foreign banks which have offices in London and, in some cases, in other cities of the United Kingdom. There are also multinational or consortium banks. Sir John Hall, the chairman of the Association of Consortium Banks, has said that the common thread of these banks is that their business is exclusively wholesale.[9] He added that he would put them broadly into two different categories: first, those which are set up by members which are not large enough 'to go it alone', and second, those which are set up to specialize in a particular type of business. The shareholders of these banks are very often an English bank and a group of overseas banks.

1-12A In its Report on 'Banking Services and the Consumer' published in 1983 the Consumer Council recommended that the banks should appoint a Banking Ombudsman who would 'be empowered to consider and adjudicate upon all complaints of a personal banking nature, including executor and trustee business'. The banks established a working party to examine the situation, and in February 1985 it was announced that they had agreed to establish and fund a Banking Ombudsman. The word 'ombudsman' was originally a Swedish word meaning a 'grievance man', that is to say, an official who is appointed to investigate complaints.

1-12B The Banking Ombudsman is Mr Laurence Shurman, and his office is at Citadel House, 5/11 Fetter Lane, London EC4 1BR. He has power to receive complaints relating to the provision of banking services within the United Kingdom. However, he will not investigate a complaint until the senior management of the bank named in the complaint have had the opportunity to consider it. His powers cover almost all banking services which are provided by the banks in the ordinary course of their business to individuals and partnerships, including advice and services relating to taxation, insurance and investment given by banks at local branch level. Complaints arising out of the provision of credit cards, and executor and trustee work also fall within his powers. The most important exclusion is that he does not have power to consider a complaint which relates to, or to any consequences of, a bank's judgment of risk and other financial or commercial criteria (including assessments of character) in making any decision concerning any advance or analogous facility, guarantee or security. He has power to make awards of up to £100,000, and any award up to that figure will be honoured by the bank concerned. However, the complainant is not bound to accept the amount awarded. Instead, he may take legal proceedings against the bank, if he wishes to do so. The Ombudsman has discretion to decide

---

9 'Consortium banks', *Banking World*, June 1985, p. 59.

whether a case requires an oral hearing or can be determined on the basis of written evidence alone. Finally, his powers relate to matters arising on or after 1 January 1986. However, an exception is made for cases where the complainant was not aware, and could not with reasonable diligence have become aware, of the circumstances giving rise to a complaint until after that date.[10]

1-12C   At any time before the Ombudsman has made an award a bank named in the complaint may give to the Ombudsman a notice in writing containing:

   (a)   a statement with reasons that, in the opinion of the bank, the complaint involves or may involve (i) an issue which may have important consequences for the business of the bank or banks generally, or (ii) an important or novel point of law; and

   (b)   an undertaking that, if within six months after the Ombudsman's receipt of that notice either the applicant or the bank institutes in any court in the United Kingdom proceedings against the other in respect of the complaint, the bank will (i) pay the applicant's costs and disbursements of the proceedings at first instance and any subsequent appeal proceedings commenced by the bank and (ii) make interim payments on account of such costs if and to the extent that it appears reasonable to do so.

Upon the Ombudsman's receiving such a notice he must consider the reasons given by the bank and if he finds them reasonable he must cease to consider the complaint and he must inform the applicant in writing of the receipt of the notice, the date of its receipt and the effect of the notice upon the complaint, and must send the applicant a copy of the notice.

(b) Merchant banks

1-13   The term 'merchant bank' is historical in origin. Many of the merchant banks started in business as merchants, buying and selling goods. Having become well known for their stability and integrity, they then began to accept bills of exchange to finance transactions of other merchants. Gradually, their own merchanting business was discontinued, and their business of accepting bills was extended. At the present day, they finance the movement of goods by acceptance credits or by short-term cash advances. Besides have extensive overseas connections (which enable them to assist in the raising of capital in a variety of over-

10   For interesting articles, see P. E. Morris, 'The Banking Ombudsman', *The Journal of Business Law*, (1987), pp. 131–6, 199–210; Graham Penn, 'The Banking Ombudsman', *Banking World*, Vol. 6 (1988), pp. 54–5.

seas markets), many of the merchant banks have important domestic activities. Thus, they receive deposits; they act as issuing houses, arranging for the provision of long-term capital and advising on company finance; they undertake the supervision of investment portfolios for investment trusts, pension funds and other big investors; and they offer equipment leasing facilities. Some are engaged in factoring and in insurance broking; and some take a direct equity stake in unquoted companies.[11] Most of the clearing banks offer the facilities of merchant banks by channelling the work to a subsidiary company which specializes in this type of work. Most merchant banks (or 'investment banks', as they are sometimes called) are members of the British Merchant Banking and Securities Houses Association, which has replaced the Accepting Houses Committee and the Issuing Houses Association.

(c) Industrial bankers

1-14 Originally the primary function of industrial bankers, or finance houses as they are generally called today, was the provision of finance by way of hire-purchase or credit sale, and for this purpose they obtain funds on deposit, usually at notice, from companies and private individuals. However, the larger finance houses diversified their activities, with the result that the Crowther Committee, which reported in 1971,[12] listed those activities as:

1. Advances for the purchase of consumer durables under hire-purchase and credit sale agreements.
2. The provision of finance for agricultural and industrial plant, machinery and equipment by way of hire-purchase and conditional sale.
3. The financing of fleets of motor vehicles under contract hire arrangements.
4. The leasing of capital equipment for industry and commerce.
5. Personal loans to consumers.
6. Activities of a banking kind, notably the issue of cheques and the maintenance of current and deposit accounts.
7. Other types of commercial financing, including the acceptance of

---

11 See T. M. Rybcyznski, 'The merchant banks', *The Bankers' Magazine*, Vol. CCXVI (1973), pp. 240–8; *Modern Merchant Banking* (1976), edited by C. J. J. Clay and B. S. Wheble; John Padovan, 'New influences in merchant banking', *Journal of the Institute of Bankers*, Vol. 98 (1977), pp. 126–8; Malcolm Craig, 'Equity finance: the next challenge', *Banking World*, Vol. 1 (1983), pp. 14–16.

12 Report of the Committee on Consumer Credit (the 'Crowther Report') Cmnd. 4596 (1971), para. 2.3.14. See also A. C. Drury, *Finance Houses: Their Development and Role in the Modern Financial Sector* (1982).

trade bills, the factoring of receivables and the provision of finance for exports.

8. Overseas business either through subsidiaries established abroad to do instalment credit business in their country of incorporation, or through international credit clubs which can provide United Kingdom exporters with a source of instalment credit for buyers of their goods in the country of importation.

1-15 Some of the functions of finance houses are similar to those of the deposit banks. Thus they borrow funds from depositors and lend or employ those funds with a view to making a profit. If banking history had developed a little differently, the work performed by the finance houses might well have been performed by the deposit banks. Most of the deposit banks now have a close association, usually as a result of a large holding of shares, in one or more of the finance companies. [13]

1-16 The Finance Houses Association was formed in 1945 and was at first made up of only the larger finance houses. In 1956 some of the medium-sized finance houses formed the Industrial Bankers Association, and in 1966 the two associations amalgamated.

Definitions of banks and banking

1-17 It will be clear from the account already given of the different kinds of banks that it would be difficult, or at least cumbersome, to formulate a definition of banking which would be wide enough to embrace the diverse activities carried on by all types of bankers; thus, the complex activities of the merchant banks have little in common with the services offered by the National Savings Bank.

1-18 One could, of course, give the word 'bank' a narrow meaning and call that a definition; or one could give it a much wider meaning, and call that a definition. [14] The truth is that before one can define a word, it is soften necessary to examine the context in which it is used. With this in mind, one may consider the definitions of bank or banker under three heads: (a) some definitions by textbook writers, (b) some statutory definitions and (c) the views expressed by the courts.

---

13 See *post*, para. 10-131.
14 In *Alice Through the Looking-Glass* (Chapter VI) Humpty Dumpty claimed to use words in unusual senses, and Alice objected. 'The question is,' she said, 'whether you *can* make words mean so many different things.' Humpty Dumpty replied, 'The question is which is to be master – that's all.'

(a) Definitions by textbook writers

1-19   The late Dr Hart defined a banker or bank as:[15]

...a person or company carrying on the business of receiving moneys, and collecting drafts, for customers subject to the obligation of honouring cheques drawn upon them from time to time by the customers to the extent of the amounts available on their current accounts.

Likewise, *Halsbury's Laws of England* defines a banker as:[16]

an individual, partnership or corporation, whose sole or pre-dominating business is banking, that is the receipt of money on current or deposit account and the payment of cheques drawn by and the collection of cheques paid in by a customer.

Both these are excellent definitions of deposit banking, but they are not wide enough to embrace, for example, the National Savings Bank.

(b) Statutory definitions

1-20   There is no United Kingdom Act of Parliament which sets out to define banking. Section 2 of the Bills of Exchange Act 1882 provides that 'in this Act, unless the context otherwise requires... "banker" includes a body of persons, whether incorporated or not who carry on the business of banking'. This curious 'definition' has been the subject of derisive comment for many years.

1-21   The Bank Act 1979 introduced the concept of 'recognized' banks, that is to say, banks recognized by the Bank of England.[17] Recognition was, however, solely for the purposes of this Act.[18] The Banking Act 1987 repealed the Banking Act 1979, and all deposit-taking institutions are now known as 'authorized institutions'.[19]

(c) Views expressed by the courts

1-22   The opinions expressed by judges concerning the essential characteristics of banking have changed over the years. The traditional view is that no one may be considered a banker unless he pays cheques drawn

15 H. L. Hart, *The Law of Banking* (4th ed., 1931), Vol. 1, p. 1, citing *Re District Savings Bank Ltd, Ex parte Coe* (1861) 31 LJ Bank 8; *Halifax Union* v. *Wheelwright* (1875) LR 10 Ex 183, at p. 193; *Re Birkbeck Permanent Benefit Building Society* [1912] 2 Ch 183; affirmed *sub nom. Sinclair* v. *Broughman* [1914] AC 398.
16 (4th ed.), Vol. 3, p. 31. See also *Paget's Law of Banking* (10th ed., 1989), pp. 124–6.
17 See *post*, paras 1-40/6.
18 S. 36(2).
19 See *post*, para. 1-41.

on himself.[20] From time to time, however, this view has been rejected; for example, Lord Goddard rejected it when delivering judgment in a case in 1954.[21] The point at issue was whether the Industrial Disputes Tribunal had power to determine a dispute between a trustee savings bank and members of the National Union of Bank Employees who were in the employment of the bank. The bank applied to the court for an order of prohibition on the ground, *inter alia*, that the tribunal had no jurisdiction. This contention failed and, in the course of his judgment, Lord Goddard said that although a trustee savings bank did more than the Post Office Savings Bank, it did not carry on the business of banking in the same way as one of the Big Five banks in the sense of issuing cheque books to its customers and performing various services for them, but it nevertheless carried on 'the business of banking'.[22]

1-23   The traditional view, namely that no one may be considered a banker unless he pays cheques drawn on himself, was re-affirmed by Mocatta J, and by the Court of Appeal in *United Dominions Trust Ltd v. Kirkwood*.[23] The decision of the Court of Appeal was by a majority,[24] but all three members of the court shared the view[25] that the usual characteristics of banking at the present time are: (a) the acceptance of money from, and collection of cheques for customers and the placing of them to the customers' credit; (b) the honouring of cheques or orders drawn on the bank by their customers when presented for payment; and (c) the keeping of some form of current or running accounts

---

20 Among the older cases usually cited in support of this view are *Re District Savings Bank Ltd, Ex parte Coe* (1861) 31 LJ Bank 8; *Halifax Union* v. *Wheelwright* (1875) LR 10 Ex 183, at p. 193; *Re Birkbeck Permanent Benefit Building Society* [1912] 2 Ch 183; affirmed *sub. nom. Sinclair* v. *Broughman* [1914] AC 398.

21 *R* v. *Industrial Disputes Tribunal, ex parte East Anglian Trustee Savings Bank* [1954] 1 WLR 1093. See also the opinion of the Judicial Committee of the Privy Council in *Bank of Chettinad* v. *Commissioners of Income Tax* [1948] AC 378, where, at p. 470, the view was expressed that the words 'banker' and 'banking' may 'bear different shades of meaning at different periods of history' and that their meaning 'may not be uniform today in countries of different habits of life and different degrees of civilisation'.

22 [1954] 1 WLR, at p. 1096. The Post Office Savings Bank is now the National Savings Bank, and the 'Big Five' are now the 'Big Four'. Trustee savings banks now issue cheque books to their customers. For other cases which support the view that a person may be a banker even though he does not operate current accounts for customers, see *Re Bottomgate Industrial Co-operative Society* (1891) 65 LT 712; an Australian case, *Commissioners of the State Savings Bank of Victoria* v. *Permewan Wright & Co. Ltd* (1914) 19 CLR 457; and two Irish cases, *Re Sheilds' Estate* [1901] IR 172, a decision of the Court of Appeal in Ireland; *Commercial Banking Co. Ltd* v. *Hartigan and Others* (1952) 86 ILTR 109, a decision of a Circuit Court.

23 [1966] 1 QBD 783; and, on appeal, [1966] 2 QBD 431.

24 See *post*, para. 1-28.

25 See [1966] 2 QBD, at pp. 447, 457 and 465.

in their books in which the credits and debits are entered. In addition to these three usual characteristics, there are, of course, others, for example the lending of money.

Some practical problems

1-24   The question, 'Who is a banker?' usually arises when one is considering the meaning of the word in an Act of Parliament. The following illustrations may be given. They are based upon a passage in the judgment of Lord Denning MR, in *United Dominions Trust Ltd* v. *Kirkwood*,[26] where attention was drawn to the privileges enjoyed by bankers.

1-25   By virtue of the Bankers' Books Evidence Act 1879, bankers cannot be compelled to produce their books in court, but may send copies.[27]

1-26   Bankers are given special protection from liability when paying a crossed cheque to another banker.[28]

1-27   Bankers are also given special protection when collecting the proceeds of cheques on behalf of customers.[29]

1-28   Bankers were given special exemption from registration under the Moneylenders Acts 1900 and 1927, and from all the stringent regulations affecting moneylenders and their contracts. Yet, as Lord Denning MR pointed out in *United Dominions Trust Ltd* v. *Kirkwood*,[30] no definition of a banking business was to be found in the Moneylenders Acts. In *Kirkwood's* case, the defendant's only defence to a claim on certain bills of exchange which he had endorsed was that the plaintiffs were moneylenders, and, as they were not registered under the Moneylenders Acts, they could not enforce their rights. The plaintiffs argued that they were bankers and accordingly had no need to register. The decision depended, therefore, upon whether or not the plaintiffs were bankers. Lord Denning MR, and Diplock LJ, held that they were bankers and therefore entitled to succeed in their claim; Harman LJ, dissented.

1-29   A year later, the Companies Act 1967 amended the law in a way which prevented this particular difficulty from arising again. It provided that a certificate given by the Board of Trade that a person was a banker

---

26 [1966] 2 QBD, at pp. 442–4.
27 *Post*, para. 1-57.
28 Bills of Exchange Act 1882, ss. 79 and 80, *post*, para. 7-79.
29 Cheques Act 1957, s. 4, *post*, para. 6-74.
30 [1966] 2 QBD, at p. 443.

is to be conclusive evidence of that fact for the purposes of the Moneylenders Acts 1900 to 1927.[31]

1-30 By virtue of the Trustee Act 1925,[32] trustees may, pending investment, pay any trust money into a bank; but the Act does not define a bank.

1-31 By virtue of the Agricultural Credits Act 1928,[33] a bank may advance money to a farmer and take a charge on all his farm stock and agricultural assets. For this purpose, a 'bank' means the Bank of England, a trustee savings bank, or the Post Office, in the exercise of its powers to provide banking services.[34]

1-32 By virtue of the Bank of England Act 1946,[35] the Bank of England may request information from bankers and make recommendations to them. For this purpose, a 'banker' means 'any such person carrying on a banking undertakings as may be declared by order of the Treasury to be a banker for the purposes of this section'.[36]

1-33 By virtue of the Companies Act 1985,[37] a banking company enjoys special privileges in making up its balance sheet and profit and loss account. The London clearing banks and the Scottish banks no longer avail themselves of these privileges.

Section 2
STARTING AND CONDUCTING A BANKING BUSINESS

1-34 There are special rules which must be observed when a partnership or a company wishes to start a banking business, and there are rules which may affect bankers in the conduct of their business.

Supervision of banks

1-35 There used to be very little legislative control of banking. In 1973 Sir Leslie (subsequently Lord) O'Brien, the Governor of the Bank of England, addressed the Scottish Institute of Bankers thus:

31 Companies Act 1967, s. 123. The Moneylenders Acts 1900 and 1927 were repealed by the Consumer Credit Act 1974, s. 192(3) and Sched. 5.
32 S. 11.
33 S. 5(1).
34 S. 5(7) as amended by the Banking Act 1979, s. 51(1) and Sched. 6, para. 2.
35 S. 4(3).
36 S. 4(6).
37 S. 228(1), Sched. 9, para. 27.

The supremacy of London as an international banking centre is founded on a freedom from vexatious banking legislation equalled in few countries in the world. Our banking system has thrived under a general rule of law and surveillance by the central bank; and generally speaking by its conduct has justified the freedom and flexibility it has been given. It would be a tragedy if this position were radically altered simply to satisfy bureaucratic tidiness.[38]

1-36 The position soon changed. One of the main reasons for this change may be found in the property boom in the early 1970s. At that time the upsurge in the property market encouraged the development of what came to be known as 'secondary banks' or 'fringe banks'. They were less conservative in their approach to financing property transactions than the clearing banks. Likewise, the secondary banks were more ready to finance share dealings than the clearing banks. The secondary banks lent money at high rates of interest, and therefore they could offer high rates of interest to those who deposited money with them. As many of these secondary banks were not regarded as banks by the Bank of England, they were not subject to its supervision. Unfortunately, some of them lent heavily (and unwisely, as it turned out) to property companies and speculators. When, in 1973/4 the property market collapsed, and then the share market, some of the secondary banks found themselves in financial difficulties. Their deposits were saved as a result of a voluntary support operation, known as the 'lifeboat', which was mounted by the Bank of England and the clearing banks.

1-37 As a result of the secondary banking crisis, the government produced a White Paper in 1976 entitled *The Licensing and Supervision of Deposit-Taking Institutions*.[39] This White Paper stated the government's intention of introducing a formal system of control and a system for licensing deposit-takers. It put forward criteria for recognition of an institution as a bank and, finally, it recommended the establishment of a Deposit Protection Fund. The Banking Act 1979 enacted the changes in the law set out in this White Paper.

---

38 *The Banker*, Vol. 123 (1973), pp. 123–5. In 1973 the only relevant statutory power which the Bank of England possessed was conferred by s. 4 of the Bank of England Act 1946, which provides that the Bank of England may, if it thinks necessary in the public interest, request information from and make recommendations to bankers, and may, if so authorized by the Treasury, issue directions to any banker for the purpose of securing that effect is given to any such request or recommendation. The powers conferred by this section still exist, but, as far as is known, they have never been exercised.

39 Cmnd. 6584. For an account of the secondary banking crisis, see Margaret Reid, *The Secondary Banking Crisis 1973–75: Its Causes and Course* (1982).

1-38 There was another event which was responsible for the passing of the Banking Act 1979. The first Banking Directive was issued by the EEC Council of Ministers in Brussels in 1977.[40] One of the requirements of this Directive was that banks and other financial institutions must be licensed. Accordingly, it was necessary for Parliament to pass an Act in order to comply with this Directive. In his Sykes Memorial Lecture in 1979, Lord O'Brien stated that 'it was our European Community obligations which were primarily responsible for the Banking Act 1979'.

1-39 The Banking Act 1979 provided for two types of deposit-taking institutions, namely, (a) recognized banks, and (b) licensed deposit-takers. This division was not required by the EEC Banking Directive. It was introduced into the law of this country in order to limit the use of banking names and descriptions to recognized banks, and also to retain for recognized banks the informal type of supervision which the Bank of England had hitherto exercised over them, whilst applying more rigorous controls over licensed deposit-takers. For reasons which are stated below, the Banking Act 1987, which repealed the Banking Act 1979, does not differentiate between recognized banks and licensed deposit-takers.

1-40 The distinction between recognized banks on the one hand and licensed deposit-takers on the other hand caused practical difficulties. One of the most serious was that the Bank of England's powers of supervision over recognized banks were inadequate. Matters came to a head in 1984, when a well-known bank, a recognized bank under the Banking Act 1979, got into financial difficulties. The bank, Johnson Matthey Bankers Limited, was one of the five main participants in the London bullion market. It was considered that if this bank failed, the stability of the banking system might have been threatened. Accordingly, the Bank of England decided to acquire Johnson Matthey. In December 1984, just three months after the Bank of England acquired Johnson Matthey, the Chancellor of the Exchequer, Mr Nigel Lawson, set up a Committee under the Chairmanship of the Governor of the Bank of England, Mr R. Leigh-Pemberton, to look into the system of banking supervision and to make recommendations. The Committee reported in June 1985,[41] and its report pointed to a number of weaknesses in the system of supervision. In December 1985 the government published a White Paper,[42] which adopted most of the recommendations of the Committee. The Banking Bill was introduced into

---

40 77/780/EEC.
41 Cmnd. 9550. *Report of the Committee set up to Consider the System of Banking Supervision.*
42 Cmnd. 9695. *Banking Supervision.*

Parliament in November 1986, and the Act received the Royal Assent in May 1987.

1-41 The Banking Act 1987[43] strengthens the system of supervision in the light of experience since 1979. Section 3(1) of the Act provides that no person shall in the United Kingdom accept a deposit in the course of carrying on (whether there or elsewhere) a business which for the purposes of the Act is a 'deposit-taking business', unless that person is authorized by the Bank of England. Section 6(1) provides that a business is a 'deposit-taking business' if '(a) in the course of the business money received by way of deposit is lent to others; or (b) any other activity of the business is financed, wholly or to any material extent, out of the capital of or the interest on money received by way of deposit.' The Act does not differentiate between recognized banks and licensed deposit-takers. All deposit-taking institutions, now known as 'authorized institutions', are subject to the same scrutiny.[44] This was an important development. The Leigh-Pemberton Committee had reported that the status of Johnson Matthey Bankers Limited as a 'recognized bank' had been 'a factor in the delay in the supervisors becoming aware of, and reacting to, its growing problems'.[45]

1-42 Section 8 of the Banking Act 1987 lays down the procedure which must be followed when an institution applies to the Bank of England for authorization to take deposits, and s. 106 defines an institution as a body corporate or a partnership. As an individual person cannot be an 'institution', he cannot apply to the Bank of England for authorization to take deposits. Schedule 3 sets out the 'minimum criteria for authorization'. Thus every person who is, or is to be, a director, controller or manager of an institution must be a fit and proper person to hold the particular position which he holds or is to hold. At least two individuals must effectively direct the business of the institution. The business of the institution must be conducted in a 'prudent manner'; for example, it must maintain adequate capital, adequate liquidity and adequate provision for bad or doubtful debts. Every institution must

---

43 See *The Banking Act 1987: A Commentary by the British Bankers' Association*. This book analyses the Act section by section. For an interesting article on the Act, see Anu Arora, 'The Banking Act 1987', *The Company Lawyer*, Vol. 9 (1988), pp. 8–13, 39–46. For a comprehensive account of the subject, see Graham Penn, *Banking Supervision* (1989). This book deals not only with the Banking Act 1987 but also with the Guidance Notes and Statements of Principle published by the Bank of England. See also Maximilian J. B. Hall, *Handbook of Banking Regulation and Supervision* (1989).

44 However, there are some institutions which are exempt from the provisions of the Act. Thus by s. 4(1) of the Act the Bank of England itself is exempt. Schedule 2 contains a list of 25 exempted persons, including the National Savings Bank, building societies and local authorities.

45 Leigh-Pemberton Committee, p. 4.

maintain adequate accounting and other records of its business and adequate systems of control of its business and records. At the time when authorization is granted, every institution must have net assets amounting to not less than £1 million, or an amount of equivalent value denominated wholly or partly otherwise than in sterling. Section 32(1) of the Act provides that the Treasury may after consultation with the Bank of England and the Building Societies Commission make regulations for regulating the issue for and content of deposit advertisements.

1-43 The Banking Act 1987 contains a number of provisions which are intended to resolve problems which the Leigh-Pemberton Committee had identified. For example, s. 39(1) gives the Bank of England power to obtain 'such information as the Bank may reasonably require for the performance of its functions' under the Act. Any person who fails to comply with the Bank's request for information is guilty of an offence under s. 39(11).

1-44 Section 12 of the Act gives the Bank of England more flexible powers of intervention. Thus the Bank has power to restrict, rather than to revoke, an authorization where the circumstances are not such as to justify revocation. A restriction can be imposed for a period of up to three years; such a limit may, in particular, be imposed where the Bank considers that an institution should be allowed time to repay its deposits in an orderly manner.

1-45 Section 47 of the Act removed the constraint which previously precluded exchanges of information between the Bank of England and the auditors of authorized institutions. This change in the law cleared the way for auditors to play a greater part in the process of supervision. The Leigh-Pemberton Committee stated that, if the Bank of England 'is not itself to carry out detailed inspections of banks' books it must be able to rely on the assistance and co-operation of the professional firms who do carry out this task: the bank's auditors'.[46] Furthermore, by s. 46(2) of the Act auditors are required to notify the Bank of England if they decide to resign or not to seek re-appointment or if they decide to include any qualification to their report on an authorized institution's accounts. Similarly, by s. 46(1) an authorized institution must notify the Bank of England if it (a) proposes to give special notice to its shareholders of an ordinary resolution removing an auditor before the expiration of his term of office, or (b) gives notice to its shareholders of an ordinary resolution replacing an auditor at the expiration of his term of office with a different auditor.

46 Leigh-Pemberton Committee, p. 3.

1-46 Another very important innovation of the Banking Act 1987 was the creation of a Board of Banking Supervision. The Board advises the Bank of England on supervisory matters in the exercise of the Bank's powers. It considers individual cases and also general matters of supervisory policy. By s. 2(2) of the Act the Board consists of three *ex officio* members, namely the Governor of the Bank of England (the Chairman of the Board), the Deputy Governor and the executive director who is responsible for the supervision of institutions. In addition to the three *ex officio* members, there are six independent members, that is to say members appointed jointly by the Chancellor of the Exchequer and the Governor, being persons having no executive responsibility in the Bank. In practice, the six independent members are senior practitioners from the fields of banking, accountancy and the law. It is the duty of the independent members to give such advice as they think fit to the *ex officio* members on the exercise by the Bank of its functions under the Act.[47] The Board prepares an annual report on its activities.[48]

1-47 Another innovation of the Banking Act 1987 relates to restrictions on the ownership of authorized institutions. The main rules are as follows:

(a) By s. 37(1), if any person becomes a significant shareholder in relation to an authorized institution, he must notify the Bank of England. By s. 37(2) a 'significant shareholder' is one who, with his associates, can exercise or control 5 per cent or more, but less than 15 per cent, of the voting power at any general meeting of the institution.

(b) By s. 21(1) a person who intends to become a minority, majority or principal shareholder controller of an authorized institution must notify the Bank of England, and he may acquire that status only if the Bank does not object within three months. By s. 105(4) a 'minority shareholder controller' is a person who, with his associates, can exercise or control at least 15 per cent but not more than 50 per cent of the voting power; a 'majority shareholder controller', more than 50 per cent but not more than 75 per cent; and a 'principal shareholder controller' more than 75 per cent. By s. 22(1) the Bank may object to a person becoming a minority, majority or principal shareholder controller unless it is satisfied that (i) he is a fit and proper person to become a controller of the description in question, (ii) the interests of present and future depositors will not be threatened by that person becoming such a controller, and (iii) the institution will continue

47 S. 2(3).
48 S. 2(6).

to fulfil the criteria for authorization notwithstanding the influence which he may exert on the institution. By s. 27(3) if the Bank objects to a person becoming a minority, majority or principal shareholder controller, he may appeal to a tribunal consisting of a chairman appointed by the Lord Chancellor and two members appointed by the Chancellor of the Exchequer.

(c) By s. 24(1), (2) and (3), if the Bank of England considers that a shareholder controller of an authorized institution is no longer a fit and proper person to have that status, it may serve preliminary notice of objection on him and after considering representations made by him, it may serve a notice of objection requiring him to cease to be a shareholder controller. By s. 27(3) he may appeal against the notice of objection to a tribunal constituted as aforesaid.

(d) By s. 26(1), (2) and (7), if a person becomes a shareholder controller of an authorized institution after the Bank of England has objected, or continues to be such a shareholder after the Bank has objected, the Bank, by serving a notice upon him, may freeze his shareholding so that he cannot transfer his shares. Furthermore, by s. 26(3) the court may, on the application of the Bank, order the sale of any such shares.

1-48 Another innovation of the Banking Act 1987 relates to the reporting of 'large exposures' by authorized institutions. The relevant provisions are intended to discourage authorized institutions from committing too large a proportion of their funds to any one customer or group of connected customers. Excessive concentrations of risk have often caused the failure of banks in the past. By s. 38(1) an authorized institution must make a report to the Bank of England if (a) it has entered into a transaction relating to any one person as a result of which it is exposed to the risk of incurring losses in excess of 10 per cent of its available capital resources, or (b) it *proposes* to enter into a transaction relating to any one person which, either alone or together with a previous transaction or previous transactions entered into by it in relation to that person, would result in its being exposed to the risk of incurring losses in excess of 25 per cent of those resources. Section 38(9) provides that an institution which fails to make a report as required by the section is guilty of an offence.

1-49 There are restrictions on the use of banking names. As regards authorized institutions incorporated in the United Kingdom, s. 67 of the Banking Act 1987 provides that only those institutions with a paid-up share capital or undistributable reserves of not less than £5 million are entitled to use any name which indicates that they are a bank or carrying on a banking business. However, s. 68(3) provides that this prohibition does not apply to an authorized institution which is a company incorporated under the law of a country outside the United Kingdom. Section 70(1) and (3) provides that where an institution applies for authorization under the Act, it must give notice to the Bank of England of any name it is using or proposes to use and the Bank may give the institution notice in writing that it objects to the notified name on the ground that it is misleading to the public or otherwise undesirable. Section 71(5) provides than an institution to which a notice of objection is given may apply to the court to set aside the objection.

1-50 The Banking Act 1979 had established a mandatory deposit insurance scheme. Section 50(1) of the Banking Act 1987 provides that the body corporate known as the Deposit Protection Board and the fund known as the Deposit Protection Fund established by the Banking Act 1979 are to continue to exist. By s. 52(1) of the Banking Act 1987 all authorized institutions are liable to contribute to the Deposit Protection Fund, and the Act contains elaborate provisions for calculating the amount of the contribution. Section 58(1) provides that if an institution becomes insolvent the Deposit Protection Board must pay out of the Fund to each depositor who has a 'protected deposit' with that institution an amount equal to three-quarters of his protected deposit. Section 60(1) provides that any reference in the Act to a depositor's protected deposit is a reference to the total liability of the institution to him immediately before the time when it becomes insolvent, limited to a maximum of £20,000. These provisions seem to provide inadequate protection to depositors. If a depositor has a deposit of, say, £50,000 with an authorized institution which becomes insolvent, the maximum amount which he can obtain from the Fund will be only £15,000.

1-51 By s. 1(3) of the Banking Act 1987 the Bank of England must prepare an annual report to the Chancellor of the Exchequer on its activities under the Act, and the Chancellor must lay copies of every such report before Parliament. By s. 2(6) the annual report of the Board of Banking Supervision must be included in the report made by the Bank of England.

The Consumer Credit Act 1974

1-52 A licence to carry on a consumer credit business is required under s. 21 of the Consumer Credit Act 1974. If, therefore, a bank wishes to carry on this type of business, a licence must first be obtained.

1-53 Section 49 of the Act provides that it is an offence to canvass debtor−creditor agreements off trade premises. If the matter had rested there, it would have been an offence for a bank manager to 'canvass' an overdraft with a customer at the golf club. Fortunately, however, the section contains a special exception for the canvassing of bank over-drafts. Accordingly, a bank manager or other officer of the bank may safely arrange an overdraft with an existing customer off the bank's premises without fear of prosecution. If, however, he canvassed an over-draft off the bank's premises with someone who was not already a cus-tomer, he would commit an offence.

1-54   Section 51(1) of the Act provides that it is an offence to supply a person with a credit card, if he has not asked for one.[49]

1-55   Regulations made under the Act[50] deal with the case where a bank is asked to quote its terms in respect of a proposed overdraft. The quotation must state:

(a)   a rate, expressed to be a rate of interest, being a rate determined as the rate of the total charge for credit calculated on the assumption that only interest is included in the total charge for credit; and

(b)   the nature and amount of any other charge included in the total charge for credit.

The overdraft limit must be stated, together with the nature and amount of any security required.

Other regulations deal with advertisements.[51] Many banks are willing to make 'personal loans'[52] which they publicize either on television, or by distributing leaflets. As a rule, these loans are repayable, together with interest, by equal monthly instalments over periods from six months to five years. Thus the rate of interest charged remains constant throughout the period of repayment. The regulations require the amount of the monthly repayments to be stated and also the total cost of the credit facility, expressed as an annual percentage rate of charge, usually known as the APR. The intimation of the APR enables a potential bor-rower to compare the cost of borrowing by way of personal loan from a bank with the cost of using hire-purchase facilities.

Other regulations deal with the form of consumer credit agree-ments.[53] If a customer enters into a consumer credit agreement with a bank by way of loan for a sum not exceeding £15,000, the agreement falls within the Act, and the Consumer Credit (Agreements) Regulations 1983 will apply to it.[54] Agreements enabling customers to overdraw on

---

49 For credit cards, see *post*, paras 10-45/50.
50 Consumer Credit (Quotations) Regulations 1980, r. 6(1) and Sched. 1.
51 Consumer Credit (Advertisements) Regulations 1980.
52 See *post*, para. 1-74.
53 Consumer Credit (Agreements) Regulations 1983.
54 Consumer Credit Act 1974, s. 8, and the Consumer Credit (Increase of Monetary Limits) Order 1983.

current account are exempt from these regulations, provided that the proper steps are taken. This is the result of a 'determination' made by the Director General of Fair Trading under s. 74(1)(b) of the Consumer Credit Act 1974 on 3 November 1983. Any bank which wishes to avail itself of the privilege exempting overdrafts must inform the Office of Fair Trading of its intention to grant overdrafts. Agreements which are not exempt must comply with the Consumer Credit (Agreements) Regulations 1983.

Considerations of space make it impossible to set out the regulations in full, but the more important requirements are as follows. The agreement must contain the following heading shown prominently on its first page: 'Credit Agreement regulated by the Consumer Credit Act 1974'.[55] It must state the APR in relation to the agreement.[56] It must contain also the following statement: 'YOUR RIGHT TO CANCEL. Once you have signed this agreement, you will have for a short time a right to cancel it. Exact details of how and when you can do this will be sent to you by post by the creditor.'[57] The agreement must contain a signature box in which the following statement is printed: 'This is a Credit Agreement regulated by the Consumer Credit Act 1974. Sign it only if you want to be legally bound by its terms.'[58] The regulations further provide that the lettering of the terms of the agreement must be easily legible and of a colour which is readily distinguishable from the colour of the paper.[59]

Bankers' books in legal proceedings

1-56 The Bankers' Books Evidence Act 1879 confers certain privileges upon bankers. Prior to the passing of an Act with the same title in 1876, it was sometimes necessary for a banker to take to court one or more of his original ledgers or other books of account. This used to be very inconvenient, especially in the days when large bound ledgers containing many customers' accounts were kept by most banks. To remove these difficulties, the Bankers' Books Evidence Act 1876 was passed. That Act was repealed and its provisions were re-enacted in a somewhat extended form by the Bankers' Books Evidence Act 1879. The latter Act applies to all civil or criminal proceedings, arbitrations,[60] and proceedings before the Solicitors Disciplinary Tribunal.[61] In all such proceedings, a

---

55 Regulation 2(1) and Sched. 1.
56 *Ibid.*
57 Regulation 2(3) and Sched. 2.
58 Regulation 2(7) and Sched. 5.
59 Regulation 6(2).
60 Bankers' Books Evidence Act 1879, s. 10.
61 Solicitors Act 1974, s. 86.

copy of any entry in a banker's books, including ledgers, day books, cash books, account books and other records used in the ordinary business of the bank, whether those records are in written form or are kept on microfilm, magnetic tape or any other form of mechanical or electronic data retrieval mechanism[62] is received as prima facie evidence of such entry and of the matters, transactions, and accounts therein recorded,[63] provided that it is first proved by a partner or officer of the bank either orally or by affidavit that the book was at the time of making the entry one of the ordinary books of the bank, that the entry was made in the usual and ordinary course of business, and that the book is in the custody or control of the bank.[64] It must also be proved that the copy has been examined with the original and is correct.[65]

1-57 The provision of the Act which makes it unnecessary in many cases for a banker to bring his original books to court is contained in s. 6 of the Act of 1879, which provides that a banker or officer of a bank shall not, in any legal proceedings to which the bank is *not* a party, be compelled to produce any banker's book the contents of which can be proved under the Act, or to appear as a witness to prove the matters, transactions and accounts therein recorded, unless by order of a judge made for special cause. These rules do not apply to proceedings to which the bank is a party. In all such proceedings, a bank is in the same position as any other litigant. It, for some special reason, the bank's opponent in the proceedings wants to ensure that the actual books in the bank's possession are produced at the trial, he could include such books in his Notice to Produce, which he serves upon the bank or its solicitors.

1-58 Thus, s. 6 confers benefit upon the bank in those cases where the bank is *not* a party to the proceedings. Let it be supposed, for example, that a plaintiff in a civil action, or the police in a prosecution, want to be able to adduce in evidence the defendant's banking account. In a case of this nature, the defendant's bank will rely upon the provisions of s. 6, and it will be unnecessary for the bank to produce its original books, unless the judge for special cause so orders.

1-59 Section 7 of the Bankers' Books Evidence Act 1879 provides that, on the application of any party to a legal proceeding, a court may order that such party be at liberty to inspect and take copies of any entries in a banker's book for any of the purposes of such proceedings. A magistrate before whom criminal proceedings are being taken has power to

---

62 Bankers' Books Evidence Act 1879, s. 9, as amended by the Banking Act 1979, s. 51 (1) and Sched. 6, para. 1.
63 S. 3.
64 S. 4.
65 S. 5.

make an order under this section.[66] An order under the section is some-times obtained when the police require from a bank information concerning its customers and copies of documents in its possession *before* a criminal trial begins. In this connection, s. 9 of the Criminal Justice Act 1967 enables written evidence by a witness to be admitted to the same extent as oral evidence in all criminal trials, subject to the right of the party against whom it is tendered and the court, to require that the witness should give evidence orally. Thus, when the police are seeking information, they may serve a bank official with an order under s. 7 of the Bankers' Books Evidence Act 1879, and with a witness sum-mons.[67] The official then prepares a written statement pursuant to the 1967 Act, and if the party against whom it is tendered does not require him to give evidence orally, his attendance at the trial will be unnecessary. Of course, if a customer authorizes his bank to make dis-closure of his affairs, a written statement may be prepared without service of an order under s. 7 of the Bankers' Book Evidence Act 1879. If, however, a bank official is to attend court, a witness summons should be served. Although the Act is still in force, it is usually more convenient for the police to obtain an order under s. 9 of the Police and Criminal Evidence Act 1984.[68]

1-60 *Bonalumi* v. *Secretary of State for the Home Department*[69] revealed a surprising feature of orders made by a judge under s. 7 of the Bankers' Books Evidence Act 1879. The Home Secretary and the Government of Sweden applied successfully to the High Court for an order under s. 7 for liberty to inspect bank accounts held by the plaintiff, Sergio Bonalumi, at the London Branch of the Banco di Roma for the purpose of obtaining evidence against him in criminal proceedings in Sweden. Macpherson J ordered that the applicants should be at liberty to inspect his accounts. Bonalumi wished to appeal, but Glidewell J held that the Divisional Court had no jurisdiction to review the Order. Thereupon, Bonalumi appealed to the Court of Appeal which held that (a) the Criminal Division of the Court of Appeal had no jurisdiction within the terms of the Criminal Appeal Act 1968 to hear such an appeal, and (b) the Civil Division of the Court of Appeal was excluded from hearing such an appeal by s. 18(1)(a) of the Supreme Court Act 1981. Thus it would seem that a High Court order under s. 7 of the Bankers' Books Evidence Act 1879 is unappealable.

66 *R* v. *Kinghorn* [1908] 2 KB 949.
67 It would seem to be unnecessary to follow this procedure if a bank is merely asked to confirm that it has no account in the name of a specified person.
68 For the Police and Criminal Evidence Act 1984, see *post*, paras. 2-107A to 2-107C.
69 [1985] QB 675.

1-61 The Bankers' Books Evidence Act 1879 applies solely to books. Occasionally, it is desired that bankers should produce in court letters or other documents. In the first place, they are usually asked whether they will do so voluntarily. Sometimes, acting upon legal advice, they decline to attend court voluntarily, and then in a proper case, a *subpoena duces tecum* may be issued whereby the court orders a named official to attend court and to bring with him the relevant books and documents and be examined upon them.

1-62 Under modern conditions many statements of customers' accounts are produced by computers, and until the Civil Evidence Act 1968 was passed, there was some doubt whether or not these statements were admissible as evidence. Section 5(1) of the Act provides that in any civil proceedings a statement contained in a document produced by a computer is admissible as evidence of any fact stated therein of which direct oral evidence would be admissible. Certain conditions must be satisfied. Thus, a certificate must be given by a person occupying a responsible position in relation to the management of the computer. This certificate should identify the document containing the statement and describe the manner in which it was produced. It should also certify that at the relevant time the computer was operating properly, or if it was not operating properly, the certificate should state that this did not affect the production of the document or the accuracy of its contents.[70]

Payment and collection of cheques and other instruments

1-63 There are special statutory provisions which apply only to bankers when they collect and pay cheques and analogous instruments.[71]

Section 3
MEANING OF CUSTOMER

1-64 There is no statutory definition of a banker's customer, and so one has to refer to the decisions of the courts in order to discover the principles which determine whether or not a person is a customer.[72] The subject is of practical importance, chiefly because the special protection afforded to bankers by s. 4 of the Cheques Act 1957 applies only when

---

70 For other requirements, see the Civil Evidence Act 1968, s. 5(2), (4) and (5).
71 See Chapters 6 and 7.
72 In the United States, s. 4-104(1)(e) of the Uniform Commercial Code defines a customer as 'any person having an account with a bank or for whom a bank has agreed to collect items and includes a bank carrying an account with another bank'.

a collecting banker is acting on behalf of a customer.[73] The position today may be summarized as follows.

1-65 The relationship of banker and customer does not come into existence unless both parties intend to enter into it.[74]

1-66 As stated by Lord Davey in *Great Western Railway Co.* v. *London and County Banking Co. Ltd,*[75] 'there must be some sort of account, either a deposit or a current account or some similar relation, to make a man a customer of a banker'. Possibly that general rule should be qualified to the extent that a person who is about to open an account may sometimes be regarded as a customer. Thus, in *Woods* v. *Martins Bank Ltd and Another,*[76] a man who had been introduced to a bank manager was given certain advice by the manager about investing money. The manager then dictated a letter addressed to the bank for this man to sign instructing the bank to deal in a specified way with the proceeds of the repayment of an investment with a building society. The letter authorized the bank to apply the greater part of the proceeds in making the investment which the manager had advised, and the balance was to be retained by the bank to the order of the person signing the letter. It was held by Salmon J that the relationship of banker and customer existed as from the date when the bank accepted the instructions contained in the letter, even though an account was not opened until about three weeks after that date.

1-67 If a person has no account with a bank and is not about to open an account, the fact that a bank renders some casual service for him will not make him a customer. The leading case which established this principle is *Great Western Railway Co.* v. *London and County Banking Co. Ltd,*[77] where a bank had cashed cheques for about twenty years for a man who had no account with the bank. Both the trial judge and the Court of Appeal held that he was a customer, but the House of Lords took the opposite view.[78] It is debatable whether or not the decision of the House of Lords would have been different if the cheques had been lodged for collection (instead of being cashed) and if the payments out had not been made until after the proceeds of the cheques had been

73 See *post*, para. 6-74.
74 See *Robinson* v. *Midland Bank Ltd* (1925) 41 TLR 402, *post*, para. 11-2.
75 [1901] AC 414, at pp. 420–1.
76 [1959] 1 QB 55.
77 [1899] 2 QB 172; on appeal [1900] 2 QB 464; reversed [1901] AC 414.
78 See also the earlier case of *Lacave & Co.* v. *Crédit Lyonnais* [1897] 1 QB 148, where a bank on only one occasion collected cheques for a man who had no account; it was held that he was not a customer.

received by the bank. The better view would appear to be that the decision would have been the same.[79]

1-68 A person becomes a customer immediately he opens an account: he does not need to have habitual dealings with a banker in order to rank as a customer.[80] The Judicial Committee of the Privy Council summed up the position as follows:[81]

> Their Lordships are of the opinion that the word 'customer' signifies a relationship in which duration is not of the essence. A person whose money has been accepted by a bank on the footing that they undertake to honour cheques up to the amount standing to his credit is, in the view of their Lordships, a customer of the bank ... irrespective of whether his connection is of short or long standing.

1-69 One bank will itself be a customer of another bank if the first bank has an account with the second and sends to it cheques for collection.[82]

Section 4
TYPES OF ACCOUNT

The following are the principal types of account available to customers of the clearing banks.

Current accounts

1-70 The distinguishing features of a current account are as follows:

(a) The balance standing to a customer's credit on current account is repayable on demand and he has the right to draw cheques.

---

79 See the opinion of the Privy Council in *Commissioners of Taxation* v. *English, Scottish and Australian Banking Ltd* [1920] AC 683, at p. 687; but, for a different view, see Lord Brampton in *Great Western Railway Co.* v. *London and County Banking Co. Ltd* [1901] AC 414, at pp. 422–3. In *Matthews* v. *Williams, Brown & Co.* (1894) 10 TLR 386 the device of collecting a cheque for a person by crediting it to 'Sundry Customers' Account' failed to make that person a customer, but the decision was based upon the view (which is now discredited) that the word 'customer' involves something of use and habit.

80 *Ladbroke* v. *Todd* (1914) 111 LT 43; *Commissioners of Taxation* v. *English, Scottish and Australian Bank Ltd* [1920] AC 683. The contrary view to the effect that the word 'customer' involves something of use and habit was expressed by a Divisional Court in *Matthews* v. *Williams, Brown & Co. (supra)* but this can no longer be regarded as sound in law.

81 *Commissioners of Taxation* v. *English, Scottish and Australian Bank Ltd* [1920] AC 683, at p. 687.

82 *Importers Co. Ltd* v. *Westminster Bank Ltd* [1927] 2 KB 297.

(b) A customer may be granted an overdraft, that is to say he may be permitted to draw cheques up to an agreed figure beyond the amount standing to the credit of his current account. It is often said that overdrafts are repayable upon demand. Thus, a leading work[83] states that 'an overdraft is repayable on demand and forms of charge over security invariably provide accordingly'. This assumption is probably justified in the case of *temporary* advances, but, in fact, many bank advances are continued for a long period, subject to review and renewal each year, or at more frequent intervals. The practice was clearly stated in a letter from Mr D. J. Robarts, Chairman of the Committee of London Clearing Bankers, to the Governor of the Bank of England:[84]

> Bank advances in this country are controlled, in the main, by pre-arranged overdraft limits. This means that customers are given a permitted limit of overdraft up to which they may draw at any time while the agreement is in being. These limits usually run for a year, and it therefore follows that major customers can without notice draw on us in very large sums.

In cases where this practice is adopted and a limit has been agreed to a specified date, it is probably not open to the bank to demand repayment of the whole or any part of the advance prior to the agreed date, unless it had been made clear to the customer, when the advance was granted or last renewed, that the bank nevertheless reserved the right to cancel the limit and demand repayment of the advances at any time. Moreover, the detailed arrangements which are sometimes included in a facility letter addressed by a bank to a customer may lead to the result that the advance is not repayable on demand.[85]

(c) If a bank manager who has received a request for an overdraft submits an application to his head office or to his regional office, he should be very careful not to say anything to the customer regarding the outcome of the application which might mislead the customer. If he does mislead the customer and the customer suffers loss, the bank may be liable in damages for the manager's negligence.[86]

(d) If a customer overdraws his current account without the bank's permission, he may thereby commit an offence under the Theft

---

83 *Paget's Law of Banking* (10th ed., 1989), pp. 182–3.
84 See *The Times*, 5 June 1969. Mr Robarts was explaining to the Governor of the Bank of England why it was difficult for the banks to reduce their total lending as requested by the government.
85 *Williams and Glyn's Bank Ltd.* v. *Barnes* [1981] Com LR 205.
86 *Box* v. *Midland Bank Ltd.* [1979] 2 Lloyd's Rep. 291; [1981] 1 Lloyd's Rep. 434, CA.

Act 1968.[87] This was decided in *Halstead* v. *Patel*,[88] where a customer deliberately overdrew his account with the National Giro although he knew that he was not permitted to do so.

(e) The bank normally allows no interest on sums standing to the customer's credit. However, there are exceptions. The Building Societies Act 1986[89] enabled building societies to offer most retail banking services. Many societies now offer current accounts, cash machine cards and credit cards. They also pay interest on current accounts. In order to compete with building societies, some banks pay interest on current accounts.

(f) The bank charges interest on a day-to-day basis on overdrafts on current account. The rate of interest is a matter for agreement, but is very frequently between one per cent and five per cent above the bank's base rate.

(g) The bank usually charges commission for services rendered, whether the account is in credit or is overdrawn. Commission is normally debited half-yearly or quarterly. As a general rule, the commission charges on the accounts of personal customers are calculated in accordance with published tariffs, whilst the charges in respect of the accounts of corporate customers are negotiated. As regards the accounts of personal customers, some banks charge no commission if an account is kept in credit; other banks charge no commission if the balance of the account does not fall below a specified sum.

(h) The bank supplies its customers with periodical loose-leaf statements setting out the debit and credit entries in their accounts.

Deposit accounts

1-71 The distinguishing features of a deposit account are as follows:

(a) The balance standing to a customer's credit on deposit account is repayable upon personal application after a stated period of notice, which at the present time is usually seven days.[90] Some deposits are made for fixed terms, such as one, two, three, six or twelve months.

(b) The customer has no right to draw cheques.

---

87 S. 15.
88 [1972] 1 WLR 661. See also *Director of Public Prosecutions* v. *Turner* [1974] AC 357. where it was held by the House of Lords that a person who paid a debt by drawing a cheque which he knew would be dishonoured had committed an offence under s. 16 of the Act.
89 S. 34 and Sched. 8, Part I.
90 Banks will also accept term deposits at a fixed rate of interest: see *post*, para. 10-136.

(c) The bank allows interest on sums standing to the customer's credit at a rate which varies with its base rate.[91]

(d) The bank does not usually charge commission on a deposit account. If services, such as the collection of dividends or the payment of standing orders, are undertaken, the customer will normally have a current account as well as a deposit account, and commission will therefore be charged in the current account.

(e) The bank supplies its customer with a passbook setting out the debit and credit entries in the account. Alternatively, if a fixed sum is to be deposited, it is still the practice in some parts of the country for the bank to issue to its customer a 'deposit receipt'.

Savings accounts

1-72 These accounts are a special type of deposit account which are intended primarily for small savers. The rate of interest on savings accounts is usually a little lower than that on deposit accounts, but the rate is fairly static, that is to say, it does not vary with every change in base rate. Some banks allow the full deposit account rate of interest on savings account balances in excess of a certain figure, e.g. £200.

Loan accounts

1-73 The most usual method of lending money to a customer is by way of overdraft on current account. However, there are cases where it is desirable to advance a fixed sum by way of loan account, the proceeds being credited to the customer's current account. This occurs, for example, when the borrowing powers of the customer are limited by law.[92] Interest is calculated on the amount of a loan outstanding on a daily basis. Sometimes, repayment is effected by periodic transfers of fixed amounts from current account to loan account.

Personal loan accounts

1-74 These accounts were introduced by some banks in 1958. The special features of such accounts are that no security is required, and that arrangements are made for repayment of the loan together with interest by equal monthly instalments over periods from six months to five years. In this way the total amount to be paid by way of charges is known at the outset. As a general rule, the loans range from a minimum

---

91 The base rates of the clearing banks are fixed by the banks individually and, although they tend to coincide, they do occasionally diverge.

92 See *post*, para. 11-280.

of £50 to a maximum of about £5000. As the name 'personal loan' implies, this service is intended primarily for financing items of domestic expenditure, for example, the purchase of furniture or a car. The agreement in respect of a personal loan usually provides that, if the borrower dies before completing his repayments, the debt will be cancelled, provided that the instalments have previously been kept up to date. Partly because of this insurance cover and partly because no security is required, a higher rate of interest is charged in respect of personal loans than the rates which apply to the more usual types of bank lending.

Other loans repayable by instalments

1-75 Some banks offer other types of loans repayable by monthly instalments, such as business development loans, house improvement loans and farm development loans. These may be either secured or unsecured. Secured loans attract a slightly lower rate of interest than unsecured loans.

Revolving credit schemes

1-76 Some banks offer revolving credit schemes. These normally involve loans repayable by regular monthly instalments, but they differ from other loans payable by instalments in two respects. First, the borrower need not take up the full amount of the loan at the outset. Secondly, as his repayments reduce his indebtedness, he can 'top up' his loan by borrowing more, provided that the total debt outstanding does not exceed his agreed credit limit.

Budget accounts

1-77 In 1967 some banks introduced a new form of account called a 'budget account'. The object is to allow personal customers to spread the incidence of normal personal and household expenditure, such as fuel bills, season tickets, car insurance and school fees. The total amount of these recurring items for the year is estimated, and the customer transfers this amount by twelve equal monthly instalments into his budget account. He then makes the payments out of this account as and when they fall due. Thus, budget accounts may at times be overdrawn when payments out of the account exceed the amounts transferred into it.

Section 5
THE FINANCIAL SERVICES ACT 1986

Professor Gower's Report

1-78   The events leading up to the passing of the Financial Services Act 1986 were clearly, and entertainingly, described in a lecture by Professor L. C. B. Gower in June 1987 and published about six months later.[93] He outlined the history of investor protection starting with the Prevention of Fraud (Investments) Act 1939. That Act was intended to deal with the outbreak of share-pushing that had occurred in the late 1930s. The basic principle of the Act was similar to that adopted in the Financial Services Act 1986. Those who undertook the business of dealing in securities were required to be licensed, unless they were members of a recognized stock exchange or of a recognized association of dealers in securities or were exempted. The intention was that there should be one powerful recognized association of dealers who would effectively regulate dealers who were not Stock Exchange members. Unfortunately, because of the outbreak of war in September 1939, the Act was not brought into operation until 1944 when the initial enthusiasm for that association had died. The provisions of the Act, as amended in various minor respects, were subsequently re-enacted in the Prevention of Fraud (Investments) Act 1958.

In 1977 the government announced its intention to amend this Act. In a consultative document published in 1977[94] it was proposed that the scope of the Act should be widened to include investment advisers and consultants, that the number of exemptions should be reduced, that fuller information should be required from applicants for licences, that power should be taken to suspend as well as to revoke licences, and that the enforcement provisions of the Act should be strengthened.

With the change of government in 1979 preliminary work on the amending legislation was shelved, but in July 1981 the government decided that reforms could not be put off any longer. Their decision resulted from the collapse of two medium-sized investment advisory firms, one an insurance and investment management firm and the other a commodity futures broker. Each failure involved about £5 million, as a result of which many investors lost their life savings. In both cases the firm had mixed clients' money with its own, and in both cases the firm had put clients' money into investments in which they themselves had

---

93 L. C. B. Gower, '"Big Bang" and City regulation', *The Modern Law Review*, Vol. 51, (1988), pp. 1–22.
94 Cmnd. 6893.

conflicting interests. Neither firm was subject to any form of regulation, and there was no compensation fund to help the investors. The government decided, as a stop-gap measure, to revise the rules and regulations made under the Prevention of Fraud (Investments) Act 1958, and to have a wide-ranging review of the whole field. In his lecture Professor Gower explained the government's policy as follows:

> They took the view that the latter might be better undertaken by one man rather than by a twelve-man Departmental Committee. And I was invited to be the one man. You may well ask, as I did, why me? The answer is that I happened to be on the spot as a part-time adviser to the Department on company law matters and they could not think of anyone else who might be foolish enough to accept. I tried to wriggle out of such an unexpected and onerous assignment by pointing out that I was unlikely to be *persona grata* with the City Establishment and by laying down conditions which I expected to be rejected. But apparently the Establishment failed to black-ball me – probably, in the light of their subsequent reactions, because they had failed to recognize that the wide terms of reference covered their operations and not merely those of the small fry. And the government accepted all my conditions – albeit after a heated argument.

The result was, therefore, that the Secretary of State appointed Professor Gower to undertake a review of the protection required by investors and to advise on the need for new legislation. In his lecture Professor Gower continued as follows:

> I had a pretty clear idea of what I thought was needed but I knew that this would only be achieved (if at all) after a prolonged exercise of persuasion – or traumatic City scandals. For what I believed was needed was something similar to the system adopted in the United States some 50 years earlier and later copied, with modifications, by many Commonwealth and foreign countries. I wanted statutory control of investment business, widely defined, under which all those conducting that business would be authorized by, and regulated through, membership of a few self-regulatory organizations recognized by, and under the surveillance of, a governmental or quasi-government body which ideally should be a self-standing Commission.
>
> The difficulties about getting this accepted were pretty obvious. The City would welcome continued self-regulation, for which it believed it had a genius. But self-regulation to most of the City then meant leaving everybody to regulate himself in his own interests subject only to a possible unpublicized reproof from his professional or trade association if he transgressed too blatantly. To me, and to a growing number of others, it meant much more – the establishment by the industry of bodies pledged to regulate their members in the interests of the public.

Professor Gower held some initial informal consultations, and then he outlined his suggestions in a Discussion Document.[95] In his lecture he stated that his suggestions aroused a mixed reception:

> Consumer groups and the media were quite enthusiastic. But the main City bodies were livid. They denounced me for having, in their view, exceeded my brief by suggesting regulation of the elite merchant banks and Stock Exchange member firms when all that was needed was effective regulation of the fringe operators. And they argued that self-regulation (in their sense) was the panacea and that it works only when it is left free from any form of governmental surveillance.

Another round of consultations ensued, and at that time certain events occurred which were a godsend to Professor Gower's cause. There were scandals at Lloyd's misdeeds by some Stock Exchange members, and the collapse of certain commodity firms. These events tarnished the City's reputation both nationally and internationally. In November 1983 Professor Gower delivered his recommendations.[96] His principal recommendation was that the Prevention of Fraud (Investments) Act 1958 should be replaced by a new Investor Protection Act. This would provide the framework for a comprehensive system for the regulation of investment business 'based so far as possible on self-regulation subject to governmental surveillance'.

The government's proposals

1-79 It soon became clear that the government would introduce legislation which would adopt the basic framework of Professor Gower's recommendations. However, as was stated by Professor Gower in his lecture, there were still two major questions on which opinion was deeply divided. The first was what should be the precise nature and number of the self-regulating organizations (the SROs). The second was whether the governmental regulator should be a government department

95 *Review of Investor Protection: A Discussion Document* (HMSO January 1982).
96 *Review of Investor Protection: Report Part I.* This report was published in 1984: Cmnd. 9125. Four years later Sir Mark Weinberg, Chairman of Allied Dunbar Assurance plc, in a lecture which he delivered to the Royal Society of Arts, paid a fitting tribute to Professor Gower. He said: 'It is often said that one man does not change history, and it is fairly certain that there would have been some legislation whatever form of enquiry had been set up, but I would guess that the resulting legislation would have been far less comprehensive if the government had appointed a committee rather than one man – and if the one man had been anyone other than Professor Gower. For he did what no one had attempted before (as far as I am aware, anywhere in the world) which is to look at investment markets in the round.' See the *Journal of the Royal Society for the Encouragement of Arts, Manufactures and Commerce*, June 1988, p. 479.

or a self-standing Commission. On the first question the City bodies had persuaded Professor Gower that, if they were to collaborate, it was essential, at any rate in the first instance, that the SROs should be based on existing trade associations and that firms should have the option of obtaining authorization either through membership of an SRO or through direct authorization by the governmental body. On the second question a majority in the City had probably reconciled themselves to a self-standing Commission. The Government's proposals were published in January 1985 in a White Paper entitled *Financial Services in the United Kingdom: A New Framework for Investor Protection.*[97] The White Paper stated that new legislation would be introduced which would make it an offence to carry on investment business without authorization or exemption. The power of authorization would be assumed by the Secretary of State, but he would be empowered to delegate this and other functions to a practitioner-based body designated by him which matched a number of criteria laid down in the Act. That body would operate in turn through a number of self-regulating organizations recognized by it.

The Securities and Investments Board

1-80   The Financial Services Act 1986 duly enacted the government's proposals.[98] Section 114(1) provided that, if it appeared to the Secretary of State that a body corporate had been established which was able and willing to discharge his functions under the Act and that certain specified requirements were satisfied, he could make an order transferring all or any of those functions to that body, which the Act referred to as a 'designated agency'. Section 114(2), which was introduced as a result of back-bench pressure at the Committee stage in the House of Commons, provided that the body, known as the Securities and Investments Board Limited, was to be the designated agency if those conditions were fulfilled. In May 1987 the Secretary of State, with an affirmative resolution of both Houses of Parliament, delegated most of his functions to the Securities and Investment Board which (as permitted by para. 2 of Sched. 9) dropped the word 'Limited' from its name.

---

97 Cmnd. 9432.
98 See Eva Z. Lomnicka and John L. Powell, *Encyclopedia of Financial Services Law* (two volumes in loose-leaf); Andrew Whittaker and Geoffrey Morse, *The Financial Services Act 1986: A Guide to the New Law* (1987); David F. Lomax *London Markets After the Financial Services Act* (1987). For an excellent account of the legislation, see four articles by Derrick Hanson published in *Banking World*, Vol. 5, May 1987, pp. 26–30, June 1987, pp. 24–5, July 1987, pp. 24–5, and August 1987, pp. 33–4. Mr Hanson is a retired director and general manager of Barclays Bank Trust Company and Chairman of Barclays Unicorn.

1-81   The Securities and Investments Board (or SIB as it is commonly known) is, in effect, a self-standing Commission. It is a private company limited by guarantee. Its members and directors are the same persons, and they are appointed and removable by the Secretary of State and the Governor of the Bank of England, acting jointly, neither of whom is a member of the company. Its costs (and also those of the whole regulatory scheme) are borne by the financial services industry and its customers, except for the residuary costs of the Department of Trade and Industry and of the Financial Services Tribunal to which those refused authorization, or whose authorization is revoked, may appeal. The high cost of administering the whole regulatory scheme was stressed by Lord Bruce-Gardyne in a lecture which he delivered to the Royal Society of Arts in March 1988. He said:[99]

> I must at once declare an interest, because I am a director of the TSB; and the TSB, like all the clearing banks − and many others − frankly finds the new regime horrendous. Of course, I know its theme is consumer protection. But my, will the consumer pay for it! I notice that Sir Mark Weinberg dismissed the estimates of compliance costs running to one hundred million pounds a year as inventions of the press and producers interests, other of course than his own.[1] I am bound to say that, judging from the TSB's experience to date, I would guess that those estimates in the end will turn out to be conservative.
>
> You may say, however, that at least the little man will be more effectively protected from shocks. I wonder. What we already know is that a great many of the genuine independent intermediaries . . . will be unable to afford the cost of compliance − quite apart from being able to understand it − and will go out of business.

In the course of his Annual Statement published in the Report and Accounts of National Westminster Bank PLC for 1988, the Chairman, Lord Boardman said:

> The Financial Services Act came into force in April 1988. It has an important role in promoting investor confidence by attacking bad practices and codifying good ones.
>
> However, the regulatory blanket that has been thrown over the investment industry is a heavy one. The costs of compliance which the industry must bear could well exceed £100 million a year. The estimated costs for us to establish Group-wide compliance were in the region of £5 million, and may run to £2 million annually.

---

99 See the *Journal of Royal Society for the Encouragement of Arts, Manufactures and Commerce*, August 1988, at p. 671. The abbreviation TSB refers to Trustee Savings Bank.

1 Sir Mark Weinberg is Chairman of Allied Dunbar Assurance plc. He is also a Deputy Chairman of the SIB.

In an industry in which competition is truly global, such additional costs may put London and British financial institutions at a disadvantage. I therefore welcome the comprehensive review now underway to analyse how thick that regulatory blanket needs to be.

Although the SIB is, in effect, a self-standing Commission, it is accountable for its actions to the Secretary of State, and he is accountable for the SIB to Parliament.

Authorization under the Act

1-82 The most important requirement of the Financial Services Act 1986[2] is that no person may carry on an investment business in the United Kingdom, unless he is either authorized or exempted under the Act. By virtue of Sched. 1 of the Act, investment business includes five types of activity, namely (a) dealing in investments, (b) arranging deals in investments, (c) managing investments, (d) giving investment advice, and (e) establishing collective investment schemes. Also by virtue of Sched. 1, the word 'investment' includes shares or stock in a company, but not in a building society or in an industrial and provident society. Debentures and government and public securities are within the definition, and debentures include 'bonds, certificates of deposit and other instruments creating or acknowledging indebtedness'. Warrants and other instruments entitling the holder to subscribe for any of these investments are also investments, and so are certificates and other instruments conferring rights of property in them. The definition also includes units in a collective investment scheme (for example a unit trust); options to acquire other investments; currency (including sterling) and gold and silver; certain futures, that is to say agreements for the sale of a commodity or property under which delivery is to take place at a future date at a price agreed upon when the contract is made; and long-term insurance contracts, with the exception of those contracts which are designed purely for protection against risk without containing an investment element.

1-83 As stated above, the Financial Services Act 1986 provides that a person carrying on an investment business in the United Kingdom must be either authorized or exempted. He may be authorized in one of three ways:

(a) He may be authorized by the Securities and Investments Board, though in practice this is rarely necessary.

(b) He may be authorized by a self-regulating organization (SRO).

2 S. 3.

Five SROs have been recognized by the SIB, each covering a particular area of investment business.

(c) He may be authorized by a recognized professional body (RPB). These bodies are the Law Society of England and Wales, the Law Society of Scotland, the Law Society of Northern Ireland, the Institute of Chartered Accountants in England and Wales, the Institute of Chartered Accountants of Scotland, the Institute of Chartered Accountants of Ireland, the Chartered Association of Certified Accountants, the Insurance Brokers Registration Council and the Institute of Actuaries. Members of these bodies apply to their appropriate RPB for a certificate which enables them to carry on the specific type of authorized investment business which is appropriate. The RPBs charge an annual fee for issuing these certificates.

The alternative to authorization is exemption, and the following institutions are exempted persons under the Act: the Bank of England; recognized investment exchanges, for example the Stock Exchange; the Society of Lloyd's and Lloyd's underwriting agents; money market institutions included in a list maintained by the Bank of England; appointed representatives who will be regulated through the principals in question; and persons acting as manager of a fund established under the Charities Act 1960, the Trustee Investments Act 1961 or the Administration of Justice Act 1982.

Any person who carries on an investment business without authorization or exemption is liable to both civil and criminal sanctions. The SIB has a formidable armoury of regulatory sanctions ranging from reprimands, public or private; civil actions to obtain restitution of client funds; suspension; and finally – the ultimate sanction – withdrawal of authorization from an investment business. There is a right of appeal to the Financial Services Tribunal, an independent body whose remit is to re-examine the case.[3]

The cost of operating the system is very substantial.[4] The financial structure is that the SIB receives fees from those whom it authorizes, including the SROs and the RPBs. In turn the SROs and the RPBs obtain fees from their own members to cover both their own costs and their contribution to the SIB.

1-83A As stated above, s. 3 of the Financial Services Act 1986 imposes a prohibition on carrying on an investment business in the United Kingdom in the absence of authorization or exemption. By way of enforcement, s. 6 confers upon the Secretary of State the power (which

---

3 Financial Services Act 1986, ss 96/101.
4 See the statements by Lord Bruce-Gardyne and Lord Boardman, *ante*, para. 1-81.

has been delegated to the SIB) to obtain an injunction to restrain breaches of s. 3 and to obtain a restitution order requiring that the profits of an unauthorized investment business be paid into court. In *Securities and Investment Board* v. *Pantell SA*[5] one of the issues was whether the Board could obtain an interim Mareva injunction, preserving the assets of the defendants pending the hearing of proceedings under s. 6. Sir Nicolas Browne-Wilkinson V-C held that he had jurisdiction to make this order. Although s. 6 did not specifically authorize the granting of a Mareva injunction, the judge had no doubt that such an order might be essential in order to prevent the frustration of any restitution order which might subsequently be made under s. 6.

The Central Register

1-84   The SIB is required by the Financial Services Act 1986[6] to maintain a Central Register of all authorizations to carry on an investment business. The entry for each firm gives: (a) its name, address and telephone number; (b) its SIB reference number; (c) its authorization status (e.g. whether it is authorized or suspended); (d) the name of its regulatory body (e.g. its SRO or its RPB); and (e) a brief description of the main type of investment business which it conducts.

The names of 'appointed representatives', who are agents of authorized firms, do not appear on the register. They do not need authorization, because an authorized firm takes full responsibility for their investment business activity.

In order to find out whether a firm is authorized, members of the public may gain access to the Central Register (a) by using Prestel, the electronic information service, or (b) by writing to the SIB at 3 Royal Exchange Buildings, London EC3V 3NL, or (c) by telephoning the SIB on a number reserved for Register enquiries, namely 071-929 3652.

The Self-Regulating Organizations

1-85   The Securities and Investments Board has recognized five self-regulating organizations (SROs), namely:

(a)   The Securities Association (known as TSA);
(b)   The Financial Intermediaries, Managers and Brokers Regulatory Association (known as FIMBRA);
(c)   The Association of Futures Brokers and Dealers (known as AFBD);

---

5 [1989] 2 All ER 673.
6 S. 102.

(d)   The Investment Management Regulatory Organization (known as IMRO);

(e)   The Life Assurance and Unit Trust Regulatory Organization (known as LAUTRO).

The rules made by the relevant SRO are binding upon its members. It was originally provided that the rules of the SROs had to provide protection for investors which was at least as effective as those of the SIB.[7] This was known as the 'equivalence test', and it has been replaced by the 'adequacy test'.[8]

The Securities Association

1-86 In 1986 The Stock Exchange merged with the International Securities Regulatory Organization (ISRO), which had been set up in 1985 by the big international investment houses with the main object of regulating their activities in the Eurodollar market. It was decided to change the structure of the old Stock Exchange and to form two limited liability companies, namely the International Stock Exchange of the United Kingdom and the Republic of Ireland Limited, and the Securities Association Limited (known as TSA).

TSA authorizes its members to carry on investment business, including dealing and arranging deals in shares, debentures, government and other public securities, warrants, certificates representing securities, rights and interests in securities, and financial futures and options on securities and on foreign currency. Its members may also be concerned with advising clients on deals in investments, with managing such investments, and with arranging and advising on transactions in life assurance and collective investment schemes.

TSA can refuse membership to firms which do not meet its criteria for being 'fit and proper', which basically means that they are considered honest, competent and solvent. It has approximately 1,000 member firms, of which less than half are British. There are also about 30,000 registered individuals. Almost all International Stock Exchange member firms are TSA members: they account for one third of TSA's membership. TSA's Board chiefly consists of representatives from member firms, though there are some independent members to ensure that the interests of the public are represented. Any employee of a member firm who is likely to be advising clients must be a TSA 'registered representative'. This involves passing an examination, through which TSA ensures high standards of professional competence.

7 Financial Services Act 1986, Sched. 2.
8 See *post*, para. 1-92.

TSA members must comply with TSA rules, which cover two main areas, namely financial regulations and conduct of business. The financial regulations are intended to ensure that a firm remains financially sound and has enough capital to support its activities. This involves proper record keeping, and the segregation of clients' money and stock from that of the firm. The conduct of business rules are designed to ensure that customers get the best possible treatment. For example, the firm must always try to obtain the best price for its clients. It must act quickly after receiving their instructions, and it must not give any advice which enables the firm to benefit at the expense of clients.

Where a client requires an advisory rather than a simple execution service, the firm asks him about his financial circumstances and gives him a 'client agreement letter' to complete. Although the client is under no obligation to complete it, the benefit is twofold. First, the agreement letter sets out the terms on which the firm will deal with his business. Secondly, the agreement letter asks for details of his financial affairs, because the firm needs to 'know its customer', if it is to give him sound advice. If a client is not satisfied with the service which he receives from a TSA member firm, he should first try to resolve the problem with the firm. If he is still not satisfied, he may write to the Complaints Bureau, The Securities Association, The Stock Exchange Building, Old Broad Street, London EC2N 1EQ.

If TSA discovers that something is amiss within a member firm, it can take disciplinary action. This can range from a reprimand, an order to the firm to put right what is wrong, to a fine or even withdrawal of authorization, which has the effect of preventing the firm from doing any further investment business. Whilst TSA is carrying out an investigation, if it considers that investors' funds may be at risk, it has power to order the firm not to dispose of its assets and to cease trading until the issue has been resolved. If TSA discovers that fraud appears to have been committed by a member firm, it will report the matter to the police. If the firm is insolvent and is in liquidation, the investor may make a claim under the Investors' Compensation Scheme.[9]

TSA's role may be compared with that of the International Stock Exchange. TSA's main function is to protect investors by regulating the relationship between member firms and their clients and by monitoring the financial stability of member firms. The International Stock Exchange still has the responsibility for regulating the market. This includes, for example, monitoring erratic movements in the price of shares prior to a takeover which may be the result of insider dealing. The Stock Exchange also ensures the proper settlement of transactions.

9 See *post*, para. 1-91.

The Financial Intermediaries, Managers and Brokers Regulatory Association

1-87 FIMBRA is a company limited by guarantee, whose members are its shareholders. It is concerned primarily with regulating firms which offer independent investment advice and services to the general public. These range from life insurance advice to arranging transactions in shares. Its members include independent advisers on life insurance, pensions and unit trusts, firms offering personal portfolio management services and firms publishing magazines and newsletters whose main purpose is to offer investment advice.

Most FIMBRA members act as an agent for their clients, that is to say they arrange an investment with a third party. However, some FIMBRA members deal in investments as a principal, that is to say they buy investments in their own name and then sell them to their clients. It is important to know in which capacity a firm is acting. The firm must make this clear to its clients. Where firms manage investments for their clients, this service must be covered by a management agreement between the firm and the client.

A firm which wishes to join FIMBRA must show that it is honest, solvent and competent. FIMBRA makes detailed enquiries about the people running the business and about the staff who advise clients.

Once a firm becomes a member it must comply with the FIMBRA rulebook. It must report its financial position at least once a year, and its accounts must be checked by an independent, qualified auditor. Its rulebook must offer investors protection equivalent to that offered by the Securities and Investments Boards rulebook.

FIMBRA carries out random checks on all its members. The frequency of these checks depend upon the type of business which a firm undertakes. A firm which handles clients' money is visited more often than one which does not. These visits are not simply to check that the accounting rules are being followed. FIMBRA also looks at the way a firm conducts its business. There are detailed rules on advertising, on the information which must be given to the client, and on recording the advice which has been given. The rules are designed to ensure that clients are offered suitable, independent and competent advice, and to minimize the chances of a firm collapsing thereby causing financial loss to its clients.

In *R* v. *Financial Intermediaries Managers and Brokers Regulatory Association, ex parte Cochrane*[10] it was held that judicial review could not succeed against an appellate tribunal's decision to expel a business

10 *The Times*, 23 June 1989.

from a self-regulatory body, where the tribunal had concluded on lawful evidence that the proprietor of the business did not intend to comply with the body's rules. The court refused an application by Colin Stafford Cochrane for judicial review of the decisions of the Council of FIMBRA to adopt the recommendation of its disciplinary committee to terminate the membership of Family Insurance Services (FIS) and of the appeal tribunal to uphold that resolution. FIS was an unincorporated business owned and run by Mr Cochrane. It had been accepted as a member by FIMBRA on 28 January 1986. FIMBRA had considered it desirable that members of its governing body should have a record of compliance with its rules. Therefore, it arranged for compliance reviews to be conducted on its behalf of each candidate for election to the council. On Mr Cochrane becoming a candidate such a review disclosed ten breaches of the rules, which were drawn to Mr Cochrane's attention and which he admitted. By the time of the full meeting of the council which considered Mr Cochrane's case on 17 February 1988, none had been remedied, although he had twice assured the council that they would be. The council decided to terminate the membership of FIS. Mr Cochrane's appeal from that decision had been heard on 26 April 1988 by a duly constituted appeal tribunal. By that time, with minor exceptions, satisfactory remedial steps had been taken by Mr Cochrane to rectify the continuing breaches. The tribunal rejected his appeal. An affidavit sworn by the chairman of that tribunal stated that, while they accepted that no client of FIS had suffered any loss and that Mr Cochrane was guilty of no dishonesty of any kind, they had rejected the views that no harm had been done to anyone, that Mr Cochrane had seen the error of his ways, that he was not guilty of an irregularity save late filing of records and documents, and that his promise to comply with the rules in future was sincere. That there was no reflection on Mr Cochrane's honesty or competence was shown by FIMBRA's willingness in September 1988 to accept him as a registered individual which would allow him to carry on as a financial adviser. However, in the light of the tribunal's conclusions, it was quite impossible for the court to detect any error in the decisions of which Mr Cochrane now sought judicial review, and his application must be refused.

The Association of Futures Brokers and Dealers

1-88 AFBD's member firms carry on business in connection with dealing and arranging and advising on deals in futures, options and contracts for differences, and managing portfolios of these types of investments.

The Investment Management Regulatory Organization

1-89 IMRO is a company limited by guarantee. It is concerned with regulating the following investment activities: (a) managing investments, (b) management and operation of unit trusts, (c) investment management of occupational pension funds and investment trusts, and (d) investment advice to institutional or other corporate customers.

IMRO will also regulate investment business which is ancillary or incidental to the main business of the member including (a) money market dealing, (b) management of portfolios comprising futures, options and contracts for differences, (c) advising on, and arranging, deals as an independent intermediary in life assurance and unit trusts and other collective investment schemes, (d) providing investment advisory services to retail customers, and (e) engaging in corporate finance activities.

The Life Assurance and Unit Trust Regulatory Organization

1-90 LAUTRO is a company limited by guarantee. Its member firms are life assurance companies, unit trust management companies, and friendly societies engaged in retail marketing of life insurance products.

In the case of life assurance companies, LAUTRO must ensure that they have the requisite authorization under the Insurance Companies Act 1982, but does not have to satisfy itself that they are managed by fit and proper persons. Similar considerations apply to friendly societies. LAUTRO must ensure that they are registered by the Chief Registrar of Friendly Societies.

In the case of unit trust management companies, different considerations apply. LAUTRO must ensure that managers of unit trust schemes are fit and proper to market their products.

Aspects of investor protection

1-91 The following principles are derived partly from the provisions of the Financial Services Act 1986 and partly from the Rules issued by the Securities and Investments Board:

    (a) Investment business, with the exception of those which are specifically exempted, must be authorized, usually through membership of the appropriate SRO or RPB, or, occasionally, by the SIB.[11] This requirement is intended to ensure that only firms which conduct their activities competently and honestly are

11 See *ante*, para. 1-82.

allowed to operate investment businesses. All authorized investment businesses must state the name of their regulatory body clearly on their advertisements and business stationery.

(b) Firms which conduct investment businesses are required to have proper regard for a client's best interests in any advice given. Accordingly, they must make sure that they are aware of the client's circumstances; for example, a widow with limited capital would invest it for a steady income and with minimum risk to the capital, whereas a wealthy person might be quite willing to invest part of his capital in commodity futures in the hope of a short-term gain.

(c) An investment firm selling, or advising on, unit trusts or life assurance must act as either (i) an impartial agent, that is to say, as an independent intermediary, selecting the product from all those available in the market, or (ii) a 'tied' company representative, selecting the product only from those produced by that company or group. This concept, which is known as 'polarization', is of considerable importance to banks and building societies, as well as to other investment advisers. [12]

(d) Investment firms transacting business for clients must take all reasonable steps to do so on the best terms available. There are record-keeping requirements in the rules which, with the help of computerized trading systems where appropriate, will show if deals were done in good time and at the best available prices.

(e) In most cases outside the areas of life assurance and unit trusts, firms providing investment services are required to set out the terms and conditions of their relationship with their clients in a customer agreement letter listing the services which are to be provided and the charges for those services. One of the few instances in which a customer agreement is not required is that of an 'execution-only' client who specifies exactly what he wants and merely requires that those instructions are carried out.

(f) Uninvited approaches to sell investments, including telephone 'cold-calls', doorstepping and street-selling are banned, except in the case of life assurance and unit trusts. Where a sale of any investment is made by means of an unpermitted cold-call, the transaction will be unenforceable by the investment firm. Where a sale of a life policy or units in a unit trust is made by a permitted call, the investor must be informed that he has a 14-day (increased to 28 days in some circumstances) 'cooling-off' period during which he is free to cancel the transaction.

(g) With regard to advertising, the rules contain strict requirements

---

12 For its application to banks, see *post*, para. 1-93.

about the contents of both press advertisements and marketing devices such as investment 'junk mail'. The contents must be accurate and relevant. They must not misuse graphs or charts to compare the performance of completely different products, and they must not misuse statistics to avoid bad periods. They must also, where relevant, contain a clear warning about the price volatility or marketability of the product. Finally, all advertisements must state that the advertiser is authorized.

(h)   All published recommendations, including those in investment tipsheets, must be researched and capable of substantiation. This requirement is intended to ensure that proper care has been taken, and is not a guarantee that the recommended product will rise in value or even maintain its value. These rules do not relate to publications such as daily newspapers whose main purpose is not to induce investors to make specific investments.

(i)   Authorized firms must keep investors' funds segregated from other money used in the business. If an investor leaves money with a firm other than in readiness for some immediate transaction, the firm must pay interest on it, unless the investor agrees otherwise.

(j)   Authorized firms must have a proper procedure for investigating complaints from clients. They must keep records of such investigations, and, if a client is not satisfied with a firm's own investigation, he is entitled to take the matter to the relevant SRO.

(k)   There is a compensation scheme which affords limited protection to investors. It is operated by a company, Investors Compensation Scheme Limited, which is funded by the businesses authorized by the SIB and the SROs. The scheme provides that, if an authorized firm is indebted to an investor and cannot meet its obligations, the investor is entitled to claim compensation – once the claim has been validated – for the whole of amounts up to £30,000. It also gives an investor the right to claim for 90 per cent of up to a further £20,000. In the result, therefore, there is a ceiling of £50,000 for each individual claim, and the scheme will normally be able to pay up to £48,000 to each investor. Although the scheme has very substantial funding, it is not unlimited and, if compensation claims in a year exceed £100 million, the payments to claimants will need to be scaled down. Members of recognized professional bodies – such as solicitors and accountants – have their own compensation schemes, and so do insurance companies and building societies.

Effect of the Companies Act 1989

1-92 In order to assist the SIB to achieve a new approach to its rule-books, the Companies Act 1989[13] amended the Financial Services Act 1986 in six main ways. In an authoritative article on the subject,[14] Mr David Walker, Chairman of the SIB, referred to the relevant clauses in the Companies Bill, which was then before Parliament. The Bill was duly passed, and the six ways in which the Act amended the Financial Services Act 1986 are as follows:

(a) The SIB has power to issue statements of principle, setting out the conduct and financial standing expected of authorized firms. Further, in order to enable the principles to be a universal statement of conduct expected, without needing to be incorporated into a series of rulebooks, the principles apply directly to all authorized persons, including members of SROs and firms certified by RPBs. Although the SIB has a duty to exercise its powers to secure compliance with the principles, the primary enforcement authority for the principles continues to be the SRO or RPB concerned.

(b) The SIB has power to *designate* particular rules or regulations within its rulebook. The effect of designation is that the rules concerned apply directly to members of an SRO, though not to firms certified by a RPB.

(c) The SIB has power to issue codes of conduct. These codes amplify the principles or rules in the same way that the Highway Code amplifies the requirements of road traffic law.

(d) There is a new basis of assessment for the rulebooks of SROs and RPBs. Under the old system involving an 'equivalence test', the SIB had to be satisfied that the rulebook of an SRO or RPB provided 'protection at least equivalent' to that provided by the SIB rulebook. The new 'adequacy test' substitutes a judgment on overall adequacy. It is a broader test than the equivalence test. It brings into the SRO or RPB side of the balance not merely its own rules, but also the statements of principle and any designated rules and codes of conduct applying to its members. It counts not only investor protection delivered by the contents of the rulebook, but also the nature of the investment business carried on by members of the organizati┄ ┄ind of investors likely to deal with them, the effectiveness ᴏ┄ ┄ organization's arrangements for enforcing compliance and the effect of any other controls to which its members are subject. In operating this

13 Ss 72–76.
14 Published in *The Law Society's Gazette*, 26 July 1989, pp. 19–20.

new basis of assessment, the SIB expects to be guided, at any rate for SROs, by the proposition that its new power to write the essential elements of regulation in a clear and enforceable way by designating rules means that it can, without impairment to investor protection, properly stand back from the detail of an SRO's own rules.

(e)　In his article Mr David Walker wrote:

> The fifth change is to be a requirement for the designation of the SIB, and also for the recognition of a self-regulating organization or professional body, that it has satisfactory arrangements for taking into account, in framing rules, both the costs of complying with them, and other controls applying to the firms concerned. In addition, the SIB itself needs to *consult* about the cost of compliance before issuing statements of principle, rules, regulations or codes of conduct. Although costs of compliance are an issue to which we have been giving increasing attention, we think it reasonable that there should be an express requirement to show the importance of considering costs to the industry.

(f)　With regard to the sixth change, Mr Walker wrote as follows:

> While the first five changes made relate to the rulebooks, the last deals with the more general issue of regulatory overlap by means of a series of changes concerning relations with other regulators. The SIB, in assessing an SRO or RPB, would be required to have regard to other controls applying to its members. If, for example, some of its members were authorized banking institutions, this would provide express sanction for reliance on the controls operated by the banking regulator, whether in the UK or overseas. Indeed, it is probably in relation to prudential supervision that this provision will be of greatest value where problems of overlap are most likely to arise.

Bankers and investment business

1-93　The rules and principles considered above apply to those banks which are in any way involved in investment business.

(a)　Each bank must decide upon its membership of SROs. In practice, the work of a large bank is often conducted through a number of subsidiary companies; for example, one subsidiary company (or possibly the parent company) may give general investment advice and will be a member of FIMBRA, a second subsidiary may be concerned with the management and operation of unit trusts and will be a member of IMRO, a third subsidiary may give advice on life policies and will be a member of

LAUTRO, a fourth subsidiary may advise on deals in futures and will be a member of AFBD, and a fifth subsidiary may be dealing in stocks and shares and will be a member of TSA.

(b) If a bank sells, or advises on, unit trusts or life assurance (as most banks do), it must make it clear to potential investors whether it acts as either (i) an independent intermediary, or (ii) a company representative. This is the result of 'polarization'.[15] No person or institution may act in both roles. Some banks, including the Clydesdale Bank and the National Westminster Bank, have elected to act as independent intermediaries. They believe that in so doing they are acting in the best interests of their customers, and they must select the product (unit trust or pension plan or life assurance policy) from all those available in the market. Most of the large banks, however, have chosen the other course. Their own unit trusts are very profitable to the bank, and they quite understandably wish to be able to sell their products to their customers as 'company representatives'. Thus, as Mr Derrick Hanson has written,[16] '. . . most banks operate unit trust groups but do not necessarily own life companies. A branch of a bank, if designated as a company representative, may sell the in-house unit trusts but may not adopt the posture of an independent intermediary in recommending another group's life assurance contracts or pensions plans.' Can this problem be resolved?

It seems that it can, because Mr Hanson continued as follows:

> However, there is a legitimate way round this problem. Whilst a branch bank may act as a company representative *another part of the group* may act as independent intermediary. Thus a bank branch may sell investment products as company representative and may introduce the customer to, for example, the bank's insurance broking subsidiary for 'advice' in the role of independent intermediary . . . As a company representative the manager of a branch will be able to sell the in-house products but beyond that any 'advice' must come from an independent intermediary within the group. The branch may act as a 'post office' for that advice but may not qualify it in any way nor advise on the merits of the intermediary's recommendations.

(c) As noted already,[17] any institution which gives investment advise must make sure that it is aware of its client's circumstances. For

15 See *ante*, para. 1-91.
16 *Banking World*, Vol. 5 (1987), p. 25.
17 See *ante*, para. 1-91.

this purpose each of the major banks has prepared a printed form of questionnaire, sometimes called a Customer Profile form, or a Fact Find. It asks for information on, for example, the customer's date of birth, marital status, occupation, name of employer, children, grandchildren, dependants, professional advisers, value of house, building society deposits, National Savings investments, unit trusts, life assurance policies, liabilities (including mortgages and hire-purchase commitments), guarantees given, gross annual earnings, and the names of beneficiaries under the customer's will. Finally, there will be questions relating to the customer's investment objectives, for example increase of income, capital appreciation, providing for school fees, paying less income tax, or minimizing inheritance tax. If this questionnaire is completed carefully by the customer before investment advise is sought, it should enable the bank's officials, including perhaps the officials in the investment department (or subsidiary company) of the bank, to have a complete picture of the financial and other circumstances affecting the customer. This should improve the quality of the advice given to the customer. There are, of course, cases where the customer knows exactly what he wants to do; for example, he may wish to invest £10,000 in the shares of a well-known public limited company. In this type of case, there is no need for the customer to complete the form of questionnaire.

(d)　Finally, each of the major banks has appointed a Compliance Officer. It is beyond the scope of this book to give a full account of his duties, which are numerous and far-reaching. Briefly, his main task is to ensure that the bank and its subsidiary companies comply with the provisions of the Financial Services Act 1986 and with the rules of the Securities and Investment Board and the SROs of which the bank or its subsidiaries are members. He arranges for the issue of instructions and guidance to senior supervisory staff. He monitors compliance with the assistance of internal audit staff. He reviews the content of all investment business advertising and promotional material in order to ensure that it complies with the regulations of the SROs. He ensures that a proper complaints procedure is in operation. When a complaint is made by a customer, it must be put into writing and sent to him.

2

Contract between banker and customer

The relationship between banker and customer is a contractual one, and in this chapter the various aspects of that relationship will be considered.

Section I
GENERAL RELATIONSHIP BETWEEN BANKER AND CUSTOMER

2-1 A remarkable feature of the creation of the contract between banker and customer is that the terms of the contract are not usually embodied in any written agreement executed by the parties. Thus, there is no formal agreement which provides that a banker must maintain strict secrecy concerning his customers accounts or that customers must exercise care when drawing cheques so as to prevent the amounts from being fraudulently increased. It is true, of course, that when certain accounts are opened, e.g. joint accounts or the accounts of limited companies, a mandate is executed which gives the bank express instructions concerning operations on the account, but even in those cases no attempt is made to prepare a comprehensive list of the respective rights and duties of banker and customer.

2-2 The contractual relationship which exists between banker and customer is a complex one founded originally upon the customs and usages of bankers. Many of those customs and usages have been recognized by the courts, and, to the extent that they have been so recognized, they must be regarded as implied terms of the contract between banker and customer. It follows, therefore, that this is a branch of the law where implied terms are of vital importance. Little does a new customer realize when, with a minimum of formality, he opens a bank account that he is entering into a contract the implied terms of which would, if reduced to writing, run into several pages.

The early bankers

2-3 Historically, deposit accounts and loans preceded current accounts. Probably the scriveners were the first bankers in England. Scriveners were scribes or clerks who wrote contracts, bonds and other documents for their clients. Thus they were in a very favourable position to become acquainted with mercantile transactions and to discover opportunities of borrowing and lending money. During the first half of the seventeenth century there was a prominent scrivener named Humphrey Shalcrosse, and an examination of his manuscript account book, covering the period 1638–56, leaves one in no doubt that he was borrowing and lending on a fairly large scale.[1] Even before that period, the Jews and the Lombards had been lending money, but they had been using merely their own capital, whereas the scriveners started the practice of borrowing at interest from some people in order to lend, at a higher rate of interest, to others. Thus they were the first true 'middlemen' in money, and for that reason they may be regarded as our first bankers. They continued to act in this way until at least the beginning of the eighteenth century. There is, however, no evidence to suggest that the scriveners allowed their clients to draw cheques or drafts upon them.

2-4 The cheque system originated with the goldsmiths. For various reasons which cannot be explained here,[2] merchants began to leave their money in the hands of the goldsmiths and to receive interest upon those sums. They appear to have started this practice shortly before the outbreak of the Civil War of 1642–9. Moreover, they soon looked to the goldsmiths to assist them in making payments to third parties. This was the origin of the cheque system. At first, the depositor would address to his goldsmith a short letter of request authorizing the payment to his creditor of the sum due. The creditor would take this authority to the goldsmith's 'shop' and there receive the sum in specie.[3] Before long, the merchant debtor drew his 'bill' or 'note' in favour of his creditor 'or order' or in favour of him 'or bearer', and the goldsmith duly honoured it upon presentation, even though it was not presented by the original payee. The accounts of those merchants, which nowadays would be called 'current accounts', were usually known as 'running cashes', and they soon became popular. By 1677 there were fifty-eight goldsmiths in London who 'kept running cashes', thirty-eight of whom lived in

---

1 For further details see J. Milnes Holden, *The History of Negotiable Instruments in English Law* (1955), p. 206; and for an interesting biography of this scrivener, see Max Beloff, 'Humphrey Shalcrosse and the Great Civil War', *English Historical Review*, Vol. LIV, pp. 686–95.
2 See J. Milnes Holden, *op cit.*, pp. 70–2.
3 See J. Marius, *Advice concerning Bills of Exchange* (1656), p. 6.

Lombard Street.[4] Furthermore, there is clear evidence that the gold-smiths employed the funds left with them by making loans to others. Thus they made loans to Cromwell and also to merchants who were in need of money.[5] In short, the goldsmiths performed the basic functions of modern bankers by accepting sums at interest, by making loans and by providing their customers with facilities for making payments to third parties.

Debtor and creditor relationship established

2-5 Although the business of banking had been firmly established before the end of the seventeenth century, there does not appear to be any reported case in either that or the eighteenth century in which the court had to consider the legal relationship between banker and customer. Possibly the earliest case in which this matter arose was one decided in 1811.[6] A testator had made a bequest of 'whatever debts might be due to him ... at the time of his death', and one of the questions to be decided was whether 'a cash balance due to him on his banker's account' passed by this bequest. Sir William Grant MR, after some hesitation, held that it did. In the course of his judgment, the learned Master of the Rolls said that this was not a *depositum*; a sealed bag of money might, indeed, be a *depositum*, but money paid in generally to a banker could not be so considered. His Lordship further observed that money had no earmark and that 'when money is paid into a banker's, he always opens a debtor and creditor account with the payor. The banker employs the money himself, and is liable merely to answer the drafts of his customer to that amount.'[7] In another case, decided a few years later, counsel argued before the same judge that 'a banker is rather a bailee of his customer's funds than his debtor', but Sir William Grant rejected that argument and held that 'money paid into a banker's becomes immediately a part of his general assets; and he is merely a debtor for the amount'.[8] Both those decisions were cited with approval in 1833 by the Chief Justice of the Queen's bench, who said in the course of his judgment that 'sums which are paid to the credit of a customer with a banker, though usually called deposits, are, in truth, loans by the customer to the banker'.[9]

4 *London Directory of 1677* (reprinted 1878), Introduction, p. viii.
5 See *The Mystery of the New fashioned Goldsmiths or Bankers* (1676). This is a very rare tract; it is reproduced in *The Grasshopper in Lombard Street* (1892) by J. B. Martin, at pp. 285–95.
6 *Carr* v. *Carr* (1811) 1 Mer 541n.
7 *Ibid.*, at p. 543. See also *Vaisey* v. *Reynolds* (1828) 5 Russ 12; *Parker* v. *Marchant* (1843) 1 Ph 356 (both these cases likewise involved bequests in wills).
8 *Devaynes* v. *Noble* (1816) 1 Mer 529, at p. 568.
9 *Sims* v. *Bond* (1833) 5 B & Ad 389, *per* Denman CJ, at pp. 392–3.

2-6 This legal principle received the *imprimatur* of the House of Lords in *Foley* v. *Hill and Others*,[10] the relevant facts of which were as follows. In 1829, the appellant opened an account with the respondent bankers, the initial credit being for £6,117 10s. It was agreed that interest at 3 per cent per annum should be allowed on this account. There were two items debited to the account in 1830, one for £1,700 and the other for £2,000. There were also entries, in a separate column, of interest up to December 1831, but not afterwards. In 1838 the appellant began certain proceedings against the respondent in Chancery, seeking to recover all sums owed to him, with interest. Counsel for the plaintiff argued that it was the duty of the respondents to keep the accounts with the appellant clear and intelligible, to calculate the interest on the balances in their hands from time to time, to make proper entries of it in the account, and to preserve all vouchers and other evidence of their transactions with him. It was further argued that these duties and transactions constituted a relation more complex than that of mere debtor and creditor, and that an account of them was a fit subject for the Court of Chancery.

2-7 The House of Lords rejected these arguments and held that the relation between a banker and his customer who pays money into the bank is the ordinary relation of debtor and creditor, with a superadded obligation arising out of the custom of bankers to honour the customer's cheques. Lord Cottenham LC said:[11]

> Money, when paid into a bank, ceases altogether to be the money of the principal; it is then the money of the banker, who is bound to return an equivalent by paying a similar sum to that deposited with him when he is asked for it. The money paid into a banker's is money known by the principal to be placed there for the purpose of being under the control of the banker; it is then the banker's money; he is known to deal with it as his own; he makes what profit of it he can, which profit he retains to himself, paying back only the principal, according to the custom of bankers in some places, or the principal and a small rate of interest, according to the custom of bankers in other places. The money placed in the custody of a banker is, to all intents and purposes, the money of the banker, to do with it as he pleases; he is guilty of no breach of trust in employing it; he is not answerable to the principal if he puts it into jeopardy, if he engages in a hazardous speculation; he is not bound to keep it or deal with it as the property of his principal; but he is, of course, answerable for the amount, because he has contracted, having received that money, to repay to the principal, when demanded, a sum equivalent to that paid into his hands.

10 (1848) 2 HLC 28.
11 (1848) 2 HLC, at pp. 36–7.

That has been the subject of discussion in various cases, and that has been established to be the relative situation of banker and customer. That being established to be the relative situations of banker and customer, the banker is not an agent or factor, but he is a debtor.

Although Lord Cottenham stated that a banker is not an agent, this statement should be read in its context. The Lord Chancellor was referring to the relationship arising out of the deposit of money with a banker. When a banker is performing certain duties, he frequently acts as an agent.[12] Thus, he often collects the proceeds of cheques as agent for his customers; and he acts as agent when accepting customers' instructions in regard to the purchase and sale of stocks and shares. Moreover, there is authority for the view that, as regards the drawing and payment of cheques, the relationship between customer and banker is that of principal and agent.[13]

2-7A   In *Space Investments Ltd* v. *Canadian Imperial Bank of Commerce Trust Co. (Bahamas) Ltd*[14] the Judicial Committee of the Privy Council, allowing an appeal from the Court of Appeal of the Commonwealth of the Bahamas, held that where a bank, as trustee, lawfully deposits trust money with itself as banker pursuant to express authority conferred by the trust instrument, the beneficiaries under the trust do not become entitled to any interest in the assets of the bank but merely to a sum equal to the amount standing to the credit of the trust deposit account. The Judicial Committee held, therefore, that if the bank became insolvent and went into liquidation, the beneficiaries were entitled to prove in the winding up of the bank only for the amount standing to the credit of the trust with the bank in the trust deposit account at the date of the liquidation. Thus the beneficiaries were unsecured creditors whose claims ranked *pari passu* with, and not in priority to, the claims of customers of the bank and other unsecured creditors.

2-8   In *Balmoral Supermarket Ltd* v. *Bank of New Zealand*[15] the plaintiff's employee entered the defendant bank's premises intending to deposit some cash and cheques. The cash was emptied out of a bag on to the counter midway between the employee and the teller. The teller took a small bundle of notes from the counter and proceeded to count them. After these notes had been counted and put to one side, robbers entered the bank and took the uncounted cash from the counter. The plaintiff

12 For a case where a banker was held not to be his customer's agent, see *Midland Bank Ltd* v. *Conway Corporation* [1965] 1 WLR 1165.
13 *Per* Lord Atkinson in *Westminster Bank Ltd* v. *Hilton* (1926) 43 TLR 124, at p. 126.
14 [1986] 3 All ER 75.
15 [1974] 2 NZLR 155.

brought an action against the bank claiming the amount of the cash taken by the robbers and alleging that the possession of and property in the cash on the counter had passed to the bank. This claim failed. The Supreme Court of New Zealand held that, until the money to be deposited had been checked and the bank had signified its acceptance thereof, the money had not been deposited and the bank had not become the debtor of the customer in respect of that money.

Terms of contract between banker and customer

2-9 *Foley* v. *Hill and Others*[16] was, of course, a most important decision in the development of the law governing the relationship between banker and customer, but in the period which has elapsed since that decision of the House of Lords was given, the courts have had to resolve many other problems concerning the relationship between banker and customer. In the result, the implied terms of the contract between banker and customer in the ordinary course of business when a current account is opened, may be stated as follows.

2-10 The banker must receive cash and collect the proceeds of such items as cheques, postal orders, money orders and bills of exchange for his customer's account.[17]

2-11 The money so received becomes at once the property of the banker, and he is thereupon indebted to his customer for an equivalent sum; hence the banker does not hold the money as his customer's agent or trustee.[18]

2-12 Although the banker becomes indebted to his customer as explained above, the ordinary rule that a debtor must seek out his creditor does not apply; the banker's duty is to repay the money or any part of it upon demand being made by the customer at the branch of the bank where the account is kept[19] and during business hours. It follows, therefore, that the customer has no right of action against his banker in respect of money deposited until after a demand has been made, and so time does not begin to run against the customer under the Limitation Act 1980, until such demand.[20] Usually, the customer's demand is made in writing by means of a cheque as indicated below, but it would seem that an oral demand by the customer at the branch where his account

---

16 *Supra*, paras 2-6/7.
17 *Cf.* Atkin LJ, in *Joachimson* v. *Swiss Bank Corporation* [1921] 3 KB 110, at p. 127.
18 *Foley* v. *Hill* (1848) 2 HLC 28; *Joachimson* v. *Swiss Bank Corporation (supra)*; *R* v. *Davenport* [1954] 1 All ER 602.
19 *Clare & Co.* v. *Dresdner Bank* [1915] 2 KB 576.
20 *Joachimson* v. *Swiss Bank Corporation (supra)*.

is kept is sufficient. There is no direct authority on this point, but Parker J adverted to it in his judgment in *Arab Bank Ltd* v. *Barclays Bank (Dominion, Colonial and Overseas) Ltd*.[21] After referring to a certain Palestinian Ordinance, Parker J said:

> Quite apart, however, from his Ordinance it was contended that under English law ... a written demand is necessary. There is no express authority on the point, and the question was specifically left open by Atkin, LJ, ... in *Joachimson* v. *Swiss Bank Corporation*,[22] where after defining the relation of banker and customer on current account he added 'Whether he must demand it in writing it is not necessary to determine.' Equally, it is not necessary for me to determine the question, and I would only say that as at present advised I see considerable difficulties in accepting the defendants' contention. The necessity for a demand at all only results from implying a term, and there seems little necessity in going further and implying that such demand must be in writing.

2-13   The banker must pay cheques drawn on him by his customer in legal form[23] on presentation during banking hours or within a reasonable margin after the bank's advertised closing time[24] at the branch of the bank where the account is kept,[25] provided that (a) the customer has there sufficient funds to his credit,[26] or the cheques are within the limits of an agreed overdraft,[27] and (b) there are no legal bars to payment. The obligation to honour cheques is the most important of the banker's duties. The breach of this duty may involve the banker in a claim for damages.[28]

2-14   The banker has the right to charge his customer a reasonable sum for services rendered.[29]

2-15   If a customer maintains two or more accounts with his banker (a) it is usually an implied term of the contract between banker and

---

21 [1952] WN 529; [1952] 2 TLR 920. The passage cited above was not reported and has been taken from a transcript. The observations of the learned judge were *obiter*, because he had found as a fact that no oral demand had been made. The point was not considered by the Court of Appeal or by the House of Lords; see [1953] 2 QB 527; [1954] AC 495.

22 [1921] 3 KB 110, at p. 127.

23 This means, *inter alia*, that cheques must not be post-dated, words and figures must agree and, as a general rule, cheques must not be crossed to more than one banker.

24 *Baines* v. *National Provincial Bank Ltd* (1927) 96 LJKB 801.

25 *Clare & Co.* v. *Dresdner Bank* [1915] 2 KB 576.

26 *London Joint Stock Bank* v. *Macmillan and Arthur* [1918] AC 777, at p. 789, *per* Lord Finlay LC; *Joachimson* v. *Swiss Bank Corporation* [1921] 3 KB 110, at p. 127, *per* Atkin LJ.

27 *Rouse* v. *Bradford Banking Co. Ltd* [1894] AC 586; at p. 596, *per* Lord Herschell LC.

28 *Post*, para. 2-140.

29 *Post*, para. 2-44.

customer that the banker will keep the accounts separate;[30] and
(b) if the customer makes a payment to credit, he has the right to
appropriate the funds to whichever account he chooses.[31]

2-15A   The banker does not owe a duty to his customer, who is seeking
to borrow money from him, to advise the customer as to the wisdom of
borrowing the money for the specified purpose.[32]

2-16   The banker must not disclose to third persons, without the
consent of the customer express or implied, either the state of the customer's account, or any of his transactions with the banker, or any
information relating to the customer acquired through the keeping of his
account, unless the banker is compelled to do so under the provisions
of an Act of Parliament or by order of a court, or the circumstances give
rise to a public duty of disclosure, or the protection of the banker's own
interest requires it.[33]

2-16A   A bank is under an obligation to supply to its customers a
printout of any information relating to them which is held in the bank's
computer.[34] In the case of most banks, the only information held in the
computer relates to the customers' accounts, and customers are supplied
with statements of account at regular intervals. Therefore, a customer
cannot really learn anything of any significance by asking for a printout
of information held in the computer. Some banks keep confidential
information about their customers on cards, which are prepared manually. Customers are not entitled to see these records.

2-17   The customer must exercise reasonable care in drawing his
cheques so as not to mislead his banker or to facilitate forgery.[35]

2-18   If the customer discovers that cheques purporting to have been
signed by him have been forged, he must inform his banker,[36] and likewise it would seem that if the banker becomes aware that forged cheques
are being presented for payment, he must inform his customer.[37]

2-19   There is probably an implied term in the contract between banker

---

30 *Post*, para. 2-67.
31 *Post*, para. 2-74.
32 *Williams & Glyn's Bank Ltd* v. *Barnes* [1981] Com LR 205.
33 *Tournier* v. *National Provincial and Union Bank of England* [1924] 1 KB 461; see
post, para. 2-100.
34 Data Protection Act 1984, s. 21. A fee is payable.
35 *London Joint Stock Bank* v. *Macmillan and Arthur* [1918] AC 777; see *post*, para.
2-125.
36 *Greenwood* v. *Martins Bank Ltd* [1932] 1 KB 371, at p. 381, *per* Scrutton LJ; affirmed
[1933] AC 51.
37 *Greenwood* v. *Martins Bank Ltd* [1932] 1 KB 371, at p. 381, *per* Scrutton LJ. See
post, para. 2-128.

and customer that the banker will supply his customer with either a pass-book or statements containing a copy of the customer's account with the banker.[38]

2-20   The relationship between banker and customer may be terminated by mutual consent, or unilaterally, by either party.[39]

2-21   Finally, there are certain events which affect, to a greater or lesser degree, the relationship between banker and customer: the death,[40] mental incapacity[41] or bankruptcy[42] of the customer; the winding up of a company customer;[43] the winding up of the bank;[44] the service of a garnishee order or summons;[45] the issue of a writ of sequestration;[46] and the outbreak of war.[47]

Section 2
LIMITATION OF ACTIONS

2-22   Lapse of time does not generally put an end to a contract or expunge a debt, but for very many years it has been part of the policy of our law to prevent the enforcement by legal action of long-dormant claims. As long ago as 1825, Best CJ observed:[48] 'Long dormant claims have often more of cruelty than of justice in them.' The law relating to the limitation of actions affects several aspects of the relationship between banker and customer.

Limitation Act 1980

2-23   Section 5 of this Act provides that 'an action founded on simple contract shall not be brought after the expiration of six years from the date on which the cause of action accrued'. The operation of this provision may be illustrated by the following example. C lends a sum of money to D, and D promises to repay the loan upon demand. The general rule in such a case is that no demand is necessary before an action is brought, because the debt which constitutes the cause of action

---

38 For passbooks and statements, see *post*, para. 2-132.
39 *Post*, paras 3-1/14.
40 *Post*, para. 3-17.
41 *Post*, para. 3-29.
42 *Post*, para. 3-39.
43 *Post*, paras 11-321/35.
44 *Post*, para. 3-45.
45 *Post*, paras 3-46/79.
46 *Post*, para. 3-81.
47 *Post*, para. 3-82.
48 *A'Court* v. *Cross* (1825) 3 Bing 329, at pp. 332–3.

arises instantly on the loan;[49] as Chitty J said, '... where there is a present debt and a promise to pay on demand, the demand is not considered to be a condition precedent to the bringing of the action'.[50] Thus, the six-year period begins to run against C as from the date of his loan and not from the date when he makes a demand upon D for repayment.

2-24   However, the Limitation Act 1980[51] provides that where any right of action has accrued to recover any debt or other liquidated pecuniary claim and the debtor 'acknowledges the claim or makes any payment in respect of it, the right shall be treated as having accrued on and not before the date of the acknowledgment or payment'. Every such acknowledgment must be in writing and signed by the person making the acknowledgment,[52] or by his agent.[53] It must be made to the person, or to an agent of the person, whose claim is being acknowledged.[54] Likewise, part payments must be made by the debtor or his agent, and to the creditor or his agent.[55] In short, therefore, the limitation period starts again upon written acknowledgment of the debt, or upon part payment. However, once a right of action is barred, it is not revived by any subsequent acknowledgment or payment.[56] When applying these rules to transactions between banker and customer it is necessary to distinguish between a customer's accounts which are in credit and those which show a debit balance.

Credit accounts

2-25   For the reasons stated above, the Limitation Act 1980 applies only when an account has been dormant. If an account is dormant and the customer is unable to show any acknowledgment of the debt by the bank during the preceding six years, the question arises whether the customer's claim against the bank for repayment of the balance may be statute-barred.

Deposit accounts

2-26   The balance standing to a customer's credit on deposit account is

---

49 *Norton* v. *Ellam* (1837) 2 M & W 461, at p. 464; *Walton* v. *Mascall* (1844) 13 M & W 452, at p. 458.
50 *Re Brown's Estate* [1893] 2 Ch 300, at p. 305.
51 S. 29(5).
52 S. 30(1).
53 S. 30(2).
54 S. 30(2).
55 S. 30(2).
56 S. 29(7).

repayable after a stated period of notice.[57] Accordingly, the customer does not have any cause of action against the bank in respect of money on deposit until notice has been given and the prescribed period of notice has expired. Therefore, the six-year period under the Limitation Act 1980 does not begin to run against the customer until that time.[58]

Current accounts

2-27 A customer may withdraw his balance on current account without giving notice, and accordingly one might have thought that the six-year period would have begun to run from the date of payment in, or from the honouring of the last cheque drawn by the customer, or from the last acknowledgment in writing by the banker of his indebtedness to the customer, whichever of these events happened last. This view was widely held[59] until 1921, when the Court of Appeal, in effect, reached a different conclusion, in *Joachimson* v. *Swiss Bank Corporation*.[60]

2-28 *Joachimson's* case was not directly concerned with any period of limitation. The plaintiff firm was a partnership between two Germans and a naturalized Englishman, carrying on business in Manchester. On 1 August 1914, one of the Germans died, and so the partnership was dissolved. On the outbreak of war three days later, the other German became an enemy alien. On 1 August a sum of £2,321 was standing to the credit of the partnership on current account with the defendant bank. No money was paid out of the account after that date. On 5 June 1919, the naturalized partner started an action in the name of the firm, for the purpose of winding up the affairs of the partnership, to recover from the bank this sum of £2,321. The cause of action was alleged to have arisen on or before 1 August 1914. The firm had not made any demand on or before that date for payment of the sum in question, and the bank pleaded, *inter alia*, that there had thus accrued no cause of action to the firm on 1 August 1914, and that therefore the cause of action was not maintainable.[61] Thus, the issue was whether or not a

---

57 See *ante*, para. 1-71.

58 There is no banking case on this point, but see *Atkinson* v. *Bradford Third Equitable Benefit Building Society* (1890) 25 QBD 377; *Re Tidd, Tidd* v. *Overell* [1893] 3 Ch 154, at p. 156.

59 See, for example, *Halsbury Laws of England* (1st ed., 1911) Vol. 19, p. 47, where it was stated that 'in the case of money on current account, time runs from the payment in'.

60 [1921] 3 KB 110.

61 It does not appear from the report why the bank resisted the plaintiff's demand on this ground. A footnote to the report indicates, however, that 'other points' were raised before the trial judge and the Court of Appeal. Furthermore, the bank raised a counterclaim against the plaintiff, the nature of which is not reported: see [1921] 3 KB 111n.

demand was necessary to create a cause of action against the bank. The Court of Appeal, reversing the decision of Roche J, held that a previous demand was necessary. Atkin LJ said:

> The question appears to me to be in every case, did the parties in fact intend to make the demand a term of the contract? If they did, effect will be given to their contract ... In the case of such a contract as this ... it appears to me that the parties must have intended that the money handed to the banker is only payable after a demand. The nature of the contract negatives the duty of the debtor to find out his creditor and pay him his debt. If such a duty existed and were performed, the creditor might be ruined by reason of outstanding cheques being dishonoured.

As there had been no demand upon the bank by the plaintiff firm, the firm had no properly constituted cause of action against the bank, and its claim failed. This result may appear strange, and it is perhaps not surprising that a judge in Scotland once referred to *Joachimson's* case as 'this remarkable English decision, which appears to have startled writers in England at its date'.[63] However that may be, there is no doubt that the principle laid down by the Court of Appeal in *Joachimson's* case is firmly established, and it is unlikely that the decision will ever be overruled by the House of Lords.

2-29 One of the results of the decision is that, in the case of a current account, the six-year period under the Limitation Act 1980 does not begin to run against the customer until the customer has made a demand and such demand has not been complied with. As Atkin LJ said:[64]

> The result of this decision will be that for the future bankers may have to face legal claims for balances on accounts that have remained dormant for more than six years. But seeing that bankers have not been in the habit as a matter of business of setting up the Statute of Limitations against their customers or their legal representatives, I do not suppose that such a change in what was supposed to be the law will have much practical effect.

2-30 By a coincidence, only a few years later a bank was faced with a claim for a balance that was alleged to have remained dormant on a deposit account for very many years.[65] The decision in that case, *Douglass* v. *Lloyds Bank Ltd*,[66] is instructive, because it shows how a bank may sometimes be able to resist such a claim, although it cannot

---

62 [1921] 3 KB, at p. 129.
63 *Macdonald* v. *North of Scotland Bank*, 1942 SC 369, at p. 379 *per* Lord Mackay.
64 [1921] 3 KB, at p. 131.
65 Although the case involved a deposit account, the result would have been the same if the money had been left on current account.
66 (1929) 34 Com Cas 263.

adduce positive evidence of the repayment of the money. Briefly, the facts were as follows. In May 1866, a Mr Fenwicke deposited £6,000 with a Birmingham branch of Lloyds Bank, upon the terms that he could withdraw the money at any time on giving fourteen days' notice, and that interest should be paid at a certain rate. In August 1866, the bank repaid £2,500 with interest to date, and a note of the payment was endorsed on the deposit receipt. In November 1866, a further indorsement was made showing that all interest then due had been paid, but after that date there was no record of any further payment by the bank of either principal or interest and no record of any demand by the customer for payment. The customer died in 1893. In 1927 one of the customer's relatives found the deposit receipt amongst some old papers, and sent it to the customer's surviving executor and trustee. He gave Lloyds Bank fourteen days' notice to pay £3,500, being the balance of the principal, together with interest from November 1866. The bank refused to pay. It had no books prior to 1873 relating to the branch which had issued the deposit receipt, but all the deposit ledgers from 1873 were available, and there was no record of the deposit in any of them, although deposits of an earlier date than 1866 were carried forward in those ledgers. Accordingly, when sued for the money, the bank argued that it must be assumed that the money had been repaid before 1873. Having regard to all the surrounding circumstances, which it is impossible to state fully here, Roche J decided that the debt must have been repaid prior to 1873, and judgment was accordingly given in the bank's favour.

Debit accounts

2-31   As in the case of customers' accounts which are in credit, so too with debit accounts, the effect of the Limitation Act 1980 calls for consideration only in those cases where accounts have been dormant for a number of years. If an overdrawn account − whether it be a loan account or an overdraft on current account − is dormant and the bank is unable to show any acknowledgment of the debt by the customer during the preceding six years, the question arises whether the bank's claim against the customer may be statute-barred.

2-32   There is no hard-and-fast rule which one can apply when considering this type of problem.[67] The rule is that no action may be brought by the bank 'after the expiration of six years from the date on

---

67 According to *Preston and Newson on Limitation of Actions* (3rd ed, 1953), p. 29, 'a bank cannot recover a dormant overdraft more than six years after the last advance'. This statement is too sweeping and is not supported by the authority cited, namely *Parr's Banking Co.* v. *Yates* [1898] 2 QB 460.

which the cause of action accrued'.[68] This rule may be applied as follows.

2-33 If a bank makes a loan to a customer to be repaid on a specified date, and the loan is not repaid on that date, a cause of action will then accrue and the six-year period will start to run.

2-34 If a bank makes a 'Personal Loan'[69] to a customer repayable, together with interest, by twenty-four equal monthly instalments and, if the customer fails to repay the loan, then in the absence of agreement to the contrary, a separate cause of action will accrue to the bank upon each of the instalment dates. However, the agreements relating to 'Personal Loans' very often expressly provide that, if default is made in the payment of any one instalment, all subsequent instalments immediately become due and payable. In that type of case, the six-year period begins to run in respect of all outstanding instalments as soon as default is made in the payment of any one instalment.

2-35 If accommodation is granted without any specific agreement concerning a date for repayment, the loan is repayable on demand. In this connection, Parke B said that, in the case of money lent payable upon request, with interest, no demand is necessary before bringing the action.[70] He continued:

> There is no obligation in law to give any notice at all; if you choose to make it part of the contract that notice shall be given, you may do so. The debt which constitutes the cause of action arises instantly on the loan.

In *Joachimson* v. *Swiss Bank Corporation*,[71] Bankes LJ quoted that passage from Parke B's judgment and continued:

> In every case, therefore, where this question arises the test must be whether the parties have, or have not, agreed that an actual demand shall be a condition precedent to the existence of a present enforceable debt. In the ordinary case of banker and customer their relations depend either entirely or mainly upon an implied contract.

Bankes LJ then considered the problem before the court, which related to a customer's account which was in credit.[72] The same principle must be applied to a debit account in respect of which no specific agreement has been made concerning the date for repayment of the advance. It is thought that, in the majority of cases, the real understanding between

---

68 Limitation Act 1980, s. 5; see *ante*, para. 2-23.
69 For 'Personal Loans', see *ante*, para. 1-74.
70 *Norton* v. *Ellam* (1837) 2 M & W 461, at p. 464; and see *ante*, para. 2-23.
71 [1921] 3 KB 110, at pp. 116–17.
72 *Ante*, para. 2-28.

a bank and its customer is that the bank will demand repayment when it requires repayment to be made and before bringing proceedings against the customer. It is a matter of common knowledge that, in the type of case under consideration, a bank always writes to a customer before bringing proceedings, and this practice appears to be soundly based upon legal considerations. In other words, the debt does not become, in the words of Bankes LJ 'a present enforceable debt' until the bank chooses to take the initiative and to demand repayment. If that demand is not complied with, a cause of action accrues to the bank and the six-year period begins to run. As a general rule, therefore, a bank does not need to concern itself with the Limitation Act 1980 until it makes a demand. However, from the purely practical aspect, a bank would not normally allow a dormant debit balance to remain on its books for a period of anything like six years without taking steps to obtain repayment.

2-36 If in any case the six-year period has started to run and the customer subsequently acknowledges the debit or makes any payment in respect thereof, the six-year period starts again.[73] A *payment* of interest by the customer is sufficient for this purpose, but the mere debiting of interest by the bank to the customer's account is not, of course, a 'payment' by the customer and does not cause the period to start afresh.

Securities for advances

2-37 When, in the preceding paragraphs, the application of the Limitation Act 1980 was considered in regard to debit accounts, the way in which the bank's right to sue the customer might become statute-barred was examined, but no attention was paid to the more complex situation where securities are deposited, either by the customer himself or by a third party, in order to secure the customer's indebtedness. It is not proposed to consider this aspect of the law relating to the limitation of actions in detail,[74] and the following summary is intended merely as a guide to the leading principles.

2-38 As between banker and customer, there is generally no occasion to apply the ordinary rule, namely that where a debtor, who owes an existing simple contract debt, gives security for the payment of it by means of a covenant under seal and a charge on his property, the simple contract debt is merged in the specialty, unless there is an express provision to the contrary. An attempt was made in *Barclays Bank* v. *Beck*[75]

---

73 Limitation Act 1980, s. 29(5); see *ante*, para. 2-24.
74 The reader is referred to specialized works on the subject, e.g. *Preston and Newson on Limitation Actions*.
75 [1952] 2 QB 47.

to persuade the Court of Appeal to apply the ordinary rule to the relationship between banker and customer, but it failed. Briefly, customers of Barclays Bank, whose joint account was overdrawn, executed an agricultural charge in favour of the bank. Later, the customers paid off the greater part of the overdraft and obtained the discharge of the agricultural charge. The customers refused to pay off the remainder of the overdraft amounting to £582 19*s.*, and, when sued, they alleged that the right of the bank to recover the overdraft had been merged in the bank's right under the charge and that, the charge and all liabilities under it having been discharged, including the obligation to repay the overdraft, the bank had no claim. If this argument had succeeded, many other similar bank overdrafts might have become irrecoverable by legal action, but it did not succeed, chiefly because the agricultural charge executed by the customers indicated that there was to be no merger. In clause 1 of the charge the customers had promised to repay moneys then due and all other moneys to become due thereafter; hence, as Somervell LJ said, clause 1 made it clear that, notwithstanding the acceptance of the charge, the contractual rights of the bank against the customer were preserved. Although this decision did not turn upon the Limitation Act 1939 (which was the Act then in force), it is mentioned here in order to show that, even in cases where security is obtained for an overdraft, the simple contract debt remains. Sometimes, as in *Beck's* case, this is vitally important to the bank. In most cases, however, the limitation periods applicable to actions to recover money charged on property are longer than the six-year period applicable to simple contract debts, and these longer periods may sometimes be relied upon by bankers.

2-39 The main limitation provision applicable to actions to recover money charged on property is that contained in s. 20 (1) of the Limitation Act 1980. The effect of this provision is that no action may be brought to recover any *principal sum*[76] secured by a mortgage or other charge on property, whether real or personal, after the expiration of twelve years 'from the date when the right to receive the money accrued'. The practical effect of this provision may be illustrated by an example. A bank makes a loan to a customer, the loan to be repaid at the end of six months and, by way of security, the customer executes a mortgage of 'Blackacre'. There can be no doubt that, when the six months expire, the bank's 'right to receive the money' accrues, and so the twelve-year period starts to run. If, for some reason, the bank discharges its mort-

---

76 Interest is dealt with separately by s. 20(5), which lays down a limitation period of six years. In *Barclays Bank plc* v. *Walters and another, The Times,* 20 October 1988, the Court of Appeal held that this period runs from the date when, on a true construction of the loan agreement, the lender could first have brought an action to recover the interest, not from the date when, under the agreement, it was due to have been paid.

gage of 'Blackacre' before the loan is repaid, the bank will still be able to rely upon the entirely separate and independent six-year period applicable to the simple contract debt.

2-40 There is a special rule laid down in s. 20 (3) of the Limitation Act 1980 with regard to mortgages or charges of any future interest in property or of any life insurance policy. The twelve-year period begins to run from the date when the future interest falls into possession, or the policy money becomes payable, or the policy is surrendered or is otherwise determined.

2-41 Separate provisions are made with regard to a mortgagee's remedy by way of foreclosure, under which the relevant period is normally twelve years.[77] These provisions may be illustrated by referring to *Lloyds Bank Ltd* v. *Margolis and Others*.[78] Briefly, in 1936 Lloyds Bank took a legal charge secured on a farm as security for a customer's overdraft on current account. The charge provided, in effect, that the customer would repay his indebtedness to the bank 'on demand'. On 19 December 1938, the bank made a demand, and on 29 November 1950 (a few weeks before the twelve-year period would have expired), the bank issued an originating summons to enforce its security by foreclosure or sale. Having stated the facts and the relevant provisions of the Limitation Act 1939, Upjohn J said:[79]

I have to determine what is the date on which the right to bring a foreclosure action first accrued to the bank. The rival contentions are these. The bank says that the time runs for twelve years from demand. That was December 19, 1938, and, therefore, they are just in time. The defendants, however, say that the time runs, in the case of advances made before the date of the deed, from the date of the deed, and in the case of subsequent advances, it runs from the date of the subsequent advances, and, as no claim is made to any advance made after October 14, 1938 ..., all of those sums have become irrecoverable, and, therefore, there is no debt in respect of which an action to foreclose can be brought.

The learned judge decided that the bank's contentions were sound. He said:[80]

In my judgment, where there is the relationship of banker and customer and the banker permits his customer to overdraw on the terms of entering

77 Limitation Act 1980, ss 15(1) and 20(2) and (4).
78 [1954] 1 All ER 734.
79 [1954] 1 All ER, at pp. 736–7.
80 [1954] 1 All ER, at p. 738.

into a legal charge which provides that the money which is then due or is thereafter to become due is to be paid 'on demand', that means what it says. As between the customer and banker, who are dealing on a running account, it seems to be impossible to assume that the bank were to be entitled to sue on the deed on the very day after it was executed without make a demand and giving the customer a reasonable time to pay. It is, indeed, a nearly correlative case to that decided in *Joachimson* v. *Swiss Bank Corporation*[81] ... In this case the agreement has provided quite clearly what is to be done before the bank can sue. They must demand the money.

2-42 There are no special limitation provisions applicable to actions against guarantors. Most guarantees taken by banks to secure their customers' accounts are under hand. In relation to them the usual rule relating to simple contracts applies, and so no action may be brought 'after the expiration of six years from the date on which the cause of action accrued'.[82] In cases where a guarantee is under seal, the limitation period is twelve years.[83] There is usually no difficulty in deciding when the appropriate limitation period starts to run, because a well-drafted guarantee invariably provides that the guarantor will pay 'on demand in writing' being made to him, and so the cause of action accrues when a written demand is served upon him.[84]

2-43 Finally, the cause of action against a customer is quite separate and distinct from the cause of action against a guarantor or other third party who has deposited security for the customer's indebtedness. One claim may be statute-barred, and the other may not. The following illustration may be given. A bank makes a loan to a customer, the loan to be repaid at the end of six months, and a guarantee under hand is executed by way of security, the guarantor undertaking to pay 'on demand in writing' being made to him. The customer fails to repay the loan, but the bank does not demand payment from the guarantor until two years after the customer's default. In this situation, the cause of action against the customer accrued when he made default, and the cause of action against the guarantor accrued when demand was made upon him. In both cases the limitation period is six years, but the bank's right to sue the customer will, of course, be barred two years before its right to sue the guarantor is barred. If the bank neglects to sue the customer until the statute has run, the guarantor is not thereby discharged.[85]

---

81 [1921] 3 KB 110, *ante*, para. 2-28.
82 Limitation Act 1980, s. 5, *ante*, para. 2-23.
83 S. 8(1).
84 *Bradford Old Bank Ltd* v. *Sutcliffe* [1918] 2 KB 833.
85 *Carter* v. *White* (1883) 25 ChD 666; *Curwen* v. *Milburn* (1889) 42 ChD 424, at pp. 434–5.

Section 3
BANKER'S RIGHT TO CHARGE FOR HIS SERVICES

2-44 From an early date bankers have made a charge for the services which they provide for their customers.[86] The legal considerations governing their right to charge commission will first be examined; this will be followed by a brief account of modern banking practice.

Legal basis for charging commission

2-45 First, the customer may have made an express agreement with his bank concerning the charging of commission.

2-46 Secondly, if there is no express agreement, an agreement may often be implied from a previous course of dealing between the bank and its customer. Thus, if a bank has habitually charged a customer commission and the customer has acquiesced in the charge, a right to charge commission arises from the course of dealing between the parties. An old case[87] illustrates how a customer may be held to have acquiesced in a charge for commission. In that case the plaintiff obtained an advance from the defendant bankers in 1874, and they issued a passbook to the plaintiff in which they made half-yearly rests and entered charges for interest and commission. The plaintiff from time to time paid in sums to the credit of the account, but never drew on it. The passbook was received by the plaintiff from time to time, and he twice wrote to the defendants acknowledging the accounts to be correct. In 1884 the plaintiff paid the balance appearing in the passbook to be due to the defendants and closed the account. Two years later the plaintiff sued the defendants to recover the sum of £95, being the aggregate amount of commissions charged, alleging that commission was not chargeable on a single advance with gradual repayments. Judgment was given for the bankers on the ground of the customer's acquiescence. The learned judge indicated that, apart from the special circumstances of acquiescence, he would have been disposed to think that it was fair to charge interest, but not commission. The reason was, apparently, that interest was being charged for the loan; no other services were being rendered and, therefore, it was not reasonable to charge commission.

2-47 Thirdly, even if there has been no express agreement concerning commission and no agreement can be implied from a previous course of

---

86 The earliest case on this point seems to be *Benson* v. *Parry* (1780) cited 2 TR 52 and 15 Ves 121, where it was held, on appeal, that a country banker who discounted bills payable in London was entitled to a fair and reasonable commission.
87 *Spencer* v. *Wakefield* (1887) 4 TLR 194.

dealing, because, for example, the account has only recently been opened, the bank will still usually have a right to charge a reasonable sum for its services. This right is based upon the principle that where one persons requests another to perform services of a professional or business nature, the law implies a promise on the part of the first person to pay a reasonable sum for services rendered.[88] Section 15(1) of the Supply of Goods and Services Act 1982 provides that where, under a contract for the supply of a service, the consideration for the service is not determined by the contract, left to be determined in a manner agreed by the contract or determined by the course of dealing between the parties, there is an implied term that the party contracting with the supplier will pay a reasonable charge. Section 15(2) provides that what is a reasonable charge is a question of fact. Furthermore, s. 13 provides that, in a contract for the supply of a service where the supplier is acting in the course of a business, there is an implied term that the supplier will carry out the service with reasonable care and skill.

2-48   As a general rule, a bank will have an undoubted right to charge commission on current accounts under one of the three heads set out above, and in practice it is very rare for a customer to challenge this right. There is, however, one type of case where it is desirable to obtain the customer's consent to the charging of commission. Let it be supposed that a customer who has maintained a steady credit balance of £400/£500 for the past three or four years has not previously been charged commission. Owing to rising costs, the bank may desire to make a charge, although it is merely rendering the same services as before. In this type of case it is desirable to obtain the customer's express agreement. In the absence of agreement, he would be able to challenge a debit to his account for commission, because he could point to a previous course of business whereby the bank's services were rendered without charge.

Practical considerations

2-49   Most banks conduct the current accounts of personal customers without charging any commission, provided that the customer maintains a stated minimum balance, though some banks have regard to the average balance. As regards the accounts of other customers, the method of charging commission is frequently the subject of an express agreement between the bank and its customer. There are three principal methods of calculating commission.

---

88 See, for example, *Price* v. *Hong Kong Tea Co.* (1861) 2 F & F 466 (accountant's remuneration); *Gibbon* v. *Budd* (1863) 2 H & C 92 (medical practitioner's remuneration).

(a) Percentage on turnover

2-50 When this method is adopted, a certain percentage is charged on the aggregate of all sums debited to the account during the accounting period, other than sums transferred to another account of the same customer; this sum is usually called 'the turnover'. In addition to charging a flat rate of commission on turnover, some banks charge a certain sum in respect of other services; for example, there may be a charge in respect of each cheque credited to the account and another charge in respect of each item debited to the account under a standing order.

(b) Cost per entry

2-51 This involves a fixed sum in respect of each item debited or credited to the customer's account. A variation of this method is adopted by some banks: different charges are made in respect of different types of transactions.

(c) Fixed charge

2-52 Sometimes a fixed charge of so much per half-year is agreed. This method should be employed only in those cases where the amount of work to be done each half-year remains fairly steady.

2-53 Whichever method is adopted, it is always necessary to take into consideration all the services rendered by the bank for the particular customer. For example, some customers may avail themselves of the bank's safe-custody services; others may use night safe facilities; others again may have large numbers of representatives in different parts of the country who make use of the services offered by the bank's branches and agents. Sometimes, a specific charge is made for some of these services, especially for safe-custody services and night safe facilities. Another factor to be taken into consideration when reviewing the overall picture is the size of the customer's balance on current account: a substantial balance on current account is clearly worth more to the bank than an account which is only a few hundred pounds in credit.

Prices and Incomes Board

2-54 In 1967 the Prices and Incomes Board reported upon bank charges made by the clearing banks, the Scottish banks and the Northern Ireland banks.[89] They summarized their conclusions as follows:[90]

89 National Board for Prices and Incomes Report No. 34, *Bank Charges*, Cmnd. 3292 (1967).
90 See para. 131 of the Report.

We have received no information to indicate that commission charges are generally too high and we do not see that the banks should be asked to subsidise them. It is not so much the actual level of charges which concerns us, as the system of charging. In the interests of more effective competition, we think that the banks should desist from collective agreements and should publish individual tariffs of charges. So far as concerns charges for handling current account transactions, such tariffs should at a minimum indicate the charge per entry or as a percentage of turnover together with the rate of offsetting allowance.[91]

The Prices and Incomes Board were not required to report upon the charges made by the trustee savings banks. In this connection it should be stated that these banks do publish tariffs of charges in respect of current accounts. Most of the other banks likewise publish their tariffs.

Section 4
BANKER'S RIGHT OF SET-OFF

2-55 If a customer has more than one account at the same branch of a bank, or at two or more branches of the same bank, the question may arise whether the bank has the right to set off what is due to the customer on one account against what is due from him on another account, and to have regard only to the ultimate or net balance when deciding what sum is available to the customer for drawing purposes. It is convenient to discuss this question under two main headings: first, where any event has occurred which has stopped the accounts, and secondly, where no such event has occurred.

Where accounts are stopped

2-56 Where any event occurs which determines a bank's duty to pay a customer's cheques, then, as a general rule, the bank is entitled to set off what is due to a customer on one account against what is due from him on another account, in order to ascertain the net amount owing to or by the customer. The various events which determine a bank's duty to pay a customer's cheques are considered in Chapter 3. The following are the more important of those events which require to be examined when considering the problem of set-off.[92]

---

91 The offsetting allowance refers to the rebate of charges which is related to the average credit balance in the account.

92 Another problem, which is sometimes regarded as one of set-off, arises where a customer who has two or more accounts with his bank creates a second mortgage or charge over property which is already mortgaged or charged to the bank.

(a) The customer's death

2-57   It is obvious that, if a customer dies at a time when he owes £400 to his bank on current account and when he has a credit balance of £100 on deposit account, the net sum (ignoring interest) which the bank will claim from his personal representative will be £300.

(b) The customer's mental incapacity

2-58   In this event, similar considerations would appear to apply as those which arise when a customer dies.

(c) The customer's bankruptcy

2-59   Section 323(1) and (2) of the Insolvency Act 1986 provides that where before the commencement of the bankruptcy there have been mutual credits, mutual debts or other mutual dealings between the bankrupt and any creditor of the bankrupt proving for a bankruptcy debt, an account must be taken of what is due from each party to the other in respect of the mutual dealings, and the sums due from one party must be set off against the sums due from the other. However, s. 323(3) of the Act provides that sums due from the bankrupt to another party must not be included in the account taken under this provision if the other party had notice at the time they became due that a bankruptcy petition relating to the bankrupt was pending. Finally, s. 323(4) provides that only the balance of the account taken under subsection (2) is provable as a bankruptcy debt, or, as the case may be, is to be paid to the trustee as part of the bankrupt's estate.

(d) The customer's liquidation

2-60   In the winding up of companies, the rules as to set-off in bankruptcy apply.[93] Thus, in one case, a company which was indebted to a bank on current account, opened another current account under a written agreement which provided that the bank would not, without the knowledge and consent of the company, appropriate any of the funds which might at any time be standing to the credit of the new account in reduction of the debt then due to the bank. A few years later the company was wound up. A substantial sum was still owing on the original account, and there was a substantial balance in favour of the company on the second account. The Judicial Committee of the Privy Council held that the bank had the right to set off the one sum against

---

93 Insolvency Rules 1986, r. 4.90; and see *Mersey Steel and Iron Co.* v. *Naylor, Benzon & Co.* (1884) 9 App Cas 434, a decision under the Supreme Court of Judicature Act, 1875, s. 10.

the other.[94] The date to which one has to look in ascertaining whether there is a right of set-off is the date of the petition for winding up.[95]

2-60A If, however, a bank has notice that an account contains money held by a customer on trust, the bank will have no right to set off this money against a debit balance on another account. Thus, in one case, a lender lent money to a company for the specific purpose of enabling the company to pay a dividend which it had declared. The company paid the money into a separate account at its bank, and the bank accepted the money with knowledge of the facts. Before the dividend was paid, the company went into liquidation. The lender sought to recover the money from the bank, but the bank claimed a right to set off the account containing the money against the company's overdrawn current account. The House of Lords held that the terms on which the loan was made were such as to impress on the money a trust in favour of the lender in the event of the dividend not being paid, and that the bank had sufficient notice of the trust. Accordingly, the bank was not entitled to retain the money against the lender.[96]

Where accounts are not stopped

The following cases arise frequently in practice.

(a) Customer has two current accounts

2-61 Assume, first, that there is no agreement for overdraft and that No. 1 account is £500 in credit and No. 2 account is £400 overdrawn. If the customer issues a cheque for any sum in excess of £100, the bank may quite properly dishonour it. Similarly, if the customer demands to be paid his credit balance, the bank may retain £400 of it as cover for the £400 debit in No. 2 account. Moreover, there is authority for the view that the same considerations apply even if the accounts are kept at two different branches of the bank. Thus, in *Garnett* v. *M'Kewan*[97] a

---

94 *British Guiana Bank* v. *Official Receiver* (1911) 104 LT 754. See also *National Westminster Bank Ltd* v. *Halesowen Presswork and Assemblies Ltd* [1972] AC 785, where the House of Lords held that the statutory set-off provisions in bankruptcy and winding up cannot be excluded by agreement.

95 *Per* Lord Hanworth MR in *Re City Equitable Fire Insurance Co.* [1930] 2 Ch 293, at p. 310.

96 *Barclays Bank Ltd* v. *Quistclose Investments Ltd* [1970] AC 567; see also *Re Kayford Ltd* [1975] 1 WLR 279.

97 (1872) LR 8 Ex 10. Although certain passages in the judgments in this case conflict with *dicta* of Swift J in *W. P. Greenhalgh and Sons* v. *Union Bank of Manchester* (*infra*), it is submitted that the principle laid down in *Garnett's* case is still the law today. For another case where the bank's right to combine accounts of a customer at two different branches of the bank was upheld, see *Barclays Bank Ltd* v. *Okenarhe* [1966] 2 Lloyd's Rep 87.

customer had an account at the Buckingham branch of the London and County Bank, and another account at their Leighton Buzzard branch. The former was overdrawn £42 15s. 11d., and the latter showed a credit balance of £42 18s. 10d. Three cheques amounting to £23 3s. were then drawn on the credit balance and were dishonoured by the bank. There was no overdraft agreement in existence, and four judges of the Court of Exchequer were unanimous in saying that the bank was justified in dishonouring the cheques.[98]

2-62 If a customer with two or more current accounts is granted an overdraft, the usual arrangement is that the *net* debit balance on his accounts must not exceed a certain figure. If the agreement is made in this way, the intention of the parties is clear; so, when the overdraft limit is reached, the bank will obviously be entitled to retain the credit balances, should the customer demand them.

(b) Customer has a deposit account and a current account

2-63 If the customer draws a cheque on his current account and his balance on that account is insufficient to meet it, but the customer also has a deposit account balance which provides sufficient cover, it is the usual practice to pay the cheque. In other words, the bank relies on its right of set-off against the deposit account.

(c) Customer has a loan account and a current account

2-64 This is the case which may give rise to difficulty. In *Buckingham & Co.* v. *London and Midland Bank Ltd*[99] the bank had lent money to the plaintiff on loan account. The plaintiff also had a drawing or current account with the bank. Eventually, the bank became dissatisfied with the value of the security which had been deposited for the loan account, and they informed the customer that his account was closed and that they could not pay any more cheques or honour any more of his acceptances. At that time there was a credit balance of £160 in the current account. On the following day two cheques and two bills of the plaintiff were presented and were dishonoured. The jury found that, in the course of dealing between the plaintiff and the bank, the plaintiff was entitled to draw on his current account without reference to his loan account, that he was entitled to reasonable notice discontinuing this course of business, and that no such notice had been given. The plaintiff was awarded £500 damages against the bank.

---

98 It has been held that a bank is entitled to charge interest on a customer's overdrawn current account at one branch of the bank, although the customer has a credit balance on current account at another branch of the same bank: *National Bank of New Zealand* v. *Grace* (1890) 8 NZLR 706.
99 (1895) 12 TLR 70.

2-65 In cases where customers maintain two or more accounts, one or more being in credit and one or more being overdrawn, some banks make a practice of obtaining from such customers a 'letter of set-off' authorizing the bank to combine the accounts at any time without notice. Such an authority is sometimes useful, but it seems doubtful whether it would afford a defence to a bank which acted as arbitrarily as the defendant bank in the *Buckingham* case. A letter of set-off is exempt from stamp duty as an agreement under hand.[1]

No right of set-off

A bank is not entitled to right of set-off in the following cases.

(a) Unmatured or contingent liabilities

2-66 As Wood V-C observed in *Jeffryes* v. *Agra and Masterman's Bank Ltd*,[2] 'you cannot retain a sum of money which is actually due against a sum of money which is only to become due at a future time'. Sometimes, for example, a bank accepts a foreign currency deposit from another bank for a fixed period, and subsequently makes a loan in the same currency and to the same bank but for a different period. If the deposit is due to be repaid on, say, 15 December, the bank holding the deposit is not entitled to retain it against a loan which is due to be repaid on, say, 31 December. Likewise, in the absence of some special agreement, a bank is not entitled to retain a customer's credit balance to secure itself against a contingent liability on bills which it has discounted for the customer.[3] However, if the customer is bankrupt, the position is different. The rule in bankruptcy is that all debts and liabilities, present or future, certain or contingent, may be the subject of set-off.[4]

(b) Express or implied agreement

2-67 There are many cases where, as a result of an agreement between the bank and the customer, there is no right of set-off. A common illustration is provided by the type of case, of which *Buckingham & Co.* v. *London and Midland Bank Ltd*[5] is an example, where the customer has a loan account and a current account and the agreement is that the customer is to be allowed to draw upon his credit balance on current

1 Finance Act 1970, s. 32 and Sched. 7.
2 (1866) 35 LJ Ch 686.
3 *Bower* v. *Foreign and Colonial Gas Co. Ltd, Metropolitan Bank, Garnishees* (1874) 22 WR 740.
4 Insolvency Act 1986, ss 323, 382(3).
5 See *ante*, para. 2-64.

account without reference to his loan account. It is quite clear that in such a case there will be no right of set-off, unless some event occurs to stop the accounts.

2-68 A decision which is often discussed in this connection is *W. P. Greenhalgh & Sons* v. *Union Bank of Manchester*.[6] That decision is considered more fully elsewhere.[7] The question of set-off did not arise directly, but it could have arisen if the bank had not paid the proceeds of the bills into the general account. If the bank had paid the proceeds into the 'bill provisional account', as it ought to have done, and if the bank had claimed the right to retain the proceeds against the debit balance in the general account, it would have failed, because the customer (with the bank's assent) had specifically appropriated the proceeds for some other purpose.

(c) Account contains trust funds

2-69 Very often the title of an account indicates that it contains moneys belonging to other people, e.g. John Jones, 'Tennis Club Account', or Benjamin L. Gross, 'Police Account',[8] or John Smith, Sole Executor of William Robinson. A bank is not entitled to set off a credit balance on such accounts against a debit balance on the customer's private account.[9] Similarly, professional men often maintain separate banking accounts for clients' moneys. Where it is known to a bank that a particular account is used for this purpose, no right of set-off can arise. There are statutory provisions which compel a solicitor to keep a separate banking account for the money of his clients, and the word 'client' must appear in the title of the account.[10] A bank cannot have any recourse or right, whether by way of set-off or otherwise, against moneys standing to the credit of such account.

2-70 In some cases, it is not easy for a bank to decide whether or not an account consists of funds held by a customer in trust for someone else, and great care must be exercised in such cases. *Union Bank of Australia Ltd* v. *Murray-Aynsley*[11] is an illustration of a borderline case. The plaintiffs, who were trustees under a marriage settlement, employed in connection with the investment of their trust funds a firm of agents and general merchants trading as Miles & Co., who afterwards transferred their business to a joint stock company incorporated as

---

6 [1924] 2 KB 153.

7 *Post*, para. 2-84.

8 *Re Gross, Ex parte Kingston* (1871) 5 Ch App 632.

9 *Ibid*.

10 *Post*, para. 11-147. See also *Barclays Bank Ltd* v. *Quistclose Investments Ltd* [1970] AC 567, *ante*, para. 2-60A.

11 [1898] AC 693.

Miles & Co. Ltd. Both the firm and their successors, the company, were customers of the Union Bank of Australia. The firm, and (later) the company, had three accounts: No. 1, which was the general account, No. 2, which was known as the stock account, and No. 3, all of which continued down to the time when the company failed. The plaintiffs had invested £1,800 through the agency of Miles & Co., and subsequently, when the loans were repaid, Miles & Co. Ltd received payment of that amount and paid it into their No. 3 account, where it stood when the company failed. At the date when the company failed, there was a large sum owing by the company to the bank, and the bank claimed a right of set-off in respect of the credit balance on the No. 3 account. The plaintiffs sued the bank for £1,800 out of the money standing to the credit of the No. 3 account.

2-71 The question was whether the bank had had notice that the moneys standing to the credit of that account were trust moneys. The evidence of the bank manager concerning the opening of the No. 3 account was as follows: 'Mr Banks saw me about opening No. 3 account. He said he wished to open a separate account. That he had received a large amount of money which was to be invested or remitted to London ... He did not say whom these moneys belonged to, said nothing about a trust account. I had no idea whom they belonged to.'

2-72 The court of first instance and, on appeal, the Supreme Court of New Zealand by a majority, decided the case in favour of the plaintiffs; but the Judicial Committee of the Privy Council gave judgment in favour of the bank, on the ground that the plaintiffs had failed to prove that the moneys for which they sued, were, to the bank's knowledge, trust funds. In the result, therefore, the bank was able to exercise a right of set-off. But a very slight variation of the facts would clearly have deprived the bank of such a right. If the bank had been told: 'These are clients' moneys which are to be invested or remitted to London', the decision would have been adverse to the bank. It follows, therefore, that whenever a customer opens a No. 2 account or a No. 3 account and gives any indication that the funds to be paid into the account are trust moneys, the bank should record this information and never regard the balance on the new account as being available to set off against a debit balance on the customer's other accounts.

(d) Accounts of different customers

2-72A In *Uttamchandami* v. *Central Bank of India*[12] the defendant bank sought to set off accounts held in different names on the ground

12 (1989) 139 NLJ 222.

that in each case the accounts were 'nominee' accounts and that in each case the customer was in reality a Mr Vaswani. The Court of Appeal, affirming the decision of Hobhouse J, held that the bank had no such right. Lloyd LJ said:

> Now the banker's right of set-off between accounts is a well-established part of our law of banking. But so far as I am aware, set-off has never been allowed save where the accounts are of the same customer, held in the same name, and in the same right. Even then, the right of set-off may be excluded by agreement express or implied. What is unusual about the present case is that the bank is seeking to set off accounts held in different names, on the ground that in each case the accounts are so-called 'nominee' accounts, and that in each case the customer is in reality Mr Vaswani.

The bank had relied not on the ordinary banker's right of set-off at common law, but on set-off in equity. Having examined the authorities, Lloyd LJ said: 'As I understand the old cases on this topic, set-off in equity was never allowed save where a court of equity could see that the person claiming to rely on set-off was the beneficial owner of the debt in question, either on the face of it, or by distinct admission, or otherwise without the need for any further enquiry.' Accordingly, the Court of Appeal dismissed the bank's appeal.

Section 5
APPROPRIATION OF PAYMENTS

2-73 The subject of appropriation of payments is a large one, and some of the older textbooks on the law of banking examined its implications in considerable detail.[13] In this book it is proposed to confine attention to those aspects of the subject which are of greatest interest in modern banking practice.

Rules governing appropriation of payments

2-74 'The general rule is, that the party who pays money has a right to apply that payment as he thinks fit. If these are several debts due from him, he has a right to say to which of those debts the payment shall be applied.'[14]

2-75 'If he does not make a specific application at the time of payment,

---

13 See, for example, Chapter XXIII of *Grant on the Law Relating to Bankers and Banking Companies* (7th ed., 1923).
14 *Per* Bayley J in *Simson* v. *Ingham* (1823) 2 B & C 65, at p. 72.

then the right of application generally devolves on the party who receives the money.'[15]

2-76 The debtor's intention to appropriate may be shown by the course of dealing or other circumstances,[16] but an entry in the debtor's books is not of itself evidence of appropriation by him.[17]

2-77 If the right of appropriation devolves on the creditor, he may appropriate to a debt which is statute-barred, though such appropriation will not revive the debt.[18] He may not, however, appropriate to an illegal debt.[19]

2-78 The creditor need not exercise his right of appropriation at the time of payment. Thus, it has been held that he may make an appropriation when he is being examined as a witness in an action by him against the debtor.[20] But once the creditor has made an appropriation, 'it is made once for all, and it does not lie in the mouth of the creditor afterwards to seek to vary that appropriation.'[21]

2-79 Money paid into a bank account to meet a particular bill or cheque must be applied accordingly.[22]

2-80 In the absence of any specific appropriation, it is presumed, in the case of a current account, (a) that the first sum paid in is first drawn out, and (b) that the first item on the debit side of the account is discharged or reduced by the first item on the credit side. This is known as the rule in *Clayton's* case.[23]

Importance of the rules in banking practice

2-81 It is proposed to give a number of illustrations in order to show how the rules relating to appropriation of payments affect the banks, their customers and third parties at the present day. The Rule in

15 *Ibid.*
16 *Marryatts* v. *White* (1817) 2 Stark 101; *Peters* v. *Anderson* (1814) 5 Taunt 596; *Burn* v. *Boulton* (1846) 2 CB 476; *Shaw* v. *Picton* (1825) 4 B & C 715; *Nash* v. *Hodgson* (1855) 6 De GM & G 474, at pp. 486, 487.
17 *Manning* v. *Westerne* (1707) 2 Vern 606.
18 *Mills* v. *Fowkes* (1839) 5 Bing NC 455; *Williams* v. *Griffith* (1893) 5 M & W 300; *cf.* *Friend* v. *Young* [1897] 2 Ch 421.
19 *Ex parte Randleson* (1833) 2 Deac & Ch 534; *Wright* v. *Laing* (1824) 3 B & C 165; *Lamprell* v. *Guardians of Billericay Union* (1849) 3 Exch 283, at p. 307.
20 *Seymour* v. *Pickett* [1905] 1 KB 715.
21 *Per* Lord Shaw in *Deeley* v. *Lloyds Bank Ltd* [1912] AC 756, at pp. 783–4.
22 *Farley* v. *Turner* (1857) 26 LJ Ch 710; *W. P. Greenhalgh & Sons* v. *Union Bank of Manchester* [1924] 2 KB 153.
23 (1816) 1 Mer 572.

Clayton's case, which impinges upon banking practice in very many ways, will be considered separately.

2-82 If a customer who maintains two or more accounts at his bank makes a payment to credit, he has the right to appropriate the funds to whichever account he chooses. If he fails to do so, then in theory the bank may appropriate, though in practice no doubt the bank would usually inquire which account was to be credited.

2-83 A customer whose credit balance is exhausted or whose account has reached the limit of the permitted overdraft, informs the bank that he has issued three cheques, each for ten pounds, in favour of Jones, Brown and Robinson respectively. He pays in ten pounds only, and instructs the bank to pay the cheque in favour of Robinson. The bank must do so. If the bank pays the cheque in favour of Jones and dishonours the cheque in favour of Robinson, the customer will be entitled to sue the bank for damages for wrongful dishonour. Robinson, however, will have no cause of action against the bank, because there is no contract between him and the bank.

2-84 *W. P. Greenhalgh & Sons* v. *Union Bank of Manchester*[24] was an exceptional case where a third party in fact succeeded in an action against a bank as a result of an appropriation made in his favour by a customer. In that case, customers of the Union Bank of Manchester maintained two accounts with the bank, known respectively as the 'general account' and the 'bill provision account'. The customers handed certain bills of exchange to the bank for collection. It seems that the bills were held in the 'bill provisional account' and that the intention was that the proceeds thereof were to be specifically appropriated to meet other bills drawn by W. P. Greenhalgh & Sons and accepted by the customers. Messrs Greenhalgh knew of the intended appropriation, and the bank knew of their interest in the proceeds of the bills paid in by the customers. Those bills were duly paid, and the bank, without their customers' consent, paid the proceeds into the customers' general account where, as Swift J said, 'they were swallowed by a large debit balance awaiting them there'.[25] In the result, Messrs Greenhalgh's bills, which the customers had promised and intended should be met by those proceeds, were dishonoured. Messrs Greenhalgh brought an action against the bank, and succeeded. The learned judge found that before the bank paid the proceeds of the bills into the customers' general account, the bank 'had received notice of a specific appropriation and of an equitable assignment of the proceeds',[26] and he accordingly gave judgment for Messrs Greenhalgh.

24 [1924] 2 KB 153.
25 [1924] 2 KB, at p. 159.
26 [1924] 2 KB, at p. 165.

Rule in *Clayton's* case

2-85 The facts of *Clayton's* case[27] were that a customer named Mr Clayton had a current account with a banking partnership. One of the partners died, and at the date of his death there was a balance standing to the credit of the customer's account. At a later date the bank failed, and between the date of the partner's death and the date of the failure the customer withdrew sums in excess of the credit balance, but he also paid in sums sufficient to put the account more in credit than it had been when the partner died. The customer claimed that the payments in should be appropriated against the withdrawals so as to leave intact the balance at the partner's death as a claim against the partner's estate. It was held, however, that the credit balance, being a liability of the continuing firm, had been extinguished by the withdrawals, since the items in the current account were presumed to be set against each other chronologically. Thus, the customer was left with no claim against the estate of the deceased partner.

2-86 The following extract from the judgment of Sir William Gant MR embodies the principle which has become known as the Rule in *Clayton's* case:[28]

> This is the case of a banking account where all the sums paid in form one blended fund, the parts of which have no longer any distinctive existence. Neither banker nor customer ever thinks of saying, this draft is to be placed to the account of the £500 paid in on Monday, and this other to the account of the £500 paid in on Tuesday. There is a fund of £1,000 to draw upon, and that is enough. In such a case, there is no room for any other appropriation than that which arises from the order in which the receipts and payments take place, and are carried into the account. Presumably, it is the sum first paid in that is first drawn out. It is the first item on the debit side of the account that is discharged, or reduced, by the first item on the credit side. The appropriation is made by the very act of setting the two items against each other.

2-87 The type of situation which arose in *Clayton's* case is not likely to arise again in this country: it is many years since a banking partnership failed. Nevertheless, the principle laid down in the judgment is one of great practical importance. For example, banks frequently lend money on current account by way of fluctuating overdraft. If in such cases security is deposited, it is the invariable practice for the instrument of charge to provide that the security is to be a continuing security. A common form of words is: 'This security shall be a continuing security

27 (1816) 1 Mer 572.
28 (1816) 1 Mer 572, at p. 608.

and extend to cover any sums of money which shall for the time being constitute the balance due from the chargor to the bank.' In the absence of a clause to that effect, the Rule in *Clayton's* case would apply, and so payments in would be treated as payments towards the discharge of the secured debt and payments out would constitute unsecured advances.

Clayton's case inapplicable

The following are the principal cases where the Rule does not apply.

(a) Between trustee and beneficiary

2-88   Let it be supposed that a trustee paid £2,000 of trust money into his personal account at a time when that account was £200 in credit. He then paid in £1,000 of his own money, and subsequently withdrew for his own use £2,000, leaving a final balance of £1,200. If the Rule in *Clayton's* case applied, the withdrawal of £2,000 would have extinguished the original credit of £200 and would have reduced the trust money to £200. Hence the final balance of £1,200 would comprise £200 of trust money and £1,000 of the trustee's own money. This result would be unjust to the beneficiaries. However, the Rule in *Clayton's* case does not apply to this situation. Equity gives priority to the beneficiaries in the resulting balance, on the basis that the customer must be taken to have drawn out his own money in preference to the trust money. This is known as the Rule in *Hallett's* case. [29] Thus, in the illustration given above, the final balance of £1,200 would represent trust money, and the beneficiaries could claim a charge on that sum in the hands of the bank.

(b) Contrary intention

2-89   The Rule in *Clayton's* case may be displaced by contrary intention, because it is not an absolute rule but a presumption of fact. [30] By way of illustration, let it be supposed that a customer who has a loan of £1,000 is debited with interest in the sum of £50 at the end of December. At the beginning of January he pays in £50 or more and asks the bank to supply him with a certificate stating the amount of interest paid, in order that he may obtain a repayment of tax on the amount of the interest paid. If the Rule in *Clayton's* case applied, he would not be entitled to a certificate, but, by asking for a certificate, it would seem that he has impliedly appropriated the sum paid in at the beginning of

29 *Re Hallett's Estate, Knatchbull* v. *Hallett* (1880) 13 Ch D 696.
30 *Cory Brothers & Co.* v. *Mecca Turkish S.S. (Owners) The Mecca* [1897] AC 286.

January to discharge the interest debited to his account at the end of December.

Clayton's case: Two or more accounts

2-90　If a customer keeps two or more accounts at the bank, it will not be presumed that credits in one of those accounts will extinguish debits in his other account or accounts in order of time. Thus, in *Bradford Old Bank Ltd* v. *Sutcliffe*[31] a customer had a loan account and a current account, and it was held that payments to the credit of the current account must be appropriated to that account, and accordingly a guarantor for the loan account could not claim that such payments should be taken in reduction of the loan. As a general rule, therefore, if a customer has more than one account, the Rule in *Clayton's* case must be applied to each account separately.[32]

2-91　However, there are exceptional cases where this general rule does not apply. Thus, in *Re E. J. Morel (1934) Ltd*,[33] a company maintained a No. 2 account and a Wages account, and the arrangement was that the credit balance on the No. 2 account would always be sufficient to cover the debit balance on the Wages account. In those special circumstances, it was held that the No. 2 account and the Wages account were in substance one account as between the bank and the company. In the result, the bank could not claim as preferential creditor in respect of payments for wages debited to the Wages account under the provisions of s. 319(4) of the Companies Act 1948. Another way of looking at the transactions was that 'even if at any time payments were made out of the Wages account which could properly be described as advances, those advances would have been repaid by credits paid into the No. 2 account before the winding up commenced'.[34] That way of viewing the transactions meant that it was necessary to merge the two accounts rather like the two halves of a pack of cards, and then to apply the Rule in *Clayton's* case to the amalgam of the two accounts.

Clayton's case: 'stopping' an account

2-92　The Rule in *Clayton's* case applies only where payments into or out of an account continue to be made. This may be illustrated by considering the position of Mr Clayton.[35] After one of the partners in the

---

31　[1918] 2 KB 833.
32　*Re Yeovil Glove Co. Ltd* [1965] Ch 148.
33　[1962] 1 Ch 21.
34　[1962] 1 Ch, at p. 33 *per* Buckley J.
35　See *ante*, para. 2-85.

banking firm had died, Mr Clayton continued to operate his account in the usual way by making payments into and out of his account. He thereby lost his claim against the deceased partner's estate. If, when the partner had died, Mr Clayton had left his account dormant and had opened a new account for future transactions, he would have preserved his rights against the deceased partner's estate.

2-93 There are numerous cases in modern banking practice where it is in a bank's interest to prevent the operation of the Rule in *Clayton's* case by breaking or 'stopping' an overdrawn account. The following are some of the more important instances which vigilant bank officers will have in mind.

(a) Death, etc., of joint account holder

2-94 If a partner or a joint account holder dies, or is made bankrupt, the account should be stopped, and future transactions passed through a new account. Failure to observe this precaution involved a bank in loss in the Scottish case of *Royal Bank of Scotland* v. *Christie*.[36] A partnership was borrowing from a bank, and a partner had executed a mortgage of land of his own by way of security. That partner died, and then further advances were made to the partnership, which continued in business. Furthermore, sums were paid into the account sufficient to cover the indebtedness at the date of death. The House of Lords held that, by virtue of the Rule in *Clayton's* case, the payments in had repaid the debt outstanding at the partner's death, and that the security executed by the deceased partner was not available in respect of the advances made after his death.

(b) Notice of second mortgage

2-95 If a bank as first mortgagee receives notice of a second mortgage, the customer's account should be stopped and future transactions passed through a new account. Failure to adopt this course involved a bank in loss in *Deeley* v. *Lloyds Bank Ltd*.[37]

(c) Determination of guarantee

2-96 If a guarantee is determined, the usual practice is to stop the principal debtor's account and to pass future transactions through a new account. If this is not done and sums continue to be paid into the original account, prima facie the Rule in *Clayton's* case will apply, with the

36 (1840) 8 Cl & Fin 214.
37 [1912] AC 756. See J. Milnes Holden, *The Law and Practice of Banking*, Vol. 2, *Securities for Bankers' Advances* (7th ed., 1986), para. 5-14.

result that payments in will reduce or extinguish the liability of the guarantor, whilst payments out will create new advances for which he will not be liable. It is possible, however, to incorporate a special clause in a guarantee, the object of which is to prevent the Rule in *Clayton's* case from operating in this case. The efficacy of such a clause was upheld in *Westminster Bank Ltd* v. *Cond.*[38]

Clayton's case operating in bank's favour

In the following instances the Rule in *Clayton's* case may operate in favour of a bank.

(a) Creation of floating charge

2-97 By virtue of s. 245 of the Insolvency Act 1986, where a company creates a floating charge at a time when it is unable to pay its debts, the charge may be invalid if it was created within twelve months prior to the commencement of winding up or the presentation of a successful petition for an administration order. The floating charge will be invalid, except to the extent of the aggregate of (a) the value of so much of the consideration for the creation of the charge as consists of money paid, or goods or services supplied, to the company at the same time as, or after, the creation of the charge, (b) the value of so much of that consideration as consists of the discharge or reduction, at the same time as, or after, the creation of the charge, of any debt of the company, and (c) the amount of such interest (if any) as was agreed to be paid on the amount falling within (a) or (b).

2-97A It follows that, if an insolvent company creates a floating charge in favour of its bank in order to secure an existing advance, every endeavour should be made to keep the company out of liquidation until twelve months have expired. However, even if this is impossible, the Rule of *Clayton's* case may operate in favour of the bank, because all moneys paid into the account after the charge is executed will be deemed to have been appropriated to reduce the debt outstanding at the time of execution and all subsequent drawings will amount to new lendings secured by the charge. Therefore, if the amount so paid in equals or exceeds the debt outstanding at the time of execution, the charge will be fully effective, even if the company goes into liquidation within the year.[39]

---

38 (1940) 46 Com Cas 60. See J. Milnes Holden, *op. cit.*, para. 19-33.
39 *Re Thomas Mortimer Ltd* (1925), reported in a Note in [1965] Ch 186, a case decided under s. 212 of the Companies (Consolidation) Act 1908; *Re Yeovil Glove Co. Ltd* [1965] Ch 148.

(b) Advances for wages and salaries

2-98   In *Re Primrose (Builders) Ltd*,[40] a company maintained an over-drawn current account with the National Provincial Bank Ltd. During the months prior to winding up, various cheques were drawn on the account to obtain cash for the payment of wages and holiday remuner-ation. Upon each occasion when a cheque was paid, the bank insisted that a payment or payments substantially equal to or exceeding the amount of the cheque would shortly be paid into the account. When the company was ordered to be wound up, the bank claimed as preferential creditor in respect of wages advances under the provisions of s. 319(4) of the Companies Act 1948. The liquidator rejected this claim and argued that the various cheques for wages and holiday remuneration constituted separate advances made by the bank, and that they had been repaid by the credits which were paid into the account after each cheque was honoured. The court refused to accede to this argument and held that the company's account was a 'true current running account', to which the Rule in *Clayton's* case applied. Therefore, the bank's claim to be a preferential creditor succeeded.

Section 6
BANKER'S DUTY OF SECRECY

2-99   For very many years it has been established that a bank is under a legal obligation to keep its customers' affairs secret.[41] At the present day banks often include in their passbooks and in their brochures a statement that the officers of the bank are bound to secrecy as regards the transactions of their customers.

2-100   The leading case on the duty of secrecy is *Tournier* v. *National Provincial and Union Bank of England*,[42] which is important not only because of the particular point that arose but also because of the general principles laid down in the judgments in the Court of Appeal. The plain-tiff was a customer of the defendant bank. In April 1922, his account was £9 8s. 6d. overdrawn, and he signed a document agreeing to pay off this amount by weekly instalments of one pound. The plaintiff wrote on the document the name and address of a certain company, whose employment he was about to enter as a traveller on a three-months con-

---

40   [1950] 1 Ch 561; see also *National Provincial Bank Ltd* v. *Freedman and Rubens* (1934), *Journal of the Institute of Bankers*, Vol. LV, p. 392; *Re James R. Rutherford & Sons Ltd* [1964] 1 WLR 1211; *Re Rampgill Mill Ltd* [1967] Ch 1138.
41   *Tassel* v. *Cooper* (1850) 9 CB 509; *Foster* v. *Bank of London* (1862) 3 F & F 214; *Hardy* v. *Veasey* (1868) LR 3 Exch 107.
42   [1924] 1 KB 461.

tract. When the agreement to repay was not observed, the acting manager of the branch telephoned the company in order to find out the plaintiff's private address, and he spoke to two of the company's directors. The plaintiff alleged that in those conversations the acting manager had disclosed that his account was overdrawn and that promises for repayment were not being carried out, and had expressed the opinion that the plaintiff was betting heavily, the bank having traced a cheque or cheques passing from the plaintiff to a bookmaker. The acting manager's version of the telephone conversation did not differ substantially from that of the plaintiff. As a result of those conversations, the company refused to renew the plaintiff's employment when the three months had expired. The plaintiff brought an action against the bank for damages for slander and for breach of an implied term of the contract between him and the bank that the bank would not disclose to third persons the state of his account or any transactions relating to it.[43] The trial took place before Avory J and a jury, and judgment was entered for the bank. The plaintiff appealed.

2-101   The Court of Appeal allowed the appeal and ordered a new trial. There is nothing in the law reports to indicate whether or not a new trial ever took place; possibly the action was settled. All three members of the Court of Appeal, Bankes, Scrutton and Atkin LJJ held that a bank does owe a duty of secrecy to its customers. There was, however, some divergence of opinion between the learned lords justices concerning the type of information which is covered by the duty of secrecy. Thus Atkin LJ said:[44]

> The first question is: To what information does the obligation of secrecy extend? It clearly goes beyond the state of the account, that is, whether there is a debit or a credit balance, and the amount of the balance. It must extend at least to all the transactions that go through the account, and to the securities, if any, given in respect of the account; and in respect of such matters it must, I think, extend beyond the period when the account is closed, or ceases to be an active account. It seems to me inconceivable that either party would contemplate that once the customer had closed his account the bank was to be at liberty to divulge as it pleased the particular transactions which it had conducted for the customer while he was such. I further think that the obligation extends to information obtained from other sources than the customer's actual account, if the occasion upon

43 Although the plaintiff pleaded an *implied* term, it is worth noting that the passbooks issued by the bank to its customers, including the passbook of the plaintiff, stated: 'The officers of the Bank are bound to secrecy as regards the transaction of its customers.' Accordingly, it would seem to have been strongly arguable that the duty of secrecy in this case was an express, rather than an implied, term of the contract.
44 [1924] 1 KB, at pp. 473–4.

which the information was obtained arose out of the banking relations of the bank and its customers – for example, with a view to assisting the bank in conducting the customer's business, or in coming to decisions as to its treatment of its customers.

2-102 Scrutton LJ considered that the implied legal duty towards the customer to keep his affairs secret did not apply to (a) knowledge which the bank acquired before the relation of banker and customer was in contemplation, or after it ceased, or (b) knowledge derived from other sources during the continuance of the relation.[45] However, Bankes LJ agreed with Atkin LJ in thinking that the duty of secrecy does extend to knowledge acquired in both (a) and (b),[46] and so their opinions must be regarded as authoritative.

2-103 Another question which the members of the Court of Appeal considered in *Tournier's* case was whether the duty of secrecy is 'absolute', or whether there are any occasions when a bank is justified in making disclosure concerning its customers' affairs. Bankes LJ said:[47]

> At the present day I think it may be asserted with confidence that the duty is a legal one arising out of contract, and that the duty is not absolute but qualified. It is not possible to frame any exhaustive definition of the duty. The most that can be done is to classify the qualification, and to indicate its limits ... On principle I think that the qualifications can be classified under four heads: (a) Where disclosure is under compulsion by law; (b) where there is a duty to the public to disclose; (c) where the interests of the bank require disclosure; (d) where the disclosure is made by the express or implied consent of the customer.

These four heads are of considerable practical importance, and it is proposed to examine each of them in turn.

Disclosure under compulsion by law

The following illustrations may be given of cases where a bank may be compelled by process of law to disclose its customers' affairs.

(a) Banker's Books Evidence Act 1879

2-104 Section 7 of the Bankers' Books Evidence Act 1879 provides that, on the application of any party to a legal proceeding, a court may order that such party be at liberty to inspect and take copies of any

45 [1924] 1 KB, at pp. 473–4.
46 [1924] 1 KB, at p. 481.
47 [1924] 1 KB, at pp. 471–3.

entries in a banker's books for any of the purposes of such proceedings. As a general rule, an order for inspection under this section will be made only where the entries relate to an account which is in form or substance the account of one of the parties to the litigation.[48] The application of the section to criminal proceedings was not tested until 1972 when the Divisional Court, in *Williams and Others* v. *Summerfield*,[49] stated that an order under the section could be a very serious interference with the liberty of the subject. It was an order which should be made only after the most careful thought and on the clearest grounds. In the result, the Divisional Court upheld the decision of justices who had made an order enabling a police inspector to inspect and take copies of certain bank accounts. In a subsequent case, *R.* v. *Andover Justices, Ex parte Rhodes*[50] the Divisional Court upheld the decision of justices who had made an order authorizing the inspection of a husband's bank account. His wife had been charged with the theft of money, and she had told the police that the money was in her husband's bank account. The magistrate's order was upheld, even though the husband was not a party to the proceedings.

2-104A In *Barker* v. *Wilson*[51] the Divisional Court held that microfilm records were within the scope of the Bankers' Books Evidence Act 1879. This point received statutory force in the Banking Act 1979, which provided in para. 1 of Sched. 6 that the expression 'bankers' books' includes 'ledgers, day books, cash books, account books and other records used in the ordinary business of the bank, whether those records are in written form or are kept on microfilm, magnetic tape or any other form of mechanical or electronic data retrieval mechanism'.[52] In *Williams* v. *Williams*[53] Mrs Williams petitioned for judicial separation from her husband. The Court of Appeal held that, as paid cheques and paying-in slips retained by a bank are not bankers' books, they could not be the subject of an order requiring Barclays Bank to allow Mrs Williams and her solicitors to inspect and take copies of her husband's paid cheques and paying-in slips. However, Sir John Donaldson MR said that it was not clear to him why, if this had not already been done, the court should not make a specific order requiring Mr Williams to obtain the cheques and paying-in slips relating to his account or accounts with Barclays Bank and to disclose them to Mrs Williams and her solicitors.

48 *Howard* v. *Beall* (1889) 23 QBD 1; *Pollock* v. *Garle* [1898] 1 Ch 1. See also *ante*, para. 1-59.
49 [1972] 2 QB 512.
50 (1980) *The Times*, 14 June.
51 [1980] 2 All ER 81.
52 This Schedule was not repealed by the Banking Act 1987.
53 [1987] 3 All ER 257.

(b) Other orders of the court

2-105   Sometimes a bank official is served with a *subpoena duces tecum* ordering him to attend court and to bring with him books, letters or other documents relating to a customer's affairs. Occasionally, a customer consents to his affairs being divulged in court but, if he does not consent, the bank should refuse to attend court unless one of its officials is served with a *subpoena duces tecum* ordering him to attend court and to bring with him the relevant books and documents.

2-105A   The court has power under the Rules of the Supreme Court to order discovery of documents which would normally be subject to the obligation of confidentiality owed by a bank to its customer.[54] Thus in *Bankers Trust Company* v. *Shapira and Others*,[55] the plaintiff bank claimed that it had been fraudulently deprived of US $1 million by two men, who then placed the money on deposit at the Hatton Garden branch of the Discount Bank (Overseas) Ltd. The plaintiff bank brought an action against the two men and against the Discount Bank. The defendant bank was duly served with the proceedings, but it was impossible to serve the individual defendants, both of whom were said to be on the Continent, one of them being in jail in Switzerland during a fraud investigation by the Swiss police. The plaintiff bank claimed as against the defendant bank an order for discovery of the documents relating to these sums of money. In his judgment in the Court of Appeal, Lord Denning MR said that the Discount Bank had got mixed up with the wrongful acts of the two men. The bank was under a duty to assist the plaintiff bank by giving them full information and disclosing the position of the wrongdoers. Though banks had a confidential relationship with their customers, it did not apply to conceal the fraud and iniquity of wrongdoers. In the result, the Court of Appeal made an order for discovery (i.e. disclosure) of the relevant documents.

(c) Stock in name of bank's nominees

2-106   The Commissioners of Inland Revenue may require a bank, under s. 13 of the Taxes Management Act 1970, to prepare and deliver a list of persons beneficially entitled to stocks registered in the name of the bank or its nominees. In *Attorney-General* v. *National Provincial Bank Ltd*[56] the Commissioners of Inland Revenue, purporting to act under s. 103 of the Income Tax Act 1918 (now replaced by s. 13 of the 1970 Act), had required the defendant bank to prepare and deliver lists

54 Order 24.
55 [1980] 3 All ER 353. See also *A and another* v. *C and others* [1980] 2 All ER 347.
56 (1928) 44 TLR 701.

containing true and correct statements of the names and addresses of all persons on whose behalf the bank had received interest on certain specified government stocks registered or inscribed in the name of the bank or its nominees, either as trustees, or by way of security, or at the mere request of the owner. The bank was unwilling to comply with this requirement unless the court so decided, with the result that this friendly action was instituted. It was held that the Commissioners' claim was well founded.

(d) Interest exceeding fifteen pounds

2-107 The Commissioners of Inland Revenue may require a bank, under s. 17 of the Taxes Management Act 1970, to make and deliver a return disclosing bank interest exceeding fifteen pounds per annum paid or credited to any one customer.

(e) Police and Criminal Evidence Act 1984

2-107A Section 9(1) of the Police and Criminal Evidence Act 1984 enables a police constable to obtain access to 'special procedure material' by making an application under Sched. 1 of the Act. Section 14 of the Act defines 'special procedure material' in very wide terms. Thus it includes material, other than items subject to legal privilege, in the possession of a person who acquired it or created it in the course of any trade, business, profession or other occupation and who holds it subject to an express or implied undertaking to hold it in confidence. Clearly, this definition includes 'material' held by bankers relating to their customers. By virtue of Sched. 1, a police constable may obtain access to this material by applying to a circuit judge. When the rules laid down in that Schedule have been complied with, a circuit judge has power to make an order that the person in possession of the material must (a) produce it to a constable for him to take it away, or (b) give a constable access to it. The Schedule requires that an application for an order must be made *inter partes*.

2-107B In *R* v. *Leicester Crown Court, ex parte Director of Public Prosecutions*[57] the Divisional Court decided an important point under this Act. The police in Leicestershire were making investigations into the suspected criminal activities of F. It was suspected that he was living on the earnings of prostitution. In order to help their investigations, the police required to see the accounts which they thought were held in F's name at branches of Barclays Bank, the National Westminster Bank, the

---

57 [1987] 3 All ER 654.

Halifax Building Society and the Citibank Savings Trust. Accordingly, the Crown Prosecutor on behalf of the police applied for an order allowing a constable to obtain access to 'special procedure material' under s. 9(1) of the Police and Criminal Evidence Act 1984. As stated in the preceding paragraph, an application for such an order must be made *inter partes*. The view of the circuit judge was that a necessary party for the purposes of an application of this kind was the person either charged with, or suspected of, the crime being investigated. Accordingly, he ruled that he was not competent to entertain the application made by the Crown Prosecutor unless notice of the application had been served on F.

That ruling caused some consternation, because both the Crown Prosecutor and the police were of the view that the only parties referred to in Sched. 1 were, on the one hand, the police and, on the other, the person or institution in whose custody the special procedure material was thought to be held. The Divisional Court upheld this view. Watkins LJ said that it seemed 'almost inconceivable' that Parliament could have contemplated that a suspected person should be made aware of this essential part of the activities of the police in making their investigation into criminal activity. He added that it should be noted that s. 9(1) referred to 'a criminal investigation'. It did not suggest that there was, even at the time of making the application, a suspected person, let alone a person who had in fact been charged with a criminal offence. Watkins LJ concluded: 'What is envisaged by s. 9(1) in my view is that, when the police are making investigation into a crime, they may at any stage of those investigations, before they have identified anyone as a likely perpetrator of the crime being investigated, seek access to what is called special procedure material and invoke the assistance of the courts for an order for that purpose.'

2-107C In *R* v. *Crown Court at Manchester, ex parte Taylor*[58] the police were investigating offences of fraud which they suspected had been committed by the applicant and others. A police officer visited the head office of a bank in Manchester and spoke to the Chief Inspector and Assistant General Manager, S, and told him that he suspected that a conspiracy to obtain by deception had been committed against the bank in relation to dealings of companies controlled by the applicant, and that he wished to inspect the accounts and other documents relating to the applicant and named companies. S confirmed that the bank would not allow him to see accounts without the consent of the account holders. The police officer told S that the police would apply for an order under s. 9 of the Police and Criminal Evidence Act 1984, but that as they suspected that a member of the bank's staff might also be

58 [1988] 2 All ER 769.

involved, neither the names of the account holders nor the offences suspected would be specified in the notice.

Subsequently, the Recorder of Manchester made an order addressed to the bank giving the police access to certain special procedure material, namely, ledger accounts, accounting documents, correspondence, minutes and business records relating to the applicant. The bank complied with the order. The applicant applied for judicial review. He sought a declaration that the order had been invalidly made, because no proper notice of intention to apply for it had been given to the bank. The Divisional Court dismissed the application. The court held that, although it was preferable for the identity of the documents sought and the alleged offence being investigated to be set out in either the notice under s. 9 of the Act or in a separate document delivered before or at the time of the notice, it was sufficient if that information was conveyed orally to the person affected and that, accordingly, the order was valid.

2-107D In *Barclays Bank plc (trading as Barclaycard)* v. *Taylor, Trustee Savings Bank of Wales and Border Counties* v. *Taylor*[59] both banks had received notices of applications by the police for orders under s. 9 of the Police and Criminal Evidence Act 1984 relating to the accounts of a Mr and Mrs T. It was argued on behalf of Mr and Mrs T that the banks were subject to an implied contractual obligation to take action in support of the confidentiality of their customers' affairs by resisting the making of an order and by informing Mr and Mrs T that the order was being sought. The Court of Appeal rejected these submissions. Lord Donaldson MR said that the real question was whether, to give business efficacy to the banker–customer relationship, there was to be an implied obligation to contest the s. 9 application or to probe it or to inform the customer. The Master of the Rolls said that since the responsibility for deciding whether the necessary conditions were fulfilled was placed on the circuit judge, he could see no reason for implying an obligation to contest the application, unless the bank knew something relevant to it, which was not likely to be apparent on the face of the application or the notice or might not be known to the police. While the banks were no doubt free to ignore a request that Mr and Mrs T should not be informed of the application, his Lordship would have been surprised and disappointed if they had done so in the context of a criminal investigation, unless they were under a legal duty to do so. There was a public interest in assisting the police in the investigation of crime and his Lordship could think of no basis for an implied obligation to act in a way which, in some circumstances, would without doubt hinder such enquiries.

Accordingly, the Master of the Rolls concluded that (a) the banks

59 *The Times*, 23 May 1989.

were obliged to comply with the s. 9 orders, and in doing so were not in breach of their duty to maintain confidentiality; (b) they were under no obligation to oppose or probe the evidence given in support of the applications; and (c) they were not obliged to inform Mr and Mrs T that the applications were being made in respect of their accounts.

(f) Companies Act 1985

2-108 In certain circumstances which are defined in the Companies Act 1985,[60] the Secretary of State has power to appoint one or more inspectors to investigate the affairs of a company and to report thereon in such manner as he directs. It is then the duty of all officers and agents of the company, including the company's bankers, to produce to the inspectors all books and documents relating to the company and to give to the inspectors all assistance in connection with the investigation which they are reasonably able to give.[61] However, it is expressly enacted that nothing in those provisions requires disclosure by the company's bankers of 'any information as to the affairs of any of their customers other than the company'.[62]

2-109 Section 218 of the Insolvency Act 1986 defines the circumstances in which certain matters must be referred to the Director of Public Prosecutions when a company is wound up. Section 219 provides that when any such matter is referred to him and he considers that the case is one in which a prosecution ought to be instituted, he must institute proceedings accordingly, and it is then the duty of the liquidator and of every officer and agent of the company, including the company's bankers, to give him all assistance in connection with the prosecution which they are reasonably able to give.

(g) Drug Trafficking Offences Act 1986

2-110 Sections 7 and 8 of the Drug Trafficking Offences Act 1986 enable the prosecution to obtain a 'restraint order' from the High Court prohibiting any person from dealing with the defendant's property in any case where the court is satisfied that there is reasonable cause to believe that the defendant has benefited from drug trafficking. The defendant's property includes any debts owing to him, and thus the expression includes his bank accounts. In the result, therefore, the court may make a restraint order preventing the defendant's bank from paying money out of the defendant's accounts.

60 Ss 431 and 432.
61 Ss 434(1) and (4).
62 S. 452.

2-110A Section 24 of the Act creates a new offence of assisting drug traffickers. If a bank fails to disclose to the police its suspicions that a customer is a drug trafficker, it may be guilty of an offence under this section. However, no offence is committed if the bank discloses its suspicions to the police as soon as possible. The Act provides that this disclosure will not be treated 'as a breach of any restriction upon the disclosure of information imposed by contract'. In the result, therefore, if a bank manager suspects that sums paid in by a customer are the proceeds of drug trafficking, he should report the matter forthwith to his head office. If the official who deals with these matters at head office considers that there are proper grounds for suspicion, he will send a report to the National Drugs Intelligence Unit at Scotland Yard.

2-110B Section 27 of the Act provides that a constable may, for the purpose of an investigation into drug trafficking, apply to a circuit judge for an order in relation to particular material or material of a particular description. The court may make an order that the person who appears to be in possession of the material must (a) produce it to a constable for him to take away, or (b) give a constable access to it. The order may be made against any person holding the material, not necessarily the person who is suspected of having carried on or benefited from drug trafficking. The order has effect notwithstanding any obligation as to secrecy or other restriction upon the disclosure of information imposed by statute or otherwise. Section 31 provides that where such an order has been applied for and has not been refused, any person who, knowing or suspecting that the investigation is taking place, makes any disclosure which is likely to prejudice the investigation is guilty of an offence. In the result therefore, the police are able to examine the suspect's bank account, and to do so without his knowledge. Anyone who told the customer that he was under suspicion would be guilty of an offence.

(h) Financial Services Act 1986

2-111 Section 105 of the Financial Services Act 1986 enables the Securities and Investments Board to investigate the affairs of a person who is, or was, or appears to be carrying on an investment business. The Board may require the person under investigation or any other person to produce any specified documents which appear to the Board to relate to any matter relevant to the investigation. The Board may take copies or extracts from them. As far as bankers are concerned, the confidentiality of a customer's affairs may be overridden in cases where the Board considers that it is necessary for the purpose of investigating any investment business carried on, or appearing to the Board to be carried on or to have been carried on, by the bank, institution or customer.

2-111A Section 117 of the Act relates to investigations into insider dealing. It enables the Secretary of State to appoint inspectors to investigate and report on suspected contraventions of the insider dealing legislation. The inspectors can compel the production of documents and examine on oath any persons who possess relevant information. As far as bankers are concerned, the confidentiality of a customer's affairs may be overridden in cases where the Secretary of State is satisfied that the disclosure or production is necessary for the purposes of the investigation.

(i) Criminal Justice Act 1987

2-112 Section 1 of the Criminal Justice Act 1987 established a Serious Fraud Office presided over by a Director who is appointed by and acts 'under the superintendence' of the Attorney-General in order to investigate any suspected offence which appears to the Director 'on reasonable grounds to involve serious or complex fraud'. The words 'serious or complex fraud' are not defined in the Act. The members of the Serious Fraud Office include accountants, lawyers, police officers and civil servants. By virtue of s. 2 of the Act, any person may be required to answer questions, to provide information and to produce documents with respect to any matter relevant to an investigation. Without obtaining an order of the court, the Director may authorize a member of the Office to issue the requisite notice. This notice is signed by him and countersigned by the Director. The notice gives the names of the persons under investigation and, in a typical case where it is directed to a bank, it continues as follows:

1. The Director of the Serious Fraud Office has decided to investigate suspected offences which appear to him to involve serious or complex fraud.
2. I am a member of the Serious Fraud Office who has been authorized by the Director of the Serious Fraud Office to exercise on his behalf all the powers conferred by s. 2 of the Criminal Justice Act 1987.
3. There appears to me, for the purposes of investigation referred to at 1 above, to be good reason to exercise the powers conferred by s. 2(2) and (3) of the Act for the purpose of investigating the affairs of the persons . . . also known as . . . and others under investigation.
4. I have reason to believe that you have relevant information about the affairs of the persons under investigation, and I therefore require you to attend at . . . on . . . to answer questions or otherwise furnish information to me with respect to matters relevant to the investigation. I also require you to produce to me at the same place, on the same date and at the same time the following documents which appear to me to relate to matters relevant to the investigation:

All mandates, books of account, bank statements, paid cheques, vouchers, transfer slips, agreements, correspondence, attendance notes and other documentation relating to all accounts held at the Bank to which persons known as . . . are known or believed by Officers of the Bank to be a party of signatory, together with details of all items of property both real and personal deposited with or charged to the Bank in connection with any of the above accounts including the instruments of deposit or charge.

2-112A   As stated above, the Director of the Serious Fraud Office may, without any order of the court, authorize a member of his Office to issue a notice requiring the production of documents. If, however, it is desired to authorize a police officer to enter and search premises, s. 2 of the Criminal Justice Act 1987 provides that a member of the Serious Fraud Office must apply to a justice of the peace for a warrant. A police officer who executes such a warrant may, in addition to searching for and seizing documents, take steps to preserve them. This power of preserving documents is useful in cases where the volume of documents prevents their immediate removal. The police officer who executes the warrant must, if practicable, be accompanied by a member of the Serious Fraud Office, or by some other person authorized by the Director.

(j) Prevention of Terrorism (Temporary Provisions) Act 1989

2-113   Section 1(1) of the Prevention of Terrorism (Temporary Provisions) Act 1989 provides that any organization for the time being specified in Sched. 1 to the Act is a proscribed organization for the purposes of the Act. The Schedule specifies just two organizations, namely the Irish Republican Army and the Irish National Liberation Army. However, s. 1(2) provides that the Secretary of State may by order made by statutory instrument add to Sched. 1 'any organization that appears to him to be concerned in, or in promoting or encouraging, terrorism occurring in the United Kingdom and connected with the affairs of Northern Ireland'.

2-113A   Section 9(1) and (2) provides that a person is guilty of an offence if, *inter alia*, he enters into or is otherwise concerned in an arrangement whereby money or other property is or is to be made available to another person, 'knowing or having reasonable cause to suspect that it will or may be applied or used' for the commission of, or in furtherance of or in connection with, acts of terrorism to which the section applies. By subs. (3) the acts of terrorism to which the section applies are (a) acts of terrorism connected with the affairs of Northern Ireland, and (b) acts of terrorism of any other description except acts connected solely with the affairs of the United Kingdom or any part of the United Kingdom other than Northern Ireland.

2-113B Section 10 of the Act provides that a person is guilty of an offence if, *inter alia*, he gives, lends or otherwise makes available or receives or accepts, whether for consideration or not, any money or other property for the benefit of a proscribed organization.

2-113C Section 11(1) of the Act provides that a person is guilty of an offence if he enters into or is otherwise concerned in an arrangement whereby the retention or control by or on behalf of another person of terrorist funds is facilitated, whether by concealment, removal from the jurisdiction, transfer to nominees or otherwise. Subsection (2) provides that in proceedings against a person for an offence under the section, 'it is a defence to prove that he did not know and had no cause to suspect that the arrangement related to terrorist funds'.[63] These provisions could be very important to bank officials who unwittingly dealt with terrorist funds.

2-113D Section 12(1) of the Act provides that a person may, notwithstanding any restriction on the disclosure of information imposed by contract, disclose to a constable a suspicion or belief that any money or other property is or is derived from terrorist funds or any matter on which such a suspicion or belief is based. Subsection (2) provides that a person who enters into or is otherwise concerned in any such transaction or arrangement as is mentioned in ss 9, 10 or 11 does not commit an offence if he is acting with the express consent of a constable, or if (a) he discloses to a constable his suspicion or belief that the money or other property concerned is or is derived from terrorist funds or any matter on which such a suspicion or belief is based, and (b) the disclosure is made after he enters into or otherwise becomes concerned in the transaction or arrangement in question but is made on his own initiative and as soon as it is reasonable for him to make it. In the result, therefore, if a bank manager suspects that any of these matters are taking place, he should report forthwith to his head office. If the official who deals with these matters at head office considers that there are proper grounds for suspicion, he will send a report to Scotland Yard.

(k) Garnishee orders

2-114 The procedure relating to garnishee orders is described later.[64]

---

63 For a criticism of these provisions, see Derek Wheatley QC, 'Guilty . . . said the Red Queen?', *New Law Journal*, Vol. 139 (1989), pp. 499–500.
64 *Post*, para. 3-47.

(l) Writ of sequestration

2-114A The issue of this writ may sometimes require disclosure by a bank of the balance of a customer's account.[65]

Duty to the public to disclose

2-115 Cases where a bank is justified in disclosing its customers' affairs on the ground that there is a duty to the public to do so are difficult to define. In his judgment in *Tournier's* case Bankes LJ said that 'many instances' might be given, though the learned lord justice did not indicate specifically what they were. He continued:[66]

> They may be summed up in the language of Lord Finlay in *Weld-Bundell* v. *Stephens*,[67] where he speaks of cases where a higher duty than the private duty is involved, as where 'danger to the State or public duty may supersede the duty of the agent to his principal'.

Scrutton LJ, in his judgment in *Tournier's* case, said that a bank 'may disclose the customer's account and affairs ... to prevent frauds and crimes',[68] and Atkin LJ considered that the right to disclose exists 'to the extent to which it is reasonably necessary ... for protecting the bank, or persons interested, or the public, against fraud or crime'.[69]

Interests of bank require disclosure

2-116 The interest of the bank will involve disclosure of some details of the customer's account whenever there is litigation between the bank and its customer. 'A simple instance ... is where a bank issues a writ claiming payment of an overdraft stating on the face of the writ the amount of the overdraft.'[70] Likewise, disclosure may be necessary where a bank makes a claim or brings an action against someone other than the customer, e.g. against a guarantor.

2-117 In *Sunderland* v. *Barclays Bank Ltd*[71] the defendant bank successfully defended an action for wrongful disclosure, and one of the grounds of the decision was that it was in the bank's interests to make the disclosure. A Mrs Sunderland had an account at Barclays Bank, and

---

65 *Post*, para. 3-81.
66 [1924] 1 KB, at p. 473.
67 [1920] AC 956, at p. 965.
68 [1924] 1 KB, at p. 481.
69 [1924] 1 KB, at p. 486.
70 *Per* Bankes LJ in *Tournier* v. *National Provincial and Union Bank of England* [1924] 1 KB 461, at p. 473.
71 (1938) *The Times*, 24 and 25 November.

she drew a cheque in favour of her dressmaker, which was dishonoured for lack of funds. Although there were insufficient funds to meet the cheque, the real reason for the non-payment of the cheque was that Mrs Sunderland had drawn cheques in favour of bookmakers, and the bank thought that it was not the type of account on which an overdraft should be permitted. Mrs Sunderland complained to her husband about the dishonour of the cheque. He told her to take up the matter with the bank, and so she telephoned the manager. After a while, her husband interrupted the conversation to add his own protest. The manager informed him that most of the cheques which had been drawn on his wife's account were in favour of bookmakers. Mrs Sunderland brought an action against the bank, alleging that, in breach of the bank's duty not to disclose information about her account without her consent, the bank manager had informed her husband that cheques drawn on her account were going to a bookmaker. Judgment was given in the bank's favour by du Parcq LJ, sitting as an additional Judge in the King's Bench Division. His Lordship thought that in the present case the interests of the bank required disclosure, and that it might be said that the disclosure was made with the implied consent of the customer. The husband having taken over the conduct of the matter, the manager was justified in thinking that the wife did not object to his offering to the husband the explanation which might satisfy him that the complaint made was unjustified.

Disclosure with consent of customer

(a) Express consent

2-118 Cases where a customer expressly authorizes his bank to disclose his affairs to a third party do not usually give rise to any difficulty. In *Tournier's* case[72] Atkin LJ said:

> A common example of such consent would be where a customer gives a banker's reference. The extent to which he authorizes information to be given on such a reference must be a question to be determined on the facts of each case.

Other common examples would be where a customer authorizes his bank to make disclosure to his wife or to his accountant.

---

72 [1924] 1 KB, at p. 486; see also p. 473 *per* Bankes LJ. Likewise in *Parsons* v. *Barclay and Co. Ltd and Goddard* (1910) 103 LT 196, Cozens-Hardy MR referred at p. 199 to 'that very wholesome and useful habit by which one banker answers in confidence and answers honestly, to another banker, the answer being given at the request and with the knowledge of the first banker's customer'.

(b) Implied consent

2-119 Cases where disclosure is justified by reason of the implied consent of the customer arise less frequently, though it will be recalled that this was one of the grounds upon which du Parcq LJ based his decision in the bank's favour in *Sunderland v. Barclays Bank Ltd (supra).*

2-120 Occasionally, an intending guarantor calls at the customer's bank for the purpose of signing a form of guarantee and asks questions concerning the ways in which the customer's account has been conducted. Sir John Paget expressed the view that the surety's questions might be answered on the ground that the customer had impliedly authorized disclosure by introducing the surety to the bank.[73] Lord Chorley QC, however, expressed the view that 'this seems doubtful'.[74] Clearly, it is safer to assume, in the present state of the law, that there is no implied consent by the customer to disclose his affairs under those circumstances. Without doubt, the safest course – and, indeed, the usual course – is to arrange a joint meeting between the guarantor, the customer and the banker at which the guarantor may, in the customer's presence, ask for information on any matters concerning the customer's affairs.

2-121 Sometimes it is said that the practice of bankers of giving opinions concerning their customers' creditworthiness without express authority is based upon the implied consent of the customers concerned.[75] In many cases the customer whose creditworthiness is the subject of enquiry does not know what opinion his own banker has given or is proposing to give, and quite often he does not even know that the enquiry has been made. Atkin LJ adverted to this matter in *Tournier's* case as follows:[76]

> I do not desire to express any final opinion on the practice of bankers to give one another information as to the affairs of their respective customers, except to say it appears to me that if it is justified it must be upon the basis of an implied consent of the customer.

Another argument which is sometimes advanced in support of the prac-

---

73 *Paget's Law of Banking* (10th ed., 1989), p. 592.
74 Lord Chorley, *Law of Banking* (6th ed., 1974), p. 335.
75 See also *post*, para. 10-59.
76 [1924] 1 KB, at p. 486. Referring to this passage, Lord Morris of Borth-y-Gest, in the course of his opinion in *Hedley Byrne & Co. Ltd v. Heller & Parnters Ltd* [1963] 2 All ER 575, at p. 588, observed: 'The present appeal does not raise any question as to the circumstances under which a banker is entitled (apart from direct authorisation) to answer an enquiry. I leave that question as it was left by Atkin, LJ, in *Tournier v. National Provincial & Union Bank of England.*'

tice is that it is justified as being 'in the interests of the customer'. Presumably this argument would be of no avail if the opinion which was given was an unfavourable one. Moreover, Scrutton LJ in the course of his judgment in *Tournier's* case, said:[77]

> I doubt whether it is sufficient excuse for disclosure, in the absence of the customer's consent, that it was in the interests of the customer, where the customer can be consulted in reasonable time and his consent or dissent obtained.

2-122 Authors on the subject are divided in their views. Thus Mr L. C. Mather, a very experienced banker, states that 'it is widely held that the established practice of answering enquiries received from other banks and certain trade protection societies concerning the financial position of customers is justified by the implied consent of the customer, on the assumption that most people are aware of this banking service when the account is first opened.'[78] His review may be contrasted with that of Lord Chorley QC who, when referring to the practice of giving opinions, states that 'it is to be feared that this is sometimes done without the knowledge or consent of the customer, and if so it would appear to be a breach of the duty which the banker owes to his customer of treating the account as confidential'.[79]

2-123 Accordingly, the position may be summed up by saying that the question whether or not a banker is justified in law in giving to another banker an opinion concerning a customer's creditworthiness without the express authority of the customer is an open one at the present day. Perhaps on some future occasion it will be fully tested in the courts.

2-123A The Report of the Committee on Privacy[80] (the 'Younger Committee') recommended that 'the banks should make clear to all customers, existing or prospective, the existence and manner of operation of their reference system, and give them the opportunity either to grant a standing authority for the provision of references or to require the bank to seek their consent on every occasion'.[81] The Committee made this recommendation, because they did not believe that the practice of giving references without the customer's knowledge was as well known and accepted among customers, particularly individuals, as the banks had asserted in their evidence.

---

77 [1924] 1 KB, at p. 481.
78 L. C. Mather, *Banker and Customer Relationship and the Accounts of Personal Customers* (5th ed., 1977), p. 32. Mr Mather was a director and former Chief General Manager of the Midland Bank.
79 Lord Chorley, *op. cit.*, p. 248.
80 Cmnd. 5012 (1972).
81 Para. 307.

Section 7
CUSTOMER'S DUTIES TO HIS BANKER

2-124 The principal duties owed by a customer to his bankers are (a) the customer must exercise reasonable care in drawing his cheques so as not to mislead his banker or to facilitate forgery, and (b) if the customer discovers that cheques purporting to have been signed by him have been forged, he must inform his banker.

Duty to draw cheques carefully

2-125 The leading case in which this duty was considered by the House of Lords is *London Joint Stock Bank Ltd* v. *Macmillan and Arthur*.[82] A firm of general merchants named Macmillan and Arthur had an account at the London Joint Stock Bank. One of the merchants' clerks, whose duty it was to prepare cheques for signature by his employers, drew a cheque payable to the firm or bearer. He filled in the amount in figures as £2 but he left a space between '£' and the figure '2'. At that stage the amount in words was not filled in at all. He then had the cheque signed by a partner. Next, he fraudulently raised the amount of the cheque. He placed the figures '1' and '0' on either side of the figure '2', thus producing a figure of £120. He filled in the amount in words as 'one hundred and twenty pounds' presented the cheque at the bank on which it was drawn, received payment, and absconded with the money. Macmillan and Arthur maintained that their account ought not to have been debited with that amount.

2-126 The House of Lords decided the case in the bank's favour. Dealing with a customer's duty Lord Finlay LC observed:[83]

> It is beyond dispute that the customer is bound to exercise reasonable care in drawing the cheque to prevent the banker being misled. If he draws the cheque in a manner which facilitates fraud, he is guilty of a breach of duty as between himself and the banker, and he will be responsible to the banker for any loss sustained by the banker as a natural and direct consequence of this breach of duty.

---

82 [1918] AC 777, approving *Young* v. *Grote* (1827) 4 Bing 253. The principles laid down in the *Macmillan* case were applied by the Supreme Court of Ceylon in *Kulatilleke* v. *Mercantile Bank of India* (1958) 59 Ceylon NLR 190, noted in *The Banker's Magazine*, Vol. CLXXXVII (1959), p. 423, and in the *Journal of the Institute of Bankers*, Vol. 80 (1959), p. 348.

83 [1918] AC, at p. 789. See also Viscount Haldane's speech at pp. 814–15, Lord Shaw's speech at p. 824, and Lord Parmoor's speech at pp. 830 and 834.

Applying those principles to the facts of the particular case, Lord Finlay said:[84]

> In the present case the customer neglected all precautions. He signed the cheque, leaving entirely blank the space where the amount should have been stated in words, and where it should have been stated in figures there was only the figure '2' with blank spaces on either side of it. In my judgment, there was a clear breach of the duty which the customer owed to the banker.

Accordingly, it was held that the bank was entitled to debit Macmillan and Arthur's account with the full amount of the cheque. It should be noted, however, that, as Viscount Haldane stressed in his speech,[85] there was nothing on the face of the cheque to awaken any doubt in the minds of the officials of the bank that the cheque was in order. If the alteration had been apparent, the bank would have had to suffer the loss.

2-127 Although it is now firmly established that a customer is bound to exercise reasonable care in drawing his cheques, it does not follow that a customer will be in breach of that duty if he leaves a space after the name of the payee. Thus in a later case,[86] it was unsuccessfully argued that the drawers of a cheque had been negligent in not drawing a line after the payee's name and so had enabled a fraud to be committed. The Court of Appeal rejected that argument on the ground that it was not at that time a 'usual precaution' to draw lines before or after the payee's name; but Scrutton LJ added that, if that type of case became frequent, it might become a 'usual precaution'.[87]

Duty to disclose forgeries

2-128 It is well established as a result of the decision in *Greenwood* v. *Martins Bank Ltd*[88] that if a customer discovers that cheques purporting to have been signed by him have been forged, he must inform his bank. The plaintiff had an account with Martins Bank. His wife kept the passbook and cheque book, and she gave him cheque forms from the cheque book when he asked for them, In October 1929, he asked her to bring him a cheque, saying that he wanted to draw £20. She told him that there was no money in the bank, as she had drawn it all out to help her sister in certain legal proceedings. She begged him not to inform the bank of the forgeries, and he agreed not to do so. No signatures were forged

---

84 [1918] AC, at p. 811.
85 [1918] AC, at p. 820.
86 *Slingsby* v. *District Bank Ltd* [1932] 1 KB 544.
87 [1932] 1 KB, at p. 560.
88 [1932] 1 KB 371, CA; [1933] AC 51, HL.

thereafter. In June 1930, he discovered that no legal proceedings had been instituted by his wife's sister and that his wife had deceived him. Thereupon he told his wife that he would go at once to the bank. He returned home that evening without having gone to the bank; on his return his wife shot herself. A few months later he brought an action against the bank for a declaration that he was entitled to be credited by the bank with the amount of the forged cheques.

2-129   At the trial of the action it was held that the plaintiff was entitled to succeed, but this decision was reversed by the Court of Appeal. It was held that there was a duty on the plaintiff to disclose the forgeries and that in the circumstances the failure to disclose gave rise to an estoppel.

2-130   The plaintiff's appeal in the House of Lords was dismissed. Lord Tomlin's closely reasoned speech may be summarized as follows. The sole question was whether in the particular circumstances the bank was entitled to set up an estoppel. The essential factors giving rise to an estoppel are (a) a representation or conduct amounting to a representation intended to induce a course of conduct on the part of the person to whom the representation is made, (b) an act or omission resulting from the representation, whether actual or by conduct, by the person to whom the representation is made, and (c) detriment to such person as a consequence of the act or omission. The bank's case was that the plaintiff's duty to disclose the forgeries to the bank ought to have been discharged by the plaintiff immediately upon his discovery in October 1929; and that if the plaintiff had disclosed the forgeries at that date, the bank could have sued the plaintiff's wife in tort and the plaintiff himself would have been responsible for his wife's tort.[89] The bank maintained that the plaintiff's silence until after his wife's death amounted to a representation that the cheques were not forgeries and so deprived the bank of its remedy. These arguments on behalf of the bank were upheld by Lord Tomlin and by the other law lords.

2-131   Thus in *Greenwood's* case the plaintiff's failure to inform his bank promptly of his wife's forgeries precluded him from successfully suing the bank.[90] Curiously enough, however, it would seem that even if the plaintiff had informed the bank forthwith, he would have fared no better, because the bank would then have had a valid claim against the plaintiff's wife in tort, and the plaintiff (as the law then stood) would have been liable for his wife's tort; and so the ultimate result would have

---

89 A husband is no longer liable for his wife's torts; see the Law Reform (Married Women and Tortfeasors) Act 1935, s. 3.

90 For another case where the plaintiff's failure to inform her bank of forgeries precluded her from successfully suing the bank, see *Brown* v. *Westminster Bank Ltd* [1964] 2 Lloyds List 187.

been that the plaintiff, and not the bank, would still have suffered the loss.

Section 8
STATEMENT OF ACCOUNT OR PASSBOOK

2-132 There is probably an implied term in the contract between banker and customer that the banker will supply his customer either with a passbook or with statements containing a copy of the customer's account with the banker. In cases where passbooks are still in use, the customer generally retains the book and presents it to the bank from time to time to be brought up to date. The more modern practice, however, is for the bank to supply customers with loose-leaf statements at regular intervals. The entries in passbooks were (and still are) handwritten, whereas statements are usually computerized.

2-133 The banks maintain a high standard of accuracy in their bookkeeping and in the writing up of passbooks or the preparation of statements. Nevertheless, a prudent customer will check the entries in his passbook or statement and, if any error is detected, he will bring this to the notice of the bank. In the vast majority of cases, any errors are corrected without difficulty, and certainly without resort to litigation. From time to time, however, the courts have had to resolve problems arising out of errors in passbooks or statements. These will now be considered under two main headings: first, where the customer's account has been over-credited, and secondly where his account has been over-debited.

Over-crediting a customer's account

2-134 The legal effect of over-crediting a customer's account is now well established. If the customer honestly believes that the entries are correct and alters his position in reliance upon them, the bank will thereafter be estopped from claiming to have the mistake put right. Thus in *Lloyds Bank Ltd* v. *Brooks*,[91] the plaintiff bank unsuccessfully claimed the sum of £1,108 from a customer, the Honourable Cecily Brooks, under the following circumstances. The customer was entitled under a trust to the income from 2,170 preference shares in a colliery company, but as the result of a mistake in the bank's investment department, an entry was made in the bank's records which showed that she was entitled also to the income from 4,000 second preference shares in the same company; the income from the 4,000 shares ought to have been paid to

---

91 (1950) *Journal of the Institute of Bankers*, Vol. LXXII, p. 114. See also *Skyring* v. *Greenwood* (1825) 4 B & C 281; *Holland* v. *Manchester and Liverpool District Banking Co.* (1909) 14 Com Cas 241; *Holt* v. *Markham* [1923] 1 KB 504.

another beneficiary. For many years the bank credited Miss Brooks' account with the dividends on the 4,000 second preference shares to which she was not entitled. When the mistake was discovered, the bank claimed from Miss Brooks the amount of those dividends, amounting in all to £1,108. Her defence was that, relying upon the bank's representations, she had altered her position to her detriment in that she had been led to believe that her income was greater than it was, and that she had spent more money than she would otherwise have done in each year since 1941; under those circumstances she maintained that the bank was estopped from alleging as against her that the sums in question were not received on her behalf. Her defence succeeded. Dealing with the bank's duties, Lynskey J said:[92]

> It seems to me in this case there was a duty on the bank to keep the defendant correctly informed as to the position of her account, and there was a duty on the bank not to over-credit her statement of account, and there was a duty on the bank also, for that matter, not to authorize her or induce her by faithful representations contained in her statement of account to draw money from her account to which she was not entitled.

The learned judge said he was satisfied that Miss Brooks had acted to her detriment as a result of the bank's action, and so the bank's claim failed.

2-135 If a customer has not acted to his or her detriment as a result of the wrong entry in the passbook or statement, the legal position is quite different. Thus in *British & North European Bank* v. *Zalstein*,[93] a customer of the bank was overdrawn £900 in excess of the agreed limit, and, in order to conceal this fact from the bank's auditors, the bank manager transferred £2,000 from another source to the credit of the customer's account. Later, the manager debited the customer's account with the same sum. At the time, the customer was unaware of the entries. Eventually, the bank sued the customer for the overdraft, and the customer contended that the debt had been extinguished *pro tanto* by the amount falsely credited by the manager. In effect, the customer wanted to claim the benefit of the credit entry and to disregard the debit entry. Sankey J had no hesitation in holding that he was not entitled to do so.

Over-debiting a customer's account

2-136 Over-debiting a customer's account usually occurs when a fraudulent person forges cheques purporting to be drawn on the

---

92 *Journal of the Institute of Bankers*, Vol. LXXII, pp. 121–2.
93 [1927] 2 KB 92. See also *United Overseas Bank* v. *Jiwani* [1977] 1 All ER 733.

account. Forgery of a cheque is often carried out so skilfully that a comparison of the signature with the customer's specimen signature in the bank's possession fails to disclose the forgery. Thus the payment of forged cheques by a bank is not necessarily the result of any carelessness on the part of the bank.[94] However, the customer ought to know what cheques he has issued, and when he receives his passbook or statement, he ought as a prudent man to check the entries therein. Accordingly, one would have thought that the law would imply a duty on his part to check the entries in his passbook or statement within a reasonable period after receiving it, and this appears to be the law in the United States.[95] Yet in England the generally accepted view at the present day is that there is no such duty on the customer's part. The late Dr Hart wrote:[96]

> It is clear that the receipt by the customer of the passbook containing an entry of the balance together with the cashed cheques debited therein, and the return of the former to the banker without objection being raised to any of the entries, does not amount to a settlement of account in respect of those entries; and that the mere omission on the part of the customer to examine the entries and cheques with businesslike promptitude and care does not constitute negligence.

In *Chatterton* v. *London and County Bank*[97] a customer had had his passbook and paid cheques from his bank week by week, usually fetching them himself. He went through the passbook, ticking the debit items (which were called out to him from his ledger by a confidential clerk), and returned the book to the bank. After about eleven months he discovered that twenty-five of those cheques had not been drawn by him, his signature having been forged by his clerk, and he claimed to have the sums in question credited to his account. At the first trial, the jury came to the conclusion that the cheques had not been forged. The Divisional Court ordered a new trial, and the bank appealed against this order to the Court of Appeal. The proceedings were brief, and the bank's appeal was dismissed. In the course of the argument, Lord Esher MR expressed the view that customers were not bound to examine their

---

94 See, for example, *Brewer* v. *Westminster Bank Ltd and another* [1952] 2 All ER 650, where 279 cheques were so skilfully forged that McNair J found as a fact that no negligence could be imputed to the officials of the defendant bank in failing to detect them.

95 For a more detailed account of the subject than is possible here, see J. Milnes Holden, 'Bank Passbooks and Statements', *The Modern Law Review*, Vol. 17 (1954), pp. 41–56.

96 H. L. Hart , *The Law of Banking* (4th ed., 1931), Vol. 1, p. 262.

97 The first trial is reported in *The Miller* newspaper for 5 May 1890; the proceedings in the Divisional Court in the same newspaper for 7 July 1890, and in *The Times* for 27 June 1890; the proceedings in the Court of Appeal, in *The Miller* for 3 November 1890; and the second trial in *The Miller* for 2 February 1891, and in *The Times* for 21 January 1891.

passbooks. A new trial took place, and on this occasion the jury found for the plaintiff.

2-137 Lord Esher's observation that customers were not bound to examine their passbooks was approved and applied by Bray J in *Kepitigalla Rubber Estates Ltd* v. *National Bank of India Ltd.*[98] In that case the secretary of a company forged cheques drawn on the company's account over a period of two months. Although the passbook had been written up several times during that period, the directors had not examined it. It was held that the bank could not charge the company with the amounts paid out on the forged cheques.

2-138 In 1985 the Judicial Committee of the Privy Council applied the same rule to bank statements. In *Tai Hing Cotton Mill Ltd* v. *Liu Chong Hing Bank Ltd and Others*[99] a fraudulent accounts clerk who was employed by a company engaged in business as textile manufacturers forged the signature of the company's managing director on some 300 cheques to the value of $HK 5.5 m drawn on the company's accounts at three banks over a period of about five years. The banks were Liu Chong Hing Bank Ltd, the first respondent; the Bank of Tokyo Ltd, the second respondent; and the Chekiang First Bank Ltd, the third respondent. The company did not learn about the frauds until a newly appointed accountant entered upon the task, not previously undertaken, of reconciling the bank statements with the company's account books. The company requested each bank to credit its account with the amounts of the forged cheques, but the banks declined to do so. They submitted that a customer owes a duty of care to his bank to take such precautions as a reasonable customer would take to prevent forged cheques being presented to his bank for payment, and to check his bank statements for unauthorized debit items. The Judicial Committee of the Privy Council rejected these submissions and allowed the company's appeal from the decision of the Court of Appeal in Hong Kong. The Judicial Committee held that banks which had paid out on forged cheques were not entitled to debit their customers' accounts with these amounts since, unless it was otherwise agreed, the duty of care owed by a customer to his bank in the operation of his current account was limited to a duty to refrain from drawing a cheque in such manner as to facilitate fraud or forgery and a duty to inform the bank of any forgery of a cheque purportedly drawn on the account as soon as he became aware of it.

98 [1909] 2 KB 1010; followed in *Walker and Another* v. *Manchester and Liverpool Banking Co. Ltd* (1913) 29 TLR 492. See also *Lewes Sanitary Steam Laundry Co. Ltd* v. *Barclay, Bevan & Co. Ltd* (1906) 11 Com Cas 255, at pp. 268–9 from which it appears that the bank had alleged want of care in the examination of the passbook. Kennedy J, as reported, omitted to deal with this argument.
99 [1985] 2 All ER 947.

2-139   The three banks further submitted that, if they failed on the general point of principle, they were entitled to rely on their contracts with the company. It had operated its current accounts with each bank pursuant to the bank's printed terms and conditions, and in each case there was a provision which purported to impose an express obligation on a customer to examine his monthly statements and to make those statements, in the absence of query, unchallengeable by the customer after the expiry of a time limit. For example, in the case of the Chekiang First Bank Ltd, the relevant term read: 'A monthly statement for each account will be sent by the Bank to the depositor by post or messenger and the balance shown therein may be deemed to be correct by the Bank if the depositor does not notify the Bank in writing of any error therein within ten days after the sending of such statement ...' The Judicial Committee held that, in order to impose an express obligation on a customer to examine his monthly statements and to make those statements, in the absence of query, unchallengeable by the customer after the expiry of a time limit, the burden of the obligation and of the sanction imposed had to be brought home to the customer. In the view of the Judicial Committee, the banks had not met 'this undoubtedly rigorous test'.

Section 9
WRONGFUL DISHONOUR OF CHEQUES

2-140   A banker must pay cheques drawn on him by his customer in legal form on presentation during banking hours or within a reasonable margin after the bank's advertised closing time at the branch of the bank where the account is kept, provided that (a) the customer has there sufficient funds at his credit, or the cheques are within the limits of an agreed overdraft, and (b) there are no legal bars to payment. A customer whose cheque has been wrongfully dishonoured is entitled to claim damages against his banker. The claim may be on one or both of two grounds: for breach of contract, and for libel.

Damages for breach of contract

2-141   Where in an action for damages for breach of contract a plaintiff fails to prove that he has sustained any actual damage the general rule is that he is entitled to recover only nominal damages.[1] In practice, the sum of £2 is usually awarded. However, where a customer brings an action against his bank for wrongfully refusing to pay a cheque which he has drawn, this general rule does not necessarily apply, and the

1 For the authorities, see *Halsbury's Laws of England* (4th ed.), Vol. 12, p. 147.

damages for breach of contract will depend upon whether or not the customer is a trader.

(a) Where customer is a trader

2-142 It is a well-established rule that in an action for breach of contract against a bank for wrongfully dishonouring a trader's cheque, the plaintiff is entitled to recover substantial, though temperate and reasonable, damages for injury to his commercial credit, without the necessity of alleging and proving any actual damage. In a leading case, *Rolin* v. *Steward*,[2] three cheques and a bill were dishonoured in error. They were presented again the next day, and paid. No actual loss was proved. The jury awarded the plaintiff, who was a trader, £500 damages. On appeal it was held that, although in the circumstances this amount was excessive, he was entitled to substantial damages, and the sum of £200 was substituted. There does not appear to be any judicial authority in English law which defines who is a 'trader' for the purpose of this rule. The expression would clearly include all merchants who buy and sell goods, and also commercial agents and brokers. A New Zealand court has held that a lady who was a substantial shareholder and a director of a company and who was actively employed as office manager of the company was not a trader.[3]

(b) Where customer is not a trader

2-143 A customer who is not a trader is entitled to recover substantial damages for breach of contract in respect of the wrongful dishonour of his cheque if, and only if, he alleges and proves special damage. The leading case is *Gibbons* v. *Westminster Bank Ltd*[4] where the plaintiff, who was not a trader, brought an action against the defendant bank for damages for breach of contract arising out of the wrongful dishonour of a cheque which she had drawn in favour of her landlord. The cheque was dishonoured owing to a mistake. The plaintiff had paid in previously a sum of money and this had been credited, by a slip, to a wrong account, and the bank was therefore under the impression that the plaintiff had no funds to meet her cheque. The bank contended that, as the plaintiff was not a trader, she was entitled to only nominal damages, because she had not pleaded any special or actual damage. This contention was upheld by Lawrence J. Accordingly, the plaintiff recovered only nominal damages of £2.

---

2 (1854) 14 CB 595. See also *Wilson* v. *United Counties Bank Ltd.* [1920] AC 102, at pp. 112, 133.
3 *Baker* v. *Australia and New Zealand Bank* [1958] NZLR 907, *post*, para. 2-147.
4 [1939] 2 KB 882.

2-144   In most cases, however, the distinction between a trader and a non-trader is not of practical importance, because if a non-trader's cheque is wrongfully dishonoured, he will usually be able to claim damages for libel against the drawee bank. In *Gibbons'* case there was no claim for libel.

Damages for libel

2-145   In *Sim* v. *Stretch*[5] Lord Atkin formulated the following test for determining whether or not words are libellous, namely, 'Would the words tend to lower the plaintiff in the estimation of right-thinking members of society generally?' If a bank writes such words as 'Refer to drawer' or 'Not sufficient' upon a cheque drawn by a customer and the customer has in fact sufficient funds in his account or is within his overdraft arrangement, the question arises whether the words are libellous. According to Scrutton J in *Flach* v. *London and South Western Bank*,[6] the words 'Refer to drawer' in their ordinary meaning amount to a statement by the bank 'we are not paying; go back to the drawer and ask why', or else 'go back to the drawer and ask him to pay'. The learned judge did not think it was possible to extract a libellous meaning from the use of the words 'Refer to drawer'. However, the case was an unusual one because the bank was justified in refusing to pay the cheque as a result of a war-time moratorium.

2-146   In a later case, *Plunkett* v. *Barclays Bank Ltd*,[7] du Parcq J adopted the language of Scrutton J, quoted above, and held that in the circumstances of the case, the words 'Refer to drawer' were no libel. Again, however, circumstances were unusual because the bank was justified in refusing to pay the cheque since a garnishee order had been served on the bank and this order had attached the customer's balance. A few years later in *Davidson* v. *Barclays Bank Ltd*,[8] the defendant bank wrongfully dishonoured the plaintiff's cheque with the answer 'Not sufficient', and Hilbery J had no hestitation in holding that the words were libellous. In an Irish case,[9] one cheque was marked 'Refer to drawer: present again', and two other cheques were marked 'Present again'. The learned judge held that the words were reasonably capable of a defamatory meaning, and allowed the case to go to the jury who found a verdict for the plaintiff. The case went to appeal, when two judges held that the words in question were reasonably capable of a

5 [1936] 2 All ER 1237, at p. 1240.
6 (1915) 31 TLR 334, at p. 336.
7 [1936] 2 KB 107.
8 [1940] 1 All ER 316.
9 *Pyke* v. *Hibernian Bank Ltd* [1950] IR 195.

defamatory meaning, and two judges held that they were not. The court being evenly divided, the judgment of the court below stood.

2-147 An illuminating judgment on this subject was delivered by the Supreme Court of New Zealand in 1958. That decision, *Baker* v. *Australia and New Zealand Bank*, [10] is not binding upon English courts, but the reasoning of the learned judge, Shorland J, is so compelling that it is likely to be cited with approval by the courts of this country. The plaintiff claimed damages from the defendant bank in respect of the wrongful dishonour of three cheques which the bank had returned unpaid with the answer 'Present again'. The plaintiff, who was held to be a non-trader, claimed damages (a) for breach of contract, and (b) for libel. She was awarded £6 nominal damages for breach of contract, being £2 nominal damages in respect of each cheque, and damages amounting to £100 for libel.

2-148 Dealing with the claim for damages for libel, Shorland J said that he had to decide whether or not the words 'Present again' were reasonably capable of a defamatory meaning. Having made a detailed analysis of the English and Irish cases, the more important of which have already been cited above, his Lordship approached the question at issue by saying:

> Whatever the answer 'Present again' may imply as to the prospects of future or later payments, it surely imports the clear intimation that the maker of the cheque so answered has defaulted as to time for performance of the legal and ethical obligation to provide for payment by the bank on presentation of a cheque issued for immediate payment. Written words which convey such meaning must, to my mind, tend to lower a person in the estimation of right-minded members of society generally.

Accordingly, the learned judge concluded that the answers 'Present again' were as a matter of law reasonably capable of conveying a defamatory meaning, and he found on the evidence that the answers did as a matter of fact in each instance libel the plaintiff.

2-149 The learned judge then turned to the assessment of damages. Before the plaintiff had commenced the action, her solicitor had written to the bank. One result of the correspondence which ensued was that it was expressly left to the defendant bank to determine what steps it would take, if any, to mitigate damages by addressing letters of retraction and apology to the payees of the cheques, or otherwise. In point of fact, no retraction or apology was made by the defendant bank.

10 [1958] NZLR 907, noted in *The Banker's Magazine*, Vol. CLXL (1960), p. 100.

Shorland J continued:

> The matters to be taken into consideration in assessing damages are the position and standing of the plaintiff, the nature of the libel, the mode and extent of the publication, the absence of any retraction or apology, and the whole conduct of the defendant from the time when the libel was published, down to the very moment of verdict ... There were three libels of limited publication upon a woman who engaged in commercial rather than domestic activities, touching her reputation in respect of financial solvency and punctiliousness in having her cheques met, an absence of retraction and apology, and a defence of no liability made in Court.[11]

As state above, Shorland J assessed the damages in respect of all three libels at a total of £100.

2-150 The decision of the Supreme Court of New Zealand in *Baker's* case is important for two reasons. First, the relevant considerations set out by Shorland J with regard to the assessment of damages are particularly helpful. Secondly, it is respectfully submitted that Shorland J applied the proper test when determining whether the answer on the cheques was defamatory, and that the view of Scrutton J in *Flach's* case[12] with regard to the answer 'Refer to drawer' must be read in the light of the special circumstances of that case. It is submitted that it makes no difference whether the answer is 'Refer to drawer' or 'Present again' or 'Not sufficient'. As a general rule, each of those answers (to borrow the words of Shorland J) 'import the clear intimation that the maker of the cheque so answered has defaulted as to time for performance of the legal and ethical obligation to provide for payment by the bank on presentation of a cheque issued for immediate payment'.[13]

2-151 Likewise, it is libellous to write upon a cheque words which state, contrary to the truth, that the drawer has no account at the drawee bank. In *Wilson* v. *Midland Bank Ltd*[14] the plaintiff's cheque for £50 2s. 5d. was wrongfully dishonoured by the Midland Bank with the answer 'No account'. Sachs J awarded the plaintiff £2 nominal damages for breach of contract, and £210 damages for libel.

---

11 Cf. *Davidson* v. *Barclays Bank Ltd* (*supra*) where the court took into consideration that the bank had omitted to write a letter acknowledging its mistake in wrongfully dishonouring a credit bookmaker's cheque for £2 15s. 8d. with the answer 'Not sufficient'. Hilbery J awarded him £250 damages for libel.

12 *Ante*, para. 2-145.

13 To the same effect, see the finding of the jury in *Jayson* v. *Midland Bank Ltd* [1967] 2 Lloyd's Rep 563; [1968] 1 Lloyd's Rep 409, CA.

14 See *The Reading Standard* for 13 October 1961; the action was tried at the Berkshire Assizes in Reading.

Practical considerations

2-152 Before a cheque is dishonoured for want of funds, it is desirable to take the following precautions with a view to ensuring that no mistakes have occurred in relation to the customer's account:

(a) The customer's paid cheques which are still in the bank's possession should be examined in order to make certain that they all appear to have been drawn by him; there is the possibility that a cheque drawn by a customer of a similar name may have been debited to the account in error.

(b) The dates on the paid cheques should be examined in order to make certain that no post-dated cheques have been paid in error.

(c) The account should be examined in order to discover whether a regular credit, such as a payment of salary, is missing; such an item may have been credited in error to the account of another customer.

(d) The bank should make certain that the cheque had not been drawn in conjunction with a cheque card.[15]

2-153 If these precautions are taken, the wrongful dishonour of a customer's cheque may be avoided. It may be impracticable to take the precautions on every occasion when a customer's cheque is dishonoured for lack of funds, but they should certainly be taken if it has not previously been necessary to dishonour any cheques drawn by the customer in question.

2-154 Finally, if a bank discovers that it has dishonoured a cheque wrongfully, it ought to act immediately with a view to minimizing the damage suffered by the customer. The mistake should be communicated by telephone to the payee or to his bankers, and this should be followed by a letter of apology to the payee. A letter of apology should also be sent forthwith to the customer. These considerations are dictated not only by the sound rule that if one makes a mistake to the detriment of others, one should as a matter of courtesy tender an apology immediately, but also by the clear indication given by the courts that any omission by the bank to acknowledge its mistake may increase the damages awarded against the bank.[16]

---

15 *Post*, para. 10-43.
16 See *ante*, para. 2-149.

3

Determination of contract between banker and customer

In this chapter it is proposed to consider the various ways in which the contract between banker and customer may be terminated, and to examine certain other problems related thereto.

Section I
CLOSURE OF ACCOUNT

3-1 In theory, the relationship between banker and customer may, like any other contractual relationship, be terminated by mutual agreement. In practice, however, it is nearly always the one party or the other who wishes to put an end to the relationship, and so the contract is usually terminated unilaterally. Accordingly, it is convenient to discuss closure of the account under two headings, namely closure by the customer, and closure by the bank.

Closure of account by customer

(a) Current accounts

3-2 One of the distinguishing features of a current account is that the balance standing to a customer's credit on such account is repayable on demand.[1] Accordingly, a customer may close a current account which is in credit by demanding repayment of the balance due, less accrued bank charges. It is prudent for the bank to ensure that the customer states in writing that he is in fact closing the account, and not merely withdrawing the available balance. If he withdraws the balance in cash, it is sound practice to obtain his signature to a cheque for the balance, made payable to 'Self, to close account'. If he withdraws the balance otherwise than in cash, some other evidence of his intention to close the

1 *Ante*, para. 1-70.

account should be obtained. Failure to take either of these precautions may sometimes involve a bank in loss. Thus in *Wilson* v. *Midland Bank Ltd*[2] the plaintiff's cheque for £50 2*s*. 5*d*. was wrongfully dishonoured by the Midland Bank with the answer 'No account'. The bank's case was that the plaintiff had had a telephone conversation with the bank manager, when the plaintiff had said he was closing his account. In evidence the plaintiff said that he had no recollection of such a conversation and at no time had any intention of closing the account. Some time after the alleged conversation, the plaintiff paid in £403 19*s*. 10*d*. at a branch of Lloyds Bank for the credit of his account at the Midland Bank. As the result of a mistake, the Midland Bank credited that sum to the joint account of other customers named Wilson. Hence, when the plaintiff's cheque for £50 2*s*. 5*d*. was presented for payment, it was dishonoured with the answer, 'No account'. Sachs J awarded the plaintiff £2 nominal damages for breach of contract, and £210 damages for libel.

3-3 If a customer wishes to close his current account at a time when it is overdrawn, he may do so by repaying the overdraft, together with accrued bank charges.

3-4 Whether the account is in credit or is overdrawn, it is always prudent to invite the customer to make provision for the payment of any outstanding cheques drawn by him; but if this is not done, the bank will be justified in dishonouring any cheques subsequently presented with the answer 'Account closed'. Another prudent step to take when the customer wishes to close a current account is to ask him to hand to the bank any unused cheque forms in his possession. Furthermore, the bank should bear in mind any engagements into which it has entered at the request of the customer, such as, for example, the purchase of stock exchange securities. Finally, credit facilities should be cancelled, and any securities or other articles held by way of security or for safe custody should be returned to him.

(b) Other accounts

3-5 One of the distinguishing features of deposit accounts is that the balance is repayable upon personal application after a stated period of notice, which at the present time is usually seven days.[3] Accordingly, the account may be closed by the giving of the relevant notice.[4] Balances on

---

2 See *The Reading Standard* of 13 October 1961; the action was tried at the Berkshire Assizes in Reading.

3 *Ante*, para. 1-71.

4 In practice, the necessity for this period of notice is often waived upon forfeiture of the appropriate number of days' interest.

savings accounts are usually repayable upon demand, and so customers may generally close such accounts without giving notice.

Closure of account by banker

3-6 *Buckingham & Co.* v. *London and Midland Bank Ltd*[5] seems to be the earliest reported case arising out of the closure of a customer's account by a bank. The customer had both a loan account and a current account, and at a time when he had a credit balance of £160 in his current account the bank informed him that his account was closed and that the bank would not pay any more cheques or honour any more of his acceptances. On the following day two cheques and two bills of the customer were presented and were dishonoured. The jury found that, in the course of dealing between the customer and the bank, the customer was entitled to draw on his current account without reference to his loan account, that he was entitled to reasonable notice discontinuing this course of business and that no such notice had been given. The customer was awarded £500 damages against the bank.

3-7 In *Joachimson* v. *Swiss Bank Corporation*,[6] Atkin LJ stated that one of the terms of the contract between banker and customer was that the banker would not cease to do business with a customer 'except upon reasonable notice'.[7] Although the existence of this implied term is now well established, the practical difficulty is to know what length of notice would be regarded as reasonable in the particular circumstances of a given case. When once a bank has decided that it wishes to cease to provide banking facilities for a customer, it usually wants to bring the relationship to an end as speedily as possible. The customer, for his part often wishes to continue the account for as long as possible, especially if he knows or thinks that other banks would not be prepared to open an account for him.

3-8 The only subsequent reported case in which a customer has challenged the sufficiency of a notice to close an account is *Prosperity Ltd* v. *Lloyds Bank Ltd*.[8] The plaintiff company had devised an ingenious scheme but, as McCardie J said, there was nothing dishonest about it. However, it is not surprising that when the senior officials of Lloyds Bank learnt about it, they decided that the bank would give notice to ter-

---

5 (1895) 12 TLR 70; *ante*, para. 2-64.

6 [1921] 3 KB 110.

7 [1921] 3 KB 110, at p. 127. Likewise, at p. 125, Warrington LJ said that '... it is well settled that a banker is not at liberty to close an account in credit by payment of the credit balance without giving reasonable notice, and making provision for outstanding cheques.'

8 (1923) 39 TLR 372.

minate the relationship of banker and customer. Briefly, the scheme was as follows.[9] Members of the public were invited to become subscribers. On payment of 35s. to the plaintiff company, a subscriber would receive a book containing ten application forms, valid for one year. Each new subscriber whom the first subscriber obtained would fill up one of the application forms, and he would go through the same process (that is, he would send 35s. to the plaintiff company and obtain a book containing ten application forms), with the result that a 'family' of subscribers was created. The maximum number of descendants in the first 'generation' succeeding the first subscriber would be ten, in the second generation one hundred, in the third generation one thousand, and so on until the seventh generation was reached, in which the maximum number of descendants would (in theory) be ten million. Each subscriber would be credited with 2s. commission in respect of every one of his descendants, and so it seems that if he had ten million descendants, he would be credited with £1 million. When the sum of eight pounds by way of commission had been credited to a subscriber the amount was to be paid to an insurance company associated with the plaintiff company as the single premium for a ten-year endowment assurance of ten pounds in favour of the subscriber, and the next eight pounds would secure a second policy of ten pounds, and so on. Of the 35s. paid by a subscriber, 16s. would be credited to him towards payment of the policy premiums, 14s. would be applied in paying the 2s. commissions, and 5s. would be paid to the plaintiff company for expenses and profit.

3-9   When the plaintiff company opened its account with Lloyds Bank, the scheme outlined above was explained to the branch manager, and he agreed, on behalf of the bank, to receive applications from subscribers. Apparently, however, senior officials of the bank read press criticisms of the scheme, and they decided that Lloyds Bank ought not to be associated with it. Accordingly, written notice was given by the bank to the plaintiff company on 14 February 1923, when there was about £7,000 standing to the company's credit, stating that the bank would cease to act as bankers to the company after 14 March 1923.

3-10   The company immediately brought an action, claiming a declaration that the bank was not entitled to close the company's account without reasonable notice and asking for an injunction restraining the bank from discontinuing the account. In the course of his judgment, McCardie J said that a banker had a right to close at any time an account which was in debit, but in the case of an account which was in credit he must give a reasonable notice, which would vary according to circumstances. The position of the bank was interwoven with the scheme

9 In addition to the report cited, see *The Times* for 13 March 1923.

of insurance evolved by the plaintiff company, which was the result of the arrangement made with the branch manager. A month's notice was not adequate in the circumstances; it did not give the plaintiff company a sufficient opportunity to make fresh arrangements. The company, therefore, was entitled to the declaration asked for, but not to an injunction, because an injunction would be in the nature of a decree for specific performance, which it would be impossible for the court to carry out. The learned judge did not indicate what period of notice would be reasonable. There followed a discussion between counsel, and it was announced that the bank had agreed to act as bankers to the plaintiff company for a further limited period.

Summary

3-11 A banker who wishes to cease transacting business for a customer must usually give that customer reasonable notice, and the period of notice must be long enough to enable the customer, having regard to all the surrounding circumstances, to make alternative arrangements.

3-12 If, however, the customer is using his account for some unlawful purpose, it cannot possibly be the law that the bank is under an obligation to give him sufficient notice to enable him to make other arrangements to carry out that unlawful purpose; either no period of notice at all, or a purely nominal period of twenty-four hours' notice, would suffice to put an end to the relationship of banker and customer in a case of that sort.

3-13 The view of McCardie J in *Prosperity Ltd* v. *Lloyds Bank Ltd* (*supra*) that a banker has a right to close at any time an account which is in debit is, with respect, one which may require further consideration. Depending upon the circumstances, a bank may be entitled to demand repayment of an overdraft forthwith, but this is very different from closing the account. A banker would be very imprudent if he called in an overdraft to close an account and then, prior to the expiry of a proper period of notice, he dishonoured cheques which the customer was prepared to cover by paying in cash. It is one thing to call in an overdraft; it is quite another matter to withdraw banking facilities without giving the customer sufficient notice to enable him to make other arrangements.

Effect of closure of account

3-14 When the customer's account has been closed, either by the customer or by the bank, the relationship of banker and customer is at an end, and neither party is under any contractual obligation to the other, save only in one respect, namely that the banker's duty of secrecy still subsists. This was the view taken by the majority in the Court of Appeal in *Tournier* v. *National Provincial and Union Bank of England.*[10]

Section 2
DEATH OF CUSTOMER

3-15   The general rule is that the rights and liabilities under a contract pass, on the death of a party to the contract, to his personal representatives. There are certain exceptions to the general rule; for example, contracts of personal service expire with either of the parties to them.[11]

3-16   There is no reported case in English law in which the effect of the customer's death upon the contractual relationship between banker and customer has been fully investigated. It is thought that the law and practice may be stated as follows.

3-17   Upon the customer's death, the right to receive any sums owing to him, including bank balances, passes as a general rule to his personal representatives. If he leaves a will and appoints executors, those balances will vest in the executors as from the date of death;[12] the probate of the will is a mere authentication of the executors' title.[13] If, however, the customer dies intestate, all his property, including his bank balances, will vest in the President of the Family Division of the High Court[14] until administrators are appointed.

3-18   In general, credit balances and securities or other articles deposited with a bank by a customer who has died ought not to be paid or delivered to his executors or administrators until a grant of probate or administration, sealed in England or Wales, is produced to the bank. In one case,[15] a testatrix delivered a bill of exchange to her bankers for collection, and died before the bill became due. Before obtaining probate of her will, her executors sued the bank for the return of the bill or its value, but it was held that all proceedings in the action ought to be stayed until the executors had obtained probate. A few months after that case had been decided, Parliament enacted that the production of probate or of letters of administration is necessary to establish the right

---

10 *Ante*, para. 2-100.
11 *Farrow* v. *Wilson* (1869) LR 4 CP 744.
12 *Woolley* v. *Clark* (1822) 5 B & Ald 744.
13 *Smith* v. *Milles* (1786) 1 Term Rep 745, at p. 480.
14 Administration of Estates Act 1925, ss 9 and 55(1)(xv); Administration of Justice Act 1970, s. 1(6).
15 *Tarn* v. *The Commercial Banking Company of Sydney* (1884) 12 QBD 294, following *Webb* v. *Adkins* (1854) 14 CB 401.

to recover or receive any part of the personal estate and effects of a deceased person.[16] Thus the matter is now beyond all doubt.

3-19 If the will of a deceased customer is found to have been deposited with his bank, the will should be delivered to the executors named in it or to their solicitors. This is the only article which should normally be delivered up prior to the production of probate.

3-20 As a matter of practice, bankers do occasionally pay small balances of deceased customer's accounts to the persons who appear to be entitled to them under the customer's will or on his intestacy, without insisting that a grant of probate or letters of administration be obtained. This should be done only in those cases where it is thought that the deceased's estate is small. An indemnity should be taken from the persons receiving the payment. In addition, banks sometimes require an insurance company to join in the indemnity.

3-21 If a bank in good faith makes payments or delivers securities or other articles to personal representatives who have obtained a grant of probate or letters of administration, the effect of the Administration of Estates Act 1925[17] is that the bank is protected 'notwithstanding any defect or circumstance whatsoever affecting the validity of the representation'. The Act also provides[18] that where a representation is revoked, all payments and dispositions made in good faith to a personal representative under the representation before the revocation thereof shall be a valid discharge to the person making the same. These statutory provisions emphasize the importance of insisting upon the production of a grant of probate or letters of administration as a matter of general practice.

3-22 Section 75 of the Bills of Exchange Act 1882 provides that the duty and authority of a banker to pay a cheque drawn on him are determined by notice of the customer's death. It would seem that if the bank pays a customer's cheque after the customer's death but before receiving notice thereof, the bank may properly debit the cheque to the customer's account, because the correct interpretation of the section would appear to be that the bank's authority to pay is not determined until it receives notice of the death. The section does not indicate what constitutes notice. Obviously, mere rumour would not suffice, but an announcement in a newspaper presumably would. When a cheque has to be returned unpaid by reason of the customer's death, the correct answer on the cheque is 'Drawer deceased'. Occasionally a customer accepts

16 Revenue Act 1884, s. 11.
17 S. 27(1).
18 S. 27(2).

bills of exchange payable at his bank; the courts would probably decide, by parity of reasoning, that the bank's authority to pay bills is determined by notice of the customer's death.

3-23 The customer's right to draw cheques does not devolve upon his personal representatives. As Rowlatt J said, 'If the executors want to become customers of the bank, they must start *de novo.*'[19]

3-24 In certain matters, a bank acts as agent for its customers; for example, a bank normally acts as agent when collecting the proceeds of customers' cheques, and it acts as agent when making payments to third parties under standing orders. Subject to exceptions, depending upon the special terms of the appointment, the death of the principal at once puts an end to the authority of his agent even though the agent was not aware of his death.[20] It has never been decided whether this general rule applies to the agency relationship between banker and customer. Perhaps the court would decide that, as regards payments under standing orders, the bank's authority is not determined until the bank receives notice of the customer's death; this result could be achieved by applying the rule regarding the payment of cheques laid down in s. 75 of the Bills of Exchange Act 1882. Although mandates for the payment of dividends to a bank are probably determined, like other mandates, by the death of the person who signed them, it is a common, but not universal, practice for banks to continue to receive the dividends, crediting them either to the account of the deceased, or to a new account to be operated upon by the executors or administrators after production of the grant.[21] This practice is a convenient one, and it appears to be free from risk.

3-25 Subject to what has been stated in the preceding paragraphs, it would appear that, on the death of a customer, his remaining contractual rights and liabilities *vis-à-vis* his banker pass to his personal representatives. The matter may be tested in the following way. Let it be supposed that a customer has two accounts, a current account and a deposit account, the balance on the latter account being repayable after seven days' notice. The customer dies at a time when the credit balance on his current account is £1,000 and that on his deposit account is £10,000. His executors obtain probate of his will which they bring to the bank and thereupon demand payment in cash of £11,000. It is submitted that the bank would be obliged to repay the balance on current account forthwith, but would be entitled to require seven days' notice before

19 *Deutsche Bank und Disconto-Gesellschaft* v. *Banque des Marchands de Moscou* (1931), *Legal Decisions Affecting Bankers*, Vol. 4, p. 293.
20 *Blades* v. *Free* (1829) 9 B & C 167; *Smout* v. *Ilbery* (1842) 10 M & W 1; *Pool* v. *Pool* (1889) 58 LJP 67; *Re Overweg, Haas* v. *Durant* [1901] 1 Ch 209.
21 *Questions on Banking Practice* (11th ed., 1978), p. 43, Question 110.

repaying the £10,000 standing to the credit of the deposit account, on the basis that the rights and liabilities under the contracts relating to both accounts had passed to the executors, who would have precisely the same rights as regards obtaining repayment as the deceased customer had. If this reasoning is correct, it would also resolve the question which is sometimes posed,[22] namely whether interest on credit balances ceases to be payable on the death of the customer. The answer would be that, if the customer had a right to be paid interest, that same right would vest in his personal representatives.

Section 3
MENTAL INCAPACITY OF CUSTOMER

3-26 Persons of unsound mind used to be known as lunatics. The Mental Treatment Act 1930[23] expressly provided that the word 'lunatic' must cease to be used in relation to any person of or alleged to be of unsound mind. That Act was repealed by the Mental Health Act 1959,[24] which replaced a great deal of complicated law and procedure with a much simplified system in keeping with modern ideas on the subject.[25] The Act of 1959 was amended by the Mental Health (Amendment) Act 1982, and the law was consolidated by the Mental Health Act 1983.

3-27 One of the complicated procedures under the old law was the solemn enquiry known as the 'inquisition', as a result of which a subject could be found to be of unsound mind. An individual known as a 'committee' was appointed to whom the management of the subject's affairs, and perhaps also of his person, was committed. The last inquisition was held in 1959. Even prior to 1959, however, it was much more usual to seek the appointment of a receiver rather than a committee when a subject was incapable of managing his own affairs. The method of appointing a receiver, which is simple and inexpensive, will be explained subsequently.

3-28 The Mental Health Act 1959 introduced the term 'patient' when referring to persons suffering or appearing to be suffering from mental disorder.[26] Under the old law, there were several different classes of patients; under the 1959 Act, instead of different categories of patients,

22 See, for example, *Questions on Banking Practice* (11th ed., 1978), p. 43, Question 111.
23 S. 20(5).
24 S. 149(2) and Sched. VIII.
25 For three excellent contributions on the Act by J. E. Hall Williams, T. C. N. Gibbens, and Raymond Jennings QC, see *The Modern Law Review*, Vol. 23 (1960), pp. 410, 416 and 421.
26 S. 147(1).

a simple test was introduced, namely whether a person is, by reason of mental disorder, incapable of managing and administering his property and affairs. Under the old classification, some patients were known as 'certified patients', that is to say, patients who had been certified insane. Certification, as such, finds no place in the modern system, though provision is of course still made for the detention, against their will, of persons suffering from mental disorder. One of the main objects of the 1959 Act, however, was to provide as much treatment as possible, both in hospital and outside, on a purely voluntary basis. Under the old law, a patient who entered a mental hospital without any application, order or direction rendering him liable to be detained, was known as a 'voluntary patient'. That term was not used in the 1959 Act. The marginal note to s. 5 of the Act referred to 'informal admission of patients', and patients who used to be known as 'voluntary patients' under the old law are now often referred to as 'informal patients'.

3-29 It is convenient to consider the question whether the contract between banker and customer is determined by reason of the customer's mental disorder under two headings, first where a receiver has been appointed, and secondly where a receiver has not been appointed.

Where a receiver has been appointed

3-30 There is an office of the Supreme Court called the Court of Protection 'for the protection and management ... of the property of persons under disability'.[27] The functions of that office, which are normally discharged by the Master of the Court of Protection, are exercisable where, after considering medical evidence, he is satisfied 'that a person is incapable, by reason of mental disorder, of managing and administering his property and affairs'.[28] Having reached that conclusion, the Master is given very wide statutory powers to ensure the maintenance or other benefit of the patient and members of his family.[29] Furthermore – and this point will interest a banker in cases where the patient's account is overdrawn – the Master, in administering the patient's affairs, must have regard to the interests of creditors.[30]

3-31 An important power possessed by the Master is the power to appoint a receiver for a patient.[31] The receiver's powers and duties are specified in the Master's order by which he is appointed, and the bank

27 Mental Health Act 1983, s. 93.
28 S. 94.
29 S. 95(1).
30 S. 95(2).
31 S. 99(1).

should ask to see a copy of the order.[32] A relative of the patient is usually appointed as his receiver. Henceforth the banker should treat the contract between himself and the customer as determined. As a general rule, the customer's account will be closed and any credit balance will be transferred to a new account in the name of the receiver. If the patient's business is to be carried on, a separate account will usually be opened for business purposes. Sometimes, the Master's order provides that the patient's securities must be lodged in court, and the bank will be asked to supply the receiver with details of any securities which it holds. It follows, of course, that if, prior to his mental disorder, the customer had authorized a third party to act for him and to draw cheques upon his account, that authority must be treated as determined; for as Brett LJ observed in *Drew* v. *Nunn,*[33] 'where such a change occurs as to the principal that he can no longer act for himself, the agent whom he has appointed can no longer act for him'.[34]

3-32 Finally, attention may be drawn to the circumstances in which a receiver's appointment may be terminated.[35] First, it is provided that a receiver must be discharged by order of the Master if he is satisfied that the patient has become capable of managing and administering his property and affairs; in that event, the customer would be able to resume his contractual relationship with his banker. Secondly, the receiver may be discharged by order of the Master at any time if the Master considers it expedient to do so. Thirdly, a receiver is automatically discharged on the patient's death.

Where a receiver has not been appointed

3-33 There are many thousands of people who are incapable, by reason of mental disorder, of managing and administering their property and affairs, for whom no receiver has ever been appointed. This may be so for one of a number of reasons: first the patient's assets may be negligible; secondly, the patient's mental disorder may be purely temporary (for example, he may be suffering from a nervous breakdown); thirdly, he may be so ill or so old that he is not expected to live for more than a few months; and fourthly, the patient's relatives may be unwilling to apply to the Court of Protection even though it is a proper case for the appointment of a receiver.

---

32 Whenever possible, the bank should try to ensure that the court order contains clear instructions concerning the patient's banking accounts and securities.
33 (1879) 4 QBD 661, at p. 666.
34 See, however, the Enduring Powers of Attorney Act 1985 *post*, paras 11-38A et seq.
35 Mental Health Act 1983, s. 99(3).

3-34 Occasionally, a bank may be in some difficulty in these cases because the bank may not know for certain whether or not it is under a duty to continue to honour cheques drawn by the customer. When the bank receives reliable information that the customer is mentally disordered, it would seem that the duty to pay cheques is determined; there is no statutory provision to this effect and there is likewise no reported case on the subject, but the absence of a consenting mind would seem to invalidate the order to pay contained in a cheque, at any rate in cases where the customer's state of mind is known to the bank.[36] Furthermore, a bank sometimes acts as agent for its customers, as for example when it makes payments to third parties under standing orders, and it is well established that when a principal can no longer act for himself, his agent can no longer act for him.[37] For these reasons, therefore, when a bank learns that one of its customers is suffering from some form of mental disorder, enquiry should be made in order to ascertain whether the customer is well enough to attend to his own financial affairs. If the customer is in hospital, the enquiry should be addressed to the medical superintendent, and if the customer is at home, to his own medical adviser. If the reply is affirmative, the customer's account may be continued as in the past, but in the event of a negative reply the account should be stopped and any cheques subsequently presented for payment should be returned with the answer 'Insufficient mandate'.[38] At the same time, the customer's relatives should be urged to apply to the Court of Protection for the appointment of a receiver. If the bank pays the balance of the account to the relatives without the authority of the Court of Protection or of the receiver, it will act at its peril. The following decisions of the courts indicate the risks which a bank may run if it pays away a customer's funds without lawful authority in cases of mental disorder.

3-35 In *Re Beavan, Davies, Banks & Co.* v. *Beavan*[39] a customer of a bank had a paralytic seizure which rendered him incapable both physically and mentally of managing his affairs. With the approval of other members of the family, the bank allowed the customer's eldest son to sign cheques drawn on his father's account. For two years the account was operated by the eldest son for the maintenance of the household in its accustomed manner. Then the customer died. At that time the account was overdrawn, and the bank claimed the amount of the over-

---

36 For the effect of mental disorder on a person's capacity to enter into contracts, see *Halsbury's Laws of England* (4th ed., 1980), Vol. 30, pp. 566-9.

37 *Drew* v. *Nunn* (*supra*).

38 This answer is probably more appropriate than 'Refer to drawer', which usually signifies lack of funds.

39 [1912] 1 Ch 196.

draft from the executors. Two of the four executors resisted the claim. It was held that, by virtue of the doctrine of subrogation, the bank was entitled to recover all amounts paid out for necessaries, but that the bank's interest and commission charges could not be recovered.

3-36 In *Scarth* v. *National Provincial Bank Ltd*[40] a customer had a credit balance of £194 1s. 7d. with the defendant bank. In 1919 he was certified as a lunatic. The bank was notified, and it quite properly refused to allow further transactions or to honour cheques drawn by the customer's wife, who had previously been authorized to draw cheques on the account. The wife opened a separate account in her own name, and the bank transferred the balance of her husband's account to her account, against an indemnity executed by the wife and another person. In 1925 the husband recovered his sanity, and in 1928 he brought an action against the bank claiming the sum of £194 1s. 7d. being the balance transferred from his account to his wife's account without his authority. His wife had used the money to pay her husband's debts, and the bank in its defence relied upon the equitable doctrine whereby a person who has paid the debts of another without authority is allowed to take advantage of his payment. The bank's defence succeeded.

3-37 Although the banks in the above-mentioned cases did not suffer any substantial loss, there would seem to be no good reason why banks should be expected to incur unnecessary risks when dealing with the accounts of customers who are suffering from mental disorder. If in such cases the bank quite properly refuses to pay out any money, this will often persuade the relatives that they should take the appropriate steps to have a receiver appointed. Any departure from this general rule, save in cases of purely temporary incapacity, should be regarded as quite exceptional.

Section 4
BANKRUPTCY OF CUSTOMER

3-38 The first step in bankruptcy procedure is the presentation to the court of a petition for a bankruptcy order under the provisions of s. 264 of the Insolvency Act 1986. As a general rule, the petition is presented either (a) by one or more of the individual's creditors, or (b) by the individual himself on the ground that he is unable to pay his debts. By virtue of s. 267 a creditor's petition may be presented if the debt is one which the debtor 'appears either to be unable to pay or to have no reasonable prospect of being able to pay'. This will usually be evidenced by the

40 (1930) 4 LDB 241.

debtor's failure to satisfy a statutory demand pursuant to s. 268. In the case of a creditor's petition, the amount of the debt, or the aggregate amount of the debts, must be £750 or more. The presentation of a creditor's petition will not necessarily result in the making of a bankruptcy order, because the debtor may be able to find the money to pay off the creditor.

3-39 In most cases, however, the presentation of a petition will result in the making by the court of a bankruptcy order. Section 278 of the Insolvency Act 1986 provides that the bankruptcy of an individual against whom a bankruptcy order has been made commences with the day on which the order is made and continues until the individual is discharged. As soon as a bank learns that a bankruptcy order has been made against a customer, no cheques drawn by the customer should be paid. They should be returned unpaid with the answer 'Refer to drawer'.

3-40 A question for consideration is whether a bank should continue to pay its customer's cheques after it learns that a petition has been presented to the court but before it learns that a bankruptcy order has been made. The answer to this question seems to depend upon the correct interpretation of s. 284 of the Insolvency Act 1986. The provisions of this section are complex, but it is suggested that the effect of the section may be summarized as follows. Where a person is adjudged bankrupt, any disposition of property made by that person in the period to which the section applies is void, except to the extent that it is or was made with the consent of the court, or is or was subsequently ratified by the court. The period to which the section applies is the period beginning with the day of the presentation of the petition for the bankruptcy order and ending with the vesting of the bankrupt's estate in a trustee. If a bank paid a customer's cheque after it had learnt that a petition had been presented and if in due course a bankruptcy order is made, the trustee in bankruptcy might obtain an order from the court ordering the bank to refund the money to him on the ground that the payment of the cheque was a 'disposition of property' and was void. Therefore, as a matter of banking practice, bankers decline to pay cheques after they have received notice of the presentation of a petition for a bankruptcy order, unless the court gives its consent. Finally, the legal position is different if the customer's account is overdrawn. The payment of the cheque could not amount to a 'disposition' of the bankrupt's property. The question is whether the debit to the customer's overdrawn account was validly made, so that the bank could prove for the debt. Section 382 of the Insolvency Act 1986 defines 'bankruptcy debt' in relation to a bankrupt as 'any debt or liability to which he is subject at the commencement of the bankruptcy'. Thus it would seem that the bank could prove for the debt. Of course, in practice it is most unlikely that a bank would wish to see a customer's overdraft increased after it had learnt that a petition had been presented, and therefore the practical result would be the same, that is to say, once a bank receives notice of a bankruptcy petition no further cheques will be paid irrespective of whether the account is in credit or is overdrawn.

3-41 By virtue of s. 306 of the Insolvency Act 1986 the bankrupt's estate vests in his trustee in bankruptcy immediately on his appointment taking effect. Under s. 283 the bankrupt's estate includes all property vested in him at the commencement of the bankruptcy. Furthermore, s. 307 enables the trustee by notice in writing to claim for the bankrupt's estate any property (known as his 'after-acquired property') which has been acquired by the bankrupt since the commencement of the bankruptcy. Section 312(3) provides that a bank which holds any property for the bankrupt must pay or deliver to his trustee in bankruptcy all property in his possession or under his control which forms part of the bankrupt's estate.

3-42 Occasionally, a bank discovers that a customer is an undischarged bankrupt. The bank should notify the customer's trustee in bankruptcy of the existence of the account, because the trustee may wish to claim the money in the account. In practice, however, the trustee may be willing to allow the bankrupt to operate a bank account. If the bankrupt is employed, it may be that his wages are being paid into the account. The wages will be 'after-acquired property', and the trustee would be entitled to claim these sums by notice under s. 307 of the Insolvency Act 1986. In practice, the trustee often applies to the court for an 'income payments order' under s. 310 of the Act claiming for the estate any payment in the nature of income, including any payment in respect of the carrying on of any business or in respect of any office or employment. No order may be made which would reduce the bankrupt's income below what appears to the court to be necessary for meeting the reasonable domestic needs of the bankrupt and his family. An income payments order will either (a) require the bankrupt to pay to the trustee an amount equal to so much of that payment as is claimed by the order, or (b) require the person making the payment to pay so much of it as is so claimed to the trustee, instead of to the bankrupt.

3-42A Sometimes, the wife of an undischarged bankrupt applies to a bank to open an account. If the account is to be used for carrying on the business formerly carried on by her husband, the bank should ask his trustee in bankruptcy to confirm that the business has been regularly transferred to the wife of the bankrupt.

Section 5
WINDING-UP OF COMPANY CUSTOMER

3-43   When a company is wound up, it ceases to have any legal existence and all its contractual relationships come to an end. In that respect, the winding-up of a company may be likened to the death of an individual.

3-44   Winding-up, however, is a procedure which may take months, or, in complicated cases, several years. It is during the intermediate period between the commencement of the winding-up and the final dissolution that certain problems may arise. During that period the company remains in being, and any existing relationship of banker and customer will continue, though there will come a time when the control of the company and of its bank account will pass from the directors to the liquidator.[41]

Section 6
WINDING-UP OF BANK

3-45   The winding-up of a bank will likewise put an end to the contract between banker and customer. Interesting problems may arise if the bank is incorporated in a foreign country. Thus in *Re Russian Commercial and Industrial Bank*,[42] a bank incorporated in Russia which also carried on business at an English branch, was dissolved under Russian law in 1917 or 1918; yet the English branch continued for a time to carry on banking business. A petition for the compulsory winding-up of the bank in England was presented in 1922, and a compulsory order was made. A customer, who at all material times had a credit balance on current account of 36,430 roubles with the English branch, sought to prove in the winding-up by converting the roubles into sterling at the rate of exchange (360 roubles to £1 sterling) current at the date of the dissolution of the bank in Russia on the ground that the debt became due at that date. The English court held, however, that although in general the relationship of banker and customer ceased and the debt became payable at that date, yet for the purposes of the distribution of assets among the creditors in a winding-up in England, the previous dissolution of the bank in Russia had to be ignored. So, for those purposes, the relationship of banker and customer must be deemed to have continued until the commencement of the winding-up in England, at

41 See *post*, paras 11-343/59.
42 [1955] 1 Ch 148.

which date the debt to the customer became due. By that time, Russian roubles were virtually worthless in terms of sterling (400,000 roubles to £1), so the customer was only able to prove in the liquidation for about two shillings.

Section 7
GARNISHEE ORDERS AND SUMMONSES

3-46 A garnishee order is an order of the court, obtained by a judgment creditor, attaching funds in the hands of a third person who owes money to the judgment debtor; the third person is called the 'garnishee'. By way of illustration, let it be supposed that D owes money to C. C obtains judgment against D in respect of the debt. D fails to pay the judgment debt. D has a credit balance with his bank. By following the procedure outlined below, C may obtain a garnishee order attaching D's credit balance at the bank. In that way, C will obtain payment of the judgment debt, either in whole or in part, as the case may be. Service of a garnishee order upon a bank may, therefore, determine – or at least suspend – the bank's duty to honour cheques drawn by the customer. As explained below, the effect of such an order upon the bank's duty to pay cheques depends upon the terms of the order.

'Unlimited' garnishee orders

3-47 The steps to be taken in order to obtain a garnishee order are set out in Order 49 of the Rules of the Supreme Court. Briefly, the judgment creditor must swear an affidavit (a) identifying the judgment or order to be enforced and stating the amount remaining unpaid under it at the time of the application, (b) stating that to the best of the information or belief of the deponent the garnishee (naming him) is within the jurisdiction and is indebted to the judgment debtor and stating the sources of the deponent's information or the grounds for his belief, and (c) stating, where the garnishee is a bank having more than one place of business, the name and address of the branch at which the judgment debtor's account is believed to be held or, if it be the case, that this information is not known to the deponent. Having sworn that affidavit, the judgment creditor must then apply to a Master for an order *nisi* attaching the debt owed by the garnishee and calling upon him to appear on a day named in the order and show cause why he should not pay the debt alleged to be due from him to the judgment creditor. This application to the Master is made *ex parte*, i.e. neither the judgment debtor nor the garnishee is required to attend. In fact, secrecy is usually essential: if the judgment debtor learnt what was taking place, he might try to ensure that the third person paid the amount of the debt to him prior to the service of the garnishee order. If the third person was a bank, the judgment debtor could easily withdraw his bank balance and so prevent the judgment creditor from serving an effective garnishee order upon the bank.

3-48   To continue with the procedure, if the Master is satisfied with the judgment creditor's affidavit, he will make the order *nisi*. The order will immediately be served upon the garnishee and, in the case of an 'unlimited' order, it will bind 'all debts owing or accruing' to the judgment debtor; but until service, any payment to the judgment debtor by the garnishee will discharge him.[43] If the garnishee is a bank having more than one place of business, the order will give the name and address of the branch at which the judgment debtor's account is believed to be held, provided that the relevant details were stated in the affidavit sworn by the judgment creditor. As already indicated, the order *nisi* calls upon the garnishee to show cause why he should not pay the debt alleged to be due from him to the judgment creditor. In the vast majority of cases, there is no lawful reason why he should not do so. In the result, the order of the court is made absolute, and thereupon the garnishee becomes liable to pay to the judgment creditor the amount due from him to the judgment debtor, or as much as may be sufficient to pay the judgment debt and the costs of the garnishee proceedings.[44] In that way, the judgment creditor eventually obtains payment of the judgment debt, either in whole or in part.

3-49   It was established by the House of Lords in *Rogers* v. *Whiteley*[45] that, when served with an 'unlimited' garnishee order *nisi*, a bank may, and should, refuse to pay *any* cheques drawn by the customer, even though it is known that the amount of the judgment debt is less than the balance standing to the customer's credit. In *Rogers* v. *Whiteley*, a customer had standing to his credit on current account and deposit account a sum of over £6,800. In those days a deposit account balance was not usually attachable by service of a garnishee order,[46] because, being subject to notice, it was not 'owing or accruing' to the customer. However, in this particular case the customer had given notice to transfer his deposit account balance to his current account. That notice had expired. Therefore, as Lindley LJ said in the Court of Appeal, 'the plaintiff had in effect both accounts to draw on'.[47] A creditor of the customer

---

43 *Cooper* v. *Brayne* (1858) 27 LJ Ex 446.
44 Rules of the Supreme Court, Order 49, rule 4.
45 [1898] AC 118.
46 At the present day such a balance is usually attachable by virtue of the Administration of Justice Act 1956, s. 38, *post*, para. 3-68.
47 23 QBD 236, at p. 238.

obtained a judgment against him for £6,000. The creditor then obtained a garnishee order *nisi* which ordered that 'all debts owing or accruing' from the bank to the customer be attached to answer the judgment recovered against him. That order was served on the bank, and thereafter the bank refused to honour *any* cheques drawn by the customer. The House of Lords held that the bank had acted correctly. Lord Watson said:[48]

> The effect of an order attaching 'all debts' owing or accruing due by him to the judgment debtor is to make the garnishee custodier for the court of the whole funds attached; and he cannot, except at his own peril, part with any of those funds without the sanction of the court.

The hardship resulting from the making of 'unlimited' garnishee orders, especially in cases where the garnishee is a bank, will be apparent. The judgment debt may be small in comparison with the customer's credit balance, and yet an 'unlimited' garnishee order will attach the whole balance. The bank must not permit any drawings from the attached balance: to do so would amount to a failure to comply with the order of the court.

3-50 The customer should be notified of the situation immediately, and he should be informed that, if he wishes to do so, he may open a new account for future transactions. The bank may even be prepared in some cases to permit this new account to become overdrawn, especially in those cases where the balance on the original account exceeds the amount of the garnishee order together with the costs which are likely to be incurred in the garnishee proceedings. Any credit balance on the new account would not be attached by the existing garnishee order, though it would be possible for the judgment creditor to obtain a second garnishee order to attach the balance on the new account, i.e. in cases where the balance on the original account was less than the judgment debt.

3-51 If a new account is not opened and it becomes necessary to refuse payment of cheques because the original account has been attached by a garnishee order, the cheques should be returned unpaid with the answer 'Refer to drawer'[49] or, more specifically, with the answer 'Funds attached by garnishee order'.

'Limited' garnishee orders

3-52 To overcome the hardship resulting from the making of 'unlimited' garnishee orders, the practice developed of limiting the effect of

---

48 [1892] AC 118, at pp. 121–2.
49 As advised in *Questions on Banking Practice* (11th ed., 1978), p. 134, Question 386.

a garnishee order *nisi*. The relevant words of a 'limited' order are that 'all debts owing or accuring due from the above-named garnishee to the above-named judgment debtor not exceeding the sum of £.... be attached'. There is no separate provision in the Rules of the Supreme Court for 'limited' orders of this type, but the practice is well established and it is certainly convenient. If a banker is served with a 'limited' order, and if the amount attached is less than the customer's credit balance, the practice is to transfer from the customer's account to a suspense account a sum sufficient to satisfy the order. The balance remaining on the customer's account is at his disposal, and the relationship of banker and customer will continue. The customer should be notified that a stated sum has been debited to his account in compliance with the terms of the garnishee order.

Garnishee summonses

3-53   Garnishee proceedings may be taken in the County Court, and the procedure is set out in Order 30 of the Country Court Rules. The procedure is very similar to that already explained above. Instead, however, of making a garnishee *order*, the Registrar of the County Court issues a garnishee *summons*.

3-54   When a banker is served with a garnishee summons, he will invariably find that it is 'limited' in amount. Indeed, it would seem that the County Court Rules at present in force no longer make any provision for the issue of an 'unlimited' garnishee summons.[50] The summons recites the amount of the judgment debt and costs, and continues as follows:

> AND TAKE NOTICE, that from and after the service of this Summons upon you so much of the debts owing or accruing from you to the Judgment Debtor as will satisfy the debt due under the said Judgment and the costs entered on this Summons are attached to answer the said Judgment.

Unlike a garnishee order, a garnishee summons then continues:

> AND FURTHER TAKE NOTICE that if you pay to the Registrar of this Court the amount of such debts, or so much thereof as will satisfy the debt due under the said Judgment and the costs entered on this Summons within eight days of the service of this Summons on you, inclusive of the day of service, you will incur no further costs.

3-55   A banker on whom a garnishee summons is served should take the same steps as have already been explained in regard to 'limited' garnishee orders, the only essential difference being that the banker may,

50 See Order 30.

and usually does, pay money into court within eight days after service upon him of the summons.

Additional rules relating to garnishee orders and summonses

As a result of reported cases and relevant statutes, the following rules relating to garnishee orders and summonses may be formulated.

3-56 *Rule 1.* The garnishee order *nisi* must state the name of the customer correctly or with sufficient accuracy to enable the bank to identify an account in its books as that of the judgment debtor.

3-57 Thus, in one case,[51] the bank informed the solicitors of the judgment creditor that they had no account in the name stated in the garnishee order. The solicitors asked the bank to attach a different account, which they said was the judgment debtor's, but the bank refused. Subsequently, the order was amended, but the bank was held not liable for having paid cheques on the account in the meantime.

3-58 *Rule 2.* The moneys attached are those standing to the customer's credit at the moment of service of the garnishee order *nisi* and for which he could sue.

This rule has various applications. Thus,

3-59 (a) In one case[52] a judgment creditor argued that moneys paid into the bank account of the judgment debtor *after* service of a garnishee summons could be attached. This argument was decisively rejected by the Court of Appeal. If, therefore, shares have been sold on a customer's instructions and the proceeds have not arrived at the time when a garnishee order *nisi* is served, the proceeds will not be attached by the order.

3-60 (b) Where a customer has more than one account at his bank, the moneys attached are those for which he could sue at the moment of service of the order. This application of *Rule 2* may be illustrated as follows:

3-61 *Example 1.* A customer has two current accounts. When No. 1 account is overdrawn £700, and No. 2 account is in credit £300, a garnishee order *nisi* is served. No moneys are thereby attached, because at the relevant date the customer could not sue the bank for any sum: he was indebted to the bank in the net sum of £400.

---

51 *Koch* v. *Mineral Ore Syndicate, London and South Western Bank Ltd, Garnishees* (1910) 54 Sol Jo 600.
52 *Heppenstall* v. *Jackson, Barclays Bank Ltd, Garnishees* [1939] 1 KB 585.

3-62 *Example 2.* A customer has a loan account and a current account. When the loan account stands at £500 and the current account is in credit £300, a garnishee order *nisi* is served. If the loan has not been called in at that date, the sum of £300 is thereby attached. This was so decided by Sir John Paget sitting temporarily as judge in the City of London Court in 1912.[53] The bank had claimed the right to combine the two accounts and set off the credit balance against part of the loan, but Sir John refused to admit this right. In the course of his Gilbart Lectures in the following year, Sir John set out at length his reasons for the decision.[54] He referred to the 'well-established rule' that to entitle a garnishee to defeat the claim of a judgment creditor by means of a set-off, such set-off must be in respect of an actual, immediate, recoverable debt due to the garnishee from the judgment debtor at the date of the service of the garnishee order *nisi*, a debt which, at that moment and without any preliminaries, the garnishee could have sued for and recovered.[55] Sir John referred to the case which he decided the previous year, and said that it was 'hopeless to contend' that such loan account constituted 'an actual immediately recoverable debt, or a set-off to the current account'.

3-63 (c) A customer, who has a credit balance at his bank, has discounted with the bank two bills for a total of £500. If a garnishee order *nisi* is served, it will attach the whole of the credit balance. The bank is not entitled to a lien on the credit balance in respect of the customer's contingent liability of £500 on the bills.[56]

3-64 (d) The proceeds of uncleared cheques paid in by the customer may or may not be attached depending upon whether or not the customer has the right to draw against the cheques before they are cleared.[57] This depends upon the agreement, express or implied, between the bank and the customer.

3-65 (e) A customer's instructions to transfer his balance to another customer of the same bank will not prevent the balance being attached by a garnishee order if the transferee has not been advised of the transfer, the instructions being revocable up to that point. Thus in one case[58] the first respondents, a Russian organization, instructed the

---

53 *Journal of the Institute of Bankers*, Vol. XXXIII (1912), p. 208.

54 *Journal of the Institute of Bankers*, Vol. XXXIV (1913), pp. 252–8.

55 *Tapp* v. *Jones* (1875) LR 10 QB 591.

56 *Bower* v. *Foreign and Colonial Gas Co. Ltd, Metropolitan Bank, Garnishees* (1874) 22 WR 740.

57 *Jones & Co.* v. *Coventry* [1909] 2 KB 1029, at p. 1044; *Fern* v. *Bishop & Co. Ltd* (1980) *Guardian Gazette*, 26 November.

58 *Rekstin* v. *Severo Sibirsko Gosudarstvennoe Akcionernoe Obschestvo Komseverputj, and The Bank for Russian Trade Ltd* [1933] 1 KB 47. This case was distinguished in *Momm* v. *Barclays Bank International Ltd* [1977] QB 790.

second respondents, their bankers, to transfer the whole of their credit balance to the account of the Trade Delegation of the USSR, a body enjoying diplomatic immunity. The transfer was completed in the books of the bank, and the account was closed. About a quarter of an hour later a garnishee order *nisi* was served on the bank purporting to attach the balance which had been transferred. The bank had not communicated the transfer to the Trade Delegation. The Court of Appeal held that at the time of service of the order, the relation of banker and customer still existed between the first respondents and the bank, and that a debt from the bank to them was due upon which the garnishee order *nisi* could operate. It was further held that the instruction given by the first respondents to the bank was still revocable at the time when the garnishee order *nisi* was served, and that the order operated in law as a revocation.

3-66 *Rule 3*. By way of exception to Rule 2, a deposit account balance may be attached, even though the customer cannot sue at the moment of service of the order.

3-67 The reason why a *current* account balance may be regarded as a debt 'owing or accruing' to the customer when a garnishee order *nisi* is served is because the service of such an order is said to constitute a sufficient demand by operation of law, to satisfy any right a banker may have as between himself and his customer to a demand before payment of moneys standing to the credit of a current account can be enforced.[59] So it amounts to this: even though the customer has made no demand for his current account balance, the law makes the demand for him and therefore his balance becomes 'owing or accruing' and attachable accordingly. This process of reasoning is somewhat refined, and the courts declined to extend it to balances on deposit accounts subject to notice of withdrawal. Such balances could not conceivably be regarded as debts 'owing or accruing' unless, of course, notice had actually been given at the date when the garnishee order was served. In *Bagley* v. *Winsome and National Provincial Bank Ltd*[60] an attempt was made to attach a deposit account, one of the terms of which was that fourteen days' notice of withdrawal should be given, and another that a personal application for payment should be made and the deposit book produced on withdrawal. The depositor had actually given notice of withdrawal fourteen days before the garnishee summons was issued and so the requisite period of notice had expired, but the Court of Appeal held that, although it had been established that a garnishee order *nisi* or a garnishee summons should be treated as equivalent to a demand by the

---

59 *Joachimson* v. *Swiss Bank Corporation* [1921] 3 KB 110, at p. 121, *per* Bankes LJ.
60 [1952] 2 QB 236.

judgment debtor, this principle could not be extended to make the order of summons satisfy the other conditions precedent to payment. Accordingly, the balance was not attached.

3-68 It was considered that technical considerations of this nature should not be allowed to prevail, and therefore s. 38(1) of the Administration of Justice Act 1956 enacted that a sum standing to the credit of a person in a deposit account in a bank is deemed to be a sum 'due or accruing' to that person and is attachable accordingly, notwithstanding that any of certain specified conditions have not been satisfied. These conditions are:

(a) any condition that notice is required before any money is withdrawn;

(b) any condition that a personal application must be made before any money is withdrawn;

(c) any condition that a deposit book must be produced before any money is withdrawn; and

(d) any condition that a receipt for money deposited in the account must be produced before any money is withdrawn.[61]

3-69 The practical result of the legislation is, therefore, that, as a general rule, deposit account balances may now be attached by garnishee proceedings. However, balances on the following accounts still cannot be attached by a garnishee order:[62]

(a) accounts in the National Savings Bank;

(b) accounts in the Trustee Savings Banks;

(c) accounts in any savings bank maintained in pursuance of any enactment by any local authority; or

(d) any account in any bank with two or more places of business if the terms applicable to that account permit withdrawals on demand, on production of a deposit book, at more than one of those places of business, with or without restrictions as to the amount which may be withdrawn. (Many banks conduct savings accounts for customers, which often fall within this exemption.[63])

3-69A *Rule 4.* A sum of foreign currency standing to the credit of a judgment debtor in the jurisdiction of the court may be attached by service of a garnishee order *nisi*, even though the judgment has been given in sterling.

---

61 This last condition was added by the Rules of the Supreme Court (No. 2) Order 1956, SI 1191, and is now incorporated in Order 49, rule 1 of the Rules of the Supreme Court.

62 Administration of Justice Act 1956, s. 38(2).

63 For savings accounts, see *ante*, para. 1-72.

3-69B In *Choice Investments Ltd* v. *Jeromnimon, Midland Bank Ltd, Garnishees*[64] the plaintiffs obtained judgment against Mr Jeromnimon for a sum in sterling. He did not pay. The plaintiffs discovered that he banked at the Midland Bank, Wigmore Street, London. Accordingly, they obtained a garnishee order *nisi* against the bank. Mr Jeromnimon had three accounts at the Midland Bank, two of which were in sterling and the third was a deposit account in United States dollars. The Court of Appeal held that the balances in all three accounts were attached. As regards the account in US dollars, Lord Denning MR said that, when the bank was served with the order *nisi*, they should have ascertained the buying rate at that moment. They should then have calculated the dollar equivalent of the sterling judgment, and put a stop order preventing those dollars from being taken out of the customer's account. If the order was made absolute, they should realize the 'stopped dollars' in order to acquire sterling for the purpose of satisfying the judgment. If the amount was not sufficient to satisfy the whole of the judgment debt, they must pay over the whole to the judgment creditor. If it was more than sufficient, they should only realize so many of the 'stopped dollars' as was sufficient to satisfy the judgment debt, and return the balance of the dollars for the benefit of their customer.

3-70 *Rule 5.* A joint account cannot be attached in respect of a debt owed by one of the parties.

3-71 The same rule applies to a partnership account. In one case[65] husband and wife had a joint account at a bank. A garnishee summons served on the bank named the husband alone as judgment debtor. The bank took the view that the summons did not attach the joint account and that they could not dishonour cheques drawn on the joint account. The Court of Appeal held, by a majority, that this view was correct.

3-72 *Rule 6.* A garnishee order *nisi* naming two judgment debtors will attach a balance standing in the name of one of them.
This should be contrasted with the preceding rule.

3-73 *Rule 7.* A liquidator's account cannot be attached in respect of a debt owed by the company of which he is the liquidator.

3-74 The reasoning underlying this rule is that a company and its liquidator are separate entities, and so money standing to the credit of the liquidator's account is not a debt owing to the company.[67]

64 [1981] 1 All ER 225.
65 *Hirschorn* v. *Evans, Barclays Bank Ltd, Garnishees* [1938] 2 KB 801.
66 *Miller* v. *Mynn* (1859) 28 LJQB 324.
67 *Lancaster Motor Company (London) Ltd* v. *Bremith Ltd, Barclays Bank Ltd, Garnishees* [1941] 1 KB 675.

3-75 *Rule 8.* Moneys standing to a customer's credit are attached by service of a garnishee order *nisi*, even though they are trust moneys.

3-76 In *Plunkett* v. *Barclays Bank Ltd*[68] the plaintiff, a solicitor, had opened two accounts at Barclays Bank, one being a Client account. On 7 September 1935, £48 5s. in cash was paid into the Client account, this sum representing rent and costs payable by a client to a third party. On 6 September a cheque for the same amount was drawn on the plaintiff's account and was sent to the solicitor acting for the third party. On 9 September application was made for a garnishee order *nisi* by the plaintiff's former wife, in respect of costs in her successful divorce proceedings against him. The order was made, and served on the defendant bank. The bank informed the plaintiff that the bank must regard both his accounts as being attached by the order. On 11 September the bank dishonoured the cheque for £48 5s. drawn on the Client account, with the answer 'Refer to drawer'. The plaintiff brought an action against the bank for alleged breach of contract by the dishonour of the cheque and for alleged libel in writing 'Refer to drawer' on it. The court held that the money standing to the credit of the Client account was a debt owing from the bank to the plaintiff, and therefore the garnishee order *nisi* attached that debt in the hands of the bank.[69] Accordingly, the bank was justified in returning the cheque unpaid.

3-77 It is obviously very inconvenient for a solicitor's Client account to be attached by a garnishee order *nisi* in respect of a debt owed by the solicitor personally. In the course of his judgment in *Plunkett's* case, du Parcq J said that it would be well that judgment creditors applying for garnishee orders *nisi* should realize that they might incur costs unnecessarily if the order was so drawn as to affect a Client account. It was always open to the creditor to ask the court to restrict the terms of a garnishee order *nisi* so that such an account would not be affected by it.

3-78 *Rule 9.* Balances held at a branch of a bank abroad cannot be attached by a garnishee order *nisi* of the courts of this country.

3-79 It has been held that foreign balances cannot be attached because they do not constitute a debt recoverable within the jurisdiction of the

---

68 [1936] 2 KB 107. See also *Harrods* v. *Tester* [1937] 2 All ER 236.

69 It does not follow from this that an order absolute would be made in respect of an account, like a solicitor's Client account, which consists of money held in trust. Indeed it would not: see *Hancock* v. *Smith* (1889) 41 Ch D 456. In *Plunkett's* case the solicitors for the judgment creditor, on being informed of the facts, very properly expressed their willingness that the garnishee order *nisi* should not be operative so far as the Client account was concerned.

English courts.[70] In principle, attachment of debts is a form of execution, and the general power of execution extends only to property within the jurisdiction of the court which orders it.'[71]

Section 8
WRITS OF SEQUESTRATION

3-80 The writ of sequestration is a mode of execution which is available where the person against whom it is issued is in contempt for disobedience of the court. It is, therefore, necessary as a preliminary to its issue that the judgment or order should have been served upon him, or at least that he should have knowledge of it and have intentionally evaded such service. The writ will not issue to enforce a judgment or order for the recovery of land or money.[72]

3-81 In *Eckman and others* v. *Midland Bank Ltd and Another*,[73] a union had been fined £5,000 for failing to comply with an order of the Industrial Relations Court. The fine was not paid, and writs of sequestration were issued. The sequestrators wrote to the union's bankers, Midland Bank Ltd and Hill, Samuel & Co. Ltd, but the banks refused to pay the balance of the union's accounts to the sequestrators without further order of the court. The sequestrators asked the Industrial Relations Court to make the appropriate order, and this was duly made. Sir John Donaldson P, delivering the judgment of the court, stated that in future cases a bank should make full disclosure to sequestrators and pay over to them the sums demanded by them without a specific order to that effect. However, the attitude of the Midland Bank and of Hill, Samuel had not been unreasonable in view of the state of the law, and so no order for costs was made.

Section 9
OUTBREAK OF WAR

3-82 In the course of his speech in *Arab Bank Ltd*. v. *Barclays Bank (Dominion, Colonial and Overseas)*,[74] Lord Reid said:

---

70 *Richardson* v. *Richardson, National Bank of India Ltd, Garnishees* [1927] P 228.
71 *Ibid.*, at p. 235, *per* Hill J.
72 For further details relating to the writ of sequestration, see *Halsbury's Laws of England* (4th ed.), Vol. 17, pp. 309–16.
73 [1973] 1 All ER 609. See also *Miller* v. *Huddlestone* (1882) 22 Ch D 233; *Re Pollard, Pollard* v. *Pollard* (1902) 87 LT 61; *Guerrine (otherwise Roberts)* v. *Guerrine* [1959] 1 WLR 760; *Bucknell* v. *Bucknell* [1969] 1 WLR 1204.
74 [1954] AC 495, at p. 530. See also *Ertel Bieber & Co.* v. *Rio Tinto Co. Ltd* [1918] AC 260.

With certain exceptions the outbreak of war prevents the further performance of contracts between persons in this country and persons in enemy territory. It is not merely that an enemy cannot sue during the war, and that trading and intercourse with the enemy during the war are illegal. Many kinds of contractual rights are totally abrogated by the outbreak of war and do not revive on its termination. On the other hand, there are other kinds of contractual rights which are not abrogated; they cannot be enforced during the war, but war merely suspends the right to enforce them and they remain and can be enforced after the war.

Accordingly, the question arises whether the contractual rights between banker and customer are abrogated if the parties become separated by the line of war. The question was exhaustively explored in the *Arab Bank* case, from which the following principles emerge.

3-83 The ordinary performance of the contract between banker and customer is prevented by the outbreak of war, with the result that banking services cannot be performed.[75] Thus, no items may be paid into the account, and no cheques drawn on the account may be honoured.

3-84 A customer's right 'to be paid a credit balance on a current account is a right which survives' the outbreak of war.[76] The right is suspended, and not destroyed.[77]

3-85 Additionally, however, one often finds that when war breaks out, legislation is enacted whereby the assets (including bank balances) of enemy subjects are vested in an official described as a Custodian of Enemy Property. The legislation may provide that bank balances of enemy subjects must be paid to the Custodian, who is empowered to give a discharge therefor. If and when that happens, it is clear that the relationship between banker and customer will be determined.

3-86 In essence, that is what happened in the *Arab Bank* case. War broke out between Israel and the Arab States. The Arab Bank had a balance of over half a million pounds with the Jerusalem branch of Barclays Bank (DCO). The Arab Bank's premises in Jerusalem were in Arab-controlled territory, and Barclay's premises in Jerusalem were in Israeli territory. By virtue of Israeli legislation, the property of absentees (a term which included the Arab Bank) was vested in a custodian. He demanded payment from Barclays of the large credit balance of the

---

75 [1954] AC 495, at p. 534 *per* Lord Reid. At p. 536 Lord Tucker referred to the outbreak of war as being 'the event which closed the account'. But in view of para. 3-84, this may, with respect, be an unfortunate choice of expression.

76 [1954] AC 495, at p. 529, *per* Lord Morton of Henryton.

77 *Ibid*. See also p. 535, *per* Lord Reid, and p. 541, *per* Lord Cohen.

Arab Bank, and Barclays paid this balance to him. The Arab Bank maintained that Barclays ought to have refused payment, and they sued Barclays for this sum. Parker, J, the Court of Appeal and the House of Lords, dismissed the action on the ground that the right to be paid the credit balance, being locally situate in Israel, became subject to the legislation of that State, and vested in the custodian, and was not recoverable by the Arab Bank from Barclays.

PART 2

Banking operations

4

Negotiable instruments

The collection, discounting and payment of negotiable instruments form a substantial part of the work of a bank. This introductory chapter is concerned with their characteristics and with the principal types of negotiable and 'quasi-negotiable' instruments.

Section I
CHARACTERISTICS OF NEGOTIABLE INSTRUMENTS

4-1 The essential characteristics of a negotiable instrument are:[1]

(a) The instrument and the rights which it embodies are capable of being transferred by delivery, either with or without endorsement according as to whether the instrument is in favour of order or bearer; an instrument thus transferred is said to be negotiated.

(b) The person to whom the instrument is negotiated can sue on it in his own name.

(c) The person to whom a current and apparently regular negotiable instrument has been negotiated, who takes it in good faith and for value, obtains a good title to it, even though his transferor had a defective title or no title at all.

Unless an instrument possesses the three characteristics mentioned above, it is not a negotiable instrument. Certain points arising out of these characteristics require further comment.

Mode of transfer

4-2 If a negotiable instrument is payable simply to bearer or to a named person 'or bearer', it may be negotiated to another person by mere delivery, that is to say, by transfer of possession, actual or constructive, from one person to another.[2] If a negotiable instrument is

---

1 *Cf.* Blackburn J in *Crouch* v. *The Crédit Foncier Co.* (1873) LR 8 QB 374, at p. 381.
2 As regards instruments falling within the Bills of Exchange Act 1882, the rule stated in the text is codified in ss 2 and 31(2) of the Act.

payable to a named person 'or order', the instrument may be negotiated to another person by endorsement and delivery, that is to say, the person to whom the instrument is payable must write or 'endorse' his name upon it before delivering it to someone else.[3]

4-3 The valuable mercantile custom of negotiating bills of exchange by endorsement was adopted in England during the first half of the seventeenth century. In his book entitled *Lex Mercatoria* which was first published in 1622, Gerard de Malynes made no reference to it. Some thirty years later, John Marius wrote his *Advice concerning Bils of Exchange*, and that book was the first to explain the practice of endorsing bills of exchange.[4] An interesting feature of this development is that the merchants did not wait for Parliament to declare that bills of exchange could be negotiated by endorsement. Among themselves, the merchants began to treat bills of exchange as transferable in this manner, and subsequently judicial recognition was given to their practice.[5]

Transferee's title

4-4 If goods are stolen, the thief clearly has no title to them. If he transfers them, whether by sale or otherwise, to an innocent third party, that party does not acquire a good title to them.[6] This is the result of the application of the common law maxim *nemo dat quod non habet* – 'no one can give what he has not got'.

4-5 In regard to negotiable instruments, however, the legal position is very different. A thief or a finder or a person who obtains a negotiable instrument by fraud does not acquire a good title to it. But if he negotiates it to an innocent third party, who takes it in good faith and for value, that party will acquire a perfect title to it, provided always that the instrument is current[7] and that it appears to be regular. There is an exception to this rule where an essential signature on the instrument has been forged; in that case an innocent third party cannot thereafter acquire a good title to the instrument because, in English law, a good title cannot be acquired through a forgery.[8] By way of illustration, if a

---

3 As regards instruments falling within the 1882 Act, the rule stated in the text is codified in s. 31(3) of the Act. The Act uses the spelling *indorsement*, but *endorsement* is more usual in commercial practice today.

4 See J. Milnes Holden, *The History of Negotiable Instruments in English Law* (1955), pp. 45–6.

5 See, for example, *Clark* v. *Pigot* (1699) 1 Salk 126, probably the first reported decision on endorsements.

6 But he does get a good title if the goods are sold to him in market overt; see Sale of Goods Act 1979, s. 22.

7 This means that it must not have been in circulation for such a length of time as would make the transaction appear to be suspicious.

8 *Cf.* Bills of Exchange Act 1882, s. 24.

cheque which is payable to a named person or order is stolen before the payee has endorsed it and the thief forges the payee's endorsement, no innocent third party can ever acquire a good title to it.

4-6 The rule which enables an innocent third party to obtain a perfect title to a negotiable instrument from a person who has no title or a defective title was based upon the custom of merchants. It was first recognized by the Common Law courts and by the court of Chancery at the end of the seventeenth century. A clear illustration is provided by a case decided by Holt CJ in 1699.[9] An instrument described as a 'Bank bill' [10] payable to A or bearer had been given to A and had been lost. It was found by a stranger, who transferred it to C for value. Holt CJ held that A, the loser of the bill, could maintain an action against the stranger 'for he had no title', but that A could not maintain an action against C 'by reason of the course of trade, *which creates a property in the assignee or bearer'.* [11]

Section 2
TYPES OF NEGOTIABLE AND QUASI-NEGOTIABLE INSTRUMENTS

4-7 The list of negotiable instruments is not a closed one. It is true that no additions have been made to the list in recent years, but this is probably because most instruments which could conceivably be regarded as negotiable had been considered by the courts before the end of the nineteenth century. It is, however, always possible that new types of instrument may come into use, and it would certainly be competent for the courts to decide whether or not they were negotiable.

Negotiable instruments

The following are the principal types of negotiable instrument which may be encountered in modern practice: [12]

9 *Anon.* (1699) 1 Salk 126; 3 Salk 71. See also *Hussey* v. *Jacob* (1696) 1 Comyns 4, another decision of Holt CJ, and *Anon.* (1697) 1 Comyns 43, a decision of Lord Somers in the Court of Chancery.
10 It seems likely that the instrument had been issued by the newly established Bank of England.
11 Author's italics.
12 For a more comprehensive list of instruments which have been recognized as negotiable, see J. Milnes Holden, *The History of Negotiable Instruments in English Law* (1955), pp. 244–69.

(a) Bills of exchange

4-8   Bills of exchange include cheques. [13]

(b) Promissory notes

4-9   Promissory notes include banknotes. [14]

(c) Bankers' drafts

4-10   These drafts are not bills of exchange in cases where the same bank is both drawer and drawee. [15] Nevertheless, it is enacted that where the drawer and drawee of a 'bill' are the same person, the *holder* may treat the instrument, at his option, either as a bill of exchange or as a promissory note. [16] It would be open to the court to decide that bankers' drafts are negotiable instruments by virtue of that provision; alternatively, the court would probably have no hesitation in holding that bankers' drafts are negotiable by usage.

(d) Travellers' cheques

4-11   These cheques are frequently used by persons journeying in this country and abroad. [17] There are two types in common use. Instruments of the first type are drawn by a person, usually a customer, to whom they are issued, in favour of 'self or order'. They are countersigned by the issuing bank. Instruments of the second type are drawn by the issuing bank upon itself. Each correspondent of the bank is supplied direct with authority to cash them together with specimen instruments and facsimile signatures of its signing officials. To guard against fraud, the customer is generally required to write in his name on each travellers' cheque in the presence of the issuing bank and to countersign each instrument in the presence of the correspondent. The two signatures are then compared. Travellers' cheques have been held by courts in the United States to be negotiable, [18] but there does not appear to be any reported English decision upon this subject.

---

13 *Post*, para. 5-6.
14 *Post*, para. 9-60.
15 Bills of Exchange Act 1882, s. 3(1) and (2); *London City and Midland Bank Ltd* v. *Gordon* [1903] AC 240, at p. 250. The decision of Bailhache J to the contrary in *Ross* v. *London County, Westminster, and Parr's Bank Ltd* [1919] 1 KB 678, at p. 687, must be regarded as erroneous.
16 Bills of Exchange Act 1882, s. 5(2).
17 On the subject of travellers' cheques, see E. P. Ellinger, 'Travellers' cheques and the Law', *University of Toronto Law Journal*, Vol. 19 (1969), pp. 132–56.
18 *Mellon National Bank* v. *Citizens' Bank & Trust Co.*, 8 Cir. 1937, 88 F. 2d 128; *Emerson* v. *American Express Co.* (1952) 90 Atlantic Reporter, 2d series, 236.

4-11A In *Braithwaite* v. *Thomas Cook Travellers Cheques Ltd*[19] the plaintiff purchased £50,000 worth of travellers' cheques from Thomas Cook Travellers Cheques Ltd in Jersey on 12 February 1987. Within 24 hours he claimed that they had all been lost or stolen on the London Underground, and he asked Thomas Cook for reimbursement of the purchase price. They refused to pay, because they were suspicious of him and put him to proof of his claim.

After collecting the travellers' cheques in Jersey, the plaintiff put them in a brown envelope, which he placed in a transparent plastic bag, and flew back to London the same day. The conditions of purchase stated that the issuer would replace or refund the face value of any travellers' cheques lost or stolen provided that the purchaser had 'properly safeguarded each cheque against loss or theft'. When the plaintiff arrived in London he spent the evening drinking with friends and then took the Underground home. In the course of the journey he fell asleep, and when he got off the Underground he realized that he no longer had the plastic bag. He claimed the value of the cheques from the defendants on the ground that the cheques had been lost or stolen.

Schieman J held that where an agreement for the purchase of travellers' cheques contained an express condition that the purchaser should properly safeguard the cheques against loss or theft, the whole of the purchaser's behaviour had to be considered when determining whether he had in fact properly safeguarded them. Taking into account the facts that the plaintiff had carried the cheques in a transparent bag instead of concealing them about his person and that he had fallen asleep on the Underground because he was tired and had been drinking, the plaintiff could not be said to have properly safeguarded the cheques and, therefore, he was not entitled to reimbursement of their face value.

Nevertheless, judgment was given for the plaintiff for £16,000 with interest on certain undertakings by him to indemnify the defendants. The sum of £16,000 was in respect of three categories of cheques. In the first category were certain cheques which the defendants had recovered before any money had been paid out against them. In the second category were cheques where, although they were presented and paid, the payer had not recovered from the defendants, who had successfully argued that the payer had been negligent in making the payment. In the third category were cheques where no attempt had been made to cash them. The defendants were prepared to reimburse the plaintiff in respect of these cheques, subject to a condition that he agreed to indemnify them if they were successfully sued by the payer.

4-11B By a coincidence, another case, *Elawadi* v. *Bank of Credit and*

19 [1989] 1 All ER 235.

Commerce International SA,[20] which also arose out of the loss or theft of a large amount of travellers' cheques, was tried in the same month as the case noted in the preceding paragraph. In *Elawadi's* case the cheques were stolen from the plaintiff's unlocked car, largely as a result of his negligence, and £40,700 worth were subsequently cashed. The defendant bank refused to refund to the plaintiff the full value of the stolen cheques, agreeing only to refund the sum of £9,300 in respect of those cheques which had not been cashed. The principal issue was whether the plaintiff's negligence in safeguarding the cheques disentitled him from recovering the value of the cheques from the defendant bank. Hutchison J held that, on the true construction of the contract entered into by the plaintiff and the defendant bank, there was an obligation on the part of the bank to refund lost or stolen cheques regardless of the plaintiff's negligence in safeguarding them. Accordingly, the defendant bank was ordered to pay the £40,700 claimed.

(e) Treasury bills

4-12   These bills were first issued under the provisions of the Treasury Bills Act 1877. The practice is for the Treasury to advertise for tenders, and the bills are issued at the best price that can be obtained for them. There does not appear to be any decision of the courts recognizing Treasury bills as negotiable instruments, but they are similar in form and purpose to earlier instruments known as Exchequer bills, which were first issued in 1696[21] and were recognized in 1820 as negotiable.[22] Hence there would seem to be no doubt that Treasury bills are negotiable.

(f) Bearer bonds

4-13   A bond, in the widest legal sense, is any obligation under seal, but, for present purposes, the obligation is that of repaying a sum of money. If the bond promises payment to bearer, the instrument is a bearer bond. As early as 1824 bearer bonds issued by the king of Prussia were recognized as negotiable by the English courts.[23] The question whether English bonds were negotiable gave rise to a good deal of litigation during the second half of the nineteenth century. The outcome of this litigation was that English bonds were eventually recognized as negotiable.[24] In 1904 it was held that various bearer bonds, some issued

---

20 [1989] 1 All ER 242.
21 Their issue was authorized by an Act of Parliament, 7 & 8 Will 3. The first Exchequer bill was issued on 14 July 1696, and they became a permanent feature of English public finance. The entries of 14 July 1696, are preserved at the Public Record Office, reference *Recs. Ex. R., Certificates of Exchequer Bills*, 406/89.
22 *Wookey* v. *Pole* (1820) 4 B & Ald 1.
23 *Gorgier* v. *Mieville* (1824) 3 B & C 45.
24 The numerous decisions are examined in Holden, *op. cit.*, pp. 251–4.

by an English company in England and others by foreign companies abroad, were negotiable and that the usage was so well established that it was no longer necessary to prove it in evidence.[25]

(g) Warehousekeepers' warrants

4-14 Private Acts of Parliament have made *some* warehousekeepers' warrants fully negotiable instruments.[26]

Quasi-negotiable instruments

4-15 There are some instruments which possess the first two characteristics of a negotiable instrument, but not the third; in other words, a transferee takes them subject to any defects in the title of prior parties. Such instruments are sometimes referred to as 'quasi-negotiable' or 'semi-negotiable' in order to distinguish them from instruments which are fully negotiable. Some common examples of quasi-negotiable instruments are:

(a) Postal orders

4-16 In a case decided in 1886,[27] it was held by the Court of Appeal that 'post office orders' were not negotiable. It is considered, on the authority of that case, that postal orders of the type issued today are not negotiable. Moreover, postal orders bear on their face the words 'not negotiable'.

(b) Bills of Lading

4-17 A bill of lading is a document signed by the master of a ship or by his agent and given to the person shipping goods on board the vessel. The document performs three functions: first it is evidence of the terms of a contract of affreightment, secondly it is evidence of the shipment of goods, and thirdly it is evidence that the holder of it has the property in the goods. It states that the goods will be delivered to 'X or his assigns' or to 'X or order' and, when endorsed in blank by X, it passes by delivery. Thus, the delivery of an endorsed bill 'is equivalent to delivery of the goods themselves, and is effectual to transfer ownership if made with that intention. The bill of lading is the symbol of the

---

25 *Edelstein* v. *Schuler & Co.* [1902] 2 KB 144.
26 See Holden, *op. cit.*, pp. 261–2.
27 *Fine Art Society* v. *The Union Bank of London Ltd* (1886) 17 QBD 705.

goods.'[28] Another characteristic of a bill of lading is that an endorsee thereof 'shall have transferred to and vested in him all rights of suit'.[29] But the third characteristic of a negotiable instrument is lacking: an endorsee who gives value in good faith is unable to obtain a better title than his transferor had.[30]

28 *Per* Lord Sumner, delivering the judgment of the Privy Council in *The Prinz Adalbert* [1917] **AC** 586, at p. 589.
29 Bills of Lading Act 1855, s. 1.
30 Thus Lord Campbell CJ in *Gurney* v. *Behrend* (1854) 3 E & B 622, at pp. 633–4 said: 'A bill of lading is not, like a bill of exchange or promissory note, a negotiable instrument, which passes by mere delivery to a *bona fide* transferee for valuable consideration, without regard to the title of the parties who make the transfer.'

5

The drawing, issue and negotiation of cheques

This chapter deals with the manner in which cheques should be drawn, issued and negotiated. Then in Chapters 6 and 7 attention will be directed to the law and practice relating to the collection and payment of cheques.

Section I
ESSENTIALS OF A CHEQUE

5-1 A brief reference has already been made to the origin of the cheque.[1] It will be recalled that about the middle of the seventeenth century, merchants began to draw 'bills' or 'notes' upon their accounts with the goldsmiths and to hand these instruments to their creditors in payment of their debts. The instruments were drawn in favour of the creditor 'or order' or in favour of him 'or bearer'.

5-2 One of the earliest of these instruments still in existence today is in the collection of the Chartered Institute of Bankers, and is dated 14 August 1675.[2] The instrument was addressed to a goldsmith named Thomas Fowles, and it reads as follows:

> *Mr. Thomas ffowles*
> *I desire you to pay unto Mr. Samuel Howard or order upon receipt hereof the sume of nine pounds thirteene shillings and six pence and place it to the account of*
> *14th Aug. 1675   Yr. Servant*
> *£9 : 13 : 6   Edmond Warcupp*
> *ffor Mr. Thomas ffowles Gouldsmith at his shop betweene the two Temple gates. ffleetstreete.*

1 See *ante*, para. 2-4.
2 A photograph of the instrument was published in the *Journal of the Institute of Bankers*, Vol. LIX (1938), facing p. 415, and also in J. Milnes Holden, *The History of Negotiable Instruments in English Law* (1955), plate V*a*, following p. 350. For a photograph of an even earlier instrument of a similar character, see J. Milnes Holden, 'Cheques: Then and Now', *Progress*, Vol. 45 (1957), pp. 285–8.

It will be noticed that the form of the instrument is very similar to that of a modern cheque, even though the language employed is somewhat different: modern customers do not sign themselves 'Your servant' when writing to their bank managers.

5-3 The word 'cheque' – or rather *check* as it was spelt at first – did not come into use until the eighteenth century. The modern spelling of the word was adopted about the middle of the nineteenth century. The 1827 edition of Joseph Chitty's work on *Bills of Exchange* used the old spelling *check*. The following year J. W. Gilbart published his *Practical Treatise on Banking*. He used the modern spelling 'cheque', and he explained that he had adopted that spelling because it was free from ambiguity and was analogous to *ex-chequer*, the royal treasury.[3] One cannot say whether Gilbart's practice was a decisive factor in bringing about a change, but it is noteworthy that the 1859 edition of *Chitty* adopted the new style.

Cheques as negotiable instruments

5-4 The late Sir William Holdsworth expressed the view that, from the first, the order given by a customer to a banker to pay a sum of money was 'regarded as a bill of exchange', and therefore negotiable.[4] As will be shown presently, the courts have had no hesitation in holding that orders given by customers to their bankers to pay a sum of money were negotiable instruments, and to that extent Holdsworth's view is undoubtedly sound. It may, however, be misleading to say that the order given by a customer to his banker to pay a sum of money was *regarded* as a bill of exchange. It *was* a bill of exchange. An instrument drawn upon X ordering him to pay a sum of money on demand was a bill of exchange, and it would not cease to be a bill of exchange merely because X was a banker.

5-5 The decisions of the courts concerning the negotiability of cheques are all one way. In a case decided in 1764[5] Lord Mansfield and Wilmot and Yates JJ took the view that a bill drawn by a customer upon his banker was a negotiable instrument. In another case in 1797[6] counsel argued that banknotes and other like notes were negotiable, and were so considered by the parties, whereas a 'banker's check' was not so considered. Lord Kenyon CJ rejected this argument and said that the contention that 'banker's checks' were not considered by merchants as

3 J. W. Gilbart, *Practical Treatise on Banking* (1828), p. 14.
4 W. S. Holdsworth, *A History of English Law*, Vol. VIII, p. 190. For a different view see C. H. S. Fifoot, 'The development of the law of negotiable instruments and of the law of trusts', *Journal of the Institute of Bankers*, Vol. LIX (1938), p. 451.
5 *Grant* v. *Vaughan* (1764) 3 Burr 1516.
6 *Boehm* v. *Sterling* (1797) 7 TR 423.

negotiable instruments appeared to him to be 'most extraordinary'.[7] The last occasion when a litigant sought to argue that a cheque was not a negotiable instrument was in 1860.[8] Again, the argument failed. One of the judges in that case, Byles J, remarked that it seemed clear to him that 'a cheque falls within the class of ordinary bills of exchange'.[9] In effect, statutory recognition was given to those observations by the Bills of Exchange Act 1882, which enacted that a cheque is a bill of exchange drawn on a banker payable on demand.[10]

Definition of a cheque

5-6 If two sections of the Bills of Exchange Act 1882 are read together, a cheque may be said to be defined by the Act as an unconditional order in writing addressed by one person to another, who must be a banker, signed by the person giving it, requiring the banker to pay on demand a sum certain in money to or to the order of a specified person or to bearer.[11]

5-7 The person who draws a cheque is known as the drawer; the banker on whom the cheque is drawn is called the drawee banker or the paying banker; and the person to whom the cheque is drawn payable is known as the payee. The drawer may draw a cheque payable to himself; in that event the drawer and the payee are the same person.

The following points arising out of the definition of a cheque require consideration.

(a) Unconditional order

5-8 The question has arisen whether an instrument in the form of a cheque which includes a form of receipt to be signed by the payee complies with the definition of a cheque. The legal effect of such an instrument depends upon the construction to be placed upon the language used. If the banker is ordered to pay conditionally on the payee's signing the receipt, then the instrument is a conditional order and not a cheque, because the order is not unconditional.[12] But if the order relating to the completion of the receipt is to be construed as addressed to the payee, the instrument is a cheque.[13]

---

7 7 TR, at p. 430.
8 *Keene* v. *Beard* (1860) 8 CB (NS) 372.
9 8 CB (NS), at p. 381.
10 S. 73.
11 Ss 3(1) and 73.
12 *Capital and Counties Bank Ltd* v. *Gordon* [1903] AC 240, at p. 252; *Bavins, Junr & Sims* v. *London and South Western Bank Ltd* [1900] 1 QB 270. But the instrument would fall within the provisions of the Cheques Act 1957, ss 1(2)(a), 4(2)(b) and 5.
13 *Nathan* v. *Ogdens Ltd* (1905) 94 LT 126.

5-9 Modern cheque forms occasionally provide that the instrument must be presented for payment within a prescribed period. A provision of that nature does not make an order conditional;[14] but, as soon as the period has expired, the instrument is no longer an effective mandate to the drawee bank.

5-10 An instrument may be a valid cheque if it indicates the particular account of the drawer which is to be debited with the amount. Such an order is an unconditional order within the meaning of the Bills of Exchange Act 1882.[15]

(b) In writing

5-11 The Bills of Exchange Act 1882 provides that writing includes print.[16] Accordingly, a cheque prepared on a typewriter would be valid, but in practice bankers discourage customers from preparing their cheques in this way because of the comparative ease with which typewritten cheques can be fraudulently altered. There are special machines in use today for the preparation of cheques; they impress the characters into the paper with the result that any attempt at alteration would be obvious. As regards handwriting, customers should always be encouraged to draw their cheques in ink. Cheques drawn in indelible pencil are still paid by some bankers, especially in country districts; but cheques drawn in lead-pencil are returned unpaid.

5-12 There is a dearth of authority as to the material upon which a cheque should be written. Drawers of cheques have lacked the originality which has inspired testators. No drawer has yet baffled his banker by drawing a cheque on an eggshell, whereas an attempt was once made (unsuccessfully, as it happened) to prove a will written thereon.[17] In practice, it is desirable that bankers should make it clear, when opening a new account, that cheques should be drawn on the special forms which they provide. These forms are printed on special paper which tends to make fraudulent alteration difficult.[18]

(c) By one person to another

5-13 If an instrument is drawn by a banker upon himself, it is not a

14 *Thairlwall* v. *Great Northern Railway Co.* [1910] 2 KB 509.
15 S. 3(3).
16 S. 2.
17 *In the Goods of Barnes, Hodson* v. *Barnes* (1926) 96 LJP 26.
18 Moreover, by advising customers to use the proper forms, bankers will ensure, as far as possible, that they will not be confronted with Sir Alan Herbert's amusing problem of a cheque written on the back and sides of a cow: see A. P. Herbert, *Uncommon Law*, and *Codd's Last Case*.

cheque because it is not addressed by one person to another; it is a banker's draft. Nevertheless, the Bills of Exchange Act 1882 provides that the holder of such an instrument may treat it, at his option, either as a bill of exchange or as a promissory note.[19]

(d) Signed by person giving it

5-14 Large companies and corporations, after giving an indemnity to their bankers, sometimes issue instruments in the form of cheques which bear a printed facsimile reproduction of the signature of some official who is too busy to sign personally and who usually never sees the instruments. The questions may some day arise whether such instruments are valid cheques and whether the so-called drawers could be held liable thereon.[20]

(e) Payable on demand

5-15 An instrument is payable on demand when it is expressed to be so payable, or when it is drawn payable at sight, or on presentation, or when no time for payment is expressed.[21]

(f) Sum certain in money

5-16 There is no provision in the Bills of Exchange Act 1882 which requires the amount to be stated both in words and in figures, but in practice the cheque forms issued by the banks always contain spaces for words and figures. If the amount stated in words differs from the amount stated in figures, one might have thought that the instrument would not be a cheque, on the ground that it did not order payment of a sum *certain* in money; the amount would seem to be uncertain. However, this reasoning appears to be unsound, because the Act contemplates the possibility of a discrepancy between the words and figures, and it specifically provides that where there is such a discrepancy, the sum denoted by the words is the amount payable.[22] In practice, bankers usually return such cheques unpaid with the answer 'Words and figures differ'. If, however, the amount claimed on the cheque is the amount in figures and that is the smaller amount, some banks will pay that amount, at any rate in cases where the discrepancy between the words and figures is not large.

19 S. 5(2).
20 See *Meyappan* v. *Manchanayake* [1961] Ceylon NLR 529, a decision of the Supreme Court of Ceylon concerning cheques bearing rubber stamp endorsements, noted in the *Journal of the Institute of Bankers.* Vol. 83 (1962), pp. 178–9. See also *Goodman* v. *J. Eban Ltd* [1954] 1 QB 550; *Lazarus Estates Ltd* v. *Beasley* [1956] 1 QB 702.
21 Bills of Exchange Act 1882, s. 10(1).
22 S. 9(2).

(g) Payable to specified person or bearer

5-17   Customers sometimes fill in cheque forms by ordering payment 'to cash or order'. Such instruments are not cheques, because 'cash' (or any other impersonal payee) is not a 'specified person'.[23] They are, however, valid orders for the payment of money, and they fall within the provisions of the Cheques Act 1957.[24]

Dating a cheque

5-18   There is no legal requirement that a cheque should be dated: the Bills of Exchange Act 1882 provides that it is not invalid merely because the date is omitted.[25] In practice, however, the drawee banker sometimes refuses to pay a cheque which is not dated and returns it with the answer 'Date required'.[26] A simpler course is for the drawee banker to insert the date, and this is authorized by the Bills of Exchange Act 1882, which provides that when a bill is wanting in any material particular, the person in possession of it has a prima facie authority to fill up the omission in any way he thinks fit.[27]

5-19   Furthermore, a cheque is not invalid by reason only that it is ante-dated or post-dated, or that it bears date on a Sunday.[28] An ante-dated cheque is one that bears date before the date of issue; a post-dated cheque is one dated later than the date of issue.[29] A cheque bearing date on a Sunday should not be paid until the next business day.

Exemption from stamp duty

5-20/29   The stamp duty on cheques was abolished by the Finance Act 1970.[30]

---

23 *North and South Insurance Corporation Ltd* v. *National Provincial Bank Ltd* [1936] 1 KB 328; *Cole* v. *Milsome* [1951] 1 All ER 311; *Orbit Mining & Trading Co. Ltd* v. *Westminster Bank Ltd* [1962] 3 All ER 565.

24 Ss. 1(2)(a), 4(2)(b) and 5.

25 S. 3(4)(a). It may be, however, that an undated cheque is not 'complete and regular on the face of it' within s. 29(1), with the result that a holder could not be a holder in due course.

26 The practice was discussed in *Griffiths* v. *Dalton* [1940] 2 KB 264, but in that case the cheque had been dated before it was presented for payment.

27 S. 20(1).

28 S. 13(2).

29 For post-dated cheques, see *post*, para. 7-16.

30 S. 32 and Sched. 7. In the first edition of this book, paras 5-20/29 dealt with the stamp duty on cheques and listed the principal exemptions from duty. In view of the abolition of the duty, this material has been omitted.

Cheques bearing characters in magnetic ink

5-30   Many banks use computers for the purpose of maintaining customers' accounts. An essential part of the system is that cheque forms
supplied to customers bear upon their face in magnetic ink certain
reading characters denoting the branch of the bank upon which they are
drawn and also the particular account to be debited. It obviously creates
confusion if a customer alters in ink the name of the drawee branch,
because he has no means of altering the magnetic ink characters.

5-31   In *Burnett* v. *Westminster Bank Ltd,*[31] a customer endeavoured
to countermand payment of a cheque which he had altered in this way.
Unfortunately, he addressed his instructions to the branch as altered,
whereas the computer sent the cheque to the original branch, where
there was no record of the countermand. The cheque was paid, and the
question which the court had to decide was whether the customer or the
drawee bank must suffer the loss. Mocatta J held that the bank must be
the loser. Although the bank had printed a warning on the cover of the
cheque book warning the customer that the cheques would be applied to
the account for which they had been prepared, there was no evidence
that the customer had read the notice, which had only recently appeared
on those covers. Accordingly, the learned judge held that, as the customer had long had accounts with the bank, the notice did not bind him
to the new restricted use of the cheques for only one account.

Section 2
CROSSINGS ON CHEQUES

5-32   The general rule of English law is that the posting of a cheque,
or of money, which is lost before it reaches the creditor does not amount
to payment, unless the creditor requested the debtor to pay in that
manner, in which case he would be taken to have run the risk of its being
lost.[32] In one case,[33] the defendants had bought goods from the plaintiff
for many years, and had paid for them by means of cheques sent by
post. The plaintiff had never objected to being paid in that way. A
cheque for £503 sent by post by the defendants to the plaintiff was never
received by the plaintiff. A stranger opened a bank account with it, and
it was paid. The Court of Appeal held that it was impossible to infer that
the plaintiff had requested payment by cheque sent through the post,
and so the loss fell upon the defendants, the drawers of the cheque.

31 [1966] 1 QB 742.
32 See the authorities cited in *Halsbury's Laws of England* (4th ed.), Vol. 9, p. 346.
33 *Pennington* v. *Crossley & Son* (1897) 77 LT 43.

5-33 Thus it is clear that, in his own interests, the drawer of a cheque should take all possible precautions to ensure that persons who are not entitled to it cannot obtain value for it. If the drawer issued an open, that is to say, an uncrossed cheque a thief could present it to the drawee bank and obtain cash for it. It is true that if the cheque was payable to a named payee or order, the drawee bank would not pay it unless it purported to be endorsed by the payee; but the thief could easily forge the payee's endorsement, and as the drawee bank would be unlikely to know the genuine signature of the payee, the chances are that the thief would succeed in obtaining payment in cash from the drawee bank.

5-34 Therefore, as a general rule, the drawer should not issue an open cheque in favour of a third party, unless he is specifically requested to do so or unless he delivers the cheque to the payee or to his authorized agent, because, as Cockburn CJ said, if a cheque is delivered in payment to the payee or to his authorized agent, the cheque operates as payment and extinguishes the debt, subject only to the condition that, if upon due presentment the cheque is not paid, the original debt revives.[34] In this chapter, attention will be drawn to the various ways of crossing a cheque. The subject will be examined primarily from the point of view of the drawer. In Chapters 6 and 7 some special problems of the collecting banker and paying banker respectively will be considered.

Origin of crossings

5-35 The way in which crossings originated and the manner in which they developed — particularly the ways in which new crossings were introduced, such as the 'Not negotiable' and 'Account payee' crossings — is one of the most fascinating chapters in the history of cheques.[35] The practice of crossing cheques began towards the end of the eighteenth century. In the first place, the custom was simply part of the machinery of the bankers' Clearing House. At the Clearing House, every banker was provided with a drawer, on which his name was affixed, and each day the clerks from the other banks would deposit in that drawer cheques drawn upon that particular banker. As a means of ascertaining by whom the various cheques had been put into the drawer of any one banker, the name of the collecting banker was written across the face of each cheque by one of his clerks.

5-36 Gradually, the drawers of cheques came to know of this practice, and they thought that it would be a useful safeguard against loss or theft

---

34 *Charles* v. *Blackwell* (1877) 2 CPD 151, at p. 158.
35 For a fuller account than is possible here, see J. Milnes Holden, *The History of Negotiable Instruments in English Law* (1955), pp. 229–34.

if they wrote across the cheques which they issued the names of the payees' bankers, so that payment would be made only to the banker named in the crossing. This type of crossing came to be known as a 'special' crossing, and a cheque so crossed is said to be crossed specially to that banker. If the drawer did not know where the payee banked, he simply wrote '& Co.' between two lines across the cheque, intending thereby that the cheque should be paid only if presented through a bank and not by the holder in person. This type of crossing came to be known as a 'general' crossing.

5-37 The practice of crossing cheques had a hard struggle to win legal recognition, and it was not until the Crossed Cheques Acts of 1856, 1858 and 1876 had been passed that the modern system was firmly established. Those Acts have been repealed, and the statutory provisions currently in force which deal specifically with crossed cheques are ss 76 to 81 of the Bills of Exchange Act 1882. The distinction between general and special crossings is preserved, the essence of the distinction being that a cheque crossed generally may be collected by any banker, whereas a cheque crossed specially should be collected only by the banker named in the crossing.

Advantages of general and special crossings

5-38 By crossing a cheque generally or specially, the drawer will make it more difficult for a fraudulent person to obtain value for it than it would be if the cheque was not crossed at all. Thus, a thief could be unable to obtain payment for it by presenting it at the counter of the drawee banker. Instead, he would either have to clear the cheque through a banking account in his own name or an assumed name (the disadvantage to him being that he might be traced subsequently and prosecuted), or alternatively he would have to forge the payee's endorsement on the cheque and obtain value for it by handing it to some third party. That third party would be the person who would ultimately suffer loss (unless he could recover the money from the thief) because he would have acquired no lawful title to the cheque by virtue of the forged signature of the payee.[36] In that event, the drawer would be able to recover the cheque, or damages for its conversion, from the third party; the drawer might even be able to claim damages for conversion from the bank which collected the proceeds of the cheque for the third party.[37]

5-39 In some cases, however, an innocent third party may obtain a good title to a cheque, whether crossed or not, even though a prior party

---

36 Bills of Exchange Act 1882, s. 24.
37 See *post*, para. 6-46.

has no title, or a defective title, to it. This is the result of the doctrine of negotiability.[38] By way of illustration, let it be supposed that a clerk, whose duty it is to prepare cheque forms for his employer's signature, decides to defraud his employer. He prepares a cheque form which he makes payable to a purely imaginary person, and he persuades his employer to sign the cheque by falsely representing to him that money is owing to that person. The clerk then endorses the cheque with the name of the imaginary payee and passes the cheque to a third party, who gives value for it in good faith. In those circumstances, the innocent third party does obtain a good title to the cheque[39] and can enforce payment of it against the drawer. The absence of a genuine endorsement does not prevent the third party from obtaining a good title because the cheque was payable to a fictitious or non-existing person, and the Bills of Exchange Act 1882 provides that such a cheque may be treated as payable to bearer.[40] Hence it does not require endorsement by the payee.

5-40 In the result, therefore, the employer, that is to say the drawer of the cheque, has to suffer the loss. He could not have avoided that loss by ordering his bank not to pay the cheque. The innocent third party would still have been able to obtain judgment against him. Very often the drawer of a cheque does not realize the possible consequences of launching a negotiable instrument upon the world. His surprise, consternation and fury, when he is advised that he is liable to someone to whom he owes nothing and of whom he has never heard, leave one in no doubt as to his views on the suitability or otherwise of a negotiable instrument for the purpose of settling debts. He would unreservedly agree with Lord Chorley's view that 'there are rather weighty objections to using an instrument which is negotiable' for the purpose of making payments from one person to another.[41] The way to avoid difficulties of this sort is for the drawer to make his cheques not negotiable, as explained below.

'Not negotiable' crossing

5-41 The 'Not negotiable' crossing, as it is sometimes called, was introduced into the law by the Crossed Cheques Act 1876. At that time there was a sharp division of opinion in Parliament as to the extent to which

---

38 See *ante*, para. 4-1.
39 Provided that the other requirements laid down in s. 29 are satisfied.
40 S. 7(3).
41 'The cheque as mandate and negotiable instrument' (being the substance of the third and fourth Gilbart Lectures, 1939), *Journal of the Institute of Bankers*, Vol. LX (1939), at p. 392.

the doctrine of negotiability should be abrogated in relation to cheques. The Lord Chancellor, Lord Cairns, was in favour of abolishing the doctrine in respect only of cheques crossed specially.[42] In the House of Commons, this proposal was strenuously opposed by a former Governor of the Bank of England, Mr J. G. Hubbard, who pointed out that not one crossed cheque in a hundred was crossed specially. He was in favour of withdrawing the attribute of negotiability from all crossed cheques payable to order.[43]

5-42 The Attorney General, Sir John Holker, then intervened with what he called a compromise. He proposed the introduction of an entirely new type of crossing, involving as part of the crossing the words 'Not negotiable'. A cheque so crossed was to be shorn of the qualities of a negotiable instrument. This proposal was ultimately adopted and became s. 12 of the Crossed Cheques Act 1876; that section was replaced by s. 81 of the Bills of Exchange Act 1882, which provides that a person[44] who takes a cheque crossed 'Not negotiable' does not acquire and cannot give a better title to it than that of the person from whom he took it.[45] The practical effect of the crossing may be shown by referring back to the illustration of the fraudulent clerk. If the drawer had crossed his cheque with the words 'Not negotiable', the innocent third party could not have obtained a good title to it and could not have enforced payment of it against the drawer.

5-43 Moreover, the crossing is a valuable protection to the drawer in a case where the payee has obtained the cheque from him by fraud or false pretences; in that type of case, the payee often negotiates the cheques without delay to an innocent third party, or at any rate to a third party who is said to be innocent. If the cheque is an open one or even if it is crossed generally or specially, the innocent third party may be able to enforce payment against the drawer, whereas if the cheque is crossed 'Not negotiable', the third party will not obtain any better title to the cheque than the payee had, and so the drawer will not be liable to the third party.[46]

---

42 *Hansard*, ser. 3, Vol. CCXXVII, Cols 1106–10.
43 *Hansard*, ser. 3, Vol. CCXXXI, Col. 1213.
44 This includes the payee; see *Wilson and Meeson* v. *Pickering* [1946] KB 422. For another case where s. 81 was applied, see *Fisher* v. *Roberts* (1890) 6 TLR 354.
45 The section does not apply to bills of exchange other than cheques; see *Hilbernian Bank Ltd* v. *Gysin and Hanson* [1939] 1 KB 483, at p. 488, *per* Slesser LJ. The Cheques Act 1957, s. 5, extends the provisions of the Bills of Exchange Act 1882 relating to crossed cheques (including s. 81) to certain instruments (e.g. bankers' drafts) which are specified in the section: see *post*, para. 9-17.
46 *Union Bank of Australia Ltd* v. *Schultz* [1914] VLR 183.

5-44   The use of the 'Not negotiable' crossing does not impair the transferability of a cheque. A cheque so crossed may pass freely from one person to another, but a transferee should be cautious, because he cannot acquire a better title than his transferor had. This applies whether the cheque is payable to order or to bearer.

5-45   A cheque crossed 'Not negotiable' does not, solely by reason of the crossing, put a collecting bank upon enquiry, even though the cheque is tendered for collection by someone other than the payee.[47] As Paget rightly observed,[48] the 'Not negotiable' crossing 'has nothing to do with the collecting banker unless he takes the instrument for value, in which case he gets no better title than had the customer who paid it in'. Likewise, the crossing does not concern the paying banker.

'Account Payee' crossing

5-46   It has been observed that the 'Not negotiable' crossing was introduced by an Act of Parliament in 1876. Such evidence as is available seems to show that some years before 1876 drawers of cheques, on their own initiative, had devised another method of making cheques secure from theft and fraud. They began to cross their cheques with the words 'For the account of ...' or 'Account payee'.[49] When the Crossed Cheques Bill 1876 was being debated in Parliament, an amendment was moved which provided that where a cheque was crossed generally or specially, a lawful holder might add to the crossing the words 'for account of', or any abbreviation thereof, followed by the names of the persons or company to whose account he wished the cheque to be credited.[50] The amendment was withdrawn, and to this day there is no reference to that crossing or to the 'Account payee' crossing in any Act of Parliament.

---

47 There are some *obiter dicta* to the contrary, but they cannot be accepted as sound: see, e.g. *Great Western Railway Co.* v. *London and County Banking Co. Ltd* [1901] AC 414, at p. 422 (*per* Lord Brampton); *Morison* v. *London County and Wesminster Bank Ltd* [1914] 3 KB 356, at p. 373 (*per* Lord Reading).

48 *Paget's Law of Banking* (10th ed., 1989), p. 468.

49 See *Bellamy* v. *Marjoribanks* (1852) 7 Ex 389, where a cheque had been crossed 'Bank of England, for account of the Accountant General'. The use of the words 'Account payee' was probably a later development. The earliest cheque crossed with those words in the Cheque Collection of the Institute of Bankers is one dated 13 October 1897, drawn on Stuckey's Banking Co. Ltd, Shepton Mallet. If this practice had developed about the middle of the century, one would have expected at least some of the cheques of that period to bear the new crossing. However, it must be admitted that most of the instruments in the Collection were drawn by private individuals who, even today, use the 'Account payee' crossing less frequently than trading concerns and local authorities.

50 *Hansard*, ser. 3. Vol. CCXXX, Col. 1515.

5-47 This does not mean, however, that the crossings are without legal significance. The relevant decisions of the courts in regard to the collection of cheques so crossed are examined elsewhere.[51] The position may be summarized by stating that bankers will not usually collect cheques so crossed for someone other than the payee or the person designated in the crossing, though exceptions are occasionally made, particularly if the cheque is for a small amount and the customer is one of long standing. The paying banker, however, is not concerned with these crossings; for, as Bigham J once observed,[52] the words 'Account A.B.' are a mere direction to the receiving bank as to how the money is to be dealt with after receipt.

The 'Safest' crossing

5-48 On 3 October 1957, the Council of the Institute of Chartered Accountants in England and Wales issued a statement recommending that cheques be crossed 'Not negotiable. Account payee only.'[53] This combination of the 'Not negotiable' crossing with the words 'Account payee only' is clearly prudent. The two crossings serve different purposes. The 'Not negotiable' crossing takes the cheque out of the category of negotiable instruments with the advantage to the drawer which has already been explained. The 'Account payee' crossing does not take the cheque out of the category of negotiable instruments.[54] This crossing is addressed to the collecting banker and in effect it warns the collecting banker that if he collects the cheque for someone other than the payee and that person is not entitled to it, the banker may be liable in damages to the person who was entitled to it. The 'Not negotiable' crossing does not imply any such warning. Thus, by combining the 'Not negotiable' crossing with the words 'Account payee', the drawer enjoys a two-fold advantage.

Who may cross a cheque

5-49 The Bills of Exchange Act 1882, contains the following rules which state the persons who may make, or add to, crossings on a cheque.

---

51 *Post*, paras 6-109/11.
52 *Akrokerri (Atlantic) Mines Ltd* v. *Economic Bank* [1904] 2 KB 465, at p. 472.
53 See *The Accountant*, Vol. 137 (1957), p. 409.
54 *National Bank* v. *Silke* [1891] 1 QB 435, where a cheque crossed by the drawer, 'Account of J. F. Moriarty, Esq., National Bank, Dublin' was held to be negotiable.

5-50 'A cheque may be crossed generally or specially by the drawer.'[55] In this connection, the Act defines a general and a special crossing as follows.[56]

5-51 *General crossing.* Where a cheque bears across its face an addition of:

(a) the words 'and company' or any abbreviation thereof between two parallel transverse lines, either with or without the words 'Not negotiable'; or

(b) two parallel transverse lines simply, either with or without the words 'Not negotiable';

that addition constitutes a crossing, and the cheque is crossed generally.

5-52 *Special crossing.* Where a cheque bears across its face an addition of the name of a banker, either with or without the words 'Not negotiable', that addition constitutes a crossing, and the cheque is crossed specially and to that banker.[57]

5-53 'Where a cheque is uncrossed, the holder may cross it generally or specially.'[58]

5-54 'Where a cheque is crossed generally, the holder may cross it specially.'[59]

5-55 'Where a cheque is crossed generally or specially the holder may add the words "Not negotiable".'[60]

5-56 'Where a cheque is crossed specially, the banker to whom it is crossed may again cross it specially to another banker for collection.'[61]

5-57 'Where an uncrossed cheque, or a cheque crossed generally, is sent to a banker for collection, he may cross it specially to himself.'[62]

5-58 The Act also provides that a crossing authorized therein is a material part of the cheque, and that it is unlawful for any person to obliterate or, except as authorized by the Act, to add to or alter the crossing.[63]

---

55 S. 77(1).
56 S. 76.
57 In regard to special crossings, the Act does not require transverse lines, though these are often used in practice.
58 S. 77(2).
59 S. 77(3).
60 S. 77(4).
61 S. 77(5).
62 S. 77(6).
63 S. 78.

Section 3
ISSUING A CHEQUE

5-59 The mere fact that the drawer fills in the blank spaces on a cheque form and signs it does not make the instrument immediately operative as a valid cheque. It does not start its life as a cheque until it has been issued.

Definition of issue

5-60 'Issue' means the first delivery of a cheque, complete in form, to a person who takes it as a holder.[64] Two words in this definition themselves require definition, (a) holder, and (b) delivery.

(a) Holder

5-61 The term 'holder' is defined by the Bills of Exchange Act 1882 as the payee or endorsee of a cheque who is in possession of it, or the bearer thereof.[65] The payee is the person to whom the cheque is drawn payable. The endorsee is the person to whom the cheque is made payable by a special endorsement.[66] The bearer is the person in possession of a cheque which is payable to bearer.[67]

(b) Delivery

5-62 The term 'delivery' is defined as meaning transfer of possession, actual or constructive, from one person to another.[68]

5-63 As issue means the *first* delivery of a cheque, complete in form, to a person who takes it as holder,[69] it follows that a cheque which is

---

64 Bills of Exchange Act 1882, s. 2. A cheque is to be regarded as 'complete in form' even though it is not dated; see s. 3(4)(a). But it may be that an undated cheque is not 'complete and regular on the face of it' within s. 29, with the result that a holder could not be a holder in due course.

65 S. 2.

66 But the term 'endorsee' is sometimes regarded as including any person who makes title through an endorsement. Thus, in *Midland Bank Ltd* v. *R. V. Harris Ltd* [1963] 2 All ER 685, at p. 687, Megaw J stated that in the definition of holder in s. 2 of the Bills of Exchange Act 1882, '"indorsee" means a person who has the rights which are given by statute in respect of a bill or cheque by virtue of an indorsement'. This definition is wide enough to denote the bearer of an instrument endorsed in blank. For the difference between a special endorsement and an endorsement in blank, see *post*, paras 5-74/5.

67 S. 2.

68 Bills of Exchange Act 1882, s. 2.

69 *Ibid.*

payable to a specified person or order can only be issued by delivery to that person, i.e. to the payee. If, however, the cheque is drawn payable to bearer, it may be issued by delivery to any person.

5-64 As stated above, delivery may be either actual or constructive. Actual delivery involves the physical handing over of a cheque by one person to another. The drawer of a cheque usually issues it by handing it to the payee; this is actual delivery. Constructive delivery, however, does not require physical handing over of the instrument; it is effected by the mere intention of the transferor. Thus, if the drawer completes a cheque form and notifies the payee that he is holding it on behalf of the payee, this is constructive delivery, and accordingly the cheque is duly issued.

5-65 Delivery may be conditional or for a special purpose only, and not for the purpose of transferring the property in the cheque.[70] For example, the drawer of a cheque may hand it to the payee and inform him that it must not be presented unless a certain event happens. This is a conditional delivery of the cheque, and the property therein does not pass to the payee until the specified event happens.

5-66 If a cheque comes into the hands of a holder in due course, a valid delivery of the cheque by all parties prior to him so as to make them liable to him is conclusively presumed.[71] For example, a drawer completes and signs a cheque payable to bearer, and locks it in his desk. It is stolen by a thief, who persuades an innocent third party to cash it. That third party is a holder in due course (provided that he fulfils the other requirements of the Bills of Exchange Act 1882[72]), and the drawer of the cheque will be liable to him. Although the drawer never made an actual or constructive delivery of the cheque, delivery thereof is 'conclusively presumed' by the Act in favour of a holder in due course. This is nothing less than a fiction. The Act resorts to it in order to protect the rights of an innocent third party.

Incomplete or inchoate cheques

5-67 It is possible, though usually unwise, for a person to sign a cheque form in blank, and to hand it to someone else for completion. Such an instrument may, for convenience, be called an incomplete or inchoate cheque. An incomplete instrument of this sort cannot be 'issued' by the drawer, because, by definition, issue means the first delivery of a cheque, *complete in form*, to a person who takes it as holder.

70 Bills of Exchange Act 1882, s. 21(2).
71 *Ibid.*
72 S. 29.

5-68   The Bills of Exchange Act 1882 provides for the situation where a blank cheque or an incomplete cheque is delivered by the drawer in order that it may be completed. It is enacted that, in order that any such instrument, when completed, may be enforceable against any person who became a party thereto prior to its completion, it must be filled up within a reasonable time, and strictly in accordance with the authority given.[73] This rule is subject to an important exception that if any such instrument after completion is negotiated to a holder in due course, it is valid and effectual for all purposes in his hands, and he may enforce it as if it had been filled up within a reasonable time and strictly in accordance with the authority given.[74]

5-69   By way of illustration, let it be supposed that the drawer of a cheque fills in the name of the payee, but as he does not know the precise sum which he owes to the payee, he leaves the amount blank. He then delivers the incomplete cheque to the payee and authorizes him to fill in the amount of the debt. The payee fraudulently fills in a larger amount. Clearly, the fraudulent payee is not entitled to enforce payment of the cheque, but if he negotiates it to a holder in due course, it will be valid and effectual for all purposes in his hands. He will be able to sue the drawer for the full amount of the cheque, and the drawer must suffer the loss unless, of course, he can recover the money from the fraudulent payee.

5-70   The above-mentioned exception which protects the holder in due course has no application unless there has been actual or constructive delivery of the instrument for the purposes of completion.[75] For example, a person signs a bearer cheque in blank, and locks it in his desk. It is stolen by a thief who fills it up and persuades an innocent third party to cash it. That third party will be unable to succeed in an action against the drawer. This is one of the very rare occasions when an innocent third party is not protected by the Bills of Exchange Act 1882. The conclusive presumption of valid delivery already noted[76] is inapplicable to a document which, when it leaves the possession of the drawer, is wanting in any material particular.

---

73 S. 20(2).
74 *Ibid.*
75 *Baxendale* v. *Bennett* (1878) 3 QBD 525; although this case was decided before the passing of the Bills of Exchange Act 1882, the principle laid down therein has not been changed. See also *Smith* v. *Prosser* [1907] 2 KB 735.
76 S. 21(2), *supra.*

Section 4
NEGOTIATION OF CHEQUES

5-71   Generally, the holder of a cheque may negotiate it to another person in the manner explained below. By way of exception to this general rule, a cheque which contains words prohibiting transfer, or indicating an intention that it should not be transferable, is incapable of negotiation, though it is perfectly valid 'as between the parties thereto'. [77] Thus, if a cheque is drawn payable to a specified person followed by the word 'only', it is incapable of negotiation, though it is valid as between the drawer and the payee; cheques drawn in this manner are seldom encountered in practice. [78] A cheque which is payable simply to a specified person without the addition of the words 'or order' is, however, negotiable in the usual way. [79] Furthermore, it has been held that, even if a cheque is crossed 'Account payee', it is still negotiable. [80]

How cheques are negotiated

5-72   A cheque is negotiated when it is transferred from one person to another in such a manner as to constitute the transferee the holder of the cheque. [81] A cheque payable to bearer is negotiated by delivery alone, [82] whereas a cheque payable to order is negotiated by the endorsement of the holder completed by delivery. [83] Where the holder of a cheque payable to his order transfers it for value without endorsing it, the transfer gives the transferee such title as the transferor had in the instrument, and the transferee in addition acquires the right to have the endorsement of the transferor. [84]

Meaning of endorsement

5-73   The definition of endorsement contained in the Bills of Exchange Act 1882 is not helpful; endorsement means an endorsement completed by delivery. [85] In a South African case [86] the learned judge stated that, in regard to negotiable instruments, endorsement is capable of three

77 Bills of Exchange Act 1882, s. 8(1).
78 See *post*, para. 9-41.
79 S. 8(4).
80 *National Bank* v. *Silke* [1891] 1 QB 435.
81 Bills of Exchange Act 1882, s. 31(1).
82 S. 31(2).
83 S. 31(3).
84 S. 31(4).
85 S. 2.
86 *National Bank* v. *Paterson* [1909] TS 322 at pp. 326–7, *per* Innes CJ.

meanings. In a general sense, every signature written on the back of such an instrument is an endorsement, even if only placed there for the purpose of identification, or as a receipt; that is the literal meaning of the word. Its ordinary legal meaning is the signing of a name on the back of an instrument *animo indorsandi*, that is, with the intention of undertaking the liabilities of an endorser. The third meaning limits the term to an endorsement in the last-named sense followed by delivery of the document. It is the third meaning which the term endorsement ordinarily bears in the Bills of Exchange Act 1882. Accordingly, in its third meaning, endorsement may be defined as the signature on a cheque, usually on the back, by the holder or by his duly authorized agent, followed by delivery of the instrument, whereby the holder of a cheque payable to his order negotiates it to another person who takes it as a new holder.

Endorsement in blank and special endorsement

5-74 An endorsement may be either in blank or special. An endorsement in blank specifies no endorsee and its effect is to make the instrument payable to bearer.[87] A cheque endorsed in blank may be negotiated by delivery.[88]

5-75 A special endorsement specifies the person, to whom, or to whose order, the instrument is to be payable.[89] Thus, a cheque endorsed 'Pay to X' or 'Pay to the order of X' or 'Pay to X or order' is specially endorsed, and X, the endorsee, may further negotiate it by endorsement and delivery.[90]

5-76 When a cheque has been endorsed in blank, any holder may convert the blank endorsement into a special endorsement by writing above the endorser's signature a direction to pay the cheque to, or to the order of, himself or some other person.[91] If the holder writes a direction to pay some other person and delivers the cheque to that person, the holder has negotiated the cheque by special endorsement, but without himself endorsing the instrument or assuming liability thereon as an endorser. Nevertheless, he may be liable as a transferor by delivery.[92]

---

87 Bills of Exchange Act 1882, s. 34(1).

88 S. 31(2).

89 S. 34(2).

90 S. 31(3).

91 This is a very old mercantile practice which was explained by Marius in relation to bills of exchange in the middle of the seventeenth century; see John Marius, *Advice concerning Bils of Exchange* (1656), p. 30. It was judicially recognized in *Clark* v. *Pigot* (1699) 1 Salk 126. The principle was reaffirmed in *Vincent* v. *Horlock* (1808) 1 Camp 442, and was codified in the Bills of Exchange Act 1882, s. 34(4).

92 *Post*, para. 5-180.

5-77 There is one case where a special endorsement does not have the effect of making a cheque payable to the named endorsee or his order, namely where the cheque was originally drawn payable to bearer. This is the result of the provision in the Bills of Exchange Act 1882[93] that a bill or cheque is payable to bearer which is expressed to be so payable, or on which the only or last endorsement is an endorsement in blank. So, if a cheque is drawn payable to bearer, it remains a bearer cheque during the rest of its life, and no special endorsement can ever make it payable to order.

5-78 If, however, a cheque which was originally drawn payable to order is endorsed in blank and is then specially endorsed, it would seem that the special endorsement is fully effective, and that it 'controls' the previous endorsement in blank. Hence the cheque becomes payable to the named endorsee or order.[94]

Requisites of valid endorsement

5-79 The signature of the holder or of his duly authorized agent is essential to the validity of an endorsement.[95]

5-80 A signature by procuration operates as notice that the agent has but a limited authority to sign, and his principal will only be bound by such signature if the agent in so signing was acting within the actual limits of his authority.[96] Thus, a person who takes a cheque endorsed *per pro* without knowing anything certain about the person who endorses it, does so at his peril.[97]

5-81 Endorsements are usually, but not necessarily, written on the back of the instrument.[98]

5-82 An endorsement must be of the entire instrument: a partial endorsement, that is to say an endorsement which purports to transfer to the endorsee a part only of the amount payable, or which purports to transfer the instrument to two or more endorsees severally, does not operate as a negotiation of the instrument.[99] For example, if the payee of a cheque for £500 writes on it the words 'Pay X £100' or 'Pay X £300

---

93 S. 8(3).
94 For a fuller examination of this problem than is possible here, see J. Milnes Holden, *The History of Negotiable Instruments in English Law* (1955), pp. 161–2.
95 Bills of Exchange Act 1882, ss 32(1) and 91(1).
96 S. 25.
97 *Employers' Liability Assurance Corporation* v. *Skipper & East* (1887) 4 TLR 55.
98 *R* v. *Bigg* (1716) 1 Str 18; *Ex p. Yates* (1857) 27 LJ Bcy 9; 2 De G & J 191; 30 LTOS 282.
99 S. 32(2).

and Y £200', these words do not constitute endorsements. An instrument may, however, be endorsed to two or more endorsees jointly,[1] as for example, 'Pay X and Y'. Moreover, it would seem that an instrument may be endorsed to alternative endorsees, as for example, 'Pay X or Y', though this is seldom, if ever, done in practice.[2]

5-83 Where an instrument is payable to the order of two or more payees or endorsees who are not partners, all must endorse, unless one has authority to endorse for the others.[3] As far as partners are concerned, the Partnership Act 1890 provides that every partner is an agent of the firm and his other partners for the purpose of the partnership.[4] Accordingly, one partner may endorse cheques payable to the partnership.

5-84 Where in an instrument payable to order, the payee or endorsee is wrongly designated, or his name is misspelt, the Bills of Exchange Act 1882 provides that he may endorse the instrument as therein described, adding, if he thinks fit, his proper signature.[5] Furthermore, the courts have held that the proper signature of the payee or endorsee by itself is valid and sufficient to pass the property in the instrument.[6] (But the discrepancy between the payee's or endorsee's name as stated on the instrument on the one hand and his signature on the other will make the endorsement 'irregular'.[7])

5-85 Where any person is under an obligation to endorse an instrument in a representative capacity, he may endorse the instrument in such terms as to negative personal liability.[8] Furthermore, *any* endorser may add an express stipulation negative or limiting his own liability to the holder,[9] for example 'without recourse to me' or '*sans recours*'. *Wakefield* v. *Alexander*[10] was an amusing case where the defendant, who was not a party to a cheque, wrote his name on the back at the request of the payee and for the obvious purpose of lending his name to the instrument; but after his signature he wrote '*sans recours*'.

1 Ss 7(2) and 34(3).
2 The argument in favour of alternative endorsees is that s. 7(2) allows alternative payees and s. 34(3) enacts that the provisions relating to a payee apply with the necessary modifications to an endorsee under a special endorsement.
3 S. 32(3).
4 S. 5.
5 S. 32(4).
6 See *Arab Bank Ltd* v. *Ross* [1952] 2 QB 216, at p. 226, *per* Denning LJ, citing *Leonard* v. *Wilson* (1834) 3 Cr & M 589, *Bird & Co.* v. *Thomas Cook & Son Ltd* [1937] 2 All ER 227.
7 See *post*, para. 5-88.
8 S. 31(5).
9 S. 16(1).
10 (1901) 17 TLR 217.

Perhaps the payee (who then took the cheque) was unfamiliar with the French language. It was held that the defendant was not liable on the instrument.

5-86 An endorser may add appropriate words to his endorsement in order to waive, as regards himself, some or all of the holder's duties. [11] For example, he may add the words 'notice of dishonour waived', meaning that, if the instrument is not duly paid, the holder need not give notice of dishonour to the endorser in order to retain his liability.

Regular and irregular endorsements

5-87 A distinction must be drawn between the *validity* of an endorsement on the one hand, and its *regularity* on the other hand. Thus, as Denning LJ pointed out in *Arab Bank Ltd* v. *Ross*, [12] an endorsement may be forged or unauthorized and, therefore, invalid under s. 24 of the Bills of Exchange Act 1882, but nevertheless there may be nothing about it to give rise to any suspicion. The endorsement may appear to be quite regular.

5-88 Conversely, an endorsement may be perfectly valid for the purpose of passing title although it is 'irregular', that is to say, it is in such a form as to give rise to doubt whether it is the endorsement of the named payee. [13] The distinction is sometimes important. If an endorsement on a cheque is irregular, an innocent third party who gives value for the instrument in good faith cannot become the holder in due course thereof, because the instrument is not 'complete and regular on the face of it' as required by s. 29 of the Bills of Exchange Act 1882. In *Arab Bank Ltd* v. *Ross*[14] two instruments payable to 'Fathi and Faysal Nabulsy Company' had been endorsed by one of the partners in that firm with the words 'Fathi and Faysal Nabulsy', the word 'Company' being omitted. The Court of Appeal held that, although the partner's endorsements were valid to pass the title in the instruments to the plaintiff bank, the omission of the word 'Company' made the endorsements irregular so as to give rise to reasonable doubt whether the payees and endorsers were necessarily the same. Therefore, the instruments were not complete and regular on the fact of them, and so the plaintiff bank could not become holders in due course thereof. [15]

5-89 The question whether any particular endorsement was or was

11 S. 16(2).
12 [1952] 2 QB 216, at p. 226.
13 [1952] 2 QB 216, at p. 227.
14 [1952] 2 QB 216. The instruments in this case were promissory notes, but the same considerations apply also to cheques.
15 Although not holders in due course, the bank succeeded as holders for value.

not regular used to loom very large in banking practice. According to the Report of the Cheque Endorsement Committee (the 'Mocatta Committee') published in 1956,[16] about 600 million cheques needing endorsement were then being issued each year, and some 13 million of the endorsements on those cheques required confirmation by the banks. One of the results of the Cheques Act 1957 is that drawee bankers do not now normally need to examine the endorsements on cheques. Accordingly, questions concerning the irregularity of endorsements do not arise as frequently as they did prior to the passing of the Cheques Act in 1957.

5-90 It is not proposed to set out a list of those endorsements which may, and those which may not, be considered as regular. Detailed and useful guidance on this subject may be obtained from *Questions on Banking Practice* published under the authority of the Council of the Institute of Bankers. Courtesy titles give rise to some peculiar points. Thus on a cheque payable to 'Mrs Helen Smith' the endorsement 'Helen Smith' is said to be regular.[17] The endorsement 'Mrs Helen Smith' is said to be irregular, even though it would not seem to give rise to doubt whether it is the endorsement of the payee. Curiously enough, if the word 'Mrs' is put in brackets thus '(Mrs) Helen Smith', the endorsement is said to be regular.[18] Whether the courts would uphold such hair-splitting distinctions is uncertain, though they will certainly take into consideration the practice of bankers when any question is raised concerning the regularity of an endorsement.[19] A cheque payable to Mrs John Smith should be endorsed 'Jane Smith, wife (or widow) of John Smith'. The endorsement 'Mrs John Smith' is said to be irregular.[20]

Conditional endorsements

5-91 The Bills of Exchange Act 1882 provides that if an endorsement is expressed to be conditional, the condition may be disregarded by the payer, and that payment to the endorsee is valid whether the condition has been fulfilled or not.[21] It would seem, however, that a conditional endorsement is valid and operative as between the endorser and the endorsee. This result seems to follow from another section of the Bills of Exchange Act 1882, which permits delivery of a cheque to be shown,

16 Cmnd. 3, paragraph 20.
17 *Questions on Banking Practice* (11th ed., 1978), p. 175, Question 523.
18 *Ibid.*
19 Thus in *Arab Bank Ltd* v. *Ross* [1952] 2 QB 216, at p. 227, Denning LJ pointed out that the law merchant is founded on the custom of merchants and added 'we shall not go far wrong if we follow the custom of bankers of the City of London on this point.'
20 *Questions on Banking Practice* (11th ed., 1978), p. 175, Question 523.
21 S. 33.

as between endorser and endorsee, or as between endorser and some subsequent holder other than a holder in due course, to have been conditional or for a special purpose only, and not for the purpose of transferring the property in the instrument.[22] If, however, the instrument is in the hands of a holder in due course, a valid delivery thereof by all parties prior to him so as to make them liable to him is conclusively presumed.[23]

Restrictive endorsements

5-92 There are two kinds of restrictive endorsements; the first prohibits the further negotiation of the instrument, and the second expresses that it is a mere authority to deal with the instrument as thereby directed and not a transfer of the ownership thereof.[24]

5-93 By the first type of restrictive endorsement, the endorser transfers ownership of the instrument to the endorsee but prevents any further negotiation, e.g. 'Pay D only', followed by the endorser's signature. Cheques are seldom endorsed in this way.

5-94 By the second type of restrictive endorsement the endorser does not transfer ownership in the instrument to the endorsee but gives him authority to deal with the instrument in a certain way. Sometimes, for example, a bank in one country restrictively endorses a cheque to a bank in another country in the following words: 'Pay the ABC Bank Ltd or order for collection', followed by the signature of the endorsing bank. The primary purpose of such an endorsement is, of course, to prevent any wrongful dealing with the instrument.

5-95 The Bills of Exchange Act 1882 contains the following provisions relating to restrictive endorsements. First, it provides that such an endorsement gives the endorsee the right to receive payment of the instrument and to sue any party thereto that his endorser could have sued, but gives him no power to transfer his rights as endorsee, unless it expressly authorizes him to do so.[25] (It will be observed that the restrictive endorsement set out above – 'Pay the ABC Bank Ltd or order for collection' – does expressly authorize the endorsee to transfer his rights.) Secondly, the Act provides that where a restrictive endorsement authorizes further transfer, all subsequent endorsees take the instrument with the same rights and subject to the same liabilities as the first endorsee under the restrictive endorsement.[26]

22 S. 21(2).
23 *Ibid.*
24 S. 35(1).
25 S. 35(2).
26 S. 35(3).

Section 5
HOLDER OF A CHEQUE

5-96   The holder of a cheque is the payee or endorsee who is in possession of it, or the bearer thereof.[27] The bearer is the person in possession of a cheque which is payable to bearer.[28] It follows that a person cannot be the holder of a cheque unless he is in possession of it.

5-97   Although every holder of a cheque is necessarily the possessor of it, the converse is not true; in other words, the possessor of a cheque is not necessarily the holder thereof. For example, if a cheque payable to 'X or order' is transferred by X to Y without endorsement, Y is the possessor, but he is certainly not the holder, because he does not fall within the definition of a holder.[29]

5-98   The owner of a cheque is not necessarily the holder. One may refer, by way of illustration, to the type of restrictive endorsement which expresses that it is a mere authority to deal with the cheque as thereby directed and not a transfer of ownership thereof, e.g. 'Pay the ABC Bank Ltd or order for collection'.[30] The ABC Bank Ltd, while in possession of the cheque, is the holder thereof, but it is clear that the bank is not the owner.

5-99   The rights and powers set out below are those of the *holder* of a cheque: those rights and powers cannot be exercised by a mere possessor (unless he is also the holder) or by the owner (unless he is also the holder).

Holder's rights and powers

The following are the more important rights and powers of the holder of a cheque.

(a) Special endorsement

5-100   The holder of a cheque endorsed in blank may convert the blank endorsement into a special endorsement by writing above the endorser's

---

27 Bills of Exchange Act 1882, s. 2. For the definitions of 'payee' and 'endorsee', see *ante*, para. 5-61.
28 *Ibid*. A cheque is payable to bearer which is expressed to be so payable on or which the only or last endorsement is an endorsement in blank: see s. 8(3).
29 However, s. 31(4) provides that where the holder of a bill payable to his order transfers it for value without endorsing it, the transfer gives the transferee such title as the transferor had in the bill, and the transferee in addition acquires the right to have the endorsement of the transferor.
30 See *ante*, para. 5-94.

signature a direction to pay the cheque to or to the order of himself or some other person.[31]

(b) Crossings

5-101 Where a cheque is uncrossed, the holder may cross it generally or specially; where it is crossed generally, the holder may cross it specially; and where it is crossed generally or specially, the holder may add the words 'Not negotiable'.[32]

(c) Duplicate of cheque

5-102 Where a cheque has been lost before it is overdue,[33] the person who was the holder of it has the right to apply to the drawer to give him another cheque of the same tenor; if required to do so (as he normally will be), he must give security to the drawer, to indemnify him against all persons whatever in case the cheque alleged to have been lost shall be found again.[34] If, on request, the drawer refuses to give a duplicate cheque, he may be compelled to do so.[35] The holder has, however, no right to apply to an endorser to make a fresh endorsement on the duplicate cheque.

(d) Negotiation

5-103 Generally, the holder of a cheque may negotiate it to another person.[36] There are exceptions: thus a cheque which contains words prohibiting transfer, or indicating an intention that it should not be transferable, is incapable of negotiation;[37] again, a cheque may be restrictively endorsed so as to prohibit its further negotiation.[38]

5-104 Usually, however, a holder has a *right* to negotiate a cheque to another person. Furthermore, a holder sometimes has *power* to negotiate a cheque even though he has no title or a defective title to it. For example, if a thief steals a cheque payable to bearer and negotiates it to someone who gives values for it in good faith, that person will become

---

31 Bills of Exchange Act 1882, s. 34(4).
32 S. 77(2), (3) and (4).
33 The meaning of 'overdue' is explained *post*, para. 5-114.
34 S. 69. Many drawers think that if they stop payment of the original cheque, a duplicate may safely be issued; this is not so, because the original may be in the hands of a holder in due course.
35 *Ibid.*
36 See *ante*, para. 5-72.
37 S. 8(1).
38 S. 35(1).

the holder in due course of the cheque, provided that he satisfies the other requirements of s. 29 of the Bills of Exchange Act 1882. In this instance, the thief, as holder, had *power* to negotiate the cheque, even though he had no *right* to do so.

(e) Presentation

5-105 If the holder of a cheque does not negotiate it to another person, he may present it for payment to the bank on which it is drawn. If the cheque is an open one, he may present it personally to the drawee bank and request payment in cash; but if the cheque is crossed, he cannot require the drawee bank to make payment in cash, and he should, therefore, present it for payment through a bank.

(f) Notice of dishonour

5-106 If the holder of a cheque presents it for payment and it is not paid, he may give notice of dishonour forthwith to prior parties in order to retain their liability to him. Prior parties comprise the drawer and the endorsers. Although it is essential for the holder to give prompt notice of dishonour to the endorsers in order to retain their liability,[39] it is unusual to have to give notice of dishonour to the drawer of a cheque. This is so because notice of dishonour is dispensed with where the drawee bank is under no obligation to pay the cheque,[40] e.g. where there are insufficient funds in the drawer's account; and the same rule applies where the drawer has countermanded payment of the cheque.[41]

(g) Right of action

5-107 It is one of the characteristics of a negotiable instrument that the holder may sue on it in his own name.[42] He may bring his action against any one or more of the prior parties. Whether his action on the cheque will succeed will very often depend upon whether he is a mere holder or a 'holder in due course'. In *Arab Bank Ltd* v. *Ross*,[43] Denning LJ stressed the essential distinction between them in the following words:

> The difference between the rights of a 'holder in due course' and those of a 'holder' is that a holder in due course may get a better title than the

---

39 The rules concerning notice of dishonour are set out in the Bills of Exchange Act 1882, s. 49; see *post*, para. 8-63.

40 Bills of Exchange Act 1882, s. 50(2)(c).

41 *Ibid.*

42 *Crouch* v. *The Crédit Foncier Co.* (1873) LR 8 QB 374, at p. 381; and see the Bills of Exchange Act 1882, s. 38(1).

43 [1952] 2 QB 216, at p. 229.

person from whom he took, whereas a holder gets no better title. In this regard a person who takes a bill which is irregular on the face of it is in the same position as a person who takes a bill which is overdue. He is a holder but not a holder in due course. He does not receive the bill on its own intrinsic credit. He takes it on the credit of the person who gives it to him ... He can sue in his own name, but he takes it subject to the defects of title of prior parties: see s. 38 of the Act.

In view of the privileged position of a holder in due course, it is essential to consider what constitutes a holder in due course.

Holder in due course

5-108 Before the Bills of Exchange Act 1882 was passed, the person who enjoyed the fullest possible rights over a negotiable instrument was known as the 'bona fide holder for value without notice before due'. The draftsman of the 1882 Act, Sir Mackenzie Chalmers, wisely substituted for this cumbrous expression the term 'holder in due course'. Section 29 of the Act defines a holder in due course as a holder who has taken a bill, complete and regular on the face of it, under the following conditions, namely:

(a) that he became the holder of it before it was overdue, and without notice that it had been previously dishonoured, if such was the fact;

(b) that he took the bill in good faith and for value, and that at the time it was negotiated to him he had no notice of any defect in the title of the person who negotiated it.

The elements of this definition will be considered.

(a) Holder

5-109 The first requirement to be satisfied before a person can be a holder in due course of a cheque is that he must be a holder.[44] Thus, if a prior essential signature has been forged or placed on the cheque without the authority of the person whose signature it purports to be, no one can thereafter become a holder, because the Bills of Exchange Act 1882 provides that a forged or unauthorized signature is 'wholly inoperative' and no right to retain the cheque or to give a discharge therefor or to enforce payment thereof against any party thereto can be required through or under that signature.[45] If, therefore, a cheque payable to P

---

44 For the definition of 'holder' see *ante*, para. 5-96.
45 S. 24. The section adds, however, that nothing in the section shall affect the ratification of an unauthorized signature not amounting to a forgery.

or *order* is stolen and P's endorsement is forged, no one can thereafter become a holder (or a holder in due course) of that cheque, because P's signature was essential to pass title and it was forged. If, however, a cheque payable to P or *bearer* is stolen and P's endorsement is forged, the position is different. P's signature was not essential to pass title, and so an innocent third party could become the holder in due course of that cheque provided that he satisfied the other requirements of the section.

5-110 Although a person in possession of a cheque on which an essential signature has been forged cannot be a holder in due course, he may sometimes have the *rights* of a holder in due course against certain parties who are estopped from setting up the forgery. The Bills of Exchange Act 1882[46] provides that an endorser is precluded from denying to a holder in due course the genuineness and regularity in all respects of the drawer's signature and all previous endorsements. Thus, if the drawer's signature, or the payee's signature, or an endorser's signature is forged, an innocent transferee is entitled to sue any endorser who became a party to the cheque subsequent to the forgery.

(b) Complete and regular

5-111 This phrase connotes two requirements, completeness and regularity. As to completeness, this expression is self-explanatory: if any essential element of form is lacking the transferee cannot be a holder in due course.[47]

5-112 As to regularity, it is clear that if a cheque bears any unauthenticated erasures or interlineations in any material particular, a transferee cannot be a holder in due course. Furthermore, it has been held that the word 'face' includes reverse, and so if an endorsement does not appear to be regular, this too will prevent a transferee from becoming a holder in due course.[48]

5-113 The effect of the expression as a whole was summed up by Denning LJ, who said it meant that, looking at the instrument front and back, without the aid of outside evidence, it must be complete and regular in itself.[49]

---

46 S. 55(2).
47 A cheque is to be regarded as complete in form even though it is not dated: see s. 3(4)(a). In spite of this, however, it may be that an undated cheque is not 'complete and regular on the face of it' within s. 29.
48 *Arab Bank Ltd* v. *Ross* [1952] 2 QB 216.
49 *Ibid.*, at p. 226.

(c) Before overdue

5-114 As a cheque is a bill payable on demand, it is deemed to be overdue when it appears on the face of it to have been in circulation for an unreasonable length of time; what is an unreasonable length of time for this purpose is a question of fact.[50] There do not appear to have been any reported High Court decisions relating to overdue cheques after the passing of the Bills of Exchange Act 1882, but there is a report of a County Court case where it was held that a cheque which had been negotiated to a publican twelve days after the date it bore was overdue with the result that the transferee failed to become a holder in due course.[51]

(d) No notice of dishonour

5-115 To qualify as a holder in due course, a transferee must have no notice of previous dishonour of the cheque. A cheque which has been previously dishonoured will usually have some answer written upon it, and in such a case a transferee will have clear notice of dishonour.

(e) For value

5-116 Value is defined as 'valuable consideration'.[52] There is a provision in the Bills of Exchange Act 1882 which states that where value has at any time been given for a bill, the holder is deemed to be a holder for value as regards the acceptor and all parties to the bill who became parties prior to such time.[53] In spite of that provision, however, it seems clear that, in order to qualify as a holder in due course, a transferee must *himself* have given value.[54]

5-117 A question which is sometimes posed is whether a transferee must give full value in order to qualify as a holder in due course. There is no provision which requires that full value must be given, and, as will be seen subsequently, there are banking cases where a bank which gave less than full value for a cheque nevertheless succeeded in establishing

50 Bills of Exchange Act 1882, s. 36(3).
51 *Legal Decisions Affecting Bankers*, Vol. III, p. 226 (the names of the parties are not stated). Cases decided before the Act was passed are probably a useful guide. Thus, in *London and County Banking Co.* v. *Groome* (1881) 8 QBD 288, the plaintiff bank, which had given value for a cheque eight days after the date it bore, recovered judgment against the drawer; whereas in *Serrell* v. *Derbyshire Railway Co.* (1850) 9 CB 811, the court decided that where a cheque was taken two months after date it was overdue.
52 Bills of Exchange Act 1882, s. 2. The meaning of valuable consideration for the purpose of the Bills of Exchange Act is explained *post*, para. 5-128.
53 S. 27(2).
54 S. 29, *ante*, para. 5-108.

itself as a holder in due course. However, it must be remembered that inadequacy of consideration may indicate bad faith. Let it be assumed, for example, that a person whose title to a cheque for £100 is defective offers to negotiate it to a transferee for £75. If the transferee agrees to this, he will almost certainly fail to become a holder in due course. This would be so because the court would infer bad faith: an honest man does not usually give £75 in exchange for a cheque for £100.

5-118　Another provision of the Bills of Exchange Act 1882 states that where the holder of a bill has a lien on it, arising either from contract or by implication of law, he is deemed to be a holder for value to the extent of the sum for which he has a lien.[55] It seems clear that a person holding by virtue of a lien may qualify as a holder in due course because he has himself given value, even though the amount of the instrument is greater than the sum for which he has a lien. This provision is sometimes of value to bankers.[56]

(f) Must be negotiated

5-119　In *R. E. Jones Ltd* v. *Waring and Gillow Ltd*[57] the House of Lords held that the payee of a cheque cannot be a holder in due course. The Lord Chancellor, Lord Cave, said:[58]

> I do not think that the expression 'holder in due course' includes the original payee of a cheque. It is true that under the definition clause in the Act (s. 2) the word 'holder' includes the payee of a bill unless the context otherwise requires; but it appears from s. 29(1), that a 'holder in due course' is a person to whom a bill has been 'negotiated', and from s. 31 that a bill is negotiated by being transferred from one person to another and (if payable to order) by endorsement and delivery. In view of these definitions it is difficult to see how the original payee of a cheque can be a 'holder in due course' within the meaning of the Act.

The decision of this point has not escaped criticism[59] but the rule must be regarded as firmly established. In the result, therefore, a holder, in order to qualify as a holder in due course, must be an endorsee of the cheque who is in possession of it, or the bearer thereof; he must not be the payee.

---

55 S. 27(3).
56 See *post*, para. 6-41.
57 [1926] AC 670, reversing [1925] 2 KB 612, CA.
58 [1926] AC, at p. 680.
59 See *The Cambridge Law Journal*, Vol 3 (1927), pp. 84–6.

(g) In good faith

5-120 A thing is deemed to be done in good faith within the meaning of the Bills of Exchange Act 1882, where it is in fact done honestly whether it is done negligently or not.[60]

(h) No notice of defective title

5-121 The Act does not define 'defect of title' but gives examples: thus the title of a person who negotiates a cheque is defective when he obtains the cheque by fraud, duress,[61] or force and fear,[62] or other unlawful means, or for an illegal consideration, or when he negotiates it in breach of faith, or under such circumstances as to amount to a fraud.[63] Notice of defects of title may be either particular or general. Particular or express notice is where the holder had notice of the particular facts avoiding the cheque.[64] General or implied notice is where the holder had notice that there was *some* defect affecting the cheque, though he did not know exactly what it was.[65] Furthermore, a failure to enquire into the circumstances, when they are known to be such as to invite enquiry, in order to avoid possible actual knowledge will amount to general or implied notice.[66]

Deriving title through holder in due course

5-122 Probably the most cogent illustration of the favoured position occupied by the holder in due course is provided by a rule laid down before the Bills of Exchange Act 1882 was passed[67] and subsequently incorporated in s. 29(3) of the Act. The rule applies where a cheque, affected by some fraud or illegality, is negotiated to a person who has no knowledge of such irregularity and who becomes a holder in due course. He then negotiates the cheque to someone who *has* knowledge of the fraud or illegality, but is not himself a party thereto. Under those circumstances, the rule is that, although this transferee has knowledge of the irregularity and even though he has not given value for the cheque, he has all the rights of the original holder in due course as

---

60 S. 90.

61 For the meaning of duress, see *post*, para. 5-157.

62 'Force and fear' is the Scottish equivalent of the English term 'duress'.

63 S. 29(2).

64 For a case where a bank failed to establish its position as a holder in due course because it had notice, see *Midland Bank Ltd* v. *Reckitt* [1933] AC 1.

65 *Oakley* v. *Ooddeen* (1861) 2 F & F 656; *May* v. *Chapman* (1847) 16 M & W 355; *Raphael* v. *Bank of England* (1855) 17 CB 161.

66 *Jones* v. *Gordon* (1877) 2 App Cas 616.

67 See, for example, *May* v. *Chapman* (1847) 16 M & W 355.

regards all parties prior to that holder. If it were otherwise, the holder in due course might be prejudiced, for, in order to dispose of the cheque, he would have to find a transferee who knew nothing of the irregularity.

Presumption as to holding in due course

5-123   The Bills of Exchange Act 1882 provides that every holder is prima facie deemed to be a holder in due course.[68] If, however, it is admitted or proved in an action on the cheque that the issue or subsequent negotiation of the cheque was affected with fraud, duress,[69] or force and fear,[70] or illegality, the burden is shifted to the holder of proving that, subsequent to the alleged fraud or illegality, value has been given for the cheque in good faith.[71]

5-124   The effect of these provisions may be restated thus. First, there is a presumption that every holder is a holder in due course. Secondly, the presumption may be rebutted by an admission or proof that fraud, etc., affected the issue or subsequent negotiation of the cheque. Thirdly, if such fraud, etc., is admitted or proved, the onus is shifted to the holder to establish either that he himself gave value in good faith or that some previous holder who took subsequent to the fraud, etc., did so. Fourthly, if the holder succeeds in discharging the onus of proving that value has been given in good faith, the original presumption that the holder is a holder in due course is restored.

5-125   Even though the holder succeeds in getting the original presumption restored in the manner outlined above, this is still only a prima facie presumption, i.e. it is not conclusive. If, for example, the court came to the conclusion that he took the cheque when it was overdue, he could not qualify as a holder in due course because he would not have satisfied one of the requirements laid down in s. 29(1) of the Act.

Section 6
DEFENCES TO A CLAIM ON A CHEQUE

The principal defences which may be raised in answer to a claim on a cheque are as follows.

68 S. 30(2).
69 *Post*, para. 5-157.
70 *Ibid.*
71 S. 30(2).

(a) Absence or failure of consideration

5-126 Valuable consideration is necessary under English law for the validity and enforceability of all contracts except those under seal. Accordingly, a promisee who sues on an oral undertaking of another person, or on a written undertaking not under seal, will be unable to enforce it unless he gave consideration, i.e. some *quid pro quo*, in return for the promise. The *quid pro quo* may consist of (a) an act or forbearance on the part of the promisee, [72] or (b) another promise made by the promisee. In general, therefore, consideration is present when a promise is exchanged for an act or forbearance, or a promise is exchanged for another promise.

5-127 The *quid pro quo* may not consist of a past act or forbearance on the part of the promisee by which the promisor benefited; in other words 'past consideration' cannot be relied upon as valuable consideration in order to support a later promise. Thus in *Roscorla* v. *Thomas*, [73] B bought a horse from S who *subsequently*, but in consideration of the previous sale, promised that the horse was sound and free from vice. The horse proved to be vicious, and the court held that the promise was independent of the sale and, being based on a past transaction, lacked the valuable consideration necessary for its enforceability.

5-128 In effect, the Bills of Exchange Act 1882 codifies, in regard to bills of exchange, the common law rules relating to valuable consideration, subject to certain modifications. The Act provides that valuable consideration may be constituted by (a) any consideration sufficient to support a simple contract (i.e. a contract not made under seal), or (b) an antecedent debt or liability. [74] As an illustration of (a), suppose that P, the payee of a cheque, negotiates it to a transferee in exchange for the transferee's promise to do something for P. That consideration would be sufficient to support a simple contract, and so the transferee could sue successfully upon the cheque. The result would be the same if P negotiated the cheque to the transferee in payment of an outstanding (i.e. antecedent) debt owed by P; this would be an illustration of (b).

5-129 The Act, however, did not provide that past consideration is sufficient to support an action on a cheque. Suppose that whilst P was on holiday, his neighbour voluntarily mowed his lawn for him and that,

---

72 Any lawful act on the part of the promisee will suffice. As regards forbearance, if a creditor forbears to sue for a debt, this is a valid consideration: *Crears* v. *Hunter* (1887) 19 QBD 341.
73 (1842) 3 QB 234.
74 S. 27(1).

when P returned, he said to his neighbour, 'In consideration of your having mown my lawn, here is my cheque for five pounds.' In this case, the consideration would be past, and the neighbour would not be able to sue P successfully upon the cheque.

5-130 The Bills of Exchange Act 1882 contains other provisions relating to valuable consideration. Thus there is a provision that every party whose signature appears on a bill is prima facie deemed to have become a party thereto for value.[75] This presumption may, of course, be rebutted. Thus, in the illustration given above, there would be a presumption in favour of the neighbour that P (whose signature appeared on the cheque as drawer) had become a party thereto for value; but this presumption would be rebutted, when P satisfied the court that the consideration was past and, therefore, insufficient to support an action on a cheque.

5-131 The Act further provides that where value has at any time been given for a bill, the holder is deemed to be a holder for value as regards the acceptor and all parties to the bill who become parties prior to such time.[76] The effect of this section may be illustrated as follows. Suppose that A draws a cheque in favour of B as a gift. B then endorses it to C, also as a gift. The drawer A will incur no legal liability to either B or C because of the absence of consideration. If C endorses the cheque to D, who gives value for it, D may enforce payment against A, B or C. If D endorses the cheque to E as a gift, the effect of the section is that E may enforce payment against A, B or C, but not against D.

(b) Failure to present cheque in proper time

5-132 The availability of this defence depends upon whether the defendant is the drawer of the cheque or an endorser. As far as an endorser is concerned, the Bills of Exchange Act 1882 provides that where a bill is payable on demand (as is always the case with a cheque), presentment for payment must be made within a reasonable time after its endorsement in order to render the endorser liable.[77] In determining what is a reasonable time, regard must be had to the nature of the instrument, the usage of trade, and the facts of the particular case.[78] If the cheque is not so presented, the endorser is discharged from liability.

5-133 The drawer's position is different. Failure to present a cheque for payment within a reasonable time of issue will only discharge the

75 S. 30(1).
76 S. 27(2).
77 S. 45.
78 *Ibid*.

drawer to the extent of any actual damage which he suffers as a result of such failure.[79] It is clear that the drawer will not be discharged merely because of delay in presenting a cheque for payment.[80] There must be actual damage to the drawer, and it seems that he will only suffer damage by a failure to present a cheque within a reasonable time of issue if, when presentment should have taken place, he had sufficient funds in the bank to meet it, and after that time but before presentation of the cheque, the bank suspends payment, so that the drawer is a creditor of the bank to a larger amount than he would have been if the cheque had been paid. In cases where the drawer of a cheque *is* discharged, either wholly or partially, the holder of the cheque is given a right against the drawee bank by being substituted as creditor of the bank, in lieu of the drawer, to the extent of the discharge.[81]

5-134 Of course, it is rare nowadays for a bank to suspend payment, and it seems that, in the absence of this event, the drawer of a cheque will remain liable thereon until the right of action becomes statute-barred, i.e. six years after the issue of the cheque.[82]

(c) No notice of dishonour

5-135 The availability of this defence likewise depends upon whether the defendant is the drawer of the cheque or an endorser. If the holder of a cheque presents it for payment and it is not paid, he should give prompt notice of dishonour to the endorsers in order to retain their liability; if the holder fails to do so, any endorser to whom prompt notice of dishonour is not given is discharged from liability.[83] Notice of dishonour may be given as soon as the cheque is dishonoured, and must be given within a reasonable time thereafter.[84] In the absence of special circumstances, notice is not deemed to have been given within a reasonable time, unless:

(a) where the person giving and the person to receive notice reside in the same place, the notice is given or sent off in time to reach the latter on the day after the dishonour;

(b) where the person giving and the person to receive notice reside in different places, the notice is sent off on the day after the dishonour, if there be a post at a convenient hour on that day, and

---

79 S. 74(1).
80 *King and Boyd* v. *Porter* [1925] NI 107, where the cheque was not presented for payment for nearly three years.
81 S. 74(3).
82 Limitation Act 1980, s. 5.
83 Bills of Exchange Act 1882, ss 48 and 55(2)(a).
84 S. 49(12).

if there be no such post on that day, then by the next post thereafter.[85]

These time limits are rigidly adhered to by the courts, with the result that
a holder who fails to observe them may find himself completely without
remedy against an endorser, even though the endorser may have
sustained no prejudice whatever by the delay.[86]

5-136   If the cheque is in the hands of an agent when it is dishonoured,
he may either give notice direct to the parties liable thereon or give
notice to his principal; if he gives notice to his principal, he must do so
within the same time as if he were the holder, and the principal upon
receipt of such notice has himself the same time for giving notice as if
the agent had been an independent holder.[87] This provision is important
to bankers. If a banker, acting as his customer's agent, presents a
cheque for payment and it is dishonoured for any reason, the banker
should give immediate notice of dishonour to his customer. He usually
does this by returning the dishonoured cheque to his customer, but there
are circumstances in which it would be unwise to part with the cheque.[88]

5-137   The question whether one ought to give notice of dishonour to
the drawer of a cheque is governed by different considerations. Notice
of dishonour is dispensed with where the drawee bank is under no obligation to pay the cheque,[89] e.g. where there are insufficient funds in the
drawer's account; and the same rule applies where the drawer has
countermanded payment of the cheque.[90] Accordingly, it is not usually
possible for a drawer of a cheque to plead by way of defence that notice
of dishonour was not given to him.

(d) Defendant's contractual incapacity

5-138   The general rule laid down by the Bills of Exchange Act 1882 is
that capacity to incur liability as a party to a cheque is coextensive with
capacity to contract.[91] Accordingly, when a person who does not
possess full contractual capacity signs a cheque as drawer or endorser
and is sued on the instrument, he may plead his incapacity as a defence
to the same extent as if he was being sued on any other contract.

---

85 *Ibid*. As regards computation of time, see s. 92.
86 For an illustration, see *Yeoman Credit Ltd* v. *Gregory* [1963] 1 WLR 343.
87 Bills of Exchange Act 1882, s. 49(13).
88 *Post*, para. 6-35.
89 S. 50(2)(c).
90 *Ibid*.
91 S. 22(1).

Minority

5-139 If a person under the age of eighteen[92] is sued on a cheque, either as drawer or endorser, he may always plead his contractual incapacity by way of defence. In spite of the rule that a minor is bound to pay a reasonable price for necessaries ordered by and supplied to him,[93] it has been held that he cannot be sued successfully upon a cheque given by him in respect of those necessaries, for, as Lord Esher observed, 'he is not liable upon a bill of exchange or a promissory note under any circumstances'.[94] In another case a minor drew and issued a post-dated cheque, dating it some sixteen days after his twenty-first birthday. It was held that he was not liable on the cheque, because he was a minor at that time when he drew it.[95] Moreover, a person of full age who gives a bill of exchange or a cheque in respect of the repayment of a loan obtained during minority cannot be held liable upon it.[96]

5-140 In spite of these very stringent rules for the benefit of minors, the mere fact that a minor is a party to a bill of exchange or a cheque does not usually invalidate the instrument; the holder may still receive payment thereof and enforce it against any other party thereto.[97] There appears to be one exception to this rule. If a minor borrows money and agrees after coming of age to repay it, any instrument, whether negotiable or not, given in pursuance of that agreement, is declared by statute to be 'void absolutely as against all persons whomsoever'.[98]

Mental incapacity

5-141 When a person is sued on a contract and he defends the action on the ground of mental incapacity, he must prove not only his incapacity, but also the other party's knowledge of his incapacity.[99] In one case, it was proved that the defendant, as the result of senile degeneration, was incapable of understanding the true nature and effect of the

---

92 Eighteen was substituted for twenty-one by the Family Law Reform Act 1969; see *post*, para. 11-39.

93 Sale of Goods Act 1979, s. 3(2).

94 *Re Soltykoff, Ex parte Margrett* [1891] 1 QB 413, at 415.

95 *Hutley* v. *Peacock* (1913) 30 TLR 42.

96 *Smith* v. *King* [1892] 2 QB 543, applying the provisions of the Infants' Relief Act 1874, s. 2. An Irish court, however, has held that a holder in due course may sue the acceptor of a bill for a debt incurred during minority, but accepted by the latter after attaining full age: *Belfast Banking Co.* v. *Doherty* (1879) 4 LR (Ireland) 124.

97 Bills of Exchange Act 1882, s. 22(2).

98 Betting and Loans (Infants) Act 1892, s. 5. Yet in *Wauthier* v. *Wilson* (1912) 28 TLR 239, a minor and his father made a joint and several promissory note in consideration of money advanced to the minor, and the father was held liable on this note as principal debtor.

99 *Imperial Loan Co. Ltd* v. *Stone* [1892] 1 QB 599.

transaction for which she had given her cheque, and that the plaintiff was aware of her condition; judgment was given for the defendant.[1]

Drunkenness

5-142 The same rules apply as in the case of mental incapacity.[2]

(e) Cheque incomplete when signed

5-143 If a person signs a blank cheque in the space provided for the drawer's signature but never delivers it for the purpose of completion, he will not be liable on it even to a holder in due course.[3]

(f) Cheque delivered upon a condition

5-144 It is possible for delivery of a cheque to be conditional or for a special purpose only, and not for the purpose of transferring the property in the cheque.[4] Therefore, if the condition is not fulfilled, the drawer is entitled to plead the non-fulfilment of the condition by way of defence. However, this defence will not succeed as against a holder in due course, because a valid delivery of the cheque by all parties prior to him so as to make them liable to him is conclusively presumed.[5]

(g) Forged signature

5-145 If a prior essential signature has been forged or unauthorized, no one can thereafter become a holder, because the Bills of Exchange Act 1882 provides that, as a rule, a forged or unauthorized signature is 'wholly inoperative'.[6] No right to retain the cheque or to give a discharge therefor or to enforce payment thereof against any party thereto can be acquired through or under that signature.[7] But if the signature which was forged or unauthorized was not essential to pass title, an innocent third party may become the holder in due course of the cheque and may, therefore, sue all parties thereto except the person whose signature was forged or unauthorized. Thus, if a cheque is payable to P or bearer and P's endorsement is forged, a holder in due course could sue the drawer, but not P.

5-146 Sometimes, the party against whom it is sought to enforce

---

1 *Manches* v. *Trimborn* [1946] WN 62.
2 *Gore* v. *Gibson* (1845) 13 M & W 623; *Molton* v. *Camroux* (1849) 4 Ex 17.
3 *Ante*, para. 5-70.
4 Bills of Exchange Act 1882, s. 21(2).
5 *Ibid.*
6 S. 24 *ante*, para. 5-109.
7 *Ibid.*

payment is precluded from setting up the forgery or want of authority. There are two cases to consider: first there is the case where a party is precluded from alleging that what purports to be his own signature is forged or unauthorized, and secondly there is the case where a party may be precluded from alleging that the signatures of other parties are forged or unauthorized. *Greenwood* v. *Martins Bank Ltd*[8] is an illustration of the former: in that case the plaintiff was estopped from asserting that what purported to be his signature as drawer on certain cheques was forged. As an illustration of the latter, there is the rule that an endorser is precluded from denying to a holder in due course the genuineness and regularity in all respects of the drawer's signature and all previous endorsements.[9]

(h) Material alteration

5-147 The general rule laid down in the Bills of Exchange Act 1882 is that where a cheque is materially altered without the assent of all parties liable thereon, the cheque is 'avoided' (that is to say, it becomes completely void), except as against a party who has himself made, authorized, or assented to the alteration, and subsequent endorsers.[10] This is a very odd rule which leads to occasional injustice, and it can only be justified historically.[11] One might have expected that persons who had become parties prior to the alteration, and who did not assent to it, would have been liable as if the alteration had not been made.[12]

5-148 The Bills of Exchange Act 1882 does, however, afford some special protection for the holder in due course, by providing that, if the alteration is not apparent, and the cheque is in the hands of a holder in due course,[13] such holder may avail himself of the cheque as if it had not been altered, and may enforce payment of it according to its original tenor.

5-149 The commonest type of material alteration to a cheque is the fraudulent raising of the sum payable. This is usually done by the insertion of an additional digit, e.g. £20 raised to £120, £69 raised to £690,

---

8 [1932] 1 KB 371 CA; [1933] AC 51 HL. For the facts of this case, see *ante*, para. 2-128.

9 Bills of Exchange Act 1882, s. 55(2).

10 S. 64(1).

11 See *Master* v. *Miller* (1791) 4 TR 320; affirmed 5 TR 367; *Burchfield* v. *Moore* (1854) 23 LJQB 261.

12 See the provisions of the South African Bills of Exchange Act 1893, s. 62(1), where this rule is applied.

13 The words 'if the alteration is not apparent' seem to be unnecessary because, if the alteration *was* apparent, no subsequent holder could be a holder in due course: the instrument would not be complete and regular on the face of it as required by s. 29(1).

and so on. If one applies the rules stated above, the legal position may be summarized as follows. Where the raising of the amount is not apparent and the cheque is in the hands of a holder in due course, it can be enforced against non-assenting parties to the extent of the original sum for which it was drawn, and against assenting parties or those who became parties after the alteration to the extent of the raised amount. Where, however, the alteration is apparent or the cheque is not in the hands of a holder in due course, the non-assenting parties are completely discharged; but the assenting parties and those who become parties after the alteration are liable to the extent of the raised amount.

5-150 Although the alteration of the sum payable is the commonest type of material alteration, the Act gives the following as additional illustrations of material alterations to bills; any alteration of the date, the time of payment, the place of payment, and, where a bill has been accepted generally, the addition of a place of payment without the acceptor's assent. [14] Even this list is not exhaustive. The most important omission from it, as far as cheques are concerned, is any alteration of a crossing. This would clearly be a material alteration, because the Act declares that a crossing is a material part of the cheque. [15] However, not every alteration will be a material one. For example, the conversion of a blank endorsement into a special endorsement pursuant to s. 34(4) of the Bills of Exchange Act 1882 [16] has been held to be an immaterial alteration. [17]

(i) Fraud

5-151 If the plaintiff himself obtained the cheque by fraud, this would be a defence to any action brought by him.

5-152 If a prior holder had obtained a party's signature by fraud, the present holder's rights would depend upon whether the fraud rendered the contract (i) void, or (ii) voidable.

(i) Fraud rendering the contract void

5-153 A party whose signature has been obtained by fraud would be able to escape all liability by proving that his signature was a nullity. He would be able to do this if, *without any negligence on his part*, he had been fraudulently induced to sign the document, not knowing that it was, or would subsequently be converted into, a negotiable instrument,

---

14 S. 64(2).
15 S. 78. But a holder is permitted to make certain additions to a crossing: see Bills of Exchange Act 1882, s. 77, *ante*, paras 5-53/7.
16 *Ante*, para. 5-100.
17 *Bird & Co. (London) Ltd* v. *Thomas Cook & Son Ltd* [1937] 2 All ER 227.

but believing that it was a document of a different kind. In such circumstances he would not be liable on the instrument even to a bona fide transferee for value. This results from the application of the principle of *non est factum*, in accordance with which a signature by a person whose mind does not accompany his pen is a nullity.

5-154 The leading case is *Foster* v. *Mackinnon*,[18] where an old man was induced to sign his name upon the back of a bill of exchange by the fraudulent representation that he was signing a guarantee. The jury found as a fact that there was no negligence on his part in so signing. Later, the instrument was endorsed and delivered for value to a transferee who took it in good faith. On the assumption that there had been no negligence, it was held that the transferee could not succeed in an action against the old man.[19]

5-155 A person who pleads *non est factum* as a defence must show that he thought the document was of a different *kind* from that which it was.[20] If he signs without having any idea as to its contents, he cannot plead *non est factum*.[21] Moreover, the effect of the decision of the House of Lords in *Saunders (Executrix of the Will of Rose Maude Gallie, deceased)* v. *Anglia Building Society*[22] is that only in very exceptional circumstances can a person of full age and understanding successfully plead *non est factum*. In the course of his opinion Lord Hodson said: 'Want of care on the part of the person who signs a document which he afterwards seeks to disown is relevant. The burden of proving *non est factum* is on the party disowning his signature; this includes proof that he or she took care.'[23]

(ii) Fraud rendering the contract voidable

5-156 In most cases, fraud merely makes the fraudulent person's title defective and affords no defence to a claim brought by a holder in due course.[24] Thus if P fraudulently induced D to draw a cheque in his favour by falsely pretending that he was the owner of a certain car and that he would sell it to D, there is no doubt that P's title to the cheque

---

18 (1869) LR 4 CP 704.

19 The transferee asked for and obtained an order for a new trial on the ground that the jury's verdict of 'no negligence' was against the evidence. It is not known whether a new trial took place; possibly the claim was compromised.

20 *Howatson* v. *Webb* [1907] 1 Ch 537; affirmed [1908] 1 Ch 1.

21 *Gillman* v. *Gillman* (1946) 174 LT 272.

22 [1971] AC 1004.

23 [1971] AC, at p. 1019. See also *Foster* v. *Mackinnon* (*supra*), where a new trial was ordered on the question of negligence; *Krige* v. *Willemse* (1908) 25 Cape SC 180, where negligence was proved and the defendant was held liable to a bona fide transferee for value.

24 Bills of Exchange Act 1882, s. 38(2).

would be defective. D could successfully defend any action on the cheque brought by P. But if P negotiated the cheque to T, who gave value for it in good faith, T would become a holder in due course of the cheque and would obtain a perfect title thereto[25] provided that the other requirements of s. 29(1) of the Bills of Exchange Act 1882 were satisfied. Hence his claim against D would succeed.

(j) Duress

5-157 By 'duress' is meant the compulsion under which a person acts through fear of personal suffering, as from injury to the body or from confinement, actual or threatened.[26] 'Force and fear' is the Scottish equivalent of the English term 'duress'.

5-158 If the plaintiff himself obtained the cheque by duress, this would be a defence to any action brought by him. If, however, the duress resulted from pressure, not by the plaintiff himself, but by a third party, this would have no effect on the contract unless the plaintiff was shown to have knowledge of the facts.[27]

5-159 If a prior holder had obtained a party's signature by duress, the present holder's legal rights are perhaps not free from doubt. On principle, one would expect that the problem would be resolved by applying the same rules as those outlined above in regard to fraud. In other words, just as the courts have drawn a distinction between fraud which renders a contract void, and fraud which renders a contract voidable, so too one would expect the same distinction to be drawn in regard to duress.

(k) Undue influence

5-160 Courts of equity have evolved a doctrine, known as the doctrine of undue influence, which has been concisely stated as follows:[28]

In a court of equity, if A obtains any benefit from B, whether under a contract or as a gift, by exerting an influence over B which, in the opinion of the court, prevents B from exercising an independent judgment in the matter in question, B can set aside the contract or recover the gift. Moreover, in certain cases the relation between A and B may be such that A has peculiar opportunities of exercising influence over B. If under such

---

25 Unless it was crossed 'not negotiable', see *ante*, para. 5-42.
26 *Halsbury's Laws of England* (4th ed.), Vol. 9, p. 172.
27 *Talbot* v. *von Boris* [1911] 1 KB 854. This was an action on a promissory note, but the result would presumably have been the same if the instrument had been a cheque.
28 *Ashburner's Principles of Equity* (2nd ed., 1933), p. 299.

circumstances A enters into a contract with B, or receives a gift from B, a court of equity imposes upon A the burden, if he wishes to maintain the contract or gift, of proving that in fact he exerted no influence for the purpose of obtaining it.

Thus, contracts which are voidable for undue influence are of two kinds: (a) those in which there is a special relationship between the parties (e.g. between a trustee and his beneficiary, an agent and his principal, a solicitor and his client, a physician and his patient, a spiritual adviser and those under his control, a parent and a child who has recently come of age) where the influence is *presumed* to exist, and (b) those in which there is no special relationship between the parties where undue influence must be proved as a fact. There is no presumption of undue influence as between husband and wife, though transactions between spouses may, of course, be avoided if affirmative proof of undue influence is adduced.

5-161 If the plaintiff himself obtained the cheque as a result of undue influence, this would be a defence to any action brought by him.

5-162 If a prior holder had obtained the cheque as a result of undue influence, but the instrument has come into the hands of a holder in due course, he may enforce payment against all prior parties.[29]

(l) Illegal consideration

5-163 If the plaintiff himself obtained the cheque by theft or for illegal consideration, this would be a defence to any action brought by him.

5-164 If a prior holder had obtained the cheque by theft or for an illegal consideration, the general rule is that if the instrument comes into the hands of a holder in due course, he may enforce against all prior parties.[30]

5-165 A consideration may be illegal either at common law or by statute. Illegality of the consideration at common law arises where the consideration is founded upon a transaction which is against sound morals, public policy, public rights, or public interests.[31] Thus, an instrument given in consideration of stifling a criminal prosecution is given for an illegal consideration.[32]

---

29 Bills of Exchange Act 1882, s. 38(2). For a case where a wife unsuccessfully pleaded undue influence by her husband in answer to a claim on a promissory note, see *Howes* v. *Bishop* [1909] 2 KB 390.
30 Bills of Exchange Act 1882, s. 38(2).
31 *Halsbury's Laws of England* (4th ed.), Vol. 4, p. 167.
32 *Jones* v. *Merionethshire Building Society* [1892] 1 Ch 173.

5-166 As an illustration of a statute which makes the consideration given for negotiable instruments illegal, reference may be made to the Gaming Act 1835. One effect of this Act is that a cheque given for money lost at gaming or betting upon games is deemed to be given for an illegal consideration. Thus, no action can successfully be brought on the cheque by a holder who has notice of the consideration, but if the cheque comes into the hands of a holder in due course having no knowledge of the illegal consideration, he may enforce payment against prior parties. In one case,[33] the defendant lost money to a person on bets made on a horse race, and he drew a cheque for his losses in favour of the winner. The winner endorsed the cheque to the plaintiff for value, the plaintiff having notice of the consideration for which the cheque had been drawn. The Court of Appeal held that the plaintiff's claim must fail.

5-167 Sometimes, the transactions in respect of which a negotiable instrument is given is made null and void by statute. There is no illegality in this type of transaction, and so there is merely a failure of the consideration. Thus, although an instrument given in respect of it cannot be enforced as between immediate parties, it is enforceable in the hand of a holder for value, even though he has knowledge of the original transaction. An example is provided by the Gaming Act 1845, one effect of which is that cheques drawn for money lost by *bets which are not upon games* are given for no consideration, the bet being null and void, but not illegal.[34] In one case,[35] the defendant made a promissory note for gambling losses on the Stock Exchange. The payee endorsed it to a person who took it for value, but with knowledge of the transaction. It was held that he was entitled to judgment against the maker of the note.

(m) Cheque overdue

5-168 By virtue of the Bills of Exchange Act 1882, where an overdue cheque is negotiated, it can only be negotiated subject to any defect of title affecting it at its maturity, and thenceforward no person who takes it can acquire or give a better title than that which the person from whom he took it had.[36]

(n) Cheque previously dishonoured

5-169 By virtue of the Bills of Exchange Act 1882, where a bill which is *not* overdue has been dishonoured, any person who takes it with

33 *Woolf* v. *Hamilton* [1898] 2 QB 337. See also *Hay* v. *Ayling* (1851) 16 QB 423.
34 S. 18.
35 *Lilley* v. *Rankin* (1886) 56 LJQB 248.
36 S. 36(2). For the meaning of 'overdue', see *ante*, para. 5-114.

notice of the dishonour takes it subject to any defect of title attaching thereto at the time of dishonour.[37]

Section 7
LIABILITIES OF PARTIES TO A CHEQUE

5-170 Under this heading it is intended to deal with the liabilities of the ordinary parties to a cheque, namely the drawer and the endorsers (if any), as well as the liabilities of persons who occasionally 'back' a cheque (sometimes called 'quasi-endorsers') and the liabilities of the holder of a bearer cheque who negotiates it by delivery alone, without endorsement. Strictly speaking, a person who negotiates a cheque in this way is not a party to the instrument because he has not signed it, but it is convenient to consider his legal position under the present heading. Certain other related topics will also be discussed, such as the liability of agents and the special provisions relating to accommodation cheques.

Liability of drawer

5-171 When the drawer of a cheque issues it to the payee, he naturally anticipates that it will be presented for payment to the bank on which it is drawn. In the vast majority of cases the cheque is so presented, and is duly paid. The Bills of Exchange Act 1882 provides, in effect, that by the very act of drawing the cheque, the drawer engages that on due presentation it will be paid according to its tenor, and that, if it is dishonoured, he will compensate the holder or any endorser who is compelled to pay it.[38] It follows, therefore, that the drawer's liability only becomes an actual liability when the cheque is dishonoured; unless and until the instrument is dishonoured, no one can successfully bring an action against him.

5-172 When once the cheque has been dishonoured, the drawer must, as stated above, compensate the holder or any endorser who is compelled to pay it. But this general rule is subject to many exceptions. The drawer may be able to defend an action brought against him by pleading one or more of the defences already explained.[39] Thus, he may be able to resist the claim on the ground that he was a minor, and so was incapable of incurring liability on the cheque, or on the ground that there has been an absence or failure of consideration for the cheque.

5-173 The drawer may be liable on the cheque to one person but not to another. Let it be supposed, for example, that he draws and issues his

37 S. 36(5).
38 S. 55(1)(a).
39 *Ante*, paras 5-126/69.

cheque in favour of P in consideration of P's promise to render some service to him and that P fails to render that service. It is quite clear that if the drawer countermanded payment of the cheque and it was dishonoured, P would not be able to sue the drawer successfully on the cheque, because there had been a failure of the consideration for which the cheque had been drawn. But if P had negotiated the cheque to T, who took it as a holder in due course, T would be able to sue the drawer successfully: the failure of the consideration as between the drawer and P would be no defence to an action by T, who himself gave value for the cheque.

5-174   The Bills of Exchange Act 1882 further provides that the drawer of a cheque is precluded from denying to a holder in due course the existence of the payee and his then capacity to endorse.[40]

Liability of endorser

5-175   The endorser's liability is similar to that of the drawer. By the very act of endorsing the cheque, he engages that on due presentation it will be paid according to its tenor, and that, if it is dishonoured, he will compensate the holder or any endorser who is compelled to pay it.[41] The principal difference between the liability of an endorser of a cheque and that of the drawer is that an endorser will usually be discharged from liability if prompt notice of dishonour is not given to him, whereas it is usually unnecessary to give notice of dishonour to the drawer of a cheque in order to retain his liability. The relevant rules relating to the giving of notice of dishonour have already been stated.[42]

5-176   Furthermore, the Bills of Exchange Act 1882 provides that an endorser is precluded from denying to a holder in due course the genuineness and regularity in all respects of the drawer's signature and all previous endorsements.[43] He is also precluded from denying to his immediate or a subsequent endorsee that the cheque was at the time of his endorsement a valid and subsisting cheque, and that he had then a good title thereto.[44]

5-177   It has already been observed that where any person is under an obligation to endorse an instrument in a representative capacity, he may endorse the instrument in such terms as to negative personal liability.[45]

---

40 S. 55(1)(b).
41 Bills of Exchange Act 1882, s. 55(2)(a).
42 *Ante*, para. 5-135.
43 S. 55(2)(b).
44 S. 55(2)(c).
45 S. 31(5); *ante*, para. 5-85.

Furthermore, *any* endorser may add an express stipulation negativing or limiting his own liability to the holder,[46] for example, 'without recourse to me' or '*sans recours*'.

Liability of quasi-endorser

5-178   The Bills of Exchange Act 1882 provides that where a person signs a bill otherwise than as drawer or acceptor, he thereby incurs the liability of an endorser to a holder in due course.[47] The object of 'backing' a bill in this way is to increase its value by reason of the additional credit which it derives from the signature of the person concerned. This section of the Act which imposes liability upon the quasi-endorser, as he is sometimes called, has given rise to a considerable amount of litigation.[48] However, all the reported cases have been concerned with bills of exchange other than cheques, and it would not seem appropriate to analyse them here. Furthermore, it is very unusual indeed in modern business practice for cheques, as opposed to other bills of exchange, to be endorsed by a quasi-endorser. One point, however, which may be mentioned is that, as a quasi-endorser incurs the liability of an endorser only to a holder in due course, it would seem that he cannot be held liable to the payee of a cheque, because it has been held by the House of Lords that the payee of a cheque cannot be a holder in due course.[49]

Liability of transferor by delivery

5-179   Although only those persons who have signified their consent to incur liability on a cheque by signing it are properly described as parties, a certain responsibility is undertaken by a person who, being in possession of a bearer cheque (that is to say, a cheque which originally or by endorsement is payable to bearer), negotiates it without endorsing it.

5-180   The holder of a bearer instrument who negotiates it in this way is referred to in the Bills of Exchange Act 1882 as a 'transferor by delivery'.[50] He incurs no liability on the instrument,[51] but when he negotiates it, he warrants to his immediate transferee, if the latter is a holder

46 S. 16(1); *ante*, para. 5-85.
47 S. 56.
48 See the cases cited in *Halsbury's Laws of England* (4th ed.), Vol. 4, pp. 211–12.
49 *R. E. Jones Ltd* v. *Waring and Gillow Ltd* [1926] AC 670; see *ante*, para. 5-119.
50 S. 58(1).
51 S. 58(2).

for value, three distinct things in regard to it:[52]

(a) He warrants that the instrument is what it purports to be; if, therefore, it is discovered that the instrument is a forgery, he is liable under this warranty of genuineness.

(b) He warrants that he has a right to transfer it; thus, he warrants that he has a good title to the instrument.

(c) He warrants that at the time of transfer he is not aware of any fact which renders it valueless; for example, he warrants that he does not know that there has been a material alteration to the instrument.

5-181 Quite apart from these warranties, it should be noted that if the transferor by delivery transfers a cheque to a creditor in payment of a debt and the cheque is not duly paid, the debt is usually revived, because a cheque is presumed to have been accepted as conditional payment of a debt, unless the parties agree that it shall operate as a complete satisfaction of the debt.[53]

5-182 Sometimes a customer negotiates a bearer cheque to his bank in exchange for cash without endorsing it. The customer thereby becomes a transferor by delivery, and he is not liable to the bank on the cheque. In view of the limited nature of the warranties given by a transferor by delivery, it would be prudent for the bank either to require the customer's endorsement, or to embody in the exchange form to be signed by the customer a suitable indemnity in the event of the cheque being unpaid.[54]

5-183 It may be noted that the payee of an order cheque who transfers it without endorsement is not a transferor by delivery. His transferee for value (for example, a bank which cashes the cheque) acquires such title as the transferor had in the cheque, and the transferee in addition acquires the right to have the endorsement of the transferor.[55]

---

52 S. 58(3).

53 *Currie* v. *Misa* (1875) LR 10 Ex 153, at p. 163, *per* Lush J; and, on appeal, (1876) 1 App Cas 554; *Charles* v. *Backwell* (1877) 2 CPD 151, at p. 158; *Felix Hadley & Co.* v. *Hadley* [1898] 2 Ch 680; *Bolt & Nut Co. (Tipton) Ltd* v. *Rowlands Nicholls & Co. Ltd* [1964] 2 QB 10.

54 The following would be appropriate: 'Please exchange the above-mentioned cheques and drafts with recourse to me/us in the event of any of them being returned unpaid, or of any claim being made against the bank in respect of this transaction.'

55 S. 31(4). Furthermore, the Cheques Act 1957, s. 2, provides that where a banker gives value for a cheque payable to order which the holder delivers to him *for collection* without endorsing it, the banker has the same rights as he would have had if the holder had endorsed it in blank. See *post*, para. 6-37.

Agent's personal liability

5-184 The Bills of Exchange Act 1882 provides that where a person signs a bill as drawer, endorser or acceptor, and adds words to his signature indicating that he signs for or on behalf of a principal or in a representative character, he is not personally liable thereon; but the mere addition of his signature of words describing him as an agent or as filling a representative character does not exempt him from personal liability.[56] The Act further provides that in determining whether a signature on an instrument is that of the principal or that of the agent by whose hand it is written, the construction most favourable to the validity of the instrument must be adopted.[57] This latter provision is nearly always useless as a guide to the construction of the instrument, because in most cases the instrument is equally 'valid' in either event.[58]

5-185 The test to be applied when determining whether or not a person who signs a bill is personally liable upon the bill was clearly formulated by Lord Ellenborough as follows:[59]

> It is not a universal rule that a man who puts his name to a bill of exchange thereby makes himself personally liable, unless he states upon the face of the bill that he subscribes it for another, or by procuration of another, which are words of exclusion? Unless he says plainly 'I am the mere scribe', he becomes liable.

Although Lord Ellenborough was giving judgment in a case prior to the 1882 Act, it would seem that the same test must be applied at the present day.

5-186 The most difficult cases which the courts have had to decide are those concerning limited companies, and some of the decisions are difficult to justify, at any rate from a commercial aspect. Thus, in *Landes* v. *Marcus and Davids*,[60] a cheque had stamped across the top the words 'B. Marcus and Co. Ltd.' and was signed at the foot 'B. Marcus, Director. S. H. Davids, Director.—Secretary', the space for the signature of the secretary being left blank. The evidence showed that two directors had authority to sign cheques on behalf of the company and that the cheque had been drawn for goods supplied by the plaintiff to

---

56 S. 26(1).

57 S. 26(2).

58 The provision was, however, applied in *Elliott* v. *Bax-Ironside* [1925] 2 KB 301 in order to arrive at the correct construction of an endorsement on a bill of exchange.

59 *Leadbitter* v. *Farrow* (1816) 5 M & S 345, at p. 349. This passage from Lord Ellenborough's judgment was cited by Scrutton LJ, in *Elliott* v. *Bax-Ironside* [1925] 2 KB 301, at p. 308.

60 (1909) 25 TLR 478, following *Dutton* v. *Marsh* (1871) LR 6 QB 361. See also *Elliott* v. *Bax-Ironside* [1925] 2 KB 301.

the company. From a commercial aspect, there would seem to have been little doubt that this cheque was the company's cheque; yet the court held that the two directors were personally liable upon it. Accordingly to Jelf J, the directors, in drawing the cheque, had not said that they did so on behalf of the company, but they had added words showing that they signed in a representative capacity, and that brought them within the words of s. 26(1) of the Bills of Exchange Act 1882. Thus, the mere addition of words showing that they signed in a representative capacity was insufficient to enable them to escape liability.

5-187 The facts in the above-mentioned case may be compared with those in *Chapman* v. *Smethurst*,[61] a case decided by the Court of Appeal a few weeks before the trial of the action in *Landes* v. *Marcus and Davids*. A promissory note read as follows: 'Six months after demand I promise to pay to Mrs M. Chapman the sum of £300 for value received together with 6 per cent interest per annum. J. H. Smethurst's Laundry and Dye Works Limited. J. H. Smethurst, Managing Director.' The note had been made in respect of a loan by Mrs Chapman to the company for the purpose of improving the company's premises. The trial judge held Mr J. H. Smethurst personally liable upon the note on the ground that the word 'I' was 'very strong to show that the promissor was a person in the ordinary sense, an individual, and not the legal *persona* of a company . . .' The Court of Appeal had no difficulty in reversing this decision. Vaughan Williams LJ considered that anyone reading the promissory note would at once say that it was one which made the company liable.

5-188 The Companies Act 1985[62] provides, *inter alia*, that every company must have its name mentioned in legible characters in all bills of exchange, promissory notes, endorsements, cheques and orders for money purporting to be signed by or on behalf of the company. Any officer of a company or any person acting on its behalf who is party to a breach of these provisions is liable to a fine, and is further personally liable to the holder of any such bill of exchange, promissory note, cheque or order for money, unless the same is duly paid by the company.[63]

---

61 [1909] 1 KB 73; reversed [1909] 1 KB 927; followed in *Kettle* v. *Dunster and Wakefield* (1927) 43 TLR 770; *Britannia Electric Lamp Works Ltd* v. *D. Mandler and Co. Ltd* [1939] 2 KB 129. See also *Alliston Creamery* v. *Grosdanoff and Tracy* (1962) 34 DLR (2d) 189; *H. B. Etlin Co. Ltd* v. *Asselstyne* (1962) 34 DLR (2d) 191; both cases were noted in the *Journal of the Institute of Bankers*, Vol. 84 (1963), pp. 133–4.

62 S. 349(1).

63 S. 349(4). See *Scottish and Newcastle Breweries Ltd* v. *Blair and Others*, 1967 SLT 72; *Durham Fancy Goods Ltd* v. *Michael Jackson (Fancy Goods) Ltd and another* [1968] 2 All ER 987.

Accommodation cheques

5-189   The Bills of Exchange Act 1882[64] defines an accommodation party to a bill as a person who has signed the instrument as drawer, acceptor or endorser, without receiving value therefor, and for the purpose of lending his name to some other person. The Act provides that an accommodation party is liable on the instrument to a holder for value, and that it is immaterial whether, when such holder took the instrument, he knew such party to be an accommodation party.[65]

5-190   Occasionally, a cheque is drawn by an accommodation party. Suppose, for example, that B is short of funds and that he asks two of his friends, D and P, to help him. P has ready cash available, but he will only help B if D accepts responsibility for any assistance given to B. D draws a post-dated cheque for £1,000 and hands it to B, but makes it payable to P. (In the words of the Act, D signs the cheque as drawer, without receiving value therefor, and for the purpose of lending his name to B.) B takes the cheque to P, who gives him £1,000 in cash in exchange for the cheque. When the due date of the cheque arrives, P will present it for payment and, if it is dishonoured, he will be able to sue D on the cheque successfully. This is so, because the Act provides, as shown above, that an accommodation party (D) is liable on the instrument to a holder for value (P), even though P knew that D was an accommodation party.

64 S. 28(1).
65 S. 28(2).

6

Collection of cheques

In this chapter it is proposed to outline the methods for collecting the proceeds of cheques, and to examine some of the problems to which this work gives rise.

Section I
THE CLEARING SYSTEM

6-1 So many cheques and other instruments are received by banks every day for collection that it would clearly be a very cumbersome process if every cheque had to be sent by the collecting bank to the bank upon which it was drawn. For this reason, the clearing system has been devised. This enables cheques to be taken or sent to clearing centres, there to be sorted and dispatched to the drawee banks.

Categories of cheques

6-2 Cheques which are collected by bankers may be divided into three categories, namely (a) cheques drawn on the collecting branch, (b) cheques drawn on other branches of the collecting bank, and (c) cheques drawn on other banks.

(a) Cheques drawn on collecting branch

6-3 In this case the collecting bank and the paying bank are the same. When a cheque falling into this category is received at the counter, it is the usual practice for the cashier to examine it and to cancel the drawer's signature with his initials if the cheque is properly drawn. If, however, the drawer's account is not in funds, this will be brought to the cashier's notice, and he will 'remove' his cancellation by writing under the drawer's name the words 'cancelled in error' followed by his initials.[1] The cheque will then be dealt with in the usual way as an unpaid item:

---

1 See *Fernandey* v. *Glynn* (1808) 1 Camp 426n.; *Warwick* v. *Rogers* (1843) 15 M & G 340, approved by the Privy Council in *Prince* v. *Oriental Bank* (1878) 3 App Cas 325.

usually, it will be debited to the account of the customer who paid it in, and the cheque itself will be returned to him.

(b) Cheques drawn on other branches of collecting bank

6-4 These cheques are first crossed with the crossing stamp of the collecting bank and, as a general rule, the amounts are MICR[2] encoded before the cheques are remitted to the bank's clearing department. They are then sorted. The MICR code line printed along the foot of the cheques, including the amount of each cheque, is recorded on magnetic tape for updating customers' accounts on computers. The cheques themselves are sent to the branches upon which they are drawn.

(c) Cheques drawn on other banks

6-5 These cheques also are crossed with the crossing stamp of the collecting bank, the amounts are MICR encoded, and then the cheques are usually cleared through the Clearing House in London.

London Bankers' Clearing House

6-6 The first Clearing House in London seems to have been established about 1770 in a private room in a public house in Lombard Street. The way the Clearing House gradually developed and expanded is a most interesting chapter of banking history, but it is outside the scope of the present work.[3] It is proposed to examine briefly the functions of the following clearings, namely (a) the Town Clearing, (b) the Cheque Clearing, (c) the Credit Clearing and (d) BACS Clearing.

(a) The Town Clearing

6-7 This deals with articles *drawn upon and paid into* a Town office or branch of the Settlement Members.[4] (Articles drawn on Town offices or branches but paid into branches outside the Town Clearing area must be passed through the Cheque Clearing.) The Town offices and branches of the Settlement Members are situated in the City area around the Bank

2 Magnetic ink character recognition.
3 See P. W. Matthews, *The Bankers' Clearing House* (1921); W. Howarth, *Our Clearing System and Clearing Houses* (1884); W. J. Lawson, *The History of Banking* (1855), pp. 215–16; J. W. Gilbart, *The History and Principles of Banking* (1866), pp. 77–8; J. B. Martin, *The Grasshopper in Lombard Street* (1892), p. 168; J. Milnes Holden, *The History of Negotiable Instruments in English Law* (1955), pp. 214–15.
4 Now that the Clearings are open to financial institutions other than banks, members of a particular clearing are referred to as 'Settlement Members' of that Clearing.

of England; there are over one hundred offices and branches of these Settlement Members in the Town Clearing area.

6-8 There is a session of the Town Clearing each afternoon. The clearing is limited to:

(a) cheques for £100,000 or over, drawn on and paid into one of the Town offices or branches that day;

(b) clean due bills of exchange for any amount;

(c) walks payments for any amount. These are in payment of cheques, etc., drawn on non-settlement members which have not appointed an agent for clearing, and collected under walks arrangements,[5] and payments in respect of special collections between Settlement Members;

(d) payments in settlement of Credit Clearing transactions of any amount, including payments given by Settlement Members to non-settlement members and to Scottish and Irish banks;

(e) payments of any amount in settlement of Scottish and Irish Clearing.

6-9 Articles for less than £100,000 drawn on and paid into Town branches, must be passed through the Cheque Clearing.

6-10 Articles may have to be returned unpaid, either because of a technical irregularity or because there are not sufficient funds on the customer's account. Such items, with the reason for non-payment clearly marked thereon, must be returned to the Settlement Member at the Clearing House by 4.45 p.m. the same day.

(b) The Cheque Clearing

6-11 Articles to be passed through the Cheque Clearing include:

(a) all cheques drawn on a branch or office of a Settlement Member;

(b) all cheques drawn on or payable by non-settlement members which maintain either a debit or a full agency with a Settlement Member. These cheques must bear a sorting code number within a Settlement Member's range;

(c) claims for unpaid vouchers;

(d) bankers' payments;

(e) direct debit vouchers.

All cheques etc. presented in the Clearing must conform to the standards laid down from time to time.

5 *Post*, para. 6-18.

6-12   The following items should not be passed through the Cheque Clearing:

(a)   cheques drawn on Scottish or Irish branches or offices of those Settlement Members which participate also in the Scottish and/or Irish Cheque Clearing;

(b)   cheques drawn in currency other than sterling even if converted into sterling;

(c)   cheques with any attachments;

(d)   cheques to which charges or expenses have been added;

(e)   cheques drawn on non-settlement members other than those referred to in the preceding paragraph.

6-13   The Cheque Clearing takes place in the mornings only. Far more items pass through this clearing than through the Town Clearing. Cheques are sent to the Clearing House in trays transported on trolleys in electrically propelled vehicles. All the Settlement Members have installed computer equipment for the purpose of listing and sorting the cheques by electronic reader/sorters. After the cheques have been processed, they are sent to the branches on which they are drawn. Items exchanged in one day's Cheque Clearing do not, as a general rule, reach the drawee until the following day. Any article which cannot be paid is returned direct by post to the branch of the Settlement Member shown on the crossing. A computer programme allows the returning Settlement Member to input the details of the returned cheque through its computer terminal. The information is collected on magnetic tape which is passed to Bankers' Automated Clearing Services who provide the debit entries. Non-settlement members use an unpaid claim form, which is passed through the Cheque Clearing, in order to debit the collecting bank. Generally, unpaid cheques must be returned on the day of presentation. Where, however, the need to return a cheque has not been noticed on the day of presentation, a rule of the Clearing House, known as the 'Inadvertence Rule', usually allows the cheque to be returned unpaid on the next working day. If the cheque is over £500, advice of such non-payment must be given by telephone to the presenting bank not later than noon on the day of return.

(c) The Credit Clearing

6-14   This will be considered in Chapter 10.[6]

6 See *post*, paras 10-23/25.

(d) BACS Clearing

6-15 BACS Limited was first established as Bankers' Automated Clearing Services Limited in 1971. The company was renamed BACS Limited in 1986.[7]

Clearing agencies

6-16 Financial institutions which are not Settlement Members of a particular Clearing can avail themselves of the services of a clearing company by means of an 'agency' arrangement with a Settlement Member.

6-17 For cheque and credit clearing the 'agency' arrangements provided may be in the form of:

(a) 'full agency', which involves the allocation by the Settlement Member of one or more unique sorting code numbers from within the range of the Settlement Member and applies operationally to both credits and debits, or

(b) 'debit agency' which involves the use of the sorting code number of the branch of the Settlement Member with which the agency institution is in an account relationship, and applies operationally to debit items only.

The Walks Agency Clearing

6-18 This title is now applied to those cheques still in circulation which bear an extinct sorting code number (i.e. issued before agency arrangements were established) together with any other cheques which fall short of the standards required for automated processing. They are handled separately from the Cheque Clearing and are processed manually. This is a rapidly diminishing adjunct to the Cheque Clearing, and it will be phased out in due course.

The Daily Settlement

6-19 There used to be a daily settlement each day which took into account that day's Town Clearing, the previous day's Cheque Clearing, the previous day's Walks Agency Clearing and the previous day's BACS output. That system has been abolished. Each of the Clearings is now settled separately, and the relevant entries are passed to the Bank of England at 10.00 a.m. in respect of the Cheque Clearing and the Credit Clearing, and at the end of the day (usually 4.50 p.m.) in the case of the

7 See *post*, para. 10-32.

Town Clearing. BACS output is now settled directly from BACS to the Bank of England, and it does not enter into Clearing House figures.

Scottish and Irish collections

6-20 The Clearing banks used to present cheques drawn on the Scottish banks to the relevant London offices of the Scottish banks. The London offices used to forward them to their respective head offices in Edinburgh or Glasgow, and they used to forward the cheques to the branches on which they are drawn. However, many banks now send their Scottish cheques directly to Scotland by courier.

6-21 Cheques drawn on banks in Northern Ireland are handled on an agency basis through banks in Northern Ireland.

Special presentation of cheques

6-22 Sometimes a customer wishes to know the fate of a cheque speedily. His proper course is to instruct his bank to present the cheque 'specially'. The bank will remit the cheque by post direct to the drawee bank and will telephone the drawee bank to enquire whether the cheque has been paid. If it has, payment will be made by bank giro credit through the Credit Clearing to the collecting bank. If it has not been paid, it will be returned by post without entry. Sometimes, if the drawee bank is in the same locality as the collecting bank, the cheque is specially presented to the drawee bank by messenger.

6-23 Occasionally, a customer hands a cheque to his bank for collection and asks the bank to telephone the drawee bank in order to find out whether the cheque will be paid. This course serves only a limited purpose, because the drawee bank cannot pay the cheque until it is in their hands; their customer might stop payment of the cheque in the meantime. The most that they could be expected to say would be: 'The cheque would be paid if presented here now and in order.'

6-24 Special presentations give rise to a number of problems which are discussed later.[8]

The Association for Payment Clearing Services

6-25 A significant development took place in 1985. In that year the Association for Payment Clearing Services (APACS) was set up as the umbrella body for the payments industry to manage the development of payment clearing services and to oversee money transmission generally

---

8 *Post*, para. 7-53.

in the United Kingdom. It is an unincorporated association, and at January 1989 its members were the Abbey National Building Society, the Bank of England, the Bank of Scotland, Barclays Bank, Citibank, Clydesdale Bank, Co-operative Bank, Coutts & Co., Girobank, the Halifax Building Society, Lloyds Bank, Midland Bank, National Westminster Bank, the Nationwide Anglia Building Society, Northern Bank, Standard Chartered Bank, the Royal Bank of Scotland, Trustee Savings Bank, and Yorkshire Bank. In addition, APACS has a number of Associate Members who are not full Settlement Members of any clearing, but who provide payment services to their customers by means of agency in one or more of the clearings. Associate Members are entitled to receive information on developments in the clearings.

6-26 APACS was set up in 1985 as the result of a review of the membership, ownership and control of payment clearing systems undertaken by a Working Party under the chairmanship of Mr D. M. Child in 1984. The results of the review were published in a report in December 1984. The principal recommendation was that a new structure for the organization of payment clearing systems should be set up and that new rules regarding membership of such systems should be established. Membership of a clearing is now open to any financial institution which can demonstrate its ability to meet certain criteria.[9] These criteria include being subject to appropriate supervision, being able to meet the technical and operational requirements of membership, the maintenance of settlement account facilities at the Bank of England and accounting for at least a certain volume of items passing through the relevant clearing.

6-26A The main effect of the change in the structure of clearing systems was to divide the clearings into three groups, each owned and operated by an individual clearing company limited by shares. By separating the clearings in this way it became possible for an institution to be a member of one clearing without having to be a member of another. The three operating clearing companies are (a) the Cheque and Credit Clearing Company Limited, administering the Cheque Clearing and the Credit Clearing (the bulk paper clearings);[10] (b) the CHAPS and Town Clearing Company Limited, administering the Clearing House Automated Payments System[11] and the Town Clearing (the high-value clearings); and (c) BACS Limited, formerly Bankers Automated Clearing Services Limited.[12] APACS is at the head of this structure.

9 See the Child Committee's Report, Part 1, s. 1, para. 4.
10 For the Credit Clearing, see *post*, paras 10-23/25.
11 For the Clearing House Automated Payments System, known as CHAPS, see *post*, para. 10-32A.
12 For BACS Limited, see *post*, para. 10-32.

Membership of a clearing company carries with it membership of APACS.[13]

Section 2
COLLECTING BANKER'S DUTIES

6-27 A banker's duties in relation to the collection of cheques may be considered under the following headings, namely the choice of the correct clearing channel, the Bank of England's responsibility as a collecting bank, the time allowed for presenting a cheque for payment, and the giving of notice of dishonour.

Choice of clearing channel

6-28 As his customer's agent in regard to the collection of cheques, a banker is bound to use reasonable care and diligence in presenting and securing payment of such cheques; accordingly, a banker must always choose the speediest section of the Clearing House when presenting a customer's cheques for payment.

6-29 In *Forman* v. *Bank of England*[14] the plaintiff who was a customer of the Law Courts branch of the Bank of England, paid into his account before 3 p.m. on 21 May 1901 a cheque for £500 payable to himself and drawn by the Norwich Union Life Insurance Society upon 'Barclay & Co. Ltd., Bank Plain, Norwich, or Head Office, 54 Lombard Street, London'. When the cheque was paid in, the plaintiff had a credit balance of £103 6s. 10d. It was a rule of the defendant bank that, if cheques drawn on city banks were paid in before 3 p.m., they could be drawn against the next day. On 22 May the plaintiff drew a cheque upon the defendant bank for £239 in favour of a third person, which was presented on 23 May and dishonoured, owing to the fact that the defendants had treated the Norwich Union cheque as being payable at Norwich, as a result of which the amount had not been collected when the cheque for £239 was presented. The plaintiff brought an action against the defendants for damages for breach of contract in dishonouring his cheque for £239, or damages for delay in collecting the cheque for £500 and placing the proceeds to his credit. At the trial, expert witnesses from various banks expressed the opinion that the

---

13 EftPos UK Limited was formed in order to oversee the development of a national EFTPOS system, but it no longer performs this function.
14 (1902) 18 TLR 339.

cheque paid in was a London and not a country cheque, and stated that there was a general custom that such cheques should be treated as London cheques. Lord Alverston CJ left the following questions to the jury, '(1) Was the cheque a cheque on a city bank? (2) Is there a recognized and general custom amongst London bankers that cheques in this form should be treated as London cheques?' The jury answered both questions in the affirmative, and assessed the damages at £75.

The Bank of England's responsibility as a collecting bank

6-29A   A very interesting question was resolved in *Barclays Bank plc and Others* v. *Bank of England*.[15] Briefly, there had been a long standing disagreement between the member banks of the Committee of London Clearing Bankers (namely, Barclays Bank, Coutts & Co., Lloyds Bank, Midland Bank, National Westminster Bank and Williams & Glyn's Bank) and the Bank of England. The Bank of England clears cheques for its own customers by sending the cheques through the General Clearing or the Town Clearing in the usual way. The Clearing banks have always paid the cost of collecting these cheques. The Bank of England maintained that it did not need to pay a proportion of the cost on the ground that it had discharged its responsibility by delivering the cheques to the Clearing House. Eventually, it was agreed that the matter should be resolved by arbitration before Bingham J in accordance with s. 4 of the Administration of Justice Act 1970. Having considered the evidence and the submissions, Bingham J made the following award:

> Where bank A (the presenting bank) receives from a customer for collection a cheque drawn on bank B (the paying bank) by a person having an account at a branch of the paying bank and the cheque is dealt with through the inter-bank system for clearing cheques, the presenting bank's responsibility to its customer in respect of the collection of the cheque is discharged only when the cheque is physically delivered to the said branch for decisions whether it should be paid or not.

The practical result of this award was that the Bank of England must now pay its fair share of the cost of operating the clearing system.

Time for presenting cheque for payment

6-30   As stated above, a banker to whom a cheque is delivered for collection is under a duty to his customer to use reasonable diligence in presenting it for payment. To take an extreme case, if a banker put such

---

15 [1985] 1 All ER 385. See the helpful notes on this case by Mr Andrew Laidlaw of the Midland Bank's legal department in *Banking World*, January 1985, p. 49.

cheques into a drawer and forgot about them for several days, there would be no doubt that this would amount to a failure to use reasonable diligence in presenting the cheques for payment. Hence, the banker would be liable to the customer for any loss suffered by him; if, for example, the drawer of one of the mislaid cheques was adjudicated bankrupt with the result that the customer obtained only a dividend in the bankruptcy, the collecting banker would be liable to the customer for the amount so lost.

6-31 The time allowed for presenting a cheque for payment is not laid down by statute. The banker's duty in this respect would seem to depend upon the current usages of bankers and the facts of the particular case. [16] There is authority for the view that a collecting banker is not bound to transmit cheques on the day he receives them, but has until post time the next day for doing so. [17] If the cheque is drawn on the branch receiving the credit, that branch need not decide whether or not to pay the cheque until the day *after* it is paid in, [18] unless the customer who pays it in asks to be informed forthwith whether or not it is paid.

Giving notice of dishonour

6-32 A collecting bank must always give prompt notice to its customer if any cheque paid in by him for the credit of his account or cashed for him by the bank are dishonoured. The safest course to follow is to send written notice of dishonour to the customer on the same day as the unpaid item is received by the bank. [19] Unless the bank wishes to make a claim against the drawer of the cheque as explained below, the bank will debit the amount of the cheque to its customer's account and return the cheque to him forthwith. This constitutes notice of dishonour. [20]

6-33 The customer must then give prompt notice of dishonour to prior parties if he wishes to retain their liability. [21] Any failure to give notice of dishonour in accordance with the rules laid down in the Bills of Exchange Act 1882 will usually have the effect of releasing the person to whom proper notice should have been given from liability on the cheque. [22]

---

16 *Cf.*, ss 45(2) and 74(2), Bills of Exchange Act 1882.
17 *Hare* v. *Henty* (1861) 10 CB (NS) 65; applied by the Supreme Court of the Republic of Ireland in *Royal Bank of Ireland Ltd* v. *O'Rourke* [1962] IR 159.
18 *Boyd* v. *Emmerson* (1834) 2 A & E 184.
19 Bills of Exchange Act 1882, s. 49(12) and (14), allows notice to be given on the following day in certain circumstances; but the safest course is that stated above.
20 S. 49(6).
21 But he does not usually need to give notice of dishonour to the drawer of a cheque; see *ante*, para. 5-137.
22 S. 48.

6-34 Even if a cheque is returned unpaid and the circumstances are such that the collecting bank decides to present it again forthwith (e.g. where the answer was 'Refer to drawer, please re-present'; or 'Post-dated' and the due date has now arrived), the bank should nevertheless give notice of dishonour to its customer. The fact that the cheque has been dishonoured makes it obligatory to give notice of dishonour in accordance with the Act, and any failure to do so may result in loss.

Section 3
BANK AS HOLDER FOR VALUE

6-35 When a cheque is returned unpaid to the collecting bank, the customer's account may not be sufficiently in credit to enable the bank to debit the amount of the cheque to the account without creating an overdraft; or if the account is already overdrawn, the debiting of the unpaid cheque thereto may cause the amount of the agreed overdraft to be exceeded. In such cases, it may be open to the collecting bank to retain the cheque and to claim, as holder for value, against the drawer or some other party to the cheque, provided that the bank gives notice of dishonour where this is necessary.[23] If the bank returned the cheque to its customer, it would no longer be the holder of the cheque, and so its claim as holder for value would fail;[24] but the mere debiting of the cheque to the customer's account would not be fatal to the bank's claim as holder for value.[25]

6-36 In order to establish its rights as holder for value, a bank must first be a 'holder' as defined in the Bills of Exchange Act 1882,[26] or must bring itself within s. 2 of the Cheques Act 1957; and, secondly, it must have given valuable consideration.

6-37 By virtue of s. 2 of the Cheques Act 1957, a bank will have the same rights as a holder, even though the person who pays in the cheque does not endorse it; and the House of Lords decided in *Westminster Bank Ltd* v. *Zang*[27] that where the holder of a cheque, without endorsing it, pays it in for the credit of *someone else's account*, the bank may still enjoy the rights of a holder.

---

23 It is not usually necessary to give notice of dishonour to the drawer of a cheque; see *ante*, para. 5-137.
24 *Lloyds Bank Ltd* v. *Dolphin* (1920) *The Times*, 2nd December.
25 *Royal Bank of Scotland* v. *Tottenham* [1894] 2 QB 715. In practice, however, it is usual to debit the amount of the cheque to a suspense account or to unpaid bills account.
26 See *ante*, para. 5-61. In particular, there must be no forgery of an essential signature.
27 [1966] AC 182.

6-38   As regards valuable consideration, attention was drawn in an earlier chapter to the provisions of s. 27(1) of the Bills of Exchange Act 1882 governing valuable consideration in regard to cheques.[28] Briefly, valuable consideration may be constituted by either (a) any consideration sufficient to support a simple contract, or (b) an antecedent debt or liability. In the following cases a bank may become a holder for value of a cheque.

(a) Payment against uncleared cheque

6-39   In *National Bank Ltd* v. *Silke*[29] the defendant drew a cheque for £450 payable to the order of J. F. Moriarty and crossed it 'Account of J. F. Moriarty, Esq., National Bank, Dublin'. The payee endorsed the cheque and sent it to the National Bank directing them to credit his account with the amount of the cheque. Before the cheque was cleared, the bank allowed Moriarty to draw upon it. The cheque was dishonoured, the defendant having countermanded payment on the ground that it had been obtained by misrepresentation. The Court of Appeal held that the plaintiff bank was a holder in due course of the cheque and entitled to succeed in an action against the drawer for the amount of it, because the bank had acted in good faith, did not know of the misrepresentation, and had given value for the cheque. The Court of Appeal made it clear that the crossing 'Account of J. F. Moriarity, Esq., National Bank, Dublin' did not restrict the transferability or negotiability of the cheque. If, however, the defendant had added 'Not negotiable' to the crossing, the bank could not have claimed any better title to the cheque than the payee had.[30]

(b) Reduction of advance

6-40   In *M'Lean* v. *Clydesdale Banking Co.*,[31] a customer who had an overdraft at the Clydesdale Bank persuaded a man named M'Lean to draw a cheque for £265 in his favour. The customer paid it into his bank account, so that it might be collected in reduction of his overdraft. Almost immediately, the drawer of the cheque countermanded payment

---

28 See *ante*, para. 5-128.
29 [1891] 1 QB 435. See also *Lloyds Bank Ltd* v. *Hornby* (1933) *The Financial Times*, 5 July; *Midland Bank Ltd* v. *Charles Simpson Motors Ltd* (1961) *Journal of the Institute of Bankers*, Vol. 82, p. 38; *Barclays Bank Ltd* v. *Harding* (1962) *Journal of the Institute of Bankers*, Vol. 83, p. 109; *Midland Bank Ltd* v. *R. V. Harris Ltd* [1963] 1 WLR 1021. In all these cases the plaintiff bank had paid against uncleared effects. In *Westminster Bank Ltd* v. *Zang* [1966] AC 182, the plaintiff bank failed to establish that it had paid against uncleared effects.
30 Bills of Exchange Act 1882, s. 81; see *ante*, para. 5-42.
31 (1883) 9 App Cas 95.

of it, with the result that it was returned unpaid to the Clydesdale Bank. The bank brought proceedings against the drawer, who contended that the bank had obtained no better title to the cheque than the payee had. The House of Lords rejected this argument and upheld the decision of the Court of Session where it had been held that, as the bank had received the cheque in reduction of the balance due to it, the bank had become a holder for value. Thus the bank's claim against the drawer succeeded. (At the present day, the case would be decided under s. 27(1)(b) of the Bills of Exchange Act 1882, because the valuable consideration was constituted by an 'antecedent debt or liability', namely the bank overdraft. As, however, the transactions in *M'Lean's* case took place before the 1882 Act was passed, the House of Lords did not base its decision upon the provisions of the Act.)

(c) Lien on cheque

6-41 Section 27(3) of the Bills of Exchange Act 1882 provides that where the holder of a cheque has a lien on it, arising either from contract or by implication of law, he is deemed to be a holder for value to the extent of the sum for which he has a lien. A bank has a lien on (i.e. a right to retain) any cheques delivered into its possession by a customer, provided that the customer is indebted to the bank and that the bank has not agreed expressly or impliedly that its right shall be excluded.[32] These rules sometimes enable a bank to claim that it is a holder for value of a cheque paid in by a customer even though the bank has not allowed him to draw against it before it is cleared: the mere fact that the customer's account is overdrawn is sufficient to enable the bank to exercise its lien, and then the bank will be deemed to be a holder for value to the extent of the sum for which it has a lient.[33] If a bank has a lien on a cheque, it should not part with the cheque, otherwise the lien will be lost.[34]

(d) Encashment of third-party cheque

6-42 If a bank cashes a cheque for a customer, the cheque having been drawn in the customer's favour by a third party, the bank becomes a

---

32 For a detailed account of the banker's lien, see H. L. Hart, *The Law of Banking* (4th ed., 1931), Vol. II, pp. 843 *et seq*. For examples of cases where a bank was held to have a lien on a cheque paid in by a customer for collection, see *Re Keever (a Bankrupt), Ex parte the Trustee of the Property of the Bankrupt* v. *Midland Bank Ltd* [1957] Ch 182; and *Barclays Bank Ltd* v. *Astley Industrial Trust Ltd* [1970] 2 QB 527.

33 See, for example, *Re Keever, supra.*

34 In *Westminster Bank Ltd* v. *Zang*, the bank appears to have conceded that it had lost its lien by returning the cheque to the customer's solicitors: see *per* Danckwerts LJ [1966] AC 182, at p. 205.

holder for value. If the cheque is payable to the customer or order, the customer should endorse it for the purpose of negotiating it to the bank; if the cheque is payable to bearer, the customer's endorsement is unnecessary for this purpose, but even in this case his endorsement should be obtained for the purpose of securing his liability on the cheque.

6-43 The encashing bank does *not* become a holder for value when a cheque is encashed under an open credit established by the drawee bank; in that case the encashing bank *pays* the cheque as agent for the drawee bank and does not become a holder for value.

6-44 If in any of the four cases stated above the cheque is crossed 'Not negotiable', the bank will not obtain any better title to the cheque than the customer had.[35]

Section 4
CLAIMS BY THIRD PARTIES AGAINST COLLECTING BANKERS

6-45 There are many ways in which those who are so minded can deal wrongfully with cheques. This subject closely affects collecting bankers, because a customer who is not entitled to a cheque sometimes presents it to his bank for collection.[36] In some cases, the customer knows perfectly well that he has no right to the cheque; for example, he may have stolen it. But these cases are in a minority because, if the customer had in fact stolen the cheque, he would not usually be so naïve as to pay the cheque into an account in his own name. In many cases, the customer does not know that he has no right to the cheque. This can easily happen; for example, a cheque which was originally drawn payable to X or order may have passed through several hands, and X's endorsement may have been forged. As a general rule, no one can acquire a good title to an order cheque if the payee's endorsement has been forged.[37]

---

35 Bills of Exchange Act 1882, s. 81; see *ante*, para. 5-42.
36 On this subject generally, see Lord Chorley, 'The law relating to the collection of cheques by bankers for their customers' (being the Gilbart Lectures on Banking, 1953); Maurice Megrah, 'The decline and fall of section 82', *Journal of the Institute of Bankers*, Vol. LXXVII (1956), pp. 256–63; Maurice Megrah, 'The cheque in law and practice: an appraisal of the Bills of Exchange Act 1882' (being the Spring Lectures on Banking, 1957), *Journal of the Institute of Bankers*, Vol. LXXVIII (1957), pp. 108–42, 212–26; Gordon Borrie, 'Problems of the collecting banker', *Modern Law Review*, Vol. 23 (1960), pp. 16–30.
37 Bills of Exchange Act 1882, s. 24.

Classification of third-party claims

6-46 A person whose cheque has been stolen or obtained by other unlawful means may have to consider whether he has a valid claim against the bank which collected the proceeds of the cheque. Of course, he always has a valid claim against the wrongdoer, but wrongdoers often disappear, and in any event they are usually impecunious. Banks do not disappear, nor are they impecunious. The possible claims against collecting banks may be considered under two main headings, (a) claims at common law, and (b) claims in equity.

(a) Claims at common law

6-47 Under this heading there are two types of remedy for consideration, first, an action for damages for the tort of conversion, and, secondly, an action for money had and received by the bank to the use of the plaintiff.

(i) Conversion

6-48 'Conversion at common law may be committed in so many different ways that any comprehensive definition is probably impossible, but the connecting thread running through the cases seems to be that the wrong is committed by a dealing with the goods of a person which constitutes an unjustifiable denial of his rights in them or the assertion of rights inconsistent therewith.'[38] As Scrutton LJ observed in *Lloyds Bank Ltd* v. *The Chartered Bank of India, Australia and China*,[39] 'conversion primarily is conversion of chattels' but, as the learned lord justice went on to explain, a series of decisions has surmounted the difficulty of applying this tort to cheques 'by treating the conversion as of the chattel, the piece of paper, the cheque under which the money was collected, and the value of the chattel converted as the money received under it'.

6-49 It is usually said that the act of conversion, as far as collecting banks are concerned, consists in presenting the cheque for someone who is not entitled to it, and obtained the money.[40] There is, however, some authority for the view that the mere receipt of the instrument from a person who is not entitled to it amounts to conversion. Thus, in *Fine Art*

---

38 *Winfield and Jolowicz on Tort* (12th ed., 1984), p. 479. The tort may be committed by someone who is acting quite innocently; the mere wrongful act, without any guilty knowledge, constitutes conversion.

39 [1929] 1 KB 40, at p. 55.

40 *Kleinwort, Sons & Co.* v. *Comptoir National D'Escompte de Paris* [1894] 2 QB 157; *Lacave & Co.* v. *Crédit Lyonnais* [1897] 1 QB 148; *A. L. Underwood Ltd* v. *Bank of Liverpool and Martins* [1924] 1 KB 775.

Society v. *Union Bank of London*,[41] the plaintiffs banked with the defendants. The plaintiffs' secretary also banked with the defendants, and he paid into his own account certain post office orders belonging to the plaintiffs which he ought to have paid into their account. Two members of the Court of Appeal[42] held that when the secretary handed the post office orders across the counter for credit of his own account, and the bank clerk accepted them, the bank thereby converted them. That part of the decision has been criticized, principally on the ground that so long as an instrument remains in the hands of the bank as a mere intermediary, there is not such an interference with the property as to amount to conversion.

6-50 It is not always easy to decide whether or not a prospective plaintiff has a sufficient interest in chattels, including cheques, to enable him to bring an action for damages for conversion. The reported cases[43] seem to show that a plaintiff can maintain an action for conversion if, at the time of the defendant's act, he had (1) ownership and possession of the goods, or (2) possession of them, or (3) an immediate right to possess them, but without either ownership or actual possession: but in this third case he will lose his action if the defendant proves that the title to the goods is in some third party.

6-51 Categories (1) and (2) above do not call for comment. Category (3) is important, especially in regard to claims against collecting banks. One frequently finds that the plaintiff is not in possession of the cheque at the time when the bank is alleged to have converted it. Accordingly, the plaintiff must prove that he had an immediate right to possession of the cheque at that time. In this connection reference may be made to *Marquess of Bute* v. *Barclays Bank Ltd.*[44] In that case the instruments were actually payable to the wrongdoer, but McNair J decided that the plaintiff was entitled to immediate possession of them, because the payee had left the service of the plaintiff and the payee's only title to the instruments stemmed from the fact that he had been a servant of the plaintiff. Thus, the plaintiff was entitled to bring an action for damages for conversion against the bank which collected the proceeds of the warrants for the payee. The payee ought to have handed over the instruments to his former employer. By handing them over to the bank for the credit of an account in his own name, the payee converted them; and the bank was likewise liable for conversion.

41 (1886) 17 QBD 705.
42 Fry and Bowen LJJ. Lord Esher MR was more cautious, see (1886) 17 QBD, at p. 709.
43 The relevant authorities are examined in *Winfield and Jolowicz on Tort* (12th ed., 1984), p. 487.
44 [1955] 1 QB 202.

6-52 It is doubtful whether the drawer of a cheque, who has been induced by fraud to draw it, can be said to have an immediate right to possess it, so as to enable him to bring an action for damages for conversion. Suppose, for example, that a thief stole a car and purported to sell it to a motor dealer, who drew his cheque in favour of the thief. The thief paid the cheque into his bank account and withdrew the proceeds. Would the thief or his bank be liable to the drawer of the cheque for conversion of the proceeds? On the one hand, the old case of *Tate* v. *Wilts and Dorset Bank*[45] appears to support the view that there has been no conversion of the cheque in a case of this sort, on the ground that the cheque was given in respect of a voidable, and not a void, contract. At the time when the proceeds of the cheque were collected, the thief's title to the cheque had not been avoided. This line of reasoning leads to the conclusion that 'where the collection has been for a customer having a revocable title unrevoked at the time the money was received and handed over', an action for conversion will not lie.[46]

6-53 On the other hand, some doubt was cast upon *Tate's* case by Sankey LJ in *Lloyds Bank Ltd* v. *The Chartered Bank of India, Australia and China*.[47] Furthermore, the Bills of Exchange Act 1882 seems to have been passed on the assumption that a collecting bank would be liable to a plaintiff in cases where a customer had a voidable title to a cheque which he tendered for collection.[48] As against this, however, it could be argued that Parliament misunderstood the law, and that a mere assumption by Parliament has no legislative force. A final solution cannot be given until the courts have had the opportunity of dealing expressly with it.

(ii) Money had and received

6-54 A person whose goods have been wrongfully converted by another person has been able, for very many years, to sue for the proceeds as 'money had and received to his use', i.e. instead of suing for damages for conversion. In time, the action for money had and received was recognized as being appropriate in cases where the cheques were

---

45 (1899) *Legal Decisions Affecting Bankers*, Vol. 1, p. 286. See also *Holland* v. *Russell* (1863) 4 B & S 14; *Great Western Railway Co.* v. *London and County Banking Co. Ltd* [1901] AC 414.

46 *Halsbury's Laws of England* (4th ed.) Vol. 3, p. 82.

47 [1928] 1 KB 40, at pp. 67–8.

48 See s. 82 (now replaced by the Cheques Act 1957, s. 4(1)) where the actual words used are 'no title or a defective title'. The expression 'defective title' would seem to include a voidable title. See also s. 29(2) of the 1882 Act.

converted.[49] The earliest claims against collecting banks were actions for money had and received.[50]

6-55 A plaintiff who brings an action for money had and received is said to sue in quasi-contract.[51] In days gone by, there were procedural advantages in putting one's claim in that way,[52] but in modern times there are no such advantages, and it is usually sufficient for a plaintiff to sue for damages for conversion, although sometimes a plaintiff still claims in the alternative for money had and received.[53]

6-56 Actions for damages for conversion and for money had and received are usually statute-barred six years after the wrongful act by virtue of the Limitation Act 1980.[54]

(b) Claims in equity

6-57 There is a well-established principle that a person becomes a constructive trustee if he 'received trust property with actual or constructive notice that it was trust property and that the transfer to him was a breach of trust'.[55] Accordingly, if a bank collects a cheque in circumstances where an intelligent person should see that a breach of trust would thereby be committed, or would be likely to be committed, it would seem that the bank thereby becomes a constructive trustee of the proceeds.[56] An advantage, from the plaintiff's standpoint, of establishing that a bank is a constructive trustee is that time does not then run

---

49 *Down* v. *Halling* (1825) 4 B & C 330 is probably one of the earliest reported actions for money had and received in respect of a cheque.

50 Examples are *Ogden* v. *Benas* (1874) LR 9 CP 513; *Arnold* v. *Cheque Bank* (1876) 1 CPD 578.

51 See Sir P. H. Winfield, *The Law of Quasi-Contracts* (1952), and especially pp. 91–102.

52 For an account of these advantages, see *United Australia Ltd* v. *Barclays Bank Ltd* [1941] AC 1, p. 13, *per* Viscount Simon LC.

53 In *Bavins, Junr. & Sims* v. *London and South Western Bank* [1900] 1 QB 270, the plaintiff, who was suing in respect of the conversion of a conditional order, added an alternative claim for money had and received, because there was some doubt whether an action for conversion would lie in respect of an instrument which was not a cheque. Likewise, in *Marquess of Bute* v. *Barclays Bank Ltd* [1955] 1 QB 202, the plaintiff brought alternative claims in respect of certain payment warrants which were not cheques, but the claim for money had and received proved to have been unnecessary, because McNair J awarded damages for conversion.

54 S. 2.

55 Snell's *Principles of Equity* (28th ed., 1982), p. 194.

56 See *Coleman* v. *Bucks and Oxon Union Bank* [1897] 2 Ch 243, and the cases therein cited; in *Coleman's* case the bank escaped liability because the court found that the bank had no knowledge that the wrongdoer intended to commit a breach of trust.

against the plaintiff under the Limitation Act 1980.[57] If, therefore, a period of more than six years has elasped since the wrongful act, a plaintiff whose claim for damages for conversion or for money had and received would be statute-barred, may nevertheless be able to proceed against a collecting bank in equity in the circumstances indicated above.

Section 5
STATUTORY DEFENCE

6-58 When a claim is brought against a bank on the ground that it has collected the proceeds of a cheque or other similar instrument for someone who was not entitled to it, the commonest defence pleaded by the bank is the special statutory defence which, for very many years, Parliament has provided for the protection of collecting banks.[58] The first Act which conferred this special protection was the Crossed Cheques Act 1876.

Crossed Cheques Act 1876

6-59 Some two years before this Act was passed, a successful claim had been brought against a collecting bank. That case, *Ogden* v. *Benas*,[59] is probably the earliest reported case of this nature, and although the bank had acted very imprudently, the decision focused attention upon the risks to which collecting banks were exposed, even when they acted carefully. In *Ogden's* case, the plaintiff drew a crossed cheque in favour of Vincent Willis or order and sent it to him by post. The defendants were bankers in Liverpool, and a person who was unknown to them presented the cheque to them and asked if they would collect the proceeds from the bank in London upon which it was drawn. The defendants agreed to do so and the person presenting the cheque endorsed it with the name of Vincent Willis. The defendants sent the cheque to their agents in London, who presented it and obtained payment. The person who had presented the cheque had been told to call a few days later. He did call, and he got the money. It was proved subsequently that the name 'Vincent Willis' written on the back of the cheque was a forgery. The drawer of the cheque brought an action against the defendants for the amount of the cheque as money received by him to his use. The defendants were held liable to him.

---

57 S. 21(1) The words 'trust' and 'trustee' appearing in that section include 'constructive trust' and 'constructive trustee': see Limitation Act 1980, s. 38(1) and Trustee Act 1925, s. 68.

58 For other possible defences, see *post*, paras 6-130/9.

59 (1874) LR 9 CP 513. See also *Arnold* v. *The Cheque Bank* (1876) 1 CPD 578.

6-60   The Cross Cheques Act 1876[60] enacted, in effect, that a banker collecting a cheque crossed generally or specially to himself was in future to be relieved of all liability, provided that three requirements were satisfied, namely:

(a)   that the banker received payment of the cheque for a customer;
(b)   that the banker acted in good faith; and
(c)   that the banker acted without negligence.

6-61   Even if the 1876 Act had been in force at the relevant time, the collecting bankers in *Ogden* v. *Benas* would not have been protected by it for two reasons. First, they did not receive payment of the cheque for a customer, because 'there must be some sort of account, either a deposit or a current account or some similar relation, to make a man a customer of a banker'.[61] Secondly, the Act required the banker to act 'without negligence', and it would seem to have been the height of folly to collect the proceeds of a cheque for a stranger, without any introduction, merely on the strength of his assertion that he was the named payee. Accordingly, the defendant bankers in *Ogden* v. *Benas* could not have established that they had acted 'without negligence'.

6-62   The relevant provisions of the Crossed Cheques Act 1876 may be summed up by stating that they were designed to protect a collecting banker who acted honestly and carefully ('in good faith and without negligence'). There can be no doubt that this policy was sound in principle, but it was anomalous that the rule should have applied only to the collection of crossed cheques; in respect of uncrossed cheques there was no protection at all.

Bills of Exchange Act 1882

6-63   The Bills of Exchange Act 1882 codified the law relating to bills of exchange (including cheques) and promissory notes, and it repealed a number of earlier statutes.[62] One of the Acts that was repealed was the Crossed Cheques Act 1876. Its provisions were, however, substantially re-enacted by ss 76 to 82 inclusive of the 1882 Act. The relevant provisions relating to the protection of the collecting banker were re-enacted in s. 82 of the 1882 Act.[63] The anomalous rule was preserved that, although a banker was protected when he collected a crossed cheque for a customer 'in good faith and without negligence', he was given no protection when collecting open cheques. It was most unfortunate that,

---

60   S. 12.
61   *Great Western Railway Co.* v. *London and County Banking Co. Ltd* [1901] AC 414, *per* Lord Davey, at pp. 420–1; *ante*, para. 1-66.
62   S. 96 and Sched. II.
63   S. 82 was repealed by the Cheques Act 1957, s. 6(3) and Sched.; see *post*, para. 6-73.

when the 1882 Act was passed, the opportunity was not taken of extending the protection to all cheques, whether open or crossed: there was no logical reason for differentiating between them.

Revenue Act 1883

6-64 The provisions of the crossed cheque sections of the Bills of Exchange Act 1882, namely ss 76 to 82, were extended by s. 17 of the Revenue Act 1883 to 'any document issued by a customer of any banker, and intended to enable any person or body corporate to obtain payment from such banker of the sum mentioned in such document'. Furthermore, the section provided that, for the purposes of the section, the Paymaster-General, and the Queen's and Lord Treasurer's Remembrancer in Scotland, were to be 'deemed to be bankers' and the public officers drawing on them were to be 'deemed to be customers'.

6-65 The object of s. 17 of the Revenue Act 1883 was to extend the crossed cheque sections of the Bills of Exchange Act 1882 (including the section which provided protection for the collecting banker), to instruments which were not strictly cheques, for example, conditional orders issued by customers,[64] and warrants issued by certain government departments.[65] The section was repealed, but its provisions were substantially re-enacted, by the Cheques Act 1957.[66]

Bills of Exchange (Crossed Cheques) Act 1906

6-66 It was the celebrated *Gordon* case[67] which brought about the passing of the Bills of Exchange (Crossed Cheques) Act 1906. In that case, a fraudulent clerk had paid into his own accounts at two banks a number of crossed cheques, the endorsements on which he had forged. If those had been the only material facts, the collecting banks would have been protected by s. 82 of the Bills of Exchange Act 1882, provided (as was admitted or proved) that they had acted 'in good faith and without negligence'. However, there were two other relevant facts to be taken into consideration: first, the defendant banks had credited the cheques to the customer's account immediately they were paid in and before clearance; and, second, there was, as between the customer and the banks, an arrangement, or course of practice, under which the bank

---

64 *Post*, para. 9-34.

65 For an example, see *Marquess of Bute* v. *Barclays Bank Ltd* [1955] 1 QB 202.

66 Ss. 4(2), 6(3) and Sched. Furthermore, the 1957 Act extended the protection to *uncrossed* instruments.

67 *Capital and Counties Bank Ltd* v. *Gordon; London, City and Midland Bank Ltd* v. *Gordon* [1903] AC 240.

allowed the customer to draw against the amounts of cheques paid in and credited before they were cleared.

6-67   The decision of the House of Lords, upholding that of the Court of Appeal, was to the effect that the banks were not entitled to the protection of s. 82, because they were not (as the section required) collecting the instruments 'for a customer': they were collecting the cheques for themselves. Lord Lindley summed up the position by stating that, as long as s. 82 remained unamended, bankers who desired its protection would have to be more cautious, and not place crossed cheques paid in for collection to the credit of their customers before such cheques were paid.[68]

6-68   Few decisions of the House of Lords have caused as much controversy as that in the *Gordon* case, but it would be inappropriate to explore the arguments here.[69] The decision certainly caused consternation in the banking world.[70] As a result of pressure from the Central Association of Bankers,[71] the Bills of Exchange (Crossed Cheques) Act 1906 was passed. It enacted that a banker receives payment of a crossed cheque for a customer within s. 82 of the Bills of Exchange Act 1882, 'notwithstanding that he credits his customer's account with the amount of the cheque before receiving payment thereof'.[72]

6-69   The object of the 1906 Act was, therefore, to overcome the decision in the *Gordon* case. The Act was repealed, but its provisions were re-enacted, by the Cheques Act 1957.[73]

Bills of Exchange Act (1882) Amendment Act 1932

6-70   This Act dealt with bankers' drafts. Where the same bank is both the drawer and the drawee of a draft, the instrument is not a bill of exchange, and therefore, is not a cheque.[74] Accordingly, s. 82 of the Bills of Exchange Act 1882, which protected a banker when collecting crossed cheques, did not apply to these drafts. In order to remedy the situation, the 1932 Act provided that the crossed cheque sections of the Bills of Exchange Act 1882, namely ss 76 to 82, as amended by the Bills

---

68 [1903] AC, at p. 249.
69 For a more detailed discussion of the *Gordon* case, see J. Milnes Holden, *The History of Negotiable Instruments in English Law* (1955), pp. 271–5.
70 See, for example, the Inaugural Address of the President of the Institute of Bankers, Mr J. Herbert Tritton, in November 1903, published in *The Journal of the Institute of Bankers*, Vol. XXIV (1903), pp. 505–6.
71 For details of the steps which they took, see Holden, *op. cit.*, p. 274.
72 S. 1.
73 Ss 4(1), 6(3) and Sched.
74 Bills of Exchange Act 1882, s. 3. But see s. 5(2), *ante*, para. 5-13.

of Exchange (Crossed Cheques) Act 1906, should apply to a bankers' draft as if the draft were a cheque.[75]

6-71 The object of the 1932 Act was, therefore, to assimilate crossed bankers' drafts to crossed cheques. The Act was repealed, but its provisions were re-enacted by the Cheques Act 1957.[76]

Cheques Act 1957

6-72 The object of the Cheques Act 1957 was to implement the recommendations of the Report of the Committee on Cheque Endorsement, which had been published in November 1956.[77] This Committee, which met under the chairmanship of Mr A. A. Mocatta, OBE, QC (subsequently Mr Justice Mocatta), had recommended 'that steps should be taken to remove the need for the endorsement of cheques that are to be collected through a bank for the payee's account'.[78]

6-73 As far as collecting bankers are concerned, the Cheques Act 1957[79] made a clean sweep of the statute book by repealing all the then existing provisions which afforded protection to them.[80] The provisions of the 1957 Act which now protect collecting bankers are contained in s. 4.

6-74 Subsection 1 of s. 4 provides that where a banker, in good faith and without negligence:

   (a)   receives payment for a customer of an instrument to which the section applies; or

   (b)   having credited a customer's account with the amount of such an instrument, receives payment thereof for himself;

and the customer has no title, or a defective title, to the instrument, the banker is not to incur any liability to the true owner of the instrument by reason only of having received payment thereof. It will be observed that this subsection incorporates the provisions which were formerly

---

75 S. 1.

76 Ss 4(2), 6(3) and Sched. Furthermore, the 1957 Act extended the protection to *uncrossed* instruments.

77 Cmnd. 3. For articles on this Act, see Maurice Megrah, 'Cheques Act 1957', *Journal of the Institute of Bankers*, Vol. LXXVIII (1957), pp. 251–8; J. Milnes Holden, 'The Cheques Act 1957', *The Bankers' Magazine*, Vol. CLXXXIV (1957), pp. 101–9; E. J. W. Buckler, 'The Cheques Act 1957, in Practice', *Journal of the Institute of Bankers*, Vol. 85 (1964), pp. 145–54.

78 Para. 48.

79 S. 6(3) and Sched.

80 The following were repealed: s. 82 of the Bills of Exchange Act 1882; s. 17 of the Revenue Act 1883; the whole of the Bills of Exchange (Crossed Cheques) Act 1906; and the whole of the Bills of Exchange Act (1882) Amendment Act 1932.

contained in s. 82 of the Bills of Exchange Act 1882, and in the Bills of Exchange (Crossed Cheques) Act 1906. The word 'customer' is not defined in the Act, but judicial decisions concerning the meaning of the word in s. 82 of the 1882 Act have made a statutory definition unnecessary.[81]

6-75 Subsection 2 of s. 4 specifies the instruments to which the section applies, namely:

(a) cheques;
(b) any document issued by a customer of a banker which, though not a bill of exchange, is intended to enable a person to obtain payment from that banker of the sum mentioned in the document;
(c) any document issued by a public officer which is intended to enable a person to obtain payment from the Paymaster General or the Queen's and Lord Treasurer's Remembrancer of the sum mentioned in the document but is not a bill of exchange;
(d) any draft payable on demand drawn by a banker upon himself, whether payable at the head office or some other office of his bank.

6-76 Paragraph (a) of subs. 2 of s. 4 made a radical change in the law: cheques, whether crossed or uncrossed, are within the scope of s. 4 of the Cheques Act 1957, whereas formerly only crossed cheques fell within the ambit of s. 82 of the Bills of Exchange Act 1882. The change in the law had been recommended by the Mocatta Committee.[82]

6-77 Occasionally, a person who has stolen a cheque fraudulently raises the amount before handing it to a banker for collection. One would expect that the banker would be protected when collecting such an instrument provided, of course, that he acted 'in good faith and without negligence'. However, it was held by the Supreme Court of Ceylon in *Bank of Ceylon* v. *Kulatilleke*,[83] that the banker is not protected, because, if the amount of a cheque is fraudulently raised, the instrument is no longer a cheque within the meaning of the expression in the section. The Supreme Court agreed with the view of the learned trial judge that the section applied to cheques which did not have the taint of forgery or fraudulent alteration.

81 *Ante*, para. 1-64.
82 Para. 105.
83 (1957) 59 Ceylon NLR 188, noted in the *Journal of the Institute of Bankers*, Vol. 80 (1959), pp. 348–51. The bank had claimed that it was protected by s. 82 of the Bills of Exchange Ordinance, which was in the same terms as s. 82 of the United Kingdom Bills of Exchange Act 1882.

6-78 The decision of the Supreme Court of Ceylon is not binding upon
English courts and, moreover, there is a decision of an English court in
a case involving a claim upon an altered cheque in which judgment was
given for the defendant bank. In that case, *Slingsby* v. *Westminster
Bank Ltd*,[84] the fraudulent party made an addition to the name of the
payee, and Finlay J said that in his view when the altered cheque came
into the hands of the defendant bank, it was not a valid cheque at all:
it had been avoided by the material alteration. That being so, it seemed
to him that no action could be brought upon it against the collecting
bankers: they had not dealt either with a cheque or the money of the
plaintiffs, and on that short ground he thought that the action must
fail.[85]

6-79 Paragraphs (b) and (c) of subs. 2 of s. 4 cover the instruments
which were formerly included in s. 17 of the Revenue Act 1883 with this
difference, namely that the specified instruments, whether crossed or
uncrossed, are within the scope of s. 4 of the Cheques Act 1957, whereas
formerly the instruments only fell within the ambit of s. 17 of the
Revenue Act 1883 if they were crossed.

6-80 Paragraph (d) of subs. 2 of s. 4 covers bankers' drafts, whether
crossed or uncrossed. Formerly, bankers' drafts were covered by the
Bills of Exchange Act (1882) Amendments Act 1932, but only if they
were crossed.

6-81 The following types of warrant have been brought within the
protection afforded to collecting bankers:

- (a) *crossed* warrants issued in respect of Premium Savings Bonds;[86]
- (b) *crossed* warrants issued in respect of the repayment of Savings
  Certificates;[87]
- (c) warrants, whether open or crossed, issued in respect of interest
  on certain stocks on the National Savings Stock Register;[88]
- (d) *crossed* warrants issued in respect of National Savings annu-
  ities;[89] and
- (e) *crossed* warrants issued by the National Savings Bank.[90]

84 [1931] 2 KB 583. The decision was criticized by Scrutton LJ in *Slingsby* v. *District Bank Ltd* [1932] 1 KB 544, at p. 558.
85 [1931] 2 KB 583, at p. 585. See also *Gregory-Salisbury Metal Products, Inc.* v. *Whitney National Bank* (1964) 160 So 2d 813, a decision of the Court of Appeal of Louisiana noted in the *Journal of the Institute of Bankers*, Vol. 85 (1964), p. 476, where the fraudulent party erased the names of the payees and substituted his own name; judgment was given for the defendant bank.
86 Premium Savings Bonds Regulations 1972, r. 8(2).
87 Savings Certificates Regulations 1972, r. 7(2).
88 National Savings Stock Register Regulations 1976, r. 22(2).
89 Post Office Annuity Amendment (No. 1) Regulations 1957, r. 2.
90 National Savings Bank Regulations 1972, r. 21(5).

6-82   Subsection 3 of s. 4 provides that a banker is not to be treated for the purposes of the section as having been negligent by reason only of his failure to concern himself with absence of, or irregularity in, endorsement of an instrument. This is a vague provision; it refers simply to endorsement, without saying whose endorsement. When the Cheques Bill was debated in the House of Lords, the provision was strongly criticized by Lord Chorley, who had been one of the members of the Mocatta Committee.[91] The position was clarified to some extent, at any rate as far as banking practice is concerned, by a circular dated 23 September 1957, issued by the Committee of London Clearing Bankers shortly before the Cheques Act 1957 came into operation. The text of the circular is set out in Appendix 1. The relevant rules of banking practice are as follows.

6-83   Except as stated in para. 6-89, cheques and other instruments, including dividend and interest warrants collected for the account of the ostensible payee, do not require examination for endorsement.

6-84   Cheques and other instruments payable to a bank to be applied after collection for the credit of a customer's account do not require endorsement.

6-85   Endorsement is required if a cheque or other instrument is tendered for the credit of an account other than that of the ostensible payee.[92] If a cheque is specially endorsed to the customer for whose account it is tendered for collection, no further endorsement is necessary.

6-86   If the payee's name is misspelt or he is incorrectly designated, the instrument may be accepted for collection without endorsement, unless there are circumstances to suggest that the customer is not the person to whom payment is intended to be made.

6-87   Instruments payable to one or more of a number of joint account holders may be collected for the credit of the joint account without endorsement. For this purpose, joint accounts include accounts of partners, trustees, etc.

6-88   Instruments payable to joint payees require endorsement if tendered for the credit of an account to which all are not parties.

6-89   There are some instruments which, in spite of the above rules, still require endorsement, e.g. combined cheque and receipt forms marked

---

91 See *Hansard*, Lords Debates, Vol. 204, col. 687.
92 Nevertheless, it has been held by the House of Lords that a bank may become a holder for value of such a cheque even though it is not endorsed: *Westminster Bank Ltd* v. *Zang* [1966] AC 182, *ante*, para. 6-37.

with a large 'R' close to the £ sign in the amount box; bills of exchange other than cheques; promissory notes; travellers' cheques; instruments payable by banks abroad; and drafts drawn on the Crown Agents and ·other paying agents.

Summary

6-90 Section 4 of the Cheques Act 1957 abolished the necessity for a collecting bank to examine endorsements, subject to the qualifications listed above, and the section affords protection to bankers who collect the proceeds of most types of instruments (whether crossed or not) handed to them by their customers. But there is still no protection for bankers who collect bills of exchange (other than cheques) or promissory notes for customers who are not entitled to them.

6-91 In order to qualify for protection under s. 4, a banker must act (a) in good faith, and (b) without negligence. These twin requirements have existed ever since statutory protection for collecting bankers was first introduced by the Crossed Cheques Act 1876.

Meaning of good faith

6-92 The Bills of Exchange Act 1882[93] provides that a thing is deemed to be done 'in good faith' where it is in fact done honestly, whether it is done negligently or not. The Cheques Act 1957[94] provides that the Cheques Act must be construed as one with the Bills of Exchange Act 1882, and so the words 'in good faith' have the same meaning in both Acts.

6-93 The requirement of acting 'in good faith' is easily satisfied by the collecting bank: it is satisfied if the employees of the bank act honestly in regard to the collection of the instruments paid in by the customer. Thus the protection would be lost if an employee knew that the customer's title thereto was defective.

Meaning of negligence

6-94 The word 'negligence' is not defined by Act of Parliament, and so one has to turn to reported cases on the subject in order to determine what standard of care a bank must exercise before it can be said to have collected the proceeds of a cheque 'without negligence'. In this connection, the onus of proving the absence of negligence is plainly cast upon the bank: if the bank is seeking to rely upon the special defence afforded

93 S. 90.
94 S. 6(1).

by s. 4(1) of the Cheques Act 1957, it is for the bank to prove that it has satisfied the requirements of the section.[95]

6-95   If a banker fails to establish that he has acted 'without negligence', his statutory defence may not succeed, even though it may seem probable that the exercise of care would not have enabled him to discover the defective title of his customer.[96] However, there is no rigid rule to this effect, and if a banker can show that in all probability a particular precaution would have been unavailing, the failure to take that precaution may not deprive him of his statutory defence.[97]

6-96   The standard of care required of a collecting banker is difficult to state. On the one hand, 'it is not to be expected that the officials of banks should also be amateur detectives';[98] on the other hand, a banker must certainly not assume that everyone who comes to his counter is necessarily an honest man. The difficulty of defining the standard of care briefly and accurately stems in part from the fact that the courts have not always been consistent in their approach to this problem. Broadly speaking, two different tests or standards for determining whether a collecting banker's conduct is negligent have been formulated by the courts, and the application of the one or the other can lead to different results in borderline cases. For convenience, the tests may be described as (a) the 'ordinary practice of bankers' test, and (b) the 'protection against fraud' test.

(a) 'Ordinary practice of bankers'

6-97   This test received the blessing of the Judicial Committee of the Privy Council in *Commissioners of Taxation* v. *English, Scottish and Australian Bank Ltd.*[99] The Privy Council, whose judgment was delivered by Lord Dunedin, considered that a test which had been formulated by the High Court of Australia in a previous case[1] was an

---

95 *Midland Bank Ltd* v. *Reckitt* [1933] AC 1, at p. 14, *per* Lord Atkin; *Lloyds Bank Ltd* v. *E. B. Savory and Co.* [1933] AC 201, at p. 229, *per* Lord Wright.

96 *E. B. Savory & Co.* v. *Lloyds Bank Ltd* [1932] 2 KB 122, at p. 148, *per* Greer LJ; *Lloyds Bank Ltd* v. *E. B. Savory & Co.* [1933] AC 201, at p. 233, *per* Lord Wright; *Baker* v. *Barclays Bank Ltd* [1955] 2 All ER 571, at p. 583, *per* Devlin J.

97 *Marfani & Co. Ltd* v. *Midland Bank Ltd* [1968] 2 All ER 573, at p. 582, *per* Diplock LJ and p. 584, *per* Cairns J.

98 *Lloyds Bank Ltd* v. *The Chartered Bank of India, Australia and China* [1929] 1 KB 40, at p. 73, per Sankey LJ; see also *Penmount Estates Ltd* v. *National Provincial Bank Ltd* (1945) 173 LT 344, where at p. 346, MacKinnon LJ said '... in my opinion the officials of the bank, doing their duty under s. 82, have not to be abnormally suspicious'.

99 [1920] AC 683.

1 *Commissioners of State Savings Bank* v. *Permewan, Wright & Co.* (1914) 19 CLR 457.

accurate statement of the law if certain words were added. In its amended form, the test is as follows:[2]

> The test of negligence is whether the transaction of paying in any given cheque, coupled with the circumstances antecedent and present, was so out of the ordinary course that it ought to have aroused doubts in the bankers' mind, and caused them to make inquiry.

6-98 Lord Dunedin added that if a standard were sought, 'it must be the standard to be derived from the ordinary practice of bankers...'[3] This reference to the 'ordinary practice of bankers' was repeated by Scrutton LJ in the Court of Appeal in 1924,[4] and the same test is still applied from time to time,[5] even though it would seem to be inconsistent with a decision of the House of Lords in 1933, *Lloyds Bank Ltd* v. *E. B. Savory & Co.*[6] In that case, the House of Lords held that, although the ordinary practice of bankers had been followed, this was defective, and so the defendant bank had not acted 'without negligence'.

6-99 In 1968 Diplock LJ said that the facts which ought to be known to a banker must depend on 'current banking practice, and change as that practice changes'.[7] He added that cases decided thirty years ago, when the use by the general public of banking facilities was much less widespread, might not be a reliable guide to what the duty of a careful banker is today. He upheld the view that a court is always entitled to examine current banking practice and to form its own opinion as to whether it does comply with the standard of which a prudent banker should adopt. However, he ventured to think that the Court of Appeal 'should be hesitant before condemning as negligent a practice generally adopted by those engaged in banking business'.[8]

(b) 'Protection against fraud'

6-100 This test was formulated in the following words by Lord Warrington in *Lloyds Bank Ltd* v. *E. B. Savory & Co.*:[9]

> The standard by which the absence, or otherwise, of negligence is to be determined must in my opinion be ascertained by reference to the practice

2 [1920] AC 683, at p. 688.
3 [1920] AC 683, at p. 689.
4 *A. L. Underwood Ltd* v. *Bank of Liverpool and Martins* [1924] 1 KB 775, at p. 793.
5 For example, the passage in Lord Dunedin's judgment was cited with approval by Harman LJ in *Orbit Mining and Trading Co. Ltd* v. *Westminster Bank Ltd* [1963] 1 QB 794, at pp. 823–4.
6 [1933] AC 201.
7 *Marfani & Co. Ltd* v. *Midland Bank Ltd* [1968] 2 All ER 573, at p. 579.
8 [1968] 2 All ER, at p. 581.
9 [1933] AC 201, at p. 221.

of reasonable men carrying on the business of bankers, and endeavouring to do so in such a matter as may be calculated to protect themselves and others against fraud.

In the same case, Lord Wright said: [10]

It is argued that ... a bank is not negligent, if it takes all precautions usually taken by bankers. I do not accept that latter proposition as true in cases where the ordinary practice of bankers fails in making due provision for a risk fully known to those experienced in the business of banking.

The test formulated by Lord Warrington and set out above was applied by McNair J in *Marquess of Bute* v. *Barclays Bank Ltd.* [11]

6-100A In *Thackwell* v. *Barclays Bank plc* [12] Hutchison J referred to the third edition of this book and to the two suggested tests mentioned above. He said that he had been referred to the judgment of Diplock LJ in *Marfani & Co. Ltd* v. *Midland Bank Ltd* [13] which he had found 'to be the most helpful definition of the correct approach to the consideration of the question of negligence by a collecting banker'. In that case, Diplock LJ had said: [14]

Where the customer is in possession of the cheque at the time of delivery for collection, and appears on the face of it to be the 'holder', i.e. the payee or indorsee or the bearer, the banker is, in my view, entitled to assume that the customer is the owner of the cheque unless there are facts which are known, or ought to be known, to the banker which would cause a reasonable banker to suspect that the customer is not the true owner. What facts ought to be known to the banker, i.e. what inquiries he should make, and what facts are sufficient to cause him reasonably to suspect that the customer is not the true owner, must depend on current banking practice, and change as that practice changes. Cases decided thirty years ago, when the use by the general public of banking facilities was much less widespread, may not be a reliable guide to what the duty of a careful banker, in relation to inquiries and to the facts which should give rise to suspicion, is today.

10 [1933] AC 201, at p. 232.
11 [1955] 1 QB 202, at p. 214. McNair J said that a 'somewhat lower test' had been applied by Sankey LJ in *Lloyds Bank* v. *Chartered Bank of India, Australia and China* [1929] 1 KB 40, at p. 69. Sankey LJ had said: 'I think the duty of the defendants to the true owner of the cheque was (1) to exercise the same care and forethought with regard to the cheque paid in by the customer as a reasonable man would bring to bear on similar business of his own, and (2) to provide a reasonable and competent staff to carry out this duty.'
12 [1986] 1 All ER 676. See also *post*, para. 6-139A.
13 [1986] 2 All ER 573. See also *post*, para. 11-10.
14 [1986] 2 All ER, at p. 579.

In *Thackwell's* case, Hutchison J said that the circumstances in which the cheques were presented for collection were so unusual and out of the ordinary course of business that they ought to have put the assistant manager of the New Bond Street branch of the defendant bank on enquiry. As he had made no enquiry the bank's defence that it had acted without negligence under s. 4 of the Cheques Act 1957 failed. Nevertheless, another defence which was relied upon by the bank succeeded.[15]

Illustrations of negligence

6-101 Many different acts and omissions on the part of bankers have been held to amount to negligence within s. 82 of the Bills of Exchange Act 1882, now replaced by s. 4 of the Cheques Act 1957. With those decisions of the courts in mind, one is often able to reach a firm view as to whether any particular circumstances or transactions amount to negligence at the present day.

6-102 Cases where a collecting bank has, or has not, been held to be negligent fall to be considered under three heads, namely (a) opening an account for a stranger without a satisfactory reference, (b) collection of cheques or other instruments payable to the customer, and (c) collection of cheques or other instruments payable to a third party.

(a) Opening account for a stranger without a satisfactory reference

6-103 In *Lloyds Bank Ltd* v. *E. B. Savory & Co.*[16] Lord Wright said:

> It is now recognized to be the usual practice of bankers not to open an account for a customer without obtaining a reference and without inquiry as to the customer's standing; a failure to do so at the opening of the account might well prevent the banker from establishing his defence under s. 82 if a cheque were converted subsequently in the history of the account.

If the person whose name is given to the bank as a referee is unknown to the bank, it may be prudent to enquire concerning his standing and respectability, for it sometimes happens that two dishonest persons, namely, the prospective customer and the referee, conspire to deceive the bank; and it is not unknown for the supposed referee to be none other than the new customer under another name.[17]

---

15 See *post*, para. 6-139A.
16 [1933] AC 201, at p. 231. See also *Ladbroke* v. *Todd* (1914) 30 TLR 433.
17 This happened in *Nu-Stilo Footwear Ltd* v. *Lloyds Bank Ltd* (1956) *The Times*, 19 June, *post*, paras 11-8/9.

6-103A Lord Wright's opinion was expressed over half a century ago, and banks do not now always insist upon a reference. In order to establish a person's identity when he applies to open an account, he may be asked to produce some document, such as his birth certificate, National Health medical card, passport, state pension book, or union card. If for any reason it is not possible for him to establish his identity in this way, he will usually be required to provide a reference as in the past.

(b) Collection of cheques payable to customer

6-104 Even though a cheque or similar instrument is payable to the customer for whose account the bank is asked to collect it, the customer may not have a good title thereto, and there may be special circumstances which should put the bank upon enquiry. Two reported cases may be taken by way of illustration.

6-105 In *Midland Bank Ltd* v. *Reckitt*[18] a solicitor who practised under a firm name had authority to draw cheques on the banking account of Sir Harold Reckitt. The solicitor's account was kept in the firm name at the Midland Bank, and it was overdrawn. The bank from time to time asked for reductions, and, in order to comply with those requests, the solicitor fraudulently drew cheques on Sir Harold Reckitt's account payable to the firm name, and paid them into the account at the Midland Bank. The House of Lords held that the bank was negligent in making no enquiry as to its customer's authority to make those payments.

6-106 In *Marquess of Bute* v. *Barclays Bank Ltd*,[19] a man named McGaw, who was a former employee of the plaintiff, asked the defendant bank to open an account for him with certain warrants drawn in favour of 'Mr D. McGaw (for Marquess of Bute)'. An account was opened in McGaw's name, references were taken up, and the proceeds of the warrants (which were the property of the plaintiff), were fraudulently applied by McGaw for his own purposes. Giving judgment for the plaintiff, McNair J said that the warrants bore a clear indication at least that McGaw was to receive the money as agent or in a fiduciary capacity; and the learned judge added that it was 'elementary banking practice' that such documents should not be credited to a personal account of the named payee without enquiry. As the defendant had failed to make enquiry, it had not discharged the onus of proving that it had acted without negligence.

18 [1933] AC 1.
19 [1955] 1 QB 202.

(c) Collection of cheques payable to third party

6-107   When a bank is asked by a customer to collect the proceeds of a cheque or similar instrument which was originally payable to a third party, there may be a risk that the customer is not entitled to it, even though it purports to have been endorsed by the payee. In the vast majority of such cases, of course, the customer does possess a good title to the instrument, and it would be going too far to say that a bank is put upon enquiry merely because it is asked to collect the proceeds of an instrument which had originally been drawn payable to someone other than the customer. The bank is not even put upon enquiry if the instrument is crossed 'Not negotiable'.[20]

6-108   Nevertheless, there are many reported decisions in which a bank which has collected 'third-party cheques' has failed to satisfy the court that it acted without negligence. It is impossible to devise any simple test for determining whether or not the collection of a third-party cheque would be held by the court to amount to negligence, but the reported decisions would seem to support the view that the collection of a third-party cheque may amount to negligence in any of the following cases.

(i) Cheques crossed 'Account payee'

6-109   Some reference has already been made to this crossing.[21] In *House Property Co. of London Ltd* v. *London County and Westminster Bank*,[22] a cheque so crossed had been drawn in favour of a named payee or bearer, and the defendant bank had collected it, without enquiry, for the credit of a third party. An action was brought against the bank for damages for conversion, and the bank relied upon s. 82 of the Bills of Exchange Act 1882. In view of the fact that the bank had not asked for any explanation, Rowlatt J held that it had been negligent, and so had forfeited the protection of s. 82. This decision was approved in a later case[23] by Scrutton LJ, who pointed out, however, that the crossing 'Account payee' does not affect the negotiability of a cheque, whether it is payable to order or to bearer.

---

20 *Crumplin* v. *London Joint Stock Bank Ltd* (1913) 30 TLR 99; *Penmount Estates Ltd* v. *National Provincial Bank Ltd* (1945) 173 LT 344. The contrary view put forward in Lord Brampton's speech in *Great Western Railway Co.* v. *London and County Banking Co. Ltd* [1901] AC 414, at p. 422 (which was not expressed by the other law lords) cannot be regarded as correct.

21 *Ante*, para. 5-46.

22 (1915) 84 LJKB 1846. See also *Bevan* v. *National Bank Ltd* (1906) 23 TLR 65, at p. 68.

23 *A. L. Underwood Ltd* v. *Bank of Liverpool and Martins* [1924] 1 KB 775, at pp. 793–4. In *Penmount Estates Ltd* v. *National Provincial Bank Ltd* (1945) 173 LT 344, the defendant bank did not contest liability arising out of the collection of third-party cheques crossed 'Account payee only'.

6-110 Sometimes a cheque which is crossed 'Account payee' is sent to a person who has no banking account. There is, of course, no reason why such a person should not request someone who has a banking account to present the cheque for him by paying the cheque into his account. If he does so, there is judicial authority for the view that the collecting bank is under a duty to see that, in fact, it is collecting the money for the account of the payee, and that the proceeds, when received, will go to the payee.[24]

6-111 Occasionally, a cheque is crossed 'Account A.B.' and the effect of this crossing is similar to that of the 'Account payee' crossing. Thus, in one case,[25] a customer of the Economic Bank, which carried on business as a deposit or savings bank, paid in certain cheques for collection. The Economic Bank crossed the cheques specially to Messrs Williams Deacon & Co., followed by the words 'Account Economic Bank'. It was argued in the course of the trial that the Economic Bank had made an unlawful addition to the crossing by adding the words 'Account Economic Bank', but Bigham J rejected this argument. The learned judge said that the words 'Account A.B.' were a mere direction to the receiving bank (this would be Messrs Williams Deacon & Co.) as to how the money was to be dealt with after receipt.[26]

(ii) Cheque payable to customer's employer

6-112 In *Bissell and Co.* v. *Fox Brothers and Co.*,[27] one of the earliest cases decided under s. 82 of the Bills of Exchange Act 1882, the defendant bankers allowed a commercial traveller to pay into his own account cheques which, to the banker's knowledge, were drawn in favour of the customer's employers and purported to be endorsed on their behalf by him. Denman J and, subsequently, the Court of Appeal held that the defendant bankers had not acted without negligence.

6-113 On the ground that there may be a risk that a customer will try to pay into his account cheques which are drawn in favour of his employer, the House of Lords by a majority of three law lords to two has laid down the rule in another case that, when opening an account for a new customer, a bank should ascertain the name of the prospective

24 *Importers Co. Ltd* v. *Westminster Bank Ltd* [1927] 2 KB 297, *per* Atkin LJ, at p. 309.
25 *Akrokerri (Atlantic) Mines Ltd* v. *Economic Bank* [1904] 2 KB 465.
26 *Ibid.*, at p. 472. See also *National Bank* v. *Silke* [1891] 1 QB 435, where the Court of Appeal held that the crossing 'Account of J. F. Moriarty, Esq., National Bank, Dublin' were not words prohibiting transfer within the meaning of s. 8(1) of the Bills of Exchange Act 1882.
27 (1884) 51 LT 663; on appeal (1885) 53 LT 193. See also *Lloyds Bank Ltd* v. *E. B. Savory & Co.* [1933] A. C. 201, *per* Lord Wright, at p. 229; *Australia and New Zealand Bank Ltd* v. *Ateliers de Constructions Electriques de Charleroi* [1967] AC 86 (cheques payable to the customer's principal).

customer's employer or, if the customer is a married woman, the name of her husband's employer; failure to take this precaution may amount to negligence if the customer subsequently pays into the account cheques which are the property of his employer.[28] From a practical point of view, it is difficult for a bank to scrutinize all cheques with the object of adhering to this rule, and it is not surprising that a learned lord justice once described the rule as 'a hard doctrine'.[29]

6-114 However, although it is essential for a banker to obtain the name of a new customer's employer when the account is opened, the same lord justice expressed the view that a bank is not under any obligation 'continually to keep itself up to date' as to the identity of a customer's employer.[30]

(iii) Cheque drawn by customer's employer in favour of third party

6-115 This case is very similar to (ii) above, and it is obvious that, if a customer pays into his own account a cheque drawn by his employer in favour of a third party, there is a very grave risk that the customer may have stolen it.

6-116 The leading case illustrating this risk is *Lloyds Bank Ltd* v. *E. B. Savory & Co.*[31] The case also illustrates a risk inherent in the branch credit system. Two clerks employed by a firm of stockbrokers stole cheques drawn by their employers and paid them into Lloyds Bank, in the case of one clerk for the credit of his account at Wallington, and in the case of the other clerk for the credit of his wife's account at Redhill and later at Weybridge. The fraudulent clerks made use of the branch credit system by paying in the cheques at City branches of the bank. The cheques were cleared by the City branches, and the credit slips were forwarded to the branches where the accounts were kept. As the credit slips bore no particulars of the cheques, the branches receiving the credit slips did not know the names of the drawers or the payees of

---

28 *Lloyds Bank Ltd* v. *E. B. Savory & Co.* [1933] AC 201. In this case, the cheques in question were drawn by the employer in favour of third parties.

29 *Orbit Mining and Trading Co. Ltd* v. *Westminster Bank Ltd* [1963] 1 QB 794, *per* Harman LJ, at p. 825.

30 *Ibid.*

31 [1933] AC 201. See also *Souchette Ltd* v. *London County Westminster and Parr's Bank Ltd* (1920) 36 TLR 195, and *Carpenters' Company* v. *British Mutual Banking Co. Ltd* [1938] 1 KB 511. In the former case, a customer who was known to be the secretary and managing director of a company paid into his own account with the defendant bank cheques drawn by the company in favour of one of its creditors; and, in the latter case, a customer who was known to be the assistant clerk of the Carpenters' Company paid into his own account with the defendant bank cheques drawn by his employers in favour of creditors. In both cases, it was held that the collecting banks were not entitled to the protection of s. 82 of the Bills of Exchange Act 1882; they had not acted 'without negligence'.

the cheques. Moreover, neither branch had made enquiries as to the names of the employers, in the one case of the customer, and in the other of the husband of the customer. In the House of Lords, all five law lords expressed the opinion in varying degrees that there was negligence involved in the use of the branch credit system. One result of the decision is that some banks now use a special credit slip for the branch credit system which sets out, for the benefit of the branch where the account is kept, the names of the drawers and of the payees of every cheque paid in.

(iv) Cheque drawn by customer's employer in favour of collecting bank

6-117 This is a variation of (iii) above, the difference being that the cheque is made payable to the collecting bank. In *Lloyds Bank Ltd* v. *Chartered Bank of India, Australia and China*,[32] Lloyds Bank had as its chief accountant in its Bombay office a man named Lawson, who had authority to draw cheques on behalf of his employers on the Imperial Bank of India. Cheques for over Rs 5,000 had to be countersigned by another official of Lloyds Bank. Lawson drew a series of nineteen cheques over a period of two years amounting in all to Rs 250,000 or £17,044. He induced another official of the bank to countersign the cheques, which that official did in all innocence. The cheques were payable to the Chartered Bank, and Lawson sent them to that bank, requesting it to credit the cheques to his private account. This was done. The Court of Appeal held that the Chartered Bank had not discharged the burden of proving that it had acted without negligence.

6-118 It follows from this case that, even though cheques are payable to the very bank which is asked to collect them, care should be exercised if the surrounding circumstances cast doubt upon the customer's right to have them credited to his account. In the case outlined above, the circumstances clearly called for enquiry, because Lawson, an employee of Lloyds Bank, was paying large cheques drawn on behalf of his bank into his private account at the Chartered Bank.

(v) Cheque payable to limited company is collected for the account of a director or officer of the company

6-119 This is similar to (ii) above. In *A. L. Underwood Ltd* v. *Bank of Liverpool and Martins*,[33] the sole director of a 'one-man company'[34]

---

32 [1929] 1 KB 40.

33 [1924] 1 KB 775. See also *Hannan's Lake View Central Ltd* v. *Armstrong & Co.* (1900) 16 TLR 236, where a cheque payable to the plaintiff company was collected for the account of that company's secretary; Kennedy J held that the bank's defence under s. 82, Bills of Exchange Act 1882, must fail because the bank had not acted 'without negligence'.

34 He held all the shares except one, which was held by his wife.

paid into his private account cheques which were payable to the company. Subsequently, an action was brought nominally by A. L. Underwood & Co. Ltd, though substantially by Lloyds Bank Ltd as the holder of debentures issued by that company, against the Bank of Liverpool and Martins for converting those cheques. A senior official of Martins gave evidence and admitted that in all ordinary cases where an official of a company was paying cheques made payable to the company into his private account, the bank would make enquiries and would consult the employer, but he said that where the official was a sole director of a one-man company, and himself the one man, it would not be necessary. However, the Court of Appeal rejected this view, and agreed with the decision of the trial judge that the bank was guilty of negligence.

6-120 Furthermore, it is so usual for cheques payable to a limited company to be paid into the company's account that it may amount to negligence on the part of the collecting bank, if, in the absence of special circumstances, such cheques are credited to any account other than that of the company.[35] As Lord Atkin once observed, 'in these days every bank clerk sees the red light when a company's cheque is endorsed by a company's official into an account which is not the company's'.[36]

6-121 However, the red light may occasionally change to green when enquiries are made. *Penmount Estates Ltd* v. *National Provincial Bank Ltd*[37] is an example of a case where a bank was held to have acted without negligence when it collected a cheque payable to a limited company for the credit of a solicitor's Clients' account; the bank had asked for, and had received, an explanation which satisfied MacKinnon LJ, sitting as an additional judge of the King's Bench Division, that the bank had collected the cheque without negligence. The solicitor's explanation was that his client had endorsed the cheque so that it could be paid into the Clients' account, upon which he would then draw his own cheque in favour of the company for the same amount, less his costs.

(vi) Cheque payable to partnership is collected for the account of a partner

6-122 Here, too, there is a grave risk that the cheque may have been

35 In regard to this, see the opinion of Mr Rayner Goddard, KC (later Lord Goddard CJ) published in the *Journal of the Institute of Bankers*, Vol. LIII (1932), p. 76.
36 *United Australia Ltd* v. *Barclays Bank Ltd* [1914] AC 1, at pp. 23–4. In a much earlier case, *London and Montrose Shipbuilding and Repairing Co. Ltd* v. *Barclays Bank Ltd* (1926) 31 Com Cas 67, MacKinnon J took a different view, but his decision was reversed by the Court of Appeal; it does not appear from the report what was the negligence on which the Court of Appeal decided against the bank: see 31 Com Cas 182.
37 (1945) 200 LT 150.

stolen by the partner who tenders it for the credit of his account. *Smith and Baldwin* v. *Barclays Bank Ltd*[38] is an illustration of this risk, though judgment was given in favour of the defendant bank, very largely as a result of the vigilance of some of its officials. Three men named Smith, Baldwin and Bray appeared to be partners (there was no clear evidence on this point) trading as the Argus Press. Bray fraudulently paid into his own account at Barclays Bank various cheques payable to the Argus Press. This was immediately noticed, and the bank manager sent for Bray and questioned him. Bray said that he had bought the business of the Argus Press, and in fact he produced a certificate issued under the provisions of the Registration of Business Names Act 1916, which purported to show that he was the proprietor. In fact, he was not the proprietor, and an action was brought against Barclays Bank for damages for conversion of the cheques. It was held that the bank's official had acted without negligence and that the bank was protected from liability by s. 82 of the Bills of Exchange Act 1882.

(vii) Cheque payable to holder of public office is collected for the account of a private individual

6-123   Thus, in *Ross* v. *London County Westminster and Parr's Bank*,[39] various cheques amounting to nearly £4,000 payable to 'The Officer in Charge, Estates Office, Canadian Overseas Military Forces' and endorsed by that officer under the same description, were paid into the private account of a quartermaster-sergeant at the defendant bank. It was held that the bank, which had failed to make any enquiry whether the sergeant was entitled to the cheques, was guilty of negligence and, therefore, was not within the protection of s. 82.

(viii) Payee's endorsement on an instrument payable to order appears to be irregular

6-124   Thus, in *Bavins, Junr & Sims* v. *London and South Western Bank Ltd*,[40] the defendant bank collected for a customer the proceeds of a conditional order to which the customer was not entitled, payable to J. Bavins, Junr and Sims, and endorsed and receipted 'J. Bavins, Trench, and Sim's. The Court of Appeal held that there had clearly been negligence on the part of the defendant bank in receiving the document with the endorsement and the receipt signed in a name other than that of the payee. As the instrument was a conditional order, the defendant bank had sought to rely upon the provisions of s. 17 of the Revenue Act 1883, but this defence failed as a result of the bank's negligence.

38 *Journal of the Institute of Bankers*, Vol. LXV (1944), p. 171.
39 [1919] 1 KB 678.
40 [1900] 1 QB 270.

(ix) Customer has failed to make provision for cheques

6-125   The authority for this case rests upon the decision of Goddard
J, in *Motor Traders Guarantee Corporation Ltd* v. *Midland Bank
Ltd.*[41] The defendant bank had collected a third-party cheque for a customer who was a motor dealer. The bank cashier had made enquiries of
the customer, and had received answers which seemed to be satisfactory.
The learned judge, in the course of his judgment, said that his mind had
fluctuated considerably in the course of the argument, and, had it not
been for a fact that had been disclosed at a very late stage in the case,
he thought it quite likely that his judgment would have been in the
bank's favour. That fact was that, during the six months after the
opening of the account and immediately prior to the payment in of the
cheque, thirty-five cheques drawn by the customer had been dishonoured for lack of funds. In the view of the learned judge, further
enquiries should have been made concerning the third-party cheque: the
cashier ought to have referred the matter to the manager in accordance
with the bank's regulations.

(x) Surrounding circumstances cast doubt upon regularity of transaction

6-126   An important case concerning the collection of third-party
cheques is *Baker* v. *Barclays Bank Ltd,*[42] the facts of which were as follows. A Mr Baker and a Mr Bainbridge were trading in partnership
under the name 'Modern Confections'. Bainbridge misappropriated
nine cheques amounting to about £1,160 payable to the partnership. He
endorsed the cheques and handed them to a Mr Jeffcott, an insurance
agent, who paid them into his No. 3 account at Barclays Bank. Mr Jeffcott also paid into his account other cheques payable to Bainbridge personally and endorsed by him.

6-127   When the second of the nine cheques payable to Modern Confections was paid in, the bank manager asked Mr Jeffcott why he was
paying into his own account a cheque in favour of Modern Confections.
Mr Jeffcott said that his friend Bainbridge was the sole partner in
Modern Confections and that he, Jeffcott, was helping him, with a view
to going into partnership later. The manager had other interviews with
Mr Jeffcott and was always assured that Bainbridge was the sole proprietor of Modern Confections. The manager felt that he had no reason
to distrust Mr Jeffcott, and he was satisfied with the explanations given
to him. He never asked to see Bainbridge.

---

41 [1937] 4 All ER 90.
42 [1955] 1 WLR 822. See also *Nu-Stilo Footwear Ltd* v. *Lloyds Bank Ltd* (1956), *The
Times*, 19 June, *post*, paras 11-8/9.

6-128   In the end the other partner, Mr Baker, found out what had happened, and he brought an action for damages for conversion against Barclays Bank in respect of the nine cheques payable to Modern Confections. Dealing with the collection of third-party cheques, Devlin J said:[43]

> Of course, cheques are endorsed over to third parties, but usually for small sums and only occasionally. When the bank manager sees it happening for large sums and quite regularly, I think that he is put on enquiry ... The explanation which the bank manager received when he asked for one was not, I think, one which should have satisfied a bank manager ... I do not think that he appreciated the significance of a number of endorsed cheques coming in one after the other, or also the significance that the payments out included substantial sums for cash. If he had, I think that he would have found Jeffcott's story less convincing, for within less than a month Bainbridge had received from people who were presumably his customers cheques amounting to £2,000 or £3,000. Surely a man whose business was on that scale and was done in cheques might have been expected to have a bank account of his own?

In the result, therefore, the learned judge decided that the bank's defence under s. 82 of the Bills of Exchange Act 1882 failed, because the bank could not show that it had acted without negligence.

6-129   The decision may be contrasted with that in *Crumplin* v. *London Joint Stock Bank Ltd*,[44] where nine third-party cheques, amounting in all to £324, had been collected without enquiry by the defendant bank at very considerable intervals over a period of more than two years. The learned judge gave judgment in favour of the bank, though he stated that in his opinion the case was 'very near the line'.

Section 6
DEFENCE OF ESTOPPEL

6-130   Another defence which is occasionally available to a collecting bank is the defence of estoppel: by this defence the defendant bank pleads that the plaintiff is estopped (i.e. precluded) from succeeding in his claim as a result of something which he has said or done.

6-131   The branch of estoppel which is under consideration here is generally known as estoppel by representation. The representation by the plaintiff may be either by statement or by conduct; it must be of an

43 [1955] 1 WLR, at pp. 825–6.
44 (1913) 30 TLR 99.

existing fact; it must be clear and unambiguous; there must have been an intention that the representation should be acted upon; and, finally, the representation must have been acted upon as true by the bank.[45]

6-132 The defence of estoppel might be relied on where, for example, the plaintiff had said or done something which led the collecting bank to believe on reasonable grounds that it would be in order for the bank to collect the instruments concerned for the account of its customer. Such a situation does not often arise, and the defence of estoppel does not appear to have been pleaded successfully by a collecting bank in any reported case,[46] but in principle it would seem that the defence should succeed if the facts of a particular case satisfy the requirements set out above.[47]

Section 7
DEFENCE OF CONTRIBUTORY NEGLIGENCE

6-133 Another defence which is occasionally pleaded by a collecting bank is that of contributory negligence on the part of the plaintiff. At one time, the generally accepted view was that a collecting bank, when sued for damages for conversion, could not plead that the plaintiff had contributed to the loss by his own negligence: as Lord Wright said, it was an 'immaterial averment' that the conversion was only possible because of want of ordinary prudence on the part of the true owner.[48] An argument sometimes invoked to support this view was that the true owner did not owe any duty of care to the bank.

6-134 However, as early as 1940, it was established by the House of Lords that a plaintiff who had failed to take reasonable care for his own safety against foreseeable risks could be met with a defence of contributory negligence, even though the plaintiff owed no duty of care to the defendant.[49] A few years later, the Law Reform (Contributory Negligence) Act 1945 was passed. The relevant part of s. 1 provides as follows:

---

45 See the authorities cited in *Halsbury's Laws of England* (4th ed.), Vol. 16, pp. 1068–75.
46 It was pleaded unsuccessfully by the defendant banks in *Fine Art Society Ltd* v. *Union Bank of London Ltd* (1886) 17 QBD 705, and in *Marquess of Bute* v. *Barclays Bank Ltd* [1955] 1 QB 202.
47 In *Orbit Mining and Trading Co. Ltd* v. *Westminster Bank Ltd* [1963] 1 QB 794, the defence of estoppel was pleaded by the defendant bank, but the Court of Appeal allowed the bank's appeal on other grounds and did not express any concluded view on the defence of estoppel.
48 *Lloyds Bank Ltd* v. *E. B. Savory & Co.* [1933] AC 201, at p. 229.
49 *Caswell* v. *Powell Duffryn Associated Collieries Ltd* [1940] AC 152.

Where any person suffers damage as a result partly of his own fault and partly of the fault of any other person or persons, a claim in respect of that damage shall not be defeated by reason of the fault of the person suffering the damage, but the damages recoverable in respect thereof shall be reduced to such extent as the court thinks just and equitable having regard to the claimant's share in the responsibility for the damage.

The word 'fault' is defined by s. 4 of the Act as:

... negligence, breach of statutory duty or other act or omission which gives rise to a liability in tort or would, apart from this Act, give rise to the defence of contributory negligence.

6-135 In *Lumsden & Co.* v. *London Trustee Savings Bank*,[50] the defendant bank was sued for damages for the conversion of certain cheques which it had collected for a customer. The bank had been guilty of negligence, and so was not entitled to the protection of s. 4(1) of the Cheques Act 1957. However, the plaintiffs had also been negligent, and it was held by Donaldson J that the bank was entitled to plead contributory negligence on the part of the plaintiffs. In the result, the damages awarded to the plaintiffs were reduced by ten per cent.

6-136 The law was amended by s. 11(1) of the Torts (Interference with Goods) Act 1977, which provided that contributory negligence was no longer to be a defence in proceedings founded on conversion. Then, two years later, s. 47 of the Banking Act 1979 provided that, in any circumstances in which proof of absence of negligence on the part of a banker would be a defence in proceedings by virtue of s. 4 of the Cheques Act 1957, a defence of contributory negligence was to be available to the banker notwithstanding the provisions of s. 11(1) of the Torts (Interference with Goods) Act 1977. Accordingly, a collecting bank may plead contributory negligence as a defence, as did the defendant bank in *Lumsden & Co.* v. *London Trustee Savings Bank*.

Section 8
DEFENCE THAT BANK ACQUIRED A GOOD TITLE TO CHEQUE

6-137 Another defence which may be available to a collecting bank is that, although the customer may not have possessed a good title to the

---

50 [1971] 1 Lloyd's Rep 114. See also *Helson* v. *McKenzies Ltd* [1950] NZLR 878, in which the New Zealand Court of Appeal decided by a majority that the defence of contributory negligence (based upon the New Zealand Contributory Negligence Act 1947, which appears to be in the same terms as the UK Act of 1945) was available in an action for damages for conversion.

cheques concerned, the bank itself acquired a good title to them. The bank would acquire a good title to the cheques if it became a holder in due course thereof by giving value for the cheques in good faith and by satisfying the other requirements laid down in s. 29 of the Bills of Exchange Act 1882.[51] A clear illustration of a case where a bank could acquire a good title to a cheque in this way is where the bank pays cash in exchange for a cheque drawn on another branch or on another bank.[52]

6-138 Furthermore, there may be instances where a bank can acquire a good title to a cheque which it has received from a customer *for collection*.[53] However, it was established by the Court of Appeal in *A. L. Underwood Ltd* v. *Barclays Bank Ltd*,[54] that the mere fact that 'the bank in their books enter the value of the cheques on the credit side of the account on the day on which they receive the cheques for collection does not without more constitute the bank a holder for value'.[55] In the same case, both Scrutton LJ and Atkin LJ expressed the view *obiter* that if, by agreement, the cheques had been drawn against before clearance, this would have been sufficient to constitute value. The subject is a difficult one, and there does not appear to be any reported case where a bank, when sued for damages for conversion in respect of the collection of cheques, has successfully pleaded that it had become a holder in due course of the cheques.[56] In principle, however, there does not seem to be any doubt that the defence would succeed in a proper case. The Cheques Act 1957 appears to recognize that this is so, because it provides that if a banker gives value for a cheque payable to order which the holder delivers to him *for collection* without endorsing it, the banker shall have the same rights as he would have had if, upon delivery, the holder had endorsed it in blank.[57] Prior to the passing of the Cheques Act 1957, the holder's endorsement would have been necessary in order to confer a good title upon the bank.

---

51 *Ante*, para. 5-108.
52 *Ante*, para. 6-42. But the encashing bank does not become a holder for value when a cheque is encashed under an open credit: see *ante*, para. 6-43.
53 *Ante*, para. 6-35.
54 [1924] 1 KB 775.
55 [1924] 1 KB, at p. 805, *per* Atkin LJ. See also *Importers Co. Ltd* v. *Westminster Bank Ltd* [1927] 2 KB 297, at pp. 309–10, *per* Atkin LJ; *Baker* v. *Barclays Bank Ltd* [1955] 2 All ER 571, at p. 577, *per* Devlin J.
56 The defence that the bank had become a holder in due course was unsuccessfully pleaded by the bank in *Baker* v. *Barclays Bank Ltd* [1955] 2 All ER 571. The bank argued that they had taken the cheques in satisfaction of the customer's debt, but this argument failed, because the bank knew that the cheques were not the property of the customer; he had told the bank that he was collecting the proceeds of the cheques for a friend.
57 S. 2.

6-139 The effect of the 'Not negotiable' crossing must not be overlooked. If a customer's title to a cheque crossed 'Not negotiable' is defective, the bank will be unable to obtain any better title thereto than the customer possessed; this is the effect of s. 81 of the Bills of Exchange Act 1882.[58]

Section 9
DEFENCE OF *EX TURPI CAUSA NON ORITUR ACTIO*

6-139A The availability of the defence *ex turpi causa non oritur actio* ('out of an immoral situation an action does not arise') to a collecting bank was first established in *Thackwell* v. *Barclays Bank plc*.[59] The plaintiff, Mr Thackwell, owned the rights to exploit a disused gold mine, but he was short of money to exploit it. He persuaded Riva Electronics (UK) Ltd (hereafter 'R. Ltd') to participate in the venture. As a means of raising money, he arranged with S, a director of R. Ltd, to enter into a false hire-purchase arrangement under which the plaintiff invoiced Alan Jones (Plant Sales) & Co. Ltd (hereafter 'A.J. Ltd'), a company dealing in plant and machinery, for £44,227 in respect of two items of plant supposedly sold to A.J. Ltd. In fact, one item did not exist, and the value of the other item was grossly inflated. R. Ltd then purchased from A.J. Ltd some £80,000 worth of equipment, including the two items of plant supposedly purchased by it from the plaintiff, by means of finance provided by a finance company under a hire-purchase agreement. On the day that the finance company paid a cheque for the £80,000 to A.J. Ltd to complete the purchase, a director of A.J. Ltd took the cheque to a branch of the defendant bank to bank it. While at the bank he met S who later handed to the assistant manager two cheques, one a cheque for £44,227 from A.J. Ltd made payable to the plaintiff and apparently endorsed by him, and the other a cheque from A.J. Ltd made payable to S himself and endorsed with S's own signature. S told the assistant manager that the cheque for £44,227 was to be paid into R. Ltd's account at the same branch. The assistant manager did not check the plaintiff's signature on the cheque or compare the two cheques. Such a comparison would have shown that they had obviously been endorsed by the same person. It was later found that S had forged the plaintiff's signature on the cheque for £44,227 and that it should not have been credited to R. Ltd's account. R. Ltd subsequently went into liquidation. The plaintiff brought an action for negligence and conversion against the bank in respect of the cheque. The bank's first defence,

---

58 *Ante*, para. 5-42.
59 [1986] 1 All ER 676. See *ante*, para. 6-100A.

which failed, was that it had received payment of the cheque in good faith and without negligence pursuant to s. 4 of the Cheques Act 1957.[60] The bank's second defence, which succeeded, was that the rule, *ex turpi causa non oritur actio*, prevented the plaintiff from recovering in conversion because he had been party to, or had had knowledge of, the fraudulent refinancing scheme which had caused the cheque to be made payable to him. Hutchison J added that, even if he had found that the plaintiff was innocent and that S alone was the perpetrator of the fraudulent scheme, he would still have upheld the bank's defence, *ex turpi causa non oritur actio*, because the cheque alleged to have been converted constituted in reality the very proceeds of the fraudulent conduct. The underlying crime was a serious one, and there was nothing inherently unfair in a result which deprived the plaintiff of the proceeds of the cheque. On the contrary, if the plaintiff had been permitted to recover the proceeds of the cheque from the bank, the court would, as the judge said, have been 'indirectly assisting in the commission of a crime'.

Section 10
BANK'S RIGHT TO AN INDEMNITY

6-140 If a collecting bank has no defence to a claim for damages for conversion arising out of the collection of cheques for a customer, the bank will expect to be indemnified by its customer in respect of the sum claimed. The bank acted as agent when collecting the cheques on behalf of the customer, and it is a general rule of law that an agent is entitled to be indemnified by his principal against all liabilities incurred in the reasonable performance of the agency.[61] In most cases, therefore, where a bank has to admit liability (or had judgment given against it) in a claim of this nature, it will be entitled to be indemnified by its customer against that liability.[62]

6-141 However, there are exceptional cases where the bank may not be entitled to an indemnity. Let it be supposed, for example, that a customer owns a chain of retail shops and that the manager of each shop is instructed by his employer to pay in the day's takings to the credit of the employer's account. One of the managers is dishonest. He steals a number of cheques from some third person for substantial amounts, which are not payable to his employer, and after forging the payees' endorsements, he cashes the cheques through the till of his shop. He

---

60 See *ante*, para. 6-100A.
61 *Adamson* v. *Jarvis* (1827) 4 Bing 66; *Frixione* v. *Tagliaferro & Sons* (1856) 10 Moo PCC 175.
62 See *Bavins, Junr & Sims* v. *London and South Western Bank Ltd* [1900] 1 QB 270.

then pays the cheques into his employer's account. The bank fails to make an enquiry concerning these third-party cheques. Eventually, the frauds come to light, and a claim is made against the bank by the person who was entitled to the proceeds of the cheques. Let it be assumed that the bank's defence under s. 4 of the Cheques Act 1957 fails on the ground that the bank, by omitting to make enquiry concerning the third-party cheques, had not acted 'without negligence'.[63] Depending upon the circumstances, the bank might not be entitled to an indemnity from its customer because the court might apply the rule that an agent is not entitled to an indemnity in respect of liabilities incurred in consequence of his own default or breach of duty.[64] It might well be held that the bank, in its capacity as agent, was in breach of duty to its customer, because it failed to draw his attention to the fact that third-party cheques for substantial amounts, apparently unconnected with the customer's business, were being passed through the customer's account by the manager of one of his shops.

6-142 In *Redmond* v. *Allied Irish Banks plc*[65] the plaintiff, Mr Redmond, had a deposit account with the defendant bank. In two transactions he paid into that account three cheques amounting in total to £4,300, and subsequently he drew out the value of these cheques. Each cheque was drawn by Wagon Finance Ltd on Williams & Glyn's Bank and made payable to a Mr G. Each cheque was crossed 'Not negotiable – account payee only', and each cheque appeared to bear the general endorsement of Mr G. The plaintiff endorsed the third cheque at the request of his bank. He told the bank that Mr G had explained that he did not want to put the cheques through his own account for tax reasons. As soon as the plaintiff obtained the money from his bank, he handed it over to Mr G, who eventually disappeared. It transpired that none of the holders of the cheques ever had good title, and that the cheques had got into circulation through fraud, to which it was not suggested that the plaintiff was a party. Wagon Finance Ltd brought an action against the defendant bank alleging that it had wrongly converted the cheques. The bank compromised Wagon Finance's action, and then debited the plaintiff's account with the amount of the cheques. The case proceeded on the assumption that the bank was entitled to be indemnified by the plaintiff, but as Saville J said, 'that assumption was prima facie questionable'.

What the plaintiff alleged in his action against the defendant bank was that the loss which he had sustained through the bank debiting his account resulted from its failure to warn him that dealing with such

---

63 See *Baker* v. *Barclays Bank Ltd* [1955] 1 WLR 822, *ante*, para. 6-126.
64 *Ellis* v. *Pond* [1898] 1 QB 426.
65 [1987] 2 FTLR 264.

cheques was risky. The words 'Not negotiable' on the cheques meant that he could not have or give a better title to them than the person from whom he had obtained them. He said that he was not warned that he might be liable if any of the holders up the line had no good title.

Saville J said that there was clear authority for the proposition that a bank owed its customer a duty to take reasonable care and skill in interpreting, ascertaining and acting in accordance with the customer's instructions. However, in such a case as the present there was no basis for a duty to advise or warn a customer that there were risks attendant on something which the customer wished to do. It followed that on the plaintiff's own version of the events, namely, that he had not been warned by the bank, his claim failed. However, Savile J said that he was not persuaded that the plaintiff's recollection of what had happened was correct. The judge was satisfied on the evidence that 'the bank did seek to explain to Mr Redmond the risks in dealing with such cheques'. Accordingly, judgment was given for the bank.

As the judge was satisfied that the bank had sought to explain to Mr Redmond the risks in dealing with the cheques, it follows that the judge's views on the hypothetical question of the bank's legal liability if it had not given a warning are necessarily *obiter*, and are not binding for the future. Accordingly, it will be open to a judge in a subsequent case to reconsider a bank's duty where it is asked by a customer to collect the proceeds of third-party cheques crossed 'Not negotiable – account payee only', especially if the cheques are for quite large amounts.

7

Payment of cheques

In this chapter, it is proposed to examine some of the problems which arise in regard to the payment of cheques.

Section I
PAYING BANKER'S DUTIES

7-1 The obligation of a banker to honour cheques drawn upon him by his customers is the most important of his duties. If payment of a cheque has to be refused and the cheque is presented through the London Clearing House, the rules of the Clearing House require that the 'answer' (i.e. the reason for refusing payment) must be written on the cheque; the rules further provide that answers must always be written in words without abbreviation, and not indicated by initials. It is usual to adopt the same practice when returning cheques which have been presented otherwise than through the Clearing House.

7-2 When deciding whether or not to pay cheques drawn upon him by his customers, a banker should have regard to a number of questions:

(a) Has the contractual relationship between banker and customer been terminated or suspended?[1]
(b) Is the cheque properly presented?[2]
(c) Is the cheque in proper form?[3]
(d) Does the cheque require endorsement and, if so, is it regularly endorsed?[4]
(e) Has the customer countermanded payment of the cheque?[5]
(f) Are there funds in the customer's account to meet the cheque?[6]

1 *Post*, para. 7-3.
2 *Post*, paras 7-4/11.
3 *Post*, paras 7-12/24.
4 *Post*, paras 7-25/29.
5 *Post*, paras 7-30/37.
6 *Post*, paras 7-38/40.

(g) Has a third party laid claim to the balance standing to the customer's credit?[7]

(h) Has the banker knowledge that payment of the cheque would amount to a breach of trust?[8]

(i) Has the banker notice that the person presenting the cheque has no title thereto?[9]

(j) Within what period must the banker pay or dishonour a cheque?[10]

Has the contractual relationship been terminated or suspended?

7-3 This matter was considered in Chapter 3. If the contractual relationship between banker and customer has been terminated or suspended, there is, of course, no need to enquire whether there are any additional reasons why a cheque drawn by the customer should not be paid. If, however, the cheque had been drawn in conjunction with a cheque card, the drawee bank would usually be obliged to reimburse the party who had relied upon it.[11]

Is the cheque properly presented?

One must distinguish between (a) crossed cheques, and (b) uncrossed cheques.

(a) Crossed cheques

7-4 The following rules concerning crossed cheques are derived from s. 79 of the Bills of Exchange Act 1882:

(i) If a cheque is crossed generally, it should be presented by, and paid only to, a banker.

(ii) If a cheque is crossed specially,[12] it should be presented by, and paid only to, the banker named in the crossing, or to his agent for collection being a banker.

(iii) A cheque which is crossed specially to more than one banker (except when crossed to an agent for collection being a banker), should not be paid to any one.

---

7 *Post*, paras 7-41/43.
8 *Post*, paras 7-44/45.
9 *Post*, para. 7-46.
10 *Post*, paras 7-47/53.
11 *Post*, para. 10-43.
12 For the difference between general and special crossings, see *ante*, paras 5-51/2.

254

If a banker disregards any of these rules, he will be liable to the true owner of the cheque for any loss which he may sustain,[13] In practice, it sometimes happens that the rules are not observed, either deliberately or as a result of some oversight; if, in such a case, payment is in fact made to the person entitled to the cheque, the paying bank will incur no loss.

7-5 A customer sometimes offers to indemnify his banker in respect of losses arising out of the payment in cash of crossed cheques issued by the customer. These proposals are usually made by employers who pay wages and salaries by cheque, the intention being that some of their employees, who may not be known to the drawee bank, may wish to present the cheques for payment in cash. The employer sees a protection, which may be illusory, in this method: he reasons that a thief who steals a crossed cheque would not attempt to present it for payment in cash. Bankers consider that any extension of the practice of paying crossed cheques under indemnity would be a serious embarrassment to them. Accordingly, the Committee of London Clearing Bankers resolved in 1965 'that in future no Clearing Bank shall enter into an arrangement with a customer to cash crossed cheques drawn by that customer excepting in the case of (i) a particular arrangement relating to an individual transaction, or (ii) the encashment of crossed cheques presented for payment by the drawer in person or his known agent'.

7-6 The crossings 'Account payee' and 'Account A.B.' are no concern of the paying banker; for, as Bigham J once observed,[14] the words 'Account A.B.' are a mere direction to the receiving bank as to how the money is to be dealt with after receipt.[15] Likewise, the 'Not negotiable' crossing does not concern the paying banker, who may safely pay a cheque so crossed, even though it is endorsed by someone besides the payee and therefore appears to have been negotiated by the payee to a third party.[16]

(b) Uncrossed cheques

7-7 If a cheque is uncrossed, it may be presented for payment by a banker, or it may be presented for payment in cash by the holder at the counter of the bank on which it is drawn.

---

13 S. 79(2).

14 *Akrokerri (Atlantic) Mines Ltd* v. *Economic Bank* [1904] 2 KB 465, at p. 472.

15 Regard would have to be paid to these crossings if the banker were acting in the dual capacity of paying and collecting banker; *cf. Carpenters' Company* v. *British Mutual Banking Co. Ltd* [1938] 1 KB 511, *Post*, paras 7-71/3.

16 For the 'Not negotiable' crossing, see *ante*, para. 5-42.

7-8 If a cheque payable to order is presented for payment in cash, the person who claims to be the payee or endorsee should be asked to endorse the cheque prior to payment. [17]

7-9 Payment in cash should be made during the bank's advertised hours for conducting business, or within a reasonable margin of the advertised time for closing. Failure to observe this rule might enable a customer to establish that he had been deprived of the opportunity of countermanding payment of a cheque. [18]

7-10 Payment in cash should not be made to a stranger whose appearance and demeanour raise suspicion. The reason for this rule is that a bank may find it necessary to rely upon the protection afforded by s. 60 of the Bills of Exchange Act 1882, [19] and that section requires payment to be made in the ordinary course of business. In one case, [20] Lord Halsbury said that he could well imagine that, on a person presenting himself whose appearance and demeanour were calculated to raise a suspicion that he was not likely to be entrusted with a valuable document for which he was to receive payment in cash, a banker would hesitate very much before making payment. In a later case, [21] Wright J was more specific: he referred to presentation by a tramp, or a postman or an office boy as constituting special circumstances calling for enquiry.

7-11 Payment in cash should not be made through the post. Occasionally, a person who claims to be the holder of an uncrossed cheque sends it by post to the bank on which it is drawn and asks for cash or a banker's draft to be sent to him. The Bills of Exchange Act 1882 provides that, where it is authorized by agreement or usage, a presentment through the post office is sufficient. [22] However, presentment by post in the circumstances set out above could not be regarded as authorized by agreement or usage, and the cheque should be returned to the sender with a request that he present it at the counter. If the bank paid the cheque as requested and the person to whom payment was made was not entitled to it, the bank would probably fail to obtain the protection of s. 60 of the Bills of Exchange Act 1882, as it could not claim to have paid the cheque in the ordinary course of business.

17 *Post*, para. 7-29.
18 See *Baines* v. *National Provincial Bank Ltd* (1927) 32 Com Cas 216, where, however, it was held that the cheque had been properly paid and that it was too late for the customer to countermand payment.
19 *Post*, para. 7-62.
20 *Bank of England* v. *Vagliano Brothers* [1891] AC 107, at pp. 117–18.
21 *Auchteroni and Co.* v. *Midland Bank Ltd* [1928] 2 KB 294, at p. 304.
22 S. 45(8).

Is the cheque in proper form?

When examining cheques, the paying banker should pay particular attention to (a) the customer's signature, (b) the date on the cheque, (c) the amount expressed in words and in figures, (d) any alterations to the cheque, and (e) a crossing which has been opened.

(a) Customer's signature

7-12 In the case of an account in the name of an individual, the principal matter for consideration is whether the signature is genuine; if the signature had been forged and the bank paid the cheque, then, no matter how clever the forgery, the bank would be unable to debit the customer's account, unless the customer was estopped from setting up the forgery.[23] However, the bank may be able to recover the money from the person or bank to whom it made the payment, on the ground that the money had been paid under a mistake of fact.[24] The claim will not succeed if the defendant has acted honestly and has altered his position to his detriment by spending or paying away the money in reliance on having received the payment.

7-13 In the case of joint accounts, partnership accounts, limited company accounts and other accounts where authority has been given to certain persons to draw cheques on the account, there is the additional task of ensuring that the cheque has been signed by the persons who have been duly authorized.

(b) Date on cheque

Sometimes a cheque which is presented for payment is (i) undated, (ii) out of date, or (iii) post-dated.

(i) Cheque undated

7-14 The Bills of Exchange Act 1882 provides that a cheque is not invalid merely because the date is omitted.[25] In practice, however, the drawee banker sometimes refuses to pay a cheque which is not dated and returns it with the answer 'Date required'.[26] A simpler course is for the drawee banker to insert the date himself.[27]

---

23 See *Greenwood* v.*Martins Bank Ltd* [1933] AC 51, *ante*, para. 2-128.
24 *National Westminster Bank Ltd* v. *Barclays Bank International Ltd* [1957] QB 654.
25 S. 3(4)(a). But it may be that an undated cheque is not 'complete and regular on the face of it' within s. 29, with the result that a holder could not be a holder in due course.
26 The practice was discussed in *Griffiths* v. *Dalton* [1940] 2 KB 264, but in that case the cheque had been dated before it was presented for payment.
27 See Bills of Exchange Act 1882, s. 20(1).

(ii) Cheque out of date

7-15 Bankers usually return unpaid with the answer 'Out of date' or 'Stale' those cheques which bear dates twelve months prior to presentation, though some banks treat a cheque as stale after six months.[28]

(iii) Cheque post-dated

7-16 If a post-dated cheque is presented for payment, it should be returned unpaid with the answer 'Post-dated'. There are at least three reasons why a banker should not pay a post-dated cheque: (a) if he pays it and then dishonours other cheques which would otherwise have been paid he will be liable to his customer for damages to his credit;[29] (b) even if he re-credits his customer's account with the amount of the post-dated cheque and holds the cheque until the arrival of its due date, the customer may become bankrupt in the meantime; and (c) in any event, the customer may countermand payment of the cheque before its due date.

(c) Amount in words and figures

7-17 The Bills of Exchange Act 1882 provides that where there is a discrepancy between the words and figures, the sum denoted by the words is the amount payable.[30] In practice, bankers usually return such cheques unpaid with the answer 'Words and figures differ'. If, however, the amount claimed on the cheque is the amount in figures and that is the smaller amount, some banks will pay that amount, at any rate in cases where the discrepancy between the words and figures is not large.

(d) Alterations to cheque

7-18 Any alterations to a cheque should be authenticated by the initials, or preferably by the signature, of the drawer; if there are two or more signatories to the cheque, all must join in the confirmation. Sometimes, a dishonest person alters a cheque: usually he raises the amount and forges the initials or signature of the drawer. If there is any doubt concerning the authenticity of a cheque which has been altered, a prudent banker will decline to pay the cheque until he has obtained independent confirmation from his customer. The answer written upon the cheque should be phrased so that it casts no reflection upon the customer's credit. Lord Shaw once suggested that if there was on the face of the cheque any reasonable ground for suspecting that it had been

---

28 'Out of date' should be distinguished from 'overdue': see *ante*, para. 5-114.
29 *Pollock* v. *Bank of New Zealand* (1902) 20 NZLR 174.
30 S. 9(2).

tampered with, it should be marked 'Refer to drawer'.[31] In modern usage, however, this answer may reflect adversely upon the customer's credit,[32] and it would be safer to use the phrase 'Alteration in . . . [e.g. amount] requires drawer's confirmation'.

7-19 If a bank pays a cheque which has been altered without the customer's assent, then, as a general rule, the bank will be unable to debit the customer's account and will have to suffer the loss itself, unless it can recover the money from the fraudulent person who made the alteration – a very remote possibility in most cases. The reasons why the bank cannot debit its customer's account are: (a) the instrument no longer embodies the customer's mandate, and (b) the Bills of Exchange Act 1882 provides that where a cheque is materially altered without the assent of all parties liable on the cheque, the cheque is avoided except as against a party who has himself made, authorized, or assented to the alteration, and subsequent endorsers.[33]

7-20 By way of exception to the general rule, a bank will be entitled to debit its customer's account with the amount of an altered cheque where (a) the customer did not exercise reasonable care in drawing his cheque and so facilitated an alteration of the amount, and (b) the alteration was not apparent. This is the result of the decision of the House of Lords in *London Joint Stock Bank Ltd* v. *Macmillan and Arthur*.[34]

7-21 A special rule applies to alterations to crossings in certain circumstances. The proviso to s. 79(2) of the Bills of Exchange Act 1882 enacts that where a cheque is presented for payment which does not at the time of presentment appear to be crossed, or to have had a crossing which has been obliterated, or to have been added to or altered otherwise than as authorized by the Act, the banker paying the cheque in good faith and without negligence is not to be responsible or incur any liability. This provision does not seem to extend to a case where some unauthorized person opens a crossing on a cheque, as explained below.

(e) *Opening a crossing*

7-22 Sometimes a customer who has only crossed cheque forms in his possession wishes to make a payment to a person who has no bank account. Although there is no statutory authority for the deletion or 'opening' of a crossing, a practice developed whereby the customer would write in proximity to the crossing 'Please pay cash', followed by

31 *London Joint Stock Bank Ltd* v. *Macmillan and Arthur* [1918] AC 777, at p. 824.
32 See *ante*, para. 2-150.
33 S. 64, *ante*, para. 5-147.
34 [1918] AC 777, *ante*, para. 2-125.

his signature. The payee would then treat the cheque as uncrossed and present it for payment at the counter of the drawee bank.

7-23 If a crossing is opened by some unauthorized person, and the cheque is paid over the counter to someone who is not entitled to it, the banker who paid the cheque would have no statutory protection and would, therefore, not be entitled to debit his customer's account. In order to protect themselves against the fraudulent opening of crossings, the Committee of London Clearing Bankers resolved in 1912 'that no opening of cheques be recognized unless the full signature of the drawer be appended to the alteration, and then only when presented for payment by the drawer or by his known agent'.[35]

7-24 However, if a cheque, though crossed, is paid to the true owner, the drawee banker incurs no risk in paying the cheque. Thus, if a customer tenders his own crossed cheque for payment in cash, it may safely be paid: there is no need to require him to open the crossing.

Does the cheque require endorsement?

7-25 Until the Cheques Act 1957 came into force, it was the practice of drawee banks to satisfy themselves, by careful examination, that all cheques payable to order appeared to be regularly endorsed. This precaution was considered necessary, because there was always the risk that, if payment was made to someone who was not entitled to the proceeds of a particular cheque, the drawee bank would wish to rely upon s. 60 or s. 80 of the Bills of Exchange Act 1882; and neither section would be of any avail if a bank had paid an order cheque which was irregularly endorsed.[36]

7-26 As far as the drawee bank is concerned, the Cheques Act 1957 abolished the necessity for this examination of endorsements. This important change in the law was made by s. 1(1) of the Act. The section provides that where a banker in good faith and in the ordinary course of business pays a cheque drawn on him which is not endorsed or is irregularly endorsed, he does not, in doing so, incur any liability by reason only of the absence of, or irregularity in, endorsement, and he is deemed to have paid it in due course.[37]

7-27 In two circulars dated respectively 2 and 23 September 1957, issued by the Committee of London Clearing Bankers shortly before the

---

35 *Questions on Banking Practice* (11th ed., 1978), p. 121, Question 344.
36 *Post*, paras 7-62, 7-79.
37 S. 1(2) has like effect in respect of certain instruments other than cheques.

Cheques Act 1957 came into operation, the Committee stated what the practice of the clearing banks would be when the Act came into force. [38]

7-28 The circular dated 2 September 1957 dealt at length with combined cheque and receipt forms. It stated that banks would no longer accept responsibility for examining receipts on cheques and other instruments, but an exception would be made in respect of combined cheque and receipt forms marked with a large 'R' close to the £ sign in the amount box. The circular added that the banks had agreed to encourage a reduction in the use of combined cheque and receipt forms. Customers who used these instruments were advised that s. 3 of the Cheques Act 1957 should render endorsed receipts unnecessary in most cases. That section enacted that an unendorsed cheque which appears to have been paid by the banker on whom it is drawn is to be evidence of the receipt by the payee of the sum payable by the cheque.

7-29 The circular dated 23 September 1957 was more comprehensive. It stated that paying banks would not examine instruments for endorsement, with the following exceptions, namely combined cheque and receipt forms marked 'R', travellers' cheques, bills of exchange (other than cheques), and promissory notes. [39] Dealing specifically with cheques and other instruments cashed at the counter (including those cashed under open credits), the circular added that the clearing banks had agreed to continue to require endorsement in all cases where it had previously been the practice to do so. Accordingly, the Cheques Act 1957 has not affected banking practice with regard to order cheques paid in cash over the counter of the drawee bank; they still require to be endorsed prior to payment.

Has customer countermanded payment?

7-30 The Bills of Exchange Act 1882 provides that the duty and authority of a banker to pay a cheque drawn on him by his customer are determined by countermand of payment. [40] The commonest reason why a customer wishes to countermand payment of a cheque is because the cheque has been lost or stolen. Sometimes, however, the drawer may want to countermand payment because goods supplied by the payee are defective. In this connection, however, the drawer should remember that he cannot escape liability on a cheque merely by ordering the bank not to pay it; in particular, the cheque may have come into the hands of a

---

38 For the text of these circulars, see Appendix I.
39 It was not one of the objects of the Cheques Act 1957 to abolish endorsements on bills of exchange (other than cheques) or on promissory notes.
40 S. 75.

third party who may have acquired a perfect title to it. Very often the drawer does not realize this.[41]

7-31 If a customer desires to countermand payment of a cheque, he should given written instructions to his banker, who should return the cheque, if it is presented, with the answer 'Payment countermanded by drawer'. If instructions countermanding payment of the cheque are received by telephone, the customer's written confirmation should be obtained, and if the cheque is presented in the meantime, it should be returned with the answer 'Payment countermanded by telephone and postponed pending confirmation'.

7-32 It is generally assumed that one party to a joint account, or one partner of a firm, or one director of a company has power to countermand payment of a cheque issued by another joint-account holder, partner or director, as the case may be; but this is a matter which depends upon the proper construction of the mandate in the particular case.

7-33 The countermand must be sent by the customer to the branch of the bank where his account is kept. Such notice will not usually affect any other branches of the bank. Thus, in one case,[42] the drawer of a cheque stopped payment of it by giving notice, in the usual way, to the branch of the bank on which it was drawn. The payee endorsed the cheque and took it to another branch of the same bank, which advanced money on it in good faith and without notice that the cheque had been stopped. It was held that the bank was entitled to succeed as holder for value against the drawer.

7-34 Some customers have special arrangements whereby their cheques for wages etc. are payable at various branches of the bank. It may not be possible effectively to countermand payment of these cheques, because the clearing banks have informed customers that they cannot undertake to notify all the branches concerned that a particular cheque has been countermanded.

7-35 A countermand is not effective until it actually comes to the notice of the bank. Thus, in *Curtice* v. *London City and Midland Bank Ltd*,[43] the plaintiff drew a cheque on the defendant bank on 31 October, in payment for some horses. The horses were not delivered and, later the same day, the plaintiff sent a telegram to the bank instructing them not to pay the cheque. The same evening, a telegraph messenger put the telegram into the bank's letter box. Owing to an oversight, the telegram was

---

41 *Ante*, para. 5-40.
42 *London Provincial and South-Western Bank Ltd* v. *Buszard* (1918) 35 TLR 142.
43 [1908] 1 KB 293.

not removed from the box until 2 November. Meanwhile, on 1 November, the cheque has been presented and paid. The plaintiff brought an action claiming that the bank was not entitled to debit his account with the amount of the cheque, but the Court of Appeal held that the action must fail on the ground that the cheque had not been effectively countermanded at the time when it was paid. However, if the plaintiff had pleaded his case differently, he might have succeeded in obtaining damages against his bank in respect of their negligence in failing to empty the letter box properly.[44]

7-36 Countermand of payment is effective only when it is unequivocally referable to the cheque in question. Thus, in *Westminster Bank Ltd* v. *Hilton*,[45] the drawer of a cheque for £8 1s. 6d. countermanded payment of it by telegram, the number of the cheque being given as 117283. The countermand was confirmed by telephone, though the number of the cheque was not mentioned. A cheque for the same amount and drawn in favour of the same payee, but bearing the number 117285, was presented and paid. This was the cheque which the customer had intended to stop, its number having been wrongly given in the first instance. The customer sued the bank for having paid contrary to his instructions and for having wrongfully dishonoured another cheque, which, but for such payment, could have been met. It was argued on behalf of the customer that the bank was not entitled to assume that the cheque which was presented for payment was a duplicate of the stopped cheque, because an examination of the paid vouchers would have shown that the cheque bearing the number given by the customer, namely 117283, had in fact been paid and was not drawn in favour of the payee stated in the countermand. The House of Lords, reversing the decision of the Court of Appeal, decided the case in favour of the bank, on the ground that as the number of a cheque is the one certain item of identification, the bank had not been guilty of negligence in paying the cheque numbered 117285.

7-37 The drawer may countermand payment of a cheque provided that it has not been finally and irrevocably paid. Once that has happened, it is too late for the drawer to countermand payment.[46] Moreover, the drawer cannot countermand payment of any cheques which he draws in conjunction with a cheque card.[47]

7-37A If, by mistake a bank pays a cheque after the drawer has countermanded payment, the bank may be able to recover the money,

---

44 [1908] 1 KB at p. 298, *per* Sir H. H. Cozens-Hardy MR, at p. 300, *per* Fletcher Moulton LJ.
45 (1926) 43 TLR 124.
46 *Post*, paras 7-47/53.
47 *Post*, para. 10-43.

on the ground that the money has been paid under a mistake of fact. The bank is prima facie entitled to recover the payment from the payee, unless the payee has changed his position in good faith.[48]

Are there funds in customer's account?

7-38 A banker's duty is to pay cheques drawn on him by his customers provided, *inter alia*, that (a) the customers have sufficient funds to their credit, or (b) the cheques are within the limits of an agreed overdraft.[49] It follows, therefore, that before paying a particular cheque, the drawee banker should ensure that there are funds in the customer's account to meet the cheque, unless the banker has already agreed (or is presently willing) to permit an overdraft.

7-39 If a banker has to dishonour a cheque for lack of funds, he will return it with the answer 'Refer to drawer' and, if he has reason to believe that the customer will provide funds to meet the cheque during the next day or two, he will sometimes add 'Please represent'. Before issuing a cheque a customer should allow time for the clearance of items which he has paid into his account. If he issues cheques which are presented before such items are cleared then, in the absence of any express or implied agreement to the contrary, his bank may dishonour the cheques with the answer 'Effects not cleared'. However, an implied agreement to pay cheques issued against uncleared effects may arise out of a course of dealing, i.e. in cases where the bank has made a practice of paying such cheques.

7-40 Before dishonouring a cheque for want of funds, a banker should take certain precautions with a view to ensuring that no mistakes have occurred in relation to the customer's accounts.[50]

Has a third party laid claim to the balance?

7-41 As a general rule, a banker's duty is to repay the sum standing to a customer's credit to, or to the order of, that customer, and the banker need have no regard to the claims of any third parties who say that the whole or part of the customer's balance belongs to them. In other words, the banker's primary duty is to his customer, and third parties cannot properly intervene without legal process.[51]

48 *Barclays Bank Ltd* v. *W. J. Simms Son & Cooke (Southern) Ltd and another* [1979] 3 All ER 522.
49 *Ante*, para. 2-13.
50 *Ante*, para. 2-152.
51 *Tassell* v. *Cooper* (1850) 9 CB 509; 14 LTOS 466.

7-42 The legal process which is available to a third party is to obtain an injunction from the court restraining the customer from withdrawing funds from the account, pending the determination of the ownership of the funds by the court. If such an injunction is granted and the bank is notified, the bank should dishonour cheques subsequently presented with the answer 'Injunction granted'. If the bank has notice that an application for an injunction is being made, but the injunction has not yet been granted, it would seem that the bank's duty to honour cheques still exists. However, in exceptional circumstances, the bank may be justified in dishonouring cheques with the answer 'Notice of application for injunction'.

7-42A There was a significant development in 1975 when the Court of Appeal granted an injunction, subsequently to become known as the Mareva injunction, in a case where there was a danger that the defendant might transfer assets out of the jurisdiction, so that they would not be available to the plaintiff if his claim succeeded. In that case, *Mareva Compania Naviera SA* v. *International Bulkcarriers SA*,[52] the plaintiff shipowners had issued a writ claiming against the defendant charterers unpaid hire and damages for repudiation of a charterparty. On an *ex parte* application Donaldson J granted an injunction restraining the charterers from removing or disposing out of the jurisdiction moneys standing to the credit of the charterers' account at a London bank. The Court of Appeal upheld his decision. Lord Denning MR referred to s. 45 of the Supreme Court of Judicature (Consolidation) Act 1925, which provides that 'a mandamus or an injunction may be granted or a receiver appointed by an interlocutory order of the court in all cases in which it shall appear to the court to be just or convenient ...' Lord Denning stated that, in his opinion, the principle applied to a creditor who had a right to be paid the debt owing to him, even before he had established his right by getting judgment for it. He added: 'If it appears that the debt is due and owing, and there is a danger that the debtor may dispose of his assets so as to defeat it before judgment, the court has jurisdiction in a proper case to grant an interlocutory judgment so as to prevent him disposing of those assets.'[53]

7-42B The Mareva injunction became an established feature of English law.[54] The principles applicable to it were given statutory force by s. 37(3) of the Supreme Court Act 1981, which provides that 'the power of the High Court ... to grant an interlocutory injunction restraining a party to any proceedings from removing from the jurisdiction of the

---

52 [1975] 2 Lloyd's Rep 509; also reported in a Note at [1980] 1 All ER 213.
53 [1980] 1 All ER, at p. 215.
54 See Mark Hoyle, *Mareva Injunction and Related Orders* (1985); Richard Ough, *Mareva Injunction and Anton Pillar Order: Practice and Precedents* (1987).

High Court, or otherwise dealing with, assets located within that jurisdiction shall be exercisable in cases where that party is, as well as in cases where he is not, domiciled, resident or present within that jurisdiction'.

7-42C A few months after the Supreme Court Act 1981 had been passed, the Court of Appeal in *Z Ltd* v. *A and Others*[55] held that the power of the High Court under the Act extends to cases in which there is a danger that the assets will be dissipated within the jurisdiction as well as removed out of the jurisdiction. The Court of Appeal held also that, if a bank has notice of a Mareva injunction which affects money or other assets in its hands, it would be contempt of court for it knowingly to assist in the disposal of the assets, whether or not the defendant had knowledge of the injunction. Accordingly, as soon as a bank has notice of the injunction, it must freeze the defendant's bank account or other assets, e.g. valuables in a deposit box. Additional points from this decision of the Court of Appeal are: (a) the plaintiff should inform the court of the names of the banks to whom it is proposed to given notice of the injunction; (b) although it may be necessary to seek a comprehensive order which freezes all the defendant's assets within the jurisdiction, the injunction may, where practicable, be restricted to freezing the defendant's assets up to a maximum sum, namely the amount of the plaintiff's prima facie justifiable claim, leaving the defendant free to deal with the balance; and (c) an injunction will not prevent a bank from making payments out of the defendant's bank account which the bank is obliged to honour because they involve obligations to other parties, e.g. payments under a letter of credit or under a bank guarantee.

7-42D Criminals should not be allowed to enjoy the proceeds of their crimes. The Mareva injunction is a powerful remedy which is available to the police in suitable cases. Thus, in *Chief Constable of Kent* v. *V and Another*[56] the defendant was charged with forgery and obtaining money by deception on forged instruments. It was alleged by the police that the defendant had obtained several cheque books belonging to R, forged her signature and withdrawn about £16,000 from her account which he then paid into his accounts at the Bank of Credit and Commerce International, where the money became intermingled with money belonging to other people which had possibly been obtained by deception. In order to prevent the defendant from using the money in his accounts, the police, acting in the name of the Chief Constable, issued an originating summons seeking an injunction restraining the defendant from withdrawing the money in his accounts, and the bank from carrying out any transactions in respect of the accounts. Beldam J held that he had

55 [1982] 1 All ER 556.
56 [1982] 3 All ER 36.

no jurisdiction to grant the injunction sought. The police appealed. The Court of Appeal, by a majority (Slade LJ dissenting), held that an injunction should be granted. Lord Denning MR referred to s. 37(1) of the Supreme Court Act 1981, which provides that 'the High Court may by order (whether interlocutory or final) grant an injunction or appoint a receiver in all cases in which it appears to the court to be just and convenient to do so'. Lord Denning stated that the words in brackets showed that Parliament did not like the limitation to 'interlocutory'. He added: 'It is no longer necessary that the injunction should be *ancillary* to an action claiming a legal or equitable right. It can stand on its own. The section as it now stands plainly confers a new and extensive jurisdiction on the High Court to grant an injunction. It is far wider than anything that had been known in our courts before.'[57]

7-42E In *Ninemia Maritime Corporation* v. *Trave Schiffahrtsgesellschaft m.b.h. & Co. KG, The Niedersachsen*[58] the Court of Appeal held that the test to be applied by the court when deciding whether to exercise its statutory discretion to grant a Mareva injunction to a plaintiff pursuant to s. 37 of the Supreme Court Act 1981 whenever it 'appears to the court to be just and convenient to do so' is whether, after the plaintiff has shown that he has at least a good arguable case and after considering the whole of the evidence before the court, the refusal of a Mareva injunction would involve a real risk that a judgment or award in the plaintiff's favour would remain unsatisfied because of the defendant's removal of assets from the jurisdiction or dissipation of assets within the jurisdiction. A Mareva injunction would not be granted merely for the purpose of providing a plaintiff with security for a claim, even when it appeared likely to succeed and even when the granting of the injunction would not cause hardship to the defendant.

7-42F In *Derby & Co. Ltd and Others* v. *Weldon and Another*[59] the Court of Appeal held that the court would order a pre-judgment worldwide Mareva injunction to freeze a party's assets in an exceptional case so long as, by undertaking or proviso or a combination of both: (a) oppression of the defendants by way of exposure to a multiplicity of proceedings was avoided, (b) the defendants were protected against the misuse of information gained from the ordinary order for disclosure in

---

57 [1982] 3 All ER 40.
58 [1984] 1 All ER 398.
59 [1989] 1 All ER 469 and 1002. See also *Babanaft International Co. SA* v. *Bassatne and another* [1989] 1 All ER 433, where the Court of Appeal held that a Mareva injunction in respect of overseas assets is only justifiable against the defendant personally and not against third parties outside the jurisdiction; and *Republic of Haiti* v. *Duvalier* [1989] 1 All ER 456, where the Court of Appeal granted a Mareva injunction to support an action brought in France.

aid of the Mareva, and (c) the position of third parties was protected. Where very large sums were involved, the English assets were totally inadequate to cover them, and there was a high risk of dissipation of the foreign assets, that could constitute an exceptional case.[60]

7-43 There is another form of legal process which is available when a third party claims that he is entitled to a bank balance standing to a customer's credit. The bank itself occasionally takes the initiative by applying to the court for relief by way of interpleader.[61] Interpleader is a legal proceeding by which a person (including a bank), from whom two or more persons claim the same property or debt, and who does not himself claim the property or dispute the debt, can protect himself from legal proceedings by calling upon the two claimants to interplead – that is to say, claim against one another – so that the title to the property or debt may be decided. The bank makes an application to the court by means of an originating summons, and if the Master is satisfied that the bank's application is a proper one, he will direct that the dispute between the claimants to the bank balance be tried. The bank will not be a party to those proceedings. The Master will usually order that the bank's costs in the interpleader proceedings be paid out of the bank balance.

Has banker knowledge of breach of trust?

7-44 A banker who receives into his possession money which his customer, to his knowledge, holds in trust, is under a duty not to part with such money, even at the mandate of the customer, for any purpose which he knows is inconsistent with that trust;[62] and a banker will certainly not be permitted to retain a benefit from any wrongful dealing with a fund which he knows to be affected with a trust where such benefit has been designed or stipulated for by him.[63]

7-45 *Foxton* v. *Manchester and Liverpool District Banking Co.*[64] illustrates the risk to which bankers are occasionally exposed. In that case, two executors had an account with the defendant bank, and each of them had overdrawn private accounts at the same bank. Largely as a result of pressure from the bank to reduce their overdrafts, both execu-

---

60 See Tim Taylor, 'Worldwide Marevas in the real wide world', *The Law Society's Gazette*, 3 May 1989, pp. 22–4.
61 See Order 17 of the Rules of the Supreme Court.
62 *Re Gross, Ex parte Adair* (1871) 24 LT 198; affirmed in *Re Gross, Ex parte Kingston* (1871) 6 Ch App 632. See also *Rowlandson and others* v. *National Westminster Bank Ltd* [1978] 1 WLR 798, *post*, para. 11-231A.
63 *Gray* v. *Johnston* (1868) LR 3 HL 1.
64 (1881) 44 LT 406. See also *Coleman* v. *Bucks and Oxon Union Bank* [1897] 2 Ch 243.

tors transferred substantial sums from the executors' account to their private accounts. After their deaths, some of the beneficiaries successfully brought an action against the bank for the recovery of the moneys so transferred.

7-45A   In *Lipkin Gorman* v. *Karpnale Ltd and Lloyds Bank plc*[65] Alliott J gave judgment for a firm of solicitors, Lipkin Gorman, in their claim against Lloyds Bank as constructive trustee of money stolen by a partner from their clients' accounts, though the plaintiffs were debarred by their contributory negligence from recovering the full amount from the bank. Furthermore, the plaintiffs' action against Karpnale Ltd, operator of the Playboy Club, as constructive trustee of money received by the club was dismissed, because the plaintiffs failed to prove that the club had actual or constructive knowledge of the receipt of trust funds.

In 1976 Mr C had jointed the staff of Lipkin Gorman, a firm of London solicitors. They introduced him to their bank, Lloyds Bank, and he opened a personal account there. He became a partner in 1978, and he was expelled from the partnership at the end of 1980 for 'shoddy conduct'. By that time, Mr C had misappropriated £323,222 from the firm's clients' accounts and had paid back only £100,313. Most of this money went into the coffers of the Playboy Club during July to November 1980. Mr C was extradited from Israel and sentenced to three years' imprisonment.

The plaintiffs recovered judgment for £3,735 against Karpnale Ltd in respect of the conversion of a bank draft. Their principal claim was against Lloyds Bank as constructive trustee. Their claim rested on the fact that Mr C was a compulsive gambler, and that he had access to the clients' accounts. The branch manager at Lloyds Bank knew of this propensity of Mr C, but he suppressed this knowledge from his superiors. Alliott J concluded that the bank manager, and therefore the bank, did have reasonable grounds for believing that it was probable that Mr C was operating the clients' accounts fraudulently. This was sufficient to make the bank a constructive trustee. However, there was a certain degree of contributory negligence on the part of the plaintiffs by accepting Mr C's explanations without further investigation, and for this reason the plaintiffs could not recover the full amount of their loss from the bank.

Alliott J said that the legal basis of a constructive trust claim was laid down over one hundred years ago by the then Lord Chancellor. In *Barnes* v. *Addy*,[66] Lord Selbourne said that 'strangers are not to be

---

65   [1987] 1 WLR 987. See also *Barclays Bank plc* v. *Quincecare Ltd and Unichem Ltd* [1988] FLR 166.
66   (1874) LR 9 Ch App 244.

made constructive trustees merely because they act as the agents of trustees in transactions within their legal powers, unless those agents receive and become chargeable with some part of the trust property, or unless they assist with knowledge in a dishonest and fraudulent design on the part of the trustees'. To actual receipt of trust property and actual knowledge of another's breach of trust must now be added a third category, namely 'wilfully shutting one's eyes to the obvious or wilfully or recklessly failing to make such enquiries as an honest and reasonable man would make'.[67] The knowledge of the bank manager in the present case related to Mr C's heavy drawings for gambling on his personal account. Alliott J based his decision on the fact that the bank manager had hidden from his superiors his knowledge of Mr C's gambling. The manager, and therefore the bank, had reasonable grounds for believing that it was probable that Mr C was operating the clients' accounts fraudulently.

In the Court of Appeal[68] the conversion claim against Karpnale Ltd, the operator of the club, was upheld. As regards the claim against the bank, the Court of Appeal held that Alliott J had been wrong to hold the bank liable as a constructive trustee. Moreover, the bank had not been negligent in breach of its mandate with the solicitors. Thus the claim against the bank failed. The decision of the Court of Appeal shows that a banker's potential liability as a constructive trustee and his liability for breach of contract should not be blurred. Before liability attaches as a constructive trustee, a lack of probity is required on the part of the banker, and this conduct would probably also constitute a breach of contract. However, the reverse is not true. Thus negligence being conduct constituting a mere breach of contract does not create a constructive trusteeship and does not constitute 'knowing assistance' within the Rule in *Barnes* v. *Addy*.

Has banker notice that person presenting cheque has no title?

7-46 It seldom happens that the drawee bank has notice that the person who is presenting a cheque for payment has no title to it. Occasionally, however, a person who claims to be the payee of an open cheque (who is not a customer of the drawee bank) informs the bank that he has lost it. The correct course for the bank to adopt is to advise the payee to ask the drawer to countermand payment of the cheque; but it may be that, before he can do so, the cheque is presented at the counter by a stranger

---

67 *Baden, Delvaux and Lecuit* v. *Société Générale pour Favoriser le Développement du Commerce et de L'Industrie en France SA* [1983] BCLC 325; affirmed [1985] BCLC 258n.

68 [1988] 6 JIBL N-209.

who demands payment in cash. In these circumstances, the bank should postpone payment of the cheque pending the receipt of instructions from the drawer.

Within what period must banker pay or dishonour a cheque?

7-47 There is no specific provision in the Bills of Exchange Act 1882 which prescribes the period available to the drawee bank for deciding whether to pay or dishonour cheques.[69] However, it seems safe to assume that the courts would hold that, if the rules of the London Clearing House (or a local clearing) with regard to the return of cheques are duly observed, such action could not be attacked; conversely, if the rules are not observed and a cheque is returned after the stipulated period, objection could properly be taken.

7-48 Thus in *Parr's Bank Ltd* v. *Thomas Ashby and Co.*,[70] a cheque was presented through the Clearing House by the plaintiff bank to the defendant bank. It seems that the Clearing House rules then in force required a drawee bank to return an unpaid cheque on the day of presentation.[71] Instead of doing so, the defendant bank returned the cheque one day late, and in the meantime, the plaintiff bank, acting upon the assumption that the cheque had been paid, honoured an acceptance of their customer in the sum of £65. The court held that the plaintiff bank was entitled to recover this sum from the defendant bank on the ground that their conduct amounted to a representation that the cheque which had passed through the clearing had been paid, and that the plaintiff bank had acted upon this representation.

7-49 In regard to cheques which are presented for payment otherwise than through the London Clearing House or a local clearing, the position as regards returns may be stated as follows.

7-50 If an open cheque is presented at the counter of the drawee bank, the bank must decide promptly whether or not to pay. There is no question of postponing the decision until the close of business. If payment is made, this is final and irrevocable as soon as the money is placed on the counter. Thereafter, it is too late for the bank to change its mind and to ask for the money to be returned on the ground that the customer has

---

69 A cheque is defined by s. 73 of the Act as a bill of exchange payable *on demand*, but this defines the nature of the instrument, rather than the duty of the drawee bank.

70 (1898) 14 TLR 563.

71 For the present rule, see *ante*, para. 6-13.

insufficient funds in his account;[72] and it is too late for the customer to countermand payment.

7-51 If payment is made at the counter within a reasonable margin of the advertised time for closing, this is final and irrevocable, and it is too late for the customer to countermand payment. Thus in *Baines* v. *National Provincial Bank Ltd*[73] the plaintiff, a bookmaker, drew a crossed cheque for £200 upon the Harrogate branch of the defendant bank in favour of a man named Wood, and handed the cheque to him at such a time that it was impossible for him to present it for payment before the bank's closing time at 3 p.m. Wood did in fact present it for payment at 3.05 p.m., and it was paid. On the opening of the bank the following morning, the plaintiff tried to stop payment of the cheque, but he was informed that the cheque had already been paid. He brought an action against the bank for a declaration that it was not entitled to debit his account with the amount of the cheque. Lord Hewart LCJ decided the case in the bank's favour, on the ground that it was entitled to deal with the cheque within a reasonable margin of its advertised time for closing. The cheque had been properly paid, and it was too late for the customer to countermand payment.

7-52 If a cheque is drawn by one customer on his bank and it is paid in for collection by another customer at the same branch of the same bank, there is authority for the view that the bank need not decide whether to pay or return the cheque until the next succeeding business day.[74] In practice, however, the bank usually decides on the day when the cheque is received whether to pay or return it. If the customer paying in the cheque asks whether it is paid and is told that it is, such payment is, of course, final and irrevocable.

7-53 Likewise, if a cheque is specially presented for payment by one bank to another, it seems that the drawee bank need not decide whether to pay or return the cheque until the day after receipt.[75] If, however, the drawee bank informs the collecting bank on the day of receipt that the cheque is paid, such payment is final and irrevocable. If the cheque is

---

72 See *Chambers* v. *Miller* (1862) 13 CBNS 125, where the plaintiff received cash in payment of a cheque at the defendant's bank. Whilst he was counting the money, the cashier discovered that the drawer's account was overdrawn and demanded the money back. The plaintiff refused to hand it back, whereupon the chasier detained him and took it from him by force. This cost the bank twenty pounds damages for assault and false imprisonment. In the opinion of Erle CJ, the money became the property of the plaintiff immediately he put his hand upon it.

73 (1927) 32 Com Cas 216.

74 *Boyd* v. *Emmerson* (1834) 2 A & E 184.

75 There is no direct legal authority for this proposition. See *Halsbury's Laws of England* (4th ed.), Vol. 3, p. 76; *Questions on Banking Practice* (10th ed., 1965), p. 180, Question 432. The 11th ed., 1978, does not contain this question.

being held over until the following day, then, as a matter of practice, the drawee bank informs the collecting bank accordingly.

Section 2
STATUTORY PROTECTION OF PAYING BANKER

7-54   The Bills of Exchange Act 1882[76] provides that a bill is discharged by payment in due course by or on behalf of the drawee or acceptor. 'Payment in due course' is defined as payment made at or after the maturity of the bill *to the holder* thereof in good faith and without notice that his title to the bill is defective.[77]

7-55   It follows, therefore, that if a drawee bank pays a cheque to someone other than the *holder*, as defined by the Act,[78] this will not constitute payment in due course. It would clearly be a harsh rule if a bank which paid a cheque in good faith to someone other than the holder had to suffer the loss. English law recognizes this, and provides protection for the drawee bank. The relevant statutory provisions which provide this protection will be examined.

Stamp Act 1853

7-56   This Act, as its title implies, was concerned primarily with stamp duties, but, for reasons which will be explained shortly, the Act also provided, for the first time, protection for the drawee bank. The effect of the Act,[79] as far as stamp duties are concerned, was that bearer cheques drawn within fifteen miles of the drawee bank were to continue to be exempt from stamp duty, provided, as theretofore, that the place of issuing was specified on the cheque and that the cheque was not postdated. Bearer cheques drawn beyond that limit, and *all* order cheques were to pay a duty of one penny, instead of an *ad valorem* duty which had existed for many years. It soon became clear that the great boon conferred by these provisions was the lowering of the duty on order cheques. For many years prior to the Act of 1853 it had been customary to draw cheques in favour of the payee or bearer.[80] This practice soon changed, and thenceforth most cheques were drawn payable to order.

---

76 S. 59(1).
77 S. 59(1).
78 S. 2, see *ante*, para. 5-96.
79 S. 1 and Sched.
80 An examination of the Cheque Collection of the Institute of Bankers establishes this point beyond doubt; for an analysis of cheques during the previous sixty years, see J. Milnes Holden, *The History of Negotiable Instruments in English Law* (1955), p. 220.

7-57 If special provision had not been made in the Act of 1853 for the purpose of conferring protection upon paying bankers, they would have been exposed to a grave risk which they had not encountered when dealing with bearer instruments, namely the risk of paying order cheques bearing forged endorsements. They would not have been able to debit their customers' accounts with the amounts so paid, because they would not have obtained a good discharge in respect of those cheques.[81]

7-58 The Stamp Bill, in its original form, contained no clause conferring any protection upon bankers in respect of forged endorsements upon cheques payable to order. The banking community was not slow in foreseeing the probable consequences of the new legislation,[82] and very soon a clause was introduced into the Bill with the object of affording protection. This became s. 19 of the Stamp Act 1853, which provides that 'any draft or order drawn upon a banker for a sum of money payable to order on demand which shall, when presented for payment, purport to be endorsed by the person to whom the same shall be drawn payable, shall be a sufficient authority to such banker to pay the amount of such draft or order to the bearer thereof; and it shall not be incumbent on such banker to prove that such endorsement, or any subsequent endorsement, was made by or under the direction or authority of the person to whom the said draft or order was or is payable either by the drawer or any endorser thereof.'[83] This section has never been expressly repealed, but it is of less importance than it used to be for two reasons:

7-59 Firstly, the Court of Appeal has held that the section has been impliedly repealed by s. 60 of the Bills of Exchange Act 1882, in the case of cheques.[84] The practical result is that the operation of s. 19 of the Stamp Act 1853 is confined to bankers' drafts where the same bank is both drawer and drawee.[85]

7-60 Secondly, in modern practice, very few drafts and orders are endorsed, in the words of s. 19, by the persons to whom they are drawn payable. Such instruments are usually paid into the payees' banking accounts, in which event no endorsement is required by virtue of the Cheques Act 1957.[86] It is only in rare cases that such an instrument is

---

81 *Robarts* v. *Tucker* (1851) 16 QB 560. Although this case was concerned not with a cheque, but with a bill domiciled with a banker, the principle involved is the same.

82 See *The Bankers' Magazine*, Vol. XIII, p. 698 (an editorial comment); and *The Economist*, Vol. XI, p. 754 (a letter from a banker).

83 For cases where the section was applied, see *Charles* v. *Blackwell* (1877) 2 CPD 151; *London City and Midland Bank Ltd* v. *Gordon* [1903] AC 240.

84 *Carpenters' Company* v. *British Mutual Banking Co. Ltd* [1938] 1 KB 511.

85 *London City and Midland Bank Ltd* v. *Gordon* [1903] AC 240. For a more detailed consideration of bankers' drafts, see *post*, para. 9-14.

86 S. 1(2).

endorsed by the payee; and it is only in cases where it purports to be endorsed by the payee, but in fact has been endorsed by someone else without the payee's authority, that there is any occasion for the application of s. 19 of the Stamp Act 1853.

Section 60, Bills of Exchange Act 1882

7-61 The Bills of Exchange Act 1882 codified much of the law relating to bills of exchange, including cheques. As regards the discharge of a bill, s. 59(1) of the Act provides that a bill is discharged by payment in due course by or on behalf of the drawee or acceptor. ·The section further provides that 'payment in due course' means payment made at or after the maturity of the bill to the holder[87] thereof in good faith and without notice that his title to the bill is defective.

7-62 It follows, therefore, that if a drawee bank pays a cheque to someone other than the holder, this will not amount to payment in due course under s. 59. In many cases, a drawee bank cannot be certain that it is making payment to the holder and, in order to meet this situation, s. 60 of the Bills of Exchange Act 1882 provides, in effect, that where a drawee bank, 'in good faith' and 'in the ordinary course of business' pays a cheque bearing a forged or unauthorized endorsement, the bank is 'deemed to have paid the bill in due course', notwithstanding the forged or unauthorized endorsement.

7-63 Section 60 may be further considered under seven heads, namely, (a) the meaning of 'a bill payable to order on demand drawn on a banker', (b) 'good faith', (c) payment 'in the ordinary course of business', (d) the meaning of 'endorsement', (e) the legal result where the same bank is both collecting and paying bank, (f) negligence and the paying bank, and (g) the payment of a cheque by a bank or a branch other than that named on the cheque.

(a) A bill payable to order on demand drawn on a banker

7-64 This expression clearly includes cheques, whether crossed or uncrossed.[88] It also includes bankers' drafts where such instruments are drawn by one bank on another bank, but it does not include drafts where the same bank is both drawer and drawee, because such instruments do not comply with the definition of a bill of exchange which, by

---

87 For the definition of holder, see *ante*, para. 5-96.

88 S. 73 of the Bills of Exchange Act 1882 defines a cheque as 'a bill of exchange drawn on a banker payable on demand'. If a cheque is materially altered within the meaning of s. 64 of the Act, it seems that the drawee bank will not be able to rely upon s. 60; see *Slingsby* v. *District Bank Ltd* [1932] 1 KB 544.

s. 3(1) of the Bills of Exchange Act 1882, must be addressed by one person to another.[89]

(b) Good faith

7-65　The Bills of Exchange Act 1882[90] provides that a thing is deemed to be done 'in good faith' where it is in fact done honestly, whether it is done negligently or not. The requirement of acting 'in good faith' is easily satisfied by the drawee banker: it is satisfied if the employees of the bank act honestly. Thus, the protection would be lost if an employee of the bank paid a cheque drawn by a customer although the employee knew that it was presented for payment by or on behalf of someone who was not entitled to it.

(c) Payment in the ordinary course of business

7-66　There is no statutory definition of the phrase 'ordinary course of business', but it would seem that a cheque is paid in the ordinary course of business where the usual steps are taken by the drawee bank as regards the examination and payment of the cheque. The usual steps which should be taken by a drawee bank have already been noted,[91] and there is no need to restate them here.

(d) Meaning of endorsement

7-67　In regard to negotiable instruments, three meanings of the words 'endorsement' have been noted.[92] An important question is whether the term includes the signature of the payee of a cheque written on the back of the cheque prior to payment in cash by the drawee bank. This signature is commonly called an endorsement by both bankers and customers alike, but it has been doubted whether in law it amounts to an endorsement. If these doubts were to be treated by the English courts as justified, the effect could be serious from the point of view of paying banks, because they would be deprived of statutory protection when paying open cheques at the counter.

7-68　The argument is as follows. Section 2 of the Bills of Exchange Act 1882 provides that, unless the context otherwise requires, the term 'endorsement' means 'an endorsement completed by delivery'. The same section provides that 'delivery' means 'transfer of possession, actual or

---

89 Such drafts are, however, within s. 19 of the Stamp Act 1853, *ante*, para. 7-58.
90 S. 90.
91 *Ante*, paras 7-1/52.
92 *Ante*, para. 5-73.

constructive, from one person to another'. Hence, it is argued – and this is the controversial point – that endorsement takes place only when a cheque is *negotiated* from one person to another. Those who advance this argument lay stress on the *dictum* of Byles J in *Keene* v. *Beard*[93] to the effect that the signature of a person receiving payment of a cheque is not an endorsement but a receipt. However, it should be noted that this case was decided before the 1882 Act defined endorsement.

7-69 The opposing argument is that the definition of endorsement in the 1882 Act does not preclude such a signature from being treated as an endorsement for the purposes of s. 60. This result may be achieved in one of two ways. First, it may be argued that the definition applies 'unless the context otherwise requires', and that the context does require that the word 'endorsement' in s. 60 be given a wide meaning, for otherwise paying banks would be left unprotected in the very circumstances which the Stamp Act 1853 and the Bills of Exchange Act 1882 were intended to cover. Alternatively, even if 'endorsement' means 'an endorsement completed by delivery', it may be argued that delivery (as defined) takes place when possession of the cheque is transferred from the payee to the bank.

7-70 There is an English decision which appears to support the view that the word 'endorsement' in s. 60 does include the signature of the payee written on the back of a cheque prior to payment in cash by the drawee bank. In that case,[94] the drawee bank paid in cash an order cheque drawn by the plaintiffs on which the payee's endorsement had been forged by one of the plaintiffs' servants; it was held that the bank was protected by s. 60. However, there are decisions in other countries where the law is similar to English law, and some of those decisions have been given against the paying banks on the ground that the mere writing of the payee's name on the back of a cheque payable to order does not, without more, constitute such writing an endorsement.[95]

---

93 (1860) 8 CB (NS) 372, cited by Lord Haldane in *Gerald McDonald and Co.* v. *Nash and Co.* [1924] AC 625, p. 634.

94 *Brighton Empire and Eden Syndicate* v. *London and County Bank* (1904), *The Times*, 24 March. See also *Stapelberg* v. *Barclays Bank DCO* 1963 (3) SA 120, a decision of the Supreme Court of South Africa (Transvaal Provincial Division). The judgment is in Afrikaans, but an English translation was published in *The South African Bankers' Journal*, August 1963; the case was noted briefly in the *Journal of the Institute of Bankers*, Vol. 85 (1964), pp. 42–5.

95 See *Byles on Bills of Exchange* (26th ed., 1988), p. 300. If the English courts were to take the view that the mere writing of the payee's name on the back of a cheque for the purpose of obtaining payment did not constitute an endorsement, then if the drawee bank paid an uncrossed cheque over the counter on which the payee's signature had been forged, the bank might be able to claim protection from s. 1(1), Cheques Act 1957, which applies specifically to cheques which are not endorsed or are irregularly endorsed. The protection of s. 60 would not then be required.

(e) Same bank both collecting and paying bank

7-71 In *Carpenters' Company* v. *British Mutual Banking Co. Ltd*,[96] the defendant bank, which had only one office, acted as both collecting and paying bank in the following circumstances. It conducted an account for the plaintiff company, who were the trustees of a home; it also conducted an account for the assistant clerk of the company, who acted as secretary of the committee which looked after the home. Acting fraudulently, he obtained the signatures of the Master and Warden of the company to crossed cheques which were ostensibly in payment of the accounts of tradesmen. He forged the endorsements of the payees, and paid the cheques into his own account with the defendant bank. Thus that bank acted in the capacity of collecting bank as far as his account was concerned, and as paying bank in regard to the account of the Carpenters' Company.

7-72 In an action by the company against the bank claiming damages for conversion of the cheques, Branson J found as a fact that the bank had not acted without negligence, and therefore could not rely upon the protection afforded by s. 82 of the Bills of Exchange Act 1882 (now replaced by s. 4 of the Cheques Act 1957); but that the bank had paid the cheques in good faith and in the ordinary course of business, notwithstanding that it had been negligent, and that, therefore, the bank was protected by s. 19 of the Stamp Act 1853, and by s. 60 of the Bills of Exchange Act 1882.

7-73 The Court of Appeal, by a majority, reversed this decision and held that the bank was liable to the company. As regards s. 19 of the Stamp Act 1853, it was held that this section had been impliedly repealed by s. 60 of the Bills of Exchange Act 1882. The learned lords justices expressed differing views as regards s. 60, and it is not easy to extract any general principle from their judgments. It would seem, however, that one conclusion can safely be drawn from the decision, namely that if a bank is acting as both collecting and paying bank, and it wants to obtain statutory protection in respect of a claim for damages for conversion of cheques, it must satisfy the requirements (as collecting bank) of s. 4 of the Cheques Act 1957 (which has replaced s. 82 of the Bills of Exchange Act 1882), and (as paying bank) of s. 60 or s. 80 of the Bills of Exchange Act 1882, both of which should be read in the light of s. 1 of the Cheques Act 1957.

(f) Negligence and the paying bank

7-74 One of the questions which was much discussed in the *Carpenters'*

96 [1938] 1 KB 511.

Company case was whether a bank can claim the protection of s. 60 of the Bills of Exchange Act 1882 if it has acted negligently. Although the section does not expressly require a paying bank to act without negligence, the better view would seem to be that a paying bank which has acted negligently ought not to be granted statutory protection, for two reasons.

7-75 First, a paying bank would seem to be under a common law duty to exercise care when obeying its customers' mandates, and this duty does not appear to have been abrogated by statute. Accordingly, any breach of this duty by a bank involving a customer in loss would give rise to an action for damages.[97]

7-76 Secondly, it is submitted, though this is controversial, that a bank which pays a cheque negligently is necessarily acting otherwise than 'in the ordinary course of business', and so automatically loses the protection of s. 60. The contrary view was expressed by Slessor and MacKinnon LJJ in the *Carpenters' Company* case. Thus, Slessor LJ said that, in his view, negligence did not necessarily preclude the protection of s. 60, a view made clear, in his opinion, in the case of the other requirement, namely 'good faith', by s. 90 of the Bills of Exchange Act 1882, which provides that a thing is deemed to be done 'in good faith', within the meaning of the Act, where it is in fact done honestly, 'whether it is done negligently or not'.[98] With respect, however, this reasoning is fallacious: the rule that good faith is not inconsistent with negligence has no bearing upon the question whether a negligent act can be done in the ordinary course of business. The third lord justice, Greer LJ, took the opposite view; he did not consider that a thing done negligently could be done in the ordinary course of business.[99]

(g) Payment by another bank or branch

7-77 A customer sometimes arranges to have his cheques cashed at another branch of his own bank, or even at another bank if his bank has no branch in the town concerned. The branch where he banks will give written authority to the other branch or bank to encash his cheques within clearly defined limits. This procedure is known as opening, or establishing, a credit. The question may raise whether s. 60, which

---

97 This point has never been directly decided, but in *Bellamy* v. *Marjoribanks* (1852) 7 Ex 389, pp. 403–4, and in *Carlon* v. *Ireland* (1856) 5 E & B 765, p. 770, the opinion was expressed that payment contrary to a crossing would amount to negligence; and there would seem to have been no point in discussing the matter unless negligence deprived the bank of its right to debit the account. (The bankers' duties in relation to crossed cheques are now contained in s. 79, Bills of Exchange Act 1882.)
98 [1938] 1 KB, at p. 534.
99 [1938] 1 KB, at p. 532.

applies to payment by the banker on whom a cheque is drawn, extends to the encashment of a cheque under an open credit, though the question will only arise if the payee's endorsement has been forged.

7-78 This question has never been before the courts, but it would seem on principle that the section is capable of applying to these transactions. Where a cheque is encashed by one branch of a bank at the request of another branch of the same bank, there is only one bank involved, and that bank will be protected by s. 60, provided that it acts in good faith and in the ordinary course of business. In cases where two different banks are involved, the relationship between them is that of principal and agent, the encashing bank being the agent of the drawee bank. Encashment by a duly authorized agent acting within the scope of its authority would seem to be equivalent to payment by the drawee bank itself, and therefore s. 60 would apply.

Section 80, Bills of Exchange Act 1882

7-79 Section 80 should be read in conjunction with s. 79, which sets out the duties of bankers in regard to the payment of crossed cheques.[1] Section 80 provides, *inter alia*, that where the banker on whom a crossed cheque is drawn, in good faith and without negligence, pays it, if crossed generally, to a banker, and if crossed specially, to the banker to whom it is crossed, or his agent for collection being a banker, the banker paying the cheque is to be entitled to the same rights and be placed in the same position as if payment of the cheque had been made to the true owner.[2]

7-80 As drawee bankers are protected in respect of forged endorsements on cheques, whether crossed or not, by s. 60 of the Bills of Exchange Act 1882, it is not immediately apparent why s. 80 was enacted. The reason is mainly historical. The Crossed Cheques Act 1876 was, as its title imples, an Act which was concerned exclusively with crossed cheques. Section 9 of that Act conferred protection upon a paying banker who paid a crossed cheque in good faith, without negligence, and in accordance with the crossing. The 1876 Act was repealed by the Bills of Exchange Act 1882,[3] though most of its provisions were

---

1 *Ante*, para. 7-4.
2 Section 80 also provides that if a crossed cheque which is properly paid in accordance with the crossing has come into the hands of the payee, the drawer shall be entitled to the same rights and be placed in the same position as if payment of the cheque had been made to the true owner. The practical effect of this provision is that if a crossed cheque is delivered to the payee, and it is lost or stolen, the loss must fall upon the payee. A similar provision was contained in s. 9 of the Crossed Cheques Act 1876. See, also, *Charles* v. *Blackwell* (1877) 2 CPD 151, at p. 158, from which it would appear that the same rule applies to uncrossed cheques.
3 S. 96 and Sched. II.

re-enacted in ss 76–82 of the 1882 Act. In that way, the provisions contained in s. 9 of the 1876 Act were re-enacted in s. 80 of the 1882 Act.

7-81 A practical difficulty which arises from time to time in relation to s. 80 is that, in order to secure its protection, payment must be made, in the case of a cheque crossed generally, 'to a banker'.[4] Occasionally, a company which claims to be carrying on a banking business presents a crossed cheque for payment, but the bank upon which it is drawn may not be satisfied that the company presenting the cheque is in fact carrying on a banking business. If payment of a crossed cheque was made to such a company, and the court held that the company in question was not carrying on a banking business, the drawee bank would be unable to rely on the protection of s. 80.

Sections 60 and 80 compared

7-82 Section 60 applies to all cheques payable to order, whether they are crossed or not; s. 80 applies only to crossed cheques.

7-83 In order to qualify for protection under s. 80, payment must be made 'without negligence', whereas s. 60 contains no such express provision. However, the better view would seem to be that a paying bank which has acted negligently would not be granted protection under s. 60[5] and, if this view is correct, the practical result under both sections is that a bank is entitled to protection only in cases where it has acted without negligence.

7-84 Section 60 applies only to cheques payable to order, whereas s. 80 applies also to cheques payable to bearer, provided that they are crossed. This distinction seems to be of small importance, because a banker does not require any statutory protection when paying bearer cheques.

7-85 Section 80 is capable of applying to non-transferable cheques, at any rate in those cases where such cheques bear no evidence of transfer. Section 60, however, does not afford any protection in respect thereof, because it extends only to instruments payable to order. However, non-transferable cheques are seldom issued.[6]

7-86 The provisions of s. 80 have been extended to certain instruments (for example, bankers' drafts) which are not within s. 60.[7]

4 S. 2 of the Act provides that 'in this Act, unless the context otherwise requires ... "banker" includes a body of persons, whether incorporated or not, who carry on the business of banking'. For the meaning of 'the business of banking', see *ante*, paras 1-17/23.
5 *Ante*, para. 7-76.
6 *Post*, para. 9-42.
7 *Ante*, para. 6-70.

7-87   Neither section can be relied upon by a drawee banker who pays an order cheque bearing no endorsement or an irregular endorsement. However, the Cheques Act 1957 abolished the necessity for endorsement in many cases.[8]

7-88   It seems that neither section can be relied upon by the drawee bank if a cheque has been materially altered within the meaning of s. 64 of the Bills of Exchange Act 1882.[9]

Section I, Cheques Act 1957

7-89   The Cheques Act 1957 abolished the necessity for endorsements on cheques, with certain exceptions which have already been noted.[10] This important change in the law was made by s. 1(1) of the Act. The section provides that where a banker in good faith and in the ordinary course of business pays a cheque drawn on him which is not endorsed or is irregularly endorsed, he does not, in doing so, incur any liability by reason only of the absence of, or irregularity in, endorsement, and he is deemed to have paid it in due course.

7-90   It should be noted that the Cheques Act 1957 did not repeal s. 60 or s. 80 of the Bills of Exchange Act 1882. Drawee banks still rely upon s. 60 or s. 80 of the 1882 Act in cases where they have paid cheques bearing endorsements which appear to be regular but in fact have been forged, whereas they rely upon s. 1(1) of the Cheques Act 1957, in cases where they have paid cheques bearing no endorsement or an irregular endorsement.

7-91   The provisions of s. 1(1) of the Cheques Act 1957 may be considered under three heads, namely (a) 'good faith', (b) payment 'in the ordinary course of business', and (c) payment 'in due course'.

(a) Good faith

7-92   The expression 'good faith' has the same meaning in the Cheques Act 1957 as in the Bills of Exchange Act 1882.[11] Thus, a thing is deemed to be done in good faith where it is in fact done honestly, whether it is done negligently or not.[12]

8 *Post*, para. 7-89.
9 *Slingsby* v. *District Bank Ltd* [1932] 1 KB 544.
10 *Ante*, paras 7-26/29.
11 Bills of Exchange Act 1882, s. 90; Cheques Act 1957, s. 6(1).
12 *Ante*, para. 7-65.

(b) Payment in the ordinary course of business

7-93   There is no statutory definition of the phrase 'ordinary course of business', but it would seem that a cheque is paid in the ordinary course of business where the usual steps are taken by the drawee bank as regards the examination and payment of the cheque. The usual steps which should be taken by a drawee bank have already been noted,[13] and there is no need to restate them here.

7-94   However, one matter which is occasionally overlooked should be stressed. If a cheque payable to order is presented for payment in cash at the counter, it is still the practice of bankers, in spite of the provisions of s. 1(1) of the Cheques Act 1957, to require the person who claims to be the payee or endorsee to sign his name on the back of the cheque prior to payment.[14] Departure from this practice might well make it impossible for the paying bank to establish that it had paid the cheque in the ordinary course of business, and so the bank would be unable to obtain the protection of the section if payment had been made to someone who was not entitled to the cheque, e.g. to a finder or a thief. If, however, the person who presented the cheque was the payee, or was entitled to it as a transferee without endorsement, the paying bank would not need the protection of the section, and would suffer no loss by paying the cheque without endorsement.

(c) Payment in due course

7-95   If a paying banker satisfies the requirements of s. 1(1) of the Cheques Act 1957 he is deemed to have paid the cheque 'in due course'. In this connection, s. 59(1) of the Bills of Exchange Act 1882 provides that a bill is discharged by payment 'in due course' by or on behalf of the drawee or acceptor. Therefore, if a paying banker satisfies the requirements of s. 1(1) of the Cheques Act 1957, the cheque is discharged.

Section 3
CLAIMS BY THIRD PARTIES AGAINST PAYING BANKERS

7-96   As a general rule, a paying banker's duties are owed to his own customer and to no one else. However, there are some instances where a third party may succeed in establishing a claim against a drawee bank.

---

13 *Ante*, paras 7-1/52.
14 As far as the clearing banks are concerned, this policy was announced in a circular dated 23 September 1957; see *ante*, para. 7-29.

Classification of third-party claims

Claims against drawee banks by persons other than their own customers may be considered under three heads, (a) claims under s. 74, Bills of Exchange Act 1882, (b) claims for damages for conversion, and (c) claims arising out of 'marked cheques'.

(a) Claims under s. 74, Bills of Exchange Act 1882

7-97 It has already been noted in an earlier chapter[15] that s. 74(1) of the Act provides that failure to present a cheque for payment within a reasonable time of issue will discharge the drawer to the extent of any actual damage which he suffers as a result of such failure. It is clear that the drawer will not be discharged merely because of delay in presenting a cheque for payment.[16] There must be actual damage to the drawer, and it seems that he will only suffer damage by a failure to present a cheque within a reasonable time if, when presentment should have taken place, he had sufficient funds in the bank to meet it, and after that time but before presentation of the cheque, the bank suspends payment, so that the drawer is a creditor of the bank to a larger amount than he would have been if the cheque had been paid. In cases where the drawer *is* discharged, either wholly or partially, s. 74(3) provides that the holder of the cheque shall have a right against the drawee bank by being substituted as creditor of the bank, in lieu of the drawer, to the extent of the discharge.

(b) Claims for damages for conversion

7-98 Where a drawee bank pays the proceeds of a cheque to someone who is not entitled to those proceeds in circumstances which amount to a conversion on the part of the recipient,[17] it would seem that the drawee bank, unless protected by statute, would be liable in damages for conversion to the person who was entitled to receive the proceeds. Such a claim would rarely succeed, however, because in most cases the drawee bank would be fully protected by the relevant provisions of the Bills of Exchange Act 1882 and the Cheques Act 1957.[18]

7-99 An obvious instance where a drawee bank would not be entitled to statutory protection would be where the bank paid a cheque otherwise than in accordance with its crossing. In this connection, it is specifically

---

15 *Ante*, para. 5-133.

16 *King and Boyd* v. *Porter* [1925] NI 107, where the cheque was not presented for nearly three years.

17 For an account of what constitutes conversion, see *ante*, para. 6-48.

18 Ss 60 and 80 of the 1882 Act; s. 1(1) of the 1957 Act.

provided by s. 79(2) of the Act that the true owner of a cheque which has been paid by the drawee bank otherwise than in accordance with its crossing has a right against the bank in respect of any loss sustained by such payment.

(c) Claims arising out of 'marked cheques'

7-100 The marking of a cheque by the drawee bank as good for payment is said to have been a fairly common practice at the beginning of the present century.[19] In order to give a cheque an enhanced standing, a customer would ask his banker to mark or certify it, and the banker would write on the face of the cheque some such words as, 'This cheque is good for £x', followed by an authorized signature on behalf of the bank. In 1920, The Committee of London Clearing Bankers strongly recommended the discontinuance of the practice.[20] During the Second World War, however, it was revived to a limited extent. At the present day, most banks in the United Kingdom wisely decline to mark cheques at the request of customers; instead of marking a cheque as good for payment, a banker would offer to issue a banker's draft.

7-101 There can be no doubt that if a bank, at the request of a customer, marks a cheque as good for payment, this promise or undertaking on the part of the bank can be legally enforced by the customer. The bank should protect itself as against its customer by transferring the amount of the cheque from his account to a suspense account.[21] A more difficult question could arise if a third party gave value for a marked cheque in reliance upon the bank's promise, and subsequently the bank refused to pay. It is most unlikely that a bank in the United Kingdom would refuse payment in such circumstances, because the banks concerned would usually prefer to honour their undertaking and, if necessary, to suffer a loss, rather than dishonour a cheque which they had specifically promised to pay. In *Bank of Baroda Ltd* v. *Punjab National Bank Ltd*,[22] a third party, namely a bank, gave value for a cheque which had been marked as good for payment on a specified date. The cheque was dishonoured. The bank which had given value for it brought an action in Calcutta against the bank whose manager had marked the cheque as good for payment. The Judicial Committee of the Privy Council held that the action must fail, but the circumstances of

19 R. W. Jones, *Gilbart Lectures on Banking*, 1949, p. 48.
20 *Questions on Banking Practice* (9th ed., 1952), pp. 186–7. See also 10th ed., pp. 194–5.
21 *Cf*. Lord Wright's remarks in *Bank of Baroda Ltd* v. *Punjab National Bank Ltd* [1944] AC, at p. 185.
22 [1944] AC 176.

that case were exceptional, and it does not follow that all claims by third parties in respect of marked cheques would necessarily fail. An unusual feature of the case was that the cheque which had been certified was post-dated, and the Privy Council held that the bank manager who had so certified it (and who was subsequently suspended from duty and prosecuted) had no actual or ostensible authority to certify post-dated cheques.

8

Bills of exchange

It is not one of the objects of this work to provide a detailed exposition of the law relating to bills of exchange; for this, reference may be made to the standard textbooks.[1] Nevertheless, it is essential for bank officers to be familiar with the main principles of the law relating to bills. The purpose of the present chapter is to give a short account of this branch of the law, and to indicate the principal ways in which the subject impinges upon banking practice.

Section I
LEGAL PRINCIPLES

8-1 The law relating to bills of exchange is to be found, for the most part, in the Bills of Exchange Act 1882, as interpreted by the courts.

Definition of bill of exchange

8-2 The Act defines a bill as an unconditional order in writing, addressed by one person to another, signed by the person giving it, requiring the person to whom it is addressed to pay on demand or at a fixed or determinable future time a sum certain in money to or to the order of a specified person, or to bearer.[2] An instrument which does not comply with these conditions, or which orders any act to be done in addition to the payment of money, is not a bill of exchange.[3]

8-3 An order to pay out of a particular fund is not an unconditional order for the purpose of the definition of a bill of exchange; but an unqualified order to pay, coupled with (a) an indication of a particular fund out of which the drawee is to reimburse himself or a particular account to be debited with the amount, or (b) a statement of the transaction which gives rise to the bill, is unconditional.[4]

---

1 The two standard works are *Byles on Bills of Exchange* and *Chalmers on Bills of Exchange*.
2 S. 3(1).
3 S. 3(2).
4 S. 3(3).

8-4   The Act specifically provides[5] that a bill is not invalid by reason (a) that it is not dated; (b) that it does not specify the value given, or that any value has been given therefor; (c) that it does not specify the place where it is drawn or the place where it is payable.

Specimen bills of exchange

8-5   Figures 8.1, 8.2 and 8.3 are illustrations of bills of exchange. It will be observed that there are the same parties to a bill as there are to a cheque, but a cheque is, of course, always drawn upon a banker.[6] The person who draws a bill is known as the drawer; the person on whom it is drawn is called the drawee; and the person to whom it is drawn payable is known as the payee. A bill may be drawn to, or to the order of, the drawer, or it may be drawn payable to, or to the order of, the drawee.[7]

8-6   It will be noticed that Figs 8.2 and 8.3 have been accepted by the drawee. When the drawee accepts a bill, he is known as the acceptor. The legal significance of acceptance and the different kinds of acceptance will be explained subsequently.

8-7   Figure 8.1 is an inland bill payable on demand.[8] The Bills of Exchange Act 1882[9] provides that a bill is payable on demand (a) which is expressed to be payable on demand, or at sight, or on presentation; or (b) in which no time for payment is expressed.

8-8   Figures 8.2 and 8.3 are both payable at a determinable future time; the former is an inland bill, the latter a foreign bill. The Act[10] provides that a bill is payable at a determinable future time which is expressed to be payable (a) at a fixed period after date or sight, (b) on or at a fixed period after the occurrence of a specified event which is certain to happen, though the time of happening may be uncertain. An instrument expressed to be payable on a contingency is not a bill, and the happening of the event does not cure the defect.

8-9   The Act further provides that where a bill expressed to be payable at a fixed period after date is issued undated, or where the acceptance of a bill payable at a fixed period after sight is undated, any holder may insert therein the true date of issue or acceptance, and the bill is payable accordingly.[11] In such a case, should the holder, in good faith and by

5 S. 3(4).
6 S. 73.
7 S. 5(1).
8 For the differences between inland bills and foreign bills, see *post*, paras 8-14/16.
9 S. 10(1).
10 S. 11.
11 S. 12.

```
                                              Lombard Street, London
                                                        I April 19..
  £100
  On demand pay to James Brown or order the sum of one hundred pounds.


                                    For and on behalf of John Smith Ltd,
  To J. Green Ltd,                                  John Smith
     Gracechurch Street, London                     Director
```

Fig. 8.1 Inland bill payable on demand

```
                                              Lomard Street, London
                                                        I April 19..
       X  St,  of  n,
       Z                 £100
     XY  rd  alf  ee
   at ba  eh  Gr
  e  om     .                Two months after date pay to James Brown or order the
  l  L  n b  J,
  b  ,  o d  d               sum of one hundred pounds.
  a  td  an Lt                        For and on behalf of John Smith Ltd,
  y  L  r en                                         John Smith
  a  k  o re                                         Director
  p  n  F G  r
     a  .  .  to
  d  B  n  J  ec
  e     o     ir  To J. Green Ltd,
  t     d     D
  p     n        Gracechurch Street, London
  e     o
  c     L
  c
  A
```

Fig. 8.2 Inland bill payable after date

```
                                              Fifth Avenue, New York.
                                                        I April 19..
       X  St,  of  n,
       Z                 $100
     XY  rd  alf  ee
   at ba  eh  Gr             On I October 19.. pay to James Brown or order the sum
  e  om     .
  l  L  n b  J,              of one hundred dollars with interest at five per cent per
  b  ,  o d  d
  a  td  an Lt               annum, from date hereof to date of payment.
  y  L  r en
  a  k  o re
  p  n  F G  r  To J. Green Ltd,                    H. M. Johnson
     a  .  .  to
  d  B  n  J  ec  Gracechurch Street, London
  e     o     ir
  t     d     D
  p     n
  e     o
  c     L
  c
  A
```

Fig. 8.3 Foreign bill payable on specified date with interest

mistake, insert a wrong date, the bill is not invalidated, but will operate
and be payable as if the date so inserted had been the true date.[12] Even
if a wrong date is inserted in bad faith, if the bill subsequently comes
into the hands of a holder in due course, it is not invalidated, but operates and is payable as if the date inserted had been the true date.[13]

12 S. 12.
13 S. 12.

8-10 Figure 8.3 requires the payment of interest. The Bills of Exchange Act 1882[14] provides that the sum payable by a bill is a sum certain although it is required to be paid (a) with interest; (b) by stated instalments; (c) by stated instalments, with a provision that upon default in payment of any instalment the whole shall become due; (d) according to an indicated rate of exchange or according to a rate of exchange to be ascertained as directed by the bill. Where a bill is expressed to be payable with interest, then unless the instrument otherwise provides, interest runs from the date of the bill, and if the bill is undated from the issue thereof.[15]

8-11 Figure 8.3 is a bill for one hundred dollars, drawn in New York upon a company in London. In this connection, the Bills of Exchange Act 1882[16] provides that where a bill is drawn out of the United Kingdom and the sum payable is not expressed in the currency of the United Kingdom, the amount is to be calculated, in the absence of some express stipulation, according to the rate of exchange for sight drafts at the place of payment on the day the bill is payable.

8-12 By virtue of the Finance Act 1970,[17] bills of exchange are exempt from stamp duty.

Due date

8-12A A bill payable on demand (for example, a cheque) is due on presentation at any time on or after the date of the instrument. Where a bill was not payable on demand, the Bills of Exchange Act 1882[18] made provision for three 'days of grace' to be added to the time of payment as fixed by the bill, and the bill was due and payable on the last day of grace. The Banking and Financial Dealings Act 1971[19] abolished days of grace in relation to bills drawn on or after 16 January 1972. Apart from bills drawn before that date, all bills are now due and payable on the last day of the time of payment as fixed by the bill or, if that is a non-business day, on the succeeding business day.

8-13 Where a bill is payable at a fixed period after date, after sight, or after the happening of a specified event, the time of payment is determined by excluding the day from which the time is to begin to run and by including the day of payment.[20] Where a bill is payable at a fixed

14 S. 9(1).
15 S. 9(3).
16 S. 72(4).
17 S. 32 and Sched. 7.
18 S. 14(1).
19 S. 3.
20 S. 14(2).

period after sight, the time begins to run from the date of the acceptance if the bill be accepted, and from the date of noting or protest if the bill be noted or protested for non-acceptance, or for non-delivery.[21] The term 'month' in a bill means calendar month.[22]

Inland and foreign bills

8-14 The Bills of Exchange Act 1882[23] provides that an inland bill is a bill which is or on the face of it purports to be (a) both drawn and payable within the British Islands, or (b) drawn within the British Islands upon some person resident therein. Any other bill is a foreign bill. Thus, a bill is a foreign bill if (a) it is not or does not purport to be drawn within the British Islands, or (b) being drawn with the British Islands, it is neither payable therein nor drawn upon someone resident therein. Unless the contrary appears on the face of a bill, the holder may treat it as an inland bill.[24]

8-15 The Act further provided that, for the purposes of the Act, 'British Islands' meant any part of the United Kingdom of Great Britain and Ireland, the Islands of Man, Guernsey, Jersey, Alderney and Sark, and the islands adjacent to any of them being part of the dominions of Her Majesty.[25] However, the Republic of Ireland is no longer part of the United Kingdom.

8-16 One of the principal differences between inland and foreign bills is that, upon dishonour by non-acceptance or non-payment, a foreign bill must be protested, whereas in the case of an inland bill protesting is optional, except in certain circumstances.[26] Another difference is that inland bills are almost invariably *sola* bills, i.e. drawn in one part only, whereas foreign bills are sometimes drawn in 'sets' of two or three parts. Each part is numbered and is identical with the others, except that it refers to the others. Loss is minimized by sending two parts for acceptance by different mails, whilst the third is usually retained in the drawer's country. Only one part should be accepted, or endorsed, otherwise the signer may be liable on two signatures.[27] If two or more parts are negotiated to different holders in due course, the one whose title first accrues is as between such holders deemed the true owner of the bill.

---

21 S. 14(3).
22 S. 14(4).
23 S. 4(1).
24 S. 4(2).
25 S. 4(1).
26 S. 51, *post*, paras 8-87/89.
27 For a full statement of the rules which apply when a bill is drawn in a set, see Bills of Exchange Act 1882, s. 71.

Differences between bills of exchange and cheques

8-17 There are many points of similarity between bills and cheques. This is understandable, because a cheque is a particular type of bill. However, the following points of difference may be noted.

8-18 A bill may be drawn upon any person, whereas a cheque must be drawn upon a banker.[28]

8-19 A bill may be payable on demand or at a fixed or determinable future time, whereas a cheque must be payable on demand.[29]

8-20 Unless a bill is payable on demand, it is usually accepted, whereupon the acceptor is the party primarily liable to the holder. A cheque is not usually accepted, and the drawer is the party primarily liable.[30]

8-21 A bill must be presented for payment when due, or the drawer will be discharged.[31] The drawer of a cheque is not discharged for six years, unless through the delay in presentation he has been injured.[32]

8-22 A bill drawn prior to 16 January 1972 (unless payable on demand) takes three days of grace in every case where the bill itself does not otherwise provide.[33] A cheque takes no days of grace.

8-23 There is no provision which enables bills to be crossed, whereas cheques may be crossed.[34]

8-24 There is no statutory protection for a bank which pays bills domiciled with it, whereas banks are protected, subject to certain conditions, when paying cheques drawn upon them.[35]

8-25 There is no statutory protection for a bank which collects the proceeds of bills, whereas banks are protected, subject to certain conditions, when collecting cheques for customers.[36]

8-26 The provisions of the Cheques Act 1957, relating to the abolition of endorsements, apply to cheques but not to bills.

---

28 Bills of Exchange Act 1882, s. 73.
29 Ss 3(1) and 73.
30 'It would certainly require strong and unmistakable words to amount to an acceptance of a cheque', *per* Lord Wright in *Bank of Baroda Ltd* v. *Punjab National Bank Ltd* [1944] AC 176, at p. 188.
31 S. 45.
32 S. 74(1).
33 S. 14(1). The Banking and Financial Dealings Act 1971, s. 32 and Sched. 7, abolished days of grace in relation to bills drawn on and after 16 January 1972.
34 Ss 76 and 81.
35 Ss 60 and 80, Bills of Exchange Act 1882; s. 1(1), Cheques Act 1957.
36 Cheques Act 1957, s. 4.

Collection of bills

8-27 The Bills of Exchange Act 1882 imposes certain duties upon the holder of a bill, and any neglect of these duties may have serious consequences. The principal duties of the holder are (a) to present the bill for acceptance and subsequently to present it for payment, and (b) if the bill is dishonoured by non-acceptance or by non-payment to give notice of dishonour to prior parties, and (in some cases) to have the bill noted and protested. As bankers often undertaken the collection of bills, it is essential for them to have a precise knowledge of the law and practice relating to these matters.

Presentment for acceptance

8-28 Presentment for acceptance is legally necessary in three cases: (a) where a bill is payable after sight, presentment for acceptance is necessary in order to fix the maturity of the instrument;[37] (b) where a bill expressly stipulates that it must be presented for acceptance,[38] and (c) where a bill is drawn payable elsewhere than at the residence or place of business of the drawee.[39]

8-29 Except in the three cases listed above, it is not obligatory to present a bill for acceptance. The holder may await the maturity of the bill and then present it for payment. As a rule, however, he does present it for acceptance. His object in doing so is to secure the liability of the drawee; this may make it possible to discount the bill. Alternatively, if the drawee refuses to accept the bill, the holder will then have an immediate right of recourse against prior parties if the appropriate steps are taken.

Definition and requisites of acceptance

8-30 The acceptance of a bill is the signification by the drawee of his assent to the order of the drawer.[40] An acceptance is invalid unless it complies with the following conditions, namely:

(a) It must be written on the bill and be signed by the drawee. The mere signature of the drawee without additional words is sufficient.

---

37 Bills of Exchange Act 1882, s. 39(1).
38 S. 39(2).
39 S. 39(2).
40 S. 17(1).

(b) It must not express that the drawee will perform his promise by any other means than the payment of money.[41]

8-31 A bill is, of course, usually complete when it is placed before the drawee for acceptance. However, the Bills of Exchange Act 1882 provides that a bill may be accepted before it has been signed by the drawer, or while otherwise incomplete, or when it is overdue, or after it has been dishonoured by a previous refusal to accept, or by non-payment.[42] When a bill payable after sight is dishonoured by non-acceptance, and the drawee subsequently accepts it, the holder, in the absence of any different agreement, is entitled to have the bill accepted as of the date of first presentment to the drawee for acceptance.[43]

Liability of acceptor

8-32 Unless and until the drawee of a bill accepts it, he is not liable on it at all.[44] Once he accepts it, however, he becomes the party primarily liable thereon. In this connection, the Bills of Exchange Act 1882[45] provides that the acceptor of a bill, by accepting it, engages that he will pay it according to the tenor of his acceptance, and he is precluded from denying to a holder in due course:

(a) The existence of the drawer, the genuineness of his signature, and his capacity and authority to draw the bill.

(b) In the case of a bill payable to drawer's order, the then capacity of the drawer to endorse, but not the genuineness or validity of his endorsement.

(c) In the case of a bill payable to the order of a third person, the existence of the payee and his then capacity to endorse, but not the genuineness or validity of his endorsement.

8-33 It should be observed that, although the acceptor of a bill is estopped from denying, to a holder in due course, the drawer's existence, capacity and authority to draw the bill, and the genuineness of his signature *as drawer* he may deny the genuineness or validity of the dra-

---

41 S. 17(2). The acceptance of a bill payable 'after sight' should be dated in order to fix its maturity. In this connections s. 12 provides that where the acceptance of a bill payable at a fixed period after sight is undated, any holder may insert the true date of acceptance. The section also provides that (a) where the holder in good faith and by mistake inserts a wrong date, and (b) in every case where a wrong date is inserted, if the bill subsequently comes into the hands of a holder in due course, the bill operates and is payable as if the date so inserted had been the true date.

42 S. 18.

43 S. 18.

44 S. 53(1).

45 S. 54.

wer's endorsement, if the bill is payable to his order; or, if it is payable to the order of a third person, the acceptor may deny the genuineness or validity of the latter's endorsement.

General and qualified acceptances

8-34   An acceptance is either general or qualified.[46] A general acceptance assents without qualification to the order of the drawer.[47] A qualified acceptance in express terms varies the effect of the bill as drawn. In particular, an acceptance is qualified which is:[48]

(a) Conditional, that is to say, which makes payment by the acceptor dependent on the fulfilment of a condition therein stated.

(b) Partial, that is to say, an acceptance to pay part only of the amount for which the bill is drawn.

(c) Local, that is to say, an acceptance to pay only at a specified place. An acceptance to pay at a particular place is a general acceptance, unless it expressly states that the bill is to be paid there only and not elsewhere.[49]

(d) Qualified as to time.

(e) The acceptance of some one or more of the drawees, but not of all.

8-35   The following are examples of the five classes of qualified acceptance:

(a) *Conditional*: 'Accepted payable on surrender of bills of lading evidencing shipment of 200 metric tons of jute.'

(b) *Partial*: On a bill drawn for £200, 'accepted payable for £100 only'.

(c) *Local*: An acceptance in the form 'accepted payable at XYZ Bank Ltd, Lombard Street, London' is general; but an acceptance in the form 'accepted payable only at XYZ Bank Ltd, Lombard Street, London' is qualified.

(d) *Qualified as to time*: On a bill drawn payable six months after date, 'accepted payable twelve months after date'.

(e) *Acceptance by one of several drawees*: On a bill drawn on X, Y and Z, the acceptance of X only. (However, if X had authority to accept on behalf of all the drawees, and he did so accept, the acceptance would not be qualified.)

---

46 S. 19(1).

47 S. 19(2).

48 S. 19(2).

49 See *Bank Polski* v. *K. J. Mulder and Co.* [1942] 1 KB 497, where bills drawn in Poland on the defendants, a firm in London, and expressed to be payable in Amsterdam were accepted without qualification. It was held that the acceptance was a general acceptance.

8-36 The Bills of Exchange Act 1882 provides that the holder of a bill may refuse to take a qualified acceptance, and if he does not obtain an unqualified acceptance may treat the bill as dishonoured by non-acceptance.[50] Where a qualified acceptance is taken, and the drawer or an endorser has not expressly or impliedly authorized the holder to take a qualified acceptance, or does not subsequently assent thereto, such drawer or endorser is discharged from his liability on the bill; but this does not apply to a partial acceptance, of which due notice has been given.[51] Where a foreign bill has been accepted as to part, it must be protested as to the balance.[52] When the drawer or endorser of a bill receives notice of a qualified acceptance, and does not within a reasonable time express his dissent to the holder, he is deemed to have assented thereto.[53]

8-37 Accordingly, a banker should not take a qualified acceptance (except a partial acceptance) without the consent of his customer or correspondent. If he is offered a partial acceptance, he will usually take it, because the drawer and endorsers will not be thereby discharged; but due notice must be given to them.

Presenting bills payable after sight

8-38 As the maturity of a bill payable after sight cannot be fixed until it is presented for acceptance, unreasonable delay in making presentment may sometimes prejudice the position of the drawer or of an endorser, especially in cases where the financial position of the drawee is deteriorating. Accordingly, the Bills of Exchange Act 1882[54] provides that, subject to the provisions of s. 41(2),[55] when a bill payable after sight is negotiated, the holder must either present it for acceptance or negotiate it within a reasonable time. If he does not do so, the drawer and all endorsers prior to that holder are discharged. In determining what is a reasonable time within the meaning of this provision, regard must be had to the nature of the bill, the usage of trade with respect to similar bills, and the facts of the particular case.

Rules governing presentment for acceptance

8-39 The Bills of Exchange Act 1882 provides that a bill is duly presented for acceptance which is presented in accordance with the fol-

50 S. 44(1).
51 S. 44(2).
52 S. 44(2).
53 S. 44(3).
54 S. 40(1).
55 These deal with cases where presentment for acceptance is excused.

lowing rules: [56]

- (a) The presentment must be made by or on behalf of the holder to the drawee or to some person authorized to accept or refuse acceptance on his behalf at a reasonable hour on a business day [57] and before the bill is overdue.
- (b) Where a bill is addressed to two or more drawees, who are not partners, presentment must be made to them all, unless one has authority to accept for all, in which case presentment may be made to him only.
- (c) Where the drawee is dead, presentment may be made to his personal representative. [58]
- (d) Where the drawee is bankrupt, presentment may be made to him or to his trustee. [58]
- (e) Where authorized by agreement or usage, a presentment through the post office is sufficient.

8-40 The Act makes no provision concerning the place where a bill should be presented for acceptance. Usually, the bill will be presented for acceptance at the address of the drawee as stated on the bill but, if no address is given, presentment will be excused if the holder after exercising reasonable diligence cannot find the drawee.

When presentment for acceptance excused

8-41 The Bills of Exchange Act 1882 [59] provides that presentment for acceptance is excused, and a bill may be treated as dishonoured by non-acceptance:

- (a) Where the drawee is dead or bankrupt, or is a fictitious person or a person not having capacity to contract by bill.
- (b) Where, after the exercise of reasonable diligence, such presentment cannot be effected.
- (c) Where, although the presentment has been irregular, acceptance has been refused on some other ground.

56 S. 41(1).
57 The Bills of Exchange Act 1882, s. 92, provides that 'non-business days' for the purposes of the Act mean (a) Sunday, Good Friday, Christmas Day; (b) a Bank Holiday under the Bank Holidays Act 1871, or Acts amending it; and (c) a day appointed by Royal proclamation as a public fast or thanksgiving day. The Banking and Financial Dealings Act 1971, s. 3, added Saturday to the list of non-business days.
58 Presentment for acceptance to the personal representative of a deceased drawee, or to the trustee of a bankrupt drawee, is optional. Presentment in such cases is excused by s. 41(2), and the holder may treat the bill as dishonoured by non-acceptance.
59 S. 41(2).

The Act specifically provides[60] that the fact that the holder has reason to believe that the bill, on presentment, will be dishonoured does not excuse presentment.

Presentment for payment

8-42   As a general rule, a bill of exchange must be duly presented for payment, and if it is not so presented, the drawer and endorsers are discharged.[61] This is a vitally important rule. There are many cases where the holder of a bill has lost his rights completely as against the drawer and endorsers, merely because he failed to observe the very strict rules relating to presentment for payment.[62] The acceptor, however, remains liable on a bill accepted generally, even if it is not presented for payment,[63] and if, by the terms of a qualified acceptance, presentment for payment is required, the acceptor, in the absence of an *express* stipulation to that effect, is not discharged by the omission to present the bill for payment on the day that it matures.[64]

Rules governing presentment for payment

8-43   The Bills of Exchange Act 1882[65] provides that a bill is duly presented for payment which is presented in accordance with the following rules:

(1) Where the bill is not payable on demand, presentment must be made on the day it falls due.

(2) Where the bill is payable on demand, then, subject to the provisions of the Act, presentment must be made within a reasonable time after its issue in order to render the drawer liable, and within a reasonable time after its endorsement, in order to render the endorser liable.[66] In determining what is a reasonable time, regard shall be had to the nature of the bill, the usage of trade with regard to similar bills, and the facts of the particular case.

(3) Presentment must be made by the holder or by some person authorized to receive payment on his behalf at a reasonable hour on a business day, at the proper place as defined by rule (4) below, either to the person designated by the bill as payer, or to some person authorized to pay or refuse payment on his behalf

---

60 S. 41(3).
61 Bills of Exchange Act 1882, s. 45.
62 See, for example, *Yeoman Credit Ltd* v. *Gregory* [1963] 1 WLR 343.
63 S. 52(1).
64 S. 52(2).
65 S. 45.
66 For the special rule relating to drawers of cheques, see s. 74(1), Bills of Exchange Act 1882, *ante*, para. 5-133.

if with the exercise of reasonable diligence such person can there be found.[67]

(4) A bill is presented at the proper place:

    (a) where a place of payment is specified in the bill and the bill is there presented;

    (b) where no place of payment is specified, but the address of the drawee or acceptor is given in the bill, and the bill is there presented;

    (c) where no place of payment is specified and no address given, and the bill is presented at the drawee's or acceptor's place of business, if known, and, if not, at his ordinary residence if known;

    (d) in any other case if presented to the drawee or acceptor wherever he can be found, or if presented at his last known place of business or residence.

(5) Where a bill is presented at the proper place, and after the exercise of reasonable diligence no person authorized to pay or refuse payment can be found there, no further presentment to the drawee or acceptor is required.

(6) Where a bill is drawn upon, or accepted by two or more persons who are not partners, and no place of payment is specified, presentment must be made to them all.

(7) Where the drawee or acceptor of a bill is dead, and no place of payment is specified, presentment must be made to a personal representative, if such there be, and with the exercise of reasonable diligence he can be found.

(8) Where authorized by agreement or usage a presentment through the post office is sufficient.

8-44 All the rules set out above are, of course, important to bankers, but the rule which deserves special attention is rule (1), because many losses have been suffered by failure to observe it. This rule provides that where a bill is not payable on demand, presentment must be made on the day it falls due. There is no better illustration of the rigour of this rule than the facts in *Yeoman Credit Ltd* v *Gregory*.[68] The facts, so far as are relevant, were that the plaintiffs were the holders of a bill for

---

67 In this connection, s. 52(4) of the Bills of Exchange Act 1882 provides that where the holder of a bill presents it for payment, he must exhibit the bill to the person from whom he demands payment, and when the bill is paid, the holder must forthwith deliver it up to the party paying it. It should be noted, therefore, that the holder is not obliged to deliver the bill to the acceptor until payment is actually made: when the holder presents the bill for payment, he is merely required to exhibit it to the person from whom he demands payment.

68 [1963] 1 WLR 343.

£2,000 which had been accepted by the drawees payable at the National Provincial Bank, Piccadilly, W1. The bill was payable on 9 December 1959, fixed, i.e. no days of grace were to be allowed. The plaintiffs were told by the acceptors that there were no funds at the National Provincial Bank to meet the bill and that presentment should be made at the Midland Bank, Golden Square, W1. Accordingly on 9 December the bill was presented at the Midland Bank, Golden Square, but payment was refused. On the following day, it was presented at the National Provincial Bank, Piccadilly, but payment was again refused. The plaintiffs, as holders, brought an action against the defendant, as endorser. It was held that the bill ought to have been presented at the National Provincial Bank, Piccadilly, on its due date, namely 9 December, and that, as it was not presented there until the following day, the presentment was bad. Thus, the claim against the defendant failed, even though there was no proof that he had been in any way prejudiced by the late presentation.

When delay in presentment for payment excused

8-45 It happens very occasionally that the holder of a bill, without any fault or negligence on his part, is unable to present the bill for payment on the prescribed day. In this connection, s. 46(1) of the Bills of Exchange Act 1882 provides that delay in making presentment for payment is excused when the delay is caused by circumstances beyond the control of the holder, and not imputable to his default, misconduct or negligence. It further provides that when the cause of delay ceases to operate, presentment must be made with reasonable diligence.

When presentment for payment dispensed with

8-46 Presentment for payment is dispensed with in five cases by virtue of the provisions of s. 46(2) of the Bills of Exchange Act 1882, namely:

(a) Where, after the exercise of reasonable diligence, presentment as required by the Act cannot be effected. The Act expressly provides, however, that the fact that the holder has reason to believe that the bill will, on presentment, be dishonoured, does *not* dispense with the necessity for presentment. Thus, even though the acceptor has been adjudicated bankrupt and the holder knows quite well that payment will not be made, he must nevertheless present the bill for payment.

(b) Where the drawee is a fictitious person.

(c) As regards the drawer, where the drawee or acceptor is not bound, as between himself and the drawer, to accept or pay the bill, and the drawer has no reason to believe that the bill would be paid if presented.

(d) As regards an endorser, where the bill was accepted or made for the accommodation of that endorser, and he has no reason to expect that the bill would be paid if presented.

(e) By waiver of presentment, express or implied.

8-47 It may be noted that different rules are laid down, as indicated above, in respect of different parties. The general rule is that failure on the part of the holder to present a bill for payment frees the drawer and endorsers from liability. The effect of paragraph (c) above is that the *drawer* is not released from liability by failure on the part of the holder to present the bill in the circumstances stated in that paragraph. The effect of paragraph (d) above is that an *endorser* is not released from liability by failure on the part of the holder to present the bill in the circumstances stated in that paragraph. Finally, paragraphs (a), (b) and (e) state the circumstances in which *all parties* remain liable despite the holder's failure to present the bill for payment.

Dishonour of a bill

8-48 The vast majority of bills are duly accepted when presented for acceptance, and duly paid when presented for payment. Occasionally, however, acceptance or payment is refused, and the bill is then said to be dishonoured by non-acceptance or by non-payment, as the case may be. As a general rule, the person who presented the bill (usually a banker) must give notice of dishonour to prior parties and take the appropriate steps to have the bill noted or protested. Failure to take the proper steps promptly may have serious consequences, as will be shown presently.

Dishonour by non-acceptance

8-49 The Bills of Exchange Act 1882[69] provides that when a bill is duly presented for acceptance and is not accepted within the customary time, the person presenting it must treat it as dishonoured by non-acceptance. If he does not, the holder loses his right of recourse against the drawer and endorsers. The Act does not define 'customary time'. The person who presents a bill for acceptance should deliver it up to the drawee, if asked to do so. The drawee is entitled to retain it for twenty-four hours. At the end of that time, he must re-deliver it, accepted or unaccepted. In an old case[70] which was decided before the Act was passed, the rule

69 S. 42.
70 *Jeune* v. *Ward* (1818) 1 B & Ald 653, at p. 659.

was laid down that when a bill is left for acceptance, it is the duty of the party who leaves it to call again for it, and to enquire whether or not it has been accepted. It is not the duty of the other person to send it to him, unless there is a usual course of dealing between the persons concerned to do so. The rule laid down in this case has not been altered by the Act.

8-50 The Act[71] further provides that a bill is dishonoured by non-acceptance:

(a) when it is duly presented for acceptance, and such an acceptance as is prescribed by the Act is refused or cannot be obtained; or

(b) when presentment for acceptance is excused and the bill is not accepted.

8-51 Although 'such an acceptance as is prescribed by the Act' may be either general or qualified, it is specifically provided by the Act[72] that the holder of a bill may refuse to take a qualified acceptance, and if he does not obtain an unqualified acceptance, he may treat the bill as dishonoured by non-acceptance.

8-52 The Act[73] provides that when a bill is dishonoured by non-acceptance, an immediate right of recourse against the drawer and endorsers accrues to the holder, and no presentment for payment is necessary.

8-53 The holder's 'right of recourse' should not be confused with a 'right of action'. He will only acquire a right of action if he complies with the requirements of the Act, such as giving notice of dishonour, and protesting the bill when necessary. If he complies with these requirements, he will then have an immediate right of action against the drawer and endorsers. He need not present the bill for payment before starting his action.

8-54 Summarizing the position concerning dishonour by non-acceptance, one may notice four ways in which this may happen:

(a) when acceptance is refused or cannot be obtained;[74]

(b) when the drawee does not accept within the customary time,[75]

(c) when the acceptance given is qualified and the holder refuses to take it;[76]

(d) when presentment for acceptance is excused.[77]

71 S. 43(1).
72 S. 44(1), *ante*, para. 8-36.
73 S. 43(2).
74 S. 43(1).
75 S. 42(1).
76 S. 44(1).
77 Ss 41(2) and 43(1)(b).

8-55 Finally, the Act provides that a bill may be accepted after it has been previously dishonoured; [78] but it is, of course, at the holder's discretion to permit the drawee to accept or not in these circumstances.

Dishonour by non-payment

8-56 The Bills of Exchange Act 1882 [79] provides that a bill is dishonoured by non-payment:

(a) when it is duly presented for payment and payment is refused or cannot be obtained; or

(b) when presentment is excused and the bill is overdue and unpaid.

8-57 The Act [80] provides that when a bill is dishonoured by non-payment, an immediate right of recourse against the drawer and endorsers accrues to the holder.

8-58 Thus, the consequences of dishonour by non-payment are similar to those which flow from dishonour by non-acceptance. The holder will have a right of action against the drawer and endorsers, provided that he complies with the requirements of the Act, such as giving notice of dishonour, and protesting the bill when necessary.

8-59 There is, however, this difference. When a bill is dishonoured by non-acceptance there is no right of action on the bill or right of recourse against the drawee, because he is not a party to the bill. But when an accepted bill is dishonoured by non-payment there is an immediate right of action against the drawee in his capacity of acceptor. In this connection, the Act [81] provides that in order to render the acceptor of a bill liable, it is not necessary to protest it, or that notice of dishonour should be given to him.

Notice of dishonour

8-60 An essential step which a holder is usually required to take if he wishes to preserve his rights against the drawer and endorsers of a dishonoured bill is to give due notice of dishonour to these parties. In this connection, the Bills of Exchange Act 1882 [82] provides that when a bill has been dishonoured by non-acceptance or by non-payment, notice of dishonour must be given to the drawer and each endorser, and any drawer or endorser to whom such notice is not given is discharged. The discharge is, however, not necessarily absolute, because a bill

78 S. 18(2).
79 S. 47(1).
80 S. 47(2).
81 S. 52(3).
82 S. 48.

dishonoured by non-acceptance may subsequently come into the hands of a holder in due course, and the Act expressly provides that, in this event, his rights are not to be prejudiced by the omission to give notice of dishonour.[83] Furthermore, there are several exceptional cases (which are considered below) where notice of dishonour is unnecessary.

When notice of dishonour unnecessary

8-61 It has already been observed that it is unnecessary to give notice of dishonour to the acceptor of a bill.[84] Again, where a bill is dishonoured by non-acceptance and due notice of dishonour is given, the Act[85] provides that it is unnecessary to give notice of a subsequent dishonour by non-payment, unless the bill in the meantime has been accepted.

8-62 Furthermore, the following cases also are specified in the Act[86] as being cases where notice of dishonour is dispensed with:

(a) Where, after the exercise of reasonable diligence, notice as required by the Act cannot be given to, or does not reach, the drawer or endorser sought to be charged.

(b) Where notice of dishonour has been waived expressly or impliedly, whether the waiver takes place before the time of giving notice has arrived or after the omission to give due notice.

(c) As regards the drawer of a bill:

   (i) where the drawer and drawee are the same person;[87]

   (ii) where the drawee is a fictitious person or a person not having capacity to contract;

   (iii) where the drawer is the person to whom the bill is presented for payment;

   (iv) where the drawee or acceptor is, as between himself and the drawer, under no obligation to accept or pay the bill;[88]

   (v) where the drawer has countermanded payment.[89]

---

83 S. 48(1).

84 S. 52(3).

85 S. 48(2).

86 S. 50(2).

87 Strictly, such an instrument does not comply with the definition of a bill in s. 3(1) of the Act; but the holder, by virtue of s. 5(2), has the option of treating it either as a bill or as a promissory note.

88 Thus notice of dishonour of a cheque need not be given to the drawer if the cheque is dishonoured for want of funds; but the provision does not, of course, excuse notice of dishonour to an endorser of a cheque.

89 Thus notice of dishonour of a cheque need not be given to the drawer if he had countermanded payment.

(d)   As regards the endorser of a bill:

> (i)   where the drawee is a fictitious person, or a person not having capacity to contract, and the endorser was aware of the fact at the time he endorsed the bill;
> (ii)   where the endorser is the person to whom the bill is presented for payment;[90]
> (iii) where the bill was accepted or made for his accommodation.

What constitutes valid notice of dishonour

8-63   In order to be valid, notice of dishonour must comply with the strict rules laid down in the Bills of Exchange Act 1882. The provisions may be considered under the following headings, namely (a) by whom notice must be given, (b) who benefits from the notice, (c) the form of the notice, (d) to whom notice must be given, and (e) when notice must be given.

(a) By whom notice must be given

8-64   Notice must be given by or on behalf of the holder, or by or on behalf of an endorser who, at the time of giving it, is himself liable on the bill.[91] Hence, notice cannot be given by an endorser *sans recours*,[92] or by an endorser, who has himself been freed from liability by the holder's delay in giving notice to him.

8-65   Notice of dishonour may be given by an agent either in his own name, or in the name of any party entitled to give notice whether that party is his principal or not.[93]

(b) Who benefits from notice

8-66   Notice given by or for the holder is effective not only for the benefit of the holder, but also for all subsequent holders, and for all prior endorsers who have a right of recourse against the party to whom it is given.[94] For example, A, B, C and D are successive endorsers of a bill which is dishonoured. D gives notice to A, B and C. Neither B nor C gives notice to A, but B and C each receive the benefit of D's notice,

---

90 In *Caunt* v. *Thompson* (1849) 18 LJCP 125, the endorser of a bill became the executor of the acceptor. The bill was presented to him, and he dishonoured it. It was held that he was not entitled to notice of dishonour.
91 Bills of Exchange Act 1882, s. 49(1).
92 *Ante*, para. 5-85.
93 S. 49(2).
94 S. 49(3).

because B and C are prior endorsers with a right of recourse against A. If there had been a subsequent holder (i.e. subsequent to D), that holder would have received the benefit of D's notice. Clearly, if a holder wishes to retain his rights against prior parties, it is in his own interest to give notice to *all* such parties, rather than leave it to a previous endorser to give notice to parties prior to him.

8-67   Likewise, where notice is given by or on behalf of an endorser entitled to give notice, it enures for the benefit of the holder and all endorsers subsequent to the party to whom notice is given. [95]

(c) Form of notice

8-68   The notice may be given in writing or by personal communication, and may be given in any terms which sufficiently identify the bill, and intimate that the bill has been dishonoured by non-acceptance or non-payment. [96]

8-69   The return of a dishonoured bill to the drawer or an endorser is, in point of form, deemed a sufficient notice of dishonour. [97]

8-70   A written notice need not be signed, and an insufficient written notice may be supplemented and validated by verbal communication. A misdescription of the bill does not vitiate the notice, unless the party to whom the notice is given is in fact misled thereby. [98]

(d) To whom notice must be given

8-71   Where notice of dishonour is required to be given to any person, it may be given either to the party himself, or to his agent in that behalf. [99]

8-72   Where the drawer or endorser is dead, and the party giving notice knows it, the notice must be given to a personal representative if such there be, and with the exercise of reasonable diligence he can be found. [1]

8-73   Where the drawer or endorser is bankrupt, notice may be given either to the party himself or to the trustee. [2]

95 S. 49(4).
96 S. 49(5).
97 S. 49(6).
98 S. 49(7).
99 S. 49(8).
 1 S. 49(9).
 2 S. 49(10).

8-74   Where there are two or more drawers or endorsers who are not partners, notice must be given to each of them, unless one of them has authority to receive such notice for the others.[3]

(e) When notice must be given

8-75   The provisions concerning the proper time for giving notice of dishonour are of vital importance and, as will be shown presently, they are rigidly enforced by the courts. Notice of dishonour may be given as soon as the bill is dishonoured, and must be given within a reasonable time thereafter.[4] 'Reasonable time' for this purpose is in fact a very short time indeed, for it is expressly provided that in the absence of special circumstances notice is not deemed to have been given within a reasonable time, unless:

(a)   where the person giving and the person to receive notice reside in the same place, the notice is given or sent off in time to reach the latter on the day after the dishonour of the bill;

(b)   where the person giving and the person to receive notice reside in different places, the notice is sent off on the day after the dishonour of the bill, if there be a post at a convenient hour on that day, and if there be no such post on that day then by the next post thereafter.[5]

8-76   *Yeoman Credit Ltd* v. *Gregory*[6] is an example of a case where the plaintiffs, who were holders of twelve bills amounting in all to £10,955, lost their rights completely as against an endorser, because they failed to observe the very strict rules relating to the time allowed for giving notice of dishonour. The bills were dishonoured on 28 January 1960. The holders and the endorser resided in the same place, and therefore notice of dishonour should have been given or sent off in time to reach the endorser on the day after the dishonour, namely 29 January. In fact, however, notice of dishonour was given orally on 30 January, one day late. The court held that notice of dishonour in respect of all these bills was out of time, and accordingly the claim in respect of them failed.[7]

---

3 S. 49(11).
4 S. 49(12). For a case where notice of dishonour was posted one day *before* the bill was dishonoured, see *Eaglehill Ltd* v. *J. Needham Builders Ltd*. The notice was held by a majority in the Court of Appeal to be invalid: [1972] 2 QB 8. Subsequently, the decision was unanimously reversed by the House of Lords: [1973] AC 992.
5 S. 49(12). Non-business days are excluded when making this calculation: see s. 92.
6 [1963] 1 WLR 343.
7 See also *Hamilton Finance Co. Ltd.* v. *Coverley Westray Walbaum & Tosetti Ltd, and Portland Finance Co. Ltd* [1969] 1 Lloyd's Rep 53, where Mocatta J held, *obiter*, that, for the purpose of s. 49(12), an address in Mayfair, London, W1 was 'in the same place' as Seething Lane, London, EC3.

8-77 The Act[8] further provides that where a bill, when dishonoured, is in the hands of an agent, he may either himself give notice to the parties liable on the bill, or he may give notice to his principal. If he gives notice to his principal, he must do so within the same time as if he were the holder, and the principal upon receipt of such notice has himself the same time for giving notice as if the agent had been an independent holder. In practice a bank which is collecting a bill on behalf of a customer gives notice of dishonour only to its principal, i.e. to its customer, leaving him to give notice to prior parties. If, however, the bank is a holder for value and it wants to claim against prior parties, it will endeavour to give notice to those parties.

8-78 Any party who receives notice of dishonour (and this includes a principal who receives notice from his agent) has the same time for giving notice to antecedent parties that the holder has after the dishonour.[9]

8-79 Where a notice of dishonour is duly addressed and posted, the sender is deemed to have given due notice of dishonour, notwithstanding any miscarriage by the post office.[10]

8-80 Finally, the Act[11] provides that delay in giving notice of dishonour is excused where the delay is caused by circumstances beyond the control of the party giving notice, and not imputable to his default, misconduct or negligence. When the cause of delay ceases to operate, the notice must be given with reasonable diligence.

Noting and protesting

8-81 When a bill is dishonoured by non-acceptance or by non-payment it is sometimes necessary to obtain formal proof that it has been duly presented and dishonoured.[12] The first step to this end is known as 'noting' the bill, and the second step is known as 'protesting' it.

8-82 For these purposes, it is usually necessary to employ the services of a notary public.[13] If it is desired to have a bill noted, the bill should

---

8 S. 49(13).

9 S. 49(14).

10 S. 49(15).

11 S. 50(1).

12 For the occasion when this formal proof should be obtained, see *post*, para. 8-89.

13 The office of notary is a very ancient one, and the duties attached thereto have undergone considerable change. At one time, notaries used to draft all manner of legal documents: see H. C. Gutteridge, 'The origin and historical development of the profession of notaries public in England', *Cambridge Legal Essays* (1926), pp. 123–7. Most notaries at the present day are solicitors. For an account of their duties and method of appointment, see *Halsbury's Laws of England* (4th ed., 1980), Vol. 34, pp. 89–96.

On the   day of   One thousand nine hundred and
            at the request of   bearer of the bill of exchange a true
photostat copy of which is hereunto annexed. I   of the City of
London Notary Public by Royal Authority duly admitted and sworn went to
            where the said bill of exchange is addressed to   the
drawees thereof and is payable and there in the offices of the said drawees
speaking to a gentleman I exhibited unto him the said bill of exchange and
demanded payment thereof whereunto he answered

Therefore I the said Notary at the request aforesaid have protested and by
these presents do solemnly protest as well against the drawers and endorsers
of the said bill of exchange as against all others whom it may concern for
exchange re-exchange and all costs charges damages and interest suffered and
to be suffered for want of payment of the said bill of exchange.

This done and protested in London in the presence of:

(Signature of   Dated in London this   day of   One
first witness)   thousand nine hundred and   Which I attest
(Signature of
second witness)   *(Signature)*   SEAL
                                          Notary Public

Fig. 8.4 Protest of bill of exchange

be handed to a notary. He, or his clerk, will present the bill again to the drawee for acceptance, or to the acceptor for payment, or to the bank where it was accepted payable. If acceptance or payment, as the case may be, is still refused, the bill is then noted. The notary, or his clerk, makes a note on the bill itself consisting of the notary's initials, the date, the charges for noting and a reference to the notary's register, where full particulars of the noting are kept. He also attaches to the bill a slip or ticket on which is written the answer, if any, given by the drawee or acceptor.

8-83 A protest is a declaration by a notary in a formal document under seal. A printed form is usually employed, of which Fig. 8.4 is a specimen.

8-84 It will be observed that the form of protest set out in Fig. 8.4 above states that a copy of the bill is annexed. This requirement is laid down in the Bills of Exchange Act 1882.[14] The Act also stipulates that the protest must be signed by the notary making it, and that it must specify (a) the person at whose request the bill is protested, and (b) the place and date of protest, the cause or reason for protesting the bill, the

14 S. 51(7).

demand made, and the answer given, if any, or the fact that the drawee or acceptor could not be found.

8-85 If the service of a notary cannot be obtained at the place where the bill is dishonoured, any householder or 'substantial resident' of the place may in the presence of two witnesses give a certificate, signed by them, attesting the dishonour of the bill.[15]

8-86 Where a bill is lost or destroyed or is wrongly detained from the person entitled to hold it, protest may be made on a copy or written particulars of the bill.[16]

Noting and protest of inland bills

8-87 Where an inland bill[17] has been dishonoured it may, if the holder thinks fit, be noted for non-acceptance or non-payment, as the case may be; but it is unnecessary to note or protest an inland bill in order to preserve the recourse against the drawer or endorser.[18]

8-88 As a matter of practice, it is quite usual to note and protest an inland bill if it bears foreign endorsements, so that the foreign endorsers may be provided with formal proof of dishonour. Moreover, if it is not clear whether a bill is an inland or a foreign bill, it is prudent to treat it as a foreign bill and to have it noted and protested.

Noting and protest of foreign bills

8-89 The legal requirements concerning foreign bills[19] are very different from those relating to inland bills. The Bills of Exchange Act 1882[20] provides that where a foreign bill, appearing on the face of it to be such, has been dishonoured by non-acceptance, it must be duly protested for non-acceptance, and where such a bill, which has not been previously dishonoured by non-acceptance, is dishonoured by non-payment, it must be duly protested for non-payment. If these rules are not observed, the drawer and the endorsers are discharged from all liability on the bill.

8-90 Thus, English law makes it compulsory to protest a foreign bill once only, but the Bills of Exchange Act 1882[21] does permit the holder,

15 S. 94. A suitable form of certificate is given in Sched. I of the Act.
16 S. 51(8).
17 See *ante*, para. 8-14.
18 S. 51(1).
19 See *ante*, para. 8-14.
20 S. 51(2).
21 S. 51(3).

if he wishes, to protest a bill for non-payment even though it has previously been protested for non-acceptance. This is quite often done, because the law of many foreign countries provides that protest for non-acceptance does not excuse protest on subsequent non-payment; and the holder of a bill in this country may wish to protect his position as against a foreign drawer or endorser.

8-91 Although the drawer and endorsers are discharged by failure to protest a foreign bill, the liability of the acceptor is unaffected.[22]

Time allowed for protest

8-92 Just as there are rigid rules governing the time allowed for giving notice of dishonour, so too there are similar rules governing the time allowed for protest. The Bills of Exchange Act 1882,[23] as amended by the Bills of Exchange (Time of Noting) Act 1917,[24] provides that when a bill is noted or protested, it may be noted on the day of its dishonour and must be noted not later than the next succeeding business day. When a bill has been duly noted, the protest may be later extended as of the date of noting.

8-93 Thus, noting a bill is something which must be attended to very promptly. The formal protest of the bill may be completed at a later date. In theory, a bill may be protested within the prescribed time without first having been noted, but in practice it is more convenient to have it noted first.

8-94 Finally, the Bills of Exchange Act 1882[25] provides that delay in noting or protesting is excused when the delay is caused by circumstances beyond the control of the holder, and not imputable to his default, misconduct or negligence. When the cause of delay ceases to operate, the bill must be noted or protested with reasonable diligence.

Place of protest

8-95 As a general rule, a bill must be protested at the place where it is dishonoured;[26] this will usually be the place of presentment for acceptance or payment. When, however, a bill is presented through the post office and returned by post dishonoured, it may be protested at the place to which it is returned, in which case it must be noted or protested on

22 S. 52(3).
23 S. 51(4); see also s. 93.
24 S. 1.
25 S. 51(9).
26 Bills of Exchange Act 1882, s. 51(6).

the day of its return if received during business hours, and if not received during business hours, then not later than the next business day.[27] Again, when a bill drawn payable at the place of business or residence of some person other than the drawee (for example, at his bank) has been dishonoured by non-acceptance, it must be protested for non-payment at the place where it is expressed to be payable, and no further presentment for payment to, or demand on, the drawee is necessary.[28]

When protest unnecessary

8-96 The Bills of Exchange Act 1882[29] provides that protest is dispensed with by any circumstances which would dispense with notice of dishonour.[30]

Section 2
THE BILL IN ACTION

8-97 The primary function of bills at the present day is to enable exporters of goods to obtain cash as soon as possible after they have exported their goods, and yet enable importers to defer payment at least until they receive the goods, and in many cases until they have sold the goods and obtained the proceeds.[31] This object is attained by 'discounting' or 'negotiating ' bills. Sometimes, these two terms are treated as synonymous, but the better practice is to use the term 'discounting a bill' in order to describe the sale of an *accepted* bill, by the person who is entitled to it, to a bank or discount house. If, as often happens, a bill changes hands before it has been accepted, this should properly be called the 'negotiation' of the bill. In short, a bill is not ready to be discounted until it has been accepted.[32]

Exporters and bills of exchange

8-98 Bills of exchange are now used in a smaller proportion of international transactions than in the past. In the foreign exchange market,

---

27 *Ibid.*
28 *Ibid.*
29 S. 51(9).
30 For these circumstances, see *ante*, paras 8-61/62.
31 For an admirable account of this subject, see *The Bill on London*, published for Gillett Brothers Discount Co. Ltd (4th ed., 1976). This excellent book contains many examples of specimen transactions and reproduces the bills which would be used in those transactions.
32 This use of the terms is adopted in *The Bill on London, supra*, at p. 23, and the same practice will be followed in the present work.

for example, transactions in bills constitute a small proportion of the total turnover; by far the largest proportion of foreign exchange business consists of buying and selling telegraphic transfers. Mr C. P. Lunn, a very experienced banker in the international field, has hazarded a guess that 'as much as 40–50 per cent of world trade is now settled on open account within the six-months credit period – the finance where required coming from use of overdraft facilities or Euro-currency loans'.[33] Nevertheless, bills of exchange still play a not insignificant part in the finance of foreign trade, and an exporter may use them in different ways, some of which will now be examined.

8-99 The best method, from the exporter's point of view, is for him to persuade his customer overseas to arrange for the opening of an *irrevocable* documentary acceptance credit of a London bank in favour of the exporter.[34] By the terms of this credit, the London bank gives an irrevocable undertaking to the exporter to accept bills drawn by him on the bank at (say) 90 days after sight for sums not exceeding a stated figure, provided that the bills drawn under the credit are in respect of a current shipment and are accompanied by certain specified documents relating to the goods, such as the bills of lading, the invoice(s), and the insurance policy or certificate. These are usually called the shipping documents.

8-100 As soon as the exporter's bills drawn under the credit have been accepted, he may offer the bills to a discount house or bank for discounting. In the result, the discount house or bank buys the bills from the exporter at a discount. The charge for discounting the bills is calculated by applying the appropriate rate of interest to the lifetime of the bill.

8-101 A second, and less satisfactory method from the exporter's point of view, is for his overseas buyer to arrange for the opening of a *revocable* credit by a London bank. In the absence of some special provision, a revocable credit may be cancelled at any time and is of little protection to a seller. The usual reason for employing a revocable, rather than an irrevocable, credit is because an importer wants to protect himself against a seller whom he does not trust. However, Article 9 of the *Uniform Customs and Practice for Documentary Credits (1983 Revision)* provides that the issuing bank is bound to reimburse a branch or bank with which a revocable credit has been made available for sight

---

33 C. P. Lunn, 'Recent developments', being one of the Sykes Memorial Lectures, 1972. The lectures were published under the title, *British Banks and International Trade*, and the quotation is at p. 2.

34 On the subject of bankers' credits generally, see H. C. Gutteridge and Maurice Megrah, *The Law of Bankers' Commercial Credits* (7th ed., 1984); *The Bill on London, supra*.

payment, acceptance or negotiation, for any payment, acceptance or negotiation made by such branch or bank prior to receipt by it of notice of amendment or cancellation, against documents which appear on their face to be in accordance with the terms and conditions of the credit.[35]

8-102 A third course which an exporter in the United Kingdom may adopt is to make his own arrangements with an accepting house or bank for an acceptance credit. The accepting house or bank will usually require security, such as the pledge to them of the shipping documents; and they will forward these documents to their agent in the importer's country, to be released to the importer against payment. The exporter will be able to draw bills upon a London bank, have them accepted, and then discount them with a discount house or bank.

8-103 A fourth method, which is sometimes adopted, is that whereby bills drawn by an exporter are *negotiated* under a documentary credit. The importer overseas arranges for the London branch of his bank to negotiate bills drawn by the exporter *upon the importer*, provided that the bills are accompanied by the shipping documents. The exporter draws his bills on the importer and presents them, together with the documents, to the London branch, which purchases the bills in accordance with the credit. The bank then forwards the bills and the documents to the importer's country, where the documents are surrendered to the importer either in exchange for cash or against acceptance of the bills.

8-104 Finally, if bills are drawn by an exporter upon an importer overseas and no credit has been established by a bank on behalf of either party, the bills are usually dealt with in one of three ways, namely (a) the exporter's bank may be prepared to negotiate (i.e. to purchase) the bills, (b) the exporter's bank may be prepared to make an advance against the security of the bills, or (c) the exporter's bank will merely take the bills for collection. These will be considered in turn.

(a) Negotiation of bills without a credit

8-105 If the exporter's bank is prepared to negotiate bills for a customer – and this will depend upon several factors which will be stated later – the bank will decide whether to calculate forthwith the amount of interest to be deducted from the face value of each bill, or whether

---

35 *The Uniform Customs* are a set of rules, drawn up by the International Chamber of Commerce and applied by the banks in the United Kingdom and in many other countries. They are of great importance in regard to many aspects of a bank's work relating to documentary credits, and they are reproduced in J. Milnes Holden, *Securities for Bankers' Advances* (7th ed., 1986), Appendix 1.

to handle the bills on a 'charges after payment' basis. Even in cases where bills have been accepted and one therefore knows their due dates, it is often impossible to assess accurately the intervals between negotiation and receipt of proceeds. Such cases are usually handled on a 'charges after payment' basis.

8-106 Whichever method is adopted, the bank will ask its customer to complete a printed form giving precise instructions concerning the bill. *The Uniform Rules for Collections*[36] call this form a 'remittance letter'. The Rules provide that all commercial paper sent for collection must be accompanied by a remittance letter giving complete and precise instructions, and that banks are only permitted to act upon the instructions given in such remittance letter.[37]

8-107 These instructions (which should be communicated to the bank overseas which is entrusted with the collection of the proceeds) will deal with such matters as the steps to be taken if the bill is dishonoured: whether the bill is to be protested, and whether the goods are to be stored and insured. As regards protest of a bill, the *Uniform Rules*[38] provide that, in the absence of specific instructions, the banks concerned with the collection have no obligation to have the document protested (or subjected to other legal process in lieu thereof) for non-payment or non-acceptance.

8-108 The form will usually contain a provision exempting the bank from liability for any loss which is not directly due to negligence or default of its own officers or servants. Thus the bank will not be liable for any negligence of the correspondent bank overseas. In this connection, the *Uniform Rules*[39] provide that banks utilizing the services of other banks for the purpose of giving effect to the instructions of the principal do so for the account of and at the risk of the latter.[40] They also provide that banks concerned with a collection assume no liability or responsibility for the consequences arising out of delay and/or loss in transit of any messages, letters or documents, or for delay, mutilation or other errors arising in the transmission of cables, telegrams or telex,

---

36 These are a set of rules drawn up by the International Chamber of Commerce and applied by the banks in the United Kingdom. The rules are reproduced in J. Milnes Holden, *Securities for Bankers' Advances* (7th ed., 1986), Appendix 3.
37 General Provision (C).
38 Article 17.
39 Article 3.
40 In the absence of this provision, the customer's bank would usually be liable for any negligence or breach of duty on the part of a correspondent bank: see *Calico Printers' Association* v. *Barclays Bank Ltd and Anglo-Palestine Co. Ltd* (1931) 36 Com Cas 71 and 197.

or communication by electronic systems or for errors in translation or interpretation of technical terms.[41]

8-109 The legal effect of the negotiation of the bill is that the negotiating bank becomes the holder in due course of the bill,[42] and also holds the shipping documents by way of security. Thus the bank will be a pledgee of the goods, and, if it holds, as it usually will, a 'letter of pledge' signed by the customer, it will have the rights conferred upon it by that document.

8-110 If the bill is dishonoured, the negotiating bank will look primarily to its own customer as drawer to reimburse it in respect of the amount of the bill, together with interest and charges. In this connection, the Bills of Exchange Act 1882[43] provides that the drawer of a bill engages that on due presentment it shall be accepted and paid, and that if it is dishonoured he will compensate the holder, provided that the requisite proceedings on dishonour are duly taken. Furthermore, the bank, as holder in due course, would also have the right to claim against the drawee if the latter had accepted the bill, but, as stated above, the bank looks primarily to its own customer for reimbursement.

8-111 A prudent banker will always try to avoid negotiating bills which are at all likely to be dishonoured; if bills are doubtful, they should be sent for collection. There is, of course, no infallible method for determining whether a bill is likely to be dishonoured, but the following matters are usually borne in mind by bankers when they are asked to negotiate bills.

8-112 Every bill should represent a genuine trading transaction. The documents of title relating to that transaction should be carefully scrutinized so as to ensure that they are technically in order.

8-113 As a counsel of perfection, there should be two good names to every bill, though in practice it is sometimes necessary to be content with one. The bank will know its own customer, and confidential reports as to the standing of the drawees should be obtained, and renewed from time to time.

8-114 One should enquire whether a customer's transactions are covered by an insurance policy issued by the Export Credits Guarantee Department. This Department operates under the aegis of the Department of Trade. Polices cover three main risks – the 'commercial' risk of insolvency or default by the buyer, the 'non-acceptance' risk of the

---

41 Article 4.
42 Bills of Exchange Act 1882, s. 29, *ante*, para. 5-108.
43 S. 55(1).

buyer not accepting the exported goods, and the 'political' risk arising from exchange or import restrictions or from war. A customer may assign to his bank the benefits accruing to him under his policy. Assignment is effected by completing a form issued by the Export Credits Guarantee Department, which will return to the bank a copy of the assignment as evidence that the Department has recorded the bank's interest in the policy.[44] In practice, banks are often more readily inclined to negotiate bills in cases where the shipment is covered by a policy issued by the Department, and the rate of interest charged to the customer is often slightly lower than in the case of other bills.

(b) Advance against bills

8-115 If the exporter's bank is not prepared to negotiate the bills drawn upon the importer, it may be willing to make an advance of a certain percentage of the face value of the bills. The bank will then forward the bills to its overseas correspondent for collection of the proceeds.

8-116 As in the previous case, the bank will make a careful examination of the shipping documents which accompany the bills, and the customer will complete the usual form giving precise instructions which will be passed forward to the overseas correspondent.

8-117 The legal effect of a transaction of this nature is that the bank becomes a pledgee of the goods, and, by virtue of the Bills of Exchange Act 1882,[45] it is deemed to be a holder for value of the bill to the extent of the sum for which it has a lien, i.e. to the extent of the advance.

(c) Collection of bills

8-118 Sometimes a bank simply takes bills on a collection basis without providing its customers with any finance at all. The bank remits the bills to its overseas correspondent and, when the proceeds are available, they are credited to the customer's account, after the deduction of collection charges. In this type of transaction the bank does not usually become a holder for value of the bills, unless of course it has a lien over the bills arising out of some other transaction.

8-119 As in the previous cases, the customer will complete the usual form giving precise instructions concerning the bills which will be passed forward to the bank's correspondent overseas.

---

44 Such an assignment, if executed by a company, does not require registration under s. 95, Companies Act 1948: see *Paul & Frank Ltd and Another* v. *Discount Bank (Overseas) Ltd and Another* [1967] Ch 348. Section 95, Companies Act 1948, has been replaced by s. 395, Companies Act 1985.
45 S. 27(3).

Importers and bills of exchange

8-120 An importer frequently asks his bank to open an irrevocable documentary acceptance credit in favour of an exporter overseas. For this purpose, the importer completes an application form in which he sets out a description of the goods and specifies the documents which must accompany the bill drawn by the exporter. The form embodies an agreement between the importer and his bank. The terms of this agreement will depend upon whether the credit is to be (a) covered partly by cash (in which case the customer's account will be debited forthwith with the appropriate sum), or (b) without cash cover.

8-121 The following terms would be included in an application for a credit without cash cover:

(a) The customer undertakes to provide the bank with funds to meet bills drawn under the credit.

(b) The bank and its correspondents are not to be responsible for the genuineness, correctness or form of any documents, or for any misrepresentation as to the quantity, quality or value of any goods comprised therein.

(c) If the goods are not covered by insurance to the bank's satisfaction, the bank is authorized to insure them, and the customer undertakes to repay to the bank the amount of the premiums.

(d) The goods which are the subject of the credit and the documents of title thereto are pledged to the bank as a continuing security for all advances made or to be made by the bank to the customer, and for all payments which may be made by the bank or its correspondents under the credit. In the event of a sale of the goods by the bank, the customer undertakes to pay on demand the amount of any deficiency on such sale, together with all usual commission and charges and expenses incidental thereto.

(e) The bank is not to be liable for any mistake or omission in the transmission of messages by cable.

(f) The *Uniform Customs and Practice for Documentary Credits* (*1983 Revision*) are to apply.

8-122 If the importer's bank accedes to the request contained in the application form, it issues, through its agents in the exporter's country, a letter of credit in favour of the exporter. In this letter of credit the importer's bank gives an irrevocable undertaking to accept a bill or bills drawn by the exporter on the bank at (say) 90 days sight for a sum not exceeding a stated figure, provided that the bill is accompanied by the relative shipping documents, and that the bill and the documents are presented before the expiry date of the credit.

8-123 The exporter then draws a bill on the importer's bank, and takes it, together with the shipping documents, to the local bank, which advised him of the credit. That bank buys the bill from him for cash, and forwards the bill and the shipping documents to its London correspondents for presentation to the importer's bank for acceptance. The London correspondents surrender the shipping documents to the importer's bank against their acceptance of the bill.

8-124 The importer's bank releases the shipping documents to its customer to enable him to take delivery of the goods when they arrive. In some cases the bank may require its customer to pay the amount of the bill before it releases the documents. It is more usual, however, for the bank to release the documents to its customer against a trust receipt, whereby the customer undertakes to hold the documents, the goods represented thereby, and the net proceeds thereof as trustee for the bank.

8-125 Sometimes the irrevocable undertaking by the importer's bank is confirmed by a bank in the exporter's country. The credit is then known as a 'confirmed irrevocable credit'. When a credit is confirmed in this way, it is because the exporter has requested the importer to make this arrangement. The exporter usually makes this request for one or more of the following reasons. He may regard the importer's bank as 'weak'; or he may fear that exchange control will prevent the importer's bank from carrying out its undertaking; or, finally, the government in the exporter's country, in an endeavour to increase the commissions earned by the banks in that country, may require all bankers' credits to be confirmed by a local bank.

8-126 Another course which an importer sometimes adopts in order to finance the purchase of goods from overseas is as follows. He makes arrangements with an accepting house or bank for an acceptance credit: the issuers of the credit agree to accept bills drawn on them, subject to stated conditions.

8-127 There are different ways of operating an acceptance credit. Under one method, the importer draws a bill at (say) 90 days sight a few days before he has to make payment to the seller overseas. When the bill has been accepted, the importer discounts it with a discount house or bank and remits the proceeds to the exporter. This method assumes that the issuers of the acceptance credit are prepared to offer 'clean' facilities, i.e. without security.

8-128 If the issuers of the acceptance credit require security, they may require that the proceeds of the bill, when it is discounted, are paid to them. They will remit the proceeds to their agent overseas who will pay the money to the exporter in exchange for the relative shipping documents. In this way, the issuers of the acceptance credit will obtain a pledge of the goods and of the documents of title thereto.

8-129 The following is another method of obtaining finance under an acceptance credit. It may have been agreed between the importer and the seller overseas that payment for the goods shall be by a sight bill to be drawn by the seller upon the importer. The bill will be sent to London, together with the shipping documents, where it will be presented to the importer for payment in cash, the shipping documents being then delivered to the importer. In order to obtain the necessary funds, the importer will draw a bill at (say) 90 days sight under an acceptance credit, and, as soon as this bill has been accepted, he will discount it with a discount house or bank. The issuers of the acceptance credit may or may not require the importer to deposit with them by way of security the relative shipping documents, which they may subsequently agree to release against a trust receipt signed by the importer.

8-130 Payment in respect of some transactions is made by means of a time bill at (say) 90 days sight drawn by the overseas seller *upon the importer*. The seller, however, stipulates that he requires immediate payment for his shipment, and, accordingly, the importer will arrange a credit through a bank in London which has a branch or correspondent in the foreign centre concerned.

8-131 The London office of the bank authorizes its branch or correspondent in the foreign centre to negotiate a bill drawn on the importer by the seller at 90 days sight, provided that the bill is accompanied by the shipping documents. The seller draws a bill on the importer and presents it, with the shipping documents attached, to the overseas bank, which will negotiate (i.e. purchase) it from the seller at the bank's buying rate of exchange for 90 days sight drafts on London. The bank then forwards the bill and the documents to its London office.

8-132 The London office of the bank presents the bill to the importer for acceptance. If the importer is of high standing, he may be able to arrange 'D/A terms' (Documents against Acceptance). This means that the bank will deliver the shipping documents to him against his acceptance of the bill, so that he may obtain delivery of the goods as soon as they arrive. If D/A terms are not arranged, the bank will see that, upon their arrival, the goods are warehoused and insured. All landing and warehousing charges are, of course, payable by the importer, and the goods themselves are pledged to the bank for security. The importer will pay the bill at maturity and obtain delivery of the goods. Alternatively, he may obtain early delivery of the goods by paying the bill before maturity; if he does this, he will be allowed a rebate on the amount of the bill.

Manufacturers and bills of exchange

8-133 Manufacturers often require finance for the purpose of buying raw materials. This is normally provided by a bank loan or advance. Sometimes, however, a manufacturer will apply to one of the London accepting houses for an acceptance credit. By the terms of this credit, the accepting house agrees to accept drafts up to a specified amount drawn upon them by the manufacturer, payable, for example, three months after date; and the manufacturer agrees to put the accepting house in funds at or before the maturity dates of the drafts. Having drawn a draft and had it accepted by the accepting house, the manufacturer will have no difficulty in discounting it with a bank or discount house.

8-134 Acceptance credits are frequently granted on a revolving basis; that is to say, new drafts may be drawn, up to the agreed maximum, when the original drafts mature. The procedure may be repeated again and again so long as the facility remains open. It is usually a condition of this type of credit that the value of raw materials in stock, free from any form of charge, must always exceed the total amount of acceptances outstanding under the credit, and that stocks must always be kept fully insured.

Collection of inward bills

8-135 A substantial part of the work of banks in London with overseas connections consists of the collection of 'inward bills', that is to say, bills drawn abroad on a drawee in England and remitted to banks in London by their correspondents overseas. Many such bills are drawn under bankers' credits, but others are not drawn under bankers' credits, and the procedure for dealing with them may now be noted briefly.

8-136 The legal rules governing presentment for acceptance and presentment for payment have been stated,[46] and these rules must be carefully observed. Special care is necessary in cases where a bill is accompanied by documents of title. The instructions received from overseas will indicate whether the documents are to be delivered upon acceptance of the bill, or only when the bill is paid. If the documents are deliverable upon acceptance, it is quite usual to present the bill and the documents to the drawee and leave them with him until the following day, so that he may have time to examine the documents thoroughly. If, however, the documents are to be delivered only when the bill is paid, it is usual to attach a note to the bill when the bill is presented for accept-

46 *Ante*, paras 8-39 and 8-43.

ance stating that the documents may be inspected at the office of the presenting bank.

8-137 If the drawee refuses to accept or to pay the bill, the instructions received from overseas must be followed implicitly. These instructions should state whether or not the bill is to be noted or protested upon dishonour, and whether notice of dishonour should be given by letter or by cable. If no specific instruction has been given regarding noting or protesting the bill, the collecting bank should certainly have the bill noted promptly upon dishonour, because this will enable the protest to be extended at any time thereafter if desired.

8-138 Occasionally, when a bill is dishonoured and documents of title accompany the bill, prompt action will have to be taken to warehouse the goods, or even to sell them, especially if the goods are perishable. Having obtained instructions from the remitting bank overseas, the collecting bank will deliver the documents to its shipping agent so that the appropriate steps may be taken.

Payment of domiciled bills

8-139 If a customer accepts a bill payable at his bank, the bill is said to be 'domiciled' at the bank. It constitutes an authority to the bank to pay it.[47] There is, however, no obligation upon a bank to pay a bill in these circumstances, unless there is some agreement to that effect between the bank and its customer.[48] Some banks offer this service in their advertising literature, though they often state that suitable prior arrangements should be made with the bank. The practice varies as between one bank and another. In some banks, it seems that domiciled bills are paid without any prior advice from the customer. In other banks, a customer is required to fill in a printed form giving details of bills which he has accepted payable at the bank. If a bill is presented to the bank which has not been advised to the bank in this way, it is returned unpaid with the answer 'no advice'.

8-140 There is undoubtedly some risk in paying a customer's acceptances, even under advice. Lord Macnaghten summed up the position thus:[49]

> In paying their customers' acceptances in the usual way bankers incur a risk perfectly understood, and in practice disregarded. Bankers have no

47 *Kymer* v. *Laurie* (1849) 18 LJQB 218.
48 *Bank of England* v. *Vagliano Brothers* [1891] AC 107, at p. 157, *per* Lord Macnaghten.
49 *Banker of England* v. *Vagliano Brothers* (*supra*), at pp. 157–8. See also *Robarts* v. *Tucker* (1851) 16 QB 560.

recourse against their customers if they paid on a genuine bill to a person appearing to be the holder, but claiming through or under a forged endorsement. The bill is not discharged: the acceptor remains liable; the banker has simply thrown his money away.

Although these words were spoken many years ago, they are just as true today: there is still no statutory protection in respect of the payment of bills, other than cheques. In the result, therefore, the bank's position is vulnerable, unless it pays the bill, at or after its maturity, 'to the holder thereof in good faith and without notice that his title to the bill is defective'.[50] Such a payment constitutes 'payment in due course', and the bill is thereby discharged.[51]

---

50 Bills of Exchange Act 1882, s. 59(1), *ante*, para. 7-61.
51 *Ibid*. In this connection, see *Auchteroni and Co.* v. *Midland Bank Ltd* [1928] 2 KB 294, where the defendant bank successfully resisted a claim brought by the payees of a domiciled bill, which the bank had paid in cash to a fraudulent employee of the plaintiffs, who presented it at the counter. The payee's endorsement was genuine, and therefore the employee was the 'bearer' as defined by s. 2 of the Act.

9

Other instruments handled by bankers

In this chapter attention will be directed to dividend and interest warrants, bankers' drafts, instruments payable to wages or order (or cash or order), conditional orders, non-transferable cheques, promissory notes and postal orders.

Section I
DIVIDEND AND INTEREST WARRANTS

9-1 A dividend warrant may be defined as an unconditional order[1] in writing, addressed by or on behalf of a company to its bankers, ordering them to pay on demand a sum of money to a member of the company or his agent, in respect of a dividend due to the member arising out of his holding of shares or stock in the company. Although this definition comprises what is usually understood by the term 'dividend warrant', the expression was given a wider meaning in *Slingsby* v. *Westminster Bank Ltd*,[2] where it was held that a warrant addressed to the Bank of England for the payment of interest on 5 per cent War Stock was a warrant for the payment of dividend within the meaning of s. 95 of the Bills of Exchange Act 1882.[3] The court reached this conclusion chiefly because the National Debt Act 1870 (which applied to 5 per cent War Stock), uses the word 'dividend' as meaning the sum payable on government stock.

9-2 An interest warrant may be defined as an unconditional order in writing addressed by a borrower to its bankers, ordering them to pay on demand a sum of money to a lender or his agent, in respect of interest due to the lender. The borrower is usually a company, municipality,

---

1 It is sometimes said that *conditional* orders are occasionally used, but it seems very doubtful whether they are ever employed at the present day.
2 [1931] 1 KB 173.
3 This section provides that the provisions of the Act as to crossed cheques apply to a warrant for payment of dividend.

public authority or government. However, it would seem, for the reason stated above, that warrants for the payment of interest on certain British government stocks must be regarded as *dividend* warrants.

Types of warrants

9-3 The modern practice is to make dividend and interest payments by means of cheques; in other words, most dividend and interest warrants fall within the definition of a cheque in the Bills of Exchange Act 1882.[4] Sometimes, there are words on a dividend warrant which indicate that it will not be honoured after a certain period, usually three months, from the date of issue, unless it is returned to the company for confirmation, but it has been held that such warrants are unconditional orders, and that they satisfy the definition of a cheque.[5]

9-4 When a bank pays a dividend to its own shareholders, it draws drafts upon itself for this purpose. These instruments do not satisfy the definition of a cheque, because the drawer and drawee are the same person: they are bankers' drafts.[6]

Legislation affecting warrants

9-5 As most dividend and interest warrants fall within the definition of a cheque, all the sections of the Bills of Exchange Act 1882, and the Cheques Act 1957, which apply to cheques, necessarily apply to such warrants. Furthermore, there is a provision concerning dividend warrants in s. 97(3)(d) of the Bills of Exchange Act 1882, which states that nothing in the Act or any repeal effected thereby is to affect the validity of any usage relating to dividend warrants or the endorsements thereof. This was intended, apparently, to protect the usage of paying such warrants on the endorsement of one of several payees.[7] The point is of small practical importance at the present day, because the Cheques Act 1957 abolished the necessity for endorsements on cheques in most cases.[8]

9-6 In those comparatively rare cases where dividend and interest warrants fall within the definition of a bankers' draft, all the statutory provisions which apply to bankers' drafts apply to such warrants.

---

4 *Ante*, para. 5-6.
5 *Thairlwall* v. *Great Northern Railway Co.* [1910] 2 KB 509.
6 For bankers' drafts, see *post*, para. 9-14.
7 See the notes prepared by the draftsman of the Bills of Exchange Act, Sir Mackenzie Dalzell Chalmers, in his book, *The Bills of Exchange Act, 1882* (1st ed., 1882), p. 65. The provision was not in the Bill as drafted, but was introduced in committee: see M. D. Chalmers, *Digest of the Law of Bills of Exchange* (4th ed., 1891), p. 284.
8 *Ante*, para. 7-26.

Furthermore, s. 97(3)(d) of the Bills of Exchange Act 1882 would seem to apply to bankers' drafts which fall within the ambit of the subsection, as set out in the preceding paragraph.

9-7 Section 95 of the Bills of Exchange Act 1882 provides that the provisions of the Act as to crossed cheques apply to a warrant for payment of dividend. The section is of small practical importance today, because dividend warrants fall either within the definition of a cheque or within the definitions of a bankers' draft, and both types of instrument may be crossed.[9]

Counterfoils or tax vouchers

9-8 A 'counterfoil' is the name which is commonly given to the voucher which is attached to a dividend or interest warrant. A dividend warrant shows the amount of the tax credit and the amount payable by way of dividend. An interest warrant shows the gross amount of the interest payment, the rate and amount of income tax deducted therefrom, and the net amount which is actually paid. The counterfoil or tax voucher should be retained by the person who is entitled to the dividend or interest, because it will be required if the recipient is entitled to reclaim some or all of the tax which has been deducted.

Dividend and interest mandates

9-9 A dividend or interest mandate is a written authority addressed by the person who is entitled to receive dividend or interest payments, to the company or authority making such payments, requesting and authorizing that company or authority to make the payments to the bankers of the person entitled to receive them. The system is advantageous to the shareholder or stockholder for two reasons: first, because he does not have the trouble of taking or sending the warrants to the bank, and, secondly, because there is much less risk of loss. Moreover, the system is advantageous to the company or authority concerned, because they merely issue one cheque in favour of their own bank in respect of all dividends mandated to the accounts of shareholders and stockholders; the relevant vouchers are then passed through the Credit Clearing. Finally, the system is advantageous to the banks, because less clerical work is involved when transactions are handled in this way.

9-10 When dividend or interest payments are made under mandate, the relevant counterfoils are sent to the bank, and each counterfoil bears the name of the shareholder or stockholder and the branch of the bank

---

9 See Bills of Exchange Act 1882, ss 76–81; Cheques Act 1957, ss 4(2)(d) and 5.

where his account is kept. The bank will usually forward the counterfoils to the customers concerned with their next bank statement.

9-11 Mandates for the payment of dividends or interest are probably determined, like other mandates, by the death of the customer who signed them. However, it is a common, but not universal, practice for banks to continue to receive the payments after the customer's death, crediting them either to the account of the deceased to or to a new account to be operated upon by the executors or administrators after production of the grant of probate or letters of administration.[10] This practice is a convenient one, and it appears to be free from risk. Sometimes, however, mandated dividends are received for the account of a beneficiary other than the registered owners of the securities. In the event of the death of the beneficiary, the bank should either return the dividends as 'unapplied' or seek the instructions of the registered owners.

Lost warrants

9-12 There is often some express provision which governs the payment of dividends or interest. Thus, there is a provision in Article 121 of Table A of the First Schedule to the Companies Act 1948, which declares that any dividend, interest or other moneys payable in cash in respect of shares may be paid by cheque or warrant sent through the post directed to the registered address of the holder, or, in the case of joint holders, to the registered address of the joint holder whose name appears first on the register of members. The article further provides that every such cheque or warrant must be made payable to the order of the person to whom it is sent. In regard to companies incorporated on or after 1 July 1985, regulation 106 of Table A of the Companies (Alteration of Table A etc.) Regulations 1984 contains a similar provision. Regulation 106 of the 1984 Regulations was replaced by Regulation 106 of the Companies (A to F) Regulations 1985. In the absence of any express provision in the articles, a shareholder may impliedly agree to payment by cheque or warrant sent through the post.[11]

9-13 If a cheque or warrant is sent in a manner which is expressly or impliedly authorized and the instrument is lost, it would seem that the payee's remedy is to proceed on the lines indicated by the court in *Thairlwall* v. *Great Northern Railway Co.*[12] As Lord Coleridge J pointed out in that case, s. 69 of the Bills of Exchange Act 1882 provides

10 *Questions on Banking Practice* (11th ed., 1978), p. 43, Question 110.
11 *Thairlwall* v. *Great Northern Railway Co.* [1910] 2 KB 509.
12 *Supra.*

that where a bill has been lost before it is overdue, the person who was the holder of it may apply to the drawer to give him another bill of the same tenor, giving security to the drawer, if required, to indemnify him against all persons whatever in case the bill alleged to have been lost shall be found again; and, by s. 70, in any action or proceeding upon a bill, the court may order that the loss of the instrument shall not be set up, provided that an indemnity be given to the satisfaction of the court against the claims of any other person upon the instrument in question.

Section 2
BANKERS' DRAFTS

9-14 Bankers' drafts are of two types. First, there is the type of draft which is drawn by one bank upon another. Such drafts fall within the definition of a cheque in the Bills of Exchange Act 1882.[13] Secondly, there is the type of draft where the same bank is both drawer and drawee; usually such drafts are drawn by a branch of a bank upon its head office (or vice versa) or upon another branch. These drafts do not fall within the definition of bills of exchange or cheques,[14] because both drawer and drawee are the same person, but the *holder* of such an instrument may treat it, at his option, either as a bill of exchange or a promissory note.[15]

Issuing bankers' drafts

9-15 A request to issue a bankers' draft is usually made by a customer who has to pay money to someone who is not prepared to accept his cheque; for example, a solicitor sometimes asks for a bankers' draft in order that he may complete the purchase of a property transaction on behalf of a client. The customer who requires a draft will be asked to complete an application form stating the amount of the draft, the name of the payee, and the place of payment. The application form should be signed by the customer or by those persons who have been duly authorized to act on his behalf.

9-16 The decision of the Judicial Committee of the Privy Council in *Bank of Montreal* v. *Dominion Gresham Guarantee and Casualty Co. Ltd*,[16] illustrates the danger of issuing drafts against unauthorized

---

13 *Ante*, para. 5-6.
14 Bills of Exchange Act 1882, ss 3(1) and (2), 73.
15 S. 5(2).
16 [1930] AC 659.

instructions. A Canadian company had instructed its bankers that any two of four named persons, of whom three were directors and the fourth was an accountant in the company's employment, had authority to draw cheques and sign orders on its behalf. The company from time to time required bank drafts payable in New York to remit to creditors there. The course of business was that the accountant attended at the bank with a cheque, duly signed by two of the named persons, payable to the bankers' order for the sum for which the draft was required, but without any further document or written instructions. Having completed a form giving particulars of the draft required, including the name of the payee, he was handed a draft in accordance with those particulars. On 41 out of 106 occasions upon which drafts had been so purchased, the accountant had obtained drafts payable to himself, and had misappropriated the proceeds. The respondents paid the company under a policy guaranteeing the fidelity of the accountant, and they sued the appellant bank in respect of the loss. It was held that the bank had acted negligently in issuing drafts without authority in accordance with the company's instructions, and that the bank was liable in damages.

9-17   Bankers' drafts can, and should, be crossed. If a draft is drawn by one bank upon another and, therefore, complies with the definition of a cheque, the crossed cheque sections of the Bills of Exchange Act 1882 automatically apply to it. If the same bank is both drawer and drawee of the draft, and the instrument is, therefore, not a cheque, it may be crossed by virtue of s. 5 of the Cheques Act 1957.[17] As a general rule, the safest crossing is 'Not negotiable. Account payee only.'[18]

9-18   A bankers' draft must not be drawn payable to bearer, because the Bank Charter Act 1844[19] made it unlawful for any banker to draw, accept, make or issue, in England or Wales, any bill of exchange or promissory note, or engagement for the payment of money payable to bearer on demand. Such an instrument would be a banknote. The Bank of England has the exclusive right of note issue in England and Wales.[20]

Collection of drafts

9-19   The duties of the collecting bank in relation to bankers' drafts are similar to those which govern the collection of cheques.[21] As regards

17 It was the Bills of Exchange (1882) Amendment Act 1932, s. 1, which first enabled these instruments to be crossed. The 1932 Act was repealed by the Cheques Act 1957, s. 6(3) and Sched.
18 *Ante*, para. 5-48.
19 S. 11.
20 *Ante*, para. 1-38.
21 *Ante*, para. 6-29.

statutory protection, if a draft is drawn by one bank upon another and, therefore, complies with the definition of a cheque, the collecting bank will have the same statutory protection as it has in relation to other cheques,[22] and even if the same bank is both drawer and drawee, with the result that the instrument is not a cheque, the same provisions are expressly made applicable.[23]

Payment of drafts

9-20 The duties of the paying banker in relation to bankers' drafts are similar to those which govern the payment of cheques. In particular, the necessity for requiring endorsement has been abolished to the same extent as in the case of cheques.[24] The banker on whom a draft is drawn must, of course, be satisfied that it is drawn by duly authorized officers. He must also be satisfied that the particulars of the draft correspond with those given in the advice which he will have received.

9-21 As regards statutory protection, if a draft is drawn by one bank upon another and, therefore, complies with the definition of a cheque, the drawee bank will have the same statutory protection as it has in relation to other cheques.

9-22 If, however, the same bank is both drawer and drawee, with the result that the instrument is not a cheque, the bank may be able to rely upon s. 19 of the Stamp Act 1853.[25] However, that section applies only if the draft, whether crossed or uncrossed, purports to be properly endorsed.[26] As already explained, the necessity for requiring endorsement of drafts has been abolished by the Cheques Act 1957 to the same extent as in the case of cheques, and that Act will normally protect the bank in respect of the payment of unendorsed drafts, whether crossed or uncrossed.[27]

22 Cheques Act 1957, s. 4(1) and (2)(a); see *ante*, paras 6-74/75.
23 Cheques Act 1957, s. 4(2)(d); see *ante*, para. 6-80.
24 Cheques Act 1957, s. 1(2)(b).
25 *London City and Midland Bank Ltd* v. *Gordon* [1903] AC 240.
26 *Ante*, para. 7-58.
27 S. 1(2)(b). The provisions referred to above are those which are normally invoked. For the sake of completeness, however, it may be noted that if a bankers' draft in which the same bank is both drawer and drawee is crossed, the bank may be able to rely in the alternative upon s. 5 of the Cheques Act 1957. The effect of that section is that the provisions of the Bills of Exchange Act 1882 relating to *crossed* cheques are to have effect (so far as applicable) in relation to such drafts as they have in relation to cheques. Consequently, s. 80 of the 1882 Act, which protects the paying banker when paying crossed cheques, likewise protects the paying banker when paying crossed drafts.

Lost drafts

9-23 If a customer informs his bank that a draft which has been issued to him has been lost, the drawee bank should be notified immediately, so that payment of the draft may be postponed until the title of the person presenting it has been investigated. It may be that he has a good title, in which case the draft must be paid.

9-24 Usually, the customer asks for a duplicate draft to be issued to him. The practice is to comply with such request, provided that the customer indemnifies the bank against liability in the event of the lost draft being presented by someone who has obtained a good title to it, and provided, of course, that the customer is considered to be of good standing. The indemnity should extend to the amount of the draft, together with all costs and expenses reasonably incurred by the bank in investigating the title of the person presenting the draft. This is very important, because sometimes the missing draft is presented and the bank may have to obtain legal advice with regard to the title of the person who presents it.

Section 3
INSTRUMENTS PAYABLE TO WAGES OR ORDER, OR CASH OR ORDER

9-25 Some customers make a practice of drawing cash from their bankers by filling up an ordinary cheque form so that it reads 'Pay cash or order' or 'Pay wages or order'. Furthermore, customers occasionally use the words 'Pay cash or order' when they wish to make payments to third parties, especially when they do not want to reveal the names of the payees.[28]

9-26 Instruments of this nature do not comply with the definition of a cheque. The reasoning is as follows:[29] (a) A cheque is a bill of exchange drawn on a banker payable on demand.[30] (b) A bill of exchange is an order in writing requiring the person to whom it is addressed to pay a sum to or the order of a specified person, or to bearer.[31] (c) 'Cash'

---

28 'They are used when for some special reason favouring anonymity the drawer wishes the beneficiary to be nameless', *per* MacKenna J. in *Orbit Mining and Trading Co. Ltd.* v. *Westminster Bank Ltd* [1962] 2 All ER 552, at p. 558.

29 The reasoning is that of Branson J in *North and South Insurance Corporation Ltd* v. *National Provincial Bank Ltd* [1936] 1 KB 328, as summarized by MacKenna J in *Orbit Mining and Trading Co. Ltd* v. *Westminster Bank Ltd* [1962] 2 All ER 552, at p. 559.

30 Bills of Exchange Act 1882, s. 73.

31 S. 3(1).

cannot be described as a 'specified person'. (d) As the instrument is not payable to or to the order of a specified person, it is not a bill of exchange and, therefore, not a cheque.

9-27 Although an instrument of this type is not a cheque, it has been held to be a document of the type referred to in s. 4(2)(b) of the Cheques Act 1957, namely a 'document issued by a customer of a banker which, though not a bill of exchange, is intended to enable a person to obtain payment from that banker of the sum mentioned in the document'.[32] The effect of s. 5 of the Cheques Act 1957 is that the provisions of the Bills of Exchange Act 1882 relating to *crossed* cheques are to have effect (so far as applicable) in relation to instruments of this type as they have effect in relation to cheques. This means, for example, that instruments payable to 'Cash or order' or 'Wages or order' may be crossed generally or specially or 'Not negotiable'.

9-28 As the greater part of the Bills of Exchange Act 1882 does not apply to these instruments, their position in the law is difficult to state. It would seem that they cannot be endorsed for the purpose of negotiation, because s. 31 of the Act, which deals with the negotiation of bills, is not one of the provisions of the Act relating to crossed cheques. Likewise, it would seem that no one can become a holder in due course of such an instrument, because s. 29 of the Act, which deals with this subject, is not one of the provisions relating to crossed cheques. In *Cole* v. *Milsome*[33] the court held that not even the original holder of the instrument, to whom it had been issued by the drawer, could sue on it as a bill of exchange.

Collection of 'cash or order' instruments

9-29 The collecting banker has the same statutory protection when collecting the proceeds of these instruments, whether or not they are crossed, as he has in relation to cheques. Thus, in *Orbit Mining & Trading Co. Ltd* v. *Westminster Bank Ltd*,[34] the defendant bank collected for a customer named Epstein the proceeds of crossed instruments payable to 'cash or order'. Epstein had no title thereto, and the plaintiff company, who were the drawers of the instruments, brought an action for damages for conversion against the defendant bank. The bank pleaded that it had collected the proceeds on behalf of its customer 'in good faith and without negligence', and that it was protected against the company's claim by s. 4 of the Cheques Act 1957. The trial judge,

---

32 *Orbit Mining and Trading Co. Ltd* v. *Westminster Bank Ltd* [1962] 2 All ER 552; on appeal [1963] 1 QB 794.
33 [1951] 1 All ER 311.
34 [1962] 2 All ER 552; on appeal [1963] 1 QB 794.

MacKenna J held that these instruments were documents issued by a customer of a banker which, though not a bill of exchange, were intended to enable a person to obtain payment from that banker of the sum mentioned in the document, within the meaning of s. 4(2)(b) of the Act;[35] but he took the view that the bank had failed to discharge the burden of proving that it had acted without negligence. In the result, judgment was given in favour of the plaintiff company.

9-30 The decision was reversed on appeal. The Court of Appeal upheld the view of the learned judge that the instruments fell within s. 4(2)(b) of the Act, but differed from him on the question of negligence. Sellers, Harman and Davies LJJ were unanimously of the opinion that there had been no negligence on the part of the bank, and therefore the bank's appeal was allowed.

Payment of 'cash or order' instruments

9-31 It would seem that, if the banker pays an instrument in favour of 'cash or order' or 'wages or order' to someone who is not entitled to it, the banker will be protected by s. 1(2)(a) of the Cheques Act 1957 provided that the instrument is unendorsed and that the banker makes payment 'in good faith and in the ordinary course of business'. The relevant part of the subsection provides that where a banker in good faith and in the ordinary course of business pays a document issued by a customer of his which, though not a bill of exchange, is intended to enable a person to obtain payment from him of the sum mentioned in the document, he does not, in doing so, incur any liability by reason only of the absence of, or irregularity in, endorsement, and the payment discharges the instrument. This subsection applies whether the instrument is crossed or uncrossed, but if it is crossed the usual rules relating to crossings must be observed.

9-32 These provisions seem to have effected an important change in the law, as far as instruments payable to 'cash or order' or 'wages or order' are concerned. Prior to the Cheques Act 1957, there was no statutory protection in respect of such instruments if they were uncrossed;[36] if

---

35 One of the instruments was collected shortly before the Cheques Act 1957 came into operation. The trial judge and the Court of Appeal held that this instrument fell within s. 17 of the Revenue Act 1883. That section was repealed by the Cheques Act 1957, s. 6(3) and Sched.

36 See *North and South Insurance Corporation Ltd* v. *National Provincial Bank Ltd* [1936] 1 KB 328, where Branson J held that such an instrument was not a cheque for the reasons already given, *ante*, para. 9-26. But it was held that, owing to special circumstances, the claim against the paying bank could not succeed.

they were crossed, it would seem that the paying banker would have been protected by s. 17 of the Revenue Act 1883.[37]

9-33 If such instruments are endorsed, the position of the paying bank is difficult to define. It would seem that s. 1(2)(a) of the Cheques Act 1957 does not apply to endorsed instruments. If they are crossed, it might be possible to rely upon s. 5 of the Cheques Act 1957, in conjunction with s. 80 of the Bills of Exchange Act 1882.[38] If they are uncrossed, there would seem to be no protection.

Section 4
CONDITIONAL ORDERS

9-34 A conditional order for payment is an instrument issued by a customer of a bank, ordering the bank to pay a sum of money to a named person, provided that a stated condition is fulfilled. Thus, in *Bavins, Junr & Sims* v. *London and South Western Bank Ltd*[39] the instrument in question, which had been issued by the Great Northern Railway Company, was drawn as follows: 'Pay to J. Bavins Junr & Sims the sum of sixty-nine pounds seven shillings, provided the receipt form at foot hereof is duly signed, stamped, and dated.' The Court of Appeal held that this order was not a cheque, because the payment was made conditional upon signature of the receipt.[40] Conditional orders of this type are still issued by some insurance companies, especially in respect of claims under life policies.

9-35 However, the mere fact that a form of receipt on a cheque is to be completed does not, of itself, make an order conditional. Thus in *Nathan* v. *Ogdens Ltd*[41] the instrument was drawn as follows: 'Pay Mr H. Nathan or order one hundred and twenty-six pounds five and five pence.' Printed at the foot were the words: 'The receipt at back hereof must be signed, which signature will be taken as an endorsement of this cheque.' The court expressed the view that the cheque was a negotiable instrument notwithstanding the words, above quoted, at the foot thereof; the order to pay was unconditional, as the words at the foot of

---

37 This section was repealed by the Cheques Act 1957, s. 6(3) and Sched.
38 See the reasoning in relation to crossed bankers' drafts, *ante*, para. 9-22.
39 [1900] 1 QB 270.
40 The action was a claim against a collecting bank. In the Court of Appeal, the defendant bank relied upon s. 17 of the Revenue Act 1883 (which has been repealed by the Cheques Act 1957, s. 6(3) and Sched.); but it was held that this defence failed on the ground that there had clearly been negligence on the part of the bank in receiving the document with the endorsement and the receipt signed in a name other than that of the payees.
41 (1905) 93 LT 553; affirmed 94 LT 126.

the cheque were not addressed to the bankers and did not affect the nature of the order to them.

9-36   Moreover, one sometimes find a notice on a dividend warrant indicating that it will not be honoured after a certain period, usually three months, from the date of issue, unless it is returned to the company for confirmation; it has been held that such warrants are unconditional orders, and that they satisfy the definition of a cheque.[42] Conditional orders, properly so called, are rarely issued at the present day except, as stated above, by insurance companies.

Collection of conditional orders

9-37   The collecting banker has the same statutory protection when collecting the proceeds of conditional orders, whether or not they are crossed, as he has in relation to cheques.[43] The banker must, of course, act 'in good faith and without negligence'. Accordingly, if the order to pay is conditional upon the completion of a form of receipt, the collecting banker must examine the form of receipt carefully.[44]

Payment of conditional orders

9-38   It would seem that if a banker pays an unendorsed conditional order, whether crossed or uncrossed, to someone who is not entitled to it, the banker will be protected by s. 1(2)(a) of the Cheques Act 1957, provided that he makes payment 'in good faith and in the ordinary course of business'.

9-39   If such instruments are endorsed, it would seem that the section would have no application. If they are crossed, it might be possible to rely upon s. 5 of the Cheques Act 1957, in conjunction with s. 80 of the Bills of Exchange Act 1882.[45] If they are uncrossed, there would seem to be no protection.[46]

---

42 *Thairlwall* v. *Great Northern Railway Co.* [1910] 2 KB 509.
43 Cheques Act 1957, s. 4(2)(b).
44 The defendant bank failed to do so in *Bavins, Junr & Sims* v. *London and South Western Bank Ltd, supra,* and lost the benefit of the protection of the Revenue Act 1883, s. 17. That section was repealed by the Cheques Act 1957, s. 6(3) and Sched.
45 See the reasoning in relation to crossed bankers' drafts, *ante,* para. 9-22.
46 It is sometimes suggested that s. 19 of the Stamp Act 1853 applies to conditional orders, whether crossed or uncrossed. The argument to the contrary is that an order which embodies a condition cannot be said to be payable on demand.

Section 5
NON-TRANSFERABLE CHEQUES

9-40   The Bills of Exchange Act 1882[47] makes special provision for non-transferable instruments. It enacts that when a bill contains words prohibiting transfer, or indicating an intention that it should not be transferable, it is valid as between the parties thereto, but is not negotiable.[48] It used to be possible to make a cheque non-transferable by simply omitting the words 'order' or 'bearer'. However, the Bills of Exchange Act 1882[49] altered the law in this respect by providing that a bill is payable to order which is expressed to be so payable or which is expressed to be payable to a particular person, and does not contain words prohibiting transfer or indicating an intention that it should not be transferable. Hence, if a cheque is drawn 'Pay X' with the word 'order' deleted, it is nevertheless payable to X or his order.

9-41   It is still theoretically possible to make a cheque non-transferable by drawing it 'Pay X only' or by writing across it the words 'Non-transferable'. If this is done, the word 'order' should be deleted; but even if the word is not deleted, the court would probably resolve the ambiguity or inconsistency by disregarding the printed word 'order' in favour of the written word or words prohibiting transfer, because the written words are taken as being intended to qualify a printed form.[50]

9-42   The reason why it is only theoretically possible to draw non-transferable cheques is because the clearing banks decided in 1958 that the drawing of such cheques was unacceptable to them, as such a practice created serious practical difficulties and could expose them to unreasonable risks. The principal objection is that instruments in this form would seem to impose upon the paying banker the burden of enquiry as to whether or not he was paying the one person designated as payee.[51]

Section 6
PROMISSORY NOTES

9-43   The law relating to promissory notes is to be found, for the most part, in the Bills of Exchange Act 1882, as interpreted by the courts.

---

47 S. 8(1).
48 I.e. not transferable. The words 'not negotiable' have a different meaning in s. 81: see *ante*, para. 5-42.
49 S. 8(3).
50 *Glynn* v. *Margetson & Co.* [1893] AC 351, at pp. 354, 358; *Addis* v. *Burrows* [1948] 1 KB 444, at pp. 449, 457.
51 *Byles on Bills of Exchange* (26th ed., 1988), p. 87.

£100

Lombard Street, London
1 April 19..

Six months after date we promise to pay to James Brown or order the sum of one hundred pounds.

For and on behalf of John Smith Ltd,
John Smith
Director

Fig. 9.1 Promissory note

Requirements of a valid note

9-44   The Bills of Exchange Act 1882 defines a promissory note as an unconditional promise in writing made by one person to another signed by the maker, engaging to pay, on demand or at a fixed or determinable future time, a sum certain in money, to, or to the order of, a specified person or to bearer.[52] An instrument which promises, in addition to the payment of money, the performance of some other act is not a promissory note.[53]

9-45   Figure 9.1 is a specimen note payable six months after date. John Smith Ltd are the makers of this note. The maker is the party primarily liable on the note, and corresponds with the acceptor of a bill of exchange. James Brown is the payee.

9-46   A note is inchoate and incomplete until delivery thereof to the payee or bearer.[54] Just as bills of exchange may be payable with interest or by stated instalments,[55] so too may promissory notes. In practice, it is quite common to find that the maker of a note promises to make payments monthly, quarterly or half-yearly and to pay interest at a specified rate on the amount outstanding. It is also quite usual to insert a provision that, upon default in payment of any instalment, the whole shall become due.

9-47   The Bills of Exchange Act 1882 provides that an instrument in the form of a note payable to maker's order is not a note within the definition unless and until it is endorsed by the maker.[56] A note is not invalid by reason only that it contains a pledge of collateral security with

52 S. 83(1).
53 *Dickie* v. *Singh*, 1974 SLT (Notes) 3.
54 S. 84.
55 S. 9(1), *ante*, para. 8-10.
56 S. 83(2).

authority to sell or dispose thereof.[57] A note which is, or on the face of it purports to be, both made and payable within the British Islands is an inland note. Any other note is a foreign note.[58]

9-48   A promissory note may be made by two or more makers, and they may be liable jointly, or jointly and severally, according to its tenor.[59] The usual way of establishing joint liability on the part of two or more makers is to use the words 'We promise to pay', whilst the usual way of establishing joint and several liability is to use the words 'We jointly and severally promise to pay'. The Act provides that where a note runs 'I promise to pay' and is signed by two or more makers, it is deemed to be their joint and several note.[60]

9-49   If makers are liable jointly, each is fully liable for the whole sum, but judgment against any one maker used to prevent the holder from taking further action against the others.[61] This rule was abolished by s. 3 of the Civil Liability (Contribution) Act 1978.

9-50   If the makers are only jointly liable and not severally also, then on the death of one maker his estate is not liable, and the survivor or survivors alone become liable both at law and in equity.[62] The process continues until there is but one survivor, when the obligation necessarily becomes several and, upon his death, devolves upon his personal representatives. Although this was clearly the position as established by the courts, it has been argued that the law has been changed by the Law Reform (Miscellaneous Provisions) Act 1934. The Act does not provide specifically for the case of joint obligations, but it has been argued that one effect of the Act is that the personal representatives of a deceased joint promisor are now in every case liable on the contract.[63] There is much force in this argument but, until the point has been decided by the courts, it is perhaps safer to assume that the Act has not altered the law in this respect and, therefore, that when a joint maker dies his liability ceases.

9-51   By virtue of the Finance Act 1970,[64] promissory notes are exempt from stamp duty.

57 S. 83(3).
58 S. 83(4).
59 S. 85(1).
60 S. 85(2).
61 *Re Hodgson, Beckett* v. *Ramsdale* (1885) 31 Ch D 177, at p. 188.
62 *Richards* v. *Heather* (1817) 1 B & Ald 29; *Calder* v. *Rutherford* (1882) 3 Brod & Bing 302.
63 Glanville L. Williams, *Joint Obligations* (1949), p. 72. The Act provides in s. 1(1) that 'subject to the provisions of this section, on the death of any person after the commencement of this Act all causes of action subsisting against or vested in him shall survive against, or, as the case may be, for the benefit of, his estate.'
64 S. 32 and Sched. 7.

Liability of maker

9-52 The maker of a promissory note is the principal debtor or the party primarily liable on the instrument, and in this respect he differs from the drawer of a bill. The maker's obligations correspond with those of the acceptor of a bill.

9-53 The liability of the maker of a note is defined in s. 88 of the Bills of Exchange Act 1882, which provides that the maker of a note by making it, (a) engages that he will pay it according to its tenor; and (b) is precluded from denying to a holder in due course the existence of the payee and his then capacity to endorse.[65]

9-54 Where a promissory note is in the body of it made payable at a particular place, it must be presented for payment at that place in order to render the maker liable.[66] In any other case, presentment for payment is not necessary in order to render the maker liable.[67] This is important when one is considering the position of the maker under the Limitation Act 1980. In the usual case, the maker of a promissory note payable on demand remains liable for six years from the date of the note, or of its issue, if later; after six years the right of action against him becomes statute-barred by virtue of s. 5 of the Act. However, if a note is, 'in the body of it', made payable at a particular place, the statutory period runs from the date of its presentment, because that is the date when the liability of the maker arises.

Liability of endorser

9-55 The endorser of a note engages that on due presentment it will be paid according to its tenor, and that, if it is dishonoured, he will compensate the holder or any subsequent endorser who is compelled to pay it, provided that the requisite proceedings on dishonour are duly taken. This is nowhere expressly so provided in the Bills of Exchange Act 1882, but it clearly seems to be the effect of a number of its provisions.[68]

9-56 The Act does expressly provide that presentment for payment is necessary in order to render the endorser liable.[69] It further provides that where a note is in the body of it[70] made payable at a particular

---

65 For the meaning of 'holder in due course' see s. 29(1) of the Bills of Exchange Act 1882, *ante*, para. 5-108.
66 Bills of Exchange Act 1882, s. 187(1). 'In the body of it' means in the terms of the actual contract to pay: *Re British Trade Corporation* [1932] 2 Ch 1.
67 S. 87(1).
68 See ss 55(1) and (2), and 89(1) and (2).
69 S. 87(2).
70 See *Re British Trade Corporation* [1932] 2 Ch 1, *supra*.

place, presentment at that place is necessary in order to render an endorser liable; but when a place of payment is indicated by way of memorandum only, presentment at that place is sufficient to render the endorser liable, but a presentment to the maker elsewhere, if sufficient in other respects, suffices. [71]

9-57 The Act also provides that where a note payable on demand has been endorsed, it must be presented for payment within a reasonable time of endorsement; if it is not presented, the endorser is discharged. [72] In determining what is a reasonable time, regard shall be had to the nature of the instrument, the usage of trade, and the facts of the particular case. [73] There is a similar provision in the Act with reference to bills payable on demand, [74] but in practice there is an important difference between bills and notes. A bill payable on demand is usually intended to be presented and paid immediately, whereas a promissory note payable on demand is often intended as a security. Therefore, 'reasonable time' in regard to notes usually connotes a much longer time than in regard to bills. [75]

Negotiation of notes

9-58 Promissory notes may be negotiated in the same way as bills of exchange. Thus a note payable to bearer is negotiable by delivery alone, [76] whereas a note payable to order is negotiated by the endorsement of the holder completed by delivery. [77]

9-59 There is, however, a special rule which applies to promissory notes, namely that where a note payable on demand is negotiated, it is not deemed to be overdue, for the purpose of affecting the holder with defects of title of which he had no notice, by reason that it appears that a reasonable time for presenting it for payment has elapsed since its issue. [78] This may be contrasted with the rule relating to bills, namely that where an overdue bill is negotiated, it can only be negotiated subject to any defect of title affecting it at its maturity, and thenceforward no person who takes it can acquire or give a better title than that which the person from whom he took it had. [79]

71 S. 87(3).
72 S. 86(1).
73 S. 86(2).
74 S. 45(2).
75 See, for example, *Chartered Bank* v. *Dickson* (1871) LR 3 PC 574.
76 Ss 31(2) and 89(1).
77 Ss 31(3) and 89(1).
78 S. 86(3).
79 S. 36(2).

Banknotes

9-60 A banknote is a promissory note made by a banker, payable to bearer on demand. One of the objects of the Bank Charter Act 1844 was to concentrate in the Bank of England the sole responsibility for the issue of banknotes in England and Wales. That object was eventually achieved in 1921 when Messrs Fox Fowler & Co., the last private bank having the right to issue notes, was merged in Lloyds Bank.

Modern functions of promissory notes

9-61 Many bank officers conclude their careers without ever having seen a promissory note, other than a banknote. Nevertheless, it should not be assumed that promissory notes play no part in modern commercial life. They are, for example, quite often given to motor traders by customers of theirs to whom vehicles have been let out by the traders on hire-purchase terms.

9-62 As far as bankers are concerned, the most important transactions in which promissory notes are used are those involving medium-term export credits. These credits are usually for some period between three and five years. Credits of this type were first made available about 1954, when the Export Credits Guarantee Department introduced its 'direct and unconditional guarantee', which was designed to be given to the financing bank and was intended to secure the bank against losses arising from the failure of the overseas buyer to pay. The goods which form the subject of these credits are capital goods, such as, for example, ships, aircraft and machinery. In some cases, an entire factory complete with all its equipment has been supplied and erected, and the transaction has been financed by this type of credit.

9-63 A detailed consideration of these credits is outside the scope of this book.[80] Very briefly, the financing bank addresses to the exporter a facility letter setting out the terms and conditions upon which it will make funds available to him. The bank undertakes to purchase from the exporter, subject to specified conditions, promissory notes made by the importer (or, alternatively, bills drawn by the exporter upon the importer and accepted by him) for an amount up to the equivalent of the sum guaranteed to the bank under the direct guarantee given by the Export Credits Guarantee Department. The promissory notes or bills which the bank purchases are usually drawn in series and are payable at

---

80 For an admirable account of these credits, see C. P. Lunn, 'Medium- and long-term export credit' (being the second of the Ernest Sykes Memorial Lectures, 1965), *Journal of the Institute of Bankers*, Vol. 86 (1965), pp. 356–62.

six-monthly intervals. Interest is payable at an agreed rate, and so sums in respect of principal and interest fall due for payment at regular intervals.

Section 7
POSTAL ORDERS

9-64 Postal orders are instruments embodying instructions for the payment of money deposited at one post office and payable at the same, or at a different, post office. Postal orders are issued for certain fixed amounts, ranging from 25p to £10. A small commission or poundage is charged when a postal order is issued.

9-65 A postal order has a space for the name of the payee and for his signature on receipt of the money. There is also a space for the office of payment, and if this is filled in, payment will be made only at that office, unless the order is presented through a bank.

9-66 A postal order is not a negotiable instrument; it bears on its face words stating that it is 'not negotiable'.[81] As postal orders are not negotiable, a bona fide transferee cannot obtain a better title to them than his transferor possessed. It follows, therefore, that a bank should never cash them for a stranger.

9-67 Postal orders may be effectively crossed, either generally or specially, in which case the Post Office will make payment only to a banker or to the banker named in the crossing, as the case may be.[82] If postal orders, whether initially crossed or not, are presented for payment by a bank, payment will be made even though the payees have not signed them, provided that the orders bear the crossing stamp of the bank.

9-68 A curious feature affecting postal orders is that bankers have no means of knowing whether or not they are finally paid.[83] Thus bankers sometimes find that postal orders are returned to them unpaid many months after they presented the orders for payment. The bankers' only consolation is that they will usually be entitled to debit their customers' accounts with the amount of the returned orders.[84] By that time, how-

81 See also *Fine Art Society Ltd* v. *The Union Bank of London Ltd* (1886) 17 QBD 705, where the Court of Appeal held that orders known at that time as 'post office orders' were not negotiable.

82 Post Office Scheme P5/1971, published in *The London Gazette*, 3 February 1971.

83 Post Office Scheme P5/1971, *supra*.

84 *London and Provincial Bank* v. *Golding* (1918) 3 LDB 161, a decision of the Court of Appeal upholding the bank's rights in this regard.

ever, the customer may have closed his account, or died, or emigrated, or been made bankrupt, and in any such cases the bank may have to suffer the loss.

9-69 A possible risk to which banks are exposed when collecting the proceeds of postal orders for customers is the risk of a claim for damages for conversion, i.e. in cases where a customer was not entitled to the orders. However, s. 21(3) of the Post Office Act 1953 provides that any person acting as a banker in the British postal area who, in collecting in that capacity for any principal, has received payment or been allowed by the Post Office in account in respect of any postal order, or of any document purporting to be a postal order, incurs no liability to anyone except that principal by reason of having received the payment or allowance, or having held or presented the order or document for payment.

10

Other banking operations

In this chapter it is proposed to examine a number of services provided by bankers other than the payment and collection of cheques.

Section I
THE BANK GIRO SYSTEM

10-1 Like the cheque, the transfer or 'giro' is a means of making a payment without the use of cash. For many years, giro systems have been fairly extensively employed on the Continent for the settlement of debts and for making other payments. An authoritative and impartial contribution on the subject, published in 1960, focused the attention of bankers in the United Kingdom upon these systems.[1] The author, Mr J. Kraa, whose native country is the Netherlands, observed that in countries where cheque payments predominated there had for some years been signs of a kind of propaganda for the giro system, whilst in giro countries, there was a growing awareness, especially among the banks, of the attractiveness of cheque payments. From the banks' point of view this was not hard to understand, since (as Mr Kraa pointed out) giro transfers and, through them, deposits in current accounts are to a fairly considerable extent handled by government and municipal institutions. Thus, under a giro system, funds are kept outside the banking system.

Giro transfers compared with cheques

10-2 In the case of payment by cheque, the debtor draws a cheque on his bank in favour of his creditor and sends it to him. The creditor hands the cheque to his bank, which credits his account and collects the proceeds from the debtor's bank. The bank debits the debtor's account. In exceptional cases, however, the creditor, instead of handing the cheque to his bank, negotiates it to a third party.

1 See J. Kraa, 'Giro', *Journal of the Institute of Bankers*, Vol. 81 (1960), pp. 262–71.

10-3 In the case of payment by giro transfer, the debtor writes out a giro – an order to transfer – to his bank in favour of the creditor, stating the name of the creditor's bank. The debtor's bank debits its customer's account and transfers the amount to the beneficiary's bank, under advice. That bank passes the amount to the creditor's account, also under advice. A giro transfer, unlike a cheque, cannot be negotiated to a third party, because the payment passes directly into the beneficiary's account.

10-4 In some respect, the giro procedure is simpler than payment by cheque; in other respects, payment by cheque is simpler. In the article referred to above, Mr Kraa summarized the principal differences thus:

1. With the cheque, the payer's account is debited after the payee's account has been credited; with the giro, the payer's account is debited first, and thereafter the payee's account is credited. In this respect the giro procedure is simpler than the cheque payment. An uncovered giro is simply not carried out and so does not affect the accounting of the payer's bank or the payee's bank or the payee. An uncovered cheque does.

2. When payment is made by cheque, the payer sends the cheque direct to the payee, who hands it to his bank for the credit of his account. Apart from a statement of account, the collecting bank does not send any further credit advice to the payee; nor does the paying bank send a debit advice to the payer, other than the usual statement of account, accompanied, in some cases, by the paid cheque. Thus, for the entire procedure, one single document is used. With payment by giro transfer, the payer sends an order to his bank. In due course, the payee's bank sends to the payee a specific advice of the payment; and, under some systems, the payer receives a specific advice that his order has been carried out. In this respect, the giro procedure is less simple than that followed for payment by cheque.

3. With cheque payments, the sorting of cheques has to be carried out by reference to the payer's bank. It is a simple matter to indicate this bank by means of a code number printed on the cheque in advance. With giro payments, the sorting has to be done by reference to the beneficiary's bank. This cannot, of course, be indicated by a code number printed in advance on the giro order form. In this respect, the giro procedure is less simple than that followed for payment by cheque.

10-5 Summing up the position, Mr Kraa expressed the opinion that, all in all, cheque payments are slightly simpler for the banks to handle than giro transfers; this was on the supposition that the number of uncovered cheques remained at a minimum; but, for customers, giro payments are simpler – at any rate, in cases where no cash payments are required.

'Bank Giro'

10-6 The term 'Bank Giro' was adopted by the clearing banks and the Scottish banks in 1967 to describe their established credit transfer system and their newly introduced direct debiting system. The term was devised as part of the campaign to compete effectively with the National Giro, which came into operation some twelve months later.[2]

Development of credit transfer system

10-7 Although the cheque has proved to be a convenient instrument for making payments, it has certain disadvantages:

(a) Every cheque has to be signed by or on behalf of the drawer.

(b) Most cheques are sent by post to the payees; this is costly in terms of stationery and postage.

(c) A cheque often passes through several hands, including the staff of the remitter and the staff of the recipient, and there is some risk that it may be stolen and misappropriated.

These are the considerations which induced a desire to devise a simpler, cheaper and safer method of transferring funds from one person to another.

10-8 The credit transfer system avoids those disadvantages of cheques which are listed in the preceding paragraph. The development of the system may be considered under three heads, (a) standing orders, (b) traders' credits, and (c) other credit transfer facilities.

(a) Standing orders

10-9 The system of making payments on behalf of customers by means of standing orders seems to have originated during the latter half of the nineteenth century. A standing order (or banker's order, as it is sometimes called) is a written order given by a customer to his bank to make a series of payments on his behalf. These orders are often used by customers to give instructions to their bankers to pay annual subscriptions or to make quarterly or monthly payments by way of rent, insurance premiums or hire-purchase payments.

(b) Traders' credits

10-10 It is not known precisely when the system of traders' credits originated, though it probably dates from about the beginning of the

2 See *post*, para. 10-35.

present century.[3] The system developed slowly, and it was the subject of a note in the *Journal of the Institute of Bankers* in 1930.[4] The note stated that 'for some years past' bankers had been pressed by certain of their larger customers to undertake work which would relieve the customer of the trouble and expense of drawing and posting cheques in payment of his creditors' accounts. The procedure was to draw a single cheque for the total of the bills to be paid and take it to the bank with a list of the creditors, the names of their bankers and the amounts of their debts, and to request the bank to pay over the amounts.

10-11 The note continued by stating that the spread of the procedure had been hindered by the fact that it had been commonly believed that the list of payments was subject to a stamp duty of $2d$. for each item in the list. However, one of the clearing banks had submitted the point to the Board of Inland Revenue, who had replied that in their opinion neither the list of payments to be made nor the individual credit or advice slips attracted stamp duty.

10-12 After this ruling, the system of traders' credits became more widespread during the 1930s. The practice developed of requiring customers to fill in the credit slips themselves, which they would then list by machine. Customers would hand the list and the credit slips, together with a cheque for the total amount, to their bank.

10-13 One of the first organizations to use this system on a national scale was the Milk Marketing Board, which distributed thousands of payments to farmers every month by means of this system. Each month the Board would deliver the credit slips to their own bankers, who would then distribute them to the London offices of the various banks for onward transmission to their branches. In those days, however, there was no Credit Clearing: as will be shown presently, that was a much later development.

(c) Other credit transfer facilities

(i) Interest and dividend payments

10-14 For many years, a customer has been able to have interest and dividend payments remitted to his bankers. He addresses a mandate to the authority or company concerned requesting that interest or dividend

---

3 In 1961 the chairman of one of the banks told the present writer that in 1907, when he was a junior clerk in the employment of a trading company, he used to deliver to his employers' bankers bundles of what later became known as traders' credits. The system was not at all widespread at that time.
4 Vol. LI (1930), p. 398.

payments, as the case may be, should be sent to his bankers. When the payments are made, they are accompanied by tax deduction certificates (or 'counterfoils') which the receiving bank subsequently delivers to its customers.

(ii) Payments-in by customers

10-15   Another transfer facility which has been offered to customers for many years is the facility of paying in, at *any* branch of the bank, cash and cheques for the credit of their accounts. If a customer found that there was no branch of his bank in a particular town, he could go to one of the other banks in that town and pay in there for the credit of his account at his own bank. Credit items of this nature were usually the subject of a *direct* advice; in other words, the receiving bank would send an advice slip to the customer's bank by post, together with an 'Agents' Claim Voucher', which that bank would pass through clearing channels in order to obtain reimbursement. Once again, the absence of any system of Credit Clearing may be noted.

(iii) Payments-in by non-customers

10-16   In the years which followed the 1939–45 war there was a rapid, and unprecedented, increase in hire-purchase transactions. The hire-purchase companies were dealing with many people who had no bank accounts or cheque books. Accordingly, the companies made arrangements whereby their customers could make payments to the companies' bankers, and very often this meant that cash was paid into some *other* bank for transmission to their own bankers. These transfer facilities were not, strictly speaking, granted to the payer (i.e. to the customer of the hire-purchase company); they were services specially arranged for the recipient account holder, who normally paid for them.

Credit transfer system today

10-17   The origin of the credit transfer system as it exists today was recounted by Mr D. Robson in his Sykes Memorial Lecture in 1961.[5] Mr Robson recalled that, when freedom was returned to bankers in August 1958,[6] there was a broadening in banking activity not restricted to lend-

---

5 Three lectures were delivered under the title, *Bank Transfer Systems in the United Kingdom – Developments in Law and Practice*. Mr Robson was a Joint General Manager of the Westminster Bank. His lecture was the second in the series. See also the Sykes Memorial Lectures for 1974, *Money Transmission – Today and Tomorrow*. Two lectures were delivered under this title. The first, which was by Mr G. E. K. Foster, was devoted to 'Current developments', and the second, which was by Mr Charles Read, was devoted to 'Future plans and prospects'.

6 This refers to the ending of a credit squeeze at that date.

ing. There was a general upsurge of activity. Certain banks deputed senior officers to study the workings of giro systems abroad, and their report, according to Mr Robson, proved a most stimulating document.[7] The time was ripe for change, continued Mr Robson, and it proved possible to create a general scheme, suitable to British conditions, for use by customers and non-customers alike, based upon transfers of funds by the movement of credits through the banking system.

10-18 The publication of the Radcliffe Report in 1959 had given a further stimulus to the already prepared scheme,[8] and the Payment of Wages Act 1960 for the first time had legalized the payment of wages by credit transfer, or by cheque, or by money order or postal order, provided that the employee made a written request to that effect and his employer agreed.[9]

10-19 The credit transfer system, which was brought into full effect in 1961, consists of three main services; two of those services were well known prior to 1961, and the third was an extension of an existing service. The three services which the credit transfer system provides are as follows.

10-20 First, bankers will make payments on a customer's instructions to the credit of other customers, either of the same bank or of other banks in the United Kingdom. These payments include standing-order payments and traders' credits, already described above.

10-21 Secondly, bankers will accept cash, cheques, etc., from a customer, or his representative, for the credit of his account at another branch of the bank or at another bank.

10-22 Thirdly, bankers will accept credits from non-customers for a customer's account at the receiving branch or at another branch of the same bank or at another bank. These credits are often in favour of hire-purchase companies, building societies and gas and electricity boards.

---

7 The stimulation was experienced by only a few. The report was addressed (presumably) to the banks themselves, and it has never been published.

8 The Radcliffe Committee had concluded that, in the absence of an early move on the part of existing institutions to provide the services of a giro system, there would be a case for investigating the possibility of instituting a giro system to be operated by the Post Office. See *Report of the Committee on the Working of the Monetary System*, Cmnd. 827 (1959), para. 964.

9 Prior to 1960, the effect of the Truck Acts and of certain other Acts was to prevent many employees and their employers from making agreements whereby wages could be paid otherwise than in legal tender; but these provisions of the Acts were not well known and, even when known, were often ignored. The Payment of Wages Act 1960 was repealed and replaced by the Wages Act 1986, s. 11 of which repealed the Truck Acts. Employees no longer have a statutory right to be paid in cash. The method of payment is governed by the contract between the employer and the employee.

Credit clearing

10-23   In 1960, almost two hundred years after the introduction of the cheque clearing system, a clearing for the exchange and settlement of credit vouchers was added to the functions of the Clearing House in London. This new clearing was called the Credit Clearing. [10]

10-24   At the end of each working day, branches dispatch all the relevant credit vouchers to clearing departments in London, where they are passed through the Credit Clearing. [11] In most cases, the account of the recipient is credited on the second business day after the relative voucher leaves the originating branch, except where a weekend intervenes, or when postal delays occur.

10-25   As regards settlement between the banks themselves, the general rule is that transactions in the Credit Clearing are settled the next working day after the exchange of vouchers takes place.

Direct debiting

10-26   In 1967 the clearing banks, the Scottish banks and the Northern Irish banks introduced a new service, known as 'direct debiting'. By this system, the payee or creditor claims the payment; he initiates the entry. The system may be used for fixed amounts due at fixed intervals, or for varying amounts due at varying intervals.

10-27   The company or other organization which initiates the debits (referred to hereafter as 'the creditor') is required to execute an indemnity addressed to *all* financial institutions to whom a sorting code number has been allocated. By the terms of this indemnity the creditor agrees to keep each bank indemnified against all actions, claims, damages, costs and expenses arising directly or indirectly from such debiting; and the creditor authorizes each bank to admit, compromise or reject any claims without reference to the creditor.

10-28   Having executed this indemnity, the creditor obtains the agreement of the person or persons whose accounts are to be debited. They sign an instruction addressed to their own bank. For payments of fixed

---

10 For an admirable account of this subject, see the fourth of the articles by Mr E. A. Young on 'The bankers' clearing house', published in the *Journal of the Institute of Bankers*, Vol. 81 (1960), pp. 196–204.

11 The main items which are not passed through the Credit Clearing are (a) credits passing between branches of the same clearing bank; these usually pass through that bank's own clearing department, (b) payments resulting from the majority of standing orders, and (c) credits for customers of banks other than the clearing banks; these are still settled by means of bankers' payments.

amount, it reads as follows:

> I/We instruct you until further notice in writing to charge to my/our account with you on or about the ... day of every month at the instance of the ... Company plc the sum of ... by direct debit.

For payments of varying amount, the instruction reads as follows:

> I/We instruct you to pay direct debits from my/our account at the request of the ... Company plc. The amounts are variable and may be debited on various dates. I/We will inform the bank in writing if I/We wish to cancel this instruction. I/We understand that if any direct debit is paid which breaks the terms of this instruction, the bank will make a refund.

10-29 Once a month, or at other stated times, the creditor fills in 'direct debit' forms. They are encoded in magnetic ink characters, in the same way as cheques. The basic codings are pre-printed in bulk. A further code, for the amount payable, is added when the 'direct debit' is paid into the bank by the creditor, or by the creditor's own encoding equipment. The work may be carried out by the creditor's computer.

10-30 Finally, the creditor lists the 'direct debits' and delivers them to his own bank. His account will be credited with the total amount, and the debits will be distributed to the banks to whom they are addressed. If a debit cannot be paid because of lack of funds, it is returned unpaid. The vast majority of direct debits are routed through BACS.

10-31 The system has certain obvious advantages to the creditor. It ensures the prompt payment of sums due to him, or alternatively, if a debit is returned 'unpaid', it enables him to know quickly that one of his debtors is unable to pay. As against these advantages, there is the risk that, as a result of an error, a 'direct debit' could be made out for too large a sum, and this could involve the creditor in a heavy liability, especially in view of the indemnity which he is required to sign.

BACS Limited

10-32 This company was first established as Bankers Automated Clearing Services Limited in 1971, and it was renamed BACS Limited in 1986. It provides an automated money transfer service. The transactions which it handles include the majority of standing orders, salary and pension payments and direct debits. These transactions are recorded on magnetic tape and, as a general rule, vouchers are not used, though they are still printed for some recipients at the output stage. Some customers are permitted to prepare their own tapes for transfers which they wish to make. Alternatively, customers may be permitted to send the relevant instructions to BACS over the telecommunications system, direct from their own computers. At January 1989 the company had the following members: the Abbey National Building Society, the Bank of England, the Bank of Scotland, Barclays Bank, Clydesdale Bank, Cooperative Bank, Coutts & Co., Girobank, the Halifax Building Society, Lloyds Bank, Midland Bank, National Westminster Bank, Northern Bank, the Royal Bank of Scotland, Trustee Savings Bank and Yorkshire Bank.

Clearing House Automated Payments System

10-32A This system, known as CHAPS, came into operation in 1984 for the purpose of making high-value payments of £10,000 or over anywhere within the United Kingdom very speedily. The system, which now allows for payments of £7,000 or more, provides an electronic sterling credit transfer service, with 'same-day settlement'. Instructions to issue a CHAPS payment message can be made in a number of ways, for example by writing, by telex, or by computer link-ups. The system was designed with a minimum amount of central development, essentially only the central software. Each settlement bank has, or shares, two tandem computers, of which one is for standby purposes. These are referred to as CHAPS gateways. Payment messages are transmitted between gateways across British Telecom's packet switched network, the most sophisticated method of high speed, low cost data transmission available.

Electronic funds transfer at point of sale

10-32B This system, known as Eftpos, enables a purchaser to pay for goods or services by using a plastic card in conjunction with either (*a*) a personal identification number, known as a PIN, or (*b*) a paper voucher.[12] The card is passed or 'swiped' through a card reader at the cash desk. If a PIN is to be used, the customer enters this number on a special keyboard designed to shield the operation from bystanders. If a paper voucher is to be used, the customer signs it. The information relating to the purchase is then electronically encrypted (or 'scrambled') and sent through the Eftpos delivery system to the retailer's card scheme acquirer. The acquirer, which is the financial institution dealing directly with the retailer on behalf of card schemes, then relays the information through other networks to the card issuer. The card issuer responds

---

12 See Catherine P. Smith, *Retail Banking Technology* (1987), and Anu Arora, *Electronic Banking and the Law* (1988).

through the system either authorizing or declining the transaction. If the transaction is authorized, the customer's account will be debited and the retailer's account will be credited with the amount of the purchase. Instead of instituting an on-line system (as described above), some banks in the United Kingdom use an off-line system, whereby transactions are transmitted in bulk overnight.

10-32C There are two rival systems in operation at present.[13] In June 1987 Barclays Bank launched its debit card system known as 'Connect'. This card may be used in many shops, restaurants, hotels and petrol stations, wherever the VISA sign is displayed. The customer hands the card to the supplier and signs a voucher. The Connect card may also be used as a cash dispenser card and as a cheque guarantee card. Lloyds Bank and Trustee Savings Bank also issue Visa debit cards. For this reason the system is sometimes referred to as the Visa system.

10-32D After Barclays Bank had launched its debit card system known as 'Connect', another debit card system known as 'Switch' was introduced. This rival system is operated by six banks, namely, Midland Bank, National Westminster Bank, Royal Bank of Scotland, Bank of Scotland, Clydesdale Bank and Yorkshire Bank. The Halifax Building Society is about to join, subject to approval at their annual general meeting.

10-32E The position at the date of going to press is that Barclays Bank and Lloyds Bank have applied to join the Switch system. Switch and Connect regulations prohibit banks from putting both systems on the same card. Switch regulations also stipulate that members should issue Switch as their principal (but not necessarily exclusive) debit card. Neither Barclays Bank nor Lloyds Bank is willing to do this.

Section 2
GIROBANK

10-33 On 21 July 1965, the House of Commons resolved that they would welcome the establishment of a postal giro service in the United Kingdom offering similar facilities to those given by postal giro systems in other countries.[14] Some two years earlier, the Assistant Postmaster-General, speaking on behalf of the then government, had said that they took the view that the Post Office ought not to launch into what might

13 The total number of terminals signed by both systems at the end of January 1990 was approximately 97,000. See *Banking World*, Vol. 8 (1990), p. 36.
14 *Hansard*, Commons Debates, 5th series, Vol. 716, col. 1589.

easily be a losing venture, until it was far clearer than it was then that the clearing banks' system was incapable of developing so as to meet the country's needs.[15] However, in 1965 the Post Office made a fresh review of the need for a postal giro and of its financial prospects, taking into account changes in recent years. The review showed that there had been a substantial increase in the kind of business (mail order, hire-purchase, credit-shopping, and the payment of bills by instalments) for which an inexpensive and speedy money-transfer service would be a boon.

10-34 The government set out this information in a White Paper entitled 'A Post Office Giro' published in August 1965.[16] The White Paper stated that, in the light of those studies, the government had concluded that a Post Office Giro, offering the usual facilities of the giro systems in European countries, would be a worthwhile addition to the existing media for transmitting money. For many people with simple needs and no bank accounts, it would provide a cheap and efficient service, run by a familiar institution, for the settlement of bills, the sending of money and, if desired, the receipt of their pay.

10-35 In the result, the National Giro came into operation in 1968.[17] Ten years later it was renamed the National Girobank, and in 1985 the bank was incorporated as Girobank plc. It became a wholly-owned subsidiary company of the Post Office. In 1989 it was announced that the government wanted to find a buyer for Girobank. The Alliance and Leicester Building Society, the fifth largest building society in the country, made an offer which was accepted, and completion of the sale was arranged to take place in January 1990.

10-36 Girobank is a member of the London Bankers' Clearing House. It provides a wide range of normal banking services using some 20,000 post offices as its branches. It is a recognized bank under the Banking Act 1979, a sponsoring bank in the Bankers' Automated Clearing Services (BACS), a settlement bank in the Clearing House Automated Payment System (CHAPS), a member of the Society for Worldwide Interbank Telecommunications (SWIFT), and a founder member of the Association for Payment Clearing Services (APACS) the body which is

---

15 *Hansard*, Commons Debates, 5th series, Vol. 673, cols 170–4. There was a change of government in October 1964.

16 Cmnd. 2751.

17 The Postmaster General was authorized to operate 'a banking service of the kind commonly known as a giro system'; see s. 2, Post Office (Borrowing Powers) Act 1967, replaced by s. 7(1), Post Office Act 1969. He was subsequently given wider powers, namely to operate 'banking services': see s. 1(1), Post Office (Banking Services) Act 1976.

responsible for the operation and development of inter-bank payment systems.[18]

10-37 Girobank offers to its customers current accounts, deposit accounts, personal loans, mortgage loans, overdraft facilities and revolving credits. Cash deposits may be made at most post offices, but personal customers must send cheques for collection to the Girobank centre. Business customers may, by arrangement, pay in cheques at post offices.

10-38 A customer may make a transfer of funds from his account to another customer's account by completing a transfer slip (contained in cheque books and in separate books of transfers) and sending it to the Girobank centre through the post. Payments may also be made by standing orders and by direct debits. Cheque cards are issued, and, since 1985, VISA credit cards have been provided. Since 1989 MasterCards have been available. A holder of a cheque card may cash his cheques at most post offices.

10-39 In 1985 Girobank introduced automated teller machines (ATMs) as part of a national ATM network known as 'Link'. The founding partners of Link were the bank, the Abbey National Building Society and Funds Transfer Sharing Ltd, a consortium of seventeen companies active in the retail financial sector. Other banks and building societies joined the Link network. Meanwhile, another network, known as 'Matrix' was formed, consisting of seven building societies. In 1989 both these networks merged, and a few months later the Bank of Scotland also joined the network.

10-40 Sterling travellers' cheques may be purchased from stock at most post offices or ordered direct from the bank. Foreign currency travellers' cheques and foreign bank notes may be ordered direct from the bank. In addition, the bank issues 'postcheques' which may be used with an authorizing 'postcheques card' to draw cash in local currency from many post offices in Europe and in several other countries.

10-41 Additional facilities are offered to corporate customers. These include money market deposits for short-, medium- and long-term investments; credit facilities including overdrafts, short- and medium-term loans, acceptance credits and leasing finance; payment services for employees and pensioners; and rent collection for local authorities.

18 *Ante*, paras 6-25 and 6-26.

Section 3
CHEQUE CARDS, CREDIT CARDS AND CASH DISPENSERS

10-42   Cheque cards and credit cards originated in the United States, and their use both in the United States and in the United Kingdom is now widespread.

Cheque cards

10-43   A cheque card (Americans call it a 'courtesy card') is a document issued by a bank which enables the holder to cash cheques up to a stated maximum, usually £50, at any branch of the issuing bank or of certain other banks with whom reciprocal arrangements have been made. Furthermore, the card is useful when making payments to third parties, because it contains an undertaking to the payee of a cheque that the bank will pay any cheque not exceeding the stated maximum, usually £50, provided that it is drawn by the person named on the card (a specimen of whose signature appears thereon) and provided that the cheque is drawn before a specified date. In effect, therefore, a cheque card makes cheques up to the stated amount as good as cash. These cards are now widely used by businessmen, holidaymakers and shoppers. They enable payments to be made by cheque in circumstances where, without production of a card, this method of settling a debt would not be acceptable to the creditor.

10-43A   British banks started to issue cheque cards in 1965, and as from July 1969, all the main commercial banks in Britain (with the exception of the Barclays Group) agreed to issue a standardized form of cheque card.[19] The name of the issuing bank is shown against a distinctive colour flash. When a cheque card is presented at a bank counter to support an encashment, the cheque book is stamped. After the first withdrawal in any day, a bank which receives a request for a further withdrawal telephones the account-holder's bank before allowing a further encashment. This procedure minimizes the risk of fraudulent encashments. By using their cheque cards, customers of British banks may cash their cheques in banks in most European countries.

10-43B   The application form which a customer is required to sign when he wishes to be supplied with a cheque card provides, *inter alia*, that all cheques drawn in conjunction with the card must be marked on the reverse with the card number; that the issue of the card automatic-

---

19 Barclays Bank issue 'Barclaycards'. These were originally (and still are) credit cards; see *post*, para. 10-45. However, as from September 1974, they have served also as cheque cards.

ally involves the issuing bank in paying, on first presentation, the customer's cheques of individual amount up to £50, and that the customer has no right to countermand payment of any cheque which the payee has accepted in conjunction with the use of the card.

10-44 The issuing bank's undertaking to pay, which is printed on the card, is usually expressed to be subject to the following conditions:

(a)   The cheque must be signed in the presence of the payee.

(b)   The signature on the cheque must correspond with the specimen signature on the card.

(c)   The cheque must be drawn on a bank cheque form bearing the code number shown on the card.

(d)   The cheque must be drawn before the expiry date of the card.

(e)   The card number must be written on the reverse of the cheque.

10-44A   If a customer abuses his cheque card and issues cheques which he knows that his bank would not be prepared to pay if it were not for their obligation under the cheque card, he commits a criminal offence. Thus in *Metropolitan Police Commissioner* v. *Charles*[20] the House of Lords held that, if the holder of a cheque card presents it, together with a cheque made out in accordance with the conditions of the card, it is open to the court to infer that a representation has been made by the drawer that he has authority as between himself and the bank to use the card in order to oblige the bank to honour the cheque. If that representation is false and the payee accepts the cheque, it is open to the court to find that the payee was induced to accept the cheque by reason of that false representation and that the drawer thereby obtained a pecuniary advantage by deception contrary to s. 16(1) of the Theft Act 1968.

10-44B   In *R* v. *Bevan*[21] the defendant had opened an account at a London branch of Lloyds Bank. He dishonestly obtained money by using his cheque card in Paris and in Brussels to withdraw sums in excess of that permitted by Lloyds Bank. It was held by the Court of Appeal that he was guilty of obtaining a pecuniary advantage by deception contrary to s. 16(1) of the Theft Act 1968, because the pecuniary advantage had been obtained in England.

10-44C   In *R.* v. *Navvabi*[22] the defendant had been convicted in the Crown Court at Newcastle upon Tyne of a number of offences, including eleven counts of theft of money from two banks by drawing, without funds or overdraft facilities, but with a cheque card on accounts which he had opened in false names. He used the cheques to obtain gaming

---

20   [1977] AC 177.
21   (1987) 84 Cr App R 143.
22   [1986] 3 All ER 102.

chips at a casino. The trial judge ruled that the case be left to the jury. He directed them that the delivery of each cheque and the tendering of the cheque card could amount to an appropriation of the assets of the bank for the purposes of s. 3(1) of the Theft Act 1968. The appellant was convicted, and he appealed.

The Court of Appeal Criminal Division allowed his appeal against conviction on the counts of theft. The Lord Chief Justice, Lord Lane, delivering the judgment of the court, said that the use of the cheque card and delivery of the cheque did no more than give the casino a contractual right as against the bank to be paid a specified sum from the bank's funds on presentation of the guaranteed cheque. That was not in itself an assumption of the rights of the bank to that part of the bank's funds to which the sum specified in the cheque corresponded: there was, therefore, no appropriation by the drawer either on delivery of the cheque to the casino or when the funds were ultimately transferred to the casino.[23]

Credit cards

10-45 About 1914 a number of oil companies in the United States issued the first credit cards to their customers for the purchase of gasoline, oil and accessories at the companies' stations.[24] Local department stores, air travel companies and railway companies also started to issue credit cards. In 1950 the Diners' Club, Inc., was probably the first company to issue an all-purpose card. The Franklin National Bank of New York was, in 1951, the first bank in the United States to adopt a credit card plan. About 1958, the American Express Company and two large banks, the Bank of America and the Chase Manhattan, entered the credit card field. Some of these companies introduced their cards into the United Kingdom, and in 1966 Barclays Bank was the first British bank to introduce credit cards, known as 'Barclaycards'. In 1972 'Access' cards were introduced by Lloyds Bank, the Midland Bank, the National Westminster Bank, and Williams and Glyn's Bank, together with the Clydesdale Bank, the Royal Bank of Scotland and the Northern Bank. Each of these banks is responsible for the issue of cards to its own

---

23 If the appellant had been charged with obtaining a pecuniary advantage by deception contrary to s. 16(1) of the Theft Act 1968, it may be that he would have been convicted and that this conviction would have been upheld: see *Metropolitan Police Commissioner* v. *Charles, ante*, para. 10-44A.

24 See William B. Davenport, 'Bank credit cards and the uniform commercial code', *The Banking Law Journal*, Vol. 85 (1968), pp. 941–86. This article, which is based upon American practice and was first published in the *Valparaiso University Law Review*, Vol. 1 (1967), p. 218, contains a wealth of material about credit cards. See also D. G. Hanson, *Service Banking* (3rd ed., 1987), pp. 213–41; A. C. Drury and C. W. Ferrier, *Credit Cards* (1984); Peter E. Sayer, *Credit Cards and the Law: An Introduction* (1988); Sally A. Jones, *The Law Relating to Credit Cards* (1989).

customers, and for fixing the credit limit for each customer. Since 1978 the trustee savings banks have provided VISA cards under the name 'Trustcard'. Girobank and the Bank of Scotland likewise provide VISA cards.

10-46 Credit cards operate quite differently from cheque cards. A cheque card guarantees payment of a cheque, whereas a credit card (as will be shown presently) guarantees payment against a sales voucher signed by the cardholder. Each credit card bears a specimen signature of its holder and is embossed by the issuing bank with the holder's name and number. When goods or services are supplied, the holder hands his card to a supplier who has agreed to join the scheme. The supplier places the card in a special imprinter machine, which records the holder's name and number on a sales voucher, to which are added the particulars of the transaction. The holder signs the voucher, and the supplier compares the signature with that on the card. He then sends the voucher to the issuing bank which pays the amount claimed, less a service charge of between three and seven per cent. At the end of the month, the bank sends a fully itemized statement to its cardholder. He is not required to pay any interest upon the sum due, provided that he makes payment within a specified time, usually about three weeks. Credit cards may also be used for the purpose of obtaining cash from branches of the issuing bank or branches of certain other banks with whom arrangements have been made.

10-46A It is an offence to supply a person with a credit card, if he has not asked for one. This rule was introduced by s. 51(1) of the Consumer Credit Act 1974.

10-46B In *R* v. *Lambie*[25] the House of Lords held that a customer who uses a credit card implies that he or she has the authority of the issuing bank to do so. The accused had used her Barclaycard substantially beyond her credit limit. The House of Lords held that she was guilty of obtaining a pecuniary advantage by deception contrary to s. 16(1) of the Theft Act 1968.

10-47 Some institutions make a specific annual charge to their cardholders. Bankers usually make no charge; they are content to receive as their remuneration the service charge which they deduct from each supplier's account.

10-47A If the holder of a Barclaycard or an Access card buys goods which have a cash price of more than £100 and which are discovered to

---

25 [1982] AC 449. Compare with the decision in *Metropolitan Police Commissioner* v. *Charles, supra*, para. 10-44A.

be faulty or not in accordance with the description, he may have a claim, not only against the seller of the goods, but also against the credit card company. The right to claim against the credit card company was introduced by s. 75(1) of the Consumer Credit Act 1974.[26] If the cardholder brings a claim against the credit card company, the company is entitled to be indemnified by the seller of the goods and is entitled to have the seller made a party to the proceedings.[27]

10-47B   In *Re Charge Card Services Ltd*[28] the main issue was whether the holder of a credit card was liable to the supplier if the card company became insolvent. Millett J answered this question in the negative. He recognized that payment by cheque or bill of exchange was only conditional payment, and so the supplier retained his right to sue his customer if the bank on which the cheque or bill of exchange was drawn became insolvent. In the opinion of Millett J, the position was different in a credit card transaction. He held that payment by credit card operated as an absolute payment on the part of the customer. This decision, which was upheld by the Court of Appeal, seems to be sound from the business point of view. The question is: 'To whom does the supplier look for payment?' The answer is that he looks to the card company. If the card company had not given its absolute undertaking to pay, the supplier would not have delivered the goods on credit terms. If the card company becomes insolvent, the loss should fall on the supplier.

10-48   There can be no doubt that credit cards save trouble and paperwork to travelling businessmen. They are also widely used by shoppers, who need not carry large amounts of cash or be concerned about the reluctance of suppliers to accept personal cheques. Another advantage is that a cardholder enjoys a period of 'free credit' which lasts for something between three and seven weeks.

10-49   However, credit cards have not escaped criticism. Objections have been raised by those people who prefer to make payment by cash or by cheque and who resent subsidizing those who take credit by using a card. A possible disadvantage to the cardholders is that they may tend to overspend, especially if they omit to keep a record of purchases which they make. Moreover, some shopkeepers are strongly opposed to being asked to pay a service charge in respect of each transaction. Other sup-

---

26 This right arises in cases where the agreement for the issue of the credit card was made on or after 1 July 1977. Furthermore, Barclaycard and Access have agreed, in respect of cards issued prior to that date, to meet claims up to the amount of credit extended by the card company in respect of the particular purchase. No claims can be made against American Express or Diners' Club, because their cards do not offer extended credit. Their cards are usually known as 'charge cards' rather than 'credit cards'.
27 Consumer Credit Act 1974, s. 75(2) and (5).
28 [1988] 3 All ER 702.

pliers find that the paper work is tedious, and they prefer to deal with a customer who produces a cheque card which guarantees payment of his own cheque.

10-50   Nevertheless, credit cards may bring benefits to suppliers of goods and services. The principal benefit to them is that a credit card ensures certainty of payment; suppliers no longer have to send out numerous reminders of outstanding debts. Losses through bad debts are reduced, and additional liquidity is achieved.

Cash dispensers and automated teller machines

10-50A   Cash dispensers were first introduced at a few of the larger offices of the clearing banks in 1967. The programme for installing the machines was accelerated as a result of the decision to close the banks on Saturday mornings as from July 1969. They are now known as automated teller machines (ATMs) if they provide an extra service, as explained in the next paragraph.

10-50B   In order to use the machine, a customer inserts a specially provided debit card into a terminal, punches his Personal Identity Number (PIN) into a keypad on the terminal. He can then withdraw cash up to a fixed limit. Automated teller machines provide one or more additional services. Thus a customer may find out the balance of his current account, or he may ask for a statement of account, cheque book or information leaflet to be sent to him. Some ATMs allow a customer to deposit cash and cheques in a sealed envelope for the credit of his account.

10-50C   Most ATMs are built into the walls of existing bank offices, though some have been placed specifically for the benefit of customers who are unable to visit the bank in normal working hours; for example, some have been installed in factories and in hospitals.

Section 4
STATUS OPINIONS

10-51   A service which a banker is prepared to offer to a customer is to obtain for him a status opinion concerning the creditworthiness of a third party by addressing a request to the third party's banker.[29] Conversely, a banker will provide a status opinion concerning one of his own

---

29 On this subject, see A. W. Wright, *Bankers' References* (2nd ed., 1985). See also Kelvin Williams, 'Privacy and the private bank account', *New Law Journal*, Vol. 124 (1974), pp. 613–14.

customers by communicating it to another banker. If, as sometimes happens, both customers bank at the same bank, that bank will provide a status opinion concerning one customer at the request of another customer.

10-52 The need for status opinions may be illustrated as follows. Let it be supposed that a customer is proposing to enter into an agreement, such as a hire-purchase or tenancy agreement, and that the other party to the proposed agreement asks the customer to name some person, preferably a banker, who would be prepared to give a reference concerning the customer's financial standing. The customer thereupon supplies the name and address of its bankers. The other party asks his own bankers to follow up this reference. They write to the bankers named, making use of a printed form of letter, asking for an opinion in confidence[30] as to the respectability and standing of the customer concerned and further asking whether he may be considered trustworthy, in the way of business, to the extent of £x. (This sum will either be a single amount, or alternatively may be expressed as £x per month or per annum.)

10-53 The manager, or a senior clerk, of the branch receiving the enquiry will reply to it by making use of such knowledge as the bank possesses concerning the customer's affairs: the bank is not under any duty to make outside enquiries to supplement the information which it already has.[31] The reply, or opinion (as it is usually called), will give a general indication of the creditworthiness of the customer, without, of course, giving any details of the account. A usual form of opinion is: 'Respectable, and considered good for your figures.' If, however, the customer has only recently opened an account, the opinion might be: 'Has only recently opened an account with us, and we cannot speak for your figures.' The opinion is usually typed on a printed form which is often headed: 'Confidential. For your private use only and without responsibility on the part of the bank or its officials.' The opinion is then communicated to the customer who made the enquiry. The words 'for

---

30 It is a little curious that the word 'confidence' should be used because, as soon as the opinion is received, it is communicated to the customer who initiated the enquiry. No doubt the word 'confidence' in this context is intended to indicate that the bank will use the opinion only for this purpose. Cf. the observations of Lord Morris of Borth-y-Gest in *Hedley Byrne & Co. Ltd* v. *Heller & Partners Ltd* [1964] AC 465, at p. 503. The enquiring bank had asked 'in confidence' for an opinion. Lord Morris said that he approached the case on the footing that the bank giving the opinion knew that what they said would in fact be passed on to some unnamed customer of the enquiring bank.

31 *Parsons* v. *Barclay & Co. Ltd* (1910) 103 LT 196, at p. 199, *per* Cozens-Hardy MR; *Hedley Byrne & Co. Ltd* v. *Heller & Partners Ltd* [1962] 1 QB 396, at p. 414, *per* Pearson LJ.

your private use only' are not regarded as prohibiting this communication, even though at first sight they appear to do so. The phrase is understood by bankers to mean that the opinion may be passed on to a customer. For reasons which will be given later, the words 'without responsibility on the part of the bank or its officials' are of vital importance and must never be omitted. Some banks add: 'The bank is not a credit reference agency for the purposes of the Consumer Credit Act 1974'. Section 145(8) of the Act provides that 'a credit reference agency is a person carrying on a business comprising the furnishing of persons with information collected by the agency for that purpose'. It seems clear from this definition that a bank is not a credit reference agency within the meaning of the Act, because a bank does not 'collect' information for the purpose of giving opinions.

10-54 Occasionally, status enquiries are made by telephone. The source of the enquiry should be verified. Unless this can be established by code, the safest course is to ask for the name, address and telephone number of the bank making the enquiry, ring off, *verify the number from the directory or the telephone exchange*, call that number and dictate the reply, expressly stating that the opinion is 'without responsibility on the part of the bank or its officials'. The bank which made the enquiry should be asked to confirm it in writing, and the reply should likewise be confirmed in writing.

10-55 Sometimes, business concerns such as hire-purchase finance companies and departmental stores, address status enquiries direct to a bank, that is to say without passing them through their own bankers. They request that the reply should be sent to their own bankers. Some banks comply with this request; others ask the enquirers to put their enquiry through their own bankers.

10-56 There are a few well-known trade protection societies which address their enquiries concerning customers direct to those customers' bankers. These enquiries are answered direct, just as though they had been received from banks.

10-57 Many thousands of status opinions are given by bankers every year, and it is only very rarely that any legal difficulties arise. The problems which can, and occasionally do, require consideration may be classified as follows. First, there are possible claims which a customer may make against his bank by reason of a status opinion which his bank has given about him; and, secondly, there are possible claims which a third party, who has received and relied upon a status opinion, may make against the bank which gave it.

Claims by customers against their bankers

10-58 Customers' claims may be considered under two headings, namely (a) claims whereby the customer alleges that his bank made some unauthorized disclosure of his affairs, and (b) claims where the customer alleges that the opinion was unfavourable to him, that it was not justified, and that he has suffered loss.

(a) Unauthorized disclosure

10-59 The practice of bankers of giving status opinions, when expressly authorized to do so by a customer, has received judicial commendation. The practice has been referred to as 'that very wholesome and useful habit of which one banker answers in confidence and answers honestly, to another banker, *the answer being given at the request and with the knowledge of the first banker's customer*'.[32]

10-60 However, there are many cases where a customer whose credit-worthiness is the subject of enquiry does not know that any enquiry is being made, and, in such cases, his banker provides a status opinion without his customer's express authority. The question whether a banker is justified in law in doing so is an open one at the present day.[33]

10-61 In the vast majority of cases, the practice of giving status opinions concerning a customer without that customer's express authority does no harm to the customer, though exceptional cases can, and do, arise where the customer would object most vigorously if he knew that his banker was proposing to give a status opinion about him. Take, for example, the case of a man who has a large and well-conducted account at Bank X, and has just opened a small account at Bank Y. He proposes to enter into a substantial transaction with a third party who happens to have seen the customer transacting business at the counter of Bank Y. The third party puts through a status enquiry to Bank Y, who reply (quite honestly and accurately) that they cannot speak for the figures mentioned. If the customer had been informed what was taking place, he would, of course, have given the name of Bank X as a referee. It is in a case of this nature that the customer is able to argue, with some force, that Bank Y made an unauthorized disclosure of his affairs.

10-62 Of course, if the customer had been blessed with the foresight of a prophet, he might have foreseen, when opening his account at Bank Y, the remote possibility that someone might put through a status

---

32 *Parsons* v. *Barclay & Co. Ltd* (1910) 103 LT 196, at p. 199, *per* Cozens-Hardy MR (italics added).
33 *Ante*, para. 2-123A.

enquiry to that bank concerning him. He might then have expressly instructed them not to reply, without his express permission, to enquiries concerning him. If, however, he had taken this exceptional course, he might have found that the bank would not have opened an account for him on those terms. *Questions in Banking Practice*[34] contains the following question and answer:

Question: What should be the answer of a bank which is asked:

(i) by a prospective customer;
(ii) by a customer of long standing;

not to reply without his express permission to enquiries concerning him?
Answer: (i) The prospective customer should be informed that it is normal banking practice to answer enquiries from other banks and certain trade protection societies without reference to the customer concerned. It should be pointed out to him with advantage that a refusal to answer might carry an implication detrimental to him. It would be open to the banker to refuse to accept an account on such conditions if he thought fit.
(ii) A banker, having accepted the account, would ignore at his peril his customer's instructions overriding the customary practice of bankers. Here again, the possibility of such a course being to the customer's disadvantage could be stressed. If the banker was not disposed to continue banking relations under such exceptional terms it would be open to him to arrange for the account to be closed.

(b) Unfavourable and unjustified opinion

10-63 Great care is exercised by bankers when giving status opinions, and mistakes are made only very rarely. A mistake might occur where a bank has two customers of similar name, one being wealthy and the other impecunious. An enquiry might be received concerning the wealthy customer, but, as the result of an error, the bank might give an opinion relating to the impecunious customer. There does not appear to be any reported decision on this type of problem, but on general principles it would seem that the wealthy customer would have a claim against the bank for damages for breach of duty. If a bank is prepared to give opinions concerning its customers, presumably it owes a duty to them to exercise reasonable care in so doing.

Claims by third parties

10-64 There is usually no contractual relationship between a bank giving a status opinion and the third party to whom it is communi-

34 11th ed., 1978, p. 239, Question 693.

cated.[35] Accordingly, the bank could not be sued by the third party if it refused to give any information whatever. If, however, the bank does give an opinion and that opinion is too sanguine, the third party may, in very exceptional circumstances, have a valid claim against the bank, provided that he relied upon the opinion and suffered loss as a result. The legal position of the bank and of its officials would depend upon whether the opinion was given (a) negligently or (b) fraudulently.

(a) Opinion given negligently

10-65 This branch of the law was exhaustively explored in *Hedley Byrne & Co. Ltd* v. *Heller & Partners Ltd*.[36] In that case, the plaintiffs caused enquiries to be made through their own bank from the defendants, who were merchant bankers, concerning the creditworthiness of a company, Easi-power Ltd, which had an account with the defendants. The defendants gave two references, which were acted upon by the plaintiffs, resulting in a loss to them of £15,454. The references were expressly stated to be 'without responsibility' on the part of the defendants. The plaintiffs sought to recover damages from the defendants, alleging that the references were given negligently and without reasonable care in that the expressions of opinion contained in the references were not justified by the facts as known to the defendants. The learned trial judge held that, although in his opinion the defendants had acted without reasonable care, judgment must be given for the defendants on the ground that the defendants did not owe a duty of care to the plaintiffs. There was clearly no contract between the plaintiffs and the defendants, and the learned judge said he could find no fiduciary relationship.

10-66 The plaintiffs' appeal was dismissed by the Court of Appeal and, subsequently, by the House of Lords. In the House of Lords, however, the view of the learned trial judge concerning the absence of a duty of care was not upheld. It would seem that, if there had not been an express disclaimer of responsibility by the defendants, the House of Lords would have given their decision in favour of the plaintiffs. As, however, responsibility had been disclaimed, the plaintiff's claim could not succeed.[37] In the result, therefore, the decision turned upon the express disclaimer of responsibility by the bank. However, in view of the provisions

---

35 It is otherwise where both customers bank at the same bank.

36 (1960) *The Times*, 21 December, McNair J: [1962] 1 QBD 396, CA; [1964] AC 465, HL. The earlier cases are mainly of historical interest; see, for example, *Batts Combe Quarry Co.* v. *Barclays Bank Ltd* (1931) 48 TLR 4.

37 'A man cannot be said voluntarily to be undertaking a responsibility if at the very moment when he is said to be accepting it he declares that in fact he is not.' [1964] AC, at p. 533, *per* Lord Devlin.

of the Unfair Contract Terms Act 1977,[38] it may be that banks are no longer able to rely upon such disclaimers of responsibility. It seems that such a disclaimer would be effective only if the bank could show that the exclusion of liability was reasonable.

(b) Opinion given fraudulently

10-67 It is seldom alleged that a bank or one of its officials gave a status opinion fraudulently. Such an allegation was in fact made in the pleadings in *Hedley Byrne & Co Ltd* v. *Heller & Partners Ltd*,[39] but it was withdrawn at the trial. In order to establish a claim for fraud arising out of a status opinion, it is necessary to prove that a false representation in the opinion was made knowingly or recklessly (that is to say, not caring whether it was true or false) with intent that it should be acted upon by someone who did in fact act upon it and thereby suffered damage.[40]

10-68 A plaintiff who wishes to allege that a representation in a status opinion is false and fraudulent must have in mind the provisions of s. 6 of the Statute of Frauds Amendment Act 1828, often known as Lord Tenterden's Act. The section is badly drafted,[41] but its effect is that no action may be brought against a person who makes a fraudulent representation[42] concerning another person's credit, unless such representation 'be made in writing, signed by the party to be charged therewith'. Thus, *writing* (including, of course, typescript) and *signature* are essential in order to establish liability for fraud.

10-69 The operation of the section is clearly illustrated by referring to the decision in *Hirst* v. *West Riding Banking Co. Ltd*.[43] In that case, the plaintiff claimed damages against the defendant bank for a statement, alleged to be a misrepresentation, made in writing by a branch manager, and signed by him. The bank relied upon s. 6 of Lord Tenterden's Act,

---

38 Ss 2(2) and 11(5).
39 (1960) *The Times*, 21 December.
40 *Derry* v. *Peek* (1889) 14 App Cas 337.
41 It reads as follows: 'No action shall be brought whereby to charge any person upon or by reason of any representation or assurance made or given concerning or relating to the character, conduct, credit, ability, trade, or dealings of any other person, to the intent or purpose that such other person may obtain credit, money, or goods upon [   ], unless such representation or assurance be made in writing, signed by the party to be charged therewith.' One or more words seem to have been inadvertently omitted from the section where the brackets are printed; or perhaps the word 'upon' should have been 'thereupon'.
42 It was held by the House of Lords in *Banbury* v. *Bank of Montreal* [1918] AC 626, that the section applies only to fraudulent representations.
43 [1901] 2 KB 560.

and the Court of Appeal held that the bank was protected by that section. The signature of the bank manager was insufficient to impose liability upon the bank. This was a curious result. Presumably, the bank manager could have been made personally liable, but he had not been joined as a defendant in the action. It is strange that the bank manager was not sued in that case, because the Court of Exchequer Chamber had decided in an earlier case, *Swift* v. *Jewsbury and Goddard*,[44] that the second-named defendant, Mr Goddard, who was a bank manager, was personally liable for a false representation contained in a letter signed by him concerning the status of one of the bank's customers. Section 6 of Lord Tenterden's Act protected the bank, but not the bank manager.[45]

10-70 Possibly as a result of these decisions, the modern practice is that status opinions are not signed, thus ensuring that there can be no liability for any fraudulent representations contained therein.

Section 5
SAFE CUSTODY

10-71 One of the most important services which a banker offers to his customers is that of keeping in safe custody valuables of various kinds, including jewellery, share certificates, life policies and title deeds. As a general rule, property which is thus left with a banker for safe custody is deposited in a locked box, the key of which is retained by the customer. Alternatively, items such as deeds, share certificates and life policies may be enclosed in an envelope which is sealed with sealing wax. If the customer possesses a personal seal, he will make an impression from this in the molten wax. If not, he will sign his name in ink across the wax when it has set; alternatively, he may be asked to sign his name across the flap of the envelope, the signature being then covered with a special form of sealing tape which, if removed, takes the signature with it.

10-72 *Bearer securities.* These securities are not as common as they used to be. A customer who does possess bearer securities usually leaves them with his bank for safe custody, and he authorizes the bank to detach the coupons in respect of dividend or interest and to present them

44 (1874) LR 9 QB 301.
45 In *Commercial Banking Company of Sydney Ltd* v. *R. H. Brown & Co.* [1972] ALJR 297, a status opinion had been given fraudulently. The defendant bank was held liable by the Supreme Court of Western Australia, notwithstanding an express disclaimer of responsibility by the bank. The decision was upheld by the High Court of Australia. No defence based on the Western Australian equivalent of Lord Tenterden's Act was raised.

for payment. The bank will also receive payments of capital when bonds are redeemed.

10-73 *Receipt for safe custody articles.* Most banks in England issue to their customers a form of receipt in respect of articles lodged for safe custody, and state that the receipt should be returned to them when the articles are withdrawn. Moreover, it is usually added that, if possible, the customer should attend in person in order to withdraw the articles; if he is unable to do so, he is asked to sign an order on the back of the receipt instructing the bank to deliver the articles to the bearer of the document. Some banks, however, refrain whenever possible from issuing a receipt in respect of safe custody articles on the ground that difficulties may arise if the customer calls to collect an article but cannot produce the receipt.

10-74 *Authority to have 'access'.* Occasionally, a customer who is unable to attend at the bank, signs an authority addressed to his bankers instructing them to allow a named person access to his box. The word 'access' is equivocal, and it is safe to assume that it merely confers power to inspect the contents of the box, without removing anything from it. Accordingly, if the customer desires the third party to have the right to remove items from the box, this should be expressly stated.

10-75 *Death of customer.* When a customer dies, his bank will obtain a good discharge in respect of safe custody articles by taking the receipt of his personal representatives, after they have obtained a grant of probate or administration. The grant should be exhibited to the bank. A customer's will is not infrequently deposited in his deed box, and, in order to enable probate thereof to be obtained, the bank will permit the will to be removed in exchange for a receipt signed by all the persons named therein as executors.

10-76 *Bankruptcy of customer.* If a bank receives notice of the presentation to the court of a petition for a bankruptcy order, any safe custody articles should not be released to the customer but should be held pending the appointment of a trustee in bankruptcy.[46]

10-77 *Joint accounts, partnership accounts, limited company accounts, etc.* It is the usual practice, when accepting safe-custody articles from these account holders, to obtain specific instructions concerning the persons to whom the articles may be returned.

Legal claims

10-78 Claims against banks arising out of the provision of safe-custody

46 See *ante*, para. 3-41.

facilities are very rare. Such claims may conveniently be considered under the following headings, namely (a) conversion, (b) detinue and negligence, and (c) liability for criminal acts of the bank's servants.

(a) Conversion

10-79 Liability for conversion will arise where it is proved that the bank delivered safe-custody articles to a third party without the customer's authority. Any person who wrongly disposes of another's goods so as to deprive him of possession is guilty of conversion and is liable to pay the value of the goods to the owner by way of damages.[47] This applies even though the wrongful conversion was made bona fide and without negligence.

10-80 A case which is often cited in this connection is *Langtry* v. *Union Bank of London*.[48] Although the case is a useful illustration of the sort of situation which may arise, it is of no value as a judicial precedent, because no judgment was ever delivered. The plaintiff had deposited some valuable jewellery for safe custody with the Union Bank of London. It seems that a fraudulent person stole a piece of her notepaper and forged a request to the bank to hand over the jewels to the bearer. The bank delivered the jewels to the bearer of the note, and the plaintiff brought this action against the bank. The claim was settled by judgment for the plaintiff by consent for £10,000.

(b) Detinue and negligence

10-81 It used to be said that the duty of a bailee to whom articles were entrusted for safe custody depended upon whether the bailee was a 'bailee for reward' or a 'gratuitous bailee'.[49] It was said that the duty owed by a bailee for reward was higher than that owed by a gratuitous bailee: the latter was liable only for 'gross negligence', whereas the former was liable for 'ordinary negligence'. This may well have been the correct approach at one time, based upon certain early decisions of the courts,[50] but the attitude of the judges in modern times is different.

10-82 A good illustration of the modern approach is provided by the decision of the Court of Appeal in *Houghland* v. *R. R. Low (Luxury Coaches) Ltd*.[51] In that case, the plaintiff, when returning to her home

---

47 See *Halsbury's Laws of England* (4th ed., 1985), Vol. 45, p. 650.
48 *Journal of the Institute of Bankers*, Vol. XVII (1896), p. 338.
49 See, for example, T. Beven, *Negligence in Law* (4th ed., 1928), Vol. 2, pp. 903 *et seq.*
50 See, for example, *Moore* v. *Mourgue* (1776) 2 Cowp 479; *Giblin* v. *McMullen* (1869) LR 2 PC 317.
51 [1962] 1 QB 694.

in one of the defendants' coaches, deposited her suitcase with the coach driver, who put it into the boot, which was then locked. The coach broke down, and the passengers had to wait until a relief coach came, the first coach standing unattended in the dark for about three hours. The driver of the first coach supervised the reloading and stowing of the luggage on to the relief coach, but there was no supervision of the discharge and transfer of the luggage from the first coach to the relief coach. When the plaintiff arrived at her destination, her suitcase could not be found. She claimed against the defendants in detinue for the return of the suitcase and its contents, or £82 10s 11d. their value, or alternatively for the same sum as damages in negligence. The plaintiff succeeded. The Court of Appeal held that the standard of care required of a bailee, whether gratuitous or otherwise, is the standard demanded by the circumstances of the particular case. It was further held that whether the action was brought in detinue or in negligence, the burden was on the defendants to show that there was no negligence on their part in the care which they took of the goods. As the defendants had failed to show that they had exercised reasonable care of the goods, the plaintiff was entitled to judgment.

10-83   Ormerod LJ adverted to the terms 'gratuitous bailment' and 'bailment for reward'. His Lordship said that it seemed to him that to try to put a bailment, for instance, into a watertight compartment − such as gratuitous bailment on the one hand, and bailment for reward on the other − was to overlook the fact that there might well be an infinite variety of cases, which might come into one or the other category. The question to be considered was whether in the circumstances of the particular case a sufficient standard of care had been observed by the defendants.

10-84   Turning then to the subject of bankers as bailees, one may say that the care which a banker is obliged to take is such care as an ordinarily efficient and prudent banker would take in similar circumstances. The following illustrations may be given. If a bank locks up its customers' valuables in the strongroom and if thieves succeed in breaking into that strongroom and stealing the customers' valuables, the bank will not be liable. If, however, the bank's officials carelessly leave a customer's deed box outside the strongroom and it is stolen, this will be a clear case of negligence and the bank will be liable accordingly. Again, if a bank discovers that a loss has taken place and thereupon fails to take prompt steps to recover the property by informing the owner or the police, this too will amount to negligence.[52]

52 See *Coldman* v. *Hill* [1919] 1 KB 443.

Disclaimer of liability

10-85 Some banks are content to accept articles for safe custody subject to the obligations imposed upon them at common law. In the case of other banks, their safe-custody service is the subject of a special contract in which it is stipulated that the bank will not, in any circumstances whatsoever, be liable for loss or damage to articles accepted for safe custody. However, in view of the provisions of the Unfair Contract Terms Act 1977,[53] it may be that banks are no longer able to rely upon such disclaimers of responsibility. It seems that such a disclaimer would be effective only if the bank could show that the exclusion of liability was reasonable.

10-86 The effect of a disclaimer was tested in the following case, but the case was decided before the Unfair Contract Terms Act 1977 was passed.[54] A depositor, Mrs Kesby, lodged a sealed packet with a trustee savings bank and signed a document expressly agreeing to the terms set out above. The packet was subsequently lost or stolen. According to the evidence, when a routine check of articles kept for safe custody was made in October 1956, the packet was in its place, but when the next periodic inspection was made in February 1957, it was missing. Nothing further happened until October 1957, when the branch manager asked the depositor to call. He asked her whether she could produce the receipt, and on her saying that she could, informed her that the packet had been mislaid. A further search was made, but the packet was not found. The depositor was informed. She made known the contents of the packet and asked that the police be informed. In his award, the Chief Registrar of Friendly Societies set out these facts and continued:

> There is a complete lack of evidence tending to show in what circumstances the package was taken from the strongroom. The fact that Mrs Kesby held the receipt for the package and that the register of items deposited contains no signature in the place where persons withdrawing deposited articles have to sign, is prima facie evidence that the package was not delivered in error to some person other than Mrs Kesby.
>
> The evidence given on behalf of the bank satisfied me that the bank adopted a reasonably safe system for the custody of packages left in its charge. There was no evidence of the bank having been negligent in the custody of the package up to February 1957. It may be that, on the authority of *Coldman* v. *Hill*,[55] Mrs Kesby might have established a claim for negligence arising out of the bank's delay in informing her of the loss, but for the terms of the bailment to which she agreed.

53 Ss 2(2) and 11(5).
54 Award *Kesby*: (1958) CRR 12, cited in C. L. Lawton, *Guide to the Law of Trustee Savings Banks* (3rd ed., 1962), Vol. 1, p. 339.
55 [1919] 1 KB 443, *supra*.

In my view, however, the words 'neither the trustees nor the bank will, under any circumstances whatsoever, be liable for loss of the package' cover loss by negligence. Since the bank has established, to my satisfaction, that the package is lost and has not been misdelivered, I find that it has a defence to Mrs Kesby's claim.

Insurance

10-87 A customer should insure against loss of articles, especially jewellery, which are deposited for safe custody. Many 'Householders' Comprehensive' policies include cover in respect of jewellery deposited with a bank or safe-deposit company. Valuable items of jewellery should be valued, and the value agreed with the insurance company, so that if a loss occurs, there will be no difficulty in quantifying the loss.

(c) Liability for criminal acts of the bank's servants

10-88 In practice, it is very difficult to prove that a missing safe-custody article was stolen by one of the bank's employees. Such cases, however, though rare, are not unknown. Thus, in one case,[56] a customer who owned certain railway shares deposited the certificates with his bank where they were kept in a safe to which the manager had the one and only key. There were dividend coupons attached to the certificates, and the bank was authorized to collect the coupons as and when they became due. The manager stole the certificates which he converted to his own use. This careless system – that is to say a system under which one man had uncontrolled access to a customer's valuables – was held to amount to negligence on the part of the banking company; there was 'sufficient negligence' in the performance of their duty as bailee to render the company liable for the consequences of that negligence.

10-89 Let it be supposed, however, that an employee of a bank steals a customer's valuable in circumstances where no negligence can be attributed to the bank. Is the bank vicariously liable for this wrongful act? There is no authority which directly answers this question. The governing principle, which has been accepted by the House of Lords, is that an employer is liable for the wrongful acts of his servants where they are committed in the course of their employment, even though the employer obtains no benefit from them.[57] The controversial question is whether an employee of a bank who goes to the strongroom and steals a customer's valuables is acting in the course of his employment. One view is that the employee is doing *dishonestly* something that he is employed to do *honestly*, and that the bank is liable accordingly. The

56 *Re United Service Co., Johnston's Claim* (1871) 6 Ch App 212.
57 *Lloyd* v. *Grace Smith & Co.* [1912] AC 716.

opposing view is that the employee, in such circumstances, could never be said to be acting in the course of his employment. The question must be regarded as an open one at the present day; perhaps one day it will be resolved by the courts.

Night safe facilities

10-90 A customer who uses night safe facilities is able to deposit cash and cheques for safe custody after his bank has closed for business. In order to obtain these facilities, he will sign a form in which he acknowledges receipt of a wallet, a key thereto and a key to the night safe. He agrees that he will use the night safe primarily when the bank is closed and that its use will be restricted to himself or his authorized agent. If any items are deposited during business hours, they will be dealt with on the following business day. He undertakes responsibility for any loss caused by his or his agent's omission to lock the door of the night safe. He agrees that he will deposit items in the night safe only by using the wallet, and that the wallet will not be used for any other purpose.

10-91 If the customer wants the bank to open the wallet, he undertakes to enclose in the wallet a paying-in book or a credit slip in duplicate, and to enter therein particulars of the cash, cheques, etc., placed in the wallet; and he authorizes the bank to open the wallet to pay in the contents to the credit of his account. He agrees that when the wallet is placed in the night safe, it is to be held by the bank for safe custody only, and that the ordinary relationship of banker and customer is not to arise until the officers of the bank have opened the wallet and paid in the contents in the ordinary course of business. If, however, he does not want the bank to open the wallet, he will either call at the bank and open it himself, or he may wish to authorize the bank to hand it to a named person, a specimen of whose signature will be given on the form.

Section 6
CUSTOMERS' INVESTMENTS

10-92 Another service which banks offer to their customers is that of assisting them in the investment of their money. Bank officers should, therefore, possess a sound general knowledge of the different types of investments, and especially of securities quoted on a stock exchange. They are not, however, required to be specialists in this field.

Investing on the International Stock Exchange

10-93   In March 1973, the London Stock Exchange and the other stock exchanges outside London were amalgamated to form one organization called 'the Stock Exchange'. Then in 1986 the Stock Exchange decided to merge with the International Securities Regulatory Organization (ISRO) which had been set up in 1985 by the big international investment houses with the main object of regulating their activities in the Eurodollar market. The ISRO firms were also in the forefront of the global market in internationally traded securities, such as US Treasury bonds, UK gilts and shares in multinational companies. The merger between the Stock Exchange and ISRO was an event which had a wide range of implications.[58] Thus it was decided to change the structure of the old Stock Exchange and to form two limited liability companies, namely the International Stock Exchange of the United Kingdom and the Republic of Ireland Limited, and The Securities Association Limited (known as TSA). These were formed in order to comply with the Financial Services Act 1986. The Securities and Investments Board duly recognized The Securities Association as a self-regulating organization, and its principal functions have been noted in Chapter 1.[59]

10-94   It is no part of the purpose of this book to give a detailed account of stock exchange procedure.[60] Attention will, however, be directed to (a) the different types of quoted securities, (b) the difference between 'shares' and 'stock', and (c) some practical and legal considerations affecting the purchase and sale of securities.

(a) Types of quoted securities

The principal types of securities which are dealt in on a stock exchange are as follows.

(i) British government and government guaranteed stocks

10-95   These represent loans to the British government and compensatory stocks issued in exchange for the capital of the nationalized industries. A distinction should be drawn between short- and long-dated stocks. Those which are redeemable many years hence or are irredeemable (such as $2\frac{1}{2}$ per cent Consols) fluctuate in price with changes in the level of interest rates. Thus, when interest rates rise the price of long-

---

58 See Sir Nicholas Goodison, 'All change at the Stock Exchange', *The Law Society's Gazette* (1987), pp. 1721–2. At the time when he wrote this article, Sir Nicholas was Chairman of the International Stock Exchange of the United Kingdom and the Republic of Ireland Limited.

59 See *ante*, para. 1-86.

60 On this subject see N. Whetnall, *How The Stock Exchange Works* (6th ed., 1987).

dated government stock falls, and vice versa. Short-dated stocks, i.e. those which are drawing near to their redemption dates, are naturally much more stable in value.

(ii) Commonwealth government and foreign government stocks

10-96 These fluctuate in value more than British government stocks. The value of a particular security depends upon the political and financial conditions in the country concerned.

(iii) Municipal stocks

10-97 The stocks of many local authorities in the United Kingdom are quoted on the Stock Exchange. For all practical purposes, they are as 'safe' as British government stocks. There has been no default by a local authority in Britain this century.

(iv) Stocks of public boards and authorities

10-98 These include, for example, the stocks of the Port of London Authority. These stocks rank almost as high as those of the British government.

(v) Industrial and commercial stocks and shares

10-99 There are different types of stocks and shares which companies offer to the investing public. Some of these investments appeal to the investor who wants security of capital and income, whereas others appeal to the person who is prepared to take a risk and hopes to earn a large return on his investment. The principal types of industrial and commercial stocks and shares may be classified as follows.

10-100 *Debenture stocks.* The company security which offers the highest degree of safety is debenture stock. This is not part of a company's share capital. Persons who subscribe for debenture stock are in no sense the owners or part-owners of the company. They have made a loan to the company – a loan which is generally secured by a charge on the company's assets. If unsecured, the stock is usually called 'unsecured loan stock' rather than debenture stock. It is a rule of the Stock Exchange that an official quotation will not be granted for a stock which constitutes an unsecured liability unless the stock is entitled 'unsecured'.[61] In return for their loan the lenders receive a fixed rate of interest and, no matter how prosperous the company may become, they can never receive more than that agreed rate. Very occasionally, however, one comes across participating debentures, the holders of which are entitled to a further payment of interest over and above the agreed rate if the shareholders receive more than a certain rate on their capital.

61 Admission of Securities to Listing Rules, s. 9, para. 6.1.

Sometimes 'convertible debenture stock' or 'convertible unsecured loan stock' is issued. The holder has the option of surrendering his debenture or loan stock in exchange for ordinary stock at one or more stated dates and at stated rates. As long as their interest is paid to them, debenture holders have no control over the company's affairs or policy. If however, their interest is not paid or their security can be shown to be in jeopardy, they are usually entitled to appoint a receiver, who has very extensive powers of management; in fact, effective control of the company then passes from the directors to the receiver.

10-101 *Preference shares or stock.* These rank before the ordinary shares or stock with regard to the payment of dividend, and very often they carry a preferential claim to return of capital in the event of the company's liquidation. Usually, preference shareholders receive a fixed rate of dividend. Occasionally, however, a company issues participating preference shares. The holders of these shares are entitled to a higher rate of dividend if the ordinary shareholders receive more than a stated return on their capital. All preference shares are either cumulative or non-cumulative, the distinction being important if in any particular year the company earns insufficient profits to enable the preference dividend to be paid. If the shares are non-cumulative, that year's dividend will never be paid, but if they are cumulative, the dividend will be paid when profits are available. When preference shares are issued, it is usually stated whether they are cumulative or non-cumulative, but in the absence of any definite provision, they are presumed to be cumulative.[62] Unlike debenture holders, preference shareholders cannot appoint a receiver, though if their dividend is not paid, they are sometimes given the right to vote at the company's general meeting.

10-102 *Ordinary shares or stock.* These rank for dividend and often for capital repayment after the preference shares, and accordingly they carry most of the risk. If a company prospers, the dividend on the ordinary share is likely to show a steady increase. In this respect ordinary shares (or 'equities' as they are often called) provide a valuable hedge against inflation. If, however, a company is unsuccessful, the ordinary shareholders will suffer a reduction in their income, and they may lose a part or even all of their capital. Prices of ordinary shares may fluctuate widely: from May 1972 to December 1974 prices fell by over seventy per cent, and from July to November 1987 prices fell by approximately thirty-five per cent. The ordinary shareholders have most of the voting rights in general meetings.

10-103 *Deferred shares or stock.* Occasionally, a company would issue deferred shares. These shares were usually held by the founders of a

62 *Webb* v. *Earle* (1875) LR 20 Eq 556.

business or by their descendants. They ranked last for payment of dividend after the claims of all other types of shares had been satisfied. The deferred capital would usually be comparatively small but would carry extensive voting rights and receive a high rate of dividend. Deferred shares are not usually issued at the present day, and most public companies which had deferred shares have converted them into ordinary shares or stock.

(b) Difference between 'Shares' and 'Stock'

10-104   Reference has been made above to preference shares or stock, to ordinary shares or stock, and so on. The Companies Act 1985 provides that once shares are fully paid, a company may convert them into stock, provided that it is authorized to do so by its articles of association.[63] This means that the shares may be treated as merged into one fund of a nominal value equivalent to that of the total of the shares. Thus, instead of holding 100 shares of £1 each, a member will hold £100 stock.

10-105   The main difference between stock on the one hand and shares on the other is that, subject to the company's articles, stock may be transferred in any fractional amount, whereas a share cannot be subdivided. In practice, however, the articles of most companies do in fact provide that the stock is not to be transferred in less than units of a prescribed amount. For example, in the illustration given above, the articles may provide that the stock shall be in units of £1 each, and that fractions of units may not be transferred. For all practical purposes, therefore, a member who used to hold 100 shares of £1 each and who now hold 100 stock units of £1 each is in just the same position as he was previously.

10-106   Shares were often converted into stock to save clerical work in the company's office. Shares always had to be numbered – a rule inapplicable to stock – and, in a transfer of shares, it was necessary to specify all the numbers of the shares transferred. The registration of transfers of shares was, therefore, much more cumbersome than the registration of transfers of stock. Nowadays, however, fully paid up shares are no longer required by statute to be numbered,[64] and this advantage of stock over shares has gone. In spite of this, some companies still convert their shares into stock units. There seems to be no advantage in so doing. Some companies which had previously con-

---

63 S. 121. A company is not permitted to issue share capital in the form of stock in the first instance, though it may, of course, raise loan capital by issuing debenture stock.
64 Companies Act 1985, s. 182(2).

verted their shares into stock units have converted their stock units back into shares.

(c) Purchase and sale of stock exchange securities

10-107   Under the single capacity dealing system which ended in the 'Big Bang' on 27 October 1986,[65] members of the Stock Exchange were divided into jobbers and brokers. Jobbers made markets and were only allowed to deal as principals with brokers, never directly with investors. Brokers, on the other hand, were only allowed to deal as agents on behalf of investors and could not themselves make markets. They were obliged to take their clients' order to the jobbers.

10-108   Under the single capacity dealing system, an investor who wanted to invest in stocks and shares could either instruct a stockbroker directly, who would then transact the business with a jobber as stated above, or he could instruct his bank, which would pass on the instruction to a broker, who would then transact the business with a jobber. The jobber used to earn his living by dealing in investments: he hoped to sell securities at a higher price than that at which he bought them. The broker used to earn his living by charging a commission on each transaction, and there used to be a scale of minimum commissions. When the broker received his instructions through a bank, he used to share the commission with the bank.

10-109   The events which led up to the 'Big Bang' started in 1979 when the Office of the Director General of Fair Trading initiated litigation under the Restrictive Trade Practices Act 1976 in order to challenge a number of key features of the Stock Exchange, in particular the rule that all stockbrokers must charge minimum commissions fixed by the Stock Exchange on the sale and purchase of shares for their clients. This litigation was ended in 1983 by the historic agreement between Sir Nicholas Goodison, the then Chairman of the Stock Exchange, and Mr Cecil Parkinson, the then Secretary of State for Trade and Industry. Mr Parkinson agreed to drop the case, and in return Sir Nicholas had to concede that outsiders could own stockbroking and jobbing firms, and that the minimum commission scales would be scrapped within three years. The members of the Stock Exchange insisted on a third change, namely that brokers and jobbers – to be known respectively as broker-dealers and market-makers – could merge and do one another's jobs. In this way the single capacity dealing system came to an end, and the

---

65   The 'Big Bang' is a colloquial reference to the reorganization of the Stock Exchange which took place on 27 October 1986: see Sir Gordon Borrie, QC, Director General of Fair Trading, 'Effective marketing and a fair deal for the consumer', *Journal of Business Law*, March 1987, pp. 86–93.

present dual capacity system came into existence, whereby market-makers can deal directly with clients. There are still many broker-dealers who are not market-makers. In June 1989 there were 393 members of the International Stock Exchange. Of these, 127 were market-makers and 266 were broker-dealers.

10-110 The changes described in the preceding paragraph have increased the capital requirements of the members of the International Stock Exchange, as it is now called[66] because they now have to take positions in stock. Many members are now joint stock companies in place of the previous partnerships. The banks themselves have played an active part in these developments. Even before the 'Big Bang' on 27 October 1986, British and overseas banks had bought or agreed to buy existing firms of brokers and jobbers.

10-111 As far as private investors are concerned, the changes which have occurred since the 'Big Bang' on 27 October 1986 are not very substantial. The principal change which a private investor may notice is that, if his transaction relates to a small amount of money, the minimum commission which he will be charged has increased sharply. If he wishes to invest, for example, £1,000 in shares, he will probably find that the commission will be £30/£40. This charge is justified on the grounds that overheads have increased and that payments have to be made under the Financial Services Act 1986. If the investor goes direct to a firm of stockbrokers, they may be acting solely as agents, or they may be market-makers, in which case they may buy or sell as principals. If the investor places the order to buy or sell shares with his bank, the bank may have a subsidiary company which deals in securities. In this way the bank will earn more money than it did under the old single capacity system when the bank used to pass on the instructions to a broker and receive a share (about 25 per cent) of the commission charged by the broker.[67]

Other investments

(a) Unit trusts

10-112 A wealthy investor will usually invest in a wide range of securities with the object of spreading his risks. An investor of modest means who wishes to spread his risks will often purchase units in a unit trust. Briefly, a unit trust operates in the following way.[68] The savings of a large number of investors who subscribe to the initial issue are

66 See *ante*, para. 10-93.
67 For the implications of the Financial Services Act 1986, see *ante*, paras 1-91/93.
68 On the subject of unit trusts, see Christine Stopp, *Unit Trusts* (1988).

placed with the managers of the trust, who invest the funds in a wide cross-section of securities.[69] The trust is divided into units, and each investor applies for a certain number of units. He may send his application direct to the managers, or through his bank or stockbroker, in which case they will receive a small commission from the managers. The issue is made at an advertised price per unit. This price includes an initial charge levied by the managers. Thereafter, it is still possible to apply for units, and the price of each unit depends upon the prices of the investments included in the portfolio.

10-113 The investments are registered in the name of a trustee, usually a bank or an insurance company, and the dividends from investments are, of course, received by the trustee. After the charges and expenses of the managers and the trustee have been deducted, distributions are made at stated intervals, usually half-yearly, to the holders of the units. Income tax is deducted at source, and therefore the sum which each investor receives is a net sum. If he is not liable to tax at the basic rate, he may submit a claim for refund to his Inspector of Taxes.

10-114 An investor may always realize his units, because the managers undertake to purchase all units offered to them. The price to be paid will depend upon the prices of the underlying investments. There is a difference between the price at which the managers buy back units (the 'bid price') and the price at which they sell them on again to new investors (the 'offer price'). Managers can, and do, make substantial profits from dealing in their units in this way, especially when the prices of the underlying securities are rising. The units are not usually saleable on a stock exchange, though the Stock Exchange does permit units to be granted an official quotation.[70]

10-115 Thus, the managers of a unit trust derive their profits from three sources: first from the initial charge which is made on newly created units, secondly from the annual service charge which is usually deducted from revenue before a distribution is made to unit-holders, and thirdly from dealing in their own units. The principal expenses incurred by the managers are in respect of office accommodation, salaries and wages, advertising, and the payment of commissions to banks, solicitors and other agents through whom applications for the purchase of units are submitted.

10-116 In October 1966, Lloyds Bank introduced its own unit trust. The managers of the trust are a wholly-owned subsidiary of the bank,

---

69 Some unit trusts, however, specialize in a particular industry, e.g. the Bank Unit Trust which, as its name implies, invests in bank shares.

70 See the Admission of Securities to Listing Rules, s. 10, para. 1. The first unit trust to be granted an official quotation (on 1 May 1951) was the 'M & G' General Trust Fund.

and the trustee is an insurance company. No commission is payable by the managers to agents in respect of the sale of these units. Most of the units are sold at branches of the bank, though investors may, if they wish, apply direct to the managers of the trust. Applications by unit-holders to sell their units may likewise be sent to any branch of the bank or direct to the managers.

10-116A Other clearing banks subsequently acquired interests in unit trusts. Thus the Westminster Bank, in association with Hambros Bank, established a unit trust management company. Martins Bank acquired a controlling interest in the Unicorn Unit Trust Group, and, after the merger between Barclays Bank and Martins Bank, this was renamed Barclays Unicorn Ltd. Unit trusts are also provided by the Trustee Savings Banks.

(b) Investment trusts

Unit trusts should not be confused with investment trusts. There are the following differences between them.

10-117 First, investment trusts are companies registered under the Companies Acts. They are formed for the purpose of holding a widespread range of investments. Unit trusts *are* trusts: the investments are registered in the name of a trustee.

10-118 Secondly, unlike unit trusts, investment trusts may have several classes of capital, such as debentures, preference shares and ordinary shares, which are usually quoted on the stock exchanges. This produces what is called 'gearing' in the case of the capital of an investment trust. 'Gearing' is a term used to describe the proportionate relationship between the fixed-interest securities (debentures and preference shares) and the ordinary shares of an investment trust. Suppose that there are £100 of ordinary shares, and £100 of debenture stock in an investment trust. The total investments held by the trust will be worth initially about £200, and the net assets, after deducting the debentures, will amount to about £100. If the value of the trust's investments rises by 50 per cent, so that they become worth £300, the whole appreciation will be attributable to the ordinary shareholders. The net assets, after deducting the debentures, will amount to £200. Therefore, the shareholders will see an increase of about 100 per cent in the value of their shares. By contrast, a unit-holder in a unit trust would see an increase in the value of his investment of only 50 per cent, because there is no gearing in a unit trust. Of course, if prices of investments fall, the value of investment trust shares will fall much more than the value of units in a unit trust.

10-119 Thirdly, the managers of a unit trust distribute the whole of the available income to unit-holders. Investment trusts are obliged to distribute not less than 85 per cent of their available income to shareholders;[71] they may retain up to 15 per cent for the purpose of re-investment or for equalizing fluctuations in future income.

10-120 Finally, shares of most investment trusts are quoted on the Stock Exchange. The price depends upon supply and demand, and it bears no fixed relation to the value of the underlying securities in which the capital is invested. With unit trusts, the price depends upon the value of the underlying securities and is calculated according to a formula laid down by the Department of Trade.

(c) National savings certificates

10-121 These certificates are a government security. Although no interest is actually remitted to the holder, the certificates increase in value, and this increase is free of income tax and capital gains tax. Whenever a new issue is made, the terms are altered in order to bring the effective return on the certificates into line with market rates of interest on government securities. The certificates are attractive to small savers who may wish to buy one or two certificates weekly or at other intervals. As the steady increase in the value of the certificates is not subject to tax, they are also attractive to wealthy investors who pay tax at a high rate. The certificates are sold by post offices, trustee savings banks and the joint-stock banks. There is a limit to the number of each issue of certificates which a person may hold. The certificates may always be encashed at short notice, together with any interest that may have accrued.

(d) Income bonds

10-122 These bonds, which are a government security, are subject to a minimum purchase of £2,000, and thereafter purchases may be made in multiples of £1,000. The maximum holding is £100,000. A certificate is issued in respect of each purchase. Interest is paid monthly without deduction of income tax, but is subject to income tax and must be included in the holder's tax return. A holder may have all or part of his holding repaid by giving three months' notice, provided that the amount to be repaid is a multiple of £1,000 and at least £2,000 remains invested.

(e) Capital bonds

10-122A These bonds, which are a government security, may be

71 Income and Corporation Taxes Act 1970, s. 359(1).

bought in multiples of £100, with no upper limit. They grow at fixed rates for five years. On each anniversary of purchase, interest is added to the value of the bond. At the end of five years the capital is repaid with all the added interest. The interest is taxable each year – even though the holder does not receive the interest each year – and the interest must be included in the holder's tax return. A holder may have all or part of his holding repaid by giving three months' notice, but the rate of return will be lower than it would have been if the holder had kept his bonds for the full five years.

(f) Premium bonds

10-123 These bonds are a government security. The minimum purchase is £100. The maximum holding is £10,000. Unlike other National Savings investments, they do not bear interest for the individual owners. Instead, a sum equivalent to interest is put into a prize fund and distributed by weekly and monthly prize draws. A bond first becomes eligible for the draw after it has been held for three clear months. The winning numbers are picked by 'ERNIE' (Electronic Random Number Indicator Equipment). The prizes are free of income tax and capital gains tax. The purchase price of a bond is repayable in full at short notice.

(g) 'Yearly Plan'

10-123A The Department for National Savings operates a contractual savings scheme whereby any person aged 7 or over may agree to save regular monthly sums, up to a maximum of £200 per month. He enters into an agreement to pay twelve monthly contributions. He will then be issued with a Yearly Plan Certificate. The rate of interest for the first year, and a higher rate of interest for the next four years, are notified to the investor on the day when his application is received by the Department. Thus rates of return are guaranteed over a period of five years, and interest is free of income tax and capital gains tax. The monthly payments may be made only under standing order mandate. The investor can carry on investing from year to year for as long as the Yearly Plan is on offer. Each year the Department writes to the investor quoting the relevant rates of interest, i.e. for the first twelve months and for the succeeding four years.

Investment advice

10-124 Customers sometimes ask bank officials to give them advice in regard to investment matters. In this connection, it is important to appreciate what a banker's duties are in this field. [72] A banker is expected to have a good, general knowledge of investment matters. For example, he is expected to be able to discuss the relative merits, on the one hand, of government securities and other similar securities which provide a fixed return on capital and, on the other hand, of good-class industrial shares which may be expected to provide a hedge against inflation. In this way, he will be able to bring to his customer's notice the different types of investment which are available. The customer may be seeking a short-term investment where security of capital is the paramount consideration, or he may be looking for a long-term investment which may be expected to increase in value over a period of years.

10-125 A preliminary discussion along these lines is valuable, because it enables the customer to indicate, with the banker's guidance, what his particular requirements are and what type of investment he is seeking. It may be that the customer will then ask for the names of *specific* stocks or shares which would meet his requirements. A bank does not usually hold itself out to give specific advice of this nature, and, for this reason, it is the practice to say that the bank will pass forward a statement of the customer's requirements to a firm of stockbrokers for attention. Stockbrokers are in much closer touch with market trends than are bank officials, and it is right that a customer should have the benefit of expert advice. Some banks have a subsidiary company which deals in stocks and shares, and a customer's business will usually be conducted by that company.

10-126 There is one type of investment which a banker should never, under any circumstances, bring to his customer's attention, namely the shares in a private company which are not quoted on any stock exchange. The risk of so doing may be illustrated by referring to the facts of two decided cases. In the first case, *Dunnicliffe* v. *Johnson and Another*, [73] the plaintiff sought to hold Barclays Bank and one of their cashiers named Mr Johnson liable for the latter's negligent advice. The plaintiff had placed her life's savings, about £1,130, on deposit with Barclays Bank, and Mr Johnson had advised her in regard to the investment of this money. He advised her to invest the money in a concern managed by a customer of the bank, and the plaintiff's life savings were lost. One of the questions which arose was whether Mr Johnson was acting in the course of the business of the bank when he gave this advice. It was held that he was not so acting, and therefore the bank was not

---

72 The Financial Services Act 1986 applies to all types of investment business. See *ante*, para. 1-93.

73 This case, which is unreported, was discussed by the late Mr Bernard Campion, KC in a lecture published in the *Journal of the Institute of Bankers*, Vol. LV (1934), p. 129.

liable in respect thereof. However, Mr Johnson was held personally liable for the negligent advice which he gave.

10-127   In a later case, *Woods* v. *Martins Bank Ltd and Another*,[74] the plaintiff asked one of the branch managers of Martins Bank for financial advice. The advice which he gave to the plaintiff was that a company called Brocks Refrigeration Ltd (which was a customer of the bank) was financially sound, and that an investment in its shares would be a wise one. There were in fact no grounds on which the manager could reasonably have advised that the company was in a sound or strong financial position, and still less could an investment in its shares be reasonably recommended as a wise one. Unknown to the plaintiff, the company had a considerable overdraft at the bank, and the District Head Office of Martins Bank had been pressing the manager to get it reduced. The plaintiff lost the sum of £14,800 which he invested in the company, and he claimed this sum from the bank and from the manager. Both defendants denied liability. One of the arguments advanced on behalf of the bank was that it was no part of its business as bankers to advise upon such financial transactions as the plaintiff had entered into. The learned judge, Salmon J, rejected this argument, and in doing so, referred to a booklet issued by Martins Bank, part of which read:

> If you want help or advice about investments, our managers will gladly obtain for you advice from the best available sources in such matters.

The learned judge observed that the 'best available source' in the present case was the bank itself, for they were the bankers for Brocks Refrigeration Ltd. The booklet continued:

> You may consult your bank manager freely and seek his advice on all matters affecting your financial welfare. All these advantages are yours as the possessor of a bank account. ...

10-128   Salmon J had no hesitation in finding, partly as a result of this booklet and partly for other reasons, that it was within the scope of the business of Martins Bank to advise on all financial matters. The advice to the plaintiff had been given without the ordinary care and skill that a bank manager should possess, and so both defendants, Martins Bank and the manager, were held liable for the loss arising from the investment in Brocks Refrigeration Ltd, namely £14,800.

10-129   The decision in the above-mentioned case holds no terrors for bank officials who act prudently. In the course of their duties, they quite frequently learn that some customers are in need of funds, and that

---

74 [1959] 1 QB 55; approved by Lord Devlin in *Hedley Byrne & Co. Ltd* v. *Heller & Partners Ltd* [1964] AC 465, at p. 530.

other customers have funds for investment. In essence, that was what had happened in *Woods'* case. The temptation to introduce a customer who is seeking capital to a customer who has funds to invest should be resisted.

10-129A   Section 13 of the Supply of Goods and Services Act 1982 provides that 'in a contract for the supply of a service where the supplier is acting in the course of a business, there is an implied term that the supplier will carry out the service with reasonable care and skill'. This provision applies to a bank when its officials give advice on investments.

Investment management service

10-130   Some banks offer to their customers an investment management service, which is available for investment portfolios above a prescribed minimum size, e.g. £10,000 or £50,000. Specialist officials in the bank are responsible for providing this service. The customer may elect whether the bank is to make purchases and sales of investments with his consent, or whether such changes are to be made without reference to him. In some instances, the customer's investments are transferred into the name of the bank's nominee company so that all communications from company registrars may be sent to the nominee company, which is thus able to deal with such matters as new issues of shares on the customer's behalf. The service is particularly useful for customers who are likely to reside overseas for a number of years. It is also utilized by wealthy investors at home who, for a variety of reasons, do not wish to be troubled with investment problems. The skilled management of the portfolio is an added attraction. A special fee is, of course, payable for this service, depending upon the size of the fund. Some of the merchant banks make a special feature of this type of work.

Section 7
ANCILLARY FINANCIAL SERVICES

In addition to the services already described in this book, many bankers provide a number of additional financial services, sometimes through subsidiary or affiliated companies.[75] It is convenient to classify these services under the following heads.

(a) Hire-purchase, credit sales, etc.

10-131   During the 1950s, hire-purchase finance companies expanded rapidly, and from time to time the banks were criticized for not making

75 See D. G. Hanson, *Service Banking* (3rd ed., 1987).

hire-purchase facilities available to their customers. In 1954, however, a solution was found. A Scottish bank purchased the entire share capital of a hire-purchase finance company. Then, in 1958, one of the clearing banks acquired a substantial interest in a hire-purchase finance company, and thereafter other banks quickly acquired similar interests. In the result, most of the clearing and Scottish banks, and some of the merchant banks, can provide their customers with the full range of services offered by hire-purchase finance companies, by referring the customer to the bank's own subsidiary or affiliated company. Those services include the hire-purchase of domestic goods and industrial equipment, credit sale of goods, finance for business expansion and for certain domestic purposes (such as, for example, the installation of central heating), and the leasing of industrial equipment. It is outside the scope of this book to describe these facilities in detail.

(b) Factoring

10-132 Factoring is a means of financing traders and manufacturers by taking over the collection of their customers' bills.[76] The factor either buys the book debts of his client or makes an advance against a charge over the debts. He then collects the money from his clients' customers direct. Sometimes the factor assumes the whole of the credit risk, but in other cases he stipulates for a right of recourse against his clients in case the debtors fail to pay. The factor receives a service charge for his services. This charge varies with the average number and value of the invoices, and the degree of credit risk. It is usually between one-half and two per cent on turnover, though it may be a little higher than this in the case of goods which are exported. As with hire-purchase, so too with factoring, the banks have refrained from offering these services themselves, but have preferred to acquire interests in factoring companies.

(c) Leasing

10-133 Leasing is a financial service whereby a bank or finance company buys a capital asset at a customer's request and hires or leases it to him at an agreed rental. The customer usually pays a rental for a 'primary' period which is related to the estimated working life of the equipment. The primary period may be as short as three years or as long as fifteen years, even longer in exceptional cases. At the end of the primary period the customer continues to use the equipment for a

---

76 On this subject, see F. R. Salinger, *Tolley's Factoring: A Guide to Factoring Practice and Law* (1984); F. R. Salinger, *Tolley's Factoring and the Lending Banker* (1986).

nominal rent. Some banks have established subsidiary 'leasing companies', whereas others offer the facility through their hire-purchase finance company.[77]

(d) Share registration services

10-134 Some banks are prepared to act as registrars to companies. They keep the share registers of the companies concerned, and they pay dividends to the shareholders.

(e) Estate agency

10-135 Some banks have acquired firms which conduct business as estate agents. This is often a useful introduction to other services, because a customer who has agreed to buy a house which was offered for sale by a bank through a subsidiary company may need to borrow money on mortgage and may also require insurance services.

---

77 Malcolm Craig, 'Lending? Why not lease?', *The Bankers' Magazine*, Vol. CCXXI (1977), pp. 41–7.

PART 3

Accounts of customers

11

Accounts of customers

In this chapter the various categories of customers will be considered, with special reference to the opening and operation of their accounts.

Section I
ACCOUNTS OF INDIVIDUAL CUSTOMERS

11-1   When application is made to a bank to open an account in the name of a private individual, there are four principal matters for consideration regarding the prospective customer, namely (a) whether he has authorized the opening of an account in his name, (b) whether he is the person he claims to be, (c) whether he is a proper person to conduct a banking account, and (d) whether he is employed by someone else and, if so, the name of his employers.

(a) Authority to open account

11-2   Usually, a prospective customer calls at the bank when he wishes to open an account. Occasionally, however, some third party states that he has been authorized to open an account for him. Requests of this nature should always be treated with caution. In this connection reference may be made to *Robinson* v. *Midland Bank Ltd*,[1] the amazing case concerning the Eastern potentate, whose name was a carefully guarded secret at the trial of the action, though it subsequently became known that he was Sir Hari Singh, a man of great wealth and the heir of the Maharajah of Kashmir.[2] Sir Hari had been found in 'compromising circumstances' in a Paris hotel with a Mrs Robinson. Her husband was a bookmaker, and it was he who brought these proceedings against the Midland Bank. Three persons conspired to obtain, and did obtain, from

---

1 (1925) 41 TLR 170, and, on appeal, 402. For some of the details, the present writer has drawn upon the daily report of the case published in *The Times*. For a somewhat similar case, see *Stoney Stanton Suppliers (Coventry) Ltd* v. *Midland Bank Ltd* [1966] 2 Lloyd's Rep 373, at pp. 382, 384 and 385.
2 See (1925) 41 TLR, at p. 403.

Sir Hari a cheque for £150,000, because of the circumstances referred to above. The jury found that Mr and Mrs Robinson were not parties to this conspiracy. It was stated during the hearing that the conspirators had obtained a second cheque, also for £150,000, but that cheque was never presented. The first cheque was an open one payable to a firm of solicitors, Appleton and Co. One of the conspirators, H, was a clerk employed by that firm. Although he had no authority from his employers to do so, he endorsed this cheque 'Pay to the order of Mr C. Robinson, Appleton & Co.' He then took it to the Kingsway, London, branch of the Midland Bank, where his employers banked, and said that he wanted to open an account with it for C. Robinson. He was allowed to do this. The cheque was specially cleared and paid. The following day, H presented for payment at the counter a cheque for £130,000 purporting to have been drawn by C. Robinson, but not in fact signed by him. The bank paid the cheque in £1,000 notes. The balance of the account was paid out later by cheques similarly drawn. H paid £25,000 of this money to Robinson, the plaintiff. Robinson said in evidence that he handed the money to his wife and left the room, saying that he would have nothing more to do with her. He said that he had instructed H, who had represented himself to be a solicitor, to institute proceedings for divorce, and he supposed that the £25,000 had been paid by way of compromise. When he discovered that the conspirators had in fact received a cheque for £150,000, and that an account had been opened in his name at the Midland Bank with this cheque, he sued the bank for the balance, namely £125,000, as money had and received to his use, or as damages for negligence.

11-3   The trial judge gave judgment for the defendant bank on the ground that the cheque for £150,000 was obtained by menaces, and belonged always to the drawer, and that it could not have become the property of the plaintiff. The Court of Appeal dismissed the plaintiff's appeal. Atkin LJ said that he thought that the cheque had never come into the possession of Appleton and Co. at all; but even if it had done so, that in itself did not give any right to the plaintiff, and it was necessary to show that Appletons had in fact endorsed the cheque to the plaintiff. The jury had been asked whether the endorsement to C. Robinson was written by some person as agent for Appleton and Co., and the answer was 'No'. The sole partner in Appleton and Co. had given evidence that he had no knowledge of the cheque, and the evidence was irresistible that the cheque had been endorsed by someone for the purpose of committing a fraud. It seemed clear that it was not an endorsement which was intended to pass any right to the plaintiff at all.

11-4   Although the Midland Bank succeeded in defeating the enormous claim brought against them, the case was a costly one so far as they were concerned: it was stated in court that they had paid £3,000 to one of the conspirators to persuade him to come to this country in order to give evidence of the conspiracy. The case stands as a warning against opening an account without taking steps to make certain that the prospective customer has *authorized* the opening of the account in his name. The bank should have required to see Robinson.

(b) The customer's identity

11-5 There have been very many cases where a dishonest person has succeeded in opening an account in an assumed name for the purpose of obtaining money to which he was not entitled. Thus, in *Ladbroke and Co.* v. *Todd*,[3] an account was opened by a banker for a stranger, who claimed to be the payee of a cheque which he produced. In fact, however, he had stolen an envelope containing the cheque from a pillar-box in which the letter had been posted. The banker did not ask for an introduction. The cheque was cleared, and the proceeds were withdrawn. The plaintiffs, who were the drawers of the cheque, took an assignment from the payee of his rights, if any, in the stolen cheque, and brought an action against the defendant banker to recover the proceeds as money had and received to their use. The claim succeeded; it was held that the defence based upon s. 82 of the Bills of Exchange Act 1882[4] failed, because the defendant had not taken reasonable precautions to safeguard the interests of persons who might be the true owners of the cheque.

11-6 A few years later, there was another case, *Hampstead Guardians* v. *Barclays Bank Ltd*,[5] where the bank was more cautious, yet still lost the action. A man who said he was Donald Stewart opened an account with £15 in cash at the Oxford Street branch of the defendant bank. Having been asked for a reference, he gave the name of a Mr Woolfe, with whom the bank communicated. A reply was received which purported to come from him and appeared to be satisfactory, but was in fact a forgery. Later, instruments payable to D. Stewart and Co. were paid into the account; the customer said that he traded under that name. In fact, they had been stolen from the plaintiffs by a temporary employee. The bank relied, by way of defence, upon s. 82 of the Bills of Exchange Act 1882, but the court held that the bank had been negligent in omitting to verify that the person describing himself as Donald Stewart was in reality Donald Stewart. The learned judge said that a mere reference to the London directory would have shown that there was no Donald Stewart at the address given.

3 (1914) 30 TLR 433.
4 See *ante*, para. 6-63.
5 (1923) 39 TLR 229.

11-7   At the present day, it is certainly the usual practice to try to verify the identity of a new customer if he wants to be permitted to pay in cheques for collection. It is, however, extremely difficult to check a person's identity, unless one employs an enquiry agent to visit the supposed addresses of the new customer and of his referee. Ideally, the prospective customer should be introduced by an established customer, upon whom the bank may rely. Often, however, this is impracticable. Accordingly in order to establish a person's identity when he applies to open an account, some banks ask him to produce a document such as his birth certificate, National Health medical card, passport, state pension book, or union card.[6] If for any reason it is not possible for him to establish his identity in this way, he will usually be required to provide a reference as in the past. However, this practice is well known to those who seek to open bank accounts for the purpose of clearing stolen cheques, and they experience no difficulty in providing a bogus referee. In order to try to combat these frauds, some banks require the referee to be vouched for by his bankers. Even this precaution may fail to reveal the frauds where the fraudulent party and his referee are one and the same person.

11-8   Thus, in *Nu-Stilo Footwear Ltd* v. *Lloyds Bank Ltd*[7] a man named Gerald Trevelyan Montague was employed by the plaintiffs as their secretary and accountant. He opened an account with Lloyds Bank in the fictitous name of 'Bauer'. He said that he was a freelance agent, and he gave the name of G. T. Montague as a referee. The bank subsequently telephoned Montague and asked whether 'Bauer' was a suitable person to have a banking account. Not surprisingly, Montague gave 'Bauer' a highly satisfactory reference. Lloyds Bank also telephoned Montague's bankers, who stated that Montague was a suitable person to give a reference. Lloyds Bank then wrote to Montague for confirmation, and Montague gave a written reply stating that 'Bauer' was a fit and proper person to conduct a banking account. Thus Lloyds Bank had done everything that they could reasonably have been expected to do when opening the account for 'Bauer'. The stage was now set for the frauds to begin. 'Bauer' proceeded to pass nine cheques for a total sum of £5,027 odd through his account. The cheques were all drawn by his employers, Nu-Stilo Footwear Ltd, and they were signed on behalf of the company by Montague and by a co-signatory. They were payable, in some cases to 'Bauer', and in other cases to third parties. 'Bauer' had no title to the cheques. The company claimed damages from the collecting bank, Lloyds Bank, for the conversion of the nine cheques. The

6 See *ante*, para. 6-103A.
7 (1956) *The Times*, 19 June 1956.

bank admitted the conversion, but they relied upon s. 82 of the Bills of Exchange Act 1882 by way of defence.

11-9 Sellers J gave judgment for the plaintiffs in respect of eight out of the nine cheques. He held that the bank had acted without negligence in opening the account and also in the collection of the first cheque. The cheque was apparently correct; it was made payable to the customer, was endorsed by him and, though for a substantial amount, it was not so large as to raise suspicion. The second cheque was for £550, and it was payable to a third party, who had apparently endorsed it to 'Bauer'. Without enquiry, the bank had credited that cheque to his account. In so doing, the learned judge had no hesitation in finding that the bank had departed from the ordinary standards of good banking. If the bank had made proper enquiry before collecting that cheque, the fraud of the customer would probably have been exposed, and so no further frauds could have been committed by the presentation of the further seven cheques.[8]

11-10 *Marfani & Co. Ltd* v. *Midland Bank Ltd*[9] was another case where, in spite of proper precautions taken by a bank, a dishonest person succeeded in opening an account in an assumed name. A Pakistani named K opened an account at the Midland Bank. He pretended that he was a Pakistani named E. He did this because he had in his possession a cheque for £3,000 payable to E, and he wanted to persuade the bank to collect the proceeds of the cheque for him. He realized that he would stand a much better chance of persuading the bank to do this for him if he pretended to be E, the payee of the cheque. The bank opened an account for him. He gave the bank the names of two Pakistanis as referees. The bank wrote to both, but only one replied, and his reply was favourable. K had introduced himself to that referee as E, so that the referee genuinely believed that he was E, and when the bank enquired of the referee concerning E, he still thought that K was E. When the proceeds of the cheque had been collected, K misappropriated them. The drawers of the cheque brought an action against the bank, which set up a defence under s. 4 of the Cheques Act 1957, alleging that they had received the proceeds of the cheque in good faith and without negligence. Both Nield J and the Court of Appeal decided this case in favour of the bank. They held that the bank had discharged the onus of showing that the bank had acted without negligence. It had been argued on behalf of the plaintiffs that the bank had not taken proper steps to identify the proposed customer, e.g. by asking to see the

---

8 For another case which emphasizes the danger of collecting third-party cheques without proper enquiry, see *Baker* v. *Barclays Bank Ltd* [1955] 1 WLR 822, *ante*, para. 6-126.
9 [1968] 1 WLR 956.

customer's passport. However, it was held that this was unnecessary.[10] As regards the failure of the second referee to reply, the court accepted the evidence of the securities clerk who opened the account. He said that the fact that only one referee replied did not cause him suspicion, because of the good standing of the one who did reply, and very often letters to Pakistanis were not replied to.

(c) The customer's integrity

11-11 The referee or person introducing the new customer should be in a position to identify him, and to say whether he is a fit and proper person to have a bank account. However, a trickster always seems to be able to provide a 'satisfactory', though bogus, reference, and so, from a purely practical standpoint, the main purpose of going through the motions of obtaining a 'satisfactory' reference concerning a trickster is to help the bank (if it is subsequently sued for damages for conversion of cheques paid into the account) to satisfy the court that it acted 'without negligence' when opening the account. By so doing, it may be able to defend the action successfully by pleading that it collected the proceeds of the cheques 'in good faith and without negligence' as required by s. 4 of the Cheques Act 1957.[11] If it fails to obtain what appears to be a satisfactory reference, this may well prevent the bank from establishing this defence.[12]

11-12 A secondary purpose of obtaining a satisfactory reference is to try to ensure that the new customer is a suitable person to be entrusted with a cheque book. It must be admitted, however, that a small proportion of new customers, even though properly introduced, do attempt to overdraw their accounts without permission. After first giving an appropriate warning to such a customer, the bank, as a last resort, may find it necessary to require him to close his account.[13]

(d) The customers' employers

11-13 The new customer should be asked whether he or she is employed and, if so, the nature of the employment and the name of the employers. If the new customer is a married woman, she should also be

---

10 In a later case, *Lumsden & Co.* v. *London Trustee Savings Bank* [1971] 1 Lloyd's Rep 114, Donaldson J commented adversely upon the failure of the defendant bank to request a customer 'newly arrived from abroad and to that extent liable to be more of an unknown quantity' to produce his passport for the purpose of obtaining confirmation of his identity.
11 See *ante*, para. 6-74.
12 *Lloyds Bank Ltd* v. *E. B. Savory & Co.* [1933] AC 201, at p. 221, *per* Lord Wright.
13 *Ante*, paras 3-6/13.

asked, in addition, whether her husband is employed and, if so, the name of his employers. The reason for these detailed enquiries is to put the bank on guard if the new customer should try to pay into his account cheques *payable to* his or her employers, or cheques *drawn by* the employers in favour of third parties, or if the new customer (being a married woman) should try to pay into her account cheques payable to, or drawn by, her husband's employers. Illustrations of such cases have been given in an earlier chapter. [14] The practical result, as far as the bank is concerned, is that if the enquiries are not made and the new customer pays into his or her account any cheques falling into the above-mentioned categories, the bank will almost certainly be liable in damages for conversion of the cheques and will be unable to rely upon s. 4 of the Cheques Act 1957.

11-14 Fortunately, there are many customers whose employment does not require them to handle their employer's cheques. The accounts which require the closest scrutiny are those of clerks and other office workers who do have the responsibility of dealing with such cheques. There have been countless cases where such persons have stolen or misappropriated their employers' cheques and paid them into a bank account.

11-15 If suspicious circumstances are observed, the most careful and painstaking enquiries should be made. An illustration of the uselessness of half-hearted enquiries is provided by the facts in *Harding* v. *London Joint Stock Bank Ltd.* [15] In that case, the new customer, a man named Francom, was a cashier and book-keeper, and he was properly introduced to the defendant bank by one of its existing customers. He wished to open an account with a cheque for £92 19s. 9d. payable to J. Bland, Smith-Harding and Co. The bank manager told Francom that the bank ought to have written confirmation that he was authorized to deal with the cheque, and asked *him* to get that confirmation. This was clearly a foolish course to follow. Francom went away and wrote a letter in the name of Bland, Smith-Harding and Co., who were his employers. The letter stated that the cheque was all right, and it referred to 'our Mr Francom'. It is hardly surprising that the plaintiff, who carried on business in the name of Bland, Smith-Harding and Co., succeeded in his claim against the defendant bank. The jury decided that the bank had not taken the reasonable and proper precautions which they ought to have taken.

14 *Ante*, paras 6-112/16.
15 (1914) *The Times*, 21 January.

Mandates and powers of attorney

11-16 Sometimes a customer wishes to authorize a third party to operate upon his account. In this connection, it is important to distinguish between a mandate and a power of attorney. A mandate, in this context, is a written instruction given by a customer to his banker, instructing the latter that a named third party is duly authorized to do certain acts on behalf of the customer, such as drawing cheques on his account. A power of attorney is a document, usually executed under seal, which authorizes one person (called the attorney, or donee, or grantee) to act on behalf of another person (called the donor, or principal, or grantor). The following differences between the two types of document may be noted.

11-17 First, a power of attorney is usually addressed to the world at large, starting with he words, 'Know all men by these presents ...' A mandate is usually addressed to one particular person.

11-18 Secondly, in view of the general application of a power of attorney, the donor cannot notify his decision to revoke it to everyone who might rely upon it; in this connection, the law makes special provision in favour of persons who rely upon a power in the honest belief that it has not been revoked. By contrast, a person who has signed a form of mandate may easily inform the person to whom it was addressed that the authority of the agent has been cancelled.

11-19 Thirdly, the general rule of English law is that where an agent is authorized to execute a deed on behalf of his principal, his authority must be given by an instrument under seal.[16] Thus, an attorney under a power of attorney may be empowered to execute deeds, e.g. legal mortgages, whereas an agent whose appointment is set out in a mandate cannot do so.

11-20 Attention will be directed to the main provisions of (a) mandates, and (b) powers of attorney, with special reference to the practice of bankers.

(a) Mandates

11-21 Most banks have a printed form of mandate. In this document the customer declares that, until he gives written notice to the contrary, a named person (whose signature appears on the mandate) is authorized to draw and endorse cheques on his behalf, notwithstanding that the debiting of any such instruments to his account may cause the account

---

16 *Berkeley* v. *Hardy* (1826) 5 B & C 355.

to be overdrawn. This latter provision is important, because authority to draw cheques does not necessarily confer power to overdraw the account. [17]

11-22 A number of optional clauses, one or more of which may be deleted in order to meet the wishes of the customer, confer power upon the agent (a) to receive cheques, statements and other vouchers relating to the account, (b) to draw, accept, make and endorse bills of exchange and promissory notes on behalf of the customer, (c) to withdraw from the bank securities or other property belonging to the customer, (d) to negotiate advances whether by way of loan, overdraft, discount or otherwise, and (e) to pledge or deposit with the bank any type of security for the repayment of such advances. As already indicated, this type of authority will not enable an agent to execute a deed on behalf of the customer, and therefore he will be unable to create a legal mortgage by way of security. [18]

11-23 As a general rule, all persons of sound mind, including minors, are competent to act as agents. [19]

11-24 The death of a principal at once puts an end to the authority of his agent, even though the agent was not aware of his death. [20] Therefore, as soon as a bank receives notice of a customer's death, the authority of an agent must be regarded as having terminated. Likewise, a mandate is determined by mental incapacity of the principal, for it is well established that when a principal can no longer act for himself, his agent can no longer act for him. [21] Again, a mandate is determined by the bankruptcy of the principal. As stated in an earlier chapter, [22] a banker's duty and authority to pay cheques drawn on him are usually determined when he learns of the presentation of a bankruptcy petition against the customer who drew them. Accordingly, when a bank learns of the presentation of a petition against the customer, no further cheques drawn by the agent should be paid.

11-25 The bankruptcy of an agent does not, of itself, determine the mandate in his favour, though the principal may, of course, wish to terminate his authority and to appoint a new agent. In the event of the

---

17 Cf. *Jacobs* v. *Morris* [1902] 1 Ch 816. Some banks have two forms of mandate, one of which authorizes the drawing of cheques, but does not confer power to overdraw the account.

18 *Ante*, para. 11-19.

19 See *post*, para. 11-53.

20 *Blades* v. *Free* (1829) 9 B & C 167; *Smout* v. *Ilbery* (1842) 10 M & W 1; *Pool* v. *Pool* (1889) 58 LJP 67; *Re Overweg, Haas* v. *Durant* [1901] 1 Ch 209.

21 *Drew* v. *Nunn* (1879) 4 QBD 661.

22 *Ante*, paras 3-40/41.

agent's death, cheques signed by him, but presented for payment after his death, may be honoured. If it becomes known that an agent is mentally disordered, his principal should be consulted with a view to the appointment of a new agent.

(b) Powers of attorney

11-26 Powers of attorney are of two main types, special and general. A special power is one given for a specific purpose. A general power usually confers very extensive powers upon the grantee. Both types are usually executed under seal, thus enabling the attorney to execute deeds on behalf of the donor.

11-27 A power often opens with a *preamble*, which recites the names, addresses and occupations of the parties and states the reason for the existence of the power. The *authority* is the main part of the document, specifying the extent of the delegation. The document ends with the *attestation*, being the signatures of the donor and the witnesses.

11-28 The Powers of Attorney Act 1971[23] provides that any instrument creating a power of attorney must be signed and sealed by, or by direction and in the presence of, the donor of the power.[24] Where it is signed and sealed by someone other than the donor, two other persons must be present as witnesses and they must attest the instrument.[25] This rule which enables someone other than the donor to execute the instrument was introduced in order to assist a person 'of perfectly sound mind but physically incapable of executing any document because of paralysis or other serious bodily injury'.[26] The Act further provides that a photocopy of a power of attorney, certified by the donor or by a solicitor or stockbroker, and any copy of a photocopy likewise certified, is sufficient proof of the existence and contents of the power.[27]

11-29 The Act enables a general power of attorney to be made in a very short form set out in a schedule to the Act.[28] This authorizes the donee of the power to do on behalf of the donor anything which he can lawfully do by an attorney. However, this provision does not apply to functions which the donor has as a trustee or personal representative or as a tenant for life or statutory owner under the Settled Land Act 1925.[29]

23 The Act gave effect to the recommendations of the Law Commission's Report on Powers of Attorney: Law Com. No. 30; Cmnd. 4473.
24 S. 1(1).
25 S. 1(2).
26 Law Com. No. 30, para. 28.
27 S. 3.
28 S. 10(1) and Sched. 1.
29 S. 10(2).

11-30 When a power of attorney, or a photocopy thereof, executed by a customer is exhibited to his bankers, they will wish to satisfy themselves that the following requirements have been complied with.

11-31 First, the power must appear to have been validly executed. Occasionally, difficulties arise if the customer is old and verging on senility. It is prudent in such cases to have the power witnessed by the customer's doctor, who should certify that the customer understands the nature and effect of the document. However, it should be appreciated that the power would be revoked by the subsequent mental incapacity of the customer and that the Powers of Attorney Act 1971 did not remedy the situation. The Enduring Powers of Attorney Act 1985 established a procedure for appointing an attorney who can manage a person's affairs even after that person has become mentally incapable.[30]

11-32 Secondly, the person claiming to be the attorney must in fact be the person named in the power.

11-33 Thirdly, a true copy of the instrument creating the power must be supplied to the bank.

11-34 Finally, the powers conferred upon the attorney must cover the transaction which he wishes to enter into. This last-mentioned point occasionally gives rise to difficulty, because powers are strictly construed by the courts.[31] One way of overcoming the difficulty is by requesting the customer to execute the bank's standard form of mandate, which is specifically adapted to banking transactions. Alternatively, the customer may execute a general power of attorney under the Powers of Attorney Act 1971 which, as stated above,[32] will enable the donee of the power to do on behalf of the customer anything which he could lawfully do by an attorney.

Revocation of powers

11-35 Subject to the Powers of Attorney Act 1971, a power may be revoked (a) where any time limit is expressed in the power and that time has elapsed, (b) where the object expressed in the power has been attained, (c) when the donor revokes the power, (d) upon the death, bankruptcy or mental incapacity of the donor, (e) upon the mental incapacity of the attorney, and (f) when the attorney renounces his powers by giving notice to the donor.

11-36 The Powers of Attorney Act 1971 provides that, where a power of attorney is expressed to be irrevocable and is given to secure *either*

---

30 *Post*, paras 11-38A *et seq.*
31 See, for example, *Bryant, Powis and Bryant Ltd* v. *La Banque du Peuple* [1893] AC 170.
32 *Ante*, para. 11-29.

a proprietary interest of the donee *or* the performance of an obligation owed to him, then, so long as the interest or obligation continues, the power cannot be revoked (a) by the donor, without the consent of the donee, or (b) by the death, incapacity or bankruptcy of the donor or, if the donor is a body corporate, by its winding up or dissolution.[33] An example arises where an equitable mortgage of a legal estate is made by deposit of title deeds, accompanied by a memorandum of deposit. The memorandum frequently contains a power of attorney authorizing the lender to sell the property if the borrower defaults.[34] The lender has a proprietary interest in the land, and so the power cannot be revoked whilst the interest lasts.

11-37 As a general rule, powers which have not been given by way of security may be revoked at any time by the donor and they will be automatically revoked by his death, unsoundness of mind or bankruptcy. In order to protect the donee, the Powers of Attorney Act 1971 provides that a donee of a power who acts in pursuance of the power at a time when it has been revoked incurs no liability if at that time he did not know that the power had been revoked.[35]

11-38 Third parties are also protected. The Act provides that where a power has been revoked and a person, without knowledge of the revocation, deals with the donee of the power, the transaction between them is to be as valid as if the power had then been in existence.[36]

Enduring powers of attorney

11-38A Until the Enduring Powers of Attorney Act 1985 came into operation, it was impossible to create a power of attorney which would survive the mental incapacity of the donor. The Act, which implemented a recommendation of the Law Commission in its Report *The Incapacitated Principal*,[37] established a procedure for appointing an attorney who can manage a person's affairs even after that person has become mentally incapable. In this book it is not intended to give a full account of the provisions of the Act. The following paragraphs contain a brief account of some of its main provisions.

11-38B Section 1(1) of the Act provides that where an individual creates a power of attorney which is an 'enduring power' within the meaning of the Act, the power will not be revoked by any subsequent mental incapacity of his. Upon such incapacity supervening, the section

33 S. 4(1).
34 See J. Milnes Holden, *Securities for Bankers' Advances* (7th ed., 1986), para. 3-11.
35 S. 5(1).
36 S. 5(2).
37 Law Com. No. 122, Cmnd. 8977.

provides that the donee of the power may not do anything under the authority of the power except as directed or authorized by the court under s. 5 unless or until the instrument creating the power is registered by the court under s. 6. However, s. 1(2) provides that where the attorney has applied for registration of the instrument, then, until the application has been initially determined, the attorney may take action under the power (a) to maintain the donor or prevent loss to his estate, or (b) to maintain himself or other persons as laid down in the Act. Prior to the donor's incapacity, an enduring power will operate in the same way as an ordinary power of attorney, subject to the specific points concerning scope of authority provided by the Act.

11-38C   Section 2(1) of the Act provides that a power of attorney is an 'enduring power' if the instrument which creates it (a) is in the prescribed form, and (b) was executed in the prescribed manner by the donor and the attorney, and (c) incorporated at the time of execution by the donor the prescribed explanatory information. An enduring power of attorney must be in the exact form prescribed by the Enduring Powers of Attorney (Prescribed Form) Regulations 1986. A blank form can be purchased from any stationer who supplies legal forms. The form must be completed by the donor and by the attorney in the manner prescribed by the form. It must be signed by each of them and witnessed. The donor and the attorney do not have to sign it at the same time, but clearly the donor should sign first. Although it is not essential it is advisable for donors and attorneys to seek legal advice.

11-38D   Section 3(1) of the Act provides that an enduring power may confer general authority on the attorney to act on the donor's behalf in relation to all or a specified part of the property and affairs of the donor, or it many confer on him authority to do specified things on the donor's behalf. Section 3(4) provides that, subject to any restrictions contained in the instrument, an attorney under an enduring power, whether general or limited, may act under the power so as to benefit himself or other persons than the donor to the following extent, namely (a) he may so act in relation to himself or in relation to any other person if the donor might be expected to provide for his or that person's needs respectively, and (b) he may do whatever the donor might be expected to do to meet those needs. Section 3(5) provides that the attorney may make gifts, such as birthday or marriage gifts, to anyone, including himself, and also gifts to any charity to whom the donor might have been expected to make gifts.

11-38E   Section 4 of the Act provides that, if the attorney under an enduring power has reason to believe that the donor is or is becoming mentally incapable, the attorney must make an application for the registration of the instrument creating the power. The application is made to the Court of Protection. Before making an application for registration the attorney must comply with the provisions as to notice set out in Sched. 1. This schedule contains a list of those relatives of the donor who are entitled to receive notice of the application. Section 6 of the Act provides that if a valid notice of objection to the registration is received by the court, the court must make such enquiries as it thinks appropriate.

11-38F Bankers may be affected by the Act in at least two ways. First, an elderly customer may be advised by the members of his family or by his solicitor to make provision for his possible mental incapacity by appointing an attorney under an enduring power. If and when the power comes into operation, the customer's bank account will be conducted by his attorney. Secondly, by virtue of s. 2(7) of the Act, an attorney may be either (a) an individual who has attained eighteen years and is not a bankrupt, or (b) a trust corporation. Accordingly, a bank may be appointed as an attorney under an enduring power, though in practice the donor would usually prefer to appoint a close relative.

11-38G In two reported cases[38] the question arose whether an enduring power of attorney executed by a donor was valid. In both cases there was evidence that when they executed the powers, the donors fully understood the nature and effect of the power, but on account of recurrent mental disability, they could not be said to be capable of managing and administering their property. In the case of one donor, certain of her relatives objected to the registration of the power, and the Master refused to register it, whereupon the applicant for registration appealed. The Master also referred the application to register the other power to the judge to be heard with the appeal. It was held by Hoffman J that both powers would be directed to be registered. The judge said that an enduring power executed pursuant to the 1985 Act was not rendered invalid by reason of the fact that, at the time of execution of the power, the donor was incapable by reason of mental disorder from managing his or her property and affairs. The test of validity of the power was whether at the time of execution the donor understood the nature and effect of the power and not whether the donor would have been able to perform all the acts which the power authorized. On the facts, both donors had understood at the time when they had executed the powers of attorney the nature and effect of the power, although they were both incapable of managing their affairs.

---

38 In *re K and re F (Enduring Powers of Attorney)* [1988] Ch 310.

Section 2
ACCOUNTS OF MINORS

11-39 The Family Law Reform Act 1969 provides that the age of majority is eighteen, instead of twenty-one.[39] It also provides that a person attains a particular age at the first moment of the relevant birthday,[40] and that a person under eighteen may be termed a 'minor', rather than an 'infant'.[41]

11-40 It is beyond the scope of this book to give a full account of the contractual capacity of minors. Briefly, a minor is bound to pay a reasonable price for necessaries ordered by and supplied to him,[42] though he is not liable upon a cheque given by him in respect of those necessaries.[43] Moreover, a minor is liable upon contracts which, though not for necessaries, are nevertheless for the minor's benefit, such as service contracts.[44]

11-41 Then there are certain contracts which are declared by s. 1 of the Infants Relief Act 1874 to be 'absolutely void', namely contracts entered into for the repayment of money lent or to be lent or for goods supplied or to be supplied (other than necessaries), and all accounts stated. These contracts are, however, not entirely without effect. Thus, where goods which are not necessaries have been supplied to a minor under such a contract, the property passes to him;[45] and where a minor has paid for something and has consumed or used it, he cannot recover back the money which he paid.[46]

11-42 As regards loans, s. 5 of the Betting and Loans (Infants) Act 1892 provides that if a person who during infancy had contracted a loan which is void, agrees *after attaining full age* to pay any money which in whole or in part represents or is agreed to be paid in respect of the loan and is not a new advance, the agreement, and any negotiable or other instrument given for carrying into effect the agreement or otherwise in relation to the payment of money in respect of the loan is, so far as it represents or is payable in respect of the loan, absolutely void.

11-43 Next, there are certain contracts of continuing liability, such as contracts of tenancy or partnership or membership of a company, which

39 S. 1.
40 S. 9.
41 S. 12.
42 Sale of Goods Act 1979, s. 3(2); *Nash* v. *Inman* [1908] 2 KB 1.
43 *Re Soltykoff, Ex parte Margrett* [1891] 1 QB 413, at p. 415.
44 *Clements* v. *London and North Western Railway Co.* [1894] 2 QB 482.
45 *Stocks* v. *Wilson* [1913] 2 KB 235, at pp. 246, 247.
46 *Valentini* v. *Canali* (1889) 24 QBD 166.

bind a minor, unless he expressly repudiates them during minority or within a reasonable time after coming of age. In regard to these contracts, however, although a minor may repudiate them and so avoid a future liability, he cannot recover back money which he has paid.[47]

11-44 Finally, there is a fourth class of contracts, which is really a residuary class, comprising those contracts not falling within one of the preceding categories: for example, where a minor contracts to have a house built. Although a minor may sue upon these contracts, he may not be sued upon them. Furthermore, s. 2 of the Infants Relief Act 1874 applies to these contracts. It provides that no action may be brought to charge any person upon any promise made after full age to pay any debt contracted during infancy or upon any ratification made after full age of any promise or contract made during infancy, even though new consideration is given for such ratification. It has been held under this section that no action may be brought against a person who, after attaining full age, accepts a bill in respect of a debt incurred during infancy.[48] Likewise, no action may be brought against a person who, during infancy, drew and issued a cheque post-dated with a date subsequent to the attainment of majority.[49]

11-45 The English courts have never had to decide into which of the above-mentioned four classes of contracts the ordinary contract of banker and customer should be placed, i.e. in those cases where a minor's account is maintained in credit. Very probably, such a contract falls into the fourth class; that is to say, a minor may sue, but may not be sued upon the contract.[50] Accordingly, if a banker acts in breach of his duty of secrecy or wrongfully dishonours cheques drawn by a minor, he will be liable in damages to the same extent as if his customer was of full age. The fact that a banker is probably unable to sue a minor is of little practical importance, because, if the account is maintained in credit, there is no occasion for a banker to wish to sue him. The payment of cheques drawn by such a customer does not seem to place a banker in jeopardy, for s. 22(2) of the Bills of Exchange Act 1882 provides that where a bill (and this includes a cheque) is drawn by an infant, the drawing entitles the holder to receive payment.

---

47 *Steinberg* v. *Scala (Leeds) Ltd* [1923] 2 Ch 452.
48 *Smith* v. *King* [1892] 2 QB 543. An Irish court, however, has held that a holder in due course may sue the acceptor of a bill given for a debt incurred during infancy, but accepted by the latter after attaining full age: *Belfast Bank Co.* v. *Doherty* (1879) 4 LR Ir 124.
49 *Hutley* v. *Peacock* (1913) 30 TLR 42.
50 It is possible, however, that in modern conditions the court might regard the contract as one for necessaries. A good deal might depend on the particular circumstances.

11-46   In practice, a cheque book is not issued to a customer until he reaches about sixteen or seventeen years of age. Prior to that age, there can be no risk in conducting a deposit account or a savings account for him, provided that he has the capacity to understand the nature of the transactions. Such an account could, therefore, be opened for a child of about seven years of age and upwards. A question which has been debated is whether a customer of such tender years could give a valid receipt or discharge for money paid to him by a bank. It would clearly be inequitable if the law allowed a young person to withdraw his bank balance and then, after attaining full age, to claim the money a second time, on the ground that the receipt which he gave whilst a minor was invalid. Fortunately, the law seems to lean against such an absurdity. Thus, Lord Mansfield once observed that if an infant receives rents, he cannot demand them again when of age.[51] The same rule would probably be applied if an infant received money from his bank. There is an express statutory rule governing withdrawals from trustee savings banks.[52] It provides than an application for the withdrawal of money deposited by, or in the name of, a minor may be made by the minor, if he has attained the age of seven years.

11-47   Prior to the age of seven, an account for the benefit of a child may be opened in the name of a person of full age 'Re A.B., a minor'. The person of full age is, of course, the customer, and he is the only person who may operate the account.

Lending to minors

11-48   The position with regard to an overdrawn account in the name of a minor is clear. Repayment cannot be enforced as against him,[53] even if he obtained the advance by a false representation that he was of full age.[54] Any promise made by him after attaining full age to repay the advance is void.[55]

11-49   The general rule is that any security given by a minor for an advance is void.[56] It does not follow, however, that the security is necessarily worthless. Thus in *Nottingham Permanent Benefit Building Society* v. *Thurstan*,[57] a minor borrowed money from the society to

---

51 *Earl of Buckinghamshire* v. *Drury* (1762) 2 Eden 60, at p. 70.
52 Trustee Savings Bank Regulations 1972, r. 4.
53 Infants Relief Act 1874, s. 1.
54 *R. Leslie Ltd* v. *Sheill* [1914] 3 KB 607.
55 Betting and Loans (Infants) Act 1892, s. 5.
56 Infants Relief Act 1874, s. 1.
57 [1903] AC 6.

enable her to buy land and complete houses which were being built on it. The society discovered that she was a minor and discontinued the advances which they had been making, took possession of the property, and spent money on it. The borrower attained full age and brought an action against the society claiming a declaration that the mortgage was void, delivery of the title deeds and possession of the property. The House of Lords held that, although the Infants Relief Act 1874 rendered the loan and the mortgage absolutely void, nevertheless the society had a right, by virtue of the doctrine of subrogation, to stand in the shoes of the vendor. In the result, the society was entitled to a lien upon the houses for the amount of the purchase money and expenses paid by the society on completion of the purchase of the property, with interest at 4 per cent.

11-50 In those rare instances when an advance is made to a minor by a bank, it is usual to obtain by way of security a guarantee executed by a person of full age.[58]

11-51 If money is lent to a minor to enable him to provide himself with necessaries he cannot give a binding security for it;[59] but if the loan is actually spent upon the purchase of the necessaries, the lender is subrogated to the rights of the seller, and the lender is allowed in equity the same right of recovery as the seller would have possessed if he had not been paid.[60] No banker, however, would knowingly lend money in reliance upon this rule.

Other transactions involving minors

11-52 A minor may witness a document, provided, of course, that he is old enough to know what is required of him: he must know that the person whose signature he is witnessing is the person named in the document.

11-53 A minor may act as an agent, and in so doing may bind his principal.[61] It follows, therefore, that a minor may be authorized by a customer to operate upon his banking account, even though this causes the account to become overdrawn, or causes an existing overdraft to be

58 See J. Milnes Holden, *Securities for Bankers' Advances* (7th ed., 1986), para. 19-44.
59 *Martin* v. *Gale* (1876) 4 Ch D 428; *Walkden* v. *Hartley and Cavell* (1886) 2 TLR 767; *Walter* v. *Everard* [1891] 2 QB 369, at p. 372.
60 *Re National Permanent Benefit Building Society, Ex parte Williamson* (1869) 5 Ch App 309, at p. 313; *Lewis* v. *Alleyne* (1888) 4 TLR 560.
61 *Smally* v. *Smally* (1700) 1 Eq Cas Abr 283.

increased. However, it would be very unusual to give such authority to a person under the age at which majority is now attained. [62]

11-54 A minor may become a partner, and his acts will bind the firm of which he is a member. [63] Accordingly, he may be authorized to operate upon the firm's banking account. He does not, however, incur any personal liability, during his minority, for the debts of the firm; but the adult partner is entitled to insist that the partnership assets must be applied in payment of the liabilities of the partnership, and that until these are provided for, no part of them shall be received by the partner who is a minor. [64] It has already been observed that a minor may repudiate the partnership agreement during minority or within a reasonable time after coming of age.

11-55 A legal estate in land cannot be held by a minor. [65]

11-56 As regards stocks and shares, it has already been noted that a minor may repudiate his membership and his holding in a company, either during minority or within a reasonable time after attaining full age. [66] If shares are transferred into the name of a minor, the transferor remains liable for calls in respect of the shares, [67] whether at the time of the transfer he was aware of the minority of the transferee or not; [68] if, however, he was ignorant of it, he may claim to have his liability transferred to the person who effected the transaction. [69] It follows, therefore, that there are objections to the registration of shares in the name of a minor, more especially if the shares are partly paid. If, however, the shares are fully paid, there seems to be no good reason why they should not be transferred into the name of a minor, and this is in fact occasionally done.

11-57 A minor may be appointed executor, but cannot validly act as such and is not entitled to probate until he attains full age. If a minor is appointed sole executor, administration with the will annexed will be granted to his guardian or to such other person as the court thinks fit, until the minor attains full age. [70] If adult executors are appointed jointly with an infant, they can, of course, execute the will.

---

62 *Ante*, para. 11-39.
63 *Lovell and Christmas* v. *Beauchamp* [1894] AC 607.
64 *Lovell and Christmas* v. *Beauchamp* [1894] AC 607.
65 Law of Property Act 1925, s. 1(6).
66 *Ante*, para. 11-43.
67 *Weston's Case* (1870) 5 Ch App 614.
68 *Capper's Case* (1868) 3 Ch App 458.
69 *Brown* v. *Black* (1873) 8 Ch App 939.
70 Supreme Court of Judicature (Consolidation) Act 1925, s. 165(1).

11-58 As a general rule, a minor may not make a valid will.[71] However, soldiers, sailors and airmen while in actual military service and seamen at sea (under any conditions) enjoy special privileges. Thus, they may make wills, even though they are not of age.[72]

11-59 A minor may be made bankrupt, but only if the petition is based upon an enforceable debt.[73]

Section 3
ACCOUNTS OF MARRIED WOMEN

11-60 The old Court of Chancery used to give special protection to married women, largely because of their servile position at common law. Consequently, the older legal textbooks devoted considerable space to married women, often treating them (rather quaintly perhaps) between chapters on infants and lunatics.

11-61 During the last hundred years, however, the legal position of married women has changed radically. In general, a married woman is now:

(a) capable of acquiring, holding and disposing of any property; and
(b) capable of rendering herself, and being rendered, liable in respect of any tort, contract, debt or obligation; and
(c) capable of suing and being sued, either in tort or in contract or otherwise; and
(d) subject to the law relating to bankruptcy and to the enforcement of judgments and orders, in all respects as if she were a *feme sole*.[74]

11-62 When a bank is asked to open an account for a married woman, the usual steps should be taken in order to establish her identity and her integrity.[75] She should be asked whether she is employed and, if so, the nature of her employment and the name of her employers. In addition, she should be asked whether her husband is employed, and, if so, the name of his employers. The reason for making these enquiries has already been stated.[76]

---

71 Wills Act 1837, s. 7.
72 Wills Act 1837, s. 11; Wills (Soldiers and Sailors) Act 1918, ss 1, 2, 5(2).
73 *Re a Debtor (No. 564 of 1949), Ex parte Commissioners of Customs and Excise* v. *Debtor* [1950] Ch 282.
74 Law Reform (Married Women and Tortfeasors) Act 1935, s. 1. A *feme sole* is an unmarried woman.
75 *Ante*, paras 11-5/12.
76 *Ante*, paras 11-13/15.

11-63 Before a married women executes a guarantee or deposits security in favour of her husband or of some company in which he is interested, she should receive independent legal advice. The reason for this precaution is to make certain that the transaction will not be set aside for 'undue influence'.[77] There is no initial presumption of undue influence as between husband and wife, but the very nature of the relationship between the parties makes it far more likely that undue influence may be proved than in a transaction between, say, two businessmen. Some banks carry the matter further: they require that a married woman should receive independent legal advice when she executes a guarantee or deposits security in favour of any third party. In all cases where independent legal advice is given to a married woman, the solicitor should first explain the nature of the liability to her. He should then witness her signature to the document and add a note to the effect that he has explained to her the nature and implications of the transaction.

11-64 When a woman informs her bank of her marriage, it is usual to call for production of her marriage certificate. The reason for this precaution is to guard against the type of fraud where a spinster steals cheques payable to a married woman. The spinster calls at the bank and falsely states that she has recently married, and that the cheques which she produces and tenders for collection are payable to her in her married name.

Section 4
JOINT ACCOUNTS

11-65 A joint account, for the purpose under discussion, is a bank account conducted with two or more parties who are neither partners, nor executors, nor administrators, nor trustees. Husband and wife very frequently open a joint bank account, but joint accounts may, of course, be opened by others who may, or may not, be related to each other.

11-66 When application is made to a bank to open a joint account, the same four questions arise as have already been noted when opening an account for an individual,[78] namely the questions relating to the customers' authority, identity, integrity and employment. In practice, one often finds that one of the parties to a new joint account is already well known to the bank, in which case his introduction of the other or others will usually be considered sufficient to establish their identity and integrity.

---

77 See J. Milnes Holden, *Securities for Bankers' Advances* (7th ed., 1986), para. 20-3.
78 *Ante*, para. 11-1.

Mandate for joint account

11-67 Before a joint account is opened, it is usual for the bank to supply the proposed customers with a printed form for completion. This form will embody the instructions of the account-holders to the bank, and it is commonly referred to as a 'mandate for joint account'. Some of the clauses in this mandate contain alternative provisions, so that the customers may select those provisions which satisfy their requirements. A well-drawn mandate for joint account (for two parties) might include the following provisions, though some banks prefer to employ a much shorter document.

11-68 *Clause 1.* The customers request the bank to open or continue an account or accounts in their joint names and, at any time subsequently, to open such further account or accounts in their joint names as *both/either*[79] of them may direct.

11-69 *Clause 2.* The customers authorize the bank to debit to such account or accounts any cheques, bills of exchange, promissory notes, or order for payment drawn, accepted, or made by *both/either* of them, and to carry out any instructions in connection with the account or accounts (save as otherwise expressly provided) given by *both/either* of them, notwithstanding that this may cause such account or accounts to be overdrawn or any overdraft thereon to be increased.

11-70 *Presumption against delegation of authority.* If the parties do not expressly authorize the bank to act on one signature, cheques and other orders must be signed by all the parties to a joint account. As was said by Maule J in the course of argument in *Husband* v. *Davis*:[80]

> It is part of the law merchant that bankers shall not pay to one of several jointly interested, without the consent of the others, except by an express agreement.

Then in the course of his judgment in the same case, the learned judge said:[81]

> It is a general rule that a man may pay a debt to one of several persons with whom he has contracted jointly. In the case of a banker he cannot do so; but that arises from the particular contract which exists between him and his customer.

11-71 *Forgery of cheques drawn on joint account.* If the mandate provides that cheques etc. must be signed by two or more parties to the

79 One of these will be deleted, here and elsewhere in the mandate.
80 (1851) 20 LJCP 118, at p. 120.
81 *Ibid.*

account, and if the signature of any such party on a cheque is forged, the bank will not be entitled to debit the amount of such cheque to the account.[82]

11-72 *Clause 3.* The customers authorize the bank to carry out instructions countermanding payment of cheques, bills of exchange, promissory notes or orders for payment when such instructions are given by any one of them.

11-73 It is generally assumed that one joint account holder has power to countermand payment of a cheque drawn on the account.[83] Strictly speaking, however, this depends upon the proper construction of the mandate in the particular case, and it is prudent to deal expressly with this matter.

11-74 *Clause 4.* The customers authorize the bank to place to the credit of such account or accounts all amounts, including dividends, interest and capital sums arising from securities received or collected by the bank for the credit of *both/either* of them.

11-75 This covers the situation which arises where, for example, a husband and wife open a joint account, and dividends in favour of one or both of the parties individually are remitted direct to the bank. If it is desired that such dividends be placed to the credit of the joint account, the word 'both' in this clause should be deleted.

11-76 *Clause 5.* The customers authorize the bank to make advances, with or without security, on the request of *both/either* of them by way of overdraft, loan or in any other manner, and to discount bills and promissory notes on the request of *both/either* of them.

11-77 *Clause 6.* The customers agree that any liability whatsoever incurred by them to the bank shall be joint and several.

11-78 The alternative to 'joint and several' liability would be 'joint' liability, but joint liability would not be acceptable to the bank, because the death of a person who was jointly (as opposed to jointly and severally) liable would release him and his estate from all liability to the

---

82 *Jackson* v. *White and Midland Bank Ltd* [1967] 2 Lloyd's Rep 68. See also *Twibell* v. *London Suburban Bank* [1869] WN 127. The decision to the contrary in *Brewer* v. *Westminster Bank Ltd* [1952] 2 All ER 65 cannot be regarded as sound. It was doubted in *Welch* v. *Bank of England* [1955] Ch 508, at p. 532, and in *Arden* v. *Bank of New South Wales* [1956] VLR 569, and not followed in *Jackson* v. *White and Midland Bank Ltd., supra,* or in *Catlin* v. *Cyprus Finance Corporation (London) Ltd* [1983] 1 All ER 809. See the note by Professor A. L. Goodhart in *Law Quarterly Review*, Vol. 68 (1952), p. 446.

83 See, for example, *Questions on Banking Practice* (11th ed., 1978), p. 130, Question 373.

bank. Although this is the generally accepted view,[84] there is an argument to the contrary based upon the Law Reform (Miscellaneous Provisions) Act 1934, which provides that on the death of any person, after the commencement of the Act, all causes of action subsisting against or vested in him, survive against, or, as the case may be, for the benefit of, his estate.[85] There is much force in this argument but, until the point has been decided by the courts, it is perhaps safer to assume that when a person who is jointly liable dies, his liability ceases.

11-79   *Clause 7.* The customers authorize the bank to deliver up on the instructions of *both/either* of them any securities, deeds, boxes and parcels and their contents and property of any description held in their joint names.

11-80   *Clause 8.* The customers authorize the bank to hold, on the death of either of them, any credit balance on any account in their joint names and any securities, deeds, boxes and parcels and their contents and property of any description held in their joint names, to the order of the survivor. This clause, known as the survivorship clause, will be examined later.

11-81   *Clause 9.* The customers agree that the instructions given by them in the mandate are to remain in force until written revocation thereof by them or either of them.

11-82   This is a useful clause. It provides, among other things, for the situation which may arise when for example two persons open a joint account and authorize the bank to honour cheques and other instruments signed by either of them. Then they have some disagreement, and one of them wants to revoke this authority. He may do so, pursuant to clause 9, by giving written notice to the bank. It follows, of course, that the bank should give immediate notice to the other joint-account holder.

Death of joint-account holder

When a party to a joint account dies, the problems which may arise may be considered under two headings, (a) problems concerning the relationship of banker and customer, and (b) problems concerning the relationship of the parties to the account *inter se.*

(a) Problems concerning relationship of banker and customer

11-83   Most modern mandates for joint accounts contain a survivorship clause. The purpose of the clause is to state the terms of the contract

---

84 See, for example, *Halsbury's Laws of England* (4th ed.), Vol. 9, p. 428.
85 S. 1(1). On this point, see Glanville L. Williams, *Joint Obligations* (1949), p. 72.

governing the operation of the account, and to specify the person or persons to whom the bank may properly pay the balance when one of the joint-account holders dies.

11-84 The leading case of *McEvoy* v. *Belfast Banking Co. Ltd*[86] shows how imprudent it is for a bank to ignore the clear terms of a survivorship clause. In the result, the bank suffered no loss, but that was because of the special facts of the case. A man named John McEvoy deposited £10,000 in the joint names of himself and his son, who was then fifteen years of age. The deposit receipt bore the words 'payable to either or survivor'. The father was in failing health, and the object of the deposit in joint names – as is often the case – was to try to avoid death duties. A few months after opening the joint account the father died, leaving the residue of his estate in trust for his son upon attaining the age of twenty-five. In spite of the terms of the deposit receipt, the father's executors managed to obtain repayment from the bank of the deposit of £10,000, and then they redeposited the money in their own names. The deceased's business was carried on by the executors, and the son, who by this time had reached the age of seventeen, began to take an active part in its management. The business account of the executors was continually overdrawn, and the practice of the executors was to pay off the overdrafts out of the £10,000. They continued to do this until that fund was exhausted. On attaining twenty-five, the son claimed the sum of £10,000 from the bank, on the ground that by the terms of the deposit receipt, he was the proper person to have received payment on his father's death, and that the bank had no right to pay the money to the executors. The claim failed. The House of Lords held that the son had failed to establish his case, but the bank was nevertheless strongly criticized for its conduct. Thus Lord Warrington stated that the bank had decided the matter for themselves without taking any care to protect the interests of the deceased's infant son. The proper course, his Lordship stated, would have been either to institute proceedings making the executors and the infant by his guardian *ad litem* defendants, and asking for directions as to the disposal of the money, or to refuse to act except under the directions of the court, leaving the executors or the infant to institute the necessary proceedings.

11-85 Occasionally, a joint account is opened although no mandate has been signed; or sometimes a mandate is signed, but it does not contain a survivorship clause. In both these cases, the bank may obtain a good discharge by paying the balance to the survivor or survivors. The mere transfer of money into joint names is sufficient to constitute joint ownership with its attendant right of survivorship.[87]

86 [1935] AC 24.
87 See *Halsbury's Laws of England* (4th ed., 1981), Vol. 35, p. 380, and Vol. 39, p. 351.

(b) Problems concerning relationship of parties to the account inter se

11-86 In the vast majority of cases a bank will obtain a good discharge by paying the balance of a joint account to the survivor or survivors, either because of the express terms of a survivorship clause or because of the right of survivorship which arises when money is deposited in joint names. It does not follow, however, that the survivor or survivors are *beneficially* entitled to the money standing to the credit of the account. Sometimes, the survivor or survivors will hold the balance in trust for the personal representatives of the party who died first; sometimes the survivor or survivors will be beneficially entitled to the whole of the balance;[88] and in other cases, the balance may have to be apportioned. Fortunately, the bank is not usually concerned with these problems which, in default of agreement, may have to be resolved by the courts.[89]

11-87 It is outside the scope of this work to explore the various legal rules which determine the *beneficial* interests of the parties. However, in view of that fact that joint accounts of husband and wife provide the greatest number of these cases, it may usefully be noted that the court, when adjudicating upon contested claims of this nature, reviews the whole history and conduct of the account. In one case, for example, a husband had been in ill health and a joint account with his wife had been opened merely to enable his wife to draw money for necessaries during her husband's illness; it was held that the balance accrued to his estate upon his death.[90] In another case, however, there was nothing at all to indicate that the account had been opened for a specific or limited purpose; it was held that the balance accrued to the survivor beneficially.[91]

11-88 As stated above, the bank will obtain a good discharge by paying the balance to the survivor, unless, of course, the mandate contains an express provision to the contrary. If, however, there are exceptional circumstances (as there were, for example, in *McEvoy* v. *Belfast Banking Co. Ltd*),[92] the bank may be justified in taking the initiative and seeking an order from the court. If there are adverse claims to the balance, the appropriate procedure is for the bank to take out an interpleader summons.[93] In a proper case, the court will then make an order

---

88 For an example, see *Young and Another* v. *Sealey* [1949] Ch 278.

89 For a discussion of these and other problems relating to joint accounts, see Professor M. C. Cullity, 'Joint bank accounts with volunteers', *The Law Quarterly Review*, Vol. 85 (1969), pp. 530–47.

90 *Marshal* v. *Crutwell* (1875) LR 20 Eq 328.

91 *Re Bishop, National Provincial Bank Ltd* v. *Bishop* [1965] Ch 450; [1965] 1 All ER 249.

92 [1935] AC 24, *ante*, para. 11-84.

93 Under Order 17 of the Rules of the Supreme Court.

directing that an issue between the claimants be stated and tried. The bank will not be a party to those proceedings.

Cheques presented for payment after death

11-89   If a bank receives notice of the death of one of the parties to a joint account, any cheques presented for payment and signed by the deceased should be returned unpaid with the answer 'Drawer deceased'. If there is only one survivor, then, as the balance normally vests in him, cheques signed by him may be honoured. If, however, there is more than one survivor, a fresh mandate should be obtained from them and cheques should be drawn in accordance with the terms of that mandate.

'Stopping' an account

11-90   If a joint account holder who has undertaken joint and several liability dies at a time when the account is overdrawn, the account should be stopped, and future transactions passed through a new account. This will prevent the Rule in *Clayton's* case[94] from operating and will preserve the bank's right against the deceased's estate.[95]

Inheritance tax

11-91   Where a joint-account holder dies, and all, or a proportion of the funds in the account belonged to him, his personal representatives may be liable for inheritance tax thereon. There is no legal duty imposed upon the bank to see that the necessary steps are taken to pay this tax.

Bankruptcy of joint-account holder

11-92   Unlike death, bankruptcy does not bring the right of survivorship into operation. Consequently, as soon as a bank learns of the presentation of a bankruptcy petition against a joint-account holder, no further drawings from the account should be permitted. Any cheques presented for payment and drawn by the party involved in the bankruptcy proceedings should be dishonoured with the appropriate answer, for example 'Bankruptcy petition presented'. Cheques drawn by the other party or parties to the account should bear an answer which casts no reflection upon him or them, such as 'Joint-account customer, X, involved in bankruptcy proceedings'. Eventually, any credit balance on the account will be withdrawn upon the joint instructions of the trustee in bankruptcy or the Official Receiver on the one hand, and the remaining joint-account holder or holders on the other. Any articles which had been deposited for safe custody should likewise be the subject of joint instructions.

94 (1816) 1 Mer 572.
95 *Ante*, para. 2-94.

11-93   If the account is overdrawn, it should be stopped in order to pre-serve the bank's rights against the bankrupt's estate. The bank will prove in that estate for the entire debt, ignoring the remaining account-holder or holders an any security deposited by them. Any security depo-sited by the bankrupt must, of course, be realized or valued, and the bank will prove in his estate for the amount of the overdraft, minus the security as realized or valued.

11-93A   In *Midland Bank plc* v. *Shephard*[96] Mr Shephard had an over-drawn account with the plaintiff bank. He made arrangements with the bank to transfer the overdraft to a new joint account held by him and his wife. The mandate for the joint account was signed by him and his wife, and it included the words 'any loan or overdraft ... being our joint and several responsibility ...'. Mr Shephard subsequently required a loan for business purposes, and the bank agreed to an overdraft of £10,000 on the joint account. Mrs Shephard took no part in the arrangements, and although she was aware of her husband's intention to borrow the money, she did not know that it would be a liability on the joint account. Subsequently, Mr Shephard was unable to repay the money advanced, and he became bankrupt. The bank obtained summary judg-ment against Mrs Shephard for the sum outstanding. She appealed, con-tending that in obtaining her signature to the mandate her husband had acted as an agent for the bank and had put undue influence upon her to sign. Her appeal was dismissed, and she further appealed to the Court of Appeal. Again, her appeal was dismissed. It was held that there was no evidence that Mr Shephard had induced his wife to sign the mandate by means of fraudulent misrepresentation or by fraudulent concealment, nor that he had induced his wife to sign the mandate by exercising undue influence over her.

Mental incapacity of joint-account holder

11-94   Similar considerations apply under this heading, save that a receiver appointed by the Master of the Court of Protection will give instructions to the bank jointly with the remaining account-holder or holders.[97]

Service of a garnishee order

11-95   A balance standing to the credit of a joint account will be attached by a garnishee order *nisi* which names all the joint account holders as judgment debtors. Likewise, a garnishee order *nisi* naming

96 [1988] 3 All ER 17.
97 For the receiver's powers and duties, see *ante*, para. 3-31.

two judgment debtors will attach a balance standing in the name of one of them.[98] A joint account cannot, however, be attached in respect of a debt owed by one of the parties.[99]

Section 5
PARTNERSHIP ACCOUNTS

11-96 A detailed exposition of partnership law is outside the scope of this book.[1] Attention will be confined to those aspects of the subject which are of greatest interest to bankers.

General principles

11-97 Many aspects of the law of partnership were codified by the Partnership Act 1890. A partnership is there defined as the relation which subsists between persons carrying on a business in common with a view of profit,[2] and the expression 'business' includes every trade, occupation or profession.[3] For the purposes of the Act, persons who have entered into partnership with one another are called collectively 'a firm', and the name under which their business is carried on is called the 'firm name'.[4] The word 'firm' is often used by businessmen when referring to a limited company (e.g. 'ICI is one of the largest firms in this country'), but the word 'firm' will be employed in this book in its strictly legal meaning to connote a partnership. Curiously enough, a partnership may and often does, adopt a name which includes the word 'company' for example, 'Smith, Brown and Company'.

11-98 A person who contributes property without labour, and has the rights of a partner, is often called a sleeping or dormant partner; he is, of course, fully liable as a partner.

11-99 A person who by words spoken or written or by conduct represents himself, or who knowingly suffers himself to be represented, as a partner in a particular firm, is liable as a partner to anyone who has on the faith of any such representation given credit to the firm[5]

---

98 *Miller* v. *Mynn* (1859) 28 LJQB. 324.
99 *Hirschorn* v. *Evans, Barclays Bank Ltd, Garnishees* [1938] 2 KB 801, *ante*, para. 3-71.
1 On the subject generally, see Charles D. Drake, *Law of Partnership* (3rd ed., 1983); or for a fuller treatment, *Lindley on the Law of Partnership* (15th ed., 1984).
2 S. 1(1).
3 S. 45.
4 S. 4(1).
5 S. 14(1).

11-100 In English law, a firm is not a legal person distinct from the partners of whom it is composed.[6] In spite of this, the Rules of the Supreme Court expressly provide that a firm may sue and be sued in the firm name.[7] A judgment against a firm has the same effect as a judgment against all the partners.

11-101 *Number of partners.* The general rule is that a partnership must not consist of more than twenty members.[8] There is, however, no limit to the number of partners in the case of firms carrying on practice as either solicitors, accountants or stockbrokers,[9] or in the case of other firms exempted by regulations made by the Secretary of State.[10]

11-102 *Partnership articles.* The relations between partners are usually regulated by a partnership agreement, or by articles, as they are often called. Many provisions of the Partnership Act 1890 apply only in the absence of any agreement to the contrary, and therefore the articles may virtually supersede numerous provisions of the statute. Partnership agreements are usually made in writing, but they may be made by word of mouth. Unlike the articles of association of a limited company, partnership articles are not required by law to be registered in any public register. Accordingly, it is impossible for a third party to ascertain the terms of partnership articles merely by searching a public register.

11-103 *Authority of partners.* Every partner is an agent of the firm and his other partners for the purpose of the business of the partnership.[11] Subject to certain qualifications stated below, the acts of every partner who does any act for carrying on in the usual way business of the kind carried on by the firm of which he is a member bind the firm and his partners.[12]

11-104 *Limitations on authority of partners.* If it has been agreed between the partners that any restriction shall be placed on the power of

---

6 *Re Sawers, Ex parte Blain* (1879) 12 Ch D 522, at p. 533, *per* James LJ. In Scotland, however, a firm is a legal person: Partnership Act 1890, s. 4(2).

7 Order 81, rule 1.

8 Companies Act 1985, s. 716(1).

9 S. 716(2).

10 S. 716(3). Partnerships (Unrestricted Size) Regulations have been made for patent agents and for partnerships to carry on surveying, auctioneering, valuing, estate agency, land agency and estate managements (1968 SI No. 1222); for actuaries (1970 SI No. 835); for consulting engineers (1970 SI No. 992); for building designers (1970 SI No. 1319) and for loss adjusters (1982 SI 530). The Limited Partnerships (Unrestricted Size) No. 1 Regulations 1971, SI No. 782, were made for certain limited partnerships to carry on surveying, auctioneering, valuing, estate agency, land agency and estate management.

11 Partnership Act 1890, s. 5.

12 S. 5.

any one or more of them to bind the firm, no act done in contravention of the agreement is binding on the firm with respect to those persons who have notice of the agreement.[13] The express or implied authority of a partner cannot, however, be limited by a private arrangement between the partners, of which the person dealing with the partner has no notice, except where the limitation is imposed upon a partner who is not known or believed by such person to be a partner.[14]

11-105 *Examples of implied authority.* A partner in a mercantile or trading firm has implied authority to draw, accept and endorse bills of exchange and other negotiable instruments on behalf of his firm in the ordinary course of its business.[15] This implied authority does not extend to firms which are not mercantile partnerships, such as solicitors.[16] Furthermore, it has been held that a partner has implied authority to borrow money for the purposes of the business, where the business is of a kind that cannot be carried on in the usual way without such a power.[17] These rules are of only passing interest to bankers, because, as will be shown presently, express instructions concerning many of these matters are embodied in a mandate addressed by the partners to the bank. A guarantee signed by one partner in the name of the firm does not bind the other partners, unless the giving of guarantees is part of the firm's normal business, or unless the partner so signing had obtained the express authority of his partners.[18] Furthermore, a partner has no implied authority to execute deeds on behalf of the firm.[19]

11-106 *Liability of partners.* The Partnership Act 1890 provides that a partner in a firm is liable jointly with the other partners (and in Scotland severally also) for all debts and obligations of the firm incurred while he is a partner.[20] Thus every partner of a firm (including, of course, any sleeping or dormant partner)[21] is liable to the full extent of his private means for the debts and obligations of his firm. As will be shown presently, the rule regarding joint liability is expressly varied in the mandate which partners give to the bank: they agree therein to be jointly and severally liable for debts due to the bank. The Act also pro-

---

13 S. 8.
14 S. 5.
15 *Harrison* v. *Jackson* (1797) 7 Term Rep 207, at p. 210; *Williamson* v. *Johnson* (1823) 1 B & C 146.
16 *Hedley* v. *Bainbridge* (1842) 3 QB 316.
17 *Bank of Australasia* v. *Breillat* (1847) 6 Moo PCC 152, at p. 194; *Fisher* v. *Tayler* (1843) 2 Hare 218.
18 *Brettel* v. *Williams* (1849) 2 Exch 623.
19 *Harrison* v. *Jackson* (1797) 7 Term Rep 207; *Marchant* v. *Morton Down & Co.* [1901] 2 KB 829.
20 S. 9.
21 *Beckham* v. *Drake* (1841) 9 M & W 79; affirmed on this point (1843) 11 M & W 315.

vides that the separate estate of a deceased partner is liable jointly and *severally* for the partnership debts and obligations, subject, however, to the prior payment of his separate debts.[22]

Business Names Act 1985

11-107   The Business Names Act 1985 contains provisions relating to the choice of name by a company, and by a partnership, and by a private individual. As far as partnerships are concerned, s. 1 provides that the Act applies to every partnership which has a place of business in Great Britain and which carries on business in Great Britain under a name which does not consist of the surnames of all partners who are individuals and the corporate names of all partners who are bodies corporate without any addition except the forenames of individual partners or the initials of those forenames, or where two or more individual partners have the same surname, the addition of 's' at the end of that surname.

11-108   Section 2 of the Act provides that a partnership to which the Act applies must not, without the written approval of the Secretary of State, carry on business in Great Britain under a name which (a) would be likely to give the impression that the business is connected with the government or with any local authority, or (b) includes any word or expression for the time being specified in regulations made under the Act. The Company and Business Names Regulations 1981 contain a list of these words and expressions, for example 'British', 'Co-operative', 'English', 'International', 'Prince', 'Princess', 'Royal' and 'Scottish'. Although the regulations had been made prior to the Business Names Act 1985, they are to be treated as made and having effect under that Act.[23]

11-109   Section 4 of the Act provides that a partnership to which the Act applies must give the names and addresses of its partners on all business letters, written orders for goods or services to be supplied to the business, invoice and receipts issued in the course of the business and written demands for payment of debts arising in the course of the business. There is an exception in the case of any document issued by a partnership of more than twenty persons which maintains at its principal place of business a list of the names of all the partners if (a) none of the names of the partners appears in the document otherwise than in the text or as a signatory, and (b) the document states in legible characters the address of the partnership's principal place of business and that the list of the partners' names is open to inspection at that place.

22 S. 9.
23 Companies Consolidation (Consequential Provisions) Act 1985, s. 31(2).

Opening a partnership account

11-110 When application is made to a bank to open a partnership account, the same four questions arise as have already been noted when opening an account for an individual, [24] namely the questions relating to the customers' authority, identity, integrity and employment.

11-111 The identity and integrity of the partners should be investigated first. If at least one of the partners is already known to the bank, his introduction of the others is usually considered sufficient. If, however, none of them is known to the bank, references should be obtained and followed up.

11-112 The Partnership Act 1890 defines a partnership as the relation which subsists between persons carrying on a business in common with a view of profit, [25] and the expression 'business' includes every trade, occupation or profession. [26] Accordingly, the bank should ascertain the nature of the firm's business, and note this information in its records.

11-113 Some banks make a practice of calling for the production of the partnership agreement, i.e. the articles of partnership. The intention is to find out whether the document contains any special provisions which might affect the conduct of the bank account. Other banks do not call for the partnership agreement; they argue that if they obtain a properly executed mandate from the partners, this is sufficient protection for the bank. The latter method seems preferable.

11-114 The final question for consideration is the necessary authority to open the account. As a general rule, any one partner has implied authority to open a bank account *in the name of the partnership*. It has been held, however, that one partner does not have implied authority to open an account for the partnership *in his own name*, so as to make his co-partners liable for any overdraft on the account. [27] The normal practice of bankers is to invite all the partners to sign a mandate embodying precise instructions to the bank concerning the conduct of the partnership account.

Mandate for partnership account

A mandate for a partnership account might include the following provisions.

24 *Ante*, para. 11-1.
25 S. 1(1), *ante*, para. 11-97.
26 S. 45.
27 *Alliance Bank Ltd* v. *Kearsley* (1871) LR 6 CP 433.

11-115 *Clause 1*. The partners request the bank to open or continue an account or accounts in the name of their firm, and at any time subsequently, to open such further account or accounts as *both/all/any* ...[28] of the partners in the firm for the time being may direct.

11-116 *Clause 2*. The partners authorize the bank to debit to such account or accounts any cheques, bill of exchange, promissory notes, or orders for payment drawn, accepted, or made by *both/all/any* ... of the partners in the firm for the time being, and to carry out any instructions in connection with the account or accounts (save as otherwise expressly provided) given by *both/all/any* ... of the partners in the firm for the time being, notwithstanding that this may cause such account or accounts to be overdrawn or any overdraft thereon to be increased.

11-117 *Clause 3*. The partners authorize the bank to carry out instructions countermanding payment of cheques, bills of exchange, promissory notes or orders for payment when such instructions are given by any one of them.

11-118 It is generally assumed that one partner has power to countermand payment of a cheque drawn on the account.[29] Strictly speaking, however, this depends upon the proper construction of the mandate in the particular case, and it is prudent to deal expressly with this matter.

11-119 *Clause 4*. The partners authorize the bank to make advances, with or without security, on the request of *both/all/any* ... of the partners in the firm for the time being, by way of overdraft, loan or in any other manner, and to discount bills and promissory notes on the request of *both/all/any* ... of them.

11-120 *Clause 5*. The partners authorize the bank to accept by way of pledge or of deposit as security or for safe custody anything belonging to the firm on the instructions of *both/any/all* ... of the partners in the firm for the time being; and to deliver up anything so accepted or held by the bank on account of the firm on the said instructions.

11-121 *Clause 6*. The partners agree that any liability whatsoever incurred by them to the bank in respect of the foregoing is to be joint and several.

11-122 In the absence of this clause, the partners would be jointly liable during their lives.[30]

---

28 Here and elsewhere in the mandate, this must be completed in accordance with the wishes of the partners.
29 See e.g. *Questions on Banking Practice* (11th ed., 1978), p. 130, Question 373.
30 Partnership Act 1890, s. 9.

11-123 The principal advantage of securing the joint and several liability of partners is that, in the event of the bankruptcy of the partnership, the bank will have the right to prove, in respect of the indebtedness of the partnership, in the separate estates of the partners, as well as in the joint estate. This is sometimes known as a right of double proof.[31]

11-124 Another advantage of securing joint and several liability is that the death of a joint debtor (as opposed to a person who is jointly and severally liable) is usually considered to release him and his estate from liability.[32] In the case of a partnership, however, it is expressly provided by the Partnership Act 1890[33] that the separate estate of a deceased partner is severally liable for the partnership debts, but subject to the prior payment of his separate debts.

11-125 *Clause 7.* The partners undertake that on any change in the constitution of the firm, they will give immediate notice thereof to the bank; and that they will procure any incoming partner to sign an assent to the present mandate.

11-126 The 'assent' is a short document in which the incoming partner states that he has been taken into partnership by the firm, and that he assents and agrees to the terms of the mandate given to the bank and dated. ... He further agrees that all securities held by the bank to secure the liabilities of the firm are to apply to both existing and future liabilities of the firm. When the incoming partner has signed this assent, it must be countersigned by the existing partners.

11-127 *Clause 8.* The partners agree that the mandate is to remain in force until revoked in writing by them or by any of them, notwithstanding any change in the name of the firm and is to apply notwithstanding any change in the membership of the firm by death, bankruptcy, retirement or otherwise or the admission of any new partner or partners.

Dissolution of a partnership

11-128 If there are articles of partnership, it is almost certain that they will contain express provisions concerning dissolution. Irrespective of the terms of any agreement, however, a partnership is in every case dissolved by the happening of any event which makes it unlawful for the business of the firm to be carried on or for the members of the firm to carry it on in partnership. This appears to be the only case laid down

---

31 See *Halsbury's Law of England* (4th ed.), Vol. 2, p. 442.
32 *Ante*, para. 11-78.
33 S. 9.

in the Partnership Act 1890[34] where a partnership is automatically dissolved. Thus, if the partner is a foreigner and war breaks out, with the result that he becomes an alien enemy, the partnership is forthwith dissolved.[35]

11-129   There are, however, other events enumerated in the Partnership Act 1890, which *may* cause a partnership to be dissolved. Thus, subject to any agreement between the partners, a partnership is dissolved:[36]

(a)   if entered into for a fixed term, by the expiration of that term;

(b)   if entered into for a single adventure or undertaking, by the termination of that adventure or undertaking; and

(c)   if entered into for an undefined time, by any partner giving notice to the other or others of his intention to dissolve the partnership.

11-130   Again, subject to any agreement between the partners, a partnership is dissolved by the death of a partner.[37] As, however, it is inconvenient for a partnership to be dissolved when a partner dies, one nearly always finds that, whenever articles of partnership are drawn up, they expressly provide that the death of a partner is not to dissolve the partnership. The articles may, and frequently do, provide that the surviving partner or partners may purchase the share of the deceased partner; if they elect not to do so, the partnership is deemed to have been determined and the affairs of the partnership must then be wound up. Similar provisions are often contained in the articles of partnership respecting the retirement of a partner.

11-131   Furthermore, subject to any agreement between the partners, a partnership is dissolved by the bankruptcy of a partner.[38] It is usual for the articles of partnership to provide that a partner who is adjudicated bankrupt forthwith ceases to be a partner and is deemed to have retired from the partnership as from the date of adjudication. His share will be purchased by the continuing partners, and the purchase money will be paid to his trustee in bankruptcy. In this way, dissolution will be avoided.

---

34   S. 34.

35   *R.* v. *Kupfer* [1915] 2 KB 321; *Hugh Stevenson & Sons Ltd* v. *Aktiengesellschaft für Cartonnagen-Industrie* [1918] AC 239.

36   Partnershp Act 1890, s. 32.

37   S. 33(1).

38   S. 33(1). The statement in *Questions on Banking Practice* (11th ed., 1978), p. 20, Question 58, that a partnership is 'automatically' dissolved when a partner is adjudicated bankrupt should be considered as applying to those cases where there is no agreement to the contrary.

11-132   A bank which is owed money by a partnership sometimes presents a petition for the winding up of the firm pursuant to the Insolvency Act 1986.[39] The requirements are:

(a)   The partnership must be indebted to the bank for a sum exceeding £750.

(b)   The petition must allege that the partnership is unable to pay its debts. The partnership will be deemed to be unable to pay its debts if:

    (i)   the banker serves a written demand for the payment of the debt, and then for a period of three weeks after service of this demand the partnership neglects to pay the sum or to secure or to compound for it to the bank's satisfaction; or

    (ii)   execution or other process issued on a judgment, decree or order obtained in any court in favour of the bank against the partnership or any partner of it as such is returned unsatisfied; or

    (iii)   it is proved to the satisfaction of the court that the value of the partnership's assets is less than the amount of its liabilities, taking into account its contingent and prospective liabilities.

Each partner is, of course, personally liable for the debts of the partnership. In cases where one of the partners is financially sound, the bank will probably claim the full amount of the partnership debt from him, instead of petitioning for the winding up of the partnership.

11-133   Again, a partnership may, at the option of the other partners, be dissolved if any partner suffers his share of the partnership property to be charged under the Partnership Act 1890 for his separate debt.[40]

11-134   Finally, there are certain events specified in the Partnership Act 1890[41] which give the court power, at its discretion, to decree a dissolution of a partnership. By virtue of these provisions, a dissolution will usually be decreed (a) when a partner becomes of permanently unsound mind, or is in any other way permanently incapable of performing his part of the partnership contract; (b) when a partner has been guilty of conduct prejudicially affecting the carrying on of the business of the firm; (c) when a partner is guilty of wilful misconduct; (d) when the business can be carried on only at a loss; and (e) when circumstances have arisen which render it just and equitable that the partnership should be dissolved.

39 See ss 221/4.
40 S. 33(2).
41 S. 35.

Effect of dissolution

11-135   After dissolution, a partnership subsists merely for the purpose of completing transactions, winding up the business and adjusting the rights of the partners; and for these purposes, and these only, the authority, rights and obligations of the partners continue. The course of action to be taken by a bank in regard to the account of a partnership which has been dissolved depends upon the circumstances.

(a) Death of a partner

11-136   If a partnership is dissolved by the death of a partner, the surviving partners must wind up the affairs of the partnership, and for this purpose they may continue to operate the bank account. Cheques drawn by the deceased partner and presented for payment after his death should not be paid without the approval of the survivors, unless the mandate governing the account provides to the contrary. If the account is overdrawn and the bank wishes to preserve its rights against the estate of the deceased partner, the account must be stopped and future transactions passed through a new account. This will prevent the Rule in *Clayton's* case[42] from operating, and will preserve the bank's rights against the deceased's estate. The new account should be maintained in credit, unless the bank is satisfied that borrowing is necessary for winding up the business, in which case fresh security may be taken over partnership assets.

(b) Bankruptcy of a partner

11-137   When the bankruptcy of a partner brings about a dissolution, the partnership account should be dealt with in a manner similar to that described in the preceding paragraph. If the account is in credit, it may be continued. If it is overdrawn and the bank wishes to preserve its rights against the bankrupt partner, the account must be broken.

(c) Bankruptcy of the partnership

11-138   In this event the partnership account and the private accounts of the partners must all be stopped, whether they are in credit or overdrawn.[43]

42 (1816) 1 Mer 572, *ante*, para. 2-94.
43 *Ante*, para. 11-132.

Change in constitution of partnership

11-139 Not every change in the constitution of a partnership involves its dissolution. Thus the death of a partner, or his retirement, or the admission of a new partner to an existing firm are all common events which bring about a change in the constitution of a firm. For the reasons already given, however, they do not necessarily cause the firm to be dissolved. When there is a change in the constitution of a firm, the following matters may have to be considered.

(a) The mandate

11-140 The bank should consider whether or not any new mandate is required. If a partner has died or retired or has ceased to be a partner for any other reason, but he has not been replaced by a new partner, it should be unnecessary to obtain a fresh mandate, provided that the original mandate contains a clause stating that it is to remain in force notwithstanding any change in the membership of the firm. If, however, there is no such clause in the original mandate, a fresh mandate should be obtained. If a new partner is to be admitted to the firm, he should be asked to sign an assent to the existing mandate, such assent being countersigned by the existing partners; or, alternatively, all the partners, including the new partner, may be asked to sign a fresh mandate.

(b) Liability of incoming partner

11-141 If, when a new partner is admitted, the partnership is indebted to the bank, it may be necessary to decide whether the incoming partner should be asked to assume responsibility for that indebtedness. As far as the law is concerned, the position is quite clear: the Partnership Act 1890 provides that a person who is admitted as a partner does not thereby become liable to the creditors of the firm for anything done before he became a partner.[44]

11-142 In many cases, banks are content to rely upon the liability of the existing partners, especially as the Rule in *Clayton's* case[45] will operate against the incoming partner, in that future credits to the partnership account will reduce the old debt, for which he was not liable, and future debits to the account will create new advances for which he will be liable.

11-143 In exceptional cases, however, it may be agreed that the incoming partner is to be liable forthwith for the sum owed by the part-

44 S. 17(1).
45 (1816) 1 Mer 572.

nership to the bank. In those cases, a course which is sometimes adopted is to stop the account and obtain the signatures of all the partners to a cheque for the balance. The cheque will be credited to the old account, and debited to a new account.

(c) Liability of outgoing partner

11-144   The Partnership Act 1890 provides that a partner who retires from a firm does not thereby cease to be liable for partnership debts or obligations incurred before his retirement.[46] A bank's principal concern is often to make certain that his liability is not lost. Thus, if the partnership account is overdrawn and it is desired to retain the liability of a retiring partner, the account should be broken forthwith. If this is not done, the Rule in *Clayton's* case[47] will operate against the bank: future credits will reduce the liability of the retiring partner, and future debits will create new advances for which he will not be liable.

11-145   Similar considerations arise on the death or bankruptcy of a partner; if it is desired to retain the liability of the deceased's or bankrupt's estate, the account should be broken.

Section 6
ACCOUNTS OF CUSTOMERS IN THE PROFESSIONS

11-146   This section is concerned with the accounts of those professional men and women who, in the course of their practice, are entrusted with money belonging to their clients: in particular, solicitors, accountants, stockbrokers, surveyors, auctioneers and estate agents. There are, of course, other professional people who are not entrusted with money by those who consult them, for example, barristers, doctors, clergymen and engineers.

Accounts of solicitors

11-147   The Solicitors Act 1974[48] required the Council of the Law Society to make rules concerning the opening and keeping by solicitors of banking accounts for clients' money. The rules currently in existence are the Solicitors' Accounts Rules 1986, and the Solicitors' Trust Account Rules 1986. It is not proposed to examine these rules in detail. Their broad effect was explained as follows in notes published by the

46 S. 17(2).
47 (1816) 1 Mer 572.
48 S. 32(1). There were earlier provisions of a similar nature.

Law Society in 1967:

> Money which is received by a solicitor and which does not belong to him:
>
> (i) must be dealt with through his client account,[49] if he receives it in connection with his practice;
>
> (ii) must be dealt with either through his client account or through a separate trust bank account opened for the particular trust, if it is trust money subject to a trust of which the solicitor is sole trustee or co-trustee only with a partner, employee of his, or with more than one of such persons; and
>
> (iii) may be dealt with through his client account, if it is subject to any other trust of which he is a trustee.

11-148 Moreover, the Solicitors Act 1974[50] provided that a solicitor must place a client's money on deposit, or pay the client a sum in lieu of interest, in cases laid down by the Law Society. In cases which are specified in the Solicitors' Accounts (Deposit Interest) Rules 1988 the money must be kept in a 'separate designated account', which means a deposit account at a bank or building society in the name of the solicitor or his firm in the title of which the word 'client' appears and which is designated by reference to the identity of the client or matter concerned. Whenever client money is kept in a 'separate designated account', the solicitor must account for all interest earned. Clients' moneys which are not within the provisions relating to separate designated accounts must be paid into a general client account. The banks will accept a mandate to credit interest arising on a general client account to an office account; alternatively, such interest can be credited to the office account without first being credited to the general client account.

Banking practice in relation to solicitors' accounts

11-149 Banking practice may be considered under the following headings, namely (a) opening accounts for solicitors, (b) conduct of solicitors' accounts, (c) serious illness of a solicitor, (d) death of a solicitor, (e) bankruptcy of a solicitor, (f) service of a stop order, (g) service of a garnishee order and (h) return of paid cheques.

(a) Opening accounts for solicitors

11-150 As every practising solicitor (or firm of solicitors) must have one or more clients' accounts for the purposes set out above, it may be

---

49 The rules use the term 'client account'. In practice, it is usually designated a 'clients' account'.
50 S. 33(1).

considered prudent to ask a new solicitor customer whether he or his firm, as the case may be, wishes to open a clients' account. Of course, a clients' account may already have been opened at another bank: solicitors quite often have accounts at more than one bank. Clients' accounts must be kept at a bank as defined in the Solicitors Act 1974.[51] This provision, as amended, is that 'bank' means (a) the Bank of England, or the Post Office, in the exercise of its powers to provide banking services, or a recognized bank within the meaning of the Banking Act 1979; (b) any other company as to which, immediately before the repeal of the Protection of Depositors Act 1963, the Secretary of State was satisfied that it ought to be treated as a banking company or as a discount company for the purposes of the Protection of Depositors Act 1963; and (c) a trustee savings bank.[52] The Law Society maintains a list of banks falling within the definition. Solicitors are also permitted to open clients' accounts at building societies. In order to accept deposits of clients' money, a society must hold an authorization of the Building Society's Commission. The Law Society maintains a list of building societies holding such authorizations.

(b) Conduct of solicitors' accounts

(i) No overdraft on clients' account

11-151　As a general rule, a clients' account should not become overdrawn: this follows from the nature of these accounts, which are to be used solely for the receipt of money belonging to clients. However, many solicitors have a clients' deposit account as well as a clients' current account, and the latter account is sometimes overdrawn.

(ii) No right of set-off over clients' account

11-152　No right of set-off can ever exist over a credit balance on a solicitors' clients' account, i.e. in respect of an overdraft on any other account of the solicitor. This follows from the fact that the money standing to the credit of a clients' account is not the solicitor's money. There is, moreover, a provision in the Solicitors Act 1974[53] which expressly deprives a bank of any recourse or right against money standing to the credit of a clients' account.

---

51 Ss 32 and 87(1), as amended by the Banking Act 1979, s. 51(1) and Sched. 6, para. 9.
52 Finance (No. 2) Act 1975, s. 74.
53 S. 85.

(iii) Possible breach of trust by solicitor

11-153   The Solicitors Act 1974[54] made provision for the protection of banks with whom accounts are kept for clients' moneys. The bank is not to incur any liability or be under any obligation to make any enquiry, or be deemed to have any knowledge of any right of any person to any money paid or credited to any such account, which it would not incur or be under or be deemed to have in the case of an account kept by a person entitled absolutely to all the money paid or credited to it. As du Parcq J observed in *Plunkett* v. *Barclays Bank Ltd*,[55] this seems to be another way of saying that the bank shall not be deemed to have any knowledge which it has not in fact as to such rights: nobody can be deemed to have knowledge of rights of third persons to money in a customer's account when the customer is absolutely entitled to all the money in it. Equally, as the learned judge stated, the bank is relieved by the section from any obligation to make enquiry as to the rights of third persons in respect of a clients' account. All this, however, is subject to the proviso to s. 85 which, as du Parcq J observed, is important. The bank is not relieved by the Act from any obligation under which it would be apart from the Act. Further, as the learned judge emphasized, the section does not say that the bank is to be deemed to be ignorant of facts which are within its knowledge, or that it is to be deemed to be ignorant of the law.

11-154   In the result, therefore, bankers should exercise common sense and not close their eyes to what appears to be a breach of trust. Transfers from a solicitor's clients' account to his office account or his personal account require special mention. Such transfers are frequently made for the purpose of enabling a solicitor to receive costs to which he is entitled. In this connection, the Solicitors' Accounts Rules 1986[56] provide, in effect, that where money is due to a solicitor and the money is standing to the credit of his clients' account, he may withdraw it only by either (a) a cheque in his own favour, or (b) a transfer to a bank or building society account in the name of the solicitor not being a client account. Some banks use specially printed forms for making these transfers. It is prudent to exercise vigilance in regard to sums transferred from clients' account to other accounts in the name of the solicitor, at any rate in those cases where the circumstances are unusual. For example, if a solicitor asked for an overdraft, which was declined, and soon afterwards he attempted to transfer a large sum of money in this way, the bank would probably be put upon enquiry. An even stronger

---

54 S. 85.
55 [1936] 2 KB 107, at p. 116. The relevant section was then s. 8, Solicitors Act 1933, and is now s. 85, Solicitors Act 1974.
56 Rule 8(1).

case for enquiry would arise where a bank had been pressing a solicitor to reduce an overdraft on his private account, and the solicitor tendered, by way of reduction, a cheque for a substantial amount drawn on his clients' account.

(c) Serious illness of solicitor

11-155 A solicitor who practices on his own should have a standing arrangement with a neighbouring solicitor, who should be prepared on receipt of a call for assistance, to manage the practice until its principal returns.[57] The solicitor who is practising on his own should notify his bank of these arrangements in advance; and the solicitor who is nominated to manage the practice must be duly authorized to operate the clients' account and the office accounts, thus avoiding interruption of clients' business.

(d) Death of solicitor

11-156 Where a firm of solicitors has a banking account and one partner dies, the usual rules appertaining to the death of a partner apply.[58] No special problems are likely to arise, as far as the bank is concerned.

11-157 Special arrangements in contemplation of death ought, however, to be made by a solicitor who is practising on his own. In the first place, he ought to make a will, and he should leave clear instructions for his executors to make arrangements immediately after his death for a practising solicitor to be nominated to carry on the practice pending its sale or disposal.[59]

11-158 On the solicitor's death, the bank should be notified of the arrangements, and the executors should immediately authorize the solicitor who is nominated to manage the practice to operate new bank accounts, pending the grant of probate, to enable clients' matters to proceed and staff salaries to be paid. These accounts will usually be designated as suspense accounts. Thus the new account for clients' money will be called 'ABC (name of managing solicitor) *re* XYZ (name of the deceased solicitor) clients' suspense account'. If it is necessary to pay out clients' money which had been placed to the credit of the old clients' account, there are two ways of dealing with the situation. The more usual course is for the solicitors to apply to the bank for a temporary

---

57 *The Professional Conduct of Solicitors* (1986/7), Principle 2.03.
58 *Ante*, para. 11-130.
59 *The Professional Conduct of Solicitors* (*supra*), Principle 2.04.

advance, and to undertake that, on probate being obtained, they will repay that advance out of the old clients' account. When probate is obtained, the old clients' account (and the other balances of the deceased solicitor) will vest in the executors, and they will repay the advance. Alternatively, on the death of a sole solicitor, the Law Society possesses statutory power,[60] which it exercises only occasionally, to take possession of any money in his clients' accounts. The Society must pay the money into a special account in the name of the Society or of a person nominated on behalf of the Society. The money will be held on trust for the persons beneficially entitled to it.

11-159 During the period between the death and the sale of the practice, the solicitor who is nominated to manage the practice will do so for the executors, and he will pay the profits, less his own remuneration, to the estate. If this arrangement continues beyond the executors' year, the solicitor who is managing the practice should report the circumstances to the Law Society, and obtain authority to continue the arrangement.

11-160 In 1965 the senior registrar of the Principal Probate Registry issued a practice direction concerning the grant of representation to the estate of a solicitor who has been practising on his own account without partners, and who has made no proper arrangements for the management of his practice after his death. Briefly, the direction provides that if the persons entitled to a grant fail to apply and if the interests of the deceased solicitor's clients are jeopardized, the Law Society may obtain a grant of representation through its nominee. This person will, of course, exhibit his grant to the bank where the deceased solicitor maintained his accounts.

(e) Bankruptcy of solicitor

11-161 If a solicitor who is practising on his own is adjudicated bankrupt, the balance standing to the credit of his clients' account does not vest in his trustee in bankruptcy, because the money is held by the solicitor on trust for another person.[61] Two trustees should be appointed in place of the bankrupt solicitor, either by the bankrupt himself, or by the court. The two trustees who are usually appointed are the trustee in bankruptcy (or the Official Receiver) and a nominee of the Law Society.[62]

11-162 The bankruptcy of a solicitor used to involve his clients in financial loss. Nowadays, however, the Law Society maintains and

---

60 Solicitors Act 1974, s. 35 and Sched. 1, paras 2, 6 to 8.
61 Insolvency Act 1986, s. 283(3); *Re A Solicitor* [1952] Ch 328.
62 *Re A Solicitor* (*supra*).

administers a compensation fund and, where it is proved to the satis-faction of the Council of the Society that a person has sustained loss in consequence of dishonesty on the part of any solicitor or of his clerk or servant in connection with his practice as a solicitor or in connection with any trust of which that solicitor is trustee, the Society may, if the Council thinks fit, make a grant to such person from the fund for the purpose of relieving the loss.[63]

(f) Service of stop order

11-163   If the Council of the Law Society is satisfied that a solicitor or his clerk or servant has been guilty of dishonesty in connection with his practice as a solicitor or with any trust of which the solicitor is a trustee, the court may, on the application of the Council, order that no payment be made, without the leave of the court, by any banker named in the order, out of any banking account in the name of the solicitor or his firm.[64] Such an order is known as a 'stop order'.

(g) Service of a garnishee order

11-164   When a bank is served with a garnishee order *nisi* attaching all sums owing by the bank to a solicitor, the question whether his clients' account or accounts will be affected depends upon the terms of the gar-nishee order. The judgment creditor ought to ask the court to restrict the terms of the order, so that such an account is not affected by it.[65] If, however, he has failed to do this, the order will attach any sum standing to the credit of a clients' account.[66] The bank should inform the judg-ment creditor's solicitors of the position, and when the matter first comes before the court, the creditor or his solicitors should express their willingness that the order be drafted in terms which will exclude the clients' account. The court will give effect to this.

(h) Return of paid cheques

11-164A   Banks retain their customers' paid cheques for only a limited time – in some cases for only two years. Accordingly, the Council of the Law Society considers that, in certain circumstances, a solicitor might not be able to comply with the Solicitors' Accounts Rules 1986 if he was unable to produce, if required, all paid cheques drawn during the pre-ceding six years. For this reason the Council advises solicitors to make

---

63 Solicitors Act 1974, s. 36(1).
64 Solicitors Act 1974, s. 35 and Sched. 1.
65 *Plunkett* v. *Barclays Bank Ltd* [1936] 2 KB 107, *ante*, para. 3-76.
66 As in *Plunkett* v. *Barclays Bank Ltd* (*supra*).

arrangements with their banks for the return to them of paid cheques which would otherwise be destroyed.[67]

Accounts of other professional people

(a) Stockbrokers

11-165 As a result of the Conduct of Business Rules made by The Securities Association, stockbrokers must pay money which they hold on behalf of clients into a clients' account at a bank. The aim is to safeguard clients' money by ensuring that it is held on trust, so that if a stockbroker becomes insolvent, his clients' money cannot be used to meet the claims of creditors.

11-166 In *Thomson* v. *Clydesdale Bank Ltd*,[68] trustees instructed their stockbroker to sell certain shares with a view to another investment. The broker sold the shares and credited the proceeds to his own overdrawn account with the Clydesdale Bank. He then absconded. The question was whether the trustees were entitled to 'follow', as it is called, this sum of money and to require its payment to them by the Clydesdale Bank, or whether the bank was entitled to retain it in discharge *pro tanto* of the debt which was owing to the bank by the broker. The House of Lords decided in favour of the bank. Lord Herschell LC said:[69]

> My Lords, I cannot assent to the proposition that even if a person receiving money knows that such money has been received by the person paying it to him on account of other persons, that of itself is sufficient to prevent the payment being a good payment and properly discharging the debt due to the person who receives the money. No doubt if the person receiving the money has reason to believe that the payment is being made in fraud of a third person, and that the person making the payment is handing over in discharge of his debt money which he has no right to hand over, then the person taking such payment would not be entitled to retain the money, upon ordinary principles which I need not dwell upon.

Lord Herschell made the point that a stockbroker might have advanced money to clients in anticipation of sums which he would receive for them. In that case, his Lordship stated that it would be perfectly legitimate, the broker having obtained for that purpose an advance from his bankers, that when he received the money for his clients he should pay it to his bankers for the purpose of reinstating the account which he had overdrawn.

---

67 *The Professional Conduct of Solicitors* (*supra*), Principle 17.36.
68 [1893] AC 282.
69 [1893] AC, at pp. 287–8.

(b) Other professions

11-167   Under this heading are accountants, auctioneers, estate agents, insurance brokers and surveyors. By virtue of s. 11 of the Insurance Brokers (Registration) Act 1977 and rules made thereunder,[70] every insurance broker must maintain one or more separate bank accounts designated an 'Insurance broking account'. An insurance broker must pay into an insurance broking account all money relating to insurance transactions. By virtue of s. 14 of the Estate Agents Act 1979 and rules made thereunder,[71] estate agents must likewise maintain clients' accounts. They must pay into such accounts all money which they hold as stakeholders. Accountants, auctioneers and surveyors usually maintain clients' accounts, though they do not appear to be under a legal obligation to do so. No right of set-off exists over a credit balance on any clients' account: the bank is fixed with notice that the money standing to the credit of a clients' account is not the customer's money.

Section 7
ACCOUNTS OF EXECUTORS AND ADMINISTRATORS

11-168   An executor is a person appointed by will or codicil to administer the property of the testator, and to carry into effect the provisions of the will.[72] An administrator is a person appointed by a court of competent jurisdiction to administer the property of a deceased person.[73] The expression 'personal representative' is used to describe either an executor or an administrator.

11-169   A grant of probate to the executors, or a grant of letters of administration to administrators, is necessary in order that they may make title to the property of the deceased and thereafter administer, collect and protect it for the benefit of the persons interested in the estate, whether as creditors, legatees or next of kin. A grant is essential if the estate comprises land; as a general rule, no one except the personal representatives can convey a good title thereto. Furthermore, the production of a grant is usually necessary to establish the right to recover or receive any part of the personal estate and effects of the deceased.[74]

---

70 The Insurance Brokers Registration Council (Accounts and Business Requirements) Rules Approval Order 1979, as amended by the Insurance Brokers Registration Council (Accounts and Business Requirements) (Amendments) Rules Approval Order 1981.
71 The Estate Agents (Accounts) Regulations 1981.
72 *Halsbury's Laws of England* (4th ed.), Vol. 17, p. 373. Although a sole executor is sometimes appointed, it is usual to appoint two or more.
73 *Ibid.*
74 Revenue Act 1884, s. 11.

In some exceptional cases, however, small sums of money may be disposed of on death by nomination, and no grant of administration is required.[75] Moreover, as a matter of practice, bankers do occasionally pay small balances of deceased customers' accounts to the person who appears to be entitled to them under the customer's will or on his intestacy, without insisting that a grant of probate or letters of administration be produced.[76]

Opening an executors' account

11-170 Executors usually open a bank account soon after the testator's death, into which they should pay any money found in his house after his death. If necessary, they should be introduced to the bank by their solicitors.

11-171 They should be asked to sign a mandate which is similar in its terms to the mandate which is executed when a joint account is opened. In particular, it instructs the bank how cheques are to be signed. Executors may authorize any one or more of themselves to sign, but they may not delegate this power to third parties. In cases where executors are directed to hold the residue of the estate upon certain trusts, it is sound policy for the bank to ask *all* the executors to draw cheques together from the outset. They would normally be required to act together as soon as their work as executors was concluded and they became trustees. Accordingly, from an administrative point of view, it is good practice to ask them to sign together from the outset, rather than have to trouble them with such a request about twelve months later. Another clause in the mandate usually provides that the executors are to be jointly and severally liable for any borrowings on the account.

11-172 Sometimes the testator's will is held by the bank for safe custody, and the names of the executors may not, therefore, be ascertainable until the will is made available. The bank will usually permit the will to be removed in exchange for a receipt to be signed by all the persons named therein as executors or by their solicitors. Prior to the grant of probate, however, no other items lodged for safe custody by the testator should be released. Such items may, of course, be inspected by the executors or by their solicitor, in the presence of a bank official. Share certificates or title deeds may have been lodged for safe custody, and full details thereof will be required by the executors for the preparation of the Inland Revenue affidavit.

---

75 These cases are listed in *Halsbury's Laws of England* (4th ed.), Vol. 17, p. 505.
76 *Ante*, para. 3-20.

Advance to executors for payment of inheritance tax

11-173 Executors usually ask the bank to make an advance to them for the purpose of paying inheritance tax, and this is generally embodied in a formal request which the bank requires them to sign. The bank will usually be able to accede to this request, though it will, of course, wish to be satisfied that there appear to be sufficient readily saleable assets of the estate to enable the advance to be repaid. Moreover, the attention of the executors may usefully be drawn to the clause in the formal request which makes it plain that they are undertaking personal responsibility for the repayment of the advance. At this stage, they cannot mortgage or charge the assets; they cannot do so until probate has been granted. Hence, it is important for a bank to be fully satisfied as to their integrity before it makes an advance.

11-174 The formal request for such an advance would usually contain the following provisions:

(a) The person or persons whose names and addresses are given declare that he/they is/are the sole executor, or the executors, of .... who died on ....

(b) He/they declare that he/they intend to apply for probate of the will and request the bank to advance the sum of £... for the purpose of paying inheritance tax on the deceased's estate, the net value of which is estimated at £...

(c) They declare that they will hold themselves jointly and severally responsible for the repayment of such advances, together with interest, commission and other usual banking charges.

(d) He/they undertake to apply such advances to the above-mentioned purposes, to procure the grant of probate without delay, and to lodge the same with the bank for registration.

(e) He/they undertake to repay such advances out of the first funds coming into his/their hands from the said estate, and he/they charge with such repayment any cash and securities in the bank's hands belonging to the deceased.

Opening an administrators' account

11-175 Where a person dies without having made a will, or where he makes a will but does not appoint executors, or where he appoints executors but they are unable or unwilling to act, one or more administrators must be appointed. Although these are the usual cases where administrators are appointed, limited grants of administration are made in special circumstances. Thus, where a minor is appointed or becomes sole executor of a will, a grant to one or more administrators *durante* *minore aetate* will be made, that is to say a grant limited in time until the minor attains his majority. Likewise, if a sole executor or administrator is incapable of acting by reason of mental incapacity, a grant *durante dementia* will be made. There are other cases where limited grants may be made.[77]

11-176 The procedure to be followed when opening an account for administrators is similar to that which is adopted when opening an account for executors. If they are unknown to the bank, the persons who are applying for a grant will usually be introduced to the bank by their solicitors; and they will be asked to sign a mandate which is similar to that completed by executors.

11-177 Executors derive their title from the testator's will (probate being the legal recognition of the validity of the will); but administrators derive their title entirely from the grant of administration. For this reason, when it becomes necessary for persons who are applying for letters of administration to ask the bank to make an advance for the purpose of paying inheritance tax, the persons who make this request are required to complete a form in which they state that they 'intend to apply for letters of administration': they cannot at that stage describe themselves as administrators. They undertake to apply the advance for the purpose of paying the tax, and to lodge the grant of letters of administration with the bank without delay. They also hold themselves jointly and severally responsible for the repayment of the advance.

Conduct of accounts of personal representatives

11-178 Having obtained a grant of probate or letters of administration, as the case may be, one of the first tasks of the personal representatives is to realize sufficient assets to repay the sum which the bank advanced for the payment of inheritance tax. It may also be necessary to realize assets for the payment of debts owed by the deceased or for the payment of legacies.

11-179 If the deceased's account with the bank is in credit, the personal representatives will instruct the bank to transfer the balance to their account. If, however, the deceased's account is overdrawn, the personal representatives will repay the overdraft, either out of income or out of the proceeds of the realization of assets. When instructions to close the deceased's account are received, the bank should make certain that any safe-custody articles deposited by the deceased have been delivered to the personal representatives.

---

77 See, e.g., *Halsbury's Laws of England* (4th ed.), Vol. 17, pp. 510 *et seq.*

11-180 In the simplest type of case, where the deceased's estate has to be divided among persons of full age, the personal representatives should be able to complete their work within twelve months of their appointment. Their last act, as far as the bank is concerned, will be to ask for a statement of account, including charges, and then they will close the account by drawing cheques in favour of the beneficiaries. In many cases, however, the personal representatives are directed to hold the residue of the estate upon certain trusts. Having paid the debts and legacies, they then become trustees of the residue. Their account should be re-styled 'Trustees of ... deceased'. [78]

Advances to personal representatives

11-181 In addition to borrowing money for the payment of inheritance tax, personal representatives may wish to borrow from the bank for other purposes, e.g. in order to pay debts and legacies. They will usually have power to do so, [79] but the bank should satisfy itself that there is no express provision in the deceased's will forbidding the borrowing of money. Such a provision is rarely found.

11-182 As already stated, the bank will require the personal representatives to undertake joint and several liability for any borrowing. They have power to offer as security specific assets of the estate: usually such security will consist of land and buildings, or stocks and shares. Property which the deceased had charged to the bank by way of security may not be retained as security for any borrowing by the personal representatives; though it may, of course, be the subject of a new charge by them.

Continuing the business of the deceased

11-183 In the absence of a direction in the testator's will, executors have no power to carry on the testator's business, except for the purpose of winding it up. [80] It has been held, however, that although executors may have no express authority to continue the business, it is their duty (as it is also the duty of administrators) to do whatever may be required to be done to preserve the business as an asset, [81] and if they act bona fide and to the best of their judgment, they will not be liable for a breach of trust in continuing it for some years. [82] Executors who are authorized

---

78 For the accounts of trustees see *post*, paras 11-194/231.
79 Administration of Estates Act 1925, ss 2(1) and 39.
80 *Collinson* v. *Lister* (1855) 20 Beav 356.
81 *Strickland* v. *Symons* (1883) 22 Ch D 666, at p. 671, *per* Pollock B; on appeal (1884) 26 Ch D 245.
82 *Garrett* v. *Noble* (1834) 6 Sim 504.

to carry on the business are not entitled to employ in the business any of the general assets of the testator beyond the fund directed to be so employed.[83] Where the testator has not authorized the employment of any of his general assets, the executors are only entitled to employ the assets already embarked in the business.[84] Whenever personal representatives continue the deceased's business, the bank should require them to open a separate account for this purpose.

11-184 If the bank is asked to provide accommodation to enable the personal representatives to continue the deceased's business, there are three principal matters for consideration.

11-185 First, it is necessary to determine whether the personal representatives have power to carry on the deceased's business. The relevant rules have been stated above.

11-186 Secondly, one must consider whether the deceased's creditors have been paid or, alternatively, have assented to the carrying on of the business. If they have assented, the personal representatives are entitled to be indemnified out of the assets in priority to them; and the right of indemnity is not limited to the portion of the estate which has come into existence or changed its form after the testator's death.[85] In such a case, the business of creditors (including the bank) are, by subrogation, entitled to priority over the deceased's creditors. If, on the other hand, the deceased's creditors have not assented to the business being carried on, the bank's position as a lender to the personal representatives is unsatisfactory. The deceased's creditors would be entitled to be paid first out of the assets which existed at the death, in spite of the fact that the testator had empowered his executors to carry on his business; for the testator cannot, by any direction in his will, deprive his creditors of their right to be paid.[86]

11-187 Finally, unless the bank is content to rely upon the joint and several liability of the personal representatives, there is the question of security for the proposed advance. As a general rule, the personal representatives have no power to charge the testator's assets outside the business as security for the repayment of the loan[87] but they may give a valid charge upon the assets already engaged in the business.[88] If

---

83 *Re Ballman, Ex parte Garland* (1804) 10 Ves 110; *Cutbush* v. *Cutbush* (1839) 1 Beav 184.

84 *Re Hodson, Ex parte Richardson* (1818) 3 Madd 138; affirmed (1819) Buck 421.

85 *Dowse* v. *Gorton* [1891] AC 190.

86 *Re Oxley, John Hornby & Sons* v. *Oxley* [1914] 1 Ch 604; *Re East, London County and Westminster Banking Co. Ltd* v. *East* (1914) 111 LT 101.

87 *M'Neillie* v. *Acton* (1853) 4 De GM & G 744.

88 *Devitt* v. *Kearney* (1883) 13 LR Ir 45.

executors find it impossible to carry on the business with only those assets already engaged in it or authorized by the testator, they should apply to the court for its directions.[89]

Death of personal representative

11-188   If one of several representatives dies, the survivors may continue to act.[90] Cheques signed by the deceased representative may be paid and debited to the account. It is usual to obtain a fresh mandate from the survivors, governing the future operation of the account. If the account is overdrawn and the personal representatives had contracted to be jointly and severally liable, the account should be stopped and a new account opened, if it is desired to retain the liability of the deceased representative's estate.

11-189   Upon the death of a sole or lasting surviving executor, his executors, on proving the will, become the executors of the original testator,[91] and they may therefore continue transactions on the account after they have exhibited probate to the bank. They should, of course, be asked to sign a mandate governing operations on the account.

11-190   If a sole or last surviving executor dies intestate or fails to appoint an executor, a grant of administration *de bonis non administratis* must be obtained. The persons to whom such a grant is made will then be entitled to operate the account after completing the usual mandate.

11-191   Upon the death of a sole or last surviving administrator, whether or not he leaves a will, a grant of administration *de bonis non administratis* must be obtained.

Breach of trust by personal representatives

11-192   Personal representatives who are in financial difficulties may be tempted to misappropriate funds belonging to the estate. Bankers should be alive to this possibility. Thus, it would clearly be imprudent for a bank to collect a cheque payable to the executors for the private account of one of the executors; if the executor misappropriated the proceeds of the cheque, the bank might be liable to the honest executors in respect of the loss.

11-193   There are occasions when a bank may be justified in refusing payment of a cheque drawn on the account of personal representatives

89 *M'Neillie* v. *Acton* (*supra*).
90 *Flanders* v. *Clarke* (1747) 3 Atk 509.
91 Administration of Estates Act 1925, s. 7(1).

on the ground that the drawing of the cheque constituted the commission of a breach of trust. The leading case is *Gray* v. *Johnston*, in which Lord Cairns LC said:[92]

> In order to hold a banker justified in refusing to pay a demand of his customer, the customer being an executor, and drawing a cheque as an executor, there must, in the first place, be some misapplication, some breach of trust, intended by the executor, and there must in the second place ... be proof that the bankers are privy to the intent to make this misapplication of the trust funds. And to that I think I may safely add, that if it be shown that any personal benefit to the bankers themselves is designed or stipulated for, that circumstance, above all others, will most readily establish the fact that the bankers are in privity with the breach of trust which is about to be committed.

By way of illustration, one might instance the case of an executor who is being pressed by the bank to reduce the overdraft on his private account. He tenders for the credit of his private account a cheque drawn upon the executors' account. Unless the bank was satisfied from its knowledge of the contents of the testator's will that the payment was a proper one, there would be strong evidence on these facts of a breach of trust. Furthermore, there would, in the words of Lord Cairns, be a personal benefit to the bank, resulting from the reduction in the overdraft on the executor's private account. Accordingly, the bank should decline to pay the cheque drawn upon the executor's account unless and until a satisfactory explanation was forthcoming.

Section 8
ACCOUNTS OF TRUSTEES

11-194 A trust may be defined as 'the relationship which arises wherever a person (called the trustee) is compelled in equity to hold property, whether real or personal, and whether by legal or equitable title, for the benefit of some persons (of whom he may be one and who are termed beneficiaries) or for some object permitted by law, in such a way that the real benefit of the property accrues, not to the trustees, but to the beneficiaries or other objects of the trust'.[93]

Distinctions between private and charitable trusts

11-195 Trust may be divided, according to their purpose, into private

---

92 (1868) LR 3 HL 1, at p. 11.
93 G. W. Keeton and L. A. Sheridan, *The Law of Trusts* (11th ed., 1983), p. 3.

trusts on the one hand, and public (or charitable) trusts on the other. The following distinctions between them may be noted.

11-196   A private trust is one which exists for the benefit of an individual or class, even though it confers some benefit on the public at large; a public or charitable trust is one whose object is to promote the public welfare, even though it confers some benefit on an individual or class.

11-197   A private trust may be enforced by any of the beneficiaries, a public trust by the Attorney-General.

11-198   In regard to private trusts involving a settlement of land or a trust for sale of land, the number of trustees must not exceed four.[94] The number of charitable trustees is not limited by statute.

11-199   There is no department of state which is charged with the supervision of private trusts. Owing to the special nature of charitable trusts, and especially the usual absence of a beneficiary who can enforce the trusts, a number of official bodies are charged with the supervision of charities. Chief among them are the three Charity Commissioners who, with their staff, form a department of state responsible to the Home Secretary.[95]

11-200   Subject to exceptions which will be noted later, trustees of a private trust may not delegate their duties: they must act together. Trustees of a charity may, subject to the trusts of the charity, confer on any of their body (not being less than two in number) a general authority, or an authority limited in such manner as the trustees think fit, to execute deeds or instruments for giving effect to transactions to which the trustees are a party.[96]

11-201   The trust deed of a charitable trust often provides that trustees may be appointed or discharged by resolution of a meeting of the trustees.[97] This cannot be done in the case of a private trust.

Opening an account for trustees

11-202   If trustees who wish to open a bank account are not already known to the bank, references should be obtained and followed up in the usual way. The title of the account should indicate clearly that it is a trust account, e.g. 'Trustees of John Jones, deceased'. If the trust

94 Trustee Act 1925, s. 34(1).
95 Charities Act 1960, s. 1(1), (2), Sched. I.
96 Charities Act 1960, s. 34.
97 Cf. Charities Act 1960, s. 35(1).

instrument is produced, its main provisions should be recorded; but there is usually no necessity to require its production at the time when the account is opened.

11-203 The trustees should sign a mandate governing transactions on the account. As stated above, trustees of a charity may usually delegate the power to sign cheques drawn on their account to any of their body, not less than two.[98] They generally do so.

11-204 Subject to certain exceptions to be stated presently, a trustee of a private trust, being personally responsible for the exercise of his judgment and for the performance of his duty, cannot escape responsibility by leaving to another person the exercise of that judgment or the performance of that duty, even if he is one of several trustees and the person to whom he leaves it is his co-trustee. Kay J explained the rule thus:[99]

> The reason why more than one trustee is appointed is that they shall take care that the moneys shall not get into the hands of one of them alone, that they shall take care that the trust moneys are always under the power and control of every one of them ...

Accordingly, the mandate which is executed by trustees of a private trust should provide that cheques drawn upon the account must be signed by all trustees together. This is the normal practice.

11-205 However, there are exceptional cases where trustees who are well known to the bank are so insistent that they wish to delegate their powers that the bank may feel obliged to try to meet their requirements. In these cases, the following safeguards should be observed. First, at least two of the trustees should sign cheques together. Secondly, the trustees should open both a capital and an income account, and delegation should be permitted only in relation to the latter account. Thirdly, an indemnity protecting the bank from possible loss should always be executed by the trustees themselves and, ideally, by those beneficiaries who are of full age. Fourthly, all the trustees should be asked to verify the balances of the bank accounts at least every six months. Finally, this exceptional procedure should be permitted only in those cases where the trustees are of undoubted integrity.

11-206 The mandate which is signed by the trustees when the account is opened should provide that any liability incurred by them to the bank is to be joint and several. Another clause should authorize the bank to

---

98 See s. 34, *supra*.
99 *Re C. Flower and Metropolitan Board of Works, Re M. Flower and Metropolitan Board of Works* (1884) 27 Ch D 592, at pp. 596–7.

deliver up on the instructions of all the trustees any securities, deeds, boxes and parcels and their contents held by the bank for safe custody.

Delegation by trustees

11-207   The following are the principal cases where a trustee may delegate his authority.

(a) Provision in trust instrument

11-208   As an illustration of this type of delegation, one may refer to the appointment by a testator of a bank and a private individual as his executors and trustees. A bank will usually supply a testator with a suitable draft clause for inclusion in his will for the purpose of making this appointment. The clause frequently provides that the bank account of the trust is to be maintained in the sole name of the bank: the other trustee does not even become a party to it.

(b) Section 23, Trustee Act 1925

11-209   This section provides, *inter alia*, that, instead of acting personally, trustees may employ and pay an agent, whether a solicitor, banker, stockbroker or other person, to transact any business or do any act required to be transacted or done in the execution of the trust, including the receipt and payment of money. Trustees are entitled to be allowed and paid all charges and expenses so incurred, and are not responsible for the default of any such agent, if employed in good faith. The section does not enable trustees to delegate their duties generally, e.g. by a power of attorney.[1] It really empowers trustees to appoint agents to do particular acts.

(c) Section 25, Trustee Act 1925

11-210   This section, as amended by the Powers of Attorney Act 1971,[2] provides, *inter alia*, that a trustee may, by power of attorney, delegate for a period not exceeding twelve months the execution or exercise of all or any of the trusts, powers and discretions vested in him as trustee either alone or jointly with any other person or persons; but he may not appoint his sole co-trustee as attorney unless the co-trustee is a trust corporation. He remains liable for the acts or defaults of his attorney as if they were his own. The power of attorney must be attested by at least one witness.

1 *Green* v. *Whitehead* [1930] 1 Ch 38.
2 S. 9.

11-211   Before or within seven days after giving a power of attorney the donor must give written notice thereof to his co-trustees and to each person who has, under the trust instrument, power to appoint new trustees. The notice must specify who the attorney is, when the power takes effect, how long it is to last, why it was given and which powers and discretions are delegated.

Advances to trustees

11-212   When trustees apply to a bank for an advance, two questions to be considered are, first, whether the trustees have power to borrow money for the purpose which they have in mind and, secondly, whether they have power to give security for the proposed advance. Power to borrow and to give security may be conferred upon trustees (a) by the trust instrument, (b) by Act of Parliament, (c) by the beneficiaries, or (d) by the court.

(a) The trust instrument

11-213   The trust instrument should always be examined in order to ascertain whether it confers the relevant powers upon the trustees. It rarely does so.

(b) Act of Parliament

11-214   The Trustee Act 1925[3] provides that where trustees are authorized by the trust instrument or by law to apply *capital* money for any purpose or in any manner, they have power to raise the money by, *inter alia*, mortgage of all or any part of the trust property for the time being in possession. This applies notwithstanding a contrary direction in the instrument, if any, creating the trust, but it does not apply to trustees of a charity or to Settled Land Act trustees.[4] This statutory power to raise money is sometimes invoked when a bank is asked to lend money to trustees to enable them, in turn, to make a loan to a remainderman. As a general rule, trustees have power to apply capital money for the advancement of a remainderman, and so the above-mentioned statutory power enables them to raise the money by mortgage of any part of the trust property.

11-215   The Trustee Act 1925[5] further provides that no mortgagee advancing money on a mortgage purporting to be made under any

3 S. 16(1).
4 S. 16(2).
5 S. 17.

power vested in trustees is concerned to see that such money is wanted, or that no more is raised than is wanted. This, too, is a useful provision.

(c) The beneficiaries

11-216 If all the beneficiaries are of full age, and if they are all prepared to authorize the trustees to borrow money against specified security, there can be no risk in acting in accordance with their wishes.

(d) The court

11-217 As a last resort, application may be made to the court to sanction a mortgage of trust property. The court has statutory power to make the necessary order on such terms, and subject to such provisions and conditions, if any, as it thinks fit.[6]

11-218 Whichever of the above-mentioned powers is invoked, the lending bank will usually ensure that all the trustees undertake joint and several liability for the repayment of the advance, and that they all execute the relevant documents by way of security. The mandate which the trustees will have signed when opening the account will probably have provided that they are to be jointly and severally liable for any borrowings though sometimes trustees who execute a mortgage by way of security insist that their personal liability is to be limited to any trust funds in their hands. Finally, when securities are released and returned to the trustees, the receipt of all of them should be obtained.

Changes in trustees

11-219 The commonest events which may lead to the appointment of a new trustee are (a) the death, (b) the retirement or (c) the bankruptcy of a trustee.

(a) Death of trustee

11-220 The remaining trustee or trustees may have to seek legal advice on the question whether a new trustee should be appointed or whether it is permissible for them to continue without the appointment of a new trustee. The bank should enquire what is to be done.

11-221 In the absence of notice of any special provision in the trust deed, the bank may meanwhile rely upon the Trustee Act 1925, which provides that, if a trustee dies, any power or trust given to the trustees

---

6 S. 57(1).

jointly may be exercised or performed by the survivor or survivors of them for the time being.[7] Thus he or they may draw cheques on the account. Further, on the death of a sole or sole surviving trustee and until new trustees are appointed, his personal representatives are capable of exercising or performing any power or trust which the deceased trustee could have exercised or performed, unless the trust instrument contains a contrary direction.[8]

11-222   In any of these cases, if the account of the trustees is overdrawn and the trustees have contracted to be jointly and severally liable, the account should be stopped and a new account opened, if it is desired to retain the liability of the deceased trustee's estate.

(b) Retirement of trustee

11-223   There is no provision in the Trustee Act 1925 to the effect that, when a trustee retires, his powers may be exercised by the remaining trustees. Accordingly, when a banker learns that a trustee has retired, he must make further enquiries, because the action which he must take will depend upon the circumstances of the retirement. When a trustee retires, this usually comes about in one of the following ways.

(i) With the consent of the beneficiaries

11-224   If all the beneficiaries are *sui juris*, they may authorize a trustee to retire. This is an application of the rule that, as a beneficiary who concurs in a breach of trust cannot afterwards complain of the consequence of the act, so, if all the beneficiaries, being *sui juris*, consent to a trustee's retirement, they cannot hold him responsible on the ground of delegation of his office.[9]

(ii) Under the Trustee Act 1925, without a new appointment

11-225   The Trustee Act 1925[10] enables a trustee who wishes to do so to be discharged from the trust without the appointment of a new trustee or trustees to take his place if, after his discharge, there will still be a trust corporation or at least two individuals remaining to act as trustees.

(iii) Under the Trustee Act 1925, with a new appointment

11-226   The Trustee Act 1925[11] provides that, if a trustee desires to be discharged, or refuses or is unfit to act, or is incapable of acting, the

---

7 S. 18(1).
8 S. 18(2).
9 *Wilkinson* v. *Parry* (1828) 4 Russ 272, *per* Sir J Leach MR, at p. 276.
10 S. 39(1).
11 S. 36(1).

person or persons empowered by the trust instrument to appoint new trustees, or if there is no such person or no such person able and willing to act, the surviving or continuing trustees or trustee for the time being, or the personal representatives of the last surviving or continuing trustee may, by writing, appoint one or more persons to be a trustee or trustees in his place. The expression 'is incapable of acting' includes mental incapacity, [12] and age and infirmity. [13]

(iv) By order of the court

11-227 The court has an inherent jurisdiction to discharge a trustee without appointing a new trustee in his place. [14] It is seldom necessary to resort to this jurisdiction.

11-228 When the bank has ascertained which of the above-mentioned powers has been exercised, it will act accordingly. Thus, if the account is overdrawn, it may be necessary to stop the account for the reasons already stated. If a new trustee has been appointed, the bank should ask to see the deed of appointment; and the new trustee should join with the other trustees in giving a new mandate to the bank concerning future operations on the account.

(c) Bankruptcy of trustee

11-229 The fact that a person is adjudicated bankrupt does not automatically render him incapable of acting as a trustee. It is, however, very desirable that he should retire and that a new trustee should be appointed in his place. In the words of Sir George Jessel MR: [15]

> A necessitous man is more likely to be tempted to misappropriate trust funds than one who is wealthy; and besides, a man who has not shown prudence in managing his own affairs is not likely to be successful in managing those of other people.

In practice, a bankrupt trustee usually does retire, but if he does not do so, the bank need take no steps, except perhaps to be more than usually watchful for any attempted breach of trust by the bankrupt trustee.

Breach of trust by trustees

11-230 One of the leading cases on this subject is *Gray* v. *Johnston* [16] which has already been cited in regard to the commission of a breach of

12 *Re East, Re Trusts of Bellwood's Will* (1873) 8 Ch App 735; *Re Blake* [1887] WN 173.
13 *Re Lemann's Trusts* (1883) 22 ChD 633.
14 *Re Chetwynd's Settlement, Scarisbrick* v. *Nevinson* [1902] 1 Ch 692.
15 *Re Barker's Trusts* (1875) 1 Ch 43, at pp. 43–4.
16 (1868) LR 3 HL 1, *ante*, para. 11-193.

trust by personal representatives. The principles there stated in regard to personal representatives apply also to trustees.

11-231 In particular, if a breach of trust is committed, the bank's position is especially vulnerable if it benefits from the breach. Thus, in *British American Elevator Co. Ltd* v. *Bank of British North America*,[17] drafts drawn on the plaintiff company were cashed by arrangement for the company's agent so that he could use the proceeds to pay for grain purchased for the company. Although the bank knew this, it accepted the drafts in whole or in part for the credit of the overdrawn account of the agent. It was held that the bank was a party to the misapplication of trust funds and liable to the company for the amount of its loss.

11-231A Even if the bank does not benefit from the breach of trust, it may be held liable. Thus in *Rowlandson and Others* v. *National Westminster Bank Ltd*[18] it was held that once a bank has opened an account which is clearly a trust account, it is under a fiduciary duty to the beneficiaries of the trust, and so the bank will be liable to them if it knowingly assists in a dishonest and fraudulent design on the part of the trustees. In the present case the bank failed to question or prevent certain withdrawals from a trust account which were in breach of trust, and it was held that the bank was accountable to the beneficiaries.

Section 9
ACCOUNTS OF TRUSTEES IN BANKRUPTCY

11-232 Although two or more trustees are almost invariably appointed for the purpose of administering a trust, a sole trustee, known as a 'trustee in bankruptcy', is usually appointed for the purpose of getting in, and distributing, the assets of a bankrupt.[19] Only a person qualified to act as an insolvency practitioner in relation to the bankrupt's estate may be appointed as trustee of a bankrupt's estate.[20]

11-233 By virtue of the Insolvency Regulations 1986,[21] a trustee in bankruptcy must pay all money received by him into the Insolvency

17 [1919] AC 658.
18 [1978] 1 WLR 798.
19 Two or more persons may be appointed trustees, but such an appointment must make provision as to the circumstances in which the trustees must act together and the circumstances in which one or more of them may act for the others: Insolvency Act 1986, s. 292(3).
20 Insolvency Act 1986, s. 292(2). By virtue of ss 390 and 391, only an individual can be qualified to act as an insolvency practitioner; he must be currently authorized to act as an insolvency practitioner (usually by being a memer of a recognized professional body); and he must have provided security for the proper performance of his functions.
21 Regulation 4.

Services Account kept by the Secretary of State with the Bank of England, Threadneedle Street, London EC2R 8AH. However, Regulation 6 provides that if the trustee in bankruptcy intends to exercise his power to carry on the business of the bankrupt, he may apply to the Secretary of State for authorization to open a local bank account, and the Secretary of State may authorize him to make his payments into and out of a specified bank, instead of into and out of the Insolvency Services Account, if he is satisfied that an administrative advantage will be derived from having such an account. Accordingly, if a banker is requested to open an account for a trustee in bankruptcy, he should require to see the relevant authority.

11-234 The Insolvency Regulations 1986[22] also provide that where a responsible insolvency practitioner opens a local bank account, he must open and maintain clearly named local bank accounts in the name of each separate insolvent of which he is the responsible insolvency practitioner, and where money is provided for a specific purpose it must be clearly identifiable in a separate account.

11-235 Finally, the Insolvency Regulations 1986[23] provide that, as soon as a responsible insolvency practitioner ceases to carry on the business of the insolvent, or vacates office, or an authorization given under the Regulations is withdrawn, he must close the account and remit any balance to the Insolvency Services Account at the Bank of England.

11-236 Advances are seldom granted to trustees in bankruptcy. As regards security, the Insolvency Act 1986[24] provides that, with the permission of the creditors' committee or the court, a trustee in bankruptcy may mortgage or pledge any part of the property comprised in the bankrupt's estate for the purpose of raising money for the payment of his debts.

Section 10
ACCOUNTS OF TRUSTEES UNDER DEEDS OF ARRANGEMENT

11-237 Most debtors who are in financial difficulties would like to avoid being made bankrupt, chiefly because an undischarged bankrupt is subject to certain disabilities. Occasionally, a debtor may be able to pacify his creditors, and so avoid bankruptcy, by executing a deed of arrangement. The purpose of the debtor is to try to persuade his creditors to accept so much in the pound in full discharge of the debts which

---

22 Regulation 6(3).
23 Regulation 6(6).
24 S. 314(1) and Sched. 5.

he owes them. If they agree, the debtor assigns substantially all his assets to a trustee, who then realizes the assets and distributes the proceeds to the creditors. The deed usually gives priority to those creditors who would rank as preferential creditors in bankruptcy.

11-238 This method of avoiding bankruptcy is not employed frequently, mainly because creditors tend to be suspicious: they usually prefer to force a debtor into bankruptcy, so that his affairs may be the subject of detailed enquiry in court. If they assent to a deed of arrangement, there are no proceedings in court, and there is a risk that a debtor may fail to reveal all his assets.

11-239 The Deeds of Arrangement Act 1914 contains a detailed code of procedure governing the powers and duties of a trustee under a deed of arrangement. Most of these provisions do not concern bankers directly. The following points should, however, be borne in mind by a banker who is requested to open an account for a trustee under a deed of arrangement.

11-240 The bank should ask to be supplied with a copy of the deed, so that it may be satisfied that the person wishing to open the account is the person named in the deed. The Insolvency Act 1986 provides that a trustee under a deed of arrangement must be an 'insolvency practitioner'.[25] The account should be opened in the name of the debtor's estate,[26] e.g. 'John Smith, Trustee of James Brown under Deed of Arrangement'.

11-241 It used to be necessary for the bank to inform the trustee that no payments out of the account would be permitted until three months had elapsed after the execution of the deed. This precaution was necessary because of the doctrine of relation back whereby, under the Bankruptcy Act 1914, bankruptcy commenced at the date of the first available act of bankruptcy. The execution by the debtor of a deed of arrangement constituted an act of bankruptcy. The concept of acts of bankruptcy and the doctrine of relation back finds no place in the Insolvency Act 1986. Accordingly, it is no longer necessary for the bank to inform the trustees that no payments out of the account will be permitted until three months have elapsed after the execution of the deed.

11-242 The deed must be registered with the registrar appointed by the Department of Trade and Industry within seven days after its first execution by the debtor or any creditor.[27] If not so registered, it is void.[28]

---

25 S. 388(2). For the qualifications of an insolvency practitioner, see *ante*, para. 11-232.
26 Deeds of Arrangement Act 1914, s. 11(4).
27 Deeds of Arrangement Act 1914, s. 5; Administration of Justice Act 1925, s. 22(1).
28 Deeds of Arrangement Act 1914, s. 2.

Furthermore, the deed will be void unless, within 21 days after registration, it has received the assent of a majority in number and value of the creditors of the debtor.[29] The trustee must file a statutory declaration that the requisite majority of the creditors have assented to the deed.[30] A bank which is asked to open an account for a trustee normally assumes that he is familiar with these duties, though some banks take the precaution of enquiring whether he has filed the usual statutory declaration.

11-243 Before the trustee pays the final dividend on the estate, the bank may consider it helpful to advise hm of the bank charges which will be payable upon closing the account; otherwise, he might arrange his final distribution without having regard to bank charges.

11-244 Any credit balance on the debtor's own account at the bank is usually one of the assets which are assigned to the trustee. If follows, therefore, that no further transactions should be permitted on that account. The balance should be transferred to the account of the trustee.

11-245 The Deeds of Arrangement Act 1914 was not repealed by the Insolvency Acts of 1985 and 1986. Minor amendments were made to the 1914 Act, the principal one being the elimination of references to acts of bankruptcy, and their capacity to invalidate a deed, even though it had been duly registered and assented to by the requisite majority in number and value of the creditors. The result is that the deeds of arrangement procedure has become stronger and safer for debtors and for the majority of their creditors.

Section II
ACCOUNTS OF COMPANIES

11-246 In modern times most large bank accounts, whether in credit or overdrawn, are those of companies engaged in trade. Therefore, it is essential for bank officials to possess a general knowledge of company law as a whole and a more specialized knowledge of those aspects of the subject which are of direct concern to bankers. Accordingly, some consideration must now be given to the main types of companies, and to the steps to be taken when a bank transacts business with them. A detailed exposition of company law is, however, outside the scope of this book.[31]

29 S. 3(1).
30 S. 3(4).
31 On the subject generally, see Charlesworth and Cain, *Company Law*; or, for a fuller treatment, L. C. B. Gower, *The Principles of Modern Company Law*; *Palmer's Company Law*; Robert R. Pennington, *Company Law*; and *Gore-Browne on Companies*.

Types of company

11-247 The commonest type of company is the 'company limited by shares', in which the liability of each member is limited to the amount unpaid on the shares held by him; once his shares are fully paid, he has no further liability. Then there are companies which are 'limited by guarantee'. In contrast to these two groups, there are 'unlimited companies', in which the liability of each member for the debts and liabilities of the company is unlimited. Finally, there are 'chartered companies'. These will be considered briefly in turn.

(a) Companies limited by shares

Public and private companies

11-248 Companies may be either public or private, the latter being far more numerous than the former. A public company is a company limited by shares or by guarantee[32] and having a share capital, being a company (a) the memorandum of which states that the company is to be a public company, and (b) in relation to which the provisions of the Companies Act as to registration of a public company have been complied with.[33]

11-249 The most important provision as to registration of a public company is the rule that a public company must have a prescribed minimum amount of capital. This rule was introduced by the Companies Act 1980. The nominal value of a public company's allotted share capital must be not less than £50,000, or such other sum as the Secretary of State may by order have by statutory instrument specified instead.[34] Furthermore, a public company must not allot a share except as paid up at least to one-quarter of the nominal value of the share and the whole of any premium on it.[35]

11-250 Section 1(3) of the Companies Act 1985 provides that a private company, unless the context otherwise requires, means a company that is not a public company. The distinguishing feature of a private company is that it does not offer its shares or debentures to the public. Section 81(1) of the Act provides that a private company (other than a company limited by guarantee and not having a share capital) commits

---

32 For companies limited by guarantee, see *post*, paras 11-258/260.
33 Companies Act 1985, s. 1(3). With effect from 22 December 1980, a company cannot be formed as, or become, a company limited by guarantee with a share capital; Companies Act 1980, s. 1(2) and Companies Act 1985, s. 1(4).
34 Companies Act 1985, ss. 117(2) and 118.
35 S. 101(1).

an offence if it offers to the public (whether for cash or otherwise) any shares or debentures of the company, or if it allots, or agrees to allot (whether for cash or otherwise) any shares or debentures of the company with a view to all or any of those shares or debentures being offered for sale to the public. Nevertheless, s. 81(3) of the Act provides that any issue of shares or debentures following such an offer will not be invalid.

11-251   The articles of association of a private company usually restrict the right to transfer its shares.[36] An article which is frequently employed for this purpose provides that 'the directors may decline to register any transfer of shares to any person of whom they do not approve'. The principal advantage of having such an article is that it enables the present members to preserve the company's private character. Most private companies are formed to acquire family businesses, and the shareholders naturally wish to ensure, as far as possible, that the business is kept in the family. The shares of private companies are not quoted on the Stock Exchange: there is no market in the shares. The shares of many public companies are quoted on the Stock Exchange.

11-252   As a general rule, a private company must have the word 'limited' as the last word of its name, and the name of a public company must end with the words 'public limited company'.[37] In the case of a company whose registered office is in Wales, the Welsh equivalents may be used, namely, 'cyfyngedig' (abbreviation 'cyf.') for 'limited' (abbreviation 'ltd'.), and 'cwmni cyfyngedig cyhoeddus' (abbreviation 'c.c.c.') for 'public limited company' (abbreviation 'p.l.c.').[38]

11-253   A public company, if registered after 31 October 1929, must have at least two directors, whereas a private company need have only one.[39]

11-254   It is easier to form a private company than a public company. Since a private company must not make an invitation to the public to subscribe for its shares or debentures, a prospectus is not required. Furthermore, a private company is permitted to start business immediately it is incorporated, but a public company cannot do so until various conditions have been fulfilled and a certificate has been obtained from the registrar of companies.[40]

---

36 Under the Companies Act 1948, s. 28(1), the restriction was obligatory, but the section was repealed by the Companies Act 1980, s. 88 and Sched. 4.
37 Companies Act 1985, s. 25.
38 For the provisions relating to these companies see the Companies Act 1985, ss 25(1), 26(1) and (3), and s. 27(4).
39 Companies Act 1985, s. 282.
40 S. 117(1).

Change from private to public company, and vice versa

11-255 A private company may, and sometimes does, become a public company, for example when it wishes to offer shares to the public. Conversely, a public company may become a private company. Changes from private to public company, and vice versa, do not directly affect the relationship between a company and its bankers.

Close companies

11-256 Briefly, a close company is a company, either public or private, which is controlled by five or fewer persons termed 'participators'.[41] However, a company is not to be treated as being at any time a close company if shares in the company carrying not less than 35 per cent of the voting power in the company (and not being shares entitled to a fixed rate of dividend, whether with or without a further right to participate in profits) have been allotted unconditionally to, or acquired unconditionally by, and are at that time beneficially held by, the public, and any such shares have within the preceding twelve months been the subject of dealings on a recognized stock exchange.[42]

11-257 The concept of the close company was introduced in order to combat certain forms of tax avoidance. For example, a company would make a loan to a shareholder, and then a few years later the company would release the debt. The law now provides that loans by a close company to a participator are liable to tax. The company must pay tax at the basic rate on the 'grossed-up' amount of the loan.[43] If and when the loan or any part of it is repaid to the company, the amount of tax paid by the company, or a proportionate part of it is repaid. If, however, the company releases the debt, the participator becomes liable to tax on the 'grossed-up' amount of the loan.[44]

(b) Companies limited by guarantee

11-258 A company limited by guarantee is one wherein the liability of its members is limited, by its memorandum of association, to such amount as the members may thereby undertake to contribute to the assets of the company in the event of its being wound up.[45] In effect, therefore, they are in the position of guarantors of the company's debts up to the agreed amount. By virtue of the Companies Act 1980,[46] any

41 Income and Corporation Taxes Act 1988, s. 414.
42 S. 415.
43 S. 419.
44 S. 421.
45 Companies Act 1985, s. 1(2).
46 S. 1(1) and (2). The rule has been re-enacted in the Companies Act 1985, s. 1(3).

newly constituted companies limited by guarantee must be private companies.

11-259 Where a private company limited by guarantee is formed for promoting commerce, art, science, education, religion, charity or anything incidental or conducive thereto, and intends to apply its profits, if any, in promoting its objects, and to prohibit the payment of dividends to its members, the company may be registered with limited liability, but without the word 'limited' in its name.[47] Charitable and other non-profit-making organizations are often registered as companies limited by guarantee. Such companies are particularly suitable for non-profit-making associations, because the members may not want to put any money into the organization, as they would have to do if they subscribed for shares.

11-260 It used to be possible to form a company limited by guarantee with a share capital.[48] However, with effect from 22 December 1980, it has not been possible to form a company of this nature.[49] Those companies limited by guarantee with a share capital which had been formed prior to that date will continue as such. In the rare cases when such companies were formed, the purpose was to enable them to obtain small sums by way of capital from their members and, perhaps, to distribute profits. Theatre clubs were sometimes constituted in this way.

(c) Unlimited companies

11-261 An unlimited company (which may be either public or private) is one in which, in the event of liquidation, the liability of each member for the debts and obligations of the company is unlimited. Thus, each member is in a position which is comparable with that of a partner of a firm. However, an unlimited company does enjoy certain advantages which are not possessed by a partnership; thus an unlimited company is a legal entity with perpetual succession, and the liability of each member ceases at the end of one year from the date on which his membership is terminated.[50] One or two banking companies, e.g. Coutts & Co. and C. Hoare & Co., are still unlimited companies.

11-261A Very few unlimited companies are formed at the present day. However, a number of companies, which were formerly limited,

47 Companies Act 1985, s. 30.
48 See the specimen memorandum and articles in the Companies Act 1948, Sched. 1, Table D.
49 See the Companies Act 1980, s. 1(2), and the Companies Act 1985, s. 1(4).
50 Insolvency Act 1986, s. 74(1) and (2).

changed their constitution and became 'unlimited' as a result of the provisions in the Companies Act 1967,[51] which abolished the status of 'exempt private company'. One of the privileges which used to be enjoyed by exempt private companies was exemption from the necessity to file copies of their annual accounts with the Registrar of Companies. When the Companies Act 1967 was passed, some limited companies became 'unlimited' in order to avoid having to file their accounts with the Registrar, where they would be open public scrutiny. The effect of s. 241(4) of the Companies Act 1985 is that, as a general rule, unlimited companies still do not have to file their accounts with the Registrar.

(d) Chartered companies

11-262 The Companies Act 1985 refers to companies formed in pursuance of 'letters patent'.[52] This relates to companies which have been granted a charter by the Crown, either by virtue of the Royal Prerogative or by special statutory powers. Formerly, the Crown would grant a charter to trading concerns, e.g. the Hudson Bay Company and the British South Africa Company, but this is never done today. There are, however, about twenty chartered companies, mainly banks and insurance companies, which are still trading today. Some of these companies are now also limited by shares.

11-263 The method of incorporation by Royal Charter was also employed in the past, and is occasionally employed today, in the case of charities, learned and artistic societies, and schools and colleges. Thus, some leading public schools, as well as some universites and colleges, have been granted Royal Charters. The Institute of Bankers was awarded a Royal Charter in 1987.

11-264 The modern procedure for obtaining a charter is for the members of the body to petition the Crown, through the office of the Lord President of the Council, praying for the grant of a charter. If the petition is granted, the promoters and their successors become 'one body corporate and politic by the name of ... and by that name shall and may sue or be sued, plead and be impleaded in all courts whether of law or of equity ... and shall have perpetual succession and a common seal'.

Opening a company's account

11-265 Occasionally, a company is formed or acquired for a fraudulent purpose, and there is a risk that the directors may open a banking

51 S. 2.
52 S. 716.

account and pay into the account cheques to which the company is not entitled. If none of the directors are known to the bank, their identity and integrity should be established: references should be obtained and followed up. Where at least one of the directors is already known to the bank, his introduction of the others is usually considered sufficient.

11-266   The legal status of a company is different from that of a private individual or an English partnership in that a company is a separate entity created under the law. If certain prescribed formalities are followed, a company comes into existence, but if those formalities are not observed, there is no resulting legal entity. This is important to bankers, because they cannot transact business with 'companies' which have not been properly incorporated. Thus, any loans made by a bank to a 'company' before it comes into existence are usually irrecoverable from the company, though anyone who purports to act on behalf of the company prior to its incorporation will be personally liable on the contract.[53] Accordingly, whenever a bank is asked to open an account for a company, the following documents should be required.

(a) Certificate of incorporation

11-267   On registration of a company, the Registrar of Companies issues a certificate stating that the company is incorporated. In the case of a limited company it states that the company is limited[54] and, in the case of a public company, it states that the company is a public company.[55] This certificate is conclusive evidence that all the requirements of the Companies Act 1985 in respect of registration have been complied with.[56] When the certificate is handed to the bank, the number of the company and the date of incorporation should be noted, and the certificate should then be returned to the company.

(b) Trading certificate

11-268   A private company may commence business as soon as it is incorporated; thus it may open and conduct a banking account. A public company, however, cannot commence business until some further formalities have been complied with and the Registrar issues a further certificate, commonly called a 'trading certificate', entitling the company to commence business.[57] If a company commences business before this certificate has been issued, the company and its officers are liable to a

---

53 Companies Act 1985, s. 36(3).
54 S. 13(1).
55 S. 13(6).
56 S. 13(7).
57 S. 117(1).

fine.[58] When a newly constituted public company applies to a bank to open an account, the bank should ensure that it has obtained its trading certificate. If, however, a company has been in existence for some time, it is not the practice to require production of this certificate.

(c) Memorandum and articles of association

11-269 A copy of these two documents should be obtained from the company and retained by the bank. As amendments to the documents may have been made from time to time, it is prudent to enquire whether the copy supplied to the bank is up to date, and it is also desirable to ask the secretary to the company to advise the bank of any subsequent amendments.

(i) Memorandum of association

11-270 The Companies Act 1985[59] provides that the memorandum of every company must state:

(a) the name of the company, with 'limited' as the last word of the name in the case of a company limited by shares or by guarantee;[60]

(b) whether the registered office of the company is to be situated in England[61] or in Scotland;

(c) the objects of the company;

(d) that the liability of the members is limited, in the case of a company limited by shares or by guarantee; and

(e) in the case of a limited company having a share capital, the amount of share capital and its division into shares of a fixed amount.

In the case of a company limited by guarantee, the memorandum must also state that each member undertakes to contribute to the assets of the company in the event of its being wound up while he is a member, or within one year after he ceases to be a member, such amount as may be required, not exceeding a specified amount.

(ii) Articles of association

11-271 The articles set out the powers of the directors and of the members, and they contain many regulations governing the internal

58 S. 117(7).
59 S. 2.
60 The effect of s. 1(3) of the Act is that the memorandum of a public company must state that the company is to be a public company.
61 For this purpose, 'England' includes Wales: Interpretation Act 1978, s. 22 and Sched. 2, para. 5, replacing an earlier provision contained in the Wales and Berwick Act 1746, s. 3.

working and management of the company. However, in the case of articles of companies limited by guarantee one often finds no reference to directors. Frequently, the governing body is a council or a committee. Their powers are set out in the articles.

11-272 A bank should note especially those provisions in the memorandum and articles dealing with banking and the borrowing of money. The borrowing powers of companies and the authority of directors to borrow on behalf of their companies will be considered subsequently.[62]

Mandate for company's account

11-273 The documents already mentioned, namely the company's certificate of incorporation, its trading certificate (where appropriate), and a copy of its memorandum and articles of association, are usually handed to the bank, together with a certified copy of a resolution of the board of directors appointing the bank as bankers of the company. (In the case of a company limited by guarantee, the resolution will be passed by its governing body, usually a council or committee.) The resolution gives detailed instructions concerning operations on the company's account or accounts at the bank, and constitutes the company's mandate to the bank.

11-274 At the present day, most banks supply prospective company customers with a printed form setting out the terms of a suitable draft resolution, which may be completed by filling in the necessary details. The resolution is passed at a meeting of the board of directors. Then, the chairman and secretary sign the bank's form certifying that the resolution (which is set out in full) has been duly passed. Specimen signatures of those authorized to sign on behalf of the company are usually given on the form. The following clauses would be suitable for inclusion in a standard form of resolution, though this may, of course, require amendment to meet the needs of special cases:

1. That an account be opened with the bank.
2. That the bank be instructed to honour and debit to the company's account or accounts whether in credit or overdrawn or becoming overdrawn in consequence of any such debit, all cheques or other orders signed, bills accepted and promissory notes made on behalf of the company, provided that they are signed accepted or made by ... (*here and in clauses 3, 4 and 5 should be inserted the number of persons required to sign and their descriptions, e.g. two directors and the secretary*).

---

62 *Post*, para. 11-276.

3. That all bills of exchange and promissory notes payable to the company be endorsed on behalf of the company by ...

4. That the bank be instructed to honour the signatures of ... to all warrants issued in respect of dividend or interest.

5. That ... be and are hereby authorized on behalf of the company to withdraw any of the company's securities and to give instructions with regard to the purchase or sale of any securities of the company or any foreign exchange.

6. That any ... directors be and are hereby appointed a committee of the board with full authority to arrange with the bank from time to time for advances to the company by way of loan and/or overdraft.

7. That this resolution be communicated to the bank and remain in force until an amending resolution shall be passed by the board of directors, and a copy thereof, certified by the chairman of the meeting, shall be communicated to the bank.

8. That the bank be informed of any changes which may occur from time to time in the directors and other officers of the company.

The making of loans by a company for the purchase of its shares

11-275   The law which governs the making of loans by a company for the purchase of its own shares is complicated, and it is proposed to examine briefly the principal developments which have taken place. A convenient starting point is s. 54 of the Companies Act 1948. That section provided that, subject to certain exceptions, it was unlawful for a company to give, whether directly or indirectly, and whether by means of a loan, guarantee, the provision of security or otherwise, any financial assistance for the purchase of or subscription for, its own or its holding company's shares.

11-275A   One of the reasons for the amendment of the rule relating to 'financial assistance' was the judgment of the Court of Appeal in *Belmont Finance Corporation* v. *Williams Furniture Ltd (No. 2).*[63] The case was concerned with the situation where a company enters into a commercial transaction, for example buying goods from X, and, at the same time, X uses the proceeds of sale to buy shares in the company. The Court of Appeal held that, in such a case, if the company genuinely needed those goods, there might be no breach of s. 54. However, if the company made the purchases solely to provide X with the means to buy

63   [1980] 1 All ER 393.

its shares, then there was a breach, even if the company paid a fair price for the goods.

11-275B The law was amended by the Companies Act 1981. It is not intended to refer to the sections of the Act, because its provisions have been re-enacted in the Companies Act 1985. Section 151(1) of the 1985 Act contains the basic prohibition, and it is expressed in terms of purpose. Subject to certain exempted cases in relation to public companies, and to special provisions in favour of private companies, where a person is acquiring or is proposing to acquire shares in a company, it is not lawful for the company or any of its subsidiaries to give financial assistance directly or indirectly for the purpose of that acquisition before or at the same time as the acquisition takes place. Section 151(2) provides that it is not lawful for the company or any of its subsidiaries to give financial assistance to reduce or discharge any liability incurred by any person in acquiring shares of the company. By s. 153(1) the prohibitions do not apply where the company's 'principal purpose' is not to give financial assistance for the purpose of any such acquisition, or the giving of the assistance for that purpose is but an incidental part of some 'larger purpose' of the company, and the assistance is given in good faith in the interests of the company. The use of expressions such as 'principal purpose' and 'larger purpose' may give rise to some interesting decisions by the courts.[64] Section 153(3) and (4) refer to a total of ten specific permitted transactions, which would otherwise have been prohibited by s. 151. Thus, s. 153(4) provides that the prohibition does not apply where the lending of money is part of the ordinary business of a company; for example, a bank may make loans to its customers for the purchase of shares in the bank.

11-275C The restriction in s. 151 of the Companies Act 1985 are relaxed by s. 155 in favour of private companies. Financial assistance may be given if the private company's net assets ae not reduced thereby, or to the extent that they are reduced, if the assistance is provided out of distributable profits. This special relaxation in favour of private companies is in addition to the exceptions already mentioned which apply to all companies. The special relaxation in favour of private companies was introduced in order to provide a lawful means whereby senior officials employed by a private company may obtain financial assistance from the company for the purpose of acquiring shares in the company, thus enabling the existing owners of the shares to sell them to senior officials employed by the company. This type of transaction is sometimes referred to as a 'management buy-out'.

---

64 See the decision of the House of Lords in *Brady and another* v. *Brady and another* [1988] 2 All ER 617.

Borrowing powers of companies and directors

11-276   When a company applies to a bank for accommodation, it is imperative to ensure that the company has power to borrow the sum specified and that the directors have authority to contract the loan on the company's behalf. For these purposes it is essential to examine the company's memorandum and articles of association.

(a) Memorandum of association

11-277   As already stated,[65] the memorandum sets out, among other things, the objects for which the company was incorporated. Thus, the memorandum is the company's charter and defines the limitation of its powers.[66] Any act not authorized by the memorandum is *ultra vires* ('beyond the powers of') the company and is void. The only exception to this rule is that, when an object is set out in the memorandum, the company has implied power to do other acts which are reasonably incidental thereto.[67]

11-278   With regard to borrowing money it is firmly established that a trading company has implied power to borrow and to give security for the purposes of its business.[68] Strictly speaking, therefore, this power need not be (though it almost invariably is) expressly set out in the memorandum of a trading company. A non-trading company has no power to borrow, unless its memorandum expressly so provides.

11-279   In every case the memorandum should be carefully examined, because, even in the case of a trading company, the memorandum may, and very occasionally does, place a limit on the company's borrowing powers. The importance of this examination is apparent, for, if money is borrowed by a company in circumstances which render the borrowing *ultra vires* the company, the borrowing does not give rise to any indebtedness, either at law or in equity, on the part of the company.[69] However, a lender who finds himself in this position has not necessarily lost his money, because:

> It seems that the company, if it wishes, may voluntarily repay the loan, such repayment being regarded as simply returning to the lender

---

65   *Ante*, para. 11-270.
66   *Per* Lord Cairns L.C. in *Ashbury Railway Carriage and Iron Co* v. *Riche* (1875) LR 7 HL 653, at p. 668.
67   *Attorney-General* v. *Great Eastern Railway Co.* (1880) 5 App Cas 473.
68   *General Auction Estate and Monetary Co.* v. *Smith* [1891] 3 Ch 432.
69   *Re National Permanent Benefit Building Society, Ex parte Williamson* (1869) 5 Ch App 309; *Re Jon Beauforte (London) Ltd*, [1953] Ch 131.

the lender's own money, which never became the property of the company.[70]

If the borrowed money is applied in paying off legitimate debts of the company, the lender is entitled to rank as the company's creditor to the extent to which the money has been so applied.[71]

If the lender can identify his money or the investment of his money in the hands of the company, he may be entitled to a 'tracing order'. The principle is that the funds in question remain the property of the lender, and he can call for its return.[72]

Section 35(1) of the Companies Act 1985 provides that 'in favour of a person dealing with a company in good faith, any transaction decided on by the directors is deemed to be one which it is within the capacity of the company to enter into, and the power of the directors to bind the company is deemed to be free of any limitation under the memorandum or articles'. Section 35(2) of the Act provides that 'a party to a transaction so decided on is not bound to enquire as to the capacity of the company to enter into it or as to any such limitation on the powers of the directors, and is presumed to have acted in good faith unless the contrary is proved.'

Although these provisions modified the *ultra vires* rule very substantially, they are not in practice relied upon by bankers, because bankers usually possess a copy of a company's memorandum and articles and, therefore, have express notice of their contents. It seems doubtful whether a banker would be acting 'in good faith' within the meaning of s. 35 if he knowingly lent money to a company for a purpose which was *ultra vires* the company.[73]

11-279A In *TCB Ltd* v. *Gray*[74] the plaintiff company, a secondary bank, had lent money to two companies, one of which issued a debenture as security. The loan was guaranteed by the defendant who was a director of and principal shareholder in the companies. The defendant subsequently claimed that the debenture, and consequentially his guarantee, were invalid because, *inter alia*, the debenture had not been signed and sealed in accordance with the company's articles of association. These provided that the company's seal should only be used by the authority of the directors, and that every instrument to which the seal should be affixed 'shall be signed by a director'. What had happened was that the defendant had given a general power of attorney to his

---

70 *Sinclair* v. *Brougham* [1914] AC 398, at p. 426.
71 *Sinclair* v. *Brougham* (*supra*), at p. 440.
72 *Re Birkbeck Permanent Benefit Building Society* [1912] 2 Ch 183, at p. 232.
73 Cf. *International Sales and Agencies Ltd* v. *Marcus* [1982] 3 All ER 551.
74 [1986] Ch 621.

solicitor, and it was his solicitor who had signed the debenture to which the seal had been affixed.

Browne-Wilkinson V-C held that the debenture was binding on the company because of the provisions of s. 9 of the European Communities Act 1972, now s. 35 of the Companies Act 1985. As is stated in the preceding paragraph, this section renders a transaction entered into 'in good faith' by a third party, who was dealing with the directors of a company, binding on the company irrespective of any limitation on the capacity of the company to enter into the transaction or any limitation on the powers of the directors to bind the company. The court held that the plaintiff company had acted in good faith. It followed that the validity of the debenture could not be challenged.

11-280 If follows, therefore, that a prudent banker will take every care to ensure that advances which he makes to companies are not *ultra vires*. If the memorandum limits the company's borrowing powers, it is advisable to have the limit removed; this may be done by a special resolution of the company, unless the memorandum itself expressly prohibits such an alteration.[75] As a general rule, no application to the court is necessary, but the company must deliver to the Registrar of Companies a printed copy of its memorandum as altered. Alternatively, if it is not desired to remove the limit contained in the memorandum, the banker must, of course, make certain that his advance will not cause the company's borrowing powers to be exceeded, and then the advance should be made by way of fixed loan, so that, if the company increases its borrowings from elsewhere, there is no risk of later advances by the bank on current account being *ultra vires*.

11-281 The power to borrow contained in the memorandum is usually expressed to be 'for the purpose of the company's business'. A banker invariably enquires the purpose for which the borrowing is required, and he should ensure that the purpose is consistent with the company's objects as set out in the memorandum. In *Re Introductions Ltd*,[76] the National Provincial Bank lent £29,571 on the strength of a clause in a company's memorandum empowering the company to raise or borrow money on a security. By way of security, the company executed certain debentures in favour of the bank. The bank knew that the company was carrying on a business which was inconsistent with the company's objects as set out in its memorandum, and the bank lent the money for the purpose of that business. The company went into liquidation, and it was held that the bank could not enforce its security, even though the memorandum contained a sub-clause declaring that one of the objects

75 Companies Act 1985, ss 4 and 17.
76 [1968] 2 All ER 1221; affirmed [1969] 1 All ER 887.

of the company was to borrow or raise money in such manner as it thought fit, and this was followed by another sub-clause declaring that the objects set out in each sub-clause were 'independent objects' of the company. Counsel for the bank had conceded that, if the sub-clause relating to the borrowing of money had to be construed as a power, such a power must be for a purpose within the company's memorandum. He argued, however, that it was 'elevated into an object' by the sub-clause which declared that the objects set out in each sub-clause were 'independent objects' of the company. This submission was rejected; Harman LJ answered it by stating that one cannot convert a power into an object by saying so.

Reform of the ultra vires rule

11-281A   Reference should be made to Appendix 3 for the relevant provisions of the Companies Act 1989.

(b) Articles of association

11-282   A company's articles often provide quite shortly that the directors may exercise the company's borrowing powers, though occasionally it is provided that the borrowing powers must be exercised by the company in general meeting.

11-283   In some cases directors are given unlimited borrowing powers; in others there may be some special restriction, e.g. the articles may provide that the amount for the time being remaining undischarged of moneys borrowed by the directors for the purposes of the company shall not at any time exceed a stated sum, without the sanction of the company in general meeting.

11-284   When there is a definite limit to the directors' borrowing powers, some banks obtain periodically from the secretary a certificate that the total amount borrowed by the company does not exceed the authorized amount. If the total borrowings do, in fact, exceed this figure, the question arises whether or not it is essential for the bank to ensure that the necessary formalities (e.g. the passing of a resolution by the company) have been observed. This problem is governed by the Rule in *Turquand's* case.[77]

What constitutes borrowing

11-285   In calculating the amount which a company has already borrowed, one must include all outstanding loans (whether secured or not), overdrafts from bankers, and 'deposits' from directors and staff. Trade

77 *Post*, para. 11-292.

debts are, of course, excluded. The amount obtained by discounting trade bills of exchange should probably be excluded, though there appears to be no judicial authority on this point. Although discounting a bill is in a sense a mode of borrowing, it is usually looked upon as the realization of an asset. This does not apply to accommodation bills; if these are discounted, the sum realized should certainly be taken into account when calculating the total borrowing of the company.

Table A

11-286   A company limited by shares need not draft special articles of its own, in which case the articles contained in Table A of the appropriate Companies Act will apply.[78] Furthermore, even if a company has its own articles, Table A will apply except in so far as it is not excluded or modified by the articles.[79] If, therefore, a banker finds that a company's articles make no reference to borrowing powers, the legal position depends upon the provisions contained in the Table A in force at the date of the company's incorporation.

11-287   In regard to companies incorporated prior to 1 October 1906, Table A of the Companies Act 1862 applies to these companies and imposes no limit on the borrowing powers of the directors.

11-288   In regard to companies incorporated between 1 October 1906, and 30 June 1948, the relevant Table A[80] provides that the amount remaining undischarged of moneys borrowed by the directors for the purposes of the company (otherwise than by the issue of share capital) must not at any time exceed the issued share capital of the company, without the sanction of the company in general meetings.

11-289   In regard to companies incorporated between 1 July 1948 and 30 June 1985, article 79 of Table A of the First Schedule to the Companies Act 1948 provides that:

> The directors may exercise all the powers of the company to borrow money, and to mortgage or charge its undertaking, property and uncalled capital, or any part thereof, and to issue debentures, debenture stock, and other securities whether outright or as security for any debt, liability or obligation of the company or of any third party:

78 Companies limited by guarantee and unlimited companies must have their own articles: Companies Act 1985, s. 7. There is a specimen set of articles for a company limited by guarantee and not having a share capital in Table C of the Companies (Tables A to F) Regulations 1985.
79 Companies Act 1985, s. 8(2).
80 See Order of the Board of Trade 1906, substituting a new Table A for that contained in the Companies Act 1862; Companies (Consolidation) Act 1908, Table A, article 73; Companies Act 1929, Table A, article 69.

Provided that the amount for the time being remaining undischarged of moneys borrowed or secured by the directors as aforesaid (apart from temporary loans obtained from the company's bankers in the ordinary course of business) shall not at any time, without the previous sanction of the company in general meetings, exceed the nominal amount of the share capital of the company for the time being issued, but nevertheless no lender or other person dealing with the company shall be concerned to see or inquire whether this limit is observed. No debt incurred or security given in excess of such limit shall be invalid or ineffectual except in the case of express notice to the lender or the recipient of the security at the time when the debt was incurred or security given that the limit hereby imposed had been or was thereby exceeded.

At first sight this seems to be a welcome change in the law. However, a word of caution is necessary. The effect of article 79 is not as clear as it might have been. Thus, 'temporary loans' from bankers are excluded when ascertaining the limit to the directors' borrowing powers, but what is a *temporary* loan? Many loans to companies for trading purposes, although repayable upon demand, are renewed year after year. If a banker fails to satisfy the court that the loan is 'temporary', he will probably find himself in difficulties with the last sentence of article 79 which denies protection to lenders who have 'express notice' that the limit was being exceeded. Usually, a banker requires production of a company's balance sheet, and therefore has express notice (though often much delayed) of borrowings from sources other than the bank. In short, the value of the new provisions contained in article 79 is questionable. Whenever possible, bankers still prefer to ensure that the directors' borrowing powers are not exceeded.

11-290 Another point to note in regard to article 79 is that the opening sentence refers to securities issued by the company for the debts, liabilities or obligations of the company *or of any third party*, and the proviso refers to the amount secured by the directors *as aforesaid*. This would clearly seem to mean that in calculating the limit of the directors' powers the following transactions must be included: (a) securities (including guarantees) given by the company to secure the debts of third parties, and (b) bonds or indemnities given by the company to secure the due performance of contracts by third parties.

11-290A In regard to companies incorporated on and after 1 July 1985, regulation 70 of Table A of the Companies (Tables A to F) Regulations 1985 provides that:

Subject to the provisions of the Act, the memorandum and the articles and to any directions given by special resolution, the business of the company shall be managed by the directors who may exercise all the powers of the company. No alteration of the memorandum or articles and no such direction shall invalidate any prior act of the directors which would have been valid if that alteration had not been made or that direction had not been given. The powers given by this regulation shall not be limited by any special power given to the directors by the articles and a meeting of directors at which a quorum is present may exercise all powers exercisable by the directors.

This is a welcome change in the law. However, it applies only to companies incorporated on and after 1 July 1985. There are many companies in existence which had been incorporated prior to that date, and, in relation to those companies, the borrowing powers of the directors may be limited as already stated.

Loans in excess of directors' borrowing powers

11-291 If a banker or other lender finds that he has made a loan to a company in excess of the directors' borrowing powers, the most satisfactory way of regularizing the position is to ask the directors to call a general meeting of the company, at which a resolution may be passed ratifying the excess borrowing. This may lawfully be done, provided, of course, that the borrowing was not *ultra vires* the company.[81] Alternatively, the lender may be able to bring an action against the directors personally for breach of warranty of authority,[82] though naturally one would not wish to pursue this course if the directors are prepared to have the borrowing ratified by the shareholders in general meeting.

11-292 There is yet a third possibility. The company itself will be liable to repay the loan, if the lender can show that the transaction was within the directors' *ostensible* authority. This rule – usually referred to as the Rule in *Turquand's case*[83] – may be stated thus: 'Persons contracting with a company and dealing in good faith may assume that acts within its constitution and powers have been properly and duly performed, and are not bound to inquire whether acts of internal management have been regular'.[84]

11-293 The Rule in *Turquand's* case may be illustrated by the following example. Suppose a company's articles provide that sums borrowed by the directors shall not exceed £10,000 without the sanction of the company in general meeting. The directors, on the company's behalf, ask for banking accommodation which would increase the total

---

81 *Grant* v. *United Kingdom Switchback Railways Co.* (1888) 40 ChD 135.
82 *Weeks* v. *Propert* (1873) LR 8 CP 427.
83 *Royal British Bank* v. *Turquand* (1856) 6 E & B 327.
84 This statement of the rule, which was taken from *Halsbury's Laws of England* (2nd ed.), Vol. 5, p. 423, was cited with approval by Lord Simonds in *Morris* v. *Kanssen* [1946] AC 459 at p. 474.

borrowings of the company to more than £10,000. Under these circumstances the bank would be entitled to assume that the appropriate resolution had been passed by the company in general meeting, but the bank would usually have to be able to prove that it actually knew of the provisions in the articles at the time when it entered into the transaction.[85]

11-294 The practice of bankers in relation to the Rule in *Turquand's* case is not uniform: some bankers rely upon the Rule, whereas others require evidence that the due formalities have been observed. In the illustration, for example, one could ask the secretary for a certified copy of the resolution passed at the general meeting.

Overdraft arrangements with companies

11-295 It is the usual practice for one or two members of the board of directors, sometimes accompanied by the secretary or the general manager, to discuss their company's financial requirements with officials of the bank. The representatives of the bank will first have to be satisfied (a) that the proposed advance is a proper one from a banking standpoint, (b) that the company has power to borrow the desired sum,[86] and (c) that the directors have authority to borrow on behalf of the company.[87]

11-296 Finally, it may be necessary to decide whether or not the board of directors should be asked to pass a formal resolution requesting the accommodation. There is considerable divergence of practice between bankers in regard to the obtaining of borrowing resolutions. Some banks seem to obtain them automatically in every case; others seem to dispense with them altogether.

11-297 As regards the law, there is a general principle that agents cannot delegate their authority to others – *delegatus non protest delegare*. Since directors are themselves agents, prima facie this rule applies to them. However, a company's articles often provide that the directors may delegate any of their powers to committees consisting of

---

85 The law on this subject is difficult, and some of the cases appear to be conflicting. See *Houghton & Co.* v. *Nothard, Low & Wills Ltd* [1927] 1 KB 246, affirmed on different grounds, [1928] AC 1; *Kreditbank Cassel* v. *Schenkers Ltd* [1927] 1 KB 826; *British Thomson-Houston Co. Ltd* v. *Federated European Bank Ltd* [1932] 2 KB 176; *Rama Corporation Ltd* v. *Proved Tin and General Investments Ltd* [1952] 2 QB 147; *Freeman and Lockyear* v. *Buckhurst Park Properties (Mangal) Ltd* [1964] 2 QB 480; *Hely-Hutchinson* v. *Brayhead* [1968] 1 QB 549.

86 *Ante*, paras. 11-278/9.

87 *Ante*, paras. 11-282/4.

such member or members of their body as they think fit.[88] When there is power to delegate, delegated authority will be presumed where one or two directors act in a matter properly within the ordinary business of the company,[89] at all events in favour of those who deal with such director or directors with knowledge that the articles contain such a provision.

11-298   From a practical standpoint, there is much to be said in favour of investigating the position at the outset, when the company opens its account. If the company's articles provide that the directors may delegate any of their powers to some of their number, the directors should be invited to incorporate a suitable clause in the resolution to be passed by the board, appointing the bank as bankers to the company, to the effect that 'any ... directors be and are hereby appointed a committee of the board with full authority to arrange with the bank from time to time for advances to the company by way of loan and/or overdraft'.[91] In that way, the position may be established for the future: the specified number of directors may properly act on behalf of the company.

Advances for wages or salaries

11-299   Certain classes of creditors are, by law, treated preferentially either in the event of the company being wound up or in the event of a receiver being appointed.[92] These preferential creditors, as they are usually called, have priority over creditors holding a floating charge and over unsecured creditors, but not over creditors who hold a fixed charge on the company's assets. The following debts (which rank equally between themselves) are among those given priority in this way:[93]

(a)   Value added tax having become due within the previous six months.

(b)   Car tax, general betting and other gaming duties having become due within the previous twelve months.

(c)   Sums due from the company to the Inland Revenue as deductions from employees' salaries under PAYE for the previous twelve months.

---

88 Article 102, Table A, Sched. I. Companies Act 1948 contains such a power. See also regulation 72 of the Companies (Tables A to F) Regulations 1985.
89 *Totterdell* v. *Fareham Blue Brick and Tile Co.* (1866) LR 1 CP 674.
90 *Houghton & Co.* v. *Nothard, Lowe and Wills Ltd* (*supra*); *Kreditbank Cassel* v. *Schenkers Ltd* (*supra*).
91 *Ante*, para. 11-274.
92 Insolvency Act 1986, s. 175.
93 S. 386 and Sched. 6.

(d) Wages or salary of any employee in respect of services rendered to the company during the previous four months, not exceeding £800 in the case of any one employee.

(e) All accrued holiday remuneration payable to an employee on the termination of his employment before or as a result of the winding up.

(f) National insurance contributions due from the company as class 1 or 2 payments under the Social Security Act 1975 for twelve months before the relevant date, and certain class 4 contributions due to the Inland Revenue for the preceding tax year.

(g) Any sum which is owed by the company and is a sum to which Schedule 3 to the Social Security Pensions Act 1975 applies (contributions to occupational pension schemes and state scheme premiums).

11-300 Accordingly, if a company is being wound up and the free (i.e. uncharged) assets are insufficient to pay the preferential debts listed above, those debts must be paid out of any property comprised in a floating (but not a fixed) charge in priority to the claims of the debenture holder. Likewise, if a company is *not* being wound up but a receiver is appointed, the preferential debts which have accrued up to the date of his appointment must be paid out of the assets comprised in a floating (but not a fixed) charge in priority to the claims of the debenture holder;[94] any such payments, however, may be recouped, as far as may be, out of the assets of the company available for payment of the general creditors.[95]

11-301 Any lender who has advanced money to the company to pay wages and salaries and accrued holiday remuneration is permitted to have the same preference as the employees would have had if their wages, salaries, or holiday remuneration has not been paid.[96] A company's bankers often take advantage of this provision by making advances for the payment of wages and salaries. Furthermore, it seems that if in fact an advance is used for this purpose, the company's bankers are entitled to rank as preferred creditors whether or not they *knew* of the intended application of the advance.[97] If they decline to make advances, other persons – for example, the directors – may make these advances themselves and thus obtain priority over a floating charge in favour of the bank. If a company is getting into financial difficulties, it is usually prudent for the bank to ask the company to open a separate wages account, to which all cheques for salaries and wages should be

---

94 Companies Act 1985, s. 196(1).
95 S. 196(5).
96 Insolvency Act 1986, Sched. 6.
97 *Re Rampgill Mill Ltd* [1967] Ch 1138.

debited. The company should also be requested to keep records showing the amount of 'preferential' salaries or wages in respect of each employee. Then, from time to time, transfers should be made from the company's ordinary account to the credit of the company's wages account to wipe out those wage advances which have lost their preferential character, e.g. because they were made more than four months previously.[98] Another account should be opened for holiday pay, which should be operated on similar lines. Interest and commission charges should be debited to the company's ordinary account.

11-302 The advantages of opening separate accounts for wages and salaries and holiday pay are, first, that it enables the bank to keep the position under review, and secondly, that it prevents the Rule in *Clayton's* case[99] from operating to the detriment of the bank. Thus, in *Re Rampgill Mill Ltd*,[1] a bank made advances to a company on its ordinary account, and part of the money was used for the payment of wages. The amount which would have qualified for preferential treatment was about £5,000. However, sums credited to the ordinary account had repaid some of the earlier advances, with the result that the bank had to reduce its preferential claim to about £2,160. The bank would not have had to reduce its preferential claims if it had made the wages advances through a separate wages account.

11-303 Even if separate accounts for wages and holiday pay are not opened, a bank may sometimes be able to claim preferential status for these advances. Thus in *Re Primrose (Builders) Ltd*,[2] a company maintained an overdrawn account at its bank. During the four months prior to winding up, cheques were drawn on the account for wages and holiday pay. Upon the payment of each such cheque, the bank insisted that a payment equal to or exceeding the amount of the cheque would shortly be paid into the account. Upon the liquidation of the company, the liquidator disputed the bank's claim to be a preferential creditor. He argued that the cheques for wages and holiday pay constituted separate advances made by the bank, and that they had been repaid by the credits which were paid into the account after each cheque was honoured. The court rejected this argument, and held that the advances for wages and holiday pay were entitled to preferential treatment.

---

98 Care should be taken not to make these transfers too soon; see *Re James R. Rutherford & Sons Ltd* [1964] 1 WLR 1211, where a bank lost part of its preferential claim for this reason.

99 (1816) 1 Mer 572.

1 [1967] Ch 1138.

2 [1950] 1 Ch 561. See also *National Provincial Bank Ltd* v. *Freedman and Rubens* (1934), *Journal of the Institute of Bankers*, Vol. LV, p. 392.

11-304 A bank is only entitled to claim as a preferential creditor for amounts debited to a company's wages account if those amounts represent *genuine* advances made by the bank. Thus, if the arrangement is that wages 'advances' must be covered by a credit balance in another banking account of the company, the bank cannot claim to be a preferential creditor.[3]

11-305 Furthermore, to qualify as 'wages', the payments must be by an employer to an employee. In the building industry, there is a system whereby a main contractor enters into an agreement with a subcontractor, sometimes called a gang leader, for the supply, by him, of labour only. It was held in *Re C. W. & A. L. Hughes Ltd*[4] that, as a contract for labour only is not a contract of employment, a bank which had advanced money on a wages account for the payment of subcontractors was not entitled to claim to be a preferential creditor.

11-306 Cheques debited to wages account sometimes include sums owing to the Inland Revenue under PAYE. If these sums are duly paid by the company to the Revenue, it is said that the bank may claim as preferential creditor for the full amount debited to wages account, i.e. in respect of the gross wages earned.[5] However, this question has not yet been resolved by the courts. It is, of course, clear that if the sums owing to the Revenue are not duly paid by the company to the Revenue, the latter may claim as preferential creditor in respect of PAYE deductions for the previous twelve months, and there cannot be two preferential claims in respect of the same sum. In such cases, the bank's preferential claim has to be reduced.

11-307 Where a bank which holds certain security charged by a company makes wages advances to the company and the company goes into liquidation, the bank is entitled to appropriate the proceeds of the sale of the security in discharge of *non*-preferential advances, and then to prove as a preferential creditor in respect of the wages advances. This was so decided in *Re William Hall (Contractors) Ltd.*[6] A company which had executed four mortgages of land in favour of its bank owed the bank £7,921, of which £2,274 was a preferential debt for wages advances. The security was realized by the bank for £5,779, and the bank appropriated the proceeds of sale in discharge of all the *non*-preferential debt and claimed as a preferential creditor for the balance. A clause in each form of mortgage empowered the bank to appropriate

---

3 *Re E. J. Morel (1934) Ltd* [1962] 1 Ch 21.
4 [1966] 1 WLR 1369.
5 Se L. C. Mather, 'Wages accounts', *Journal of the Institute of Bankers*, Vol. LXXIV (1953), at p. 23.
6 [1967] 1 WLR 948.

as it wished, but quite apart from this, the court held that as a general principle of law, a secured creditor was entitled to apply his security in discharge of whatever liability of his debtor he might choose. Accordingly, the bank was entitled to appropriate the proceeds in the manner indicated.

11-307A *Re Unit 2 Windows Ltd*[7] was not a banking case. Nevertheless, the principle laid down by Walton J may affect bankers. By an originating summons the Department of Health and Social Security, which was a creditor of Unit 2 Windows Ltd, sought as against the liquidator of the company the determination whether, in the voluntary winding up of the company, the sum of £2,570 due to the company from HM Customs and Excise by way of refund of value added tax (a) could be set off first against the non-preferential part of a debt amounting to £2,708 due from the company to the Department of Health and Social Security in respect of Class 1 national insurance contributions in the year 1980–81; or (b) could only be set off against the preferential part of the debt amounting to £3,529 due from the company to the Department in respect of unpaid national insurance contributions and unpaid PAYE for the period 6 April 1980 to 5 April 1982; or (c) should only be set off rateably against the non-preferential and the preferential debt in proportion to the respective amounts; or (d) should be set off in some other way, and, if so, in what manner. Having considered the authorities on this subject, Walton J decided the question posed in the originating summons in the third sense set out above, that is to say the refund of VAT owed to the company should be set off rateably against the non-preferential and the preferential debt in proportion to the respective amounts.

11-307B The decision of Walton J in *Re Unit 2 Windows Ltd* might affect bankers in the following circumstances. Let it be assumed that a company has a credit balance of £4,000 on its current account. The company's wages account at the bank is overdrawn £6,000. Part or all of this sum may be a preferential debt.[8] Furthermore, the company has another account at the bank which is overdrawn £2,000, and this is not a preferential debt. The company goes into liquidation. The question arises as to how much of the credit balance of £4,000 should be applied to reduce the overdraft on the wages account, and how much should be applied to reduce the overdraft on the other account. If, as seems likely, the ruling by Walton J applies to this situation, the credit balance of £4,000 will be applied rateably, that is to say 75 per cent, namely £3,000, will be applied to the wages account, and the remainder to the other overdrawn account.

7 [1985] 3 All ER 647.
8 See *ante*, para. 11-301.

Special problems regarding accounts of companies

(a) Too few directors

11-308   First, let it be supposed that a company has two directors. Its articles provide that the quorum at a board meeting is two, and that both directors are required to sign cheques drawn on the company's account. One director dies. Usually, this problem may be resolved in one of two ways. If Table A of the First Schedule to the Companies Act 1948 applies, the solution is simple, because by virtue of article 100, the surviving director may appoint another director. In regard to companies incorporated on or after 1 July 1984, regulation 90 of Table A of the Companies (Alteration of Table A etc.) Regulations 1984 contains a similar provision. Regulation 90 of the 1984 Regulations was replaced by Regulation 90 of the Companies (Tables A to F) Regulations 1985, which contains a similar provision. If, however, there is no such provision in the company's articles, application should be made to the court, which may order a meeting of the company to be called, held and conducted in such manner as the court thinks fit, and may even order that one member of the company shall be deemed to constitute a meeting.[9]

11-309   Secondly, let it be assumed that a private company has two shareholders, one of whom is the only director. He dies. As there is no surviving director, article 100 of Table A is of no assistance; nor is the Companies Act 1985,[10] which provides that, unless a company's articles provide otherwise, two members shall be a quorum at a meeting of the company. Articles may, and occasionally do, provide that one member may act alone; in this event he may appoint a director in place of the deceased. If there is no such article, application should be made to the court, as in the previous illustration.

(b) Accounts of 'one-man companies'

11-310   In the typical 'one-man company', one shareholder holds all the shares except one, which is usually held by his wife or his secretary. The principal shareholder in a 'one-man company' often identifies himself with his company, and accordingly he may think that he is entitled to pay cheques drawn in favour of his company into his own personal account. In law, however, a company is a legal entity quite different from its shareholders. It follows, therefore, that cheques payable

9 Companies Act 1985, s. 371.
10 S. 370.

to 'one-man companies' should not be treated any differently from cheques payable to well-known public companies. The dangers of departing from this practice were clearly illustrated in *A. L. Underwood Ltd* v. *Bank of Liverpool and Martins*.[11]

(c) Accounts of chartered companies

11-311 As already stated,[12] Royal Charters are no longer granted to trading concerns, but the grant of a charter to a charity or learned society is not uncommon. In many instances, the charity or society will have been functioning as a company limited by guarantee. The company will be wound up, and its assets will be transferred to the new chartered body. The bankers to the charity will usually be requested to open a fresh account for that body – a fresh mandate should be obtained from its council or committee – and the liquidator of the old company will be able to give a good discharge for the balance standing to the credit of that company's account.

11-312 The early case of *Sutton's Hospital*[13] is generally cited as authority for the principle that a chartered company has all the powers of a natural person in so far as an artificial entity is physically capable of exercising them; but it may be restrained by injunction at the suit of a member from exceeding the objects in the charter and thus rendering the charter liable to be forfeited.[14] Accordingly, if a banker is asked to lend money to a chartered company, he will usually wish to satisfy himself that the proposed loan is for the pursuit of objects set out in the charter.

(d) Lending to newly constituted companies

11-312A Banks should not lend to newly constituted companies, unless they are satisfied that the directors and senior officials of the company have made a complete break with their former employers, that they are not in breach of the terms of any service contract, and that they are not making use of privileged information or trade secrets. If a bank does grant facilities in these circumstances, the former employers of the directors may bring an action, not only against their former employees, but also against the bank or the bank manager for damages for conspiracy and/or inducing a breach of contract.

---

11 [1924] 1 KB 775, *ante*, para. 6-119.
12 *Ante*, para. 11-262.
13 (1613) 10 Co Rep 1a, 23a.
14 *Jenkins* v. *Pharmaceutical Society of Great Britain* [1921] 1 Ch 392.

Determination of company's mandate

11-313   The mandate given by a company to its bankers may be determined in one of four ways, namely (a) by a resolution of the board of directors, (b) by the appointment of a receiver or an administrative receiver, or (c) by the making of an administration order, or (d) by the liquidation of the company.

(a) Resolution of board of directors

11-314   The resolution appointing a bank as bankers to a company usually provides that it is to remain in force until an amending resolution is passed by the board of directors and a copy thereof is sent to the bank.[15] Accordingly, the mandate embodied in the original resolution may be amended or determined by a subsequent resolution. Sometimes, however, a company closes its account at a bank by withdrawing its credit balance or by repaying its overdraft, in either case without formally passing a resolution determining the mandate. There would seem to be no harm in this, but written evidence should be obtained from those authorized to sign to the effect that the company's account is closed.[16]

11-314A   A problem which sometimes arises in the case of small companies is as follows. In the case of a company which has two directors, the mandate often provides that cheques may be signed by either of them. If the two directors have a disagreement, one of them sometimes writes to the bank instructing the bank that in future cheques must be signed by both directors. The bank should reply by stating (as shown in the preceding paragraph) that the resolution which appointed the bank as bankers to the company provided that it was to remain in force until an amending resolution was passed by the board and a copy thereof sent to the bank. This will usually resolve the problem. However, if the directors fail to agree to pass the appropriate resolution, one of them may succeed in obtaining an order from the court giving directions to the bank with reference to the conduct of the account.

(b) Appointment of receiver or administrative receiver

11-315   A receiver may be appointed either by the court, or by the debenture holder in accordance with the powers conferred by the debenture. Appointments by the court are infrequent at the present day because, in modern practice, a debenture almost invariably gives the

15   *Ante*, para. 11-274.
16   *Ante*, para. 3-2.

debenture holder power to appoint a receiver and expressly provides that a receiver so appointed is to have power to carry on the business of the company. The appointment must comply with any formalities required by the debenture. If none is specified, a receiver may be appointed under hand, unless he is to be authorized to execute deeds in the name of the company, when he must be appointed by deed.

11-316   Any person who obtains a court order for the appointment of a receiver or who himself appoints a receiver must have the appointment registered at Companies House within seven days; and, if he fails to do so, he is liable to a fine not exceeding five pounds for every day during which the default continues.[17]

11-317   The effect of the appointment of a receiver either by a debenture holder or by the court depends very largely upon the type of assets charged by the debenture. For example, if a debenture creates a fixed charge over the company's land and buildings and nothing else, the receiver's powers will be limited to those assets; he will have no power to receive any balance on the company's bank account or to give any instructions to the bank relating to the account.

11-318   If, however, a debenture creates, in addition, a floating charge over the remainder of the company's assets, the appointment of a receiver will crystallize the floating charge, and so the receiver will be entitled to any assets covered by such charge, including any balances standing to the company's credit at the bank. On demand, the bank must pay such balances to the receiver, after deducting therefrom, by way of set-off, any debit balances on other accounts of the company. The bank may also deduct, by way of set-off, the amount of any bills which it had discounted for the company if those bills have been dishonoured and have not already been debited to one of the company's accounts. If, however, the bills have not yet matured, the bank is probably not entitled to retain any sum in respect of the purely contingent liability of the company on the bills.[18]

11-318A   Section 7(1) of the Administration of Justice Act 1977 provides that 'a receiver appointed under the law of any part of the United Kingdom in respect of the whole or part of any property or undertaking of a company and in consequence of the company having created a charge which, as created, was a floating charge may exercise his powers in any other part of the United Kingdom so far as their exercise is not inconsistent with the law applicable there.'

17 Companies Act 1985, s. 405.
18 Cf. *Bower* v. *Foreign and Colonial Gas Co. Ltd, Metropolitan Bank, Garnishees* (1874) 22 WR 740, *ante*, para. 2-66.

11-319   When a debenture is secured by a floating charge, the appointment of a receiver will determine the mandate given by the board of directors to the bank. Any cheques drawn pursuant to the mandate, and presented for payment after the bank has notice of the receiver's appointment, should be returned unpaid with the answer 'Refer to drawer, receiver appointed', unless the receiver authorizes the bank to pay them.

11-320   A receiver is sometimes hampered in his effort to sell a business as a going concern as a result of retention or reservation of title clauses which are often incorporated in sellers' standard form contracts. The leading case dealing with reservation of title clauses is *Aluminium Industrie Vaasen BV* v. *Romalpa Aluminium Ltd*[19] (usually called the *Romalpa* case). The plaintiffs, who were Dutch manufacturers of aluminium foil, supplied foil to the defendants, an English company. Clause 13 of the contract provided that the ownership of the foil would remain with the plaintiffs until the defendants had paid all sums owing to the plaintiffs. It further provided that where the foil was used in the manufacture of other products, the ownership of such products was to be transferred to the plaintiffs as security for full payment. The defendants were entitled to sell such 'mixed' goods on condition that, while any money was owing to the plaintiffs, the defendants would on request assign to the plaintiffs the benefit of any claim against the subpurchasers.

Eventually, the defendants got into financial difficulties, and their bankers appointed a receiver pursuant to powers granted to them under a debenture which the defendants had executed. At the date when the receiver was appointed, the defendants owed over £122,000 to the plaintiffs. The receiver certified that £35,152 was held by him, representing the proceeds of sale of unmixed aluminium foil supplied by the plaintiffs to the defendants and sold by the latter to third parties. The first claim of the plaintiffs related to this sum. They claimed that, by virtue of clause 13 of the contract, they were entitled to the sum of £35,152 in priority to the secured and unsecured creditors of the defendants. The plaintiffs' second claim related to aluminium foil still in the possession of the receiver. He certified that aluminium foil to the value of £50,235 was held by him and that this originated in deliveries to the defendants by the plaintiffs. This second claim of the plaintiffs was admitted by the defendants.

The first claim of the plaintiffs was upheld by Mocatta J whose decision was affirmed by the Court of Appeal. The court held that, in order to give effect to the obvious purpose of clause 13, that clause must

---

19 [1976] 2 All ER 552.

be construed as conferring on the defendants a power to sell unmixed foil and also as imposing on them an obligation to account to the plaintiffs for the proceeds of sale unless and until all moneys owing from the defendants to the plaintiffs had been paid. Although, as far as the sub-purchasers were concerned, the defendant sold the unmixed foil as principals, as far as the plaintiffs were concerned, the foil was the plaintiff's property which the defendants were selling as agents for the plaintiffs. It followed, therefore, that the plaintiffs were entitled to trace the proceeds of sale of the unmixed foil and to recover them in priority to the secured and unsecured creditors of the defendants.

11-321 In *Borden (UK) Ltd* v. *Scottish Timber Products Ltd*[20] under a retention of title clause the suppliers of resin to chipboard manufacturers claimed to trace the resin into the manufactured chipboard. The Court of Appeal held (a) that the effect of the retention clause was to reserve property in the resin as long as it remained unused – once incorporated in the chipboard it ceased to exist as resin and there was nothing to trace; (b) that there was no fiduciary relationship between the sellers and the buyers that could create a right to trace; and (c) that even if the sellers had acquired an interest in the chipboard it would have been by way of charge requiring registration under s. 95 of the Companies Act 1948 (now s. 395 of the Companies Act 1985). Thus, in this case, the retention of title clause failed.

11-322 The title 'administrative receiver' was introduced by the Insolvency Act 1985, and the current legislation is contained in the Insolvency Act 1986 and the Regulations made under that Act. Section 29(2)(a) of the Insolvency Act 1986 provides that an administrative receiver means 'a receiver or manager of the whole (or substantially the whole) of a company's property appointed by or on behalf of the holders of any debentures of the company secured by a charge which, as created, was a floating charge, or by such a charge and one or more other securities'.[21] Most receivers who are appointed by the banks fall within the definition of administrative receivers. Since an administrative receiver (but not an ordinary receiver) is acting as an insolvency practitioner for the purposes of the Insolvency Act 1986, only a qualified insolvency practitioner may be appointed.[22] Administrative receivers

---

20 [1981] Ch 25. See also *Clough Mill Ltd* v. *Martin* [1985] 1 WLR 111; *Tatung (UK) Ltd* v. *Galex Telesure Ltd* [1989] 5 BCC 25.

21 By s. 29(2)(b) the definition of an administrative receiver also includes a person who would be such a receiver but for the appointment of some other person as the receiver of part of the company's property. This could arise, for example, where a receiver is appointed by the holder of a fixed charge and then a receiver is appointed by the holder of a floating charge.

22 For the qualifications of an insolvency practitioner, see *ante*, para. 11-232.

must be distinguished from 'administrators' whose functions will be considered later.[23]

11-323   Administrative receivers are subject to rules contained in the Insolvency Act 1986, and the Act confers certain powers upon them. Thus s. 42(1) confers upon them the powers listed in Sched. 1 to the Act, subject to any contrary express terms in the debenture. Schedule 1 sets out twenty-three powers, including (a) power to take possession of, collect and get in the property of the company, (b) power to sell or otherwise dispose of the property of the company by public auction or by private contract, (c) power to raise or borrow money and grant security therefor over the property of the company, and (d) power to carry on the business of the company. Section 42(3) provides that a person dealing with the administrative receiver in good faith and for value is not concerned to enquire whether the receiver is acting within his powers.

11-324   Section 43(1) of the Insolvency Act 1986 provides that where, on an application by the administrative receiver, the court is satisfied that the disposal of any property which is subject to a security would be likely to promote a more advantageous realization of the company's assets than would otherwise be effected, the court may by order authorize the administrative receiver to dispose of the property as if it were not subject to the security. However, by virtue of s. 43(2) this does not include property which is subject to a charge held by the person who appointed the receiver or any charge having priority over such a charge. The secured creditor whose security is disposed of is protected, because s. 43(3) provides that the net proceeds of sale must be used to discharge his debt, together with, if the court regards such proceeds as less than the open market value of the property, such additional sums as are necessary to make good the deficiency.

11-325   Section 44(1) of the Insolvency Act 1986 provides that the administrative receiver (a) is deemed to be the agent of the company unless and until the company goes into liquidation, (b) is personally liable on any contract entered into by him in the carrying out of his functions, and (c) is entitled in respect of that liability to an indemnity out of the assets of the company.

11-326   Section 46(1) of the Insolvency Act 1986 provides that where an administrative receiver is appointed, he must (a) send to the company and publish in the prescribed manner a notice of his appointment, and (b) within 28 days after his appointment, unless the court otherwise

---

23 See *post*, paras 11-329 *et seq.*

directs, send such a notice to all the creditors of the company, so far as he is aware of their addresses.

11-327   Section 47 of the Insolvency Act 1986 provides that when an administrative receiver is appointed, he must obtain 'forthwith' a statement of the company's affairs from some or all of the past or present officers of the company, its promoters (if they acted within the year prior to his appointment), its employees (if, in his opinion, they are capable of giving the required information, and are either present employees or have been employed within the preceding year) and the officers of any company which is (or had been within the previous year) an officer of the company concerned. Where any persons are required under this section to submit a statement of affairs to the administrative receiver, they must do so within 21 days. The administrative receiver, may excuse any person from this obligation or extend the time limits, although the court may intervene and exercise the power. Statements submitted under s. 47 must be verified by affidavit and contain particulars of the company's assets, debts and liabilities, the names and addresses of its creditors, any securities held by them, and such further information as may be prescribed.

11-328   Section 48(1) of the Insolvency Act 1986 provides that within three months after his appointment, an administrative receiver must send to the Registrar of Companies, to any trustees for secured creditors of the company and (so far as he is aware of their addresses) to all such creditors a report as to the following matters, namely (a) the events leading up to his appointment, (b) the disposal or proposed disposal by him of any property of the company and the carrying on or proposed carrying on by him of any business of the company, (c) the amounts of principal and interest payable to the debenture holders by whom he was appointed and the amounts payable to preferential creditors, and (d) the amount (if any) likely to be available for the payment of other creditors. By virtue of s. 48(2) the administrative receiver must, within three months after his appointment, either send a copy of his report to all the company's unsecured creditors (so far as he is aware of their addresses), or publish an address to which they may write for copies to be sent to them free of charge. In either case he must also summon a meeting of the unsecured creditors on not less than fourteen days' notice, before which he must lay a copy of his report. By virtue of s. 48(3) the court may dispense with such a meeting if the report states that the receiver intends to apply for such an order and the other requirements as to publicity are complied with at least fourteen days before the application.

(c) Making of an administration order

11-329 The Insolvency Act 1985 introduced a new concept into company law, namely the making of an administration order. This reform of the law, which had been recommended by the 'Cork Committee',[24] was intended to provide an alternative to a liquidation for those companies which are unable to pay their debts. The object of the legislation is either to rehabilitate the company so that it will continue as a going concern, or to provide a better way of realizing its assets. If an administration order is made, the company has a 'breathing space' free from a winding up order or the appointment of a receiver. The relevant legislation is contained in twenty sections of the Insolvency Act 1986 and in the Regulations made thereunder. Owing to considerations of space, it is only possible to outline the procedure and its implications for bankers. For a detailed exposition of the subject reference should be made to textbooks on company law.[25]

11-330 By virtue of s. 8 of the Insolvency Act 1986 the court may only make an administration order if it is satisfied that the company is or is likely to become unable to pay its debts,[26] and that such an order would be likely to achieve one or more of the following purposes: (a) the survival of the company, and the whole or any part of its undertaking as a going concern; (b) the approval of a voluntary arrangement with creditors; (c) the sanctioning of a scheme of arrangement under s. 425 of the Companies Act 1985; and (d) a more advantageous realization of the company's assets than would be effected on a winding up. An administration order must specify the purpose or purposes for which it is made. An order cannot be made after a company has gone into liquidation, or if it is an insurance company or a banking company.

Most petitions cite the first and/or the last of the four purposes (a), (b), (c), and (d) specified in s. 8 of the Act. *In re Harris Simons Construction Ltd*[27] is an illustration of a case where an administration order was made in order to achieve purposes (a) and (d). Hoffman J said that over the past four years there had been a spectacular increase in the company's turnover, almost all of which had come from one client, a property developer called Berkley House plc. The relationship turned sour, and there were disputes over a number of contracts. The effect on the company's cash flow was that it was unable to pay its debts as they

---

24 See the Cork Report, Cmnd. 8558 (1982), Chapter 9.
25 See *ante*, para. 11-246.
26 As defined in s. 123.
27 [1989] 1 WLR 368. See also *Re Consumer and Industrial Press Ltd* [1988] BCLC 177.

fell due. It would have had to go into liquidation more or less immediately.

If an administration order were made, the company would have a breathing space. It had been able to negotiate an armistice with Berkley House by which the latter would, conditionally on an administration order being made, provide sufficient funding to enable the company to complete four contracts. It was hoped that those contracts would produce a profit and that it might thereby be possible to stabilize and preserve a business which could either survive or be sold to a third party.

The directors of the company petitioned for an administration order to achieve two of the purposes specified in s. 8(3) of the Insolvency Act 1986: '(a) the survival of the company ... as a going concern', and '(d) a more advantageous realization of the company's assets than would be effected on a winding up'. The petition was not opposed. Hoffman J held that the requirements of s. 8 would be satisfied if the court considered that there was 'a real prospect' that one or more of the stated purposes might be achieved. The judge decided that, on the evidence, there was 'a real prospect that an administration order, coupled with the agreement with Berkley House, would enable the whole or part of the company's undertaking to survive, or at least enable the administrator to effect a more advantageous realization of assets than in a winding up. The prospects for the company, its employees and creditors looked bleak if no administration order was made and there had to be a winding up.' Accordingly, an administration order was made.

11-331 Section 9(1) of the Insolvency Act 1986 provides that an application to the court for an administration order is to be by petition presented either by the company or the directors, or by a creditor or creditors, or by all or any of them, together or separately. By virtue of s. 9(2) where a petition is presented to the court, notice of the petition must be given forthwith to any person who has appointed, or is or may be entitled to appoint, an administrative receiver of the company. By s. 9(3) where the court is satisfied that there is an administrative receiver of the company, the court must dismiss the petition, unless it is also satisfied that the person by whom the receiver was appointed has consented to the making of the administration order. By s. 9(4), on hearing a petition, the court may dismiss it, or adjourn the hearing conditionally or unconditionally, or make an interim order or any other order that it thinks fit.

In most cases the court requires the petition to be supported by the report of an independent accountant, usually the prospective administrator, specifying the purposes which may be achieved by making the order. In practice, only a creditor who is able to obtain this information is able to present a petition. Bankers rarely present a petition. Occasionally, however, when the company itself presents a petition, its bank will acquiesce. Sometimes the bank is consulted concerning the identity of the proposed administrator. When he has been appointed, he may need to borrow from the bank in order to fund his initial capital needs, particularly if the company's book debts are subject to a fixed charge.

Section 230(1) provides that where an administration order is made in relation to a company, the administrator must be a person who is qualified to act as an insolvency practitioner in relation to the company.[28]

11-332 As stated in the preceding paragraph, s. 9(2) requires that notice of the petition must be given to any person who is entitled to appoint an administrative receiver. Very frequently that person is a bank. When a bank receives notice of a petition, it must decide within five days whether or not to appoint an administrative receiver,[29] and if it does not appoint a receiver, the court will have power to make an administration order. The making of the order will prevent the bank from realizing its security.[30] The bank will not lose its rights in its security, and it will be entitled to the proceeds of realization, which will take place, if at all, at the administrator's discretion. It follows, therefore, that banks often oppose the appointment of an administrator. To enable them to do so, they now take floating charges in cases where, in the past, they might have taken a fixed charge limited to certain assets. These rules relating to the appointment of administrators sometimes produce a result which can be detrimental, because the holder of a floating charge, such as a bank, will sometimes appoint an administrative receiver precipitately and thus cause the collapse of the company, a result which the appointment of an administrator is designed to avoid.

11-333 The effect of s. 10(1) of the Insolvency Act 1986 is that during the period beginning with the presentation of a petition for an administration order and the date when the court either makes the order or dismisses the petition, (a) no resolution for the voluntary winding up of the company nor any compulsory winding up order can be made, (b) no steps may be taken to enforce any security against the company without the court's consent, and (c) no other proceedings may be commenced or enforced against the company or its property without the court's consent. However, by virtue of s. 10(2), the presentation of a petition for

---

28 For the qualifications of an insolvency practitioner, see *ante*, para. 11-232.
29 Rule 2 of the Insolvency Rules 1986. For a case where the court was asked to reduce the period of notice to a bank entitled to appoint an administrative receiver, see *Re a company (No. 00175 of 1987)* [1987] BCLC 467. Vinelott J held that the court did have jurisdiction to shorten the five day period.
30 Insolvency Act 1986, s. 11(3).

an administration order does not prevent a winding up petition being presented.

11-334 The effect of s. 11 of the Insolvency Act 1986 is that, if the court makes an administration order, (a) any petition for winding up must be dismissed, (b) any administrative receiver must vacate office (for this reason the bank or other creditor who appointed the administrative receiver should not consent to the making of an administration order), (c) no security may be enforced against the company, and (d) no proceedings may be commenced or continued against the company without the consent of the administrator or of the court. These provisions are necessary in order to give the company a 'breathing space' and to enable the administrator to try to achieve the purpose stated in the order by which he was appointed.

11-335 The effect of s. 14 of the Insolvency Act 1986 is that the administrator has the following powers: (a) to do all such things as may be necessary for the management of the affairs, business and property of the company, (b) to exercise any of the twenty-three powers listed in Sched. 1 to the Act,[31] (c) to appoint and remove directors of the company, and (d) to call meetings of the shareholders or creditors. In exercising his powers the administrator is deemed to act as the company's agent. A person dealing with the administrator in good faith and for value is not concerned to enquire whether he is acting within his powers.

11-336 The effect of s. 15 of the Insolvency Act 1986 is that the administrator has power to sell any property subject to a floating charge free of that charge.[32] The holder of the floating charge retains his priority in respect of the proceeds of the disposal. Moreover, the administrator may ask the court for authority to dispose of property free of any other existing security, on the ground that such a disposal would be likely to promote the purpose or purposes specified in the administration order. The secured creditor whose security is disposed of is protected, because s. 15(5) provides that the net proceeds of sale must be used to discharge his debt, together with, if the court regards such proceeds as less than the open market value of the property, such additional sums as are necessary to make good the deficiency.

11-337 Section 21(1) of the Insolvency Act 1986 provides that where an administration order has been made, the administrator must (a) send to the company and publish in the prescribed manner a notice of the order, and (b) within 28 days after the making of the order, unless the court

---

31 The same powers are given to an administrative receiver: see *ante*, para. 11-323.

32 An administrative receiver requires the court's consent to exercise this power: see *ante*, para. 11-324.

otherwise directs, send such a notice to all the creditors of the company, so far as he is aware of their addresses.

11-338 Section 22 of the Insolvency Act 1986 provides that where an administration order has been made, the administrator must 'forthwith' require a statement of the company's affairs to be made out by the company's officers. Where any persons are required under this section to submit a statement of affairs, they must do so within 21 days. The administrator may excuse any person from this obligation or the time limits, although the court may intervene and exercise the power. Statements submitted under s. 22 must be verified by affidavit and contain particulars of the company's assets, debts and liabilities, the names and addresses of the creditors, any securities held by them, and such further information as may be prescribed.

11-339 Section 23(1) of the Insolvency Act 1986 provides that where an administration order has been made, the administrator must, within three months (or such longer period as the court may allow) after the making of the order, (a) send to the Registrar of Companies and (so far as he is aware of their addresses) to all creditors a statement of his proposals for achieving the purpose or purposes specified in the order, and (b) lay a copy of the statement before a meeting of the company's creditors summoned for the purpose on not less than fourteen days' notice. By virtue of s. 23(2) the administrator must, within three months (or such longer period as the court may allow) after the making of the order, either send a copy of the statement of his proposals to all shareholders of the company, or publish an address to which they may write for copies to be sent to them free of charge.

11-340 Section 18(1) of the Insolvency Act 1986 provides that the administrator of a company may at any time apply to the court for the administration order to be discharged, or to be varied so as to specify an additional purpose. Section 18(2) provides that he must make an application to the court if (a) it appears to him that the purpose of each of the purposes specified in the order has been achieved or is incapable of achievement, or (b) he is required to do so by a meeting of the company's creditors.

11-341 The effect of s. 19 of the Insolvency Act 1986 is that the administrator of a company must vacate office if (a) he ceases to be qualified to act as an insolvency practitioner, (b) the administration order is discharged, (c) he is removed by the court, and (d) he resigns his office by giving notice of his resignation to the court.

11-342 A survey covering most the administrations in 1987 showed that 43 per cent of the cases ended in break-up and subsequent liquidation of the company;[33] in 8 per cent the company was restored to solvency; 11 per cent involved voluntary arrangements with creditors and the survival of all or part of the business; 36 per cent involved the going-concern sale of the business and the liquidation of the company. The remaining 2 per cent were voluntary arrangements as a quasi-liquidation. In 40 per cent of the cases surveyed, bankers with floating charges had waived their right to appoint a receiver and had allowed the administration to proceed. When deciding whether or not to waive their rights bankers will often take into consideration some of the following points:

(a) If a bank waives its right to appoint a receiver, it will lose direct control of the right to deal with its security. The administrator's duty is to the court and to the general body of creditors, whereas the receiver's primary objective is to repay the debenture holder.

(b) If a bank has already appointed a receiver under a floating charge, the withholding of the bank's consent to the making of an administration order will block the making of the order. If the bank waives its right, the receiver under the floating charge will be required to vacate office. In view of the unsatisfactory nature of the handover provisions from a receiver to an administrator, the holder of a floating charge who has appointed a receiver should not consent to the making of an administration order until the receiver's position is satisfactorily resolved.

(c) An additional disadvantage is the cost of an administration. Whereas a receiver concentrates his attention on dealing with the business and the assets, an administrator is heavily involved in making reports to the creditors. The necessity of making applications to the court also adds to the legal costs.

(d) Nevertheless, in some cases, an administration can provide certain advantages over a receivership. Thus where there are substantial reservation of title claims or where there are assets subject to leases or hire-purchase, an administrator is protected from creditors who are seeking possession. The administrator is, therefore, in a better position to preserve the business.

(e) Again, where there are substantial overseas assets, an administrator, who is of course appointed by the court, may find it easier to obtain recognition in a foreign jurisdiction than a privately appointed receiver under a debenture.

33 See Mark Homan, 'Administration – banker's dilemma', *Banking World*, February 1989, pp. 16–17, for a full account of this subject.

(d) Liquidation of company

The legal position as between a company and its bankers depends upon whether the winding up is voluntary or compulsory.

(i) Voluntary winding up

11-343   This is initated by the shareholders. The manner in which voluntary winding up is conducted and supervised depends upon whether it is a *members'* voluntary winding up, or a *creditors'* voluntary winding up. If the directors are able to make a statutory declaration of solvency, the winding up will be a members' voluntary winding up.[34] The company in general meeting will appoint a liquidator;[35] on his appointment all the powers of the directors cease, except so far as the company in general meeting or the liquidator sanctions the continuance thereof.[36]

11-344   If the directors are unable to make a statutory declaration of solvency, the winding up will become a creditors' voluntary winding up. The company must (a) call a meeting of creditors for the day not later than the fourteenth day after the day on which there is to be held the company meeting at which the resolution for voluntary winding up is to be proposed, (b) send the notices of the creditors' meeting by post not less than seven days before the day on which the meeting is to be held, and (c) cause notice of the creditors' meeting to be advertised once in the *Gazette* and once at least in two local newspapers.[37] Thus, even if the directors have not kept the bank informed of what is happening, the advertisements will usually come to the bank's notice and, in any event, if the company's account is overdrawn, the bank should receive notice of the creditors' meeting. When the members have resolved that the company is to be wound up, a liquidator must be appointed.

11-345   The creditors and the company may each nominate a person to be liquidator. If the creditors and the company nominate different persons, the person nominated by the creditors is to be the liquidator, and if no person is nominated by the creditors, the person, if any, nominated by the company is to be the liquidator. In the case, however, of different persons being nominated, any director, member or creditor of the company may, within seven days after the date on which the nomination was made by the creditors, apply to the court for an order either directing that the person nominated as liquidator by the company is to be liquidator instead of or jointly with the person nominated by the creditors, or appointing some other person to be liquidator instead of

34 Insolvency Act 1986, s. 89.
35 S. 91(1).
36 S. 91(2).
37 S. 98(1).

the person appointed by the creditors.[38] On the appointment of a liquidator, all the powers of the directors cease, except so far as the liquidation committee, or if there is no such committee, the creditors,
sanction the continuance thereof.[39]

11-346 Whether a winding up is a members' voluntary winding up or
a creditors' voluntary winding up, it is deemed to commence at the time
when the members pass the resolution for voluntary winding up.[40]
Notice of this resolution must be advertised in the *Gazette* within fourteen days.[41] As soon as the bank learns of the passing of the resolution,
the mandate relating to operations on the company's account should be
treated as determined. Thereafter, no cheques drawn pursuant to the
mandate should be paid without the consent of the liquidator, unless the
directors' powers have been continued as explained above. Cheques
should be returned unpaid with the answer 'Refer to drawer, resolution
to wind up passed'.

11-347 In the winding up of an insolvent company, the bankruptcy
rules concerning set-off and contingent liabilities apply.[42] Accordingly,
the bank should combine all accounts in the name of the company in
order to determine the net amount owing to or from the company. Any
remaining credit balance may be retained against any contingent liability
of the company to the bank, e.g. in respect of bills discounted but not
yet matured.

(ii) Compulsory winding up

11-348 A winding up by the court, usually called compulsory winding
up, is initiated by a petition to the court. The petition may be based on
one of a variety of grounds,[43] the usual one being that 'the company is
unable to pay its debts'. A company is deemed to be unable to pay its
debts if, *inter alia*, a creditor to whom the company is indebted in a sum
exceeding £750[44] serves on the company a demand requiring the
company to pay the sum so due and the company for three weeks
neglects to pay the sum or to secure or compound for it to the reasonable
satisfaction of the creditor.[45]

11-349 As far as bankers are concerned, certain aspects of the law
relating to the compulsory winding up of companies are unsatisfactory.

---

38 S. 100(2).
39 S. 103.
40 S. 86.
41 S. 85.
42 *Ante*, para. 2-60.
43 They are listed in the Insolvency Act 1986, s. 122.
44 Insolvency Act 1986, s. 123(1).
45 *Ibid*.

One must consider (a) cheques drawn by a company, and (b) cheques payable to a company.

(i) Cheques drawn by a company

11-350   By virtue of s. 129 of the Insolvency Act 1986, an order made by the court for the winding up of a company relates back to the date of the presentation of the petition for winding up; and by s. 127, any disposition of the company's property made after the commencement of the winding up is void, unless the court orders otherwise.[46] A petition for winding up must be advertised by the petitioners once in the *Gazette* so as to appear (if the company is the petitioner) not less than seven business days before the day appointed for the hearing, or (where someone other than the company is the petitioner) not less than seven business days after the service on the company nor less than seven business days before the appointed day. If compliance with these requirements is not reasonably practicable, the court may direct advertisement to be placed in a specified London morning newspaper, or other newspaper, instead of in the *Gazette*.[47] As soon as a company's bankers learn that a petition has been presented, they decline to pay cheques drawn on the company's accounts in favour of third parties, unless and until the petition is dismissed by the court. (Sometimes a petition is dismissed, because the company is able to offer cash to the petitioning creditor prior to the hearing.) Cheques which are dishonoured should be returned with the answer 'Refer to drawer, winding-up petition presented'.

11-351   Cheques drawn by a company and presented for payment in cash by one of its officials used to be treated differently from cheques drawn by the company in favour of third parties. The House of Lords held that the payment to a company of a debt owing to it was not a 'disposition' of the company's property.[48] Accordingly, it was said that the balance standing to the credit of a company's bank account might, notwithstandng the presentation of a petition, be paid to the company against the receipt of an authorized official or officials. Thus, after notice of the presentation of a petition, cheques drawn by the company *in favour of third parties* were usually dishonoured, whereas cheques drawn by the company and *presented at the bank counter* by one of its own officials were often paid. This practice is no longer followed. In view of the decision of the Court of Appeal in *Re Gray's Inn Construction Co. Ltd*,[49] it seems clear that the proper course for a bank to take

---

46 See *Re Steane's (Bournemouth) Ltd* [1950] 1 All ER 21; *Re T. W. Construction Ltd* [1954] 1 All ER 744; *Re Clifton Place Garage Ltd* [1970] 1 All ER 353.
47 Insolvency Rules 1986, rule 4.11.
48 *Mersey Steel and Iron Co.* v. *Naylor, Benzon & Co.* (1884) 9 App Cas 434.
49 [1980] 1 All ER 814, *post*, para. 11-359.

is to stop all accounts of a company as soon as the bank learns of the presentation of a petition.

(ii) Cheques payable to a company

11-352 In *D. B. Evans (Bilston) Ltd* v. *Barclays Bank Ltd*,[50] the plaintiffs, who were public works contractors, had work in progress under contracts to the value of £1m and a weekly wages bill of £8,000. They got into financial difficulties, and an application was made to the court for approval of a scheme of arrangement. At the same time, a winding-up petition was presented by a creditor of £117. The court adjourned the winding-up proceedings pending the sanctioning of the scheme. Prior to the filing of the winding-up petition, the plaintiffs had three accounts at Barclays Bank with an overall credit balance of £27,360, of which about £3,500 had been retained as a result of garnishee proceedings. Shortly after the petition was filed, a No. 4 account was opened, and cheques totalling £2,800 were placed to the credit of this account. The bank informed the plaintiffs that they would permit the plaintiffs to withdraw the available credit balance on the original three accounts, and this was done. The bank also informed the plaintiffs that the credit balance on the No. 4 account and the proceeds of any further cheques which might be placed to the credit of that account would be frozen, so long as the winding-up petition remained on the file. During the next few weeks, the plaintiffs received cheques totalling £48,000, but they were unable to utilize the proceeds for the payment of wages and materials for the reasons given above. As the plaintiffs had no cash, they were faced with the prospect of having to discharge their employees and stop work. Accordingly, they brought this action against the bank claiming damages for breach of contract and also an injunction restraining the bank from refusing to honour the plaintiffs' cheques to the extent that their account with the bank was in credit. Atkinson J refused to grant an interim injunction, and the plaintiffs appealed.

11-353 In the Court of Appeal it was argued on behalf of the plaintiffs that unless a bank had a special term in its contract with a customer, it was bound to pay its customers' cheques to the extent of the customer's credit balance, unless there was some legal bar. It was submitted that there was no legal bar in the present case. On behalf of the bank it was argued that the difficulty with which the bank was faced was that the collection of the plaintiffs' cheques would amount to a disposition of the property of the company, and that if the bank paid out the proceeds to the company, the bank would be liable to account therefor to the liquidator. To this argument the plaintiffs replied as follows: (a) the payment

50 (1961) *The Times*, 17 February. See the note in *Journal of the Institute of Bankers*, Vol. 82 (1961), p. 232.

to a company of a debt owing to it is not a 'disposition' of the company's property;[51] (b) the Companies Court would almost certainly make an order under s. 227 of the Companies Act 1948 validating the disposition, if (which was unlikely) the liquidator challenged the collection of the cheques; and (c) even if the bank was exposed to risk, this was a risk of conducting a banking business, and it afforded no excuse for refusing to collect the cheques and pay the proceeds to the plaintiffs.

11-354 The Court of Appeal adjourned for half an hour to enable the parties to try to come to some arrangement. In the result, an order was made that, by consent, the plaintiffs should be at liberty to pay to the credit of their account with the defendant bank all such cheques drawn in favour of the plaintiffs as they desired, and that the defendants should honour all such cheques drawn on the account to the extent of the credit balance from time to time, provided that (a) such cheques be drawn to cash or order of the plaintiffs, and (b) such cheques at time of presentation be certified by one director of the company and by a senior partner of the company's solicitors or by a chartered accountant (both of whom were nominees under the scheme of arrangement) as being necessary to be disbursed for the purpose of carrying on the company's business and as being for its benefit and/or the benefit of its creditors.

11-355 In 1962 the Company Law Committee (the 'Jenkins Committee') recommended[52] the following amendment to the Companies Act 1948:

Section 227[53] should be amended to empower the Court, between the date of the winding-up petition and the date of the winding-up order, if any, to validate on such terms as it may think fit a disposition of the property of the company. The section should also make clear that, during the same period, the Court is similarly empowered to sanction the carrying on of the business of the company and acts incidental thereto, such as the drawing of cheques on its bank account.

11-356 Although this recommendation has not been implemented by Parliament, there have been at least three subsequent reported cases in which orders have been made by the court after the presentation of a petition and before the petition has been heard. In the first case, *Re A. I. Levy (Holdings) Ltd*,[54] Buckley J held that a disposition could be authorized under s. 227 of the Companies Act 1948 after the presentation of a petition, notwithstanding that a winding-up order had not

---

51 *Mersey Steel and Iron Co.* v. *Naylor, Benzon & Co., supra.*
52 Cmnd. 1749, para. 503(k).
53 S. 227, Companies Act 1948 has been replaced by s. 127, Insolvency Act 1986, but the original provision has not been amended as recommended by the Jenkins Committee.
54 [1964] Ch 19.

been made, if it was clearly beneficial to the creditors. The company owned a valuable asset, and it wanted to dispose of the asset for cash whilst the petition was on the file. Buckley J decided that he had jurisdiction under s. 227 to make the necessary order.

11-357   In the second case, *Re George Grose Ltd*,[55] Megarry J made an order which enabled a company, subject to certain undertakings which it had to give, to operate its banking account pending the hearing of a petition to wind up the company. The petition was on the ground that the company was not being run for the benefit of the shareholders, but for the benefit of the directors. It was common ground that the company was solvent and was a going concern. The company's bank had indicated that in view of the presentation of the petition, it would be unable to honour the company's cheques. Accordingly, the company sought an order enabling it to sell goods for the time being constituting part of its stock-in-trade in the ordinary course of its business, and to pay all debts due or becoming due in the ordinary and proper course of that business.

11-358   In the third case, *Re Operator Control Cabs Ltd*,[56] the company's bank stopped the company's account when a petition to wind up the company was presented. On an application by the company to the vacation court it was held that as, on the evidence, it would be to the advantage alike of the petitioner, the creditors and the company that it should continue trading, payments made out of the company's bank account in the ordinary course of business, and dispositions of its property sold in the ordinary course of business to its customers at the full market price, should not be avoided by s. 227.

11-359   In *Re Gray's Inn Construction Co. Ltd*,[57] the Court of Appeal held that payments into and out of a company's bank account during the period between the date of the presentation of a petition and the date when the winding-up order was made constituted dispositions of the company's property within s. 227 of the Companies Act 1948. The bank had permitted the company to continue to operate its account without making an application to the court for an order. On an application by the liquidator, the Court of Appeal ordered the bank to repay certain sums to him. It seems clear from this decision that, as soon as a bank learns of the presentation of a petition, it should stop all the company's accounts. An application should be made to the court forthwith, and the court will allow the bank to operate a new account 'subject to safeguards directed to ensuring that it would only do so for so long as the

---

55 *The Financial Times*, 23 May 1969.
56 [1970] 3 All ER 657n.
57 [1980] 1 WLR 711.

company was trading at a profit or that continued trading would be likely to benefit the general body of creditors'.[58]

11-360 Section 227 of the Companies Act 1948 has been replaced by s. 127 of the Insolvency Act 1986 which provides: 'In a winding up by the court, any disposition of the company's property, and any transfer of shares, or alteration in the status of the company's members, made after the commencement of the winding up is, unless the court otherwise orders, void.' It seems clear from the authorities considered above – and especially from the decision of the Court of Appeal in *Re Gray's Inn Construction Co. Ltd* – that, as soon as a bank learns of the presentation of a petition, it should stop all the company's accounts. Any cheques drawn by the company should be returned unpaid marked 'Winding-up petition presented'. The bank should apply to the court forthwith for a validation order, that is to say, an order that all dealings in the ordinary course of business on the company's account or accounts pending an order for the winding up of the company should be valid. According to the judgments in the Court of Appeal in the *Gray's Inn* case, when the application comes before the judge, he should be satisfied that it would be in the interests of the general body of creditors that the company should be permitted to continue trading and to use the services of the bank for that purpose. He should 'freeze' the company's overdrawn account, which would be provable in the winding up. A new bank account should be opened in the name of the company, and the court would allow the bank to operate the new account subject to safeguards directed to ensuring that it would only do so for so long as the company was trading at a profit or that continued trading would be likely to benefit the general body of creditors.

Responsibility for wrongful trading

11-361 Section 214 of the Insolvency Act 1986 introduced a new type of liability arising from 'wrongful trading', which can occur when a company continues to trade where there is no reasonable prospect of it avoiding insolvent liquidation. The court is given power by s. 214(1), on the application of the liquidator, to declare that a director is to be liable to make such contribution (if any) to the company's assets as the court thinks proper. By virtue of s. 214(2) such declaration can be made only if (a) the company has gone into insolvent liquidation, (b) at some time before the commencement of the winding up of the company, the director knew or ought to have concluded that there was no reasonable prospect that the company would avoid going into insolvent liquidation,

58 *Per* Buckley LJ at pp. 719–20.

and (c) he was a director at that time. However, s. 214(3) provides that the court must not make a declaration under this section if it is satisfied that the director took every step with a view to minimizing the potential loss to the company's creditors as he ought to have taken.

11-361A The manner in which the court should exercise its discretion under s. 214 was considered by Knox J in *Re Produce Marketing Consortium Ltd.*[59] Two directors of the company were aware of a serious drop in turnover and of the subsequent inevitability of insolvency. Knox J decided that the directors ought, on objective grounds, to have been aware of the insolvency of the company, and that such knowledge was not negatived by the facts that the company had long-established customers, that the bank had not withdrawn overdraft facilities, and that the company's auditor – while expressing grave reservations – was nevertheless prepared to accompany the directors to the bank to seek further overdraft facilities. Knox J held that the directors had not taken every step to minimize potential losses to creditors, as they had allowed the company to trade for a further year from becoming aware of insolvency. He fixed the level of the directors' contribution in the following way. The losses due to wrongful trading were estimated by the liquidator to be some £216,000. Knox J held that the provisions of s. 214 were primarily compensatory rather than penal, so that prima facie the amount of personal liability was the amount of loss caused to the company due to wrongful trading, but that in fixing the actual amount of liability a number of factors had to be taken into account. In the present case, these included: (a) there was no deliberate course of wrong doing, but simply a failure to appreciate what was clear; (b) a number of factually untrue statements had been made by one of the directors, which indicated an unwillingness to acknowledge the precarious state of the company's affairs; (c) a solemn warning given to the directors by the auditor was ignored; (d) the last seven months of trading had been aimed at reducing the fully secured indebtedness to the bank, whereas the purpose of any order in the instant case ought to be to benefit unsecured creditors. Taking these facts into consideration, Knox J held that the directors were jointly and severally liable to contribute £75,000 to the assets of the company, although as between the directors themselves, the senior of them should be liable for the first £50,000, with joint liability being appropriate for the remainder.

11-362 It is possible that a bank may be held liable for wrongful trading on the part of one of its company customers. This liability may arise because s. 214(7) of the Insolvency Act 1986 provides that a director includes a shadow director, and s. 251 defines a shadow director as a

---

59 [1989] 1 WLR 745.

'person in accordance with whose directions or instructions the directors of the company are accustomed to act (but so that a person is not deemed a shadow director by reason only that the directors act on advice given by him in a professional capacity)'. If a company, which is in financial difficulty, asks its bank for advice, the bank should ensure that it gives advice, rather than 'directions or instructions'. It would be perfectly in order for the bank to inform the directors of the company of the terms upon which the bank is prepared to give financial support to the company, but it would be unwise for the bank to proceed to instruct the company as to how it should act. If the bank did so, it might be held by the court that the bank, or one of its officials, had become a shadow director. For example, a company may have a cashflow problem where the overdraft limit is insufficient to meet payments to pressing creditors. No instruction should be given by the bank as to which creditors should be paid. That is a management decision, and it should be left to the directors.

Section 12
ACCOUNTS OF RECEIVERS FOR DEBENTURE HOLDERS

11-363 If a lender advances money to a company which executes a debenture in his favour by way of security, the normal remedy of the lender, in the event of default by the company, is to appoint a receiver, pursuant to a power for this purpose contained in the debenture. From time to time, a banker appoints a receiver in this way in order to protect his security and to realize it. As bankers frequently lend money to companies and take a debenture by way of security, it is probable that more such appointments are made by bankers than by any other lenders.

11-364 The duties of a receiver are to realize the charged assets for the benefit of the secured creditor and of preferential creditors having legal priority to the holder of a floating charge.[60] Any surplus will be passed either to a liquidator for distribution to unsecured creditors, or to the directors for the company itself. A receiver has no duty or power to deal with the claims of unsecured creditors. His appointment operates as a suspension of payments to them.[61]

11-365 A receiver's powers are usually set out in the debenture, as follows: (a) to take possession of the charged assets and to sell them, (b) to carry on the company's business, (c) to borrow money on the security

---

60 *Ante*, para. 11-299.
61 For a useful article, see Mark Homan, 'Over to the receiver', *Banking World*, December 1984, pp. 35–7.

of the assets, (d) to appoint agents, (e) to instigate or to continue legal actions, and (f) to carry out acts incidental to the performance of his duties.

11-366 Most receivers who are appointed by the banks are 'administrative receivers' as defined by the Insolvency Act 1986.[62] They are subject to rules contained in the Act, and the Act confers extensive powers upon them.[63]

Conducting an account for a receiver or an administrative receiver

11-367 Soon after his appointment, a receiver usually desires to open a bank account. The steps to be taken depend upon whether he was appointed (a) by the court,[64] or (b) by the debenture holder pursuant to a power conferred by the debenture.

(a) Appointment by the court

11-368 When a receiver has been appointed by the court, the bank should ask him to supply a copy of the court order. This order occasionally authorizes him to borrow money and to give security on the assets of the company ranking prior to the debenture. If the order does not contain such power, and accommodation is required, application should be made to the court. Provided that the limits or conditions imposed by the court are rigidly observed, the receiver will not incur personal liability, unless he expressly agrees to do so.[65] In practice, he will not usually accept personal liability.

11-369 It is possible, though undesirable, for a receiver to borrow without obtaining the sanction of the court. If he borrows without express authority from the court or if he exceeds the borrowing powers conferred on him by the court, he will be personally liable and he may find that the court will not allow him to recoup himself out of the assets.[66]

(b) Appointment by the debenture holder

11-370 When a receiver is appointed not by the court but by the debenture holder, the document appointing him should be exhibited to the

---

62 See *ante*, para. 11-320.
63 See *ante*, para. 11-323 to 11-328.
64 Appointment by the court is infrequent at the present day: see *ante*, para. 11-315.
65 *Re Boynton (A.) Ltd, Hoffman* v. *Boynton (A) Ltd* [1901] 1 Ch 519.
66 For an example, see *Re British Power Traction and Lighting Co. Ltd, Halifax Joint Stock Banking Co. Ltd* v. *British Power Traction and Lighting Co Ltd (No. 2)* [1907] 1 Ch 528.

bank. Furthermore, a copy of the debenture should also be supplied to the bank. This will enable the bank to satisfy himself that the appointment has been properly made in accordance with the power conferred by the debenture. If, however, the bank itself appointed the receiver, the relevant information will already be within its knowledge and therefore an account may be opened for the receiver immediately.

11-371 If accommodation is requested by the receiver, the bank will want to know how and when the advance is to be repaid. It will not wish to step into the shoes of the debenture holder by lending an unduly large amount, especially if repayment depends upon the sale of certain fixed assets which it may be difficult to realize.[67]

11-372 The bank will also wish to be satisfied that the receiver has power to borrow. One should ascertain whether he has been given power to carry on the business of the company because it seems that a power to carry on a business implies a power to borrow.[68] It is a question of construction in each particular case whether a receiver is authorized to borrow money on the security of the assets in priority to the debenture holders. Thus where a receiver was authorized 'to make such arrangements as he might think expedient', he was held to have such a power.[69] For his own protection, he should see that the terms of his appointment give him express powers to borrow and to create charges for loans. If they do not, and he requires to borrow, he should apply to the court for directions.[70]

11-373 Most receivers who are appointed by the banks are 'administrative receivers' as defined by the Insolvency Act 1986.[71] Section 42(1) confers upon them the powers listed in Sched. 1 to the Act, subject to any contrary express terms in the debenture. One of the powers listed in Sched. 1 is the power to raise or borrow money and grant security therefor over the property of the company.

Effect of winding-up order upon receiver's powers

11-374 Sometimes a creditor presents a petition to wind up a company after a receiver has been appointed by a debenture holder. As a general rule, this course is only profitable to the unsecured creditors in those

---

67 For a useful article, see James Dandy, 'Finance for receivers and liquidators', *Journal of Institute of Bankers*, Vol. 80 (1959), pp. 193–202.
68 *Re General Estates Co., Ex parte City Bank* (1868) LR 3 Ch App 758; *General Auction Estate and Monetary Co.* v. *Smith* [1891] 3 Ch 432.
69 *Robinson Printing Co. Ltd* v. *Chic Ltd* [1905] 2 Ch 123.
70 See the Insolvency Act 1986, s. 35(1).
71 See *ante*, para. 11-320.

cases where there will be a surplus after the debenture holder has been paid off.

11-375 The making of a winding-up order does not usually displace a receiver. When the receiver has realized sufficient assets to extinguish the debt owing to the debenture holder, he must then hand over the remaining assets to the liquidator. When so required by the liquidator, he must also render to him proper accounts of receipts and payments. [72]

11-376 Although the making of a winding-up order does not usually displace a receiver, there are exceptional cases where the court will remove a receiver appointed before the commencement of the winding-up proceedings, or after a winding-up order has been obtained. In those cases, the court usually appoints the liquidator to act as receiver as well as liquidator. [73] In such cases, no further cheques drawn by the original receiver should be paid by the bank.

Section 13
ACCOUNTS OF LIQUIDATORS

11-377 The consideration affecting the accounts of liquidators depend upon whether the liquidation is a members' voluntary winding up, a creditors' voluntary winding up, or a compulsory winding up. [74]

Members' voluntary winding up

11-378 A liquidator in a members' voluntary winding up should be asked by the bank to supply a certified copy of the resolution of the company whereby he was appointed. An account may then be opened in his name as liquidator. He is entitled to transfer to this account the net sum, if any, standing to the company's credit at the bank.

11-379 The liquidator in a members' voluntary winding up has power, without the sanction of the company, to borrow money. Nevertheless, unless the loan is small and of a very temporary nature, it is the practice to obtain the company's approval of any borrowing; this should be given by a resolution passed in general meeting. Occasionally, the liquidator is asked to undertake personal responsibility for the repayment of

---

72 S. 41(1)(b).
73 *Re Stubbs (Joshua) Ltd., Barney* v. *Stubbs (Joshua) Ltd* [1891] 1 Ch. 475; *Willmott* v. *London Celluloid Co.* (1885) 52 LT 642.
74 *Ante*, paras 11-343 and 11-348.

the loan, particularly if the company's assets are already charged elsewhere.

11-380 The liquidator in a member's voluntary winding up also has power, without the sanction of the company, to charge the company's assets by way of security.[75] He cannot, of course, charge the company's assets in such a way as to give the bank priority over any existing chargee.

11-381 If the members decide to appoint two or more insolvency practitioners to act as joint liquidators, the resolution should state whether any act required or authorized to be done by the liquidators is to be done by all or any one or more of them.[76]

Creditors' voluntary winding up

11-382 When a liquidator in a creditors' voluntary winding up produces a certified copy of the resolution by which he was appointed, a bank account may be opened in his name as liquidator.[77] He is entitled to transfer to this account the net sum, if any, standing to the company's credit at the bank.

11-383 Although the liquidator usually draws cheques alone, it is sometimes desired that one or more members of the liquidation committee should countersign these cheques. If so, a mandate should be obtained governing operations on the account.

11-384 The liquidator in a creditors' voluntary winding up has power, without the sanction of the court or the liquidation committee or the creditors, to borrow money and to charge the company's assets by way of security.[78] Nevertheless, unless the loan is small and is of a very temporary nature, it is the practice to obtain the approval of the liquidation committee or of the creditors. The liquidator cannot, of course, charge the company's assets in such a way as to give the bank priority over any existing chargee.

11-385 If two or more joint liquidators are appointed, their powers are the same as those of joint liquidators in a members' voluntary winding up.[79]

75 Insolvency Act 1986, s. 165(3) and Part II of Sched. 4.
76 Insolvency Act 1986, s. 231.
77 For the manner of his appointment, see *ante*, para. 11-345.
78 Insolvency Act 1986, s. 165 and Part II of Sched. 4.
79 *Ante*, para. 11-381.

Compulsory winding up

11-386 By virtue of the Insolvency Regulations 1986[80] a liquidator of a company which is being wound up by the court must pay all money received by him into the Insolvency Services Account kept by the Secretary of State with the Bank of England, Threadneedle Street, London EC2R 8AH. However, if the liquidator intends to exercise his power to carry on the business of the company, he may apply to the Secretary of State for authorization to open a local bank account, and the Secretary of State may authorize him to make his payments into and out of a specified bank, instead of into and out of the Insolvency Services Account, if he is satisfied that an administrative advantage will be derived from having such an account.[81]

11-387 Where a liquidator in a compulsory winding up opens a local bank account, he must open and maintain clearly named local bank accounts for each company of which he is liquidator, and where money is provided for a specific purpose, it must be clearly identifiable in a separate account.[82] As soon as the liquidator ceases to carry on the business of the company, or vacates office, or an authorization given under the Regulations is withdrawn, he must close the account and remit any balance to the Insolvency Services Account at the Bank of England.[83]

11-388 Occasionally, a liquidator in a compulsory winding up wishes to borrow from the bank. The Insolvency Act 1986[84] gives him a general power, without the sanction of the court or of the liquidation committee, to raise money on the security of the assets of the company. However, in order to carry on the business of the company 'so far as may be necessary for its beneficial winding up', he does require the sanction either of the court or of the liquidation committee.[85] Consequently, if he wishes to borrow money for the purpose of carrying on the business of the company, it is prudent to ensure that he has obtained sanction to carry on the business. If he proposes to create a charge over certain assets of the company, it is important to make certain that those assets have not already been charged by the company. A liquidator is not personally liable for advances, unless he expressly accepts such liability; he rarely does so.

11-389 Sometimes, two or more joint liquidators are appointed by the court. The appointment must declare whether any act required or

---

80 Regulation 4.
81 Regulation 6(1).
82 Regulation 6(3).
83 Regulation 6(6).
84 S. 167(1) and Part III of Sched. 4.
85 Part II of Sched. 4.

authorized to be done by the liquidators is to be done by all or any one or more of them.[86] In practice, therefore, a bank should not allow joint liquidators to sign individually on their account at the bank, unless the court has expressly authorized this delegation.

11-390 If a liquidator in a compulsory liquidation resigns, dies, or is removed by the court, a fresh appointment will be made by the court. In those exceptional cases where the account is overdrawn and the bank is relying upon the personal liability of the liquidator, the account should be ruled off, in order to avoid the operation of the Rule in *Clayton's* case.[87] In other cases, the old account may be continued by the new liquidator. He should be asked to confirm in writing that cheques issued by his predecessor may be paid by the bank.

Section 14
ACCOUNTS OF BUILDING SOCIETIES

11-391 A building society is an association of persons formed with the primary object of subscribing funds, out of which loans may be made to members of the society for the purchase of property – usually houses. The borrowing member executes a mortgage of the house in favour of the society by way of security, and he agrees to repay the loan, with interest, by an agreed number of regular (normally, monthly) payments. Most of the legal rules concerning building societies are now contained in the Building Societies Act 1986.

11-392 Any number of persons, not less than ten, may establish a society under the Building Societies Act 1986 by (a) agreeing upon rules for the government of the society, and (b) sending to the central office of the Building Societies Commission four copies of the rules.[88] The central office returns one copy, together with a certificate of incorporation.

11-393 The Building Societies Act 1986[89] enables building societies to offer most retail banking services. Many societies now offer current accounts, cheque guarantee cards, credit cards, insurance services, personal loans, unit trusts, pension plans and estate agency.

11-394 Under the Building Societies Act 1986[90] a building society has power to shed its mutual status and to become a public limited

86 S. 231.
87 (1816) 1 Mer 572.
88 Building Societies Act 1986, s. 5(8) and Sched. 2, Part I, para. 1.
89 S. 34, and Sched. 8, Part I.
90 See s. 97(1) which provides that a building society may 'transfer the whole of its business to a company'.

company. In order to do so, a society must first ballot its members. If they are in favour of their society transferring its business to a company, the society must then obtain the confirmation of the Building Societies Commission. The Commission can refuse to confirm the transfer on the grounds that the vote did not accurately reflect the views of the members, or that the new company would be unlikely to be authorized by the Bank of England under the Banking Act 1987.[91]

11-395 In 1989 the Abbey National Building Society, which is second only in size to the Halifax Building Society, ballotted its members, who voted overwhelmingly in favour of becoming a public limited company. Nevertheless, there was vigorous opposition from a minority of the membership. After conducting a public hearing, the Building Societies Commission approved the flotation. However, in one of the strongest condemnations to date by a watchdog body of a financial institution in its charge, the Building Societies Commission accused the Abbey National of giving its members a biased view of the conversion from a mutual society to a public limited company.[92] The Commission stated that there was a 'significant deficiency' in information about flotation available to members, but that it was not material to their decision. Parts of the Abbey National's transfer statement to members were described as 'facile', 'over-sanguine' and failing to bring out key aspects of the changes. Furthermore, the Abbey National was ordered by the Commission to review arrangements for compensating children with Abbey National accounts for their loss of ownership. These criticisms should be heeded by any other building societies which wish to convert from a mutual society to public limited company.

Conducting an account for a building society

11-396 A building society must keep its surplus funds with a bank which is for the time being authorized to hold funds of building societies; these orders are made with the consent of the Treasury, and they must be published in the *London, Edinburgh* and *Belfast Gazettes*. The effect of the Banking Act 1979 is that, in future, a society may keep its funds only with a recognized bank.[93] However, banks which had already been authorized to have the accounts of building societies but which did not gain recognized status – including the Trustee Savings

---

91 See *ante*, para. 1-41.
92 See the note by David Barchard and Clare Pearson in *The Financial Times*, 7 June 1989.
93 S. 51(1) and Sched. 6, para. 5.

Banks, the Girobank and the National Savings Bank – may continue to have these accounts.[94]

11-397 When a bank is requested to open an account for a building society, it should ask to be supplied with a copy of the society's rules. Particular attention should be paid to the powers of the governing body, i.e. the directors or the committee, especially with reference to the opening of a bank account and the drawing of cheques. The secretary of the society should be asked to advise the bank of all amendments to the rules. Except in the case of well-known societies, the bank should also ask to see the society's certificate of incorporation.

11-398 The directors or the committee must pass a resolution appointing the bank as bankers to the society. Most banks supply building societies with a printed form setting out the terms of a suitable draft resolution, which may be completed by filling in the necessary details. Thus, the resolution should indicate the persons who (in accordance with the society's rules) are to draw cheques on its behalf and withdraw any securities held on its behalf by the bank. When the resolution has been passed, the chairman and secretary should sign the bank's form certifying that this has been done.

11-399 In view of the fact that building societies have power to collect cheques on behalf of their customers and to pay cheques drawn by them, the Building Societies Act 1986[95] provides that 'so far as regards the provision by it of a service which is a qualifying banking service for the purposes of this paragraph a building society shall be treated for all purposes as a bank and a banker and as carrying on the business of banking or a banking undertaking whether or not it would be so treated apart from this paragraph'.

Borrowing powers of building societies

11-400 Schedule 2 of the Building Societies Act 1986 includes a provision that a society must prepare a memorandum (similar to a company's memorandum of association) setting out its purposes and powers. One of the powers included in the memorandum is the power to borrow money. In the past, building societies have raised by far the greater part of their funds from individual shareholders and depositors. Section 7 of the Act is intended to preserve the traditional character of building societies as institutions which look to the private savings sector for the bulk of their funds, but provisions are made to enable societies

94 S. 51(1) and Sched. 6, para. 16.
95 S. 34, and Sched. 8, Part 4, para. 3.

to borrow money from other sources. Limits are imposed on the amounts which may be borrowed. Before making a loan to a society, some banks supply the society with a printed form of declaration to be completed and signed by two directors and the secretary, setting out all the relevant figures affecting the society's borrowing powers.

11-401 Having ascertained that the loan required by the society is within its unexpended borrowing powers, the bank should preferably make its advance on loan account, rather than on current account. If the bank made the advance on current account and the society increased its borrowings from other sources with the result that it exceeded its borrowing powers, subsequent items debited to the current account would constitute borrowings by the society beyond its powers. If, however, the bank advance is made on loan account, an excess borrowing elsewhere will not prejudice the bank.

11-402 The most common type of security for a loan to a building society is a sub-mortgage of some of the properties mortgaged to the society by its members.

Section 15
ACCOUNTS OF FRIENDLY SOCIETIES

11-403 Friendly societies may be registered or unregistered, though there are very few unregistered societies in existence today. Briefly, the main purposes of friendly societies are the provision of relief to members and to their dependants during unemployment, sickness and old age, and the payment of money in respect of funeral expenses and upon birth of a member's child. There are still many registered friendly societies in existence, but some of the benefits which they provide are now obtainable under the national insurance scheme, and accordingly the societies do not now play as active a part in these matters as in the past.

11-404 An application to register a society must be signed by seven members and by the secretary.[96] Every registered society and branch must have one or more trustees,[97] and they must be appointed at a meeting of the society or branch and by a resolution of a majority of the members present and entitled to vote at that meeting.[98]

96 Friendly Societies Act 1974, s. 8(1).
97 S. 24(1).
98 S. 24(2).

Conducting an account for a friendly society

11-405　When a bank is requested to open an account for a friendly society, the bank should ask to be supplied with a copy of the society's rules, and a copy of all amendments thereto in the future.

11-406　If the society is a registered society, the certificate issued by the Chief Registrar of friendly societies should be examined.

11-407　The trustees should be asked to pass a resolution appointing the bank as bankers to the society, and authorizing the bank to honour cheques drawn on behalf of the society by, for example, two trustees and the secretary. The terms of the resolution must, of course, be in conformity with the society's rules. A certified copy of the resolution should be supplied to the bank.

Lending to friendly societies

11-408　When a bank is asked to lend to a registered friendly society, the first step is to examine the society's rules. If the proposed borrowing is authorized by the rules, it is the usual practice to ask the trustees to pass a resolution requesting a loan of a specified sum.

11-409　As regards security, the Friendly Societies Act 1974[99] provides that a registered society may, if its rules so provide, acquire land in the names of its trustees, and mortgage the land; and a mortgagee is not bound to enquire as to the authority for any such mortgage by the trustees.

Section 16
ACCOUNTS OF INDUSTRIAL AND PROVIDENT SOCIETIES

11-410　Societies registered under the Industrial and Provident Societies Act 1965, or earlier Acts, are bodies corporate with limited liability.[1] These societies, which are known as industrial and provident societies, are formed for many different purposes. There are the well-known wholesale and retail co-operative societies selling a wide range of domestic and household goods. Then there are the agricultural and horticultural societies; their functions are to pool the buying requirements of their members and to co-ordinate the marketing of their produce.

99 S. 52(1).
　1 Industrial and Provident Societies Act 1965, s. 3. Unless the objects of a society are wholly charitable or benevolent, the word 'limited' must be the last word in the name of the society: s. 5(2) and (5).

Finally, there are many social clubs — especially working-men's clubs — which operate as industrial and provident societies.

11-411   The rules of an industrial and provident society must provide for the appointment of a committee or other directing body of the society, and of managers or other officers.[2] As the societies are bodies corporate, there is usually no necessity to appoint trustees; the property of each society is vested in the society, just as the property of a company is vested in the company.

11-412   When a bank is requested to open an account for an industrial and provident society, the bank should ask to be supplied with a copy of the society's rules, and a copy of all amendments thereto in the future. The committee of management, or other directing body of the society, should be requested to pass a resolution appointing the bank as bankers to the society, and authorizing the bank to honour cheques drawn on behalf of the society by, for example, two members of the committee and the secretary. The terms of the resolution must, of course, be in conformity with the society's rules. A certified copy of the resolution should be supplied to the bank.

Lending to industrial and provident societies

11-413   When a bank is asked to lend to an industrial and provident society, the first step is to examine the society's rules. If the proposed borrowing is authorized by the rules, it is the usual practice to ask the committee of management, or other directing body of the society, to pass a resolution requesting a loan of a specified amount.

11-414   As regards security, the Industrial and Provident Societies Act 1965[3] provides that a registered society may, unless its rules direct otherwise, acquire land in its own name, and mortgage the land; and a mortgagee is not bound to enquire as to the authority for any such mortgage by the society.

11-415   The Agricultural Credits Act 1928[4] enabled an industrial and provident society to issue a debenture creating in favour of a bank a floating charge on farming stock. This type of debenture must be registered within seven days of its issue as an agricultural charge at the Land Registry.[5] In addition, notice of the charge must be sent to the Chief Registrar of friendly societies.[6]

2 S. 74, and Sched. I.
3 S. 30(1), re-enacting earlier legislation.
4 S. 14.
5 Agricultural Credits Act 1928, ss 9 and 14.
6 S. 14.

11-416 The Industrial and Provident Societies Act 1967 conferred much wider powers upon societies. The Act provides that a society may create a fixed or floating charge on *any* of its assets in favour of any lender.[7] A copy of the instrument creating the charge must be sent to the Chief Registrar of friendly societies within fourteen days of its execution.[8]

Section 17
ACCOUNTS OF PAROCHIAL CHURCH COUNCILS

11-417 By virtue of the Parochial Church Councils (Powers) Measure 1956 (passed by the National Assembly of the Church of England), every parochial church council is a body corporate with perpetual succession.[9] Any act of a parochial church council may be signified by an instrument executed pursuant to a resolution of the council and under the hands (or if an instrument under seal is required, under the hands and seals) of the chairman presiding and two other members of the council present at the meeting at which such resolution is passed.[10] Among the powers and duties of a parochial church council are those relating to the financial affairs of the church, including the collection and administration of all moneys raised for church purposes and the keeping of accounts in relation to such affairs and money.[11]

11-418 The opening of a banking account for a parochial church council should be authorized by a resolution passed by the council; the resolution should embody precise instructions concerning operations on the account. A copy of the resolution, certified by the chairman, should be supplied to the bank. The account should be opened in the name of 'Parochial Church Council of ... Parish'.

11-419 Any borrowing should be authorized by a resolution of the council. Sometimes, this type of borrowing is secured by guarantees executed by a few of the parishioners. If, however, it is desired to obtain a charge upon church property, whether real or personal, it is usually necessary to seek the co-operation of the diocesan authorities. This is the effect of the Parochial Church Councils (Powers) Measure 1956,[12] which provides that where a council acquires an interest in land (other

7 S. 1(1).
8 S. 1(2).
9 S. 3.
10 S. 3.
11 S. 4(1).
12 S. 6(2).

than a short lease)[13] or any interest in personal property to be held on permanent trusts, such interest must be vested in the diocesan authority; this authority is the diocesan board of finance, or any existing or future body appointed by the diocesan conference to act as trustees of diocesan trust property.[14] The Measure provides that where any such property is vested in the diocesan authority, the parochial church council must not charge the property within the consent of the diocesan authority.[15]

Section 18
ACCOUNTS OF LOCAL AUTHORITIES

Local government areas

11-420   For the purposes of local government, the whole of England, with the exception of Greater London, is divided into counties, and in the counties there are areas known as districts.[16] Some of the very large counties are called metropolitan counties, and the districts within them are metropolitan districts.

11-421   Wales is also divided into counties and districts.[17] There are, however, no metropolitan counties or metropolitan districts in Wales.

11-422   Both in England and in Wales, each county and each district is a body corporate which is administered by a council consisting of a chairman and councillors.[18]

11-423   In England there are also parishes where there are parish councils and parish meetings.[19] In Wales, instead of parishes, there are communities where there are community councils and community meetings.[20] The powers vested in all these councils and meetings are very small.

11-424   Greater London consists of the City of London, the Inner and Middle Temples (where many barristers live and have their chambers),

---

13 This means a lease for a term not exceeding one year, and includes any tenancy from week to week, from month to month, from quarter to quarter, or from year to year: s. 6(6).

14 S. 1.

15 S. 6(3). See also *Re St Peter, Roydon* [1969] 2 All ER 1233, a decision of the Chelmsford Consistory Court in which it was unsuccessfully argued that a parochial church council had no power to borrow money.

16 Local Government Act 1972, s. 1(1).

17 S. 20(1).

18 Ss 2 and 21.

19 S. 9.

20 S. 27.

and thirty-two London boroughs, twelve of which are called inner London boroughs, and the remainder of which are called outer London boroughs.

Conducting an account for a local authority

11-425 Local authorities must make arrangements for the proper administration of their financial affairs, and they must secure that one of their officers has responsibility for the administration of those affairs.[21] He is the officer who supervises the banking accounts of the local authority.

11-426 The accounts of a local authority are opened in the name of the authority itself. The council should pass a resolution authorizing the opening of the accounts and embodying precise instructions concerning their operation. A copy of the resolution, certified by the chairman and countersigned by the clerk to the council, should be supplied to the bank. Some local authority mandates to their bankers are lengthy, because it is quite usual for these customers to maintain a number of accounts at the bank, and separate signing instructions often apply to each account.

11-427 When a new treasurer or chief financial officer is appointed by the local authority, this appointment is recorded in the council's minutes, and a copy of the relevant resolution, certified by the chairman and countersigned by the clerk, should be sent to the bank. Changes in other signing officers are usually communicated to the bank by the treasurer or the chief financial officer, but this practice should be expressly authorized by the original resolution passed by the council.

Overdraft arrangements with local authorities

11-428 One advantage of lending money to a local authority is that the financial standing of the borrower is undoubted. As against this, however, there is the disadvantage that a local authority's borrowing powers are governed by a number of statutes and by regulations made thereunder. An borrowing by a local authority in excess of, or without, statutory authority is *ultra vires*.

11-429 In this regard, the relevant statute, or the regulations made thereunder, frequently provide that, before a local authority may borrow, it must obtain the consent of one of the central government

21 S. 151.

departments.[22] The treasurer or chief financial officer to the local authority is the official who applies on behalf of his council for the necessary consent. His professional training enables him to perform this task properly, and a bank will usually be able to reply upon his carrying out the work correctly. However, in some cases, the bank may wish to obtain independent legal advice. Before an advance is made, the council should pass a suitable resolution requesting the advance, and a copy of the resolution, certified by the chairman and countersigned by the clerk, should be forwarded to the bank. Such borrowings are, however, rarely made. Most local authorities borrow money from the Public Works Loans Board, the government agency through which local authorities may borrow. They also raise money by issuing stock and negotiable bonds. Additional money is raised from 'local loans', which are of relatively small amounts for a fixed period, usually between two and seven years. Finally, for temporary funds, local authorities look to the money market rather than to their bankers.[23]

Section 19
ACCOUNTS OF CLUBS AND SOCIETIES

11-430 Clubs and societies may be divided into two main categories: (a) those which are owned or controlled by a corporate body ('incorporated clubs and societies'), and (b) those which have not been incorporated ('unincorporated clubs and societies'). When a banker is asked to open an account for a club or society, the first task is to determine into which category it falls.

Incorporated clubs and societies

11-431 As far as clubs and societies are concerned, incorporation usually takes one of two forms, (a) incorporation under the Companies Acts, and (b) incorporation under the Industrial and Provident Societies Acts.

---

22 For a summary of this branch of the law, setting out the consents required, see *Halsbury's Laws of England* (4th ed.), Vol. 28, pp. 679–92. See also W. B. Taylor, 'Borrowing by local authorities in the United Kingdom', *National Westminster Bank Quarterly Review*, August 1983, pp. 60–69.
23 For an interesting article, see W. J. Capps, 'Local government finance: the relationship of a local authority with its bankers', *Journal of the Institute of Bankers*, Vol. 101 (1980), pp. 166–8.

(a) Incorporation under Companies Acts

11-432   Many sports clubs are incorporated as limited companies, the club's assets being vested in the company. Occasionally, however, although a club is managed by a company, its assets, including possibly its grounds, are vested in trustees. Accordingly, a bank which is asked to open an account for a sports club, and possibly to make a loan to the club for extensions or improvements, should obtain a copy of the club's rules, and find out who runs the club and in whose names the assets are vested.

11-433   Some professional bodies and learned societies are incorporated as companies. In some cases, incorporation is effected under the Companies Acts, with or without power to dispense with the word 'limited' in the company's name. [24] In other instances, the body or society may have been incorporated by the grant of a Royal Charter. [25]

11-434   The steps which should be taken when opening accounts for companies limited by shares or by guarantee, [26] or incorporated by Royal Charter, [27] have been stated earlier in this chapter.

(b) Incorporation under Industrial and Provident Societies Acts

11-435   Many social clubs – especially working-men's clubs – operate as industrial and provident societies. These are bodies corporate with limited liability. Unless a society's objects are wholly charitable or benevolent, the word 'limited' must be the last word in the name of the society. The operation of bank accounts for these societies has already been considered. [28]

Unincorporated clubs and societies

11-436   There are many kinds of clubs and societies which, because they are unincorporated, are not legal entities, and therefore cannot enter into any contract. For this reason, instead of opening a bank account in the name of an unincorporated club or society, some banks prefer to open the account in the name or names of private individuals, coupled with some words to indicate that the funds do not belong to them beneficially; for example, Mary Smith and Margaret Robinson, 'Old Girls' Association Account'. An advantage of opening the account

24 *Ante*, para. 11-284.
25 *Ante*, para. 11-263.
26 *Ante*, paras 11-265/74.
27 *Ante*, para. 11-311.
28 *Ante*, para. 11-412.

in this way and obtaining the customers' signatures to the bank's usual form of joint-account mandate, is that the individual customers will be jointly and severally liable for any overdraft.[29]

11-437 In practice, however, most banks are now prepared to open an account in the name of an unincorporated club or society or group of people, even though there is no legal entity with whom a contract can be made. There would seem to be no risk in doing so, provided that the account is kept in credit. If the society has rules, the account should be opened and conducted in accordance therewith. Most banks have a printed form of mandate for use by unincorporated clubs or societies. The mandate embodies a draft resolution to be passed by the committee of the society authorizing the bank to pay cheques, provided that they are drawn, for example, 'by any two members of the committee for the time being and countersigned by the treasurer', or otherwise as may be required.

Lending on the accounts of unincorporated clubs and societies

11-438 As already stated, an unincorporated club or society is not a legal entity, and therefore it cannot enter into any contract. For this reason, the lending of money on the account of an unincorporated body demands special safeguards, partly because of the fact that it is difficult, if not impossible, to obtain redress against the association's funds, and partly because it is not easy to establish the personal liability of any particular members of the association. Professor Lord Lloyd has stated the legal position as follows:[30]

> If the society is unincorporated so that it is nothing more than a collective name for the body of members, the funds are the collective property of those members, and therefore can only be reached if the transaction in question had the authority of all the members. Without that authority the contract can at most be with such of the members as did in fact authorize it, but though their personal liability may thus be established the collective funds will not be available.

Coutts & Co. v. *Irish Exhibition in London*[31] is a useful illustration of a case where a bank did eventually succeed in establishing the personal liability of six men who had formed themselves into the executive council of an unincorporated body known as the Irish Exhibition in London. The plaintiff bank lent a large sum of money on an account

---

29 *Ante*, para. 11-77.
30 Dennis Lloyd, *The Law Relating to Unincorporated Associations* (1938), p. 134.
31 (1891) 7 TLR 313. See also *Wise* v. *Perpetual Trustee Co.* [1903] A C 139; *Bradley Egg Farm Ltd* v. *Clifford* [1943] 2 All ER 378.

opened in the name of 'the Irish Exhibition', and the six men who were held personally liable were the signatories upon the account.

11-439 In spite of that decision in favour of the plaintiff bank, it does not follow that any signatory upon the account of an unincorporated body is necessarily liable for any lending on the account: his liability depends upon whether he *authorized* the borrowing. Accordingly, the only prudent course to take when lending money on the account of an unincorporated body is to obtain a guarantee, or other security, from responsible persons. The guarantee form which is used for this purpose should contain a clause to the effect that all sums of money which may not be recoverable from the guarantor on the footing of a guarantee are to be recoverable from him as sole or principal debtor.

Circulars issued by the Committee of London Clearing Bankers

2 September 1957

CHEQUES ACT 1957

Combined cheque and receipt forms

In due course instructions will be issued by the banks as to modification of banking practice in regard to the endorsement of cheques and other instruments, consequent upon the passing of the Cheques Act 1957.

On and after the 17th October next, banks paying cheques and instruments other than bills of exchange and promissory notes will be under no legal obligation to examine endorsements. Nevertheless, the banks informed the Mocatta Committee on Cheque Endorsement that in suitable cases by arrangement with customers they would continue to examine receipts on cheques.

1. NEW ARRANGEMENTS

The banks, however, pointed out to the Mocatta Committee that they could not undertake to examine receipts on cheques without limit or regardless of circumstances. Therefore, before any request for the **extension** of the use of endorsed receipts is acceded to it has been agreed by the banks that the bank concerned must be satisfied that there is real need on the part of the customer for the facility. An endeavour should be made to limit any extension of the facility to a receipt form merely acknowledging receipt of the money; a narrative receipt connecting the payment with any specific transaction is to be deprecated and discouraged. The Insurance Companies have already intimated an intention to reduce to a minimum the use of this instrument, but receipts will still be required by them in some cases, particularly in connection with the settlement of claims when endorsement by the payee is required to show that the amount is accepted in full settlement of a claim.

2. EXISTING ARRANGEMENTS

The banks have also agreed to encourage **reduction** in the use of endorsed receipts as far as possible. In this connection each bank has undertaken to approach all customers concerned and to suggest to them that Section 3 of the Act should render an endorsed receipt unnecessary unless, as in the case of some of the Insurance Companies, Local Authorities and Building Societies, the circumstances are exceptional.

Customers' attention should be drawn to Section 3 of the Act, which states:

> An unindorsed cheque which appears to have been paid by the banker on whom it is drawn is evidence of the receipt by the payee of the sum payable by the cheque.

and to the following view expressed by the Mocatta Committee:

> We are of the opinion that in law a simple receipt for a payment by cheque, not linking the payment with the relative transaction, has no greater value as evidence of payment than the paid cheque itself. This is so whether the receipt is printed on the cheque or is issued separately.

It is hoped that, with the co-operation of customers, the number of these instruments in use will be considerably reduced.

3. DISTINCTIVE MARKING OF COMBINED CHEQUE AND RECEIPT FORMS

On and after the 17th October 1957 banks will not accept responsibility for examining receipts, as such, on cheques and other instruments unless the instrument is marked on its face in the position indicated on the specimen cheque enclosed, with a bold **outline** letter 'R' at least half-an-inch high. The letter 'R' must be as close to the '£' sign in the 'amount' box as practicable, but some discretion may be given to printers to determine the size of the letter as long as the minimum requirement is observed.

There may be in use special instruments which, as now printed, cannot be stamped or over-printed in the prescribed position. In such cases an alternative position **in proximity to the amount** must be selected but every effort should be made to standardize the instruments when new stocks are printed.

Arrangements must be made forthwith to ensure that existing stocks of combined cheque and receipt forms, whether held by customers or by the banks, are overprinted or stamped with a rubber stamp in the agreed manner as soon as possible, except in cases where the customers agree that any existing arrangements may be discontinued.

It is essential that such instruments as are issued be marked well before the 17th October to allow for delay in presentation.

These arrangements also apply to instruments in the form of a receipt payable by their bankers issued by Building Societies and others.

4. PROCEDURE

(a) ALL customers who use combined cheque and receipt forms must be approached forthwith to ascertain whether they require the facilities to be continued, notwithstanding the provisions of Section 3 of the Act.

(b) Customers who agree to discontinuance of the facility as from the 17th October should so confirm in writing. The instruments will not then be marked with an 'R' and on and after that date the form of receipt may be ignored whilst existing stocks are in use.

(c) Customers who require the facility to be continued must be informed of the arrangements which must be made to mark the instruments.

5. OPERATION OF SIGNATURE TO RECEIPT AS ENDORSEMENT

Receipts should continue to indicate that the signature thereto is intended to act as an endorsement.

6. BANKS IN ISLE OF MAN: CHANNEL ISLANDS: REPUBLIC OF IRELAND

Since the Act does not apply to the Isle of Man, the Channel Islands or the Republic of Ireland, banks situated there will continue to require endorsements or discharges, whether as collecting or as paying bankers. **These arrangements do not therefore, at present, apply to such banks or to combined cheque and receipt forms payable by them.**[1]

---

1 As a result of legislation subsequently passed in the Isle of Man, the Channel Islands and the Republic of Ireland, this paragraph of the Circular no longer applies; in general, the position in the Isle of Man, the Channel Islands and the Republic of Ireland is similar to that in England, Scotland, Wales and Northern Ireland.

CHEQUES ACT 1957

The Cheques Act 1957 applies to all banks in England, Scotland, Wales and Northern Ireland and comes into operation on the 17th October 1957. Broadly the effect of the Act is that on and after that date paying banks need not concern themselves with the endorsement or absence of endorsement upon any cheque or analogous instrument and the same applies to collecting banks unless ostensibly there is, or has been, negotiation of the cheque or instrument, for which purpose endorsement is still required.

The protection afforded to collecting banks, which heretofore has been limited to crossed instruments, is extended by the Act to open instruments.

The Act introduces a completely new system relative to endorsement and the banks must feel their way with due regard on the one hand to their own safety and protection, and on the other to the public interest. The intention of the Act is to relieve customers from the task of endorsing instruments which are to be collected for the payees' accounts and to save them and the banks the trouble caused by the return of a large number of such instruments for correct endorsement.

With these considerations in mind the following instructions have been framed for the guidance of all branches of the Clearing Banks. The instructions, however, must be regarded as prepared upon an experimental basis pending practical experience of the working of the new system. It may be necessary later to tighten the procedure at certain points, but in the meantime it is desirable that customers should, as far as practicable, derive the benefit of the new legislation without being put to unnecessary inconvenience, consistent with prudent regard for the proper and reasonable protection of the banks.

I. PAYING BANKS

(a) Cheques and other instruments presented in the clearings, or specially presented, and 'house debits'

It will not be necessary to examine instruments for endorsement unless the instruments are:

Combined cheque and receipt forms marked 'R';
Travellers' cheques;
Bills of exchange (other than cheques);
Promissory notes.

In these cases endorsement or discharge will be required as heretofore.

(b) Cheques and other instruments cashed at the counter (including those cashed under open credits)

The banks have agreed to continue to require endorsement or receipt in all cases where at present it is the practice to look for this. It is felt that the public interest would best be served by a continuance of the present practice. The Mocatta Committee attached importance to the endorsement of cheques encashed over the counter as possibly affording some evidence of the identity of the recipient and some measure of protection for the public.

2. COLLECTING BANKS

(a) With the exception of the instruments referred to in the Schedule to this Circular cheques and other instruments collected for the account of the ostensible payee will not require examination for endorsement, or in the case of dividend and interest warrants for discharge.

(b) Cheques and other instruments payable to a bank to be applied after collection for the credit of a customer's account, e.g. when dividends are mandated to a bank, will not require endorsement or discharge by the payee bank.

(c) Endorsement for discharge will be required as heretofore if the instrument is tendered for the credit of an account other than that of the ostensible payee. If a cheque is specially endorsed to the customer for whose account it is tendered for collection no further endorsement will be necessary.

(d) The banks will not be concerned with the completion of the discharge at the foot of a dividend or interest or redemption warrant unless the instrument is being collected for the account of a third party. If, as a result of the Act, such warrants cease to be printed with a space for the payee's signature, they will nevertheless require endorsement if negotiated. (It is understood that the Bank of England intend to omit the space from warrants in respect of Government, etc., Stocks issued by them.)

(e) If the payee's name is mis-spelt or he is incorrectly designated, the instrument may be accepted for collection without endorsement or discharge unless there are circumstances to suggest that the customer is not the person to whom payment is intended to be made.

(f) The instruments referred to in the Schedule to this Circular will require endorsement or discharge as heretofore.

(g) Instruments payable to one or more of a number of joint account holders may be collected for the credit of the joint account without endorsement or discharge. For this purpose joint accounts include accounts of partners, trustees, etc.
(h) Instruments payable to joint payees will require endorsement or discharge if tendered for the credit of an account to which all are not parties.
(i) The foregoing sub-paragraphs of this paragraph also apply when the account is domiciled with another branch of the collecting bank or with another bank.

3. CLEARING BANKS ACTING AS COLLECTING AGENTS FOR NON-CLEARING BANKS, THE POST OFFICE, OR TRUSTEE SAVINGS BANKS

Instruments received from a Non-Clearing Bank, the Post Office or a Trustee Savings Bank need not be examined for endorsement or discharge. It may be assumed that any requisite endorsement will have been seen to by the Non-Clearing Bank, the Post Office or the Trustee Savings Bank as the case may be, to whom the collecting bank will be entitled to have recourse.

4. EXCHANGING CHEQUES AND OTHER INSTRUMENTS

Cheques and other instruments exchanged at the counter will require endorsement or discharge as heretofore.

5. EXCHANGE CONTROL MARKINGS

All markings in connection with the Exchange Control must in future be placed upon the face of the instrument.

6. COMBINED CHEQUE AND RECEIPT FORMS

Cheques and other instruments bearing receipts which paying banks have agreed to continue to examine have been dealt with fully in the Committee of London Clearing Bankers' Circular dated 2nd September 1957. All such instruments without exception will bear a denoting 'R' on the face of them, and they will require examination by both the collecting and paying banks as heretofore.

7. BANKS IN ISLE OF MAN: CHANNEL ISLANDS: REPUBLIC OF IRELAND

Since the Act does not apply to the Isle of Man, the Channel Islands or the Republic of Ireland, banks situated there will continue to require endorsements or discharges whether as collecting or as paying bankers.[2]

Schedule

Combined Cheque and Receipt Forms marked 'R'.

Bills of Exchange (other than cheques).

Promissory Notes.

Drafts and other instruments drawn on the General Post Office or payable at a Post Office.[3]

Inland Revenue warrants.[3]

Drafts drawn on HM Paymaster General or the Queen's and Lord Treasurer's Remembrancer.[3]

Drafts drawn on the Crown Agents, High Commissioners for the Union of South Africa, Pakistan and India, the Commonwealth Relations office and other paying agents.

Travellers' Cheques.

Instruments payable by banks abroad.

Instruments payable by branches of banks situated in the Channel Islands or the Isle of Man.[4]

Instruments payable by banks situated in the Republic of Ireland.[4]

(These can be distinguished by the fact that they bear the rectangular green revenue stamp of the Republic.)

© The Committee of London Clearing Bankers

Acknowledgment is made to the Committee of London Clearing Bankers for their kind permission to reproduce the text of these Circulars.

---

2 See footnote 1, *supra*, for amending legislation.
3 In general, endorsement is no longer required in the case of these instruments.
4 See footnote 1, *supra*, for amending legislation.

Terms of Reference of, and Recommendations by, the Review Committee on Banking Services Law and the Government's Response

On 26 January 1987 Mr Nigel Lawson, the Chancellor of the Exchequer, and Mr Robin Leigh-Pemberton, the Governor of the Bank of England, appointed a Committee to review Banking Services Law. The members of the Committee were Professor R. B. Jack, CBE (Chairman), Mrs Liliana Archibald and Mr G. W. Taylor. The Report of the Review Committee (the Jack Committee) was completed on 30 December 1988 and was presented to Parliament by the Chancellor of the Exchequer as a Blue Paper, Cmnd 622, in February 1989.

The Committee's Term of Reference were as follows:

> The purpose of the review is to examine the statute and common law relating to the provision of banking services within the United Kingdom to personal and business customers, including payment and remittance services; but excluding taxation, company law and parts of the law whose relevance is to trading or to the provision of services in general, rather than particularly to banking. The objectives of the review will be:
>
> (1) To examine the law and its practical implications from the point of view of banker, customer and the general public interest in the availability, reliability, security and efficient and effective operation of payment, remittance and other banking services;
>
> (2) To have regard to:
>
>   (a) current and prospective developments in banking and payment systems, including developments in electronic data processing and electronic funds transfer technology;
>
>   (b) areas of particular difficulty in or confusion about existing law and practice and the rights and obligations of banks and their customers respectively;
>
>   (c) differences in the law and practice of different parts of the

> United Kingdom and, where relevant, other studies and reviews
> of United Kingdom law;
>
> (d) developments in the law of the European Community and in
> other relevant international laws and conventions;
>
> (e) developments and trends in international payment systems and
> reviews by international bodies;
>
> (3) To prepare a final report, and if necessary interim reports also;
>
> (4) If appropriate and after consultation to recommend the introduction
> of codes of good practice (on such matters as model contract terms,
> information for customers or new banking procedures);
>
> (5) If necessary and after consultation to make proposals for legislation.

THE COMMITTEE'S RECOMMENDATIONS

The Committee's Recommendations[1] were listed under five broad categories, namely:

A. Recommendations to banks concerning standards of banking
    practice.
B. Other recommendations to banks.
C. Recommendations to government concerning standards of
    banking practice.
D. Recommendations to government concerning legislation

    (a) Banking Services Act.
    (b) Cheques and Bank Payment Orders Act.
    (c) Negotiable Instruments Act.
    (d) Other recommendations.

E. Recommendations to government concerning issues wider than
    the Review Committee's terms of reference.

A Recommendations to banks concerning standards of banking practice

5(2) A standard of best practice should enjoin banks to explain clearly
to all their customers the rules on the banker's duty of confidentiality,
once codified in statute law. It should require banks to remind customers
of their rights of access, under the Data Protection Act 1984, to com-

---

1 The Committee made 83 Recommendations in its Report. They are numbered on the
system which the Committee used throughout the Report, that is to say the initial
number gives the Chapter of the Report where the Recommendations will be found,
and the bracketed number which follows gives its place within that Chapter's Recommendations.

puter records about themselves held by banks. It should state that express consent, in whatever form, should not be sought in such a way as puts the customer under pressure to give it. In the case of express consent to be obtained in tacit form for the giving of bankers' opinions, a letter should be sent personally by the bank to its customer, seeking his consent for this specific purpose.

6(2) As an indication of what is required for banks to secure the protection of s. 4 of the Cheques Act 1957 (under the current legislation), they should initiate procedures which allow them to establish, to their reasonable satisfaction, the identity of a person opening an account, so that if subsequently challenged they can refer to the action they took at the time.

6(3) A standard of best practice should require a bank, in any communication to its customer of the terms of the banker-customer contract, to ensure he is given a fair and balanced view of those terms, and of the rights and obligations that exist on each side; and to give him reasonable notice of any proposals for variation of those terms.

6(4) A standard of best practice should require a bank to give all its customers a clear explanation of how the system of bankers' opinions works, and to invite them to give or withhold express consent, in the way detailed in Chapter Five, for the bank to supply opinions on them in response to status enquiries.

7(14) It should be a standard of best practice that, if the necessary evidence to resolve a dispute regarding a truncated cheque or bank payment order is not produced within three working days, the customer's account should be re-credited pending final resolution.

7(15) There should be a standard of best practice to the effect that a bank should not return, within six months from the date of issue, an instrument covered by the new Cheques and Bank Payment Order Act on the grounds that it was out of date.

7(16) A standard of best practice should require banks to make available in a leaflet, or by other suitable means, an explanation of the rights and obligations of bank and customer in regard to transactions effected by Bank Giro Credit (BGC) including the rules on countermand.

10(1) A standard of best practice should translate into the context of customer-activated Electronic Funds Transfer (EFT) systems a bank's principal and general duty to observe its customer's mandate. Banks should therefore adopt the principle that an EFT system must meet certain minimum standards of security in its authorization procedures, so as to provide an acceptable degree of protection for the customer against the consequences of unauthorized instructions. In furtherance of that principle, they should accept a continuing commitment to upgrade their systems by the introduction, so far as practicable, of new technology based on the recognition of a signature or other personal characteristic.

10(3) A standard of best practice should require banks to take every reasonable care when issuing cards and Personal Identification Numbers (PINs) to their customers. It should state that that obligation should be undertaken by banks on the explicit assumption that customers for their part will take every reasonable care at all times in handling their cards and PINs. It should also ban the unsolicited mailing of PINs by banks to customers, following the principle proposed for legislation in respect of the mailing of payment cards. A customer should be required to acknowledge receipt of both card and PIN, before he can avail himself of the service for which they are needed.

10(4) A standard of best practice should require banks to ensure the maximum privacy that is reasonably possible in customers' access to EFT systems. In particular banks should aim to ensure that it is physically impossible for a customer's PIN to be read by anybody else when he is keying it in.

10(7) A standard of best practice should require banks to introduce systematic arrangements, where they have not done so already, to monitor patterns of Automated Teller Machine (ATM) withdrawals, such as might give rise to suspicion of fraudulent misuse of the system.

10(8) A standard of best practice should draw attention to customers' entitlement, under the Data Protection Act 1984, to demand a written record of an EFT transaction if they wish to have it; and should require banks to interpret this in the sense that customers are given the option of a written record at the time of the transaction rather than in due course.

10(9) A standard of best practice should require a bank, as card-issuer, to deal with its own customer, as cardholder, in case of any complaint or claim arising on the customer's part from a dispute over a banking service provided through an EFT payment system. It should be for the card-issuer to take action against any other party involved, for example in an Electronic Funds Transfer at Point of Sale (EFTPOS) system or shared ATM network.

10(13) A standard of best practice should require banks to make customers who use the relevant services aware of this rule in Recommendation 10(12) on apportionment of loss arising from a disputed EFT.

11(2) A standard of best practice on multi-function cards should establish that:

- (a) a customer should be free to choose which of the functions on his card should be available for use; a bank should not be at liberty to refuse a card for a single function if its customer does not require more;
- (b) functions that the customer does not require should be blocked off, so that the card cannot be used for those purposes in a machine;
- (c) if for whatever reason the card is nonetheless compromised, the customer should (fraud on his part excepted) have no liability on all functions that he has not authorized.

11(4) All banks as card-issuers should, as a matter of best practice, inform all customers as cardholders:

- (a) whether or not they themselves will accept notification of loss or theft of a payment card from a third party, presumably a card notification organization;
- (b) if so, the terms in which they would require cardholders to notify them, by a standard form of notice acceptable to card-issuers and signed by cardholders, of the appointment of an agent for this purpose;
- (c) the effect, if any, on the cardholder's liability if an agent is appointed, especially the matter of whether notification to the agent discharges the cardholder's obligation to the card-issuer.

12(1) A standard of banking practice should require banks, when establishing countermand rules for individual payment systems, to allow customers a period of time for countermand wherever possible, only eliminating it where that is necessary for the efficient working of the system. Banks should take steps to make customers aware of the different countermand rules applying to different payment systems.

13(1) A standard of best practice should require banks to give all their customers a simple explanation of the timing of the clearing cycle, and the concept of cleared balances. This would deal, especially, with the normal time taken to clear cheques and bank payment orders, should specify the 'hold' period the bank is applying, and should say whether the bank has a right of reversal if the cheque or bank payment order is later returned unpaid. But it would cover other payment systems as appropriate, including the timing of direct debit procedures, and the customer's right of reversal under that system. Where needed, an explanation should be given of the system of truncation of cheques and bank payment orders, and of resulting charges, if any, in the timing of the clearing cycle. Banks should consider how their customers could usefully be given more information, in periodic statements of account and in ATM slips, about cleared as well as uncleared balances on their account.

13(2) A standard of best practice should require banks to explain to their customers the basis of charging for the normal operation of the account. Where an overdraft arrangement has been agreed in advance, a bank should ensure that its customer is aware, both in advance and as and when a change occurs, of the rate over base rate that will be charged, and of the timing of the debiting of interest. The customer should also be given full details of the method of calculation of fees and charges when these are applied to his account, including charges applied where an overdraft occurs without prior agreement. The customer should also be told of any services other than lending for which he will be charged (stopping cheques, correspondence, etc.).

13(3) A standard of best practice should require a bank, when undertaking a foreign exchange transaction for its customer, to ensure that he is made aware of the basis of the exchange rate to be applied, and of any associated charges.

13(4) A standard of best practice should require banks, in the direct marketing of their services, to exercise restraint, and in particular:

    (a)   to ensure that customers are aware of the marketing purpose for which they are being approached, and

    (b)   to respect any customer's objections to the use of personal information for marketing purposes, and to desist from such activity on request.

13(5) A standard of best practice should require banks to ensure that prospective guarantors, whether or not they are not customers, are adequately warned about the legal effects and possible consequences of guarantees, and about the importance of receiving independent advice.

15(2) A standard of best practice should require banks to establish clearly defined internal procedures for handling customer complaints; to ensure in some appropriate way that customers are told how to lodge a complaint, and how it would be dealt with; and to ensure that, as and when a complaint arises, the customer is made personally aware of the existence of the bank's internal procedures, and of the relevant procedures of the Banking or Building Societies Ombudsman, as appropriate.

16(1) Banks should promulgate a Code of Banking Practice on matters that are the subject of Recommendations in this Report on standards of best practice addressed to banks, giving priority to the EFT area. If in any particular respects they can see good reason for departing significantly from the terms of the illustrative Code at Appendix L, they should consult consumer and other interests.

B Other recommendations to banks

10(5) Banks should introduce encryption in customer-activated EFT systems, where this can be operationally justified.

10(6) Banks should make customer-activated EFT systems on-line, where this can be operationally justified.

C Recommendations to government concerning standards of banking practice

16(2) The government should assess whether banks' Code of Banking Practice (see Recommendation 16(1)) constitutes an adequate response to the Recommendations of this Report. If so, it should ensure that the statement is formally presented to the Banking and Building Societies Ombudsmen as the impartial guidance on best banking practice of which they should take account on their adjudications.

16(3) Against the possibility that the banks' statement which is the subject of Recommendation 16(1) proves to be inadequate, or is not forthcoming within a reasonable timescale, the government should consider at what stage to enact enabling legislation (see Appendix S) to support a statutory Code of Banking Practice, and an associated duty on banks to 'trade fairly' with their customers.

16(4) The government should appoint the Bank of England and the Building Societies Commission to monitor the continued observance and updating by banks of their published Code of Banking Practice. In support of these arrangements, the Banking and Building Societies Ombudsmen should be required, in their terms of reference, to comment in their Annual Reports on the extent to which banks are complying with, and, where necessary, keeping up-to-date their own published standards of best practice. (For example, new standards are likely to be needed before home and office banking, or smart/laser cards, come into general use). If at any time monitoring reveals that these standards are not being complied with or updated as necessary, the government should consider whether to implement the statutory fallback as in Recommendation 16(3).

D Recommendations to government concerning legislation

(a) Banking Services Act

5(1) The Tournier rules on the banker's duty of confidentiality, suitably updated to comply with modern conditions, should be codified in statute law.

6(1) There should be a statutory provision whereby, in an action against a bank in debt or for damages, arising from an unauthorized payment, contributory negligence may be raised as a defence, but only if the court is satisfied that the degree of negligence shown by the plaintiff is sufficiently serious for it to be inequitable that the bank should be liable for the whole amount of the debt or damages.

6(5) Section 6 of the Statute of Frauds Amendment Act 1828 should be repealed.

10(2) A provision in statute law should ban the unsolicited mailing of all payment cards by banks to their customers, apart from credit cards already covered by s. 51 of the Consumer Credit Act 1974.

10(10) A provision in statute law, applicable to any customer-activated EFT system, should set the limits of legal liability for loss due to fraud on the principles established in ss 83 and 84 of the Consumer Credit Act 1974. The main provisions are that a customer should normally be liable for any losses incurred up to the point where he notifies his bank, subject to a financial limit currently fixed at £50; the bank should be liable for any losses incurred thereafter. Where gross negligence on the part of either party could be demonstrated, that party should be liable for any amount up to the full amount of the loss. The bank's duty should be in any event to its customer, but the bank should have a right of relief against a third party who could be shown to have contributed to loss by fraud through an EFT system.

10(11) A provision in statute law, applicable to any EFT system, should make the bank normally liable to the customer for any direct, or clearly consequential, loss due to the failure of EFT equipment to complete a transaction, notwithstanding the terms of any contract to the contrary. Compensation may be reduced if the failure is due to causes beyond the bank's control, or if intent or gross negligence on the customer's part has contributed to the fault. If, in the case of a customer-activated system, the customer should have been aware that the equipment was unavailable for use or malfunctioning, the bank's liabilities should be limited to the correction of any errors on the customer's account, and the refund of any charges or fees imposed on him as a result. It should be for the bank to resolve with third parties any question of liability on their part.

10(12)   A provision in statute law should apply, notwithstanding the terms of any contract to the contrary, to the apportionment of any loss arising from a transaction carried out through a customer-activated EFT, where it is in dispute whether or not that transaction was authorized. It should require that loss to be apportioned on an equitable basis, by reference to the extent to which the acts or omissions of the parties have contributed to the loss. Apportionment of the loss should take into account such factors as (i) the steps taken by the customer to protect the security of his card and PIN, (ii) the extent to which the system provided by the bank protects the customer against unauthorized transactions on his account, and (iii) the relative weight of the evidence adduced by the parties in support of their respective contentions that the transaction was, or was not, authorized.

11(3)   Legislation should be introduced requiring card notification organizations to be licensed by the Director-General of Fair Trading. It should include a power by which the Director-General, if he saw fit, could impose on such organizations a requirement to take out a fidelity bond, and an errors and omissions policy in a suitable sum, as a condition of the grant or continuance of a licence.

11(5)   Section 5(5) of the Forgery and Counterfeiting Act 1981 should be made applicable, through amending legislation, to all payment cards generically.

11(6)   A provision should be inserted in the Forgery and Counterfeiting Act 1981 to make it a specific offence to possess, or to sell, information that could be used in the manufacture of counterfeit cards, with intent to defraud.

11(7)   Consideration should be given to the creation under Scots law of statutory offences in relation to card counterfeiting on the lines provided under the 1981 Act, amended as under Recommendations 11(5) and 11(6).

12(2)   Rules to define completion of payment should be enacted in primary legislation. They should provide (i) that payment is to be regarded as complete at the point where the payee's bank (or its agent in the clearing), having actual or ostenisble authority to accept payment on behalf of the payee, accepts a transfer of funds from the paying bank (or its agent in the clearing) for the payee's account – provided that the transfer is or has become unconditional; and (ii) that, where the transfer is between two accounts at the same bank, payment should be regarded as complete when the bank has taken the decision to treat the instructions for transfer as irrevocable. The rules should be subject to modification by contractual arrangement, among parties to a contract governing a payment system.

13(6) The provisions of the Bankers' Books Evidence Act 1879 relating to the admissibility in evidence of copies of entries in bankers' books should be repealed.

13(7) Section 7 of the 1879 Act should be amended so as to permit a court to make an order for inspection and copying of entries in a banker's book if it thinks fit, whether or not legal proceedings have formally commenced. An order should be granted in such circumstances only where the court is satisfied (i) that proceedings are in serious contemplation, and (ii) that there are other grounds to support a prosecution or an action over and above what might be discovered as a result of the order.

13(8) The definition of 'bankers' books' in s. 9 of the 1879 Act should be extended to include items such as credit slips and paid cheques (but not internal reference notes), in so far as they are required to substantiate and identify a transaction recorded in those books.

13(9) The Bank of England should be included in the definition of 'bank' and 'banker' in s. 9 of the 1879 Act.

13(10) The 1879 Act should be amended so as to give a court discretion to order payment of a fee to the bank against which an order under s. 7 of the Act is made, in order to reimburse the bank for the costs of compliance.

15(1) Statutory provision should be made for comprehensive coverage of authorized banks, except those with less than a given (small) number of customers, by one or more recognized Ombudsman schemes. Statutory responsibility for granting recognition to such a statutory scheme (or schemes), and for withdrawing any recognition it has granted, should be placed on the Bank of England. The statute should lay down matters to be provided for in a statutory scheme (or schemes) and the requirements for recognized schemes as regards matters of complaint, grounds of complaint, functions of the Ombudsman, etc. There should be statutory provision for periodic review and amendment of the terms of the scheme (or schemes).

The Review Committee's preference is for a single Scheme for authorized banks based on the present Banking Ombudsman Scheme, except that responsibility for approving the Ombudsman's terms of reference, for appointing independent members of the Council, and for approving the appointment of the Ombudsman himself, or its renewal or termination, would pass from the Board to the Bank of England. The Board would remain responsible for finance. The membership of the Council should be increased to eight by the addition of one more independent member. Any individual should be precluded from serving on both the Board and Council of such a Scheme. A bank rejecting a non-mandatory award under such a Scheme should be required to publish its reasons for doing so. It should be considered whether a suitable eligibility criterion could be devised which would allow small businesses to be brought within the ambit of such a Scheme.

Under such a Scheme, the following specific amendments should be made to the Banking Ombudsman's terms of reference:

(a) The Ombudsman should be required, if a complaint has not been resolved in some other way, to make a determination by reference to what is, in his opinion, fair in all the circumstances.

(b) The Ombudsman should be given a power to compel production by a bank of any relevant documents or information.

(c) The power whereby a bank may withdraw from the Ombudsman's jurisdiction any complaint which has wide ramifications, or raises important legal issues (the 'test cases provision'), should be exercised only with the concurrence of the Ombudsman.

(d) The Ombudsman should be allowed to publish information about a complaint if the customer consents.

(e) The present requirement that complaints must in all cases be made by 'all beneficiaries' should be dropped.

(f) Banking services for bank employees and their dependants should be included within the scope of the Scheme, unless there is a disciplinary issue involved.

(b) Cheques and Bank Payment Orders Act

7(1) The law relating to cheques should be re-enacted in a new Act, to be called the 'Cheques and Bank Payment Orders Act'. It should incorporate amendments recommended in Chapter Seven as follows.

7(2) The new Act should contain a provision to the effect that nothing written on any cheque can take away the right to transfer it; this would deny legal effect to any annotation such as 'Account Payee'.

7(3) The new Act should not provide for the special crossing, though banks should continue to be permitted to stamp their name and address on the face of cheques for collection purposes.

7(4) The new Act should recognize only one cheque crossing. It should consist of two transverse parallel lines as now, the effect of which would be to make the cheque 'not negotiable' in addition to requiring payment only to a bank.

7(5) The new Act should bring together the various statutory protections available to the paying bank and each should be made subject to the condition that the bank had acted 'in good faith and without negligence'. The existing ss 60 and 80 of the 1882 Act and s. 1 of the 1957 Act should be repealed.

7(6) The new Act should contain a provision restricting, for Scotland, the banks' protection to that given for the rest of the U.K. in s. 4 of the 1957 Act.

7(7) The new Act should include provisions permitting the introduction of a new non-transferable instrument (the 'bank payment order') the proceeds of which could be collected only by a bank and solely for account of the named payee.

7(8) The new Act should amend the law, so far as cheques are concerned, to permit banks to obtain payment by presentment of electronic information rather than the instrument itself (as currently required by s. 45 of the 1882 Act). It should also accord to a photocopy, or some other reproduction in legible form, of a cheque, suitably marked as paid and authenticated by the collecting bank, the status of 'evidence of the receipt by the payee of the sum payable by the cheque' (cf. s. 3 of the 1957 Act).

7(9) In determining the amount payable on an instrument covered by the new Act, precedence should continue to be given to the amount in words over that in figures.

7(10) The 'funds attached principle' in Scots law should be abolished except in relation to negotiable instruments other than cheques. The new Act should therefore provide that presentment would not operate as an assignation of the sum for which it is drawn, in relation to any instrument covered by the new Act, to any order to pay addressed to a bank otherwise than in writing, or to any such order to pay presented to the drawee otherwise than in writing.

7(11) The definitions of a cheque and of a bank payment order should be drawn to include warrants for payment of interest or dividend or for repayment of capital and to include bankers' drafts.

7(12) The new Act should specify that its provisions as to cheques or bank payment orders, as appropriate, extend to payable orders. 'Payable Order' should be defined as 'any document issued by a government department and drawn on the same or another government department, or issued by and drawn on one of the persons or bodies specified in [a

Schedule] which, not being a cheque or bank payment order, is intended to enable a person to obtain payment from the department or body on which it is drawn of the sum mentioned in the document'.

7(13) For the avoidance of doubt, the new Act should make it clear that a transfer instruction by BGC (Bank Giro Credit) does not constitute a legal assignment of the funds involved.

(c) Negotiable Instruments Act

8(1) There should be a new Negotiable Instruments Act covering not only bills of exchange and promissory notes, but also, in so far as their negotiability is concerned, all other negotiable instruments.

8(2) The language and style of the 1882 Act should be retained in the new Act since it is clear, concise and well understood.

8(3) An instrument should be negotiable if:
   (a) it is a bill of exchange or promissory note as defined in the new Act, or
   (b) it falls into one of the categories set out in (ii)–(v) of paragraph 8.09.

8(4) The need for consideration as a test of negotiability should be abolished.

14(3) The government should institute a process of consultation with a view to introducing legislation to clarify the right of set-off, and the validity of a charge over a credit balance in favour of the person with whom the balance is held.

14(4) The government should consider options for eliminating, at least for banking purposes, the two mismatches between Bank Holiday dates in Scotland on the one hand, and England, Wales and Northern Ireland on the other. Of four options discussed in Chapter Fourteen, that favoured from the standpoint of the operational efficiency of the banking system is to harmonize dates when banks north and south of the border are open for business.

14(5) The government should consider instituting a review, similar to that recently concluded by the Scottish Law Commission, of the English law dealing with a minor's capacity to contract. They should also introduce the legislation needed to implement the recommendations of the Scottish Law Commission.

14(6) Consideration should be given to a review of the evidential requirements of the criminal law, in so far as they relate to the corroboration of computer-produced evidence in cases of fraud.

14(7) Urgent action should be taken to make it a criminal offence (i) to obtain unauthorized access to a computer by 'hacking', as recommended by the Scottish Law Commission, and (ii) to introduce a 'virus' into a computer program.

14(8) The government should keep under periodic review the scope for customer choice as between different payment systems, and the related question of the acceptability of legal tender, to ensure that there is no unfair discrimination through contractual arrangement, charging, or financial incentives.

17(1) The government should keep before them the possible need for further studies to deal with new priorities as and when they emerge, in the field of banking services law and practice.

In March 1990 the Government published a White Paper, Cm. 1026, responding to the Report of the Jack Committee. The White Paper is a lengthy document, in which the Government accepts many, though not all, of the recommendations of the Jack Report.

Paragraph 13 of the White Paper states that 'the overall approach taken is to build on competition. Where this is not feasible, non-statutory self-regulation is proposed. Legislation has only been considered where it would either aid competition, correct areas where the law is inadequate or out of date, or where it is the only means of ensuring that consumers are protected'. In para. 14 the White Paper welcomes the recent move by the banks and building societies to prepare and promulgate a code of banking practice under the independent chairmanship of Sir George Blunden. The aim is that the main sections of the code should be ready and in place early in 1991. Paragraph 28 of the White Paper states: 'The Goverment thinks it desirable that the code should specify that customers will be given information in clear and simple language about the terms of their contract with the banker and the rights and obligations that apply on both sides; customers should be told of the rights to privacy which the law already affords and the very limited circumstances in which any information about their personal finances may be passed on; how to lodge a complaint if it proves necessary, how such complaints will be dealt with, and how matters may be referred to the relevant Ombudsman; they should be told what banking charges may be levied in what circumstances; and they should be given a simple explanation of the timing of the clearing cycle and when they could normally expect a cheque to be cleared'. The particular areas of banking practice which the Government thinks should be incorporated in the code are addressed in detail in Annex 1 of the White Paper, but considerations of space do not permit their inclusion here.

Annex 2 of the White Paper deals with Confidentiality and the Disclosure of Information. Briefly, the Jack Committee had recommended statutory codification of the rules in *Tournier* v. *National Provincial and Union Bank of England*. The Government has not accepted this recommendation. Paragraph 2.12 of Annex 2 states that 'several of those consulted argued cogently that the present Tournier rules are very clear as they stand, they have worked well and they are well understood by bankers; it is unnecessary to codify them in statute, and any attempt to do so, or to refine them, risks introducing unwelcome and unintended difficulties and confusion. The Government finds these arguments persuasive... It does not therefore propose to codify the Tournier judgment in statute'.

Annex 3 of the White Paper deals with Procedures for Resolving Disputes. Paragraph 3.2 of Annex 3 states that the Jack Committee had recommended that all banks, except those with only a small number of customers, should be required by law to be a member of one or more Ombudsman schemes, much on the lines of arrangements for building societies. Building societies are already required by the Building Societies Act to belong to a recognized Ombudsman scheme which meets the minimum criteria set out in that Act and is approved by the Building Societies Commission. Paragraph 3.4 states that the Banking Ombudsman scheme has recently been modified to take account of many of the concerns raised by the Jack Committee. The revised terms of reference of the scheme are now based on similar lines to the statutory scheme for building societies, the only major difference being that the Building Societies Ombudsman's awards are not binding on the society; exceptionally, building societies can reject an award against them if they give their reasons for doing so publicly. In para. 3.6 the White Paper admits that there are 'good arguments', which the Jack Committee set out in its Report, for seeking further consistency and convergence between the two Ombudsman's schemes. Nevertheless, the conclusion reached in para. 3.7 is that 'on balance the Government believes that it is not worth disrupting two schemes which are working well, and proposes to leave the present arrangements as they are for now. The Board of the Banking Ombudsman is taking steps to encourage more banks to join the scheme. Those who are members are encouraged to inform their customers and display notices prominently in their branches stating that they are members of the scheme. The Government will keep the situation under review and discuss with the representatives of the banks and building societies whether any further steps can be usefully made in the longer term to bring the two schemes closer together'.

Annex 4 of the White Paper deals with Electronic Funds Transfer. The Consumer Credit Act 1974 provides protection to the consumer when taking credit. The Jack Committee had recommended that section

51 of the Act should be extended to cover the unsolicited mailing of all payment cards (not just credit cards), and that sections 83 and 84 which set the limits of legal liability should also be extended to cover all payment cards. As regards section 51, para. 4.5 of Annex 4 states: 'The Government intends to introduce legislation in due course to ban unsolicited mailing of all payment cards including ATM and cheque guarantee cards'. Sections 83 and 84 of the Act provide that the customer is only liable for any losses incurred as a result of the loss or theft of the card up to the point where he notifies the card issuer, subject to a financial limit which is currently fixed at £50. Again, the Act only applies to credit cards and certain other credit facilities. Paragraph 4.6 of Annex 4 states that 'the Government intends to introduce legislation in due course to provide the same protection in respect of all payment cards. The card issuer will be liable for any losses incurred after notification, but will have a right of redress against a third party who can be shown to have contributed to the loss by fraudulently using any ETF system. The card issuer should not be liable in cases where negligence on the customer's part enables a person to find out the PIN applicable to the card, for example where the number has been written on the card'.

Annex 5 of the White Paper deals with Cheques and Payment Orders. The Jack Committee had recommended a number of changes to bring the law up to date, which the Committee proposed be enacted in a new separate Cheques and Bank Payment Orders Act. The Government has not accepted this recommendation. Paragraph 5.4 of the White Paper states: 'The Government accepts that there is a need for a non-transferable instrument with a clearly established legal status and that the increased use of such an instrument should help to reduce the opportunity for fraud. It is also evident that the present legal status of the various markings and crossings is unclear and that customers believe they afford a greater measure of protection than is in fact the case. However, after detailed consultation the Government found that there was little support for the introduction of a new "bank payment order", largely because its introduction might well result in even greater confusion in the public mind about the use of cheques. On balance therefore, it has decided to tackle the problems identified by the Committee by measures designed to clarify the existing law relating to cheques'. Briefly, the Government's proposals are:

(*i*) A general crossing on a cheque, even without the words 'not negotiable', will render the cheque not negotiable within the meaning of section 81 of the Bills of Exchange Act 1882: see para. 5.5 of Annex 5.

(*ii*) Special crossings are to be abolished: see para. 5.5 of Annex 5.

(*iii*) The 'account payee' crossing is to be given statutory recognition.

On this matter para. 5.6 of Annex 5 states: 'The Government agrees that there is a need for a clear method of making cheques non-transferable and proposes that this should be met by giving legal status to the words "account payee" or "a/c payee", with or without "only", written on the face of a crossed cheque. A customer who writes these words on a cheque will make it "non-transferable" so ensuring that the cheque can only be paid into the bank account of the named payee. If a collecting bank credited the proceeds of a non-transferable cheque to the wrong account it would be unambiguously liable to the payee named on the cheque; the paying bank would not be liable. The paying bank would not know whether the cheque had been paid into the account of the named payee. The collecting bank would, however, have a defence if it could show that it had acted in good faith and without negligence, where for example, the account name was indistinguishable from that of the payee and it had taken steps to establish the identity of the customer to whose account the proceeds of the cheque had been credited'. Paragraph 5.8 of Annex 5 stated: 'It is clear that bank customers will need to be made aware of these measures. The effect of the words "account payee" and the general crossing will have to be explained so that customers can understand the purpose of a "non-transferable" cheque on the one hand, and of a cheque that is simply crossed (that is "not negotiable") on the other. Banks may feel it sensible to inform their customers through the code of practice or in cheque books. The use of open cheques will, however, still be possible for payments to individuals with neither a bank or a building society account, despite the attendant risk of fraud'.

'Cheque truncation' is another topic which is deal with in Annex 5. This is a subject which is likely to have far reaching consequences for customers and their bankers. The Jack Committee recommended legislation, and the Government has accepted the recommendation. The intention is that banks would be able to obtain payment by presentation of electronic information rather than the paper cheque itself, as currently required by the Bills of Exchange Act 1882. A photocopy or some other reproduction in legible form, suitably marked and authenticated, would also be accorded the status of 'evidence of the receipt by the payee of the sum payable by the cheque'. The truncation of cheques would eliminate the transportation of millions of cheques around the country each day. The cheques would remain at the bank branch at which they were paid in, and the relevant information to permit the debiting of accounts would be transmitted electronically. Some

European countries already have systems of truncation. Paragraph 5.13 states that the Government accepts the Jack Committee's recommendation and will introduce the necessary legislation in due course. The paragraph adds that, if banks introduce cheque truncation, it is important for there to be safeguards to ensure that the customer does not suffer as a result of this innovation. The Government proposes that there should be a provision in the code of banking practice that, unless the evidence to resolve a dispute about a truncated cheque is produced within a specific number of working days of the complaint, the bank should re-credit the customer's account that has been debited. The code should either suggest a single feasible period or make it clear that the period would be notified to customers by their bank, with the actual period being determined by the individual banks. Customers should also have the right under the code to receive, within a reasonable time, a photocopy (or the original) of any cheque which has been truncated. Banks should be required to keep the original cheques for a reasonable time.

Annex 6 of the White Paper deals with Negotiable Instruments, other than cheques. These include bills of exchange, Treasury bills, certificates of deposit and bearer shares. These instruments are used by a comparatively small number of companies, traders and banks who deal in them. The Jack Committee had recommended a new Negotiable Instruments Act. Much of the Act would have been a consolidation and codification of existing statute and case law. The Government does not believe that such an exercise would be warranted. The Bills of Exchange Act 1882 has worked well, but some limited changes are necessary in order to bring the law up to date with modern circumstances. Thus the Jack Committee had recommended that the sum payable on a negotiable instrument should no longer have to be certain at the date of issue provided that it is 'certain or ordinarily determinable' in accordance with provisions which will be set out in amending legislation. This recommendation of the Jack Committee was intended to facilitate the use of instruments denominated in units of account like the European Currency Unit. In para. 6.4 of Annex 4 it is stated that the Government accepts that bills of exchange denominated in units of accounts like the ECU should be brought within the Bills of Exchange Act 1882. The Act will therefore be modified in due course so that the expression 'a sum certain in money' is defined to include 'a monetary unit of account established by an inter-governmental institution' or by agreement between two or more states. Other amendments to the Bills of Exchange Act 1882 are proposed by the Government, but considerations of space do not permit their inclusion here.

Annex 7 of the White Paper deals with Other Aspects of Banking Law. This Annex considers the remaining aspects of banking law on which the Jack Committee had made recommendations. For example, the Jack Committee had referred to section 9 of the Bankers' Books Evidence Act 1879. The current definition of 'bankers' books' under that section encompasses ledgers, day books, cash books, accounts books and all other records used in the ordinary course of business of the bank, whether in written form or kept on microfilm, magnetic tape or any other form of mechanical or electronic medium. The Jack Committee had recommended that section 9 be extended to include credit slips and paid cheques where this is necessary to identify, confirm or provide necessary details of book entries. In para. 7.8 of Annex 8, it is stated that the Government believes that a wider definition of section 9 would be helpful and will propose legislation in due course.

APPENDIX 3

Addendum on Reform of the *Ultra Vires* Rule

The Companies Act, which received the Royal Assent on 16th November 1989, implemented, with certain modifications, the recommendations made in 1986 by Dr Dan Prentice in a Consultative Document entitled 'Reform of the *Ultra Vires* Rule'. Owing to considerations of space, it is impossible to set out in full the relevant sections, and the following account of the subject should be regarded as a guide.

Problems associated with the doctrine of *ultra vires* have long been recognized. Any act which was not authorized by a company's memorandum of association was *ultra vires* ('beyond the powers of') the company and was void. In practice, the draftsman of a company's memorandum often circumvented the doctrine by incorporating in the objects clause every conceivable object which a company might desire.

Section 35 of the Companies Act 1985[1] had modified the *ultra vires* rules very substantially, but it did not go far enough. The primary object of the Companies Act 1989 is to abolish the external aspects of the *ultra vires* rule in order to provide greater protection for third parties, whilst retaining the right of internal control by shareholders over what a company does.

Section 110 of the Companies Act 1989 provides that in the Companies Act 1985 after s. 3 (forms of memorandum) a new s. 3A is to be inserted which provides that where the company's memorandum states that the object of the company is to 'carry on business as a general commercial company' (a) the object of the company is to carry on 'any trade or business whatsoever', and (b) the company has power to do all such things as are incidental or conductive to the carrying on of any trade or business by it. It seems quite likely that, in the future, the draftsmen of memoranda of association will find it convenient to make use of this new clause.

Section 108(1) of the Companies Act 1989 provides that for s. 35 of the Companies Act 1985 dealing with a company's capacity, there shall

1. *Ante* para. 11-279.

be substituted three sections, namely, ss. 35, 35A and 35B. The new s. 35(1) provides that the validity of an act done by a company shall not be called into question on the ground of lack of capacity by reason of anything in the company's memorandum. The new s. 35(2) provides that a member of a company may bring proceedings to restrain the doing of an act which but for subsection (1) would be beyond the company's capacity; but no such proceedings shall lie in respect of an act to be done in fulfilment of a legal obligation arising from a previous act of the company. The new s. 35(3) provides that it is the duty of directors to observe any limitations on their powers flowing from the company's memorandum; and action by the directors which but for subsection (1) would be beyond the company's capacity may only be ratified by the company by special resolution. These provisions have abolished the external effect of the *ultra vires* rule, whilst retaining the right of internal control by shareholders over what a company does.

The new s. 35A deals with the power of directors to bind the company. Section 35A(1) provides that in favour of a person dealing with a company in good faith, the power of the board of directors to bind the company, or authorize others to do so, shall be deemed to be free of any limitation under the company's constitution. Subsection (2) provides that, for this purpose, (a) a person 'deals with' a company if he is a party to any transaction or other act to which the company is a party, (b) a person shall not be regarded as acting in bad faith by reason only of his knowing that an act is beyond the powers of the directors under the company's constitution, and (c) a person shall be presumed to have acted in good faith unless the contrary is proved. Subsection (3) provides that the references above to limitations on the directors' powers under the company's constitution include limitations deriving (a) from a resolution of the company in general meeting or a meeting of any class of shareholders, or (b) from any agreement between the members of the company or of any class of shareholders. Subsection (4) provides that subsection (1) does not affect any right of a member of the company to bring proceedings to restrain the doing of an act which is beyond the powers of the directors, but no such proceedings shall lie in respect of an act to be done in fulfilment of a legal obligation arising from a previous act of the company. Subsection (5) provides that subsection (1) does not affect any liability incurred by the directors, or any other person, by reason of the directors' exceeding their powers.

The new s. 35B provides that a party to a transaction with a company is not bound to enquire as to whether it is permitted by the company's memorandum or as to any limitation on the powers of the board of directors to bind the company or authorize others to do so.

INDEX

All references are to paragraph numbers of the text

Acceptance
  cheque, of, 8-20
  conditional, 8-34/5
  credit, 8-99, 8-102, 8-126/9, 8-133/4
  date of, 8-30
  defined, 8-30
  documents against, 8-132
  general, 8-34
  incomplete instrument, of, 8-31
  local, 8-34/5
  partial, 8-34/5
  presentment for. *See* Presentment for
    acceptance
  qualified, 8-34/5
  writing, must be in, 8-30
Acceptor
  contract of, 8-32
  notice of dishonour to, unnecessary,
    8-59, 8-61
Accommodation
  cheques, 5-189/90
  party, 5-189
Account
  'account A.B', crossing, 5-46, 6-11
  'account payee'. *See* 'Account payee'
  accountants', with bank, 11-167
  administrators', with bank, 11-170/93
  auctioneers', with bank, 11-167
  budget. *See* Budget accounts
  building society's, with bank, 11-385/9
  closing of, by banker, 3-6/14
  closing of, by customer, 3-2/5
  club's, with bank, 11-419/28
  combining of, banker's rights as to,
    2-56/72
  company's, with bank, 11-246/357
  current. *See* Current account
  deposit. *See* Deposit account
  estate agents', with bank, 11-167
  executors', with bank, 11-170/93
  friendly society's, with bank, 11-392/8
  industrial and provident society's, with
    bank, 11-399/405
  joint, 11-65/95
  loan. *See* Loan accounts
  local authority's, with bank, 11-409/18
  married woman's, with bank, 11-60/4

Account (*contd.*)
  minor's, with bank, 11-45/51
  mistake in. *See* Mistake
  opening of, enquiries on, 6-103,
    11-1/15
  parochial church council's, with bank,
    11-406/8
  partnership, with bank, 11-110/27
  rectification of error in, 2-134/9
  savings. *See* Savings accounts
  society's, with bank, 11-419/28
  solicitors', with bank, 11-147/64
  stated. *See* Account stated
  stockbrokers', with bank, 11-165/6
  surveyors', with bank, 11-167
  trustee in bankruptcy's, with bank,
    11-232/6
  trustees', with bank, 11-194/231
  trustees', under deeds of arrangement,
    with bank, 11-237/45
  undischarged bankrupt's, with bank,
    3-42A
'Account payee'
  addition to cheque, 5-46
  cheque crossed, effect of, 5-47/8,
    6-109/11
  collection of cheque so crossed, 5-46,
    6-109/11
  negligence in collection, 6-109/10
  negotiability of cheque so crossed, 5-48
  'or bearer', 6-109
  payment of cheque so crossed, 7-6
Account stated
  pass book or statement as evidence of,
    2-138
Accountants
  customers, as, 11-167
Action
  conversion, for, 6-48/56, 7-98/9,
    10-79
  dishonour of cheque, for, 2-141,
    2-145/51
  lost bill, on, 9-13
  money had and received, for, 6-54/6
Administration order
  discharge of, 11-340
  petition for, 11-331

Administration order (*contd.*)
  powers of administrator,
    11-335/6
  purposes of, 11-380
Administrative receiver,
  11-315/28
Advice
  payment under, 7-77/8
Advising on investments, 10-124/30
After-acquired property
  bankruptcy, in, 3-42
Agent
  banker as, for collection. *See*
    Collecting banker
  bankruptcy of, 11-25
  death of, 11-25
  director as, 11-297
  liability of, 5-184/7
  mental incapacity of, 11-25
  minor as, 11-53
  signing *per pro.*, 5-80
Agricultural charge, 1-31
Alteration
  cheque, of, 7-18/20, 7-88
  crossing, to, 5-58, 7-21
  made easy through customer's
    negligence, 2-125/7
  material, 5-147/50
  payee's name, of, 2-127
Ambiguous instrument, 5-16, 7-17
Amount
  alteration of, in cheque, 7-18/20
  uncertainty as to, 5-16, 7-17
Answer on cheque
  'alteration in amount requires drawer's
    confirmation', 7-18
  'date required', 7-14
  defamation by, 2-145/54
  'drawer deceased', 3-22
  'effects not cleared', 7-39
  'injunction granted', 7-42
  'notice of application for injunction',
    7-42
  'out of date', 7-15
  'payment countermanded by drawer',
    7-31
  'post-dated', 7-16
  'refer to dawer', 2-145/6, 2-150, 3-51,
    7-39
  'refer to drawer, resolution to wind up
    passed', 11-346
  'refer to drawer, winding-up petition
    presented', 11-350
  'words and figures differ', 5-16, 7-17
Antecedent debt, 5-128
Ante-dated, 5-19

Apparent alteration, 5-149
Appropriation of payments
  Clayton's Case, 2-80, 2-85/98
  death of joint account holder, 2-94
  floating charge, creation of, 2-97
  general rules, 2-74/80
  guarantee, determination of, 2-96
  mixed moneys, in case of, 2-88
  second mortgage, notice of, 2-95
  wages and salaries, advances for, 2-98
Articles of Association
  directors' powers, conferred by,
    11-271/2, 11-282/90
Association for Payment Clearing
  Services, 6-25/6
Attorney. *See* Power of attorney
Auctioneers' accounts, 11-167
Authority
  agent's to draw cheque, 11-16, 11-21
  agent's, notice of limited nature of, 5-80
  blank, to fill up, 5-68/9
  determination of, 11-24/5, 11-35
  per pro., to sign, 5-80
  trustees', delegation of, 11-209/11
Automated teller machines, 10-50A/50C

'Backing a bill', 5-178
BACs, 10-32
Bailment
  bailee, for reward, 10-81/4
  bailee, gratuitous, 10-81/4
  bailor, death of customer, 10-75
  banker as bailee, 10-81/4
  joint deposit, authority required in case
    of, 10-77
  misdelivery of goods, banker's liability
    for, 10-79/80
  negligence in, 10-81/6
  night safes, 10-90/1
Bank Giro
  compared with cheque system, 10-2/5
  credit clearing, 10-23/5
  credit transfers, 10-6, 10-10/22
  direct debiting, 10-26/31
  dividend payments, 10-14
  functions of, 10-1
  interest payments, 10-14
  standing orders, 10-9/11
  traders' credits, 10-10/12
Bank holidays, 8-12A, 8-39
Banknotes
  promissory notes, 9-60
Bank of England
  directions by, 1-35
  functions of, 1-1

Bank of England (*contd.*)
powers of, under Banking Act, 1-41/4
Banker
advising as to investments, 10-124/30
breach of trust, knowledge of, 7-44/5
collecting. *See* Collecting banker
constructive trustee of proceeds of cheque, 6-57
conversion by, 6-48/53, 7-98/9, 10-79
crossing of cheque by, 5-57
customer, and. *See* Banker–customer relationship
customer's account, closure of, 3-6/14
defined, 1-17/33
duties of, 2-10/21
holder for value, 6-35/44, 8-117
indemnity, right to. *See* Indemnity
investments, advising as to, 10-124/30
negligence of. *See* Negligence
opinion, by, 2-99/123, 10-51/70
paying. *See* Paying banker
reference, by, 2-99/123
secrecy, duty of, 2-99/123, 10-61/2
third parties, duty towards, 6-45/6, 6-107/29, 7-41/3
Banker–customer relationship
actions, limitations of, 2-12, 2-25/30
bailor and bailee. *See* Safe custody
bank as customer, 1-69
bankruptcy of customer, 3-38/42
closure of account, 3-1/14
commencement of, 1-68
company customer, winding up of, 3-43/4
death of customer, 3-15/25
demand necessary for repayment of debt, 1-70
dependent on implied contract, 2-2
determination of, 3-1/85
intention to create, 1-65, 11-2
investments, advising as to, 10-124/30
mental incapacity of customer, 3-26/36
nature of, 2-1/2, 2-5/8
war, effect of, 3-82/6
writ of sequestration, 3-80/1
Bankers' Books Evidence Act 1879
inspection, 1-59
provisions of, 1-25, 1-56/61
Bankers' Automated Clearing Services Limited, 6-15, 10-32
Bankers' Clearing House. *See* Clearing house
Bankers' commercial credits. *See* Documentary credits

Bankers' draft
application for, 9-15
bearer, payable to, 9-18
cheque, may be, 9-14
collection of, 6-70/1, 6-80, 9-19
crossed, 9-17
defined, 9-14
dividend warrant as, 9-6
endorsement, when unnecessary, 9-22
forged endorsement on, 9-21/2
form of, 9-14
interest warrant as, 9-6
lost, 9-23/4
must be payable to order, 9-18
negotiable, 4-10
payment of, 7-64, 7-86, 9-20
Bankers' references. *See* Status opinions
Banking
business, starting, 1-35/48
business, what is, 1-23
early history of, 2-3
hire purchase finance companies, and, 1-15/16
hours, payment after, 7-9
Ombudsman, 1-12A/C
Bankruptcy
act of, deed of arrangement as, 11-238
after-acquired property, 3-42A
customer, of, 3-38/42
drawee, of, 8-39, 8-41
income payments order, 3-42
joint account-holder, of, 11-92/3
minor, of, 11-59
partner, of, 11-131, 11-137
partnership, of, 11-132, 11-138
set-off on, right of, 2-59
solicitor, of, 11-161/2
trustee in, 3-42, 11-232/6
trustee, of, 11-229
wife of undischarged bankrupt, 3-42A
Banks
bankers' payments, 1-27
books of, as evidence. *See* Bankers' Books Evidence Act
charges, 2-44/54
clearing, 1-13A, 1-29, 1-33, 6-6
collection of cheques, etc., by, 6-1/142
defined, 1-17/36
deposit banks, 1-12
industrial bankers, 1-14/16
merchant banks, 1-13
moneylender, and, distinction between, 1-28/29
payment of, crossed cheque by, 1-26
privileges of, 1-33

Banks (*contd.*)
  Scottish banks, 1-33
  trustee savings. *See* Trustee Savings
    Banks
  unlimited companies, 1-11
  winding up of, 3-45
Bearer
  bill, payable to, 8-2
  bond, 4-13
  defined, 5-61, 5-96
Betting transactions
  bills, given in, 5-166/7
Big Bang, 10-107/12
Bill of exchange
  accepted conditionally, 8-34/5
  acceptor's duty, 8-32
  advances against, 8-115/17
  after date, undated, 8-9
  cheque and, differences between,
    8-17/26
  classes of, 8-5/11
  collection by banker of, 8-27, 8-118/19,
    8-135
  crossed 'Not negotiable', 5-42
  days of grace on, 8-12A
  defined, 8-2
  demand, payable on, 8-7
  determinable future time, payable at, 8-8
  discharge of, 7-54, 7-61, 7-95, 8-140
  discounting, 8-97
  dishonour of, 8-48
  domiciled, 8-139/40
  exporters and, 8-98/119
  foreign, 8-8, 8-14/16, 8-36, 8-89/90
  functions of, 8-97
  importers and, 8-120/32
  inland, 8-7, 8-14/16, 8-87/8
  instalments, payable by, 8-10
  interest payable on, 8-10
  inward, 8-135
  kinds of, 8-5/11
  lien on, 8-118
  lost, action on, 9-13
  manufacturers and, 8-133/4
  minor party to, 5-140
  negotiable, 4-8
  negotiation of, 8-97
  noting. *See* Noting
  order, payable to, 8-2
  overdue, 9-59
  particular fund, order to pay out of, 8-3
  payable at bank, 8-139/40
  pledge of, 8-115/17
  presentment for acceptance, 8-28
  presentment for payment, 8-21

Bill of exchange (*contd.*)
  protest of. *See* Protest
  rate of exchange, 8-11
  set, drawn in, 8-16
  sum certain, 8-10
  unconditional, 8-3
  undated, 8-9
  writing must be in, 8-2
Bill of lading, 4-17, 8-99
Blank
  cheque, 5-68
  endorsement, 5-74
Bona fides. *See* Good faith
Bonds
  capital, 10-122A
  income, 10-122
  premium, 10-123
Borrowing
  administrator by, 11-177, 11-181/2
  building society, by, 11-400
  clubs, by, 11-427/8
  companies, by, 11-276/307
  executor, by, 11-173/4, 11-181/2
  friendly societies, by, 11-408/9
  industrial and provident societies, by,
    11-413/16
  joint account holders, by 11-77/8
  local authority, by, 11-417/18
  minor, by, 11-48/51
  parochial church councils, by, 11-419
  partnerships, by, 11-121/4
  societies, by, 11-438/9
  trustee in bankruptcy, by, 11-236
  trustees, by, 11-212
Breach of trust
  administrators, by, 11-192/3
  bankers' knowledge of, 7-44/5
  executors, by, 11-192/3
  notice of, 7-44/5
  solicitor, by, 11-153/4
  trustee, by, 11-230/1
British Islands, 8-15
Budget accounts, 1-77
Building societies
  account of, 11-391/3
  borrowing powers of, 11-400
  defined, 11-391
  lending to, 11-400
  powers of, 1-70
  rules of, 11-400
  sub-mortgage executed by, 11-402
Business day, 8-12A
Business development loans, 1-75

Canvassing, 1-53

Cash
  dispensers, 10-50A/B
  instrument payable to, 9-25/33
Certificate of incorporation, 11-267
Certification of cheques, 7-100/1
Channel Islands, 8-15
CHAPS, 10-32A
Charges
  bank, 2-44/54
Cheque
  accommodation, 5-189/90
  agent, drawn by, 5-184/7
  alteration of, 7-88
  amount, alteration of, 7-18/20
  amount, uncertainty as to, 7-17
  answer on. *See* Answer on cheque
  ante-dated, 5-19
  bearer, 5-96
  bill of exchange and, differences
    between, 8-17/26
  cash, payable to, 5-17
  clearing of, *See* Clearing house
  collection of, 6-1/142
  company, payable to, collected for
    account of director, 6-119/21
  conditional, 5-144
  countermand of payment, 7-37
  crossed. *See* Crossed cheque
  date of, 5-18/19, 7-16
  defect in title, 5-121
  defined, 5-6
  demand, must be payable on, 5-15,
    8-19
  disadvantages of, 10-7
  dishonour of, 2-141/54, 5-135/7
  dividend warrant as, 9-3
  drawer, 5-7, 5-171/4
  drawer deceased, 3-22
  drunkenness, 5-142
  duplicate, 5-102
  duress, 5-121, 5-158/9
  employer, cheque drawn by, position
    of banker collecting, 6-115/18
  employer payable to, position of
    banker collecting, 6-112/14
  endorsement of. *See* Endorsement
  endorser, liability of, 5-175/7
  fictitious or non-existing person,
    payable to, 5-39
  forgery of. *See* Forgery
  form of, 5-6/19
  fraud connected with drawing of,
    5-121, 5-151/6
  gaming, effect of, 5-166/7
  holder, 5-96
  illegal consideration, 5-163/7

Cheque (*contd.*)
  inchoate, 5-67/70
  incomplete, 5-67/70, 5-143
  interest warrant as, 9-3
  issue of, 5-60, 5-63
  lost, 5-102, 9-13
  magnetic ink characters on, 5-30/1
  marked, 7-100/1
  material alteration to, 5-147/50
  mental incapacity, 5-141
  minor, drawn by, 5-139
  negotiable, when, 5-4/5
  negotiation of, 5-71/2, 5-103
  non-transferable, 9-40/2
  official, payable to, position of banker
    collecting, 6-123
  origin of, 2-4, 5-1/2
  out of date, 7-15
  overdue, 5-114, 5-168
  partnership, payable to, collected for
    account of partner, 6-122
  payee of, 5-7
  payment in cash, 7-8/10, 7-49, 7-94
  payment under advice, 7-77/8
  pencil, drawn in, 5-11
  post, presentment by, 7-11
  post-dated, 5-19, 7-16
  quasi-endorser, liability of, 5-178
  raising of, 6-77/8
  receipt attached to, 9-35
  refused payment, answer on, 7-1
  special presentment of, 6-24/6, 7-53
  spelling, of, 5-3
  stale, 7-15
  Sunday, dated on, 5-19
  theft, effect of, 5-163/4
  transferor by delivery of, 5-180/2
  unconditional, must be, 5-8/10
  uncrossed, payment of, 7-61/78
  undated, 7-14
  undue influence, 5-161/2
  words and figures differ, 5-16
  writing essential, 5-11/12
Cheque cards
  application for, 10-43A
  conditions relating to, 10-44
  defined, 10-43
  origin of, 10-42
Clayton's Case. *See* Appropriation of
    payments
Clearing banks, 1-13A, 1-29, 1-33, 6-6
Clearing house
  daily settlement, 6-19
  Credit clearing, 6-14, 9-9, 10-23/5
  general clearing, 6-11/13
  origin of, 6-6

Clearing house (*contd.*)
  return of cheque, rules for, 7-1,
    7-47/8
  Town clearing, 6-7/10
Closing of account
  banker's rights as to, 3-7/13
  customer, by, 3-2/5
Clubs. *See* Societies
Collecting banker
  bankers' drafts, 9-19
  bills of exchange, 8-118/19
  'cash or order' instruments, 9-29/30
  cheques, 6-1/141
  clearing channel, choice of, 6-28
  conditional orders, 9-37
  contributory negligence of third party,
    6-133/6
  good faith, 6-74
  holder for value, 6-35/44
  holder in due course, 6-137/9
  negligence, 6-94/129
  notice of dishonour by, 6-33/4
  paying also, 7-71/3
  postal orders, 9-68/9
  protective legislation, 6-58/91, 9-5/7,
    9-29/30, 9-37
  reasonable diligence to be exercised by,
    6-31/2
  statutory protection of, 6-58/91, 9-5/7,
    9-29/30, 9-37
  true owner, obligation to, 6-46/57
  warrants, 6-81
Combining accounts. *See* Set-off
Commercial credits. *See* Documentary
  credits
Commission. *See* Charges
Companies
  accounts of, 11-246/357
  administrative receiver, 11-315/28
  administration orders, 11-329/42
  articles of association, 11-271/2,
    11-282/90
  borrowing powers of, 11-276/90
  borrowing, what constitutes, 11-285
  certificate of incorporation, 11-267
  chartered, 11-262/4, 11-311/12
  cheque payable to, collected for
    account of director, 6-119/21
  close, 11-256/7
  countermand of cheque drawn by, 7-32
  directors, too few, 11-308/9
  lending to, 11-295/307
  limited by guarantee, 11-258/60
  limited by shares, 11-248/57
  mandate determined, 11-313/35
  mandate given by, 11-273/4

Companies (*contd.*)
  memorandum of association, 11-270
    11-277/81
  non-trading, 11-278
  'one-man', 11-310
  private, 11-250, 11-252/5
  public, 11-249, 11-255
  receiver, appointment of, 11-315/28
  registration of, 11-267
  Table A, 11-286/90
  trading certificate, 11-268
  unlimited, 11-261
  wages advances, 11-299/306
  winding up of. *See* Winding-up
Compulsory winding-up, 11-348/59
Computer services, 10-144/8
Computerized statements as
  evidence, 1-62
Conditional orders
  collection of, 9-37
  defined, 9-34
  payment of, 9-38/9
Consideration
  absence of, 5-126
  antecedent debt, 5-128
  defined, 5-128, 6-38
  doctrine of, 5-126
  failure of, 5-126, 5-167
  illegal, 5-163/7
  lien by virtue of, 6-41
  past, 5-127
  presumption as to, 5-130
  simple contract, 5-128
Contributory negligence, 6-133/6
Conversion
  banker liable for, 6-48/56, 7-98/99
    9-69/70, 10-79
  bankers' drafts, 9-19
  'cash or order' instruments, 9-29
  cheques, 6-48/53
  defined, 6-48
  money orders, 9-69
  postal orders, 9-69/70
  who may sue for, 6-50/53
Counterfoil
  dividend, 9-8
Countermand of payment
  cheque, of, 7-30/7
  joint account holder, by, 11-72
  partner by, 11-117/18
Credit cards
  defined, 10-46
  disadvantages of, 10-49
  origin of, 10-45
  unsolicited, 1-54, 10-46A
Credit clearing, 10-23/5

Crediting as cash, 6-66/9
Crossed cheque
  'account A.B.' crossing, 5-46, 6-111
  'account payee', *See* Account payee
  Crossed Cheques Act 1876, 6-60
  dividend warrants, 9-7
  generally crossed, 5-36, 5-38, 5-51, 7-4
  not negotiable crossing. *See* Not
    negotiable
  obliteration of crossing, 7-21
  opening, 7-22/4
  origin of, 5-35
  payment of, 7-4/6, 7-79/81, 7-99
  safest crossing, 5-48
  specially crossed, 5-36, 5-38, 5-52, 7-4
  who may cross, 5-49/57
Crowther Committee, 1-14
Current account
  deposit account, distinguished from,
    1-71
  features of, 1-70
  garnishee order on, 3-49/52
  loan account, distinguished from, 1-73
  personal cheque account, 1-70
Customer
  account, closure by, 3-2/5
  accountant as, 11-167
  administrator as, 11-175/93
  auctioneer as, 11-167
  bankruptcy of, 3-38/42
  building society as, 11-391/3
  club as, 11-430/4
  company as, 11-246/335
  death of, 3-15/25
  defined, 1-63/8
  duties of banker, of, 2-124/31, 2-136/8
  employers of, 11-13/15
  estate agents as, 11-167
  estoppel of, where bank misled,
    6-130/2, 7-12
  executor as, 7-45, 11-170/93
  forgery, duty to disclose, 2-128/31
  friendly society as, 11-403/7
  identity of, 11-5/10
  industrial and provident society as,
    11-410/12
  integrity of, 11-11/12
  joint account, 11-65/95
  local authority as, 11-425/7
  married woman as, 11-60/4
  mental incapacity of, 3-26/37
  minor as, 11-45/51
  negligence of, when drawing cheques,
    2-125/7
  opening account with banker, 6-103,
    11-1/15

Customer (*contd.*)
  parochial church council as, 11-417/19
  partnership as, 11-110/27
  reference as to standing, 11-6/12
  society as, 11-408/17
  solicitor as, 11-147/64
  stockbroker as, 11-165/6
  trustee as, 11-194/231
  trustee in bankruptcy as, 11-232/6
  trustees under deeds of arrangement as,
    11-237/45

Damages
  conversion for, 6-47/53
  dishonour of cheque, arising from
    2-141/54
Date
  cheque, of, 5-18/19, 7-14/16
  maturity, of, 8-12A/13
  omission of, 7-14
  out of, 7-15
  post-dating, 7-16
Days of grace, 8-12A, 8-22
Death
  administrator, of, 11-188/91
  customer, of, 3-15/25
  drawee, of, 8-39, 8-41
  executor, of, 11-188/91
  joint account-holder, of, 11-83/9
  partner, of, 11-130, 11-136
  solicitor, of, 11-156/60
  trustee, of, 11-220/2
Deed of arrangement
  registration of, 11-242
  trustee under, 11-237/45
Defamation
  answer on cheque by reason of,
    2-145/54
Delay
  notice of dishonour, 8-76/80
  noting or protesting, 8-92/4
  presentment of cheque, 5-132/4
Delivery
  actual, 5-64, 7-68
  conditional, 5-65
  constructive, 5-64, 7-68
  defined, 5-62, 7-68
  presumption, as to, 5-66
Deposit account
  bank finance company, with, 10-136/8
  current account, as distinguished from,
    1-71
  deposit receipt, 1-71
  features of, 1-71
  garnishee order on, 3-67/9
Deposit protection fund, 1-38, 1-49/50

Direct debiting, 10-26/31
Directors
    borrowing powers of, 11-282/94
    borrowing resolution by, 11-296
    determination of mandate by, 11-314
    insufficient, 11-308/9
    liability of, in case of bills, 5-188
    minimum number of, 11-253
    operation of company's account,
        11-273/4
    powers of, in winding up, 11-321,
        11-328/9
    shadow, 11-362
Discharge
    bill of exchange, of, 7-54, 7-61/2, 7-95,
        8-140
    failure to protest bill, 8-89
    non-presentment, by, 8-42
    parties, of, by failure to present, 7-97
    payment, by, 7-54, 7-61/2, 7-95,
        8-140
Disclosure. *See* Secrecy
Discounting
    meaning of, 8-97
    transactions involving, 8-100, 8-102,
        8-128/9, 8-133
Dishonour
    action for, 2-141/51
    cheque, of, 7-47/53
    damages for, 2-141/51
    defamation by reason of, 2-145/51
    negotiation after, 5-169
    non-acceptance, by, 8-48/55
    non-payment, by, 8-48, 8-56/9
    notice of. *See* Notice of dishonour
Dividend. *See also* Dividend warrants
    counterfoils, 11-15
    payments by Bank Giro, 10-15
Dividend warrants
    crossing of, 9-7
    defined, 9-1
    lost, 9-12/13
    types of, 9-3/4
    unconditional order, 9-36
Documentary bills, 8-99/138
Documentary credits
    acceptance credit, 8-99, 8-102, 8-126/9,
        8-133/4
    application for, 8-121
    confirmed, 8-125
    irrevocable, 8-99, 8-120
    revocable, 8-101
    revolving, 8-134
    shipping documents, 8-99, 8-109, 8-116,
        8-121, 8-123/4, 8-129, 8-131/2
Domiciled bill, 8-139/40

Drawee
    drawer, where same person as, 4-10,
        5-13, 6-70, 8-62, 9-14
    fictitious, 8-46
    more than one, 8-35, 8-43
Drawer
    bill, of, 8-5
    cheque, of, 5-7
    discharged in case of non-presentment
        7-97, 8-21
    drawee, where same person as, 4-10,
        5-13, 6-70, 8-62, 9-14
    liability of, 5-171/4
    notice of dishonour to, 5-137, 8-60
Drunkenness
    drawer of cheque, 5-142
Duress
    defined, 5-157
    effect of, 5-121, 5-158/9

EftPos, 10-32B/D
Employer
    cheque drawn by customer's, 6-115/18
    cheque payable to customer's, 6-112/14
Endorsee
    defined, 5-61
Endorsement
    blank, effect of, 5-74
    cheque paid at counter, 7-8/10
    conditional, 5-91
    defined, 5-73, 7-67/70
    elimination of need for, 7-89, 8-26
    forged, 5-87
    irregular, 5-88/90, 6-124, 7-87
    necessary, where, 6-82/90, 7-25/9
    origin of, 4-3
    partial, 5-82
    partner, by, 5-83
    payee's name misspelt, 5-84
    per pro., 5-80
    restrictive, 5-92/5
    sans recours, 5-85, 5-177
    special, effect of, 5-75
    special, following blank, 5-76
    types of, 5-74, 5-85/6
    unauthorized, 5-87
    unnecessary, when, 5-72
    validity of, 5-79/86
    without recourse, 5-85, 5-177
Endorser
    liability of, 5-175/7
    notice of dishonour to, 8-60
    promissory note, of, 9-55/7
Estate agents
    accounts of, 11-167
    banks acting as, 10-135

Estoppel
  customer, of, for misleading bank,
    6-130/2
  customer, of, in respect of forged
    signature, 2-128/31, 5-146, 7-12
  wife forges husband's signature, 2-128/31
Evidence
  bankers' books as, 1-56/61
  passbook as, 2-138
Exchequer bills, 4-12
Executor and administrator
  accounts of, 11-170/93
  breach of trust by, 1-192/3
  business of deceased continued by,
    11-183/7
  death of, 11-188/91
  death of customer, rights on, 3-18/19,
    3-21
  defined, 11-168
  lending to, 11-173, 11-177, 11-181/2
  minor as, 11-57
  misappropriation by, 7-45
Export Credits Guarantee Department,
  8-114

Factoring, 10-132
Farm development loans, 1-75
Fictitious payee, 5-39
Figures
  'words and figures differ,' 5-16, 7-17
Finance companies
  industrial bankers, 1-14/16, 10-131
Finance Houses, 1-14, 1-45
Force and fear
  defined, 1-157
  effect of, 5-121, 5-158/9
Foreclosure
  Limitation Act 1939, 2-41
Foreign
  trade, financing of, 8-97/132
Forgery
  cheque, of, 2-128/31, 5-145, 7-12
  endorsement, of, 7-58/95
  estoppel, operation of. See Estoppel
  raising of amount of cheque, 2-125/6
  wife, by, 2-128/31
Fraud
  cheque obtained by, 5-121, 5-151/6
  void and voidable contracts induced
    by, 5-153/6
Friendly societies
  accounts of, 11-403/7
  lending to, 11-408/9
  mortgage by, 11-409
  purposes of, 11-403
  rules of, 11-405, 11-408, 11-434, 11-437

Fund
  direction to pay out of particular, 8-3

Gaming
  cheque given in respect of, 5-166/7
Garnishee proceedings
  balances abroad, 3-78/9
  bankers' course when served with,
    3-47/52
  current account, 3-49/52
  deposit account, 3-67/9
  joint account, 3-70, 11-95
  limited order, 3-52
  partnership account, 3-71
  practice, 3-47/8
  savings account, 3-69
  solicitors' account, 11-164
  summons, 3-53/5
  trust moneys, 3-75/7
Girobank, 10-33/41
Goldsmiths, 2-4
Good faith
  collecting banker, 6-74
  defined, 5-120, 6-92, 7-65, 7-92
  negligence, compared with, 6-92
  paying banker, 7-61/3, 7-65, 7-79, 7-89,
    7-92
Gower, L. C. B.
  report by, 1-78
Gratuitous bailee. See Bailment

Hire-purchase companies, 1-14, 10-131
Holder
  action on cheque, by, 5-107
  crossing of cheque by, 5-53/5, 5-101
  defined, 5-61, 5-96
  for value, See Holder for value
  in due course. See Holder in due course
  negotiation by, 5-103/4
  rights of, 5-100/7
Holder for value
  banker as, 6-35/44, 8-117
  encashment of third-party cheque,
    6-42/4
  holder deemed to be, 5-131
  lien, 5-118, 6-41
  payment against uncleared cheque, 6-39
  reduction of advance, 6-40
Holder in due course
  bank as, 6-137/9, 8-109/10
  defined, 5-108
  delivery presumed, 5-66
  distinguished from holder for value,
    5-116
  inchoate instrument, 5-68, 5-144
  payee, not, 5-119

Holder in due course (*contd.*)
  presumption, as to, 5-123/4
  presumption of delivery, 5-66
  title through, 5-122
Holidays, 8-12A, 8-39
Hours of business, 2-13, 8-12B
House improvement loans, 1-75
Householder's protest, 8-85
Husband and wife
  forgery by wife, 2-128/131
  joint account of, 11-65, 11-87
  survivorship, rule of, 11-86/7

Identity
  customer of, 11-5/10
  payee, of, 7-58, 7-62, 7-79/91
Illegality
  consideration, 5-163/7
  knowledge of, 5-122
Immoral consideration, 5-165
Inchoate instruments, 5-68/9
Indemnity
  bankers' draft, loss of, 9-24
  collecting banker's right to, 6-140/1
Indorsee, indorsement, indorser. *See*
  Endorsee, Endorsement, Endorser
Industrial and provident societies
  accounts of, 11-410/12
  charges created by, 11-416
  lending to, 11-413/46
  purposes of, 11-410
  rules of, 11-411/12
Infant. *See* Minor
Injunction
  Mareva, 7-42A/F
  restraining customer from withdrawing
    funds, 7-42
Insanity. *See* Mental incapacity
Inspection
  banker's books, of, 1-59
Instalments
  bill, payable by, 8-10
  promissory notes, payable by, 9-46
Interest
  bill, on, 8-10
  payments by bank giro, 10-15
  promissory note, on, 9-46
Interest warrant
  defined, 9-2
  lost, 9-12/13
  types of, 9-3/4
Interpleader proceedings
  nature of, 7-43
Investment
  banker advising as to, 10-124/30
  trusts, 10-117/20

Irrevocable credit, 8-99, 8-120
Isle of Man, 8-15

Jenkins Committee, 11-355
Joint account
  bankruptcy of depositor, 11-92/3
  countermand of cheque, 7-32
  death of depositor, 11-83/9
  garnishee order, 3-70, 11-95
  husband and wife, 11-65, 11-87
  liability, joint and several, 11-77
  mandate for, 11-67/82
  mental incapacity of depositor, 11-94
  opening, 11-66
  stopping of, 11-90

Leasing, 10-133
Legal personal representative. *See*
  Executor and administrator
Letter of pledge, 8-109
Libel
  cheque, dishonour of, 2-145/54
Lien
  holder for value, 5-118, 6-41
Limitation of actions
  bankers' debt, 2-12, 2-25/30
  conversion, claim for, 6-56
  credit accounts, 2-25/30
  debit accounts, 2-31/6
  guarantee, in case of, 2-42/3
  money had and received, claim for, 6-56
  personal loan accounts, 2-34
  securities for advances, 2-37/43
Limited companies. *See* Companies
Liquidator
  compulsory winding-up, 11-386/90
  creditors' voluntary winding-up,
    11-382/5
  members' voluntary winding-up,
    11-378/81
Loan accounts
  personal loan accounts, 1-55, 1-74
  procedure relating to, 1-73
Local authorities
  accounts of, 11-420/9
  Greater London, 11-424
  lending to, 11-428/9
Lord Tenterden's Act, 10-68
Lost instruments
  bankers' draft, 9-23/4
  bill of exchange, 9-13
  cheque, 5-102, 9-13
  dividend warrant, 9-12/13
Lunacy. *See* Mental incapacity

Magnetic ink character recognition
    system, 5-30/31
Maker of promissory note
    claim against, when statute barred, 9-54
    joint and several, 9-48/9
    liability of, 9-52/4
Man, Isle of, 8-15
Mandate
    agent, bankruptcy of, 11-25
    agent, death of, 11-25
    agent, mental incapacity of, 11-25
    bankruptcy of person signing, 11-24
    company, 11-273/4, 11-313/35
    death of person signing, 11-24
    dividend, 9-9/11
    interest, 9-9/11
    joint account, 11-67/82
    mental incapacity of person signing,
        11-24
    partnership account, 11-115/27, 11-140
    trust account, 11-203/6
Mareva injunction, 7-42A/F
Marking cheques, 7-100/1
Married woman
    customer, as, 11-60/4
    forgery by, 2-128/31
    guarantor, 11-63
    introduction of, 11-62
    joint account with husband, 11-65, 11-87
    legal capacity of, 11-61
Material alteration. *See* Alteration
Maturity date of, 8-12A/13
Memorandum of association
    alteration of, 11-280
    borrowing powers conferred by,
        11-277/81
    contents of, 11-270
Mental incapacity
    customer, 3-26/37
    drawer of cheque, 5-141
    joint depositor, 11-94
    partner, 11-134
Merchant banks, 1-13
Minor
    account of, 11-45/7
    agent, as, 11-23, 11-53
    bankrupt, 11-59
    cheque book issued to, 11-46
    contracts entered into by, 11-40/4
    defined, 11-39
    drawer of cheque, 5-139
    endorser of cheque, 5-139
    executor, 11-57
    land purchase by, 11-55
    legal capacity of, 11-40/4
    lending to, 11-48/51

Minor (*contd.*)
    partner, 11-54
    security given by, 11-49
    stocks and shares purchased by, 11-56
    testator, 11-58
    witness, 11-52
Misdelivery
    safe custody, articles of, 10-79/80,
        10-85/6
Mistake
    cheque, payment of, by, 7-50
    correction of account after, 2-134/8
    forged signature on cheque, payment
        by, 7-12
    passbook, in, 2-134/8
Money had and received action for,
    6-54/6
Month
    defined, 8-13

National Savings Bank, 1-2, 1-9
National Savings Certificates, 10-121
Negligence
    'account payee' cheque, 6-109/11
    collecting banker, of, 6-94/109
    company, cheque payable to, 6-119/21
    contributory, on part of customer,
        6-133/6
    customer, of, in signing cheque, 2-125/7
    degree of care required of banker,
        6-96/100
    employer, cheque drawn by, 6-115/18
    employer, cheque payable to, 6-112/14
    endorsement irregular on cheque, 6-124
    good faith compared with, 6-92
    official, cheque payable to, 6-123
    opening account, 6-103
    ordinary course of business, relation
        to, 7-76
    ordinary practice of bankers, relation
        to, 6-97/9
    partnership, cheque payable to, 6-122
    paying banker of, 7-74/6, 7-79
    third-party cheques, collection of,
        6-107/29
    what amounts to, 6-101/29
Negotiable instruments
    bankers' drafts, 4-10
    bearer bonds, 4-13
    bills of exchange, 4-8
    characteristics of, 4-1
    cheques. *See* Cheque
    endorsement of, 4-2/3
    promissory notes, 4-9
    quasi-, position of, 4-15
    stolen, 4-5

Negotiable instruments (*contd.*)
  transfer of, 4-2/3
  travellers' cheques, 4-11
  treasury bills, 4-12
  types of, 4-8/14
  warehousekeepers' warrants, 4-14
Negotiation
  cheque, of, 5-71/2
  inchoate instrument, of, 5-68
Night safes, 10-90/1
Non-acceptance, 8-48/55
Non-business day, 8-12A, 8-39
Non-existing payee. *See* Fictious payee
Non-payment, 8-48, 8-56/9
Non-presentment. *See* Presentment
Non-transferable cheque, 7-85, 9-40/2
Not negotiable
  bill crossed, 5-42
  cheque crossed, collection of, 5-45, 6-44
  cheque crossed, effect of, 5-42/5, 5-48,
    6-139
Notary public
  function of, 8-82
  noting by. *See* Noting
  protest by. *See* Protest
  substitute for, 8-85
Notice
  account, intention to close, 3-7/13
  act of bankruptcy, of, 3-40/40A
  agent's limited authority, of, 5-80
  death of customer, of, 3-22
  dishonour, of. *See* Notice of dishonour
  mental incapacity of customer, of,
    3-29/36
  withdrawal from deposit account, 1-71
Notice of dishonour
  agent, by, 5-136, 8-65
  banker, by, 8-48
  bankruptcy in case of, 8-73
  cheque, of, 5-106, 5-135
  collecting banker, by, 6-32/3
  death, in case of, 8-72
  delay, excuses for, 8-80
  dispensed with, 8-62
  drawer, to, 5-137, 8-60
  endorser, to, 8-60
  failure to give, 5-135
  form of, 8-68/70
  holder by, 5-135, 8-48, 8-64
  parties living in different places, 5-135
  parties living in same place, 5-135
  post, by, 8-79
  return of bill, by, 8-69
  time for, 8-75/8
  unnecessary, when, 8-61/2
  waiver of, 8-62

Noting
  delay in, 8-94
  expenses of, 8-82
  protest may follow, 8-81
  purpose of, 8-81

Obliteration
  crossing of, 7-21
Official
  cheque payable to, 6-123
Ombudsman, Banking, 1-12A/C
Opening account
  administrator, for, 11-176
  building society, for, 11-384/5
  club, for, 11-419/28
  company, for, 11-273/4
  executor, for, 11-170/1
  friendly society, for, 11-392/4
  individual customer, for, 6-103, 11-1/15
  industrial and provident society, for,
    11-399
  joint, 11-67/82
  local authority, for, 11-414/16
  married woman, for, 11-62/4
  minor, for, 11-45/7
  parochial church council, for, 11-407
  partnership, for, 11-110/27
  society, for, 11-425/6
  solicitor, for, 11-147/50
  stockbroker, for, 11-165/6
  trustee, for, 11-202/6
  trustee in bankruptcy, for, 11-233/4
  trustee under deed of arrangement, for,
    11-239/41
Opening of crossing, 7-22/4
Ordinary course of business
  meaning of, 7-66, 7-93
  negligence and, 7-76
  payment after banking hours, 2-13
  payment in, 7-61/3, 7-66, 7-89
Overdue
  bill, 9-59
  cheque, 5-114, 5-168

Parochial church councils
  accounts of, 11-406/8
  duties of, 11-406
  lending to, 11-408
Partial acceptance, 8-34/5
Partners. *See also* Partnership
  authority of, 11-103/5
  bankruptcy of, 11-131, 11-137, 11-145
  death of, 11-130, 11-136, 11-145
  endorsement by, 5-83
  liability of, 11-106, 11-121/4,
    11-141/4

Partners (*contd.*)
  minor as, 11-54
  number of, 11-101
  sleeping, 11-98
  unsound mind, of, 11-134
Partnership. *See also* Partner
  account of, 11-110/27
  agreement, 11-102, 11-113
  bankruptcy of, 11-132, 11-138
  change in constitution of, 11-139/45
  cheque payable to, paid into private
    account, 6-122
  choice of name for, 11-107/8
  countermand of cheque, 7-32
  customer, as, 11-110/27
  defined, 11-97
  dissolution of, 11-128/34
  garnishee order, 3-71
  legal person, not a, 11-100
  lending to, 11-119/24
  mandate, 11-115/27, 11-140
  registration of, 11-107/9
Passbook
  account stated, as, 2-138
  acquiescence based on, 2-136/8
  degree of care required from customer,
    2-136/8
  errors in, effect of, 2-134/8
  evidence, as, 2-138
  loose sheets, 2-132
  mistake in, 2-134/8
  stated account, as, 2-138
Passport
  production of, 11-10
'Pay cash'
  instrument so drawn, 9-25/33
  opening a crossing, 7-22/4
Payee
  bill, of, 8-5
  cheque, of, 5-7
  defined, 5-61
  name misspelt, 5-84
Paying banker
  bankers' draft, 9-20/2
  collection also, 7-71/3
  good faith, 7-61/3, 7-65, 7-79, 7-89,
    7-92
  negligence of, 7-74/6, 7-79
  ordinary course of business, 7-61/3,
    7-66, 7-89, 7-93
  protective legislation, 7-56/95, 8-24,
    9-5/7, 9-21/2, 9-31/3, 9-38/9
  third party claims against, 7-96/9
Payment
  advice, under, 7-77/8
  banking hours, after, 7-51

Payment (*contd.*)
  'cash or order' instrument, 9-31/3
  cheque crossed 'account payee', 7-6
  conversion and. *See* Conversion
  crossed cheque, of, 7-4/5, 7-99
  domiciled bill, of, 8-139/40
  funds insufficient, where, 7-38/40
  good faith, in, 7-62, 7-65
  in due course, 7-54, 7-61/2, 7-95,
    8-140
  ordinary course of business, in, 7-10,
    7-61/3, 7-66
  presentment for, 8-21
  uncrossed cheque, of, 7-7/11
  'wages or order' instrument, 9-31/3
Pencil
  cheque drawn in, 5-11
Per pro.
  signature, effect of, 5-80
Personal representative. *See* Executor and
    administrator
Petition in bankruptcy. *See* Bankruptcy
Pledge of bill, 8-115/17
Post Office Giro. *See* Girobank
Post Office Savings Bank
  functions of, 1-9
  investment accounts with, 1-9
  no power to make advances, 1-9
  non-profit making, 1-2
Postal orders
  collection of, 9-68/9
  crossed, 9-67
  defined, 9-64
  not negotiable, 4-16, 9-66
Post-dated cheque, 5-19, 7-16
Power of attorney
  enduring, 11-38A
  irrevocable, 11-36
  preamble to, 11-27
  revocation of, 11-35/8
  types of, 11-26
Pre-existing debt
  consideration for bill, 5-128
Preferential creditors, 11-299
Premium bonds, 10-123
Presentment for acceptance
  bankrupt, where drawee, 8-39, 8-41
  dead, where drawee, 8-39, 8-41
  rules for, 8-28, 8-39/40
  sight, payable after, 8-38
Presentment for payment
  bill, of, 8-21, 8-42/6
  cheque, of, 5-105, 6-22, 7-11, 7-49, 8-21
  dead, where acceptor is, 8-43
  delay in, when excused, 8-45
  dispensed with, 8-46/7

Presentment for payment (*contd.*)
  drawee fictitious, 8-46
  mode of, 8-43
  place, of, 8-43
  rules for, 8-43
  several drawees, 8-43
  special presentation, 6-22
  time for, 8-43
  waiver of, 8-46
Presumption
  consideration, as to, 5-130
  delivery, as to, 5-66
Prices and Incomes Board, 2-54
Principal. *See* Agent
Promissory note
  bank note, 9-60
  defined, 9-44
  endorser of, 9-55/7
  foreign, 9-47
  form of, 9-45
  functions of, 9-61/3
  inchoate, 9-47
  inland, 9-47
  instalments, payable by, 9-46
  interest, payable with, 9-46
  joint and several, 9-48/9
  maker of, 9-52/4
  negotiable, 4-9
  negotiation of, 9-58/9
  place of presentment, 9-54
  writing, must be in, 9-44
Protection
  collecting banker, 6-74/91, 9-5/7,
    9-29/30, 9-37
  paying banker, 7-56/95, 8-24, 9-5/7,
    9-21/2, 9-31/3, 9-38/9
Protest
  delay, 8-94
  excused, 8-96
  foreign bill, 8-36
  householder's, 8-85
  inland bill, 8-87
  place of, 8-95
  time for, 8-92
Public
  company, 11-249
  holiday, 8-12A

Qualified acceptance
  assent of prior parties requisite for, 8-36
  defined, 8-34/5
  holder not bound to take, 8-36
Quasi-endorser
  liability of, 5-178
Quasi-negotiability, 4-15

Receipt on cheque, 9-35
Receiver. *See also* Receiver for debenture
    holders
  mental incapacity, in case of, 3-30/2
Receiver for debenture holders
  appointed by court, 11-315/16, 11-368/9
  appointed by debenture holders,
    11-315/17, 11-370/2
  appointment of, determines company's
    mandate, 11-315/20
  effect of winding-up order, 11-373/5
  lending to, 11-369, 11-371/2
Recognized banks, 1-39
Recognized professional bodies, 1-83
Rectification
  error in passbook, 2-134/8
'Refer to drawer'
  libel, as, 2-145/6, 2-150
Reference
  bankers', 2-99/123
  customer's standing, as to, 11-6/12
Registration
  company, of, 11-267
  deed of arrangement, of, 11-242
  friendly society, of, 11-392/4
Restrictive endorsement, 5-92/5
Retention clauses, 11-320/1
Return of bill
  dishonour, as notice of, 8-69
Revocable credit, 8-101
Revolving credit schemes, 1-76

Safe custody
  access to articles deposited for, 10-74
  banker as bailee for reward or
    gratuitous, 10-81/3
  bankruptcy of customer, 10-76
  bearer securities, 10-72
  contracting out of liability, 10-85/6
  conversion, 10-79/80
  death of customer, 3-18/9, 10-75
  death of joint bailor, 11-79
  degree of care required, 10-81/4
  delivery to authorized person, 10-79/80
  detinue, 10-81/4
  generally, 10-71/87
  liability for fraud of servants, 10-88/9
  misdelivery, 10-79/80
  negligence, 10-81/4
  night safes, 10-90/1
  receipt issued, 10-73
Sans recours, 5-85, 5-177
Saturday closing, 10-50A
Savings accounts
  garnishee order on, 3-69
  purpose of, 1-72

Savings banks. *See* Trustee Savings Banks;
    Post Office Savings Bank
Savings bonds, 10-122
Savings certificates, 10-121
Scottish and Irish collections, 6-20/1
Scriveners, 2-3
Secondary banks, 1-37
Secrecy
    banker's duty as to, 2-99/123
    bank's interest, disclosure in, 2-107,
        2-117
    Board of Trade, disclosure to, 2-108
    court order, disclosure under, 1-104/5
    Director of Public Prosecutions
        disclosure to, 2-109
    disclosure with express consent of
        customer, 2-118
    disclosure with implied consent of
        customer, 2-119/23
    insider dealing, 2-111A
    Lord Tenterden's Act, 10-68
    prevention of terrorism, 2-113
    references, 2-121/3
    Serious Fraud Office, 2-112
    writ of sequestration, disclosure
        under, 2-114A
Securities and Investment Board,
    1-80/4
Securities Association, 1-86, 10-93
Self-regulating organizations, 1-79/90
Serious Fraud Office, 2-112
Set, bill drawn in, 8-16
Set-off
    accounts must be in same right, 2-60
    bankers' right to, 2-55/65
    bankruptcy, in case of, 2-59
    contingent liabilities, 2-66
    death, in case of, 2-57
    deposit account, against, 2-63
    letter of, 2-65
    liquidation, in case of, 2-60
    loan account, in case of, 2-64
    mental incapacity, in case of, 2-58
    trust funds, 2-69/72
    unmatured liabilities, 2-66
Shadow directors, 11-362
Share registration service, 10-134
Shares, *See* Stocks and shares
Shipping documents
    bills accompanying, 8-109, 8-116,
        8-121, 8-124
    meaning of, 8-99
    tendered under credits, 8-99, 8-103,
        8-128/29
Sight
    after, bills payable, presentment for
        acceptance necessary, 8-38

Societies
    accounts of, 11-419/28
    incorporated, 11-421/4
    lending to, 11-427/8
    unincorporated, 11-425/6
Solicitor
    accounts of, 11-147/64
    bankruptcy of, 11-161/2
    breach of trust by, 11-153/4
    clients' account of, 11-147, 11-151/2
    customer, as, 11-147/64
    death of, 11-156/160
    garnishee order, 11-164
    illness of, 11-155
    stop order, 11-163
Special endorsement, 5-75/8
Spelling
    payee or endorsee, of, inaccurate, 5-84
Stale cheque, 7-15
Stamp duty
    bill of exchange, 8-12
    promissory note, 9-51
Standing orders, 10-9/11
Statement of account. *See* Passbook
Status opinions
    claims arising out of, 10-54/70
    duty of care, 10-65/6
    fraudulently given, 10-57/70
    practice as to, 10-51/7
    secrecy, bankers' duty as to, 2-121/3,
        10-60/2
    telephone, by, 10-54
    unsigned, 10-70
Stock Exchange
    investing on, 10-93
    official quotation, rule as to, 11-283
    securities quoted on, 10-94/103,
        10-120
    unsecured stock, rule as to, 10-100
Stockbrokers' accounts, 11-165/6
Stocks and shares
    British government stocks, 10-95
    broker, duty of, 10-108/10
    broker's liability, rule as to, 10-110
    Commonwealth government stocks,
        10-96
    convertible stock, 10-100
    debenture stocks, 10-100
    deferred, 10-103
    difference between, 10-104/6
    industrial and commercial, 10-99
    jobbers, 10-107/8
    market-makers, 10-109, 10-111
    minor, purchase by, 11-56
    municipal stocks, 10-97
    ordinary, 10-102
    preference, 10-101

Stocks and shares (*contd.*)
  public boards, stocks of, 10-98
  purchase of, 10-107/11
  sale of, 10-107/11
  types of quoted, 10-95/103
  unsecured loan stock, 10-100
Sum payable
  alteration of, 7-18
  difference between words and figures,
    5-16, 7-17
  sum certain, 8-2
Sunday
  bill falling due on, 8-12A
  cheque dated on, 5-19
Supervision of banks, 1-35/51
Surveyors' accounts, 11-167

Theft
  cheque obtained by, 5-163/4
Third parties
  bankers' duties towards, 6-45/6,
    6-107/29, 7-41/3, 7-96/101
Title, absence of or defect in, 5-121, 7-46
Traders' credits, 10-10/13
Trading certificate, 11-268
Transfer
  forged endorsement, 5-87
  negotiation by, 5-71
  partial, 5-82
  words prohibiting, 5-71
Transferee
  by delivery, 5-180
  entitled to endorsement, 5-183
  overdue bill, of, 9-59
Transferor by delivery
  defined, 5-180
  liability of, 5-180/2
Travellers' cheque, 4-11
Treasury
  bills, 4-12
  powers of, 1-53/4
True owner
  liability to, 6-74
Trust
  breach of. See Breach of trust
  charitable, 11-195/201
  defined, 11-194
  instrument or deed, 11-201/2, 11-208,
    11-213
  investment, 10-117/20
  private, 11-195/201
  receipt, 8-124
  unit. See Unit trusts
Trustee
  account of, 1-30, 11-194/231
  bankruptcy of, 11-299
  breach of trust by, 11-230/1

Trustee (*contd.*)
  customer, as, 1-30, 11-193/231
  death of, 11-220/2
  delegation by, 11-207/11
  lending to, 11-212
  mandate by, 11-203/6
  retirement of, 11-223/8
Trustee in bankruptcy
  account of, 11-232/6
  lending to, 11-236
Trustee Savings Banks
  current accounts with, 1-5, 1-22
  history of, 1-3
  law relating to, 1-9
  non-profit making, 1-2
  Ordinary Department, 1-4
  separate legal entities, 1-8
  Special Investment Department, 1-4
  trustees and managers of, 1-3
Trustees under deeds of arrangement,
    11-237/45

Uncleared effects
  answer on cheque, 7-39
Unconditional
  bill must be, 8-2
  promissory note must be, 9-44
Uncrossed cheque
  payment of, 7-61/78
Undated bill of exchange, 8-9
Undated cheque, 7-14
Undue influence
  defined, 5-160
  effect of, 5-161/2
Uniform customs and practice for
  documentary credits, 8-101
Uniform rules for the collection of
  commercial paper, 8-106/8
Unit trusts
  banks associated with, 10-116/116A
  purchase of units, 10-112
  purpose of, 10-112
  realization of units, 10-114
United States of America
  passbook, law relating to, 2-136

Valuable consideration. See
    Consideration
Value
  defined, 5-116
  holder for. See Holder for value
  lien as, 5-118
  presumption as to, 5-131

Wages
  advances for, 11-299/306
  instrument payable to, 9-25/33

Waiver
    notice of dishonour, of, 8-62
    presentment of, 8-46
Walks, clearing, 6-18
War
    effect on banker-customer relationship,
      3-82/6
Warehousekeepers' warrant, 4-14
Wife. *See* Married woman
Winding-up
    bank, of, 3-45
    company customer of, 3-43/4,
      11-229/307, 11-343/89
    liquidator in compulsory, 11-348/59
    liquidator in creditors' voluntary,
      11-381/84

Winding-up (*contd.*)
    liquidator in members' voluntary,
      11-377/80
    petition for, 11-348/55
Words
    difference between figures and, 5-16,
      7-17
    prohibiting transfer of bill, 5-71
Writ of sequestration, 3-80/1
Writing
    acceptance must be in, 8-30
    bill of exchange must be in, 8-2
    promissory note must be in, 9-44
Wrongful trading, 11-361/2

Yearly Plan, 10-123A
Younger Committee, 2-123A